BASEBALL

BASEBALL

An Encyclopedia of Popular Culture

Edward J. Rielly

ABC-CLIO

Santa Barbara, California
Denver, Colorado
Oxford, England

Library of Congress Cataloging-in-Publication Data
Rielly, Edward J.
Baseball : an encyclopedia of popular culture / Edward J. Rielly.
    p. cm.
Includes bibliographical references and index.
  ISBN 1-57607-103-0 (alk. paper)
  1. Baseball—Social aspects—United States. 2. Popular
culture—United States. I. Title.
GV867.64.R52   2000
796.357'0973—dc21

00-010704
CIP

06 05 04 03 02 01 00   10 9 8 7 6 5 4 3 2 1

ABC-CLIO, Inc.
130 Cremona Drive, P.O. Box 1911
Santa Barbara, California 93116-1911

Typesetting by Pro Production, Mahwah, New Jersey

This book is printed on acid-free paper ∞.
Manufactured in the United States of America.

For Jeanne, whose support is always major league

Contents

Preface

This book, as the title indicates, concerns both baseball and popular culture. Were it strictly a history of baseball, it would be a different type of book—a worthwhile book, to be sure, but a different one. The idea is to present ways in which certain aspects of baseball—individuals, teams, events, works of art, or social and technological changes within the game—affect and reflect the broader society in the United States. The focus, therefore, is twofold: baseball and society. This dual perspective can be imagined as interlocking circles that move around and through each other, with baseball altering American society and society impacting the game often known as America's national pastime. Further, baseball is not separate from popular culture but part of that culture. This book therefore explores how baseball interacts with other dimensions of popular culture.

The phrase "popular culture" requires some explanation. The term is widely used but has no definitive definition. The word "popular" generally refers to "the people," meaning the large majority of "common" people rather than the intellectual and social elite. To be popular, something must be widespread and widely accepted or practiced. Almost every statement made about popular culture, though, requires qualification. In the case of baseball, individuals who otherwise would be considered among the social elite may attend baseball games and rub shoulders with the masses. In fact, many do just that. This author not long ago sat at a minor league game immediately in front of the governor of his state. Clearly, individuals shift into and out of the category often referred to as "the common people." At the same time, an activity enjoyed or practiced by a relatively small number of people would not qualify as part of popular culture.

So what is "culture"? That term, although subject to many definitions (like all of the terms referred to here), is best defined broadly. So let us think of culture as the way of life of a group of people— a not uncommon way to use the term. In this case, the group consists of the people living in the United States, who, of course, interact through baseball and many other aspects of popular culture with people from other nations. So "popular culture," as used in this book, refers to the way of life of large numbers of people who have lived in, or are now living in, the United States. Popular culture includes both attitudes and behavior. It includes how people think about themselves and society and how they act, especially when given a choice. Popular culture includes attitudes and behavior relating to how people think, dress, enjoy leisure time, make life easier at home and away, worship, spend holidays, interact with their environment, and so forth.

Popular-culture studies have mushroomed since the 1960s, and the field of popular culture is increasingly taken seriously as a legitimate way to learn more about people and society. Studying the songs that people listen to, the brands of refrigerators they buy, the clothing styles with which they adorn themselves, the television programs they watch, and the sports that excite them, for example, can tell us much about the attitudes, patterns of behavior, psychology, and values of a society.

Until the middle of the twentieth century, however, popular culture often was set against "high culture," with the clear, often explicit understanding that the user of these terms viewed high culture as good, popular culture as bad. High culture consisted of the best that had been written, painted, composed, thought, and so forth. It represented, many people believed, the activities and inclinations of an intellectual and aesthetic elite versus the widespread enjoyments of intellectually and artistically inferior masses. That elitist distinction would appear to run counter to what citizens of the United States believe about our most sacred political institution—that freedom depends on the will and consent of the masses, in other words, on the preservation and conscientious practice of democracy. In addition, many types of activities that were (sometimes still are) associated with high culture—poetry, music, painting, and visiting

museums, to name just a few—also are part of popular culture, as certain entries in this book make clear.

Folk culture and mass culture often are associated with popular culture, sometimes identified with it. As there is no single definition of popular culture, these terms and their relationships to popular culture also admit many interpretations. One could argue, nonetheless, with perhaps only modest quibbling from scholars, that folk culture is in essence pretechnological and preindustrial popular culture, arising from the people and often communal in nature. Folk songs, common rituals, and the oral tradition in literature are examples of folk culture. Mass culture is usually viewed as modern, the product of such forces as industrialization, urbanization, technology, and mass communications (or mass media). Mass culture is often viewed as top-down, a product of mass production and careful marketing to form widespread demand for products. In the United States, the rise of the dime Western in the nineteenth century would be an early example of how mass production, improved transportation, and clever marketing created a demand that became part of popular culture. Many people, especially critics of modern society, are likely to bemoan mass culture as an ongoing manipulation of the public to buy certain appliances, watch certain television shows, purchase certain clothes, or attend concerts performed by certain singers. For such critics, popular culture is almost a type of enforced mass culture.

American popular culture, however, is perhaps best seen as a combination of folk culture and mass culture synthesized in the mind and heart of America—and that should be seen as essentially a good thing. To believe that the people are merely sheep to be tricked into adopting what the manufacturing, marketing, and communications industries want them to accept demands, logically, that one view those sheep as inadequate to form the basis of a democratic society. The history of the past two hundred–plus years in the United States tells us otherwise.

The people both respond to and dictate the forces mentioned above. If people's attitudes are somewhat shaped by what is offered to them to purchase and use, their own felt understanding of what gives them pleasure, contentment, relaxation, and intellectual stimulation also strongly influences what is offered to them.

Baseball is a vivid example of how folk culture (viewed as arising from the people themselves) and mass culture (viewed as presented to the people by others with a vested interest in having their offerings purchased or otherwise accepted) coalesce in popular culture. Baseball originally was a grassroots phenomenon, arising from groups of individuals revising an English game because they wanted increased opportunities for exercise, good friendship, and relaxation. Today, baseball is big business, served up to people by technology, marketing strategies, and mass communications. Yet all of the top-down efforts to affect fans finally yield to decisions made by those fans about whether or not to attend games in person; and whether to watch or listen to games, or read about them, through the media. Still today, young children in the United States play ball as they have since the eighteenth century. Baseball is in many respects still the same game, and it remains an important part of popular culture in this country, as it has been from the early days of the nation.

This dual and interlocking focus of the book (both baseball and popular culture) explains, at least partly, why certain topics are included and others excluded, and why some are given more attention

than others. It would be nice to argue that these decisions regarding what to include and how much space to allot to each subject derive from purely objective and quantifiable judgments. This, of course, is not the case. Subjectivity can never be entirely removed from such decisions.

So what does this mean in practice? I required two basic criteria to be met in order to discuss a particular topic in this book. First, the item (person, place, thing, or something else) must have some importance within baseball. It must have a baseball value and be of the game in a manner that at least to this author seems important. Because this book is about baseball and popular culture, however, this first criterion is less important than the second, for many players and events were important within baseball but have had little or no significant impact on the wider society.

Thus the more important criterion is the second: The item must have significance beyond the diamond. It must interface with other aspects of society in a way that makes it part of the popular culture. The extent to which the item affects and is affected by the broader popular culture is reflected in the amount of space devoted to its discussion.

A few examples may help. Many players who starred, even made the Hall of Fame, are not included. They clearly were important within the game, or they would not have been so honored. However, their impact on the broader society and its attitudes and behavior was either minimal at the time or has ceased to be important. Some players, such as Curt Flood, who probably will never be elected to the Hall of Fame, are included because of their impact on the interrelationships between baseball and society. In the case of Flood, he played a crucial role in the ultimate elimination of free agency, which led to higher salaries and greater mobility for players, affecting the way that society views the game.

Regarding baseball commissioners, A. Bartlett Giamatti receives substantial attention, but some commissioners do not. This is because he affected the way that society (or at least a large portion of society) defines baseball. No one has contributed to the mythic and metaphoric view of baseball more than has Giamatti. To a great extent because of him, baseball has become a metaphor for life.

Ernest Hemingway is another potentially controversial inclusion, especially given the length of his entry. However, a major phenomenon in popular culture in recent decades is the rise of a large body of outstanding baseball fiction. As the entry points out, Hemingway deserves significant credit for this development because he gave artistic legitimacy to baseball as a subject worthy of great literature. He and his novelistic successors have brought baseball fiction into the classrooms, libraries, bookstores, and homes—and thus into the culture—of the United States.

Everyone understands why Jackie Robinson merits serious attention, but so does Hank Greenberg, who as much as Robinson represented a large body of Americans when he stepped to the plate—in his case, Jewish Americans. Race and ethnic relations are classic examples of how sport and popular culture interact, altering both forever.

Entries have been written in three general lengths depending on the extent of their significance to baseball and popular culture: 200 to 300 words, 500 to 700 words, and 1,000 to 1,500 words. In addition, a few subjects are so important (e.g., the major leagues, women in baseball) that a special supercategory of 1,800 to 2,500 words has been created for them.

It is hoped that readers of this book will find much in it to enjoy and think about. After each entry, additional readings are suggested, usually kept to a maximum of five recommendations in order to avoid turning the book primarily into an extended bibliography, which, however useful, might not be particularly pleasurable. In many cases, there is a wealth of additional opportunities in unmentioned sources to pursue the subjects even further. Readers are encouraged to follow their interests at the nearest library or bookstore.

So many books and other materials have helped in the preparation of this book that to list all of them here would extend this preface far too long. The suggested readings are one way to express appreciation for this assistance. One book, however, deserves special mention, not only because it has been of much practical help as an extensive source of information and insights but also because it marks a path between baseball and the rest of American society, or popular culture, that this book attempts to travel as well. So with a grateful nod to *Baseball: An Illustrated History,* by Ken Burns and Geoffrey C. Ward (and the television series that it accompanied), this author invites you to step up to the plate and continue turning pages.

Additional Readings in Popular Culture:

Browne, Ray. *Popular Culture and the Expanding Consciousness.* New York: Wiley, 1973.

Handbook of American Popular Culture. 2nd ed. New York: Greenwood, 1989.

Kando, Thomas M. *Leisure and Popular Culture in Transition.* 2nd ed. St. Louis: C. V. Mosby, 1980.

Storey, John. *An Introduction to Cultural Theory and Popular Culture.* 2nd ed. Athens: University of Georgia Press, 1998.

Williams, Raymond. *Keywords.* London: Fontana, 1983.

Introduction

Baseball, in its earlier versions of rounders and townball, was played prior to the Revolutionary War. In its more modern version, it antedates the Civil War. Professional teams go back as far as the Cincinnati Red Stockings of the late 1860s, with professional leagues originating in the early 1870s. The current National League dates to 1876, the American League to 1901. Other major leagues have come and gone, and minor leagues have flourished, declined, and, recently, regained some of their earlier stature. Major league teams have even moved across borders, with Canada featuring two major league clubs, and major league teams sometimes play in other countries. A typical major league roster now has a genuine international flavor, with players from Japan, Korea, various Latin American countries, and occasionally Australia joining American and Canadian performers.

Baseball, however, is more than its professional leagues. College baseball had become popular by the middle of the nineteenth century, and during the latter decades of the twentieth century a variety of organizations arose to offer boys and girls opportunities to play organized ball, including Little League, PONY, and the Babe Ruth League. Softball, properly considered a version of baseball, also has become popular, especially, but not exclusively, with girls and young women.

Baseball has become more than a national and international phenomenon. It is part of the fabric of American life. It does not occupy merely a portion of American society but, like an ingredient in a national pot of soup, has permeated almost every aspect of society. It both affects and, in turn, is affected by virtually every other dimension of popular culture. That interdependence, however, has not been achieved without also reflecting the failures of American society. Baseball is a commentary on the American way of life, and that way of life has been both good and bad.

America, since the days of the Pilgrims, has been viewed as a land of opportunity, a land of freedom. Of course, that opportunity and freedom have been achieved too often at the expense of others. As Europeans and descendants of Europeans moved westward, conquering rivers, mountains, forests, and plains, they also conquered those Native Americans who long had lived among those same rivers, mountains, forests, and plains. As citizens of the new and growing United States built social, political, and financial success for themselves and their country, they often did so with the help of slaves. Even after the Civil War, sons and daughters of slaves were deprived of political liberty and financial opportunity throughout much of the country.

Major league baseball also excluded African Americans. The ball was white, the players were white, and that was the only color that was acceptable. African Americans who wished to play baseball were left with no alternative but to start their own teams and leagues, which they did, creating through the Negro Leagues a powerful African American business. Finally, Jackie Robinson broke the color barrier in the major leagues in 1947, but as the twenty-first century takes root, the power structure in the major leagues remains almost completely white.

Occasionally, Native Americans entered the ranks of organized baseball, but it is a sad commentary on the relationship of baseball to the nation's native population that the most famous Native American player remains the tragic Louis Sockalexis.

Women helped to build the United States but long remained limited in their opportunities by the patriarchal nature of American society. Still today, women have achieved little opportunity in baseball. Although a handful of women have played minor league ball, and during World War II they had a professional league of their own, none has performed at the major league level or umpired in the majors.

Religions long seemed much more concerned with whether baseball games should be played on Sunday, and whether alcoholic beverages ought to be sold at games, than with the determined effort of organized baseball to keep whole groups of God's children out of the game because of the color of their skin. So baseball has reflected and reinforced the bigotry, injustice, and hatred of American society.

However, baseball also has demonstrated America at its best. The game has been viewed by countless fans, from Commissioner A. Bartlett Giamatti to the most humble of spectators, as an allegory reflecting humankind's deepest aspirations—to achieve harmony and communion with others, to bind parents and children together, to participate in the universal psychic effort to return home, to aspire to a vision of an earlier, Edenic existence. Myth and ritual are part and parcel of the game of baseball, elevating the game to a sort of quasi religion.

If baseball is of the ideal, it also is earthbound, linked to practical matters of business, law, and labor. Baseball is as much about dollars as myths, which has been true since the Cincinnati Red Stockings found that the way to build a powerhouse team was to pay the players. Since then, issue after issue has revolved partly around profits for owners and players—night baseball, new leagues, free agency, expansion and relocation, and new stadiums, to name just a few. Owners attempt to gain the best possible deal with local government officials to build new revenue-enhancing stadiums, and players use free agency to seek high salaries. Of course, that same free agency gives players the same freedom enjoyed by members of most professions, that is, to search after the best available job. For much of the history of the game, players were tied for life to the team that initially signed them, until Marvin Miller and the players' union capped a long legal struggle against owners and commissioners with a series of victories starting in the 1970s.

Baseball fans who wish to forget the business and legal battles of the sport can just settle back and watch the game. But they also can enjoy baseball in a variety of media, including scores of fine baseball novels and films as well as a rich harvest of songs, poems, plays, art, and indoor games (including Rotisserie, or fantasy league, baseball). They also can attend fantasy camps to play baseball under the direction of some of their favorite former players and participate in Men's Senior and Adult Baseball Leagues.

The history of baseball is filled with individuals whose influence extended from the ball field to the encompassing society. Babe Ruth, Lou Gehrig, Jackie Robinson, Satchel Paige, Joe DiMaggio, Hank Greenberg, Ted Williams, Willie Mays, Mickey Mantle, Cal Ripken, and Mark McGwire are only a few of the players whose fame and accomplishments transcended the game itself, impacting both baseball and popular culture.

Vices that Americans encounter elsewhere are also encountered in baseball. Gambling has been a problem since the beginnings of professional baseball, reaching one climax with the Black Sox scandal of 1919 and another with the disciplinary action against Pete Rose in 1989. Substance abuse is an ongoing concern, with the original problem of excessive drinking giving way somewhat to illegal drugs and questions about performance-enhancing additives.

Yet despite the problems associated with baseball and popular culture, the positive interactions among the game and modern society are even more pronounced. Americans of all races, creeds, and ethnic backgrounds can come together on a green field that symbolizes the nation's rural origins, in front of countless parents and children who find in baseball a shared experience to pass on to their children and to their children's children. The stirring sounds of "The Star-Spangled Banner" remind spectators of wars won, ideals defended, and peace secured. The lighter "Take Me Out to the Ball Game" summons the congregation to rise during the seventh-inning stretch and sing of a past time still alive in that moment.

This is a game that is now studied more than ever before. Statisticians, historians, and multitudes of fans join the Society for American Baseball Research, read *The Sporting News* and *USA Today Baseball Weekly,* page through the statistics and narratives of *Total Baseball,* peruse the many magazines devoted to various dimensions of baseball, and prize their baseball cards stored safely from earlier decades.

All of this is because baseball is more than just a game. It is a manifestation of popular culture in the United States, as well as a shaper of that culture. That thesis, recounted in many ways, informs the following entries.

BASEBALL

A

AARON, HENRY LOUIS (HANK, HAMMERIN' HANK) (1934–)

Henry Aaron rose from the Negro Leagues and overcame virulent racism to become the greatest career home-run hitter in the history of the major leagues. Currently a vice president with the Atlanta Braves, Aaron was honored at a dinner attended by President Bill Clinton prior to the 1999 season, where it was announced that an annual award given to each league's best hitter would be named after him. Aaron had come much farther than the distance between Atlanta and his birthplace, Mobile, Alabama.

Henry Aaron began his climb toward greatness while playing with the semipro Mobile Black Bears as a teenager. Bunny Downs, business manager of the Indianapolis Clowns in the Negro American League, signed Aaron to play shortstop in 1952. Aaron did not remain long with the Clowns before coming to the attention of scouts for the Boston Braves and New York Giants. The Giants were not especially impressed, but Braves scout Dewey Griggs recognized the youngster's potential.

Signed by the Braves, Aaron joined their Northern League affiliate in Eau

Claire, Wisconsin, to finish out the 1952 season. The next year, he was assigned to the Braves' Sally League club in Jacksonville, Florida, where he helped integrate the league. He put together an awesome record that year, batting .362 with 208 hits, 115 runs scored, 125 RBIs, 36 doubles, 330 putouts, and 310 assists, all league highs; he also hit 22 home runs and 14 triples. That performance earned him promotion to the Braves, who in the meantime had moved to Milwaukee. When star outfielder Bobby Thomson broke an ankle in spring training, the rookie had a regular job.

The year 1954 was remarkable for Aaron personally and black America in general. The U.S. Supreme Court ruled in *Brown v. Board of Education* that racially separate schools are by their nature unequal, thereby laying the legal foundation for desegregation in education. Prior to 1954, only six major league teams—six years after Jackie Robinson broke the color barrier in the majors—had allowed African Americans to play for them. The Negro Leagues, however, were dying, yielding to the promise of major league opportunities for African Americans. In fact, when Hank Aaron concluded his

Baseball legend Hank Aaron swings a bat, 1950s. (Archive Photos)

playing career in 1976, he was the last remaining major-leaguer to have played in the Negro Leagues.

Henry Aaron had a promising rookie season in 1954, batting .280 with 13 home runs and 69 RBIs while establishing himself as a fixture in the outfield. The following season, his greatness shone through. He batted .314 with 27 home runs and 106 RBIs. By his third season, he was the National League's leading hitter at .328. His fourth season, 1957, included league-leading marks in home runs (44) and runs batted in (132), the National League Most Valuable Player Award, and an extraordinary performance in the World Series for the victorious Braves as he hit three home runs and batted .393.

Aaron had disciplined himself to contain his emotions and ignore distractions as well as hostility. In his early years with the Braves, as the team traveled by train through the South, teammates had to bring him food in his compartment because blacks were not permitted to eat in the dining car. When Stan Williams hit him in the head with a pitch, Aaron did not retaliate, except by stroking a home run his next time at bat. Such was his self-control that seldom did either a slump or triumph elicit much of an emotional display.

The Braves moved to Atlanta in 1966, and Aaron continued his long run of accomplishments. A complete player in his prime who hit for average and power, fielded superbly, and ran the bases effectively, Aaron reached the 1974 season at the age of 40 with four home-run and RBI titles, the distinction of having become the first player ever to collect 3,000 hits and 500 home runs, and certain selection to the Baseball Hall of Fame. One more accomplishment, though, awaited him: breaking Babe Ruth's career home-run record of 714.

Aaron entered the season needing just one home run to tie and two to break Ruth's record. Life, however, had not been easy during the past season, and the off-season had continued to be difficult. As Aaron approached Ruth's record, he was increasingly the victim of probably the most bitter hatred ever directed against an African American player, with the possible exception of Jackie Robinson during his rookie season. Aaron received death threats and vicious hate mail from those who did not want to see a black supplant the legendary Ruth. There were also kidnapping threats against the Aaron children, and bodyguards accompanied Aaron to and from the ballpark.

Fortunately, neither Aaron nor his fans had to wait long once the 1974 season began. In his first at-bat, Aaron hit home run number 714 in Cincinnati. He did not play in the second game and went homerless in the third game. The Braves had hoped to ensure that the record would be broken at home by keeping Aaron out of the Cincinnati series, but commissioner Bowie Kuhn refused to allow this ploy, deciding that the integrity of the game came before individual records.

The Braves then returned to Atlanta for the first home series of the season, and on April 8, 1974, Atlanta fans did have the good fortune to see Aaron break the record at home. Facing Al Downing of the Los Angeles Dodgers, Aaron slammed number 715 for the record.

For once, the stoic slugger permitted himself the luxury of emotion. He recalled circling the bases:

> I was in my own little world at the time. It was like running in a bubble and I could see all these people jumping up and down and waving their arms in slow motion. . . . Every base seemed crowded, like there were all these people I had to get through to make it to home plate. I just couldn't wait to get there. I was told I had a big smile on my face as I came around third. I purposely never smiled as I ran the bases after a home run, but I suppose I couldn't help it that time.

After that historic season, Aaron returned to Milwaukee to conclude his playing career, playing two years as an outfielder and designated hitter for the Brewers. He finished his career with 755 home runs, 3,771 hits, 2,297 RBIs, and a .305 batting average. He played in 24 All-Star Games and, with quiet dignity, had become a baseball immortal. Selection to the Hall of Fame came in 1982.

See also: African Americans; Home Run; Negro Leagues.

Additional Reading:

Aaron, Hank. *Aaron.* Rev. ed. New York: Crowell, 1974.

———. *I Had a Hammer: The Hank Aaron Story.* New York: HarperCollins, 1991.

Hirshberg, Albert. *The Up-to-Date Biography of Henry Aaron, Quiet Superstar.* New York: Putnam's, 1974.

Morse, Ann. *Baseball's Record Breaker, Hank Aaron.* Mankato, MN: Children's Press, 1976.

AFRICAN AMERICANS

African Americans played a version of baseball called "townball" during the era of slavery, at times using a ball made of boiled chicken feathers wrapped with cloth. Thus the history of black baseball is at least almost as old as white baseball in America. As with so many other elements of American popular culture, baseball has both its good and its bad. At its best, baseball represents some of America's most shining virtues, including the nation's democratic impulse (emphasizing, as does democracy, the importance of the individual within the framework of the commonweal) and a commitment to building teamwork, fostering good health, and providing enjoyable recreation. It also provides another avenue for ballplayers to earn a good living. At the same time, baseball reflects some of the nation's failures, including racial segregation and denial of equal opportunities for African Americans and women.

African Americans were involved during the early days of organized baseball. At least a few black players were on teams in the National Association of Base Ball Players, founded in 1858. The Civil War introduced the sport to many others, including 180,000 blacks who fought for the Union. In fact, soldiers from both sides enjoyed playing baseball for recreation when they were away from the front. The postwar period was a time of quickly expanding interest in baseball throughout American society, and newly freed slaves as well as freeborn African Americans shared that interest.

So-called colored teams sprang up as early as 1865, including the Monitor Club of Jamaica, Long Island, and the Bachelor Club of Albany. Teams blossomed throughout the 1860s. One of the most famous—and best—was the Pythian Club of Philadelphia, composed of students at Banneker Institute. Some players were members of the Knights of Pythias Lodge (hence the team's name). In one of those historical footnotes so fascinating to students of history, the Pythians in 1867 played the Alerts from the Washington, D.C., area, a team that included a third baseman named Charles Douglass, son of the famous abolitionist Frederick Douglass. The Pythians in 1869 were involved in apparently the first contest between black and white teams, losing to the Philadelphia Olympics 44-23. The Pythians shortly thereafter became the first black club to defeat a white team, the City Item Club of Philadelphia. In 1870, the black Resolutes of Boston defeated a white team by the same name, 25-15; the white Resolutes (clearly a popular name connoting determination to prevail) of Oberlin, Ohio, included a black pitcher in 1869.

These promising developments in the first decade after the Civil War were not long to continue, as racism, far from defeated with the fall of the Confederacy, was to exercise great power in the South through Jim Crow laws and in the North through more subtle forms of discrimination. Before the door of opportunity slammed completely shut on African Americans in baseball, though, a few men would leave a lasting mark on the history of the game. One of these players, Bud Fowler (born near Cooperstown, home of the Baseball Hall of Fame), joined an all-white team in New Castle, Pennsylvania, in 1872. An outstanding pitcher and then second baseman, Fowler continued playing until 1895, bouncing around among some 20 teams. His first professional club was Lynn in the International Association in

1878. Life was difficult for any African American player, as his tenure on a team often lasted only until someone complained or the team could find a replacement white player. Fowler's peripatetic career was therefore typical of African American players in the early years of baseball.

About a decade after Fowler's entry into baseball, Moses Fleetwood Walker joined Toledo (in 1883 a member of the Northwestern League, then, in the following year, of the major league American Association). Walker, like many of the early black ballplayers, was far more than a talented "ballist." Born in Ohio in 1857 and the son of a doctor (or minister—the sources are not clear), Walker attended Oberlin College and played on its baseball team, for whom he caught and served as captain. After graduating in 1882, Walker attended the University of Michigan Law School and continued his baseball career as a professional. He left school in 1884 to devote himself full-time to playing for Toledo. An accomplished catcher, Walker several times drew opposition from Cap Anson, player-manager of the Chicago White Stockings and the most prominent major league player of his time. A crucial moment in the racial history of organized baseball came in 1887, when Walker was playing for Newark of the International League. Anson's White Stockings were scheduled to play an exhibition game against Newark, and Anson vowed to keep his team off the field if Walker and another African American, pitcher George Stovey, played. The Newark club, fearing loss of revenue from several thousand seats already sold, complied. Whatever chance African Americans had in the major leagues was essentially over. The handful of black players still in organized ball had been let go by 1889, when Syracuse released Moses Walker. Except for a few black players in obscure minor league towns in the 1890s, organized baseball would not have another African American player until Jackie Robinson took the field in 1946 for the Montreal Royals.

African Americans who wished to play professional baseball—and there were many—would henceforth have to confine their playing to all-black teams, which would sometimes play exhibitions against white ballclubs. Undeterred by exclusion from white leagues, African Americans formed many outstanding teams over the next several decades and created a series of Negro Leagues. From the 1890s onward, baseball was an important part of black culture and a major part of the economy of the black community, especially in the Northeast and Midwest. Outstanding late-nineteenth-century and turn-of-the-century teams included the Cuban Giants, the first professional black team and (known by various names) one of the best and most popular of all black clubs. The Cuban Giants were organized by waiters at the Argyle Hotel in Babylon, Long Island, who tried to pass themselves off as Cubans, not only through the team's name but also by speaking nonsense language on the field, in order to lessen the impact of racism.

Black teams were usually independent through the first two decades of the twentieth century, playing against each other and sometimes competing against white teams. Loose alliances occasionally were formed, and championship tournaments were held as early as 1888. Two of the greatest stars of this era were Smokey Joe Williams and Rube Foster. Williams pitched in the Negro Leagues from 1897 to 1932. Half-black and half-Comanche, Williams had a great fastball in his prime. Against white competition he was 19-7. He defeated Hall of Famers Walter Johnson (by a score of 1-0), Grover Cleveland Alexander, Waite Hoyt, Chief Bender, Rube Marquard, and Satchel Paige (splitting two games with Paige in the 1930s, when Williams was in his mid-forties). When he faced John McGraw's Giants in 1917, he threw a 10-inning no-hitter and struck out 20, only to lose 1-0 on an error. Ty Cobb once said that if Williams pitched in the majors he would be a certain 30-game winner. A 1952 poll of former Negro League players conducted by the *Pittsburgh Courier* declared Williams the best black pitcher ever, by one vote over Satchel Paige. Rube Foster was perhaps the most important figure in black baseball during the first two decades of the century. A great pitcher, manager, and organizer of the Negro National League, Foster earned the nickname the "father of black baseball." He is discussed in greater detail elsewhere in this book.

The Negro Leagues, despite financial problems during the Great Depression, enjoyed extraordinary popularity within the black community from the 1920s through the 1940s. Stars such as pitcher Satchel Paige, third baseman Judy Johnson, catcher Josh Gibson, and center fielder Cool Papa Bell became household names, and black owners built Negro League baseball into the largest financial industry within the black community. The integration of the major leagues in 1947, however, sounded the death knell for the Negro Leagues. The Negro National League died after the 1948 season, while the American League continued through 1960. The history of the Negro Leagues, as well as Jackie Robinson's entrance into the major leagues, are discussed within other entries in this book.

At the turn of the twenty-first century, African American players fill sports pages and TV screens with great accomplishments while earning multimillion-dollar salaries. Many former African American players, including Negro League stars, have been inducted into the Hall of Fame. Even the combination of fame and fortune for players, however, has not brought equality to the majors. Few African Americans have made it into leadership positions on the field or in the front offices, and the initial exclusion of Negro League owners from the majors reverberates down to the present; there are no African American owners in the major leagues.

See also: Aaron, Henry Louis; Anson, Adrian Constantine; Banks, Ernest; Bell, James Thomas; Campanella, Roy; Chandler, Albert Benjamin; Cobb, Tyrus Raymond; Doby, Lawrence Eugene; Foster, Andrew; Gibson, Joshua; Irvin, Monford; Lacy, Samuel H.; Landis, Kenesaw Mountain; Manley, Effa; Mays, Willie Howard; Negro Leagues; Paige, Leroy Robert; Rickey, Wesley Branch; Robinson, Frank; Robinson, Jack Roosevelt; Smith, Wendell; White, William DeKova; Wilson, August.

Additional Reading:

Ashe, Arthur R., Jr. *A Hard Road to Glory—Baseball: The African-American Athlete in Baseball.* 1988. Reprint, New York: Amistad, 1993.

Gilbert, Tom. *Baseball and the Color Line.* New York: Franklin Watts, 1995.

Holway, John B. *Blackball Stars: Negro League Pioneers.* Westport, CT: Meckler, 1988.

Riley, James A. *The Biographical Encyclopedia of the Negro Baseball Leagues.* New York: Carroll and Graf, 1994.

Ryczek, William J. *When Johnny Came Sliding Home: The Post–Civil War Baseball Boom, 1865–1870.* Jefferson, NC: McFarland, 1998.

ALEXANDER, GROVER CLEVELAND (OLD PETE, ALEX THE GREAT) (1887–1950)

Grover Cleveland Alexander earned his place in public memory not only through a Hall of Fame career but also by pitching one of the most memorable games in World Series history and serving bravely in World War I. Unfortunately, he also suffered from epilepsy and was prone to heavy drinking, problems exacerbated by shell shock (a condition now known as post-traumatic stress disorder) as a result of his war service.

Alexander reached stardom in 1911 with the Phillies, setting a modern rookie record of 28 wins, one of them a 1-0 victory in 12 innings over Cy Young in the master's final game. Three consecutive years (1915–1917) saw Alexander win 30 or more games. Then came service in the U.S. Army as an artillery sergeant in France. He came home with his hearing impaired, in addition to the effects of shell shock.

Although Alexander's greatest seasons were behind, he continued to be a productive pitcher, winning 27 games for the Cubs in 1920 and accumulating a total of 373 victories, including a major league record 90 shutouts. In 1926, now with the Cardinals, he faced the Yankees in the seventh game of the World Series. Pete already had won two games when he was summoned to the mound in the seventh inning with the bases loaded, two outs, and his team ahead 3-2. He struck out Tony Lazzeri and continued to handcuff the Yankees for the World Series upset.

Alexander struggled with a variety of low-paying jobs after baseball, including working at a flea circus in Times Square; he died alone in a rented room in 1950. Having been named for one U.S. president, he was portrayed by a future president, Ronald Reagan, in the 1952 film *The Winning Team.*

See also: War.
Additional Reading/Viewing:
Holtzman, Jerome. *The Chicago Cubs Encyclopedia.* Philadelphia: Temple University Press, 1997.
Lieb, Frederick G. *The St. Louis Cardinals: The Story of a Great Baseball Club.* New York: Putnam's, 1944.
The Winning Team. Dir. Lewis Seiler. Warner Bros., 1952.

ALL-AMERICAN GIRLS PROFESSIONAL BASEBALL LEAGUE

The United States was in its second full year of warfare in 1943, and increasing numbers of major league baseball players were joining the war effort, when Chicago Cubs owner Philip K. Wrigley set out to create an all-women's league. Baseball was not alone, of course, in losing men to the war, and like other industries it turned to women to fill the void. Thus female replacements streamed into American factories, helping build the military machine that would achieve victory over the Axis powers. And some women answered the call to try out for Wrigley's new league.

Although excluded from organized baseball, many women in the 1940s had played as amateurs, and many more, perhaps as many as 40,000, played softball. Hundreds of women answered the call to try out, and the 250 best were invited to Chicago. That number finally was reduced to 4 clubs of 15 players each.

The original teams—the Kenosha Comets, Racine Belles, Rockford Peaches, and South Bend Blue Sox—were located in towns without major league clubs and were close enough to make travel relatively easy and inexpensive. In later years, additional teams were added to the league: the Battle Creek Belles, Chicago Colleens, Fort Wayne Daisies, Grand Rapids Chicks, Kalamazoo Lassies, Milwaukee Chicks, Muskegon Belles, Muskegon Lassies, Minneapolis Millerettes, Peoria Redwings, and Springfield Sallies.

Some of these team names might be considered insulting in the modern context, and indeed a primary requirement was that players never sacrifice their femininity. They were to look pretty both on and off the field and absolutely never appear masculine. Consequently, players were sent to charm school to learn how to talk and walk like ladies, wear their hair in feminine fashions, and dress appropriately. Off the field the standard uniform was high heels, makeup, and attractive but modest clothing. Chaperones made sure at all times that no improper behavior occurred. On the field, the players wore makeup and kept their hair

Composite photo of the 1947 all-star team in the All-American Girls Professional Baseball League (Racine Heritage Museum)

properly done. Their short skirts no doubt appealed to male viewers, as Wrigley and his associates sold sex appeal, but in a girl-next-door fashion. The skirts did little to protect players' legs while sliding into base or diving for a sinking liner.

The game offered women the opportunity not only to play a game they loved but also to make a good salary. Their paychecks ranged from $60 to $180 per week, well above the average weekly pay of $40 for women in factories. Some of the participants earned considerable fame along with their paychecks. Perennial All-Star Dorothy Kamenshek was a brilliant defensive first baseman famous for her splits when stretching for a throw. Sophie Kurys earned the nickname "Tina Cobb" by stealing 201 bases in 203 attempts in 1946, 1,114 for her career. Jean Faut may have been the best pitcher in the league, accumulating 132 victories

against 61 defeats. Anabelle Lee, aunt of future Red Sox pitcher Bill Lee, hurled a perfect game for the Millerettes. Joanne Weaver hit .429 one year. And each town had its home favorites. Hall of Famers Max Carey, Dave Bancroft, and Jimmie Foxx were among the former major-leaguers who managed the clubs, adding their fame to the teams' drawing power.

The league apparently never was envisioned as permanent, as organizers failed to create a farm system to replenish the talent supply. The return of male players from the war, declining promotional efforts, competition from television (which made major league games more accessible), and organized baseball's continuing view of the sport as a male domain gradually hurt attendance at games, and 1954 was the league's last season. The All-American Girls Professional Baseball League thus receded from memory until a 1992 film about the league, *A League of Their Own* (starring Tom Hanks, Madonna, and Geena Davis), ignited popular interest in and serious historical research on the league and the larger subject of women in baseball.

See also: Colorado Silver Bullets; Softball; War; Women in Baseball.
Additional Reading:
Browne, Lois. *Girls of Summer: In Their Own League.* Toronto: HarperCollins, 1992.
Galt, Margot Fortunato. *Up to the Plate: The All-American Girls Professional Baseball League.* Minneapolis: Lerner, 1995.
Hammer, Trudy J. *The All-American Girls Professional Baseball League.* New York: New Discovery Books, 1994.
Macy, Sue. *A Whole New Ball Game: The Story of the All-American Girls Professional Baseball League.* New York: Holt, 1993.
Madden, W. C. *The All-American Girls Professional Baseball League Record Book.* Jefferson, NC: McFarland, 1999.

ALLEN, MEL (1913–1996)

Melvin Allen Israel, born of Russian-Jewish immigrants, was the voice of the New York Yankees during the glory days of the Bronx Bombers, from 1940 until 1964. Probably the most recognized voice in baseball, Allen, according to Yankee owner George Steinbrenner, meant as much to Yankee tradition as DiMaggio, Mantle, and other Yankee legends. And Yankee tradition was American tradition for much of the twentieth century, embodying power and success.

Allen grew up in Alabama and graduated from the University of Alabama

Sportscaster Mel Allen looks up from his desk in the broadcasting booth of a stadium, 1950s. (Archive Photos)

(where he was cut from the baseball team but earned his letter as student manager) and, later, from the university's law school. After passing the Alabama bar exam in 1936, Allen went to New York and almost on a whim auditioned for a job at CBS. By 1940, Allen was the lead announcer for Yankee games, a position he held until the end of the 1964 season, except for four years during World War II while he served in the army.

Allen's fame was not merely the result of being with the right team at the right time. A careful professional, Allen knew baseball well and combined a keen eye for detail with genuine enthusiasm for the game. His distinctive Alabama cadence was supplemented with phrases that he repeated endlessly: "Going, going, gone!" for home runs; and most famously, "How about that!" for any exciting development, especially any good turn of fortune for the Yankees. His excitement for the game never waned, and fans responded if not to his vocabulary then to his homespun excitement, easily heard in the rising tenor of his voice.

Mel Allen also was fond of nicknames and helped popularize many for Yankee greats and near-greats: "Joltin' Joe" DiMaggio, "Steady Eddie" Lopat, Phil "Scooter" Rizzuto, and many more. A consistent promoter of his team, Allen brought the same loyalty to sponsors. Adept at working commercials into the game, he also applied his fondness for nicknames to sponsors' products. A home run, for example, was a "White Owl Wallop," named for the cigar. Sometimes they were "Ballantine Blasts" after the beer company.

One of the most controversial moments in Yankee history came at the end of the 1964 season when Allen was told that he would not be rehired. The Yankees chose not even to have him broadcast the 1964

World Series. But when George Steinbrenner took over ownership of the Yankees, Mel Allen returned. Steinbrenner had long been an admirer of Allen for personal as well as professional reasons. As a young man in 1955, the Yankee owner had been fired by Northwestern University as an assistant football coach. Although he had never met Allen, he called the broadcaster, who spoke with Steinbrenner for about 45 minutes and made a number of calls to help the fired coach find another position. Steinbrenner ultimately went in other directions, but he never forgot Allen's kindness. When he became owner, he brought Allen back as an announcer in 1976. The following year, Allen began a weekly show about baseball highlights called *This Week in Baseball,* which he continued for 17 years.

When Mel Allen died in June 1996, Steinbrenner ordered the team to wear black armbands for the remainder of the season. By that time, Allen's place in broadcasting history was secure. In 1978, shortly after his return to the Yankees, he was selected for the Hall of Fame, entering with Red Barber, his broadcasting partner with the Yankees for several years.

See also: Barber, Walter Lanier; Language, Baseball; New York Yankees; Nicknames; Radio Broadcasting; Television Broadcasting.
Additional Reading:
Allen, Mel. *It Takes Heart.* New York: Harper, 1959.
———. *You Can't Beat the Hours: A Long, Loving Look at Big-League Baseball, Including Some Yankees I Have Known.* New York: Harper and Row, 1964.
Smith, Curt. *The Storytellers: From Mel Allen to Bob Costas—Sixty Years of Baseball Tales from the Broadcast Booth.* New York: Macmillan, 1995.
White, G. Edward. *Creating the National Pastime: Baseball Transforms Itself, 1903–1953.* Princeton: Princeton University Press, 1996.

ALL-STAR GAMES

The baseball All-Star Game has been a fixture since 1933, when Arch Ward, sports editor of the *Chicago Tribune,* persuaded owners to stage the game in conjunction with Chicago's Century of Progress Exposition. Connie Mack and John McGraw managed the teams, and Babe Ruth led the American League to a 4-2 triumph with a home run, becoming the first man to homer in an All-Star Game. The opportunity to see the game's greatest stars thrilled spectators and helped usher in almost a century (and still counting) of all-star extravaganzas throughout American society, from football and basketball games to countless awards shows covering virtually the entire spectrum of public entertainment.

Although some games have been less than memorable, there have been enough exciting moments, along with the opportunity to root for one's favorite players, to keep fans watching at home and from the stands. During the second All-Star Game, in 1934, Carl Hubbell of the Giants consecutively struck out five of the game's greatest hitters: Babe Ruth, Lou Gehrig, Jimmie Foxx, Al Simmons, and Joe Cronin. Sixty-five years later, that string was very much in mind for broadcasters and fans as Pedro Martinez of the Red Sox fanned Barry Larkin, Larry Walker, Sammy Sosa, and Mark McGwire before an error ended the streak.

There have been many other highlights. Because of security concerns during World War II, no game was held in 1945. Play resumed the following year, with Ted Williams returning from the war to tally two home runs, two singles, and a walk. The 1949 game, appropriately held at Ebbets Field in Brooklyn, was the first game to include African American players (Jackie Robinson, Roy Campanella, and Don Newcombe of the Dodgers and

Larry Doby of the Indians). Ted Williams made headlines again in the 1950 contest when he broke his left elbow making a catch against the wall and remained in the game to hit a run-scoring single.

Willie Mays, Stan Musial, Ted Williams, and Mickey Mantle, All-Stars for the ages, hit home runs in 1956, three of the homers off two equally immortal pitchers—Whitey Ford and Warren Spahn. The 1957 game was one of the most controversial, as Cincinnati fans stuffed the ballot box and elected seven starters, thereby causing selection of All-Star starters to be withdrawn from the fans until 1970. The most important participant in the second 1961 game, held in San Francisco's Candlestick Park (two All-Star Games having been played from 1959 to 1962), was the wind. A gust blew Stu Miller off the mound in the ninth inning, causing him to balk and advance runners. Wind then blew a grounder away from third baseman Ken Boyer, allowing the tying run to score. But the wind was fickle in its capricious bestowing of favors, shifting to the National League's side in the tenth, rendering Hoyt Wilhelm's knuckleball ineffectual and turning the final decision in favor of sluggers Hank Aaron, Willie Mays, and Roberto Clemente.

Among baseball's All-Star Games, few have been more emotionally gripping than the 1999 game, held at historic Fenway Park. The most memorable moment—despite Pedro Martinez's heroics—came before the game was even played. Many of the previously selected top 100 players of the century had gathered on the field, to be followed by the 1999 All-Stars. Then, introduced as the "Greatest Hitter Who Ever Lived," Ted Williams was driven in. Frail, with failing eyesight, the 81-year-old Williams was helped up and steadied by Tony Gwynn as he threw the ceremonial first pitch to another former Red Sox great, catcher Carlton Fisk. Then the modern players huddled around the legendary Williams, many clearly shedding tears, delaying the start of the game because they did not want the magical moment to end. This was baseball at its best—past and present merging, nostalgia and awe replacing salary disputes, even the most famous of players childlike as they honored one of the great predecessors. If Arch Ward was watching somewhere, he must have been very pleased indeed at what his All-Star Game had become.

See also: Major Leagues.
Additional Reading:
Butler, Hal. Baseball All Star Game Thrills. New York: J. Messner, 1968.
Ivor-Campbell, Frederick. "The All-Star Game." In Total Baseball. 6th ed. Ed. John Thorn et al. New York: Total Sports, 1999, pp. 287–305.

AMERICAN LEGION BASEBALL
Baseball's connection to the military goes back as far as the Revolutionary War. One of George Washington's soldiers, George Ewing, tells in his journal of participating in a game of "base." Soldiers during the Civil War helped spread baseball throughout much of the country, and subsequent wars included service (and heroism) by many players who had traded one uniform for another.

It is appropriate, then, that the American Legion, the nation's largest veterans' organization, has sponsored American Legion Baseball since 1925. American Legion Baseball is the largest and oldest amateur baseball program in the United States, with over 8 million teenagers, ages 15 to 18, having participated. Approximately 90,000 players were part of the program in 1998. No amateur baseball program has had more graduates make the Hall of Fame in Cooperstown—more

than 30, including George Brett, Robin Yount, Reggie Jackson, Jim Palmer, Yogi Berra, Roy Campanella, Ted Williams, and Bob Feller.

Major League Baseball supports the program with annual financial contributions (recently $25,000 per year), recognition of the American Legion Player of the Year at the annual Hall of Fame induction ceremony at Cooperstown, and presentation of a plaque to the winner of the American Legion World Series by the commissioner's office during the Major League World Series. Most of the financial support, though, comes from fund-raising efforts by local Legion Posts committed to fostering sportsmanship, leadership, and strong character while helping teenagers have a lot of fun.

See also: Babe Ruth League; Little League; Pony Baseball and Softball; War.
Additional Reading:
American Legion Website (American Legion Baseball features). http://www.legion.org
Rumer, Thomas A. The American Legion: An Official History, 1919–1989. New York: M. Evans, 1990.
Seymour, Harold. Baseball: The Early Years. 1960. Reprint, New York: Oxford University Press, 1989.
———. Baseball: The People's Game. 1990. Reprint, New York: Oxford University Press, 1991.

AMYOTROPHIC LATERAL SCLEROSIS (ALS, LOU GEHRIG'S DISEASE)
Amyotrophic lateral sclerosis, or ALS, is a rare disease with no known cure. Its connection to baseball, though, is more pronounced than perhaps any of the more common diseases afflicting Americans. That association was made permanent when the great Yankee first baseman, Lou Gehrig, known as the "Iron Horse" because of his record-setting string of 2,130 consecutive games played, was

diagnosed with ALS toward the end of his Hall of Fame career. The stricken Gehrig, one of the game's most popular and respected players, further won the hearts of America with the courage he displayed while suffering from ALS. Since then, the disease has been more commonly known as Lou Gehrig's disease.

ALS affects the nervous system, specifically the motor neurons controlling muscular movement. Muscles become increasingly weaker and atrophy. The early signs of ALS usually are weakness in the hands, gradually spreading up the forearms to the shoulders. Lower limbs become weak and difficult to control. Death occurs usually within two to five years, as atrophied respiratory muscles hinder breathing.

Lou Gehrig's symptoms began when he was about 35, causing a subpar season in 1938 followed by major deterioration in his skills by spring training of 1939. Gehrig took himself out of the lineup on May 2, was diagnosed with ALS in the middle of June, and died on June 2, 1941. Many people today live much longer with Lou Gehrig's disease, and there is reason for hope. Researchers in 1993 discovered the gene responsible for hereditary ALS (5–10 percent of ALS cases involve genetic inheritance); this represented a significant step toward someday effectively combating the disease in all sufferers. The disease returned to the baseball spotlight in 1999 when Hall of Fame pitcher Jim "Catfish" Hunter shared with the public that he suffered from ALS; he died later that year.

See also: Gehrig, Henry Louis; Quisenberry, Daniel Raymond.
Additional Reading:
Amyotrophic Lateral Sclerosis: Lou Gehrig's Disease: Research Strikes Back. Rev. ed. Bethesda, MD: Department of Health, Education, and Welfare, Public Health Service, National Institutes of Health, 1977.

McGill, Frances. *Go Not Gently: Letters from a Patient with Amyotrophic Lateral Sclerosis.* New York: Arno, 1980.
Mitsumoto, Horoshi. *Amyotrophic Lateral Sclerosis.* Philadelphia: F. A. Davis, 1998.
Rabin, Roni. *Six Parts Love: One Family's Battle with Lou Gehrig's Disease.* New York: Scribner, 1985.

ANSON, ADRIAN CONSTANTINE (CAP, POP) (1852–1922)

Cap Anson has come down through American history as a complex individual,

Adrian Anson (First Base Chicago) as depicted on a Champions cigarette card (Ann Ronan Picture Library)

both hero and villain. Throughout his 27 years as a player in the big leagues, beginning in 1871, he established himself as baseball's first superstar. That is the way he was remembered until the late twentieth century, when research into the history of African Americans in baseball brought to light another side of Anson—his powerful role in excluding African Americans from organized baseball.

As a player, Anson deserves his Hall of Fame status. He was the first major league player to reach 3,000 hits, although there has been recent controversy regarding whether he should be credited with that number because he accumulated 2,995 of those hits in the National League and 423 in the earlier National Association of Professional Base Ball Players.

Anson was born in Marshalltown, Iowa, where he played baseball with his father and brother. He later sharpened his skills playing for the University of Notre Dame, where he is credited with establishing Notre Dame's first baseball team and serving as its captain and first baseman. He then played five years with the Athletics of Philadelphia before joining the Chicago White Stockings (the current Cubs) in 1876 for the inaugural season of the new National League.

In addition to playing several positions before settling in at first base, Anson managed the White Stockings from 1879 until 1897. An innovative manager, he was perhaps the first to take his team to spring training, in Hot Springs, Arkansas, in 1886. During his years as player-manager, he developed a total-team defensive concept, coordinating play between his outfielders and infielders. He was a strict disciplinarian as a manager but was respected by players and generally loved by fans. Anson led the way on the field as well, compiling four batting titles while leading his club to five pennants. He batted over .300 in each of his first 20 years in the ma-

jors and remained an effective batter even in his final year, at the age of 45.

A man of many talents, Cap Anson also fancied himself an actor. In 1895, the baseball great played himself in a Broadway play, Charles Hoyt's *A Runaway Colt*. Anson's role included persuading a father and mother to permit their son to play for Anson's White Stockings, a team sometimes referred to as the "Colts" because most of the players, with the exception of the manager, were relatively young. The play glorifies the importance of baseball, which coincided with Anson's own view of the dignity of the game. When he was let go after the 1897 season, fans collected $50,000 as a gift for Anson, but he declined the offer, stating that neither fans nor the game owed him anything, that he was indebted to baseball for the opportunity to be part of it. The play, while certainly not a masterpiece, was well received, and Anson garnered favorable reviews for his acting. Although he did not gain another Broadway role, he continued to act in local and vaudeville productions.

The most disappointing aspect of Anson's life concerns his reaction to black players. Moses Fleetwood Walker, a talented African American catcher, played baseball at the major league and minor league levels during the closing decades of the nineteenth century. When Walker was playing for Newark in the International League in 1887, his team was scheduled to compete against the White Stockings in an exhibition match. Anson vowed to keep his team off the field if Walker and his African American teammate, pitcher George Stovey, played. Several thousand tickets having already been sold, the Newark management succumbed to the threat rather than risk having to refund ticket money. The incident, and Anson's status as perhaps the most influential figure in the game, helped slam the door on African American players in organized baseball. The resulting gentlemen's agreements to exclude black players meant organized baseball would remain racially segregated until Jackie Robinson joined the Montreal Royals in 1946.

See also: African Americans; Theater.

Additional Reading:

Ahrens, Art. *The Cubs: The Complete Record of Chicago Cubs Baseball.* New York: Collier, 1986.

Anson, Adrian Constantine. *A Ball Player's Career, Being the Personal Experiences and Reminiscences of Adrian C. Anson.* Chicago: Era, 1900.

Gilbert, Tom. *Baseball and the Color Line.* New York: Franklin Watts, 1995.

Golenbock, Peter. *Wrigleyville.* New York: St. Martin's, 1996.

Holtzman, Jerome. *The Chicago Cubs Encyclopedia.* Philadelphia: Temple University Press, 1997.

ANTITRUST EXEMPTION

Baseball's antitrust exemption was long a bone of contention between management and players, raising the question of why baseball should be exempt from laws applicable to all other industries—including other sports. Antitrust legislation grew out of public indignation at the growth of monopolistic activities by big business during the nineteenth century. As Standard Oil as well as railroad, sugar, and beef trusts were established to control markets, eliminate competition, and increase profits, Congress in 1890 passed the Sherman Antitrust Act, forbidding "every contract, combination in the form of trust or otherwise, or conspiracy in restraint of trade or commerce among the several States, or with foreign nations."

As the Sherman Antitrust Act proved insufficient to deal with expanding trusts, and the American public became increasingly outraged, Congress and Presidents Theodore Roosevelt, William Howard Taft, and Woodrow Wilson succeeded in reinforcing the antitrust laws through court action, as well as the creation of the Federal Trade Commission (1914), to regulate corporations engaged in interstate or international commerce, and the Clayton Antitrust Act (1914), which clarified practices considered to be restraint of trade and gave individuals the right to sue for damages.

Major League Baseball, at least as far back as the creation of the National League in 1876, engaged in monopolistic actions in restraint of trade. William Hulbert, president of the Chicago White Stockings, led the charge, gathering together owners of eight clubs previously in the old National Association. The clubs assigned exclusive territories to the franchises, creating a monopoly within their respective regions. They extended their monopoly nationwide a few years later by reserving players for the duration of their careers (or until the players were sold, traded, or released). Other teams agreed not to negotiate with players subject to this so-called reserve system. Players had two choices: either play for their current team, or retire. This "trust" continued as corporations throughout American society established their monopolistic holds on other industries.

In the same year that witnessed passage of the Clayton Antitrust Act (1914), a rival independent league came into existence—the Federal League—and, under the antitrust laws, sued the major leagues (now comprising the National and American Leagues, the latter having become part of the trust). Ironically, the presiding judge was Kenesaw Mountain Landis, an ardent fan who within a few years would become the first commissioner of Major League Baseball. Landis delayed action while the major league owners succeeded in buying out most of the Federal League owners.

Ned Hanlon, owner of the Baltimore Terrapins, brought an antitrust suit against the major leagues. Although he won in 1919, the victory was overturned by the U.S. Court of Appeals for the District of Columbia. The case then went to the U.S. Supreme Court, headed by William Howard Taft, the former trust-busting U.S. president. Taft, however, also was a fan who in 1910 had inaugurated the custom of the president throwing out the first pitch on opening day. The 1922 ruling by the Supreme Court was unanimous in finding against Hanlon. Justice Oliver Wendell Holmes wrote the decision, asserting that baseball did not involve interstate commerce and therefore did not come under antitrust protection. Strangely enough, the ruling stated that baseball was strictly a state matter (although teams travel from state to state to play) and that baseball was not "commerce" because "personal effort, not related to production, is not a subject of commerce" (although the Supreme Court ruled in the following term that a vaudeville troupe traveling across state lines engaged in commerce).

This exemption from antitrust laws would survive additional appeals throughout the following decades, including Curt Flood's lawsuit. In that case, the Supreme Court upheld the exemption in 1972, even while acknowledging that organized baseball was involved in interstate commerce, on the grounds of congressional intent (Congress had not acted to remove the exemption). Collective bargaining finally tempered the worst aspects of the antitrust exemption in 1990, but the exemption itself was in effect reaffirmed by the Supreme Court as recently as 1996. Finally, Congress acted, and the "Curt Flood Act of 1998" was signed by Bill Clinton on October 27, 1998. The legislation states that "major league baseball players are covered under the antitrust laws," bringing to a close one of baseball's longest legal chapters.

See also: Commissioner; Flood, Curtis Charles; Free Agency; Hunter, James Augustus; Koufax, Sanford; Kuhn, Bowie K.; Labor-Management Relations; Law; Miller, Marvin James; Reserve Clause; Ward, John Montgomery.

Additional Reading:

Abrams, Roger I. Legal Bases: Baseball and the Law. Philadelphia: Temple University Press, 1998.

Markham, Jesse W., and Paul V. Teplitz. Baseball Economics and Public Policy. Lexington, MA: Lexington, 1981.

Schwartz, Bernard. A History of the Supreme Court. New York: Oxford University Press, 1993.

Waller, Spencer Weber, Neil B. Cohen, and Paul Finkelman. Baseball and the American Legal Mind. New York: Garland, 1995.

Weiler, Paul, and Gary Roberts. Sports and the Law. Westbury, NY: Foundation, 1993.

ART

The Boy's Book of Sports (1839) depicts children playing baseball. Currier and Ives lithographs from the 1860s to the 1880s represent baseball scenes. Masterful paintings by Thomas Eakins (Baseball Players Practicing, 1875) and William Morris Hunt (The Ball Players, 1877) helped to establish baseball as a serious subject for artists. Since those beginnings, baseball has become a popular subject for artists in a variety of media. Although most of these efforts may fall short of great art, there exists an impressive body of work that qualifies as outstanding art and also depicts aspects of baseball.

Among the finest painters of baseball subjects is Lance Richbourg, son of a former major league outfielder, Lance Richbourg Sr. The son initially resisted depicting baseball, perhaps because he wanted to establish an identity clearly his own. Nonetheless, he eventually turned back to the game, creating paintings of his father and other former players. One of his finest efforts is *Honus Wagner* (1979) following through in his swing. Almost devoid of background, the painting conveys the timelessness of the great hitter. Earlier in the twentieth century, another skilled artist, Paul Clemens, had turned to baseball in his paintings. Actress Ethel Barrymore purchased his painting *Two Umpires* (1938), which catches the loneliness of the two men slowly making their way toward an undefined destination. A lithograph completed by Clemens a year later, *Baseball Argument,* returns to umpires, catching a universal umpire scene in which two players (or perhaps a player and manager) vociferously dispute a call while the umpire listens in tight-lipped silence.

The most famous artistic representation of umpires, though, is Norman Rockwell's *Game Called Because of Rain* (1949), an illustration for the cover of *The Saturday Evening Post.* Three umpires stand straight as arrows, gazing at the sky, from which descend drops of rain. One umpire, as if to verify what his eyes convey (those umpire eyes everyone views with suspicion), holds out his right hand. Of all artists who have worked with baseball topics, Rockwell may be the most famous. For decades, many a cover of *The Saturday Evening Post* caught Rockwell's timeless moments from America's national pastime. Among them is a scene in which a rookie enters the Boston Red Sox clubhouse, much to the amusement of the veterans (*The Locker Room,* 1957), as well as a comic depiction of a nineteenth-century pitcher kicking high, the umpire bending to stare beneath the pitcher's left leg, both seeming to have their eyes fixed directly on the reader (*100th Year of Baseball,* 1939).

The variety in baseball art is also conveyed through such disparate creations as

Charles M. Schulz's eternal baseball games involving Charlie Brown, Lucy, and the other *Peanuts* characters; and the portfolios within *Fan: A Baseball Magazine* by Marshall Smith, Dane Tilghman, Mike Schacht (editor), and many others.

Some of the most imposing works of art depicting baseball are statues. A visitor to the Baseball Hall of Fame will see the eight-foot-tall *Babe Ruth* (1984), sculpted so realistically by Armand LaMontagne that the slugger seems ready at any moment to start his bat toward another home run. Another powerful, realistic depiction of a baseball great is Frank Vittor's statue *Honus Wagner* (1955) at Three Rivers Stadium in Pittsburgh. A wonderful porcelain piece from more than a century ago, *Baseball Figure—Pitcher* (1876), by Isaac Broome, stands in the New Jersey State Museum, ball in hand; while *Casey at the Bat* (1985), a bronze by Mark Lundeed, waits patiently across the century, left hand on hip, right hand resting on the bat that supports his weight, watching something, probably the pitcher warming up. And in Chicago, *Batcolumn,* a 100-foot steel bat created by Claes Oldenburg out of more than 1,600 pieces of steel welded into a diamond-lattice pattern, towers above mere mortal pursuits.

See also: Collectibles; *Peanuts.*
Additional Reading:
Mote, James. *Everything Baseball.* New York: Prentice Hall, 1989.
Rockwell, Norman. *Norman Rockwell: A Sixty Year Retrospective.* New York: Abrams, 1972.
———. *Norman Rockwell: My Adventures as an Illustrator.* New York: Abrams, 1988.
Shissler, Barbara Johnson. *Sports and Games in Art.* Minneapolis: Lerner, 1966.
Thorn, John, and the National Baseball Hall of Fame and Museum. *Treasures of the Baseball Hall of Fame: The Official Companion to the Collection at Cooperstown.* New York: Villard, 1998.

ARTIFICIAL TURF

Perhaps no physical detail of a baseball stadium excites more controversy about the nature of the game today, or places baseball more within the rural-urban cultural dichotomy, than artificial turf. Baseball was born on playing fields of grass, and even fans who readily accept artificial lighting and roofed stadiums tend to think that synthetic fields go too far. Players tend to agree, although it has less to do with the nature of the game than because they believe that artificial turf causes more injuries.

In 1966, the Houston Astrodome became the first baseball stadium to install artificial turf, a decision forced upon owner Roy Hofheinz when the natural grass that had been planted died. Growing grass indoors has since proved almost impossible, although the new Bank One Ballpark in Phoenix, home of the Arizona Diamondbacks, features a shade-tolerant grass (*DeAnza zoysia*) under a retractable dome. Some clubs, such as the Kansas City Royals (Kauffman Stadium) and St. Louis Cardinals (Busch Stadium) have shifted from artificial to natural turf. At the beginning of the 1999 season, nine major league stadiums had artificial turf.

Research tends to show that certain injuries are more prevalent on artificial surfaces, especially torn knee ligaments caused by catching a foot in the turf. Artificial surfaces also tend to be faster, yielding increased percentages of doubles and triples but a lower rate of singles. The ball gets by outfielders more quickly, although infielders often compensate by playing deeper. There does not seem to be a significant rise overall in batting averages on artificial turf. The primary issue for many fans, however, is their belief that the game should be played on natural grass.

See also: Ballparks; Myth.

Additional Reading:
Gmelch, George, and J. J. Weiner. *In the Ballpark: The Working Lives of Baseball People.* Washington, DC: Smithsonian Institution, 1998.
Smith, David. "The Effect of Artificial Surface." June 17, 1995. Clifford Blau's Website *Original Baseball Research.* http://users.erols.com/brak/index.html
Sports Turf Managers' Association. Website: http://www.aip.com/SIMA

AUSTRALIAN BASEBALL

Australia has had a modest, although growing, impact on American baseball. The most famous Australian-born player to perform in the major leagues is David Nilsson, a strong-hitting catcher who played for the Milwaukee Brewers from 1992 through 1999 before declaring free agency. With the growing importance of baseball in Australia and the burgeoning international scope of major league scouting, the American public will see many more Australian players in the near future.

Baseball began its growth period in Australia near the end of the nineteenth century thanks to Albert Spalding's tour in 1888–1889. Later tours included the New York Giants and Chicago White Sox in 1914, as well as American warship tours in 1905 and 1925 (with service teams playing Australian clubs). Since the 1970s, Australia has competed seriously in international baseball, winning the Bronze medal in the 1997 Intercontinental Cup held in Barcelona, Spain.

The Australian Baseball League started play in 1989, with eight current teams that feature some American players. In addition to Nilsson, other Australians have made the journey to play American baseball. The first Australian-born player in the twentieth century was Craig Shipley, who reached the majors in 1986 with the Dodgers and carved out a long, productive career as a utility infielder with several teams. Another well-known Australian player in the major leagues is relief pitcher Graeme Lloyd, traded by the Yankees to the Toronto Blue Jays after the 1998 season in the transaction that sent David Wells to the Blue Jays and Roger Clemens to the Yankees.

Additional Reading:

Adair, Daryl. *Sport in Australian History.* New York: Oxford University Press, 1997.

Cashman, Richard I. *Paradise of Sport: The Rise of Organised Sport in Australia.* New York: Oxford University Press, 1995.

Laidlaw, Robert. "Baseball in Australia." In *Total Baseball.* 6th ed. Ed. John Thorn et al. New York: Total Sports, 1999, pp. 549–558.

Vamplew, Wray. *The Oxford Companion to Australian Sport.* 2d ed. New York: Oxford University Press, 1994.

Vamplew, Wray, and Brian Stoddart, eds. *Sport in Australia: A Social History.* New York: Cambridge University Press, 1994.

AUTOGRAPHS

Autograph seekers are especially at home in popular culture. Anyone who doubts this might contrast the number of people rushing the stage after a symphony performance to get the conductor's autograph against the multitudes clamoring for the signature of a rock singer or sports star. In baseball, the tradition of seeking autographs has been long established: children waiting for players going to and from the ballpark, lining the fence separating spectators from the field to solicit autographs before the game, or mailing in requests. Players' attitudes toward signing autographs naturally vary, but most players view it as part of the job.

Youngsters—and some not so young—still succeed with such tactics, but giving autographs, like many other activities in America, has steadily yielded to the impulse to profit whenever and wherever possible. The most powerful symbol of this transformation is the sports show or convention, where current and former players sign autographs for set fees, usually after attendees have already paid for admission. Autographs, depending on the fame of the signer, can easily cost $5–10, with the price rising significantly if the signature is on a baseball rather than a photograph.

Many people find these commercial practices revolting because they contradict the perception of player-as-hero. The reality, of course, is that many children attending the show are also there for pecuniary reasons, that is, to buy autographs that may increase in value over the years—the same reason many now invest in baseball cards. This is another example of how baseball reflects change in American society.

See also: Business; Collectibles.

Additional Reading:

Baker, Mark Allen. *The Standard Guide to Collecting Autographs: A Reference and Value Guide.* Iola, WI: Krause, 1999.

Pelton, Robert W. *Collecting Autographs for Fun and Profit.* White Hall, VA: Betterway, 1987.

Zoss, Joel, and John Bowman. *Diamonds in the Rough: The Untold History of Baseball.* 1989. Reprint, Chicago: Contemporary Books, 1996.

AUTRY, ORVON GENE (1907–1998)

During his career, Gene Autry combined two aspects of our culture that are considered uniquely American and the most conducive to mythmaking: baseball and the Old West. His fame came first in Westerns as American cinema's singing cowboy. As owner of the California Angels baseball team he never enjoyed the same success as in film, yet he brought the same good-guy persona and won over the public's love and admiration a second time.

Autry began his career as a singer on the National Barn Dance radio show out of Chicago in the early 1930s but quickly traded in country for western. He achieved fame with the 1935 film *Tum-bling Tumbleweeds,* which featured a song by the same title that became an Autry hallmark hit. The film also established the musical Western, a film genre in which Autry starred through the 1950s. Autry also operated his own Wild West show, the Flying A Ranch Stampede, and recorded such famous songs as "(Spurs That) Jingle, Jangle, Jingle" (1942) and "Back in the Saddle Again" (1939), the latter enjoying a rebirth of popularity when it appeared on the soundtrack for the 1993 film *Sleepless in Seattle.*

With the advent of television, Autry had a new vehicle, which he utilized masterfully with his television series *The Gene Autry Show,* produced by Autry's own Flying A Productions. The show ran from 1950 to 1956, finally giving way to a changing audience demand for more adult Westerns such as *Gunsmoke* and *Have Gun, Will Travel.* Throughout his film and television work, Autry essentially played himself, often in a contemporary Western setting. Autry invariably was the good guy, living by a set of rules that he made explicit in his 10 "Cowboy Commandments" for the television show. Among other attributes, the cowboy-hero was always to be fair, honest, kind to children, respectful of women, tolerant of other races and religions, hard-working, free from alcohol and tobacco use, and patriotic. This "white-hatted" hero was, of course, a fictional fabrication, but the qualities were not unlike those associated in the public imagination with baseball heroes like Lou Gehrig.

Autry brought the same idealism, and his considerable wealth, to baseball in the 1960s as owner of the expansion Angels (originally the Los Angeles, later the California, Angels). The Angels began play in 1961 and moved to Anaheim in 1966. Autry sold the Angels to the Walt Disney Company at the end of 1996, and the club changed its name to the Anaheim Angels. Regrettably, Gene Autry enjoyed at best modest success with his baseball club. The Angels won three division titles in some 30 years, but they never advanced. They also tied for the division lead in 1995 but lost a one-game playoff to pitcher Randy Johnson and the Seattle Mariners. The closest that Autry's Angels came to greatness was in 1986, when after winning their division they led the Red Sox three games to one in the American League Championship Series and were within one pitch of winning the deciding fifth game and advancing to the World Series. The Angels, however, could not hold the lead and ended up losing the game and the series.

Gene Autry was a beloved figure to Angel players and fans. The team consistently wanted to win for their cowboy leader and even retired the number 26 in 1982 in honor of Autry as their "extra man" on the roster. When Autry died in 1998, he left behind an extraordinary American success story. He also left behind a long life that connected two of the most important areas of American popular culture: the Wild West and the national pastime of baseball.

See also: Connors, Kevin Joseph Aloysius; Films; Grey, Pearl Zane.

Additional Reading:

Aquila, Richard, ed. *Wanted Dead or Alive: The American West in Popular Culture.* Urbana; Chicago: University of Illinois Press, 1996.

Autry, Gene. *88 Complete Song Hits.* Chicago: Cole, 1939.

———. *Back in the Saddle Again.* Garden City, NY: Doubleday, 1978.

Green, Douglas B. "The Singing Cowboy: An American Dream." *Journal of Country Music* 7 (1978): 4–62.

Rothel, David. *The Gene Autry Book.* Rev. ed. Madison, NC: Empire, 1988.

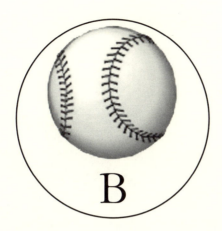

B

BABE RUTH LEAGUE

The Babe Ruth League is aptly named, for Babe Ruth sincerely enjoyed youngsters and was generous in signing autographs and otherwise interacting with them. He also was, as almost every American knows, a powerful home-run hitter, and many American boys and girls see themselves (at least in their imaginations) lofting towering drives over distant fences.

The Babe Ruth League began with players from 13 to 15 years of age in 1951, holding its first World Series in 1952. Other divisions followed: a Babe Ruth division for 16- to 18-year-old players in 1966, and in later years a 13-year-old Prep League, the Bambino Division for ages five to 12, the Rookie League (with Dr. Bobby Brown, former president of the American League, as its guiding spirit), later incorporated into the Bambino Division, and a 16-year-old Prep League. There also is an array of softball divisions for girls between the ages of five and 18.

The Bambino League consists of major, minor, rookie, and T-ball groups, the latter hitting off something like a tall tee.

Rookie League ball uses a pitching machine, softer baseballs, an extra outfielder and infielder, and 12 players per team (all of whom are in the batting order) in order to help young children overcome fear of the pitcher and the ball and to make sure that everybody plays.

Babe Ruth baseball is especially sensitive to young children with its relatively nonthreatening versions of the game. At the other end, many Babe Ruth graduates have gone on to star in the major leagues, including Bret Saberhagen, Mo Vaughn, Cal Ripken, Frank Thomas, and Paul Molitor.

See also: American Legion Baseball; Little League; Pony Baseball and Softball; Ruth, George Herman.
Additional Reading:
Babe Ruth League website: http://www.baberuthleague.org

BAKER, JOHN FRANKLIN (HOME RUN) (1886–1963)

Baseball has featured many magnificent sluggers, yet only one has had "Home Run" attached to his name: John Franklin "Home Run" Baker. Baker earned that

The Babe Ruth League was aptly named because Babe Ruth of the New York Yankees was interested in children and was always willing to talk to them and sign autographs. In this February 8, 1935, photograph, he signs autographs for two page boys on the roof of the Savoy Hotel during a visit to London. (Hulton Getty/Allsport)

nickname in the 1911 World Series. In Game 2, Baker homered off the great Giants pitcher Rube Marquard to propel his team to a 3-1 victory. The next game, against the even greater Christy Mathewson, Baker came to bat in the ninth inning, his team trailing 1-0, and hit another home run to tie the game. The Athletics eventually won 3-2 in 11 innings and went on to triumph in the World Series. From that day forward, the slugging third baseman has been known as Home Run Baker.

Baker was not a flash in the pan; his Hall of Fame credentials are real. Baker was a part of Connie Mack's talented $100,000 infield (with Stuffy McInnis, Eddie Collins, and Jack Barry) that helped the Athletics win four pennants and three World Series in five years. In the dead-ball era, Baker was home-run champion each year from 1911 to 1914, with totals of 11, 10, 12, and nine. He hit .307 over his career, with 96 home runs, hitting .363 in six World Series.

After the 1915 season, which Baker sat out in a contract dispute, Mack traded him to the Yankees. Baker played with the Yankees from 1916 to 1922 (taking off the 1920 season), a transitional time in major league history. The era of the home run was dawning, and the champion of the dead-ball years found himself on the same team with Babe Ruth, hero of the new power game. In 1921, Ruth hit 59 home runs, more than half the total that Baker accumulated in his entire career.

See also: Home Run; Mack, Cornelius Alexander.
Additional Reading:
Jordan, David M. *The Athletics of Philadelphia: Connie Mack's White Elephants, 1901–1954.* Jefferson, NC: McFarland, 1999.
Kuklick, Bruce. *To Everything a Season: Shibe Park and Urban Philadelphia, 1909–1976.* Princeton: Princeton University Press, 1991.
Mack, Connie. *My 66 Years in the Big Leagues: The Great Story of America's National Game.* Philadelphia: Winston, 1950.

BALLPARKS

The term "ballpark" reflects baseball's history, connotes certain continuing attitudes toward the game, and, for those given to critical appraisals, calls forth an ironic juxtaposition of past and present, of ideal as well as harsh reality. Now, after various images of how ballparks should be constructed, a strange, almost un-American attitude of "less is more" is shaping the nature of ballparks built for the twenty-first century.

Baseball historians usually identify the first modern baseball game as a contest between the New York Knickerbocker Base Ball Club and the New York Base Ball Club on June 19, 1846, at the Elysian Fields in Hoboken, New Jersey. The field, named for the realm of the blessed after death in Greek mythology, lay near the Hudson River, an open, grassy area among trees and bushes—an idyllic scene caught for all time in Currier and Ives and *Harper's Weekly* prints.

The rural setting of the Elysian Fields remains consistent with how Americans even today define the concept of any park. Parks, of course, are almost always urban rather than rural, because the city is where they are most needed: green oases amid urban constructions. They are therefore a metaphor for modern American life that is increasingly urban but longs to retain something of its earlier rural character and values.

The early ballparks retained a sense of the park. One of the great early ballparks was constructed for the Chicago White Stockings (the current Cubs) at the site of a former dump along the tracks of Illinois Central Railroad near Lake Michigan. The ballpark was named, not surprisingly, Lakefront Park and became for its short life (1878–1884) perhaps the finest baseball facility of its time. Lakefront included 18 luxury boxes complete with armchairs and curtains to protect fans from the elements, proving, for students of contemporary stadiums that feature high-priced skyboxes, the biblical claim that there is nothing new under the sun. When the National League set minimum distances from home plate to outfield walls, however, the White Stockings were forced to abandon the undersized Lakefront Park.

Baseball clubs came to realize that there could be more to the home-field advantage than loyal fans cheering on their favorites. Ballpark maintenance thus became a device to win games, much like pitching, fielding, and hitting. The Baltimore Orioles mastered this concept in Oriole Park. Managed by Ned Hanlon and featuring such speedy stars as John McGraw, Wee Willie Keeler, and Hughie Jennings, the Orioles emphasized the stolen base, squeeze play, and hit-and-run. The team's groundskeeper, Thomas Murphy, learned to keep the outfield grass long to slow down enemy drives, the dirt around home plate packed tight to maximize the bounce of the famous "Baltimore chops," and foul lines heavily chalked so the Oriole bunters could beat out bunts that crept along the friction-producing chalk toward frustrated infielders or veered back into play as the opponent waited fruitlessly for the bunt to slide foul.

Wooden bleachers were the standard until near the end of the first decade of the twentieth century. Although often attractive and quite serviceable, they posed certain problems. Fire was always a worry. The most famous ballpark fire may have been the conflagration that engulfed the Polo Grounds in New York in 1911, but fires had long been a hazard. Some 20 ballparks burned in the 1890s. In addition, wooden facilities always conveyed a sense of the temporary when owners wanted to secure lasting loyalties from their fans.

The first ballparks constructed of concrete and steel opened in 1909—Shibe Park, home of Connie Mack's Philadelphia Athletics; and Forbes Field, home of the Pittsburgh Pirates. The former was named after co-owner Ben Shibe and renamed Connie Mack Stadium in 1953; the latter was named after John Forbes, a Scottish general in the French and Indian War known as "Old Ironsides," a favorite military hero of Pirates owner Barney Dreyfuss. Forbes Field was especially innovative, including ramps leading to the upper-level seats, elevators to speed the wealthy to their third-story luxury boxes, spacious clubhouse facilities, and a prohibition on signs (except for war stamps and bonds during the two world wars). Shibe Park continued to house the Athletics, until they moved to Kansas City for the 1955 season, and the Phillies through the 1970 season. It now is a vacant lot. Forbes Field was home to the Pirates until June 28, 1970, also hosting the Negro League Grays from 1939 until 1948. It probably was appropriate that both of these grand ballparks, which opened in the same year, also ended their careers at approximately the same time. Mementos of Forbes Field still stand among buildings at the University of Pittsburgh.

The first two decades of the twentieth century were a golden age of ballpark construction, giving birth, in addition to Shibe and Forbes, to Comiskey Park in Chicago for the White Sox (1910); the new Polo Grounds for the New York Giants after the fire of 1911; Navin Field, later known as Tiger Stadium, in Detroit (1912); Fenway Park for the Boston Red Sox (1912); Ebbets Field, home of the Brooklyn Dodgers (1913); and the Chicago Cubs' Wrigley Field (1914). All of these stadiums continued to welcome their hometown fans until at least the late 1950s.

After the 1957 season, the Giants and Dodgers fled westward. Ebbets Field was demolished in 1960; the Polo Grounds had a brief second life featuring the expansion New York Mets in 1962 and was demolished two years later. Ironically, the same wrecking ball was used to bring down the two ballparks, in a sense uniting in death the two teams that in life had been passionate, even bitter, rivals. Comiskey Park, known in its early days as the "Baseball Palace of the World," survived through 1990. The 1999 season was the last for Tiger Stadium, leaving Fenway Park the oldest surviving park. That status, however, is likely to be short-lived, as plans are to build a replacement. In a nod to history and continuity in fan loyalty, the Red Sox management is planning to keep a "Green Monster" as the left-field wall in the new park. Someday probably even Wrigley Field, with its ivy-covered walls, will fall to the clamor for newness.

That desire for the new, however, is proving more complex than in past decades. The 1999 season witnessed the end of what had once been the most obvious example of newness in baseball parks—the Houston Astrodome. A radical construction in the mid-1960s, with its domed roof and AstroTurf, and billed as the "Eighth Wonder of the World," it increasingly fell into disfavor. Its replacement, Enron Field, harkens back to the past in a new way, as baseball executives and architects find ways to appeal to fans' continuing sense of baseball as both old and new. A retractable roof will permit real air, but on especially hot days a closed roof and air-conditioning will satisfy fans' desire for limited realism. And there is real grass. In an extraordinary trip into the past, the stadium is built next to and merges with the Union Railroad Station. Fans enter the stadium through the station's walkways, and if they want to visit the team's offices they will find them inside the station proper.

Baseball planners are also finding that small is sometimes better. The new ballpark in Houston seats about 12,000 fewer people than did the Astrodome. Other new ballparks—PacBell in San Francisco, Comerica Park in Detroit— also have decreased seating capacity. There may be fewer people at games, but the difference is more than offset by increasing the number of palatial luxury boxes, for which teams can charge high prices, knowing that many of the boxes are being paid for by companies that get tax write-offs for the expense.

Thus in a sense everybody wins—except maybe the taxpayer. A major criticism of modern ballparks is that increasingly the taxpayers, not the owners, are footing the bill for construction and that sweetheart deals permit owners to operate the ballparks virtually cost-free. The argument for such cozy deals among baseball owners and local and state politicians is that a new ballpark brings expanded revenue, new jobs, and increased prestige to the city. How much this is true continues to be debated, as each side trots out statistics to argue its side of the case. Whether owners are successful with their new-old approach to ballparks may depend on the extent to which Americans in the twenty-first century can fuse their own infatuation with the new to their psychological longing for a return to an earlier way of life symbolized by baseball—and how well owners can connect with both inclinations simultaneously.

See also: Business; Myth; Night Baseball; Polo Grounds; Ritual; Wrigley Field; Yankee Stadium.

Additional Reading:

Cagan, Joanna, and Neil deMause. *Field of Schemes: How the Great Stadium Swindle Turns Public Money into Private Profit.* Monroe, ME: Common Courage, 1998.

Gershman, Michael. *Diamonds: The Evolution of the Ballpark.* Boston: Houghton Mifflin, 1993.

Lowry, Philip. *Green Cathedrals.* Reading, MA: Addison-Wesley, 1992.

Richmond, Peter. *Ballpark.* New York: Simon and Schuster, 1993.

Ritter, Lawrence S. *Lost Ballparks: A Celebration of Baseball's Legendary Fields.* 1992. Reprint, New York: Penguin, 1994.

BANKS, ERNEST (ERNIE, MR. CUB) (1931–)

Ernie Banks joined the Chicago Cubs late in the 1953 season. The first African American in the history of the franchise, Banks came straight from the Kansas City Monarchs of the Negro American League and immediately established himself as the Cubs' regular shortstop. In 1955, his second full season, the tall, slim, right-handed hitter became the first shortstop in major league history to hit 40 home runs in a season. He produced four more seasons of over 40 home runs (1957–1960) and earned Most Valuable Player awards in 1958 and 1959. Banks also was an accomplished fielder, establishing a new record for shortstops in 1959 with a fielding percentage of .985.

Banks switched from short to first base in 1962 because of a troublesome knee and continued hitting home runs, accumulating 512 by the time he brought his 19-year career to a close in 1971. Banks spent his entire career with the Cubs, a team mired in mediocrity during most of those years, and never got to play in a

Chicago Cubs first baseman Ernie Banks (right) is presented the YMCA Athlete of the Year award by American TV show host Art Linkletter, 1967. (Archive Photos)

World Series, a great injustice for the man endeared to all as "Mr. Cub."

Ernie Banks was as much beloved for his unceasing enthusiasm for the game as for his hitting. He often announced, sincerely, that he wished he could play a doubleheader rather than the single game scheduled. The fact that he achieved such popularity in Chicago, one of the nation's more racially divided cities, was all the more striking. Banks, however, transcended racial and ethnic backgrounds and was admired by any person who considered himself a true fan of the game. While still a player, Banks even ran for Eighth Ward alderman as a Republican; although defeated, he continued to maintain his customary enthusiasm for Chicago and the Cubs. Mr. Cub was inducted into the Baseball Hall of Fame in 1977.

See also: African Americans; Negro Leagues; Wrigley Field.
Additional Reading:
Banks, Ernie, and Jim Enright. *Mr. Cub.* Chicago: Follett, 1971.
Enright, Jim. *Chicago Cubs.* New York: Macmillan, 1975.
Wilbert, Warren, and William Hageman. *Chicago Cubs: Seasons at the Summit.* Champaign, IL: Sagamore, 1997.

BARBER, WALTER LANIER (RED) (1908–1992)

Red Barber had one of the great careers in baseball broadcasting and along the way added a number of vivid phrases to American English. Always a professional and thoroughly honest, even when that honesty cost him jobs, Barber brought to his work a college degree from the University of Florida, a southern accent from his youth in Mississippi and Florida, a flair for language and vivid description, and a firm commitment to objective reporting. Never a popularizer of a specific team, he believed in neutrality. He was reporting on baseball contests, not rooting for the home team, and he wanted his audience to know the truth.

Barber began his broadcasting career with the University of Florida's radio station and was hired to announce the Cincinnati Reds games in 1934, at which time he had yet to see a major league game. Barber brought an egg timer to the broadcast booth to remind himself to give the score often for listeners who had just tuned in, just one sign of his careful preparation and attention to detail. He soon began doing pregame and postgame shows, pioneering a practice that has become commonplace. When he re-created games, he insisted on not deceiving listeners and made sure they knew precisely how he was reporting the game.

Barber's honesty led him to report as well on attendance, a practice that did not please owners and cost him his final broadcasting position, with the New York Yankees, in 1966. Barber had earlier left the Reds for the Dodgers in 1939 and joined the Yankees in 1954. He later had a radio show (having always preferred radio to television as more stimulating to the imagination), *Fridays with Red* on National Public Radio. The popular show ran for 20 years. Barber also served as director of CBS Sports for nine years.

In the popular mind, however, Red Barber remains best known for his "Barberisms"—phrases that vividly captured baseball moments. Anyone in a favorable position was "sitting in the catbird seat," and a fight or hot argument was a "rhubarb," phrases that worked their way into the popular lexicon. Barber had a keen ear for memorable phrases, and when he would hear one he would file it away mentally for later use. The "catbird seat" expression reportedly was uttered by a poker player whose two aces placed him in that advantageous position and enabled him to defeat Barber. The "rhubarb" reference came from a bartender by way of other sportswriters who did not see much use for it. The bartender later reported that a bowl of rhubarb was such a mess that it reminded him of a brawl.

The borrowing continued when the famous humorist James Thurber entitled one of his stories "The Catbird Seat." In the story, a Mrs. Ulgine Barrows so hammers a mild accountant, Mr. Martin, with questions ("Are you tearing up the pea patch?" "Are you scraping around the bottom of the pickle barrel?" "Are you sitting in the catbird seat?") that he considers suicide. A fellow employee tells Martin that Barrows must be a Dodger fan who has been listening to Red Barber. A lot of people listened to Red Barber, and both baseball and the language were the richer for his work.

See also: Brooklyn Dodgers; Language, Baseball; New York Yankees; Radio Broadcasting; Television Broadcasting.
Additional Reading:
Barber, Red. *The Broadcasters.* New York: Dial, 1970.
———. *Rhubarb in the Catbird Seat.* Garden City, NY: Doubleday, 1968.
Edwards, Bob. *Fridays with Red: A Radio Friendship.* New York: Simon and Schuster, 1993.
White, G. Edward. *Creating the National Pastime: Baseball Transforms Itself, 1903–1953.* Princeton: Princeton University Press, 1996.
Whiteford, Mike. *How to Talk Baseball.* 1983. Reprint, New York: Galahad Books, 1996.

THE BASEBALL ENCYCLOPEDIA

The Baseball Encyclopedia occupies a special place in the history of baseball statistics. It was not the first baseball encyclopedia, or even the first important one (a position filled by *The Official Encyclopedia of Baseball,* published by A. S. Barnes in 10 editions from 1951 to 1979), but it took baseball records and statistics to a new level of sophistication and accuracy when it first appeared in 1969, published by Macmillan.

Early editions of *The Baseball Encyclopedia* earned the monumental reference work an unofficial title: "The Bible of Baseball." Two early figures crucial to its birth were Lee Allen, historian of the Baseball Hall of Fame, and John Tattersall, who had accumulated voluminous records of nineteenth-century baseball. Although Allen died in 1969, the work progressed, and the first edition was published that year. This encyclopedia was the first to make use of computer technology, employing a vertical exit program that ensured accuracy by verifying individual data against a balanced bottom line. For example, individual totals of hits by batters must produce a total that equals the sum of all hits allowed by pitchers in a given year. If not, the source of the discrepancy must be tracked down. During the gathering and entering of data, "new" players were discovered, and "phantom" players (often given existence through a mistyping of an actual player's name) were discovered. In some cases, long-established records were revised.

As the editions piled up, the reputation of *The Baseball Encyclopedia* declined, with a newer competitor, *Total Baseball,* gradually supplanting it as the definitive word on baseball statistics. After the tenth edition, Macmillan sold the rights to the encyclopedia to IDG Books Worldwide, which set about completing an eleventh edition for publication in April 2000.

See also: Statistics; *Total Baseball.*

Additional Reading:

The Baseball Encyclopedia. 10th ed. New York: Macmillan, 1996.

Thorn, John, Pete Palmer, and Joseph M. Wayman. "The History of Major League Baseball Statistics." In *Total Baseball.* 6th ed. Ed. John Thorn et al. New York: Total Sports, 1999, pp. 615–629.

BAUMAN, JOE WILLIS (1922–)

Babe Ruth . . . Roger Maris . . . Sammy Sosa . . . Mark McGwire? No, Joe Bauman remains the greatest home-run hitter in the history of professional baseball. It happened in 1954. Bauman had quit professional ball after the 1948 season. Running a gas station must have seemed a more solid way to earn a living. Nonetheless, the baseball pull was strong, and he returned in 1952 with Artesia (New Mexico) in the Class-C Longhorn League. By 1954, he was playing with another New Mexico team in the same league, the Roswell Rockets.

Bauman was a superstar from the moment he first joined the Longhorn League. He hit .375 in 1952, with 50 home runs

and 157 RBIs, and followed that performance with figures of .371, 53, and 141 the following year. The 1954 season, however, put him in the record books. Bauman batted .400, scored 188 runs, walked 150 times, compiled 199 hits, drove in 224 runs, and smashed 72 homers for his Roswell team, surpassing the previous professional mark of 69 home runs set by Joe Hauser in 1933 with Minneapolis and tied by Bob Crues of Amarillo in 1948. Hauser had hit 63 homers for Baltimore (then in the minor leagues) in 1930.

Bauman never made it to the big leagues, nor did Crues. Hauser, however, had several productive years with Connie Mack's Philadelphia Athletics in the 1920s before a fractured kneecap sent him back to the minors for his greatest home-run hitting years.

So as new generations of sluggers flex their muscles and swing for the fences, they should remember that they are swinging not just against Ruth, Maris, Sosa, and McGwire but also against the often forgotten Joe Bauman.

See also: Home Run; Minor Leagues.

Additional Reading:

Salin, Tony. *Baseball's Forgotten Heroes: One Fan's Search for the Game's Most Interesting Overlooked Players.* Chicago: Masters, 1999.

Sullivan, Neil J. *The Minors: The Struggles and the Triumph of Baseball's Poor Relation from 1876 to the Present.* New York: St. Martin's Press, 1990.

BELL, JAMES THOMAS (COOL PAPA) (1903–1991)

Being "cool" in American parlance is a good quality to possess, connoting excellence accompanied by a mannered indifference, not seeming to take the matter too seriously. The term "papa," as applied to Bell, seems to have been used as a "cooler" synonym for man, something akin to "dude." Bell earned his nickname—both parts of it—as a teenager in

1922, when he coolly struck out the dangerous hitter Oscar Charleston.

A sore arm proved a blessing in disguise, turning Cool Papa from pitcher to center fielder, where he could showcase his speed. It was said of him, with some exaggeration, that he could flip the light switch and jump into bed before the room went dark. In reality, he was enormously fast, able consistently to beat out two-hoppers in the infield for hits, and capable of going from first to third on a bunt. Against Indians pitcher Bob Lemon in a game against white All-Stars, he scored all the way from first base on a bunt.

Bell played on three of the greatest teams in Negro League history: the St. Louis Stars in the late 1920s and early 1930s, the Pittsburgh Crawfords in the mid-1930s, and the Homestead Grays in the 1940s. An outstanding hitter, he was still able to bat .391 in 1946, sitting out the final game of the season in order not to qualify for the batting title, thus ensuring the title for Monte Irvin and helping the younger player to attract interest from the majors. Cool Papa was offered a playing contract by the St. Louis Browns in 1951; then in his late forties, he declined, agreeing instead to scout for them. He was elected to the Hall of Fame in 1974.

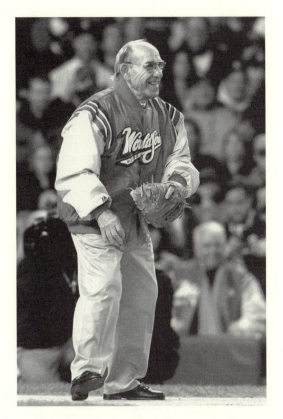

Former Yankees catcher Yogi Berra prepares to catch the ceremonial first pitch before the start of game four of the World Series between the New York Yankees and the Atlanta Braves at Yankee Stadium, October 27, 1999. (Jed Jacobsohn/ Allsport)

See also: African Americans; Irvin, Monford; Negro Leagues.

Additional Reading:

Holway, John B. *Blackball Stars: Negro League Pioneers.* Westport, CT: Meckler, 1988.

———. *Voices from the Great Black Baseball Leagues.* New York: Dodd, Mead, 1975.

O'Neil, Buck. *I Was Right on Time: My Journey from the Negro Leagues to the Majors.* 1996. Reprint, New York: Fireside, 1997.

Riley, James A. *The Biographical Encyclopedia of the Negro Baseball Leagues.* New York: Carroll and Graf, 1994.

BERRA, LAWRENCE PETER (YOGI) (1925–)

Yogi Berra was one of the great catchers in major league history. He also achieved fame beyond his considerable achievements as a player and manager, becoming something of a cult figure in American society. Not coincidentally, he followed Casey Stengel along several paths, both on the baseball field and linguistically. Both within the game itself and within the popular perception of the game, Stengel was a mentor and precursor to Berra. Although Berra never equaled Stengel's success as a manager, his effect on the English language has been more lasting.

Berra joined the Yankees in 1946, his catching skills still raw. Stengel made him the Yankees starting catcher in 1949, and Berra became one of the guiding forces behind Stengel's great teams of the 1950s. He developed into an accomplished defensive catcher and an effective handler of pitchers in addition to starring at the plate despite a habit of swinging at any pitch remotely close to the strike zone. During his 19 years as a player, he hit .285 with 358 home runs and a total of 2,150 hits. Eleven times he stroked 20 or more homers, including a span of 10 seasons in a row. Five times he drove in 100 or more runners. Berra's accomplishments did not go unrewarded, as he earned three Most Valuable Player Awards—in 1951, 1954, and 1955.

Although Berra was one of the three top stars on the 1950s Yankees (with center fielder Mickey Mantle and ace southpaw Whitey Ford), he was known as a character as much as a player. Yogi Berra delighted in reading comic books and gave the impression of having learned English at the feet of the master of mangled language, Casey Stengel. Berra's malapropisms are legion, and he has furnished the language with many memorable lines that have become permanently fixed in American syntax and semantics. The following are easily recognized as Yogiisms: "It ain't over till it's over"; "It gets late early there"; "Baseball is 90 percent mental; the other half is physical"; "I didn't really say everything I said"; and "It's déjà vu all over again."

Berra became manager of the Yankees in 1964 when his erstwhile mentor was managing the crosstown Mets. Berra guided his club to the American League pennant, although the team lost the World Series to the St. Louis Cardinals. Inexplicably, Berra was fired and replaced by Johnny Keanne, manager of the victorious Cardinals. The Yankees, however, dropped to sixth place the following year and remained among the also-rans for a decade. After his firing, Berra rejoined Stengel, remaining as a coach with the Mets through 1971, even though Stengel was pushed out as the Mets manager during the 1965 season. In 1972, Berra once again assumed a position previously held by Stengel: manager of the Mets, a position he held until 1975, winning a pennant in 1973.

Berra returned to the Yankees, serving the team as coach for eight years and becoming manager again in 1984. The Yankees finished third that year, and after the team got off to a slow start in 1985, Berra was fired just 16 games into the season. The firing was especially bitter for Berra, who remained alienated from owner George Steinbrenner and the Yankees until a reconciliation was effected in 1999.

As part of the process of welcoming Berra back, Yogi Berra Day was held at Yankee Stadium on July 18, 1999. Among those in attendance was Don Larsen, who pitched a perfect game (with Berra catching) during the 1956 World Series and threw the day's ceremonial first pitch (to Berra, of course). Both Berra and Larsen then witnessed a memorable pitching performance by Yankee right-hander David Cone, who pitched the sixteenth perfect game in major league history.

See also: Language, Baseball; New York Yankees; Steinbrenner, George Michael, III.
Additional Reading:
Berra, Yogi. *Yogi: The Autobiography of a Professional Baseball Player.* Garden City, NY: Doubleday, 1961.
———. *Yogi: It Ain't Over.* New York: McGraw-Hill, 1989.
———. *The Yogi Book: I Really Didn't Say Everything I Said!* New York: Workman, 1998.
Pepe, Phil. *The Wit and Wisdom of Yogi Berra.* New York: Hawthorn, 1974.
Schoor, Gene. *The Story of Yogi Berra.* Garden City, NY: Doubleday, 1976.

BLACK SOX SCANDAL

Perhaps the most famous baseball team in popular culture is the Chicago White

Sox of 1919, dubbed the "Black Sox" in the wake of scandal. The team achieved its notoriety by taking money (not much, it turned out) to throw the World Series to the Cincinnati Reds. What might have been just a tawdry exercise in greed and betrayal, however, proved more complex than that, and the story has taken on mythic proportions. Guilt and innocence remain difficult to apportion, and the event became the "Garden of Eden" moment in baseball history.

Eight players were involved in one way or another: pitchers Eddie Cicotte and Lefty Williams, first baseman Chick Gandil, shortstop Swede Risberg, third baseman Buck Weaver, center fielder Happy Felsch, left fielder Shoeless Joe Jackson, and utility infielder Fred McMullin. Jackson was the greatest player on the team, one of the most devastating hitters of all time and a certain Hall of Famer. Cicotte won 29 games in 1919, had won 28 in 1917, would win 21 more in 1920; he finished his career with 209 wins and a 2.38 ERA—close to Hall of Fame material. Williams was just coming into his own, winning 23 games in 1919 and 22 the following year. Weaver, an outstanding offensive and defensive player, was listed by Babe Ruth on his all-time all-star team. Felsch finished with a career .293 average, his best seasons probably still ahead of him; Gandil was a dangerous hitter; and Risberg, in his mid-twenties, was just approaching his peak. McMullin was in on the fix because he had overheard a conversation about it.

Gandil appears to have originated the idea of throwing the Series in conversations with gamblers, but other players would not have joined without their animosity toward owner Charles Comiskey. Although a former player, Comiskey was a notorious tightwad, badly underpaying his players except for second baseman

Eddie Collins. In addition, he cut financial corners any way he could where players were concerned, forcing them, for example, to pay to clean their own uniforms. Cicotte, the ace of the staff and a highly respected veteran, was the key to the fix. He was susceptible to Gandil's proposal, feeling betrayed by Comiskey, who ordered Cicotte benched during August, thereby depriving the pitcher of several starts as he inched toward the 30-win total that would have triggered a promised $10,000 bonus. He finished one win short, and Comiskey refused to pay. Most of the players felt taken advantage of by Comiskey (the reserve clause giving them no real alternative to accepting what Comiskey offered except to leave the major leagues), which absolved them in their own minds of loyalty to the club.

The machinations by gamblers remain unclear, but apparently several were involved in making arrangements, including former major league pitcher Sleepy Bill Burns, Boston bookmaker Joseph Sullivan, former featherweight champion Abe Attell, and Arnold Rothstein. History has judged Rothstein, known as "Mr. Bankroll," to be the key figure behind the fix. F. Scott Fitzgerald in *The Great Gatsby* (published in 1925) would fictionalize Rothstein as Meyer Wolfsheim, "the man who fixed the World's Series back in 1919."

The promised payoff for the players was $100,000 total, but less than half was ever paid. With the money not coming through, at least some of the conspirators gave up on the fix after the sixth game and tried to win. Rookie pitcher Dickie Kerr had kept the team in the Series by winning twice, while Cicotte and Williams each lost two games. In Game 7, Cicotte won, and the White Sox appeared ready to retrieve the Series from the Reds. Williams, however, lost again, yielding to threats made against his wife.

Gambling was pervasive in baseball, and rumors had circulated about the Series before it began. It took no longer than the first game to raise suspicions within the White Sox camp. Catcher Ray Schalk, thoroughly honest with a burning desire to win, knew something was not right about Cicotte's pitching. Manager Kid Gleason, himself a former pitcher, also sensed what was going on but did not want to admit his feelings, especially to himself. Late that night, Gleason visited Comiskey in the owner's hotel room, both men having received telegrams warning of the fix. Comiskey then talked with John Heydler, president of the National League, and the two powerful baseball men went to the room where Ban Johnson, American League president, was sleeping. Johnson and Comiskey had once been friends and partners in creating the American League but in recent years had turned into bitter enemies. Johnson insultingly dismissed Comiskey's concerns as the "whelp of a beaten cur," his feelings against Comiskey blinding him to the reality of the situation.

After the second loss, tempers flared. Schalk attacked Williams, who had kept crossing up his catcher by throwing fastballs when Schalk called for curves, and Gleason went after Gandil. Meanwhile, famed Chicago sportswriter Hugh Fullertin, sensitive to the pre-Series rumors he was hearing, had asked former baseball great Christy Mathewson to watch the first game with him, looking for indications of attempts to throw the game. After the second game, Fullerton and fellow sportswriter Ring Lardner were convinced, yet no one wanted to make public charges for fear of harming baseball.

Had the baseball owners not panicked and hired Judge Kenesaw Mountain Landis as commissioner to replace the three-man National Commission that previously had run baseball, everyone might have escaped serious consequences resulting from the thrown Series. In fact, the 1920 season began with the White Sox intact (with the exception of Gandil, who had left the team). Comiskey in fact issued some significant pay increases, perhaps fearing a repeat disaster. Even when a Chicago grand jury moved from investigating reports of Cubs throwing some games to exploring the 1919 World Series, the matter might have been contained. Indictments were issued, and Jackson and Cicotte confessed. Yet after the confessions mysteriously disappeared, the players were found not guilty at trial. Comiskey still had his team, one that would have contended for years.

Judge Landis, however, was now in place as commissioner. Despite the jury finding, Landis threw the eight players out of the game for life. Landis had been hired to clean up baseball, and he was determined to do that—as well as demonstrate his authority. The story, of course, was far from over, and it likely will never be over, so long as baseball is played.

The Black Sox remain alive in history, literature, films, and the myth of baseball. Eliot Asinof's *Eight Men Out* (1963), a careful examination of the World Series scandal, inaugurated a new era of inquiry and reassessment. Millions of Americans were introduced to the story of the Black Sox through three of the finest baseball movies ever made: *The Natural* (1984), based on Bernard Malamud's 1952 novel of the same title; *Eight Men Out* (1988), based on the Asinof book; and *Field of Dreams* (1989), a film version of W. P. Kinsella's *Shoeless Joe* (1982). In these modern retellings, Comiskey becomes more the villain than do the players, who at worst are viewed as making bad judgments. The Pete Rose case at the end of the 1980s refocused public attention on Jackson and the Black Sox, and Ted

Williams continued to stoke the fire by arguing for Jackson's reinstatement.

The story is all the more compelling for its tragic characters, especially Jackson and Buck Weaver. Weaver never took a dime, gave his best in the Series, and was guilty only of not being able to determine whether he should say anything. Like Gleason and Comiskey, he hoped that the players would turn it around, and he certainly is no more guilty than the owner who knew what was happening and later tried to cover it up. Jackson twice refused the proposal, finally received $5,000, but always claimed that he played to win. The statistics support that claim, as he set a Series record with 12 hits, drove in six runners, and committed no errors. Immediately after the Series, he tried to see Comiskey but was not admitted by the owner.

The 1919 World Series scandal changed baseball history by leading to the commissioner system, but its contribution to the myth of baseball is even greater: It was the moment when sin transformed the Elysian fields of baseball's past. In truth, gamblers and gambling had been there from the start. It's just that their corrupting influence was not openly acknowledged until the Black Sox's fall from grace.

See also: Fiction; Field of Dreams; Films; Gambling; Jackson, Joseph Jefferson; Kinsella, William Patrick; Landis, Kenesaw Mountain; Myth; Rose, Peter Edward; World Series.

Additional Reading:

Asinof, Eliot. *Eight Men Out: The Black Sox and the 1919 World Series.* New York: Holt, 1963.

Axelson, Gustaf W. *"Commy": The Life Story of Charles A. Comiskey.* Chicago: Reilly and Lee, 1919.

Gaughran, Richard. "Saying It Ain't So: The Black Sox Scandal in Baseball Fiction." In *Cooperstown Symposium on Baseball and the American Culture* (1990). Ed. Alvin L. Hall. Westport, CT: Meckler, 1991, pp. 38–56.

Gropman, Donald. *Say It Ain't So, Joe: The True Story of Shoeless Joe Jackson and the 1919 World Series.* 1979. Reprint, New York: Lynx, 1988.

Riess, Steven A. *Touching Base: Professional Baseball and American Culture in the Progressive Era.* Rev. ed. Urbana: University of Illinois Press, 1999.

BOUTON, JAMES ALAN (JIM) (1939–)

Jim Bouton's *Ball Four* was published in 1970, two years after the former star pitcher left the Yankees, and was an instant sensation.

Ball Four was one of the first tell-alls about baseball. Chronicling Bouton's 1969 season with the Seattle Pilots and Houston Astros, the book also says much about his former team, the Yankees, and some of baseball's most beloved figures, including Mickey Mantle and Whitey Ford. Bouton attempted to describe baseball the way players experience the game, in language players really use. So Bouton wrote about Mantle's drinking and how he sometimes pushed kids aside when they wanted autographs. And how Ford would cheat by scratching the ball with his wedding ring or loading it with mud. And, of course, that players sometimes cheated on their wives.

The result was a book that fascinated fans and angered many baseball people. Commissioner Bowie Kuhn tried to force Bouton to sign a statement saying that the book was false, Mickey Mantle developed a long-standing resentment against Bouton, sportswriters blasted the book, and the San Diego Padres burned a copy in the visitors' clubhouse when Bouton was pitching. The Yankees, after Bouton's retirement, routinely excluded him from Old-Timers' Day. But the book sold millions of copies, becoming the best-selling sports book ever.

If fans have a less naive view of players because of *Ball Four* and books that followed, they have a truer understanding of the game and those who play it. There is always something to be said for truth. And the Yankees have finally become reconciled with their prodigal son. On July 25, 1998, Bouton returned, at George Steinbrenner's invitation, to Yankee Stadium for Old-Timers' Day.

See also: Kuhn, Bowie K.; Mantle, Mickey Charles; New York Yankees; Steinbrenner, George Michael, III.

Additional Reading:

Anderson, Dave. "Bouton's Day Was Long Time in Coming" (syndicated column from *New York Times*). *Portland (Maine) Press Herald,* July 27, 1998, p. D-1.

Bouton, Jim. *Ball Four.* 20th anniv. ed. New York: Macmillan, 1990.

———. *I'm Glad You Didn't Take It Personally.* New York: Dell, 1972.

Bouton, Michael. "For Bouton, Let Bygones Be Bygones." *New York Times,* June 21, 1998, sec. 8, p. 13.

BRICKHOUSE, JOHN BEASLEY (JACK) (1916–1998)

Jack Brickhouse was one of the most popular, successful, and versatile sportscasters in America. An Illinois native, he made Chicago his home and broadcast various Chicago teams (White Sox, Cubs, Bears, and Bulls) plus other sports events during a career lasting more than 40 years. A man of wide interests, from Shakespeare to politics, he interviewed six U.S. presidents and Pope Paul VI, helping to establish not only his reputation as one of America's most respected broadcasters, in or out of sports, but also the reputation of the sportscasting profession.

Brickhouse was born in Peoria and briefly attended Bradley University before landing a radio job in Peoria. Bob Elson, then handling White Sox games, brought Brickhouse in to work with him at WGN in 1940. Eight years later, after serving in the Marines, Brickhouse became lead announcer at WGN-TV. He continued to broadcast White Sox games through 1967 and Cubs games until he retired following the 1981 season, when he was succeeded by his friend Harry Caray.

Always a strong booster of the home team, Brickhouse presided at the microphone during the White Sox's pennant season of 1959, their only pennant since the 1919 Black Sox scandal. He had a long-standing, if largely private, feud with manager Leo Durocher, whom he blamed for the Cubs' collapse during the stretch run of 1969, when the Cubs went from 9.5 games ahead with six weeks to play to finish eight games behind the New York Mets. Brickhouse was inducted into the Baseball Hall of Fame in 1983.

See also: Caray, Harry; Durocher, Leo Ernest; Radio Broadcasting; Television Broadcasting; Wrigley Field.

Additional Reading:

Brickhouse, Jack. *Thanks for Listening.* South Bend, IN: Diamond Communications, 1986.

Petterchak, Janice A., and Jerome Holtzman. *Jack Brickhouse: A Voice for All Seasons.* Lincolnwood, IL: NTC, 1996.

BROOKLYN DODGERS

"Dem Bums," as the Brooklyn Dodgers were lovingly called, were the source of endless frustration, despair, hope, and, occasionally, joy for those denizens of Brooklyn who frequented Ebbets Field or listened to the Dodgers on the radio. The Dodgers developed a reputation as wacky losers, entertaining but certain to fail in the end. The old saying that "hope springs eternal in the human breast" rang true for Dodger fans, who began each year, much against their better judgment, hoping that finally the Dodgers would win. "Wait 'til next year" became the autumn cry, and the spring and autumn anthems sounded across the streets and buildings of Brooklyn

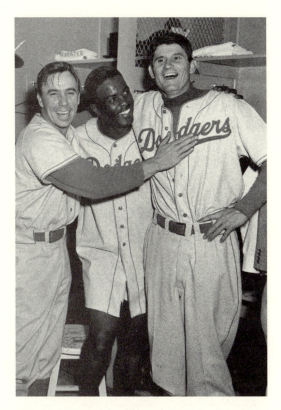

*Brooklyn Dodgers, from left, Pee Wee Reese,
Jackie Robinson, and Preacher Roe are a happy
trio in the clubhouse after the Dodgers beat the
Yankees 5-3 in the third game of the World Series
at Yankee Stadium in New York City, October 3,
1952. (AP Photo)*

for decades. Finally, in 1955 the Dodgers
won their first World Series; ironically—
and tragically, Dodger fans would say—
just two years later the beloved Bums
were heading west to Los Angeles.

Actually, the story of the Dodgers is
not really a story of losers, despite the
popular perception. Perhaps the pes-
simistic view derived from the habitual
sense of Brooklyn itself as an inferior
borough of New York City, a mere bed-
room suburb from whence middle-class
workers journeyed daily to Manhattan to
work and to which they returned at
night, removed from the places where
really important events transpired. Or it
may have been the peculiar dialect that
characterized inhabitants of Brooklyn, a

tough-guy vernacular spoken by people
for whom others were almost always social superiors—or so it seemed in the
public imagination. It also was a borough
noted for its long-lived neighborhoods
and for the tendency of Brooklynites to
spend their entire lives in the homes in
which they were born. This continuity of
place surely contributed to the enduring
loyalty through thick and thin (primarily,
of course, through thin) of Brooklyn inhabitants toward their Bums.

In reality, Brooklyn has a long tradition. It was there that Dutch colonists settled in the 1630s and in the following
decade established the hamlet of Breuck-
elen. Where baseball is concerned,
Brooklyn has an especially distinguished
history. The powerful Brooklyn Atlantics
ended the Cincinnati Red Stockings's unbeaten streak in 1870. Ten years earlier,
the Brooklyn Excelsiors had conducted
the first baseball tour, traveling by train
through several eastern states. An early
baseball observer and advocate was the
young editor of the *Brooklyn Daily
Eagle,* a man who would become the
most American of poets—Walt Whitman.
The Brooklyn entry in the American Association overcame the St. Louis Browns
to win their league championship in
1889. The following year Brooklyn
switched to the National League and won
another pennant. At this time, the nickname was the Bridegrooms, as six team
members had recently undergone their
entry into marital bliss. Brooklyn, by then
known as the Superbas after a popular
vaudeville act, added another pennant in
1899. The year 1900 brought another pennant and a sort of world championship, as
the Superbas defeated second-place Pittsburgh for the Chronicle-Telegraph Cup, a
precursor to the World Series.

As the twentieth century dawned,
Charles Ebbets, who had begun with the
team as a ticket seller, became majority

owner. Unfortunately, the team began a 12-year sojourn in the second division in 1903. The team, now called the Dodgers—apparently from the practice of dodging the omnipresent trolley cars in Brooklyn—moved into new Ebbets Field in 1913. Wilbert Robinson became manager the following year and led the Dodgers to National League pennants in 1916 and 1920, only to lose the World Series each time. For the most part, the next 20 years were marked by consistent losing, punctuated by the death of Charles Ebbets on opening day in 1925. The new Dodger president, Ed McKeever, caught a cold that turned into pneumonia and died about five weeks later.

Wilbert Robinson's tenure as manager (1914–1931) cemented the wacky reputation of the Dodgers. Newscasters loved "Uncle Robbie" because he was always good for an entertaining quote. Once, becoming a bit perturbed by their comments, he let them choose the lineup. Having Casey Stengel on the team compounded the wackiness. Robinson promised to catch a ball dropped from a plane; fortunately, Stengel intervened to turn what might have meant the demise of his manager into a great practical joke. When the "ball" struck Robbie, it was a grapefruit splattering over him, which he took for blood, much to the amusement of the players surrounding him. Robinson supposedly once played a man named Cox because he could not pronounce the name of the player he actually wanted. Afflicted by a tendency to forget people's names, he often would refer to them generically as "whosus." Strangely enough, Uncle Robbie concluded his managing career, which included an earlier season in Baltimore, one win above .500.

Outfielder Babe Herman, an outstanding hitter who batted .381 and .393 in 1929 and 1930, was just as bad a fielder.

It was a baserunning blunder on August 15, 1926, though, that made him the stuff of legend. With the bases loaded, Herman drove the ball to right field. The runner scored from third, but the other two runners, because of the fear by the player on second that the ball would be caught, ended up on third. Herman meanwhile had been charging around the bases with his head down when he also landed on third base. The incident gave rise to a vaudeville routine where one performer says that the Dodgers have three men on base. The response: "Which base?"

The player on second base during the three-men-on-third blunder was pitcher Dazzy Vance. A talented future Hall of Famer who played on terrible teams, Vance delighted in breaking team rules, even establishing a club whose membership was limited to players who could successfully break training rules without being caught. He also had a practice of slitting the right sleeve of his uniform shirt so that when he wound up and delivered the pitch, the flapping strips of cloth created an illusion of multiple arms flinging the ball.

People like Uncle Robbie, Casey Stengel, Babe Herman, and Dazzy Vance earned the love of Dodger fans even when the team was consistently losing. Perhaps the most loved of all Dodger teams, though, were those of the late 1940s and 1950s, the teams of Duke Snider, Gil Hodges, Pee Wee Reese, Roy Campanella, Don Newcombe, and Jackie Robinson. The Dodgers had been resurrected in the late 1930s by general manager Larry MacPhail and manager Leo Durocher, winning a pennant in 1941. By 1947 Branch Rickey was running the team, and Jackie Robinson was at second base, the first African American player in the modern history of major league baseball. Three years later, Rickey left for

Pittsburgh, and Walter O'Malley replaced him. The outstanding Rickey and O'Malley teams of the late 1940s and 1950s won six pennants in 10 years.

This great success of the Dodgers in the postwar years did not stop fans from still thinking of them as Dem Bums. The Dodgers were a much more serious team than the stars of the previous decades, and they were very talented. Yet they kept falling short of the mountaintop. Each year, it seemed, they led the National League only to lose the World Series, usually to the crosstown Yankees. Frustration continued—it just developed later in the season. That would change, however, in 1955, thanks to a young left-handed pitcher named Johnny Podres.

Podres twice turned back the powerful Yankees in the 1955 Series to lead his team to the world championship. It was the first victory ever for the Dodgers in the modern World Series. Even another Series loss the following year to the Yankees and Don Larsen's perfect game could not erase the feeling that an enormous corner had been turned in Dodger fortunes. And around that corner—unfortunately, for Brooklyn fans—was Los Angeles. After finishing third in the league in 1957, the Dodgers moved to California. The era of the Bums was over. They were now the glamorous Dodgers of movie stars and surfers, while Brooklyn had been spurned and deserted. One of the great baseball love affairs was over.

See also: Barber, Walter Lanier; Campanella, Roy; Durocher, Leo Ernest; Expansion; Rickey, Wesley Branch; Robinson, Jack Roosevelt; World Series.

Additional Reading:

Goodwin, Doris Kearns. *Wait Till Next Year: A Memoir.* New York: Simon and Schuster, 1997.

Holmes, Tommy. *Dodger Daze and Knights: Enough of a Ball Club's History to Explain Its Reputation.* New York: D. McKay, 1953.

Kahn, Roger. *The Boys of Summer.* New York: Harper and Row, 1972.

Kavanagh, Jack, and Norman Macht. *Uncle Robbie.* Cleveland: SABR, 1999.

Laforse, Martin W. "Baseball and Urbanism." In *Popular Culture and American Life: Selected Topics in the Study of American Popular Culture.* Martin W. Laforse and James A. Drake. Chicago: Nelson-Hall, 1981, pp. 163–228.

BROWN, MORDECAI PETER CENTENNIAL (THREE FINGER, BROWNIE) (1876–1948)

Mordecai Brown was born in Indiana in the nation's centennial year of 1876, hence his third name. He came from rural America, typical of many major-leaguers around the turn of the century, but he was atypical in both the disability and talent that he brought with him. As a boy of seven he lost most of his right index finger and had his little finger paralyzed in a corn-shredding accident on an uncle's farm. The accident gave him his nickname: "Three Finger."

It would take another accident, however, to get Brown to the pitcher's mound, this time to another person. While he was playing third base on a semipro team, the pitcher suffered an injury, and Brown was summoned to relieve. He was successful and remained a pitcher throughout his Hall of Fame career. In fact, the injury to his fingers altered his grip on the ball in such a way that his curveball broke sharply, somewhat like a knuckleball.

Brown was an ace pitcher on the great Chicago Cubs teams that featured Tinker, Evers, and Chance and won four pennants and two World Series between 1906 and 1910. He had six seasons of winning at least 20 games and compiled a lifetime 2.06 ERA. He also doubled as a relief pitcher; statistics retroactively compiled indicate that he would have led the league in saves in four of his six 20-win seasons. Other highlights included beating the Giants in 1908 in the pennant-deciding makeup game resulting from Fred Merkle's famous "boner" play; many classic matchups against Christy Mathewson, with Brown having the edge, 13-11; and helping the Chicago Whales, managed by Joe Tinker, win the Federal League championship in 1915.

See also: Hitless Wonders; Merkle Boner; Tinker to Evers to Chance.

Additional Reading:

Ahrens, Art. *The Cubs: The Complete Record of Chicago Cubs Baseball*. New York: Collier, 1986.

Brown, Warren. *The Chicago Cubs*. New York: Putnam's, 1946.

Holtzman, Jerome. *The Chicago Cubs Encyclopedia*. Philadelphia: Temple University Press, 1997.

Wilbert, Warren, and William Hageman. *Chicago Cubs: Seasons at the Summit*. Champaign, IL: Sagamore, 1997.

BUSINESS

The business of baseball is big business—make that Big Business. Those who lament that fact might not be aware that the game has been a business at least since the 1860s. The Cincinnati Red Stockings, who roared through the 1869 season undefeated, are usually credited with being the first professional team. In fact, Cincinnati's paying of players was a prime reason for the team's success. Money draws quality, and quality translates into success. Baseball is not an anomaly in this regard. Any popular activity that draws people to participate and/or watch is sure to include considerable potential for putting revenue in someone's pockets. In the nineteenth century, both baseball and most businesses were relatively small. As the twentieth century progressed, small businesses, while not dying out, gradually

yielded to ever larger enterprises. From mom-and-pop groceries to chain supermarkets, from local hardware stores to megastores. Even institutions such as hospitals and schools have moved in the same direction, growing larger and squeezing out smaller counterparts. As baseball has grown in popularity, it has also grown in size, including the quantity of money changing hands.

When they consider the financial dimensions of major league ballclubs, fans are likely to think first of player salaries, which is natural given that fans care more about the performers on the field than about owners and unfamiliar management figures. Players throughout major league history have been paid better on an annual basis than most Americans, but until recent decades their salaries were modest if one considers the short active careers of most players.

The average salary of big league players in 1898 was $2,200. That figure had jumped to $7,531 by 1929, the effect of the growing popularity of the Babe Ruth–era game and the revenue that fans brought to the owners' cash boxes. The average salary actually dropped, however, to just above $6,000 in 1933 as the country struggled with the Great Depression. By 1943, after fluctuations, compensation was not much higher than 10 years earlier—$6,423. Wartime prosperity, though, affected baseball as it did the rest of the country, increasing the mean baseball wage to $11,294 in 1946. The figure would climb gradually through the next few decades, to $13,288 in 1950; $19,000 in 1967; and $44,676 in 1975. A minimum salary had been established in 1947 at $5,500. This had increased by only $500 by 1967, then inched up until it reached $21,000 in 1978.

The arrival of free agency in 1975 had a major impact on salaries, which

Los Angeles Dodgers president Peter O'Malley congratulates Hideo Nomo of Japan after the Dodgers signed the right-handed pitcher to a minor league contract as Don Nomura, left, Dodgers general manager Fred Claire, and Director of Minor League Operations Charlie Blaney look on, February 13, 1995. Nomo is the first Japanese-born player to sign a major league contract without first playing in Japan's Central or Pacific League. (J. D. Cuban/Allsport)

both the owners (in their view negative) and the players (positive, of course) had predicted. Between 1975 and 1977, the average salary came close to doubling, jumping from $44,676 to $76,066. After arbitration decisions found that owners had colluded to inhibit movement of free agents and depress salaries, the average wage leaped from $438,729 in 1988 to $597,537 in 1990 to $1,014,947 in 1992.

Player salaries continue to rise. The average salary at the start of the 1999 season was $1,720,050, an increase of over 19 percent from the previous season. The top individual salaries were $11,949,794 (Albert Belle), $11 million (Pedro Martinez), $10,714,286 (Kevin Brown), and $10,600,000 (Greg Maddux). By comparison, Mark McGwire, who had hit 70 home runs the previous season, seemed positively underpaid at just $8,333,333.

The minimum salary by 1999 had risen to $200,000, higher than the average salary in 1981. Approximately 42 percent of players were millionaires by opening day 1999.

Teams' payrolls have therefore skyrocketed. The highest team payroll in 1999 was approximately $85,100,000 (for the World Series–champion Yankees); followed by $79,200,000 (Dodgers), $78,500,000 (Orioles), and $74,900,000 (Rangers). At the bottom in team salaries were the Expos with $17,300,000. Next lowest were the Marlins, who had engaged in a massive salary-dumping binge after winning the World Series in 1997 ($18,800,000), and the Twins ($19,100,000).

Major league owners routinely claim poverty as a result of increasing salary costs. Fourteen teams stated that they lost money in 1998. The Dodgers, for example, said that they lost approximately $11,900,000 with total revenue of $108 million. The Red Sox lost $7,600,000. The Yankees, in contrast, had revenue of $175,500,000 and showed a profit of about $23 million. Other profitable clubs included the expansion Arizona Diamondbacks ($22,500,000) and Tampa Bay Devil Rays ($20,600,000).

Profits and losses are hard to pin down, however, because many factors can increase a team's value even if it shows a loss on paper. Owners, starting with Bill Veeck, learned how to use the tax code to their advantage. The legendary former owner of the Browns, Indians, and White Sox started the practice of depreciating player contracts. An owner who also owns a television station may sell broadcasting rights to himself at below-market value, taking a supposed loss that will reduce his tax obligation. Then there are the stadiums.

From the 1970s on, there has been a steady shift from privately financed to publicly funded stadiums. State and local governments subsidized owners with as much as $11 billion dollars for stadiums in the 1990s. A variety of revenue-raising initiatives have been used to support construction of stadiums, for example, lotteries in Baltimore and cigarette and liquor taxes in Cleveland. With stadium costs running to $600 million or more, owners increasingly are finding politicians willing to foot much if not all of the bill with the hope that a new stadium will keep the team from moving to another city, draw other business investments into the city, and add more jobs to the local economy. Critics of public financing argue instead that a new stadium seldom actually boosts the local economy and is a form of corporate welfare.

New stadiums (often built with limited expense to the club owners) are a major

reason why the values of baseball teams continue to rise in the face of supposed monetary loss. The Baltimore Orioles sold for $12 million in 1979; for $70 million in 1989; and, after the new stadium opened, for $173 million in 1993. The Cleveland Indians were valued at $81 million in 1993 and, again after a new stadium, at $125 million in 1996. The profitability of ballclubs (especially when it comes time to sell) is demonstrated by expansion in the modern era. From 1903, stretching for over half a century, the number of major league clubs remained constant at 16. Today there are 30 franchises. It also is in the financial interest of owners to welcome new clubs because of the large joining fee shared by the owners—$95 million paid by the Marlins and the Rockies each in 1993, $150 million each for the 1998 Devil Rays and Diamondbacks.

In fact, there is big money to be made by club owners. Lucrative television contracts are one source. A single TV contract, negotiated with ESPN in December 1999, will eventually earn major league baseball $800 million over six years. Only about 50 percent of revenue comes from gate receipts, which are supplemented by money from food, beverages, programs, and souvenirs. A more recently developed revenue stream flows from luxury boxes, an especially good deal for the team, which can charge a high price for each box (in some cases more than $100,000 per year), knowing that the lessee usually is a corporation that will write the cost off as a business expense. Owners may also sell personal (or permanent) seat licenses, which give the purchaser the right to buy tickets for specific seats in future years. Then there is the huge income (if usually a one-time source) from selling the right to name the stadium. The rights to name the new Miller Park in Milwaukee (by

Miller Beer, whose parent company is to-bacco manufacturer Philip Morris) report-edly brought the Brewers $40 million.

Yet the basic fact is that baseball is big business, which introduces elements that were present in earlier eras but to a much lesser degree. The large stadiums may be quite appealing to fans, the food more varied and possibly more appetizing, the restrooms cleaner and more abundant. Players earn as much money as their tal-ents and the market will bear—something that other people at least theoretically have the right to do. Yet attending a game is expensive (average ticket prices having increased from $8.64 in 1991 to $14.91 in 1999), and the lure of big bucks made possible by free agency draws many players from team to team, lessening the ability of fans to identify with their home-town teams. And all of that tax-free help given to owners may mean less tax money to address problems involving education, housing, and poverty. But baseball as big business is here to stay.

See also: Autographs; Ballparks; Cards, Base-ball; Collectibles; Expansion; Free Agency; Labor-Management Relations; Law; Miller, Marvin James; Negro Leagues; Night Base-ball; Radio Broadcasting; Television Broad-casting.

Additional Reading:
Cagan, Joanna, and Neil deMause. *Field of Schemes: How the Great Stadium Swindle Turns Public Money into Private Profit.* Monroe, ME: Common Courage, 1998.
Quirk, James, and Rodney Fort. *Hard Ball: The Abuse of Power in Pro Team Sports.* Prince-ton, NJ: Princeton University Press, 1999.
Rosentraub, Mark. *Major League Losers: The Real Cost of Sports and Who's Paying for Them.* Rev. ed. New York: BasicBooks, 1999.
Scully, Gerald W. *The Business of Major League Baseball.* Chicago: University of Chicago Press, 1989.
Zimbalist, Andrew. *Baseball and Billions: A Probing Look Inside the Big Business of Our National Pastime.* Rev. ed. New York: Basic-Books, 1994.

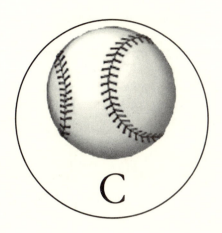

C

CAMPANELLA, ROY (CAMPY) (1921–1993)

Roy Campanella joined the Brooklyn Dodgers in 1948, one year after Jackie Robinson broke the color barrier with the same club, and became one of the great catchers in the major leagues. Even more significantly, he was the first African American catcher to make it in the big leagues, establishing himself at a position analogous to quarterback in football. The catcher calls all the pitches, and Campanella's pitchers were white in his first year, although Don Newcombe joined the team in 1949. To assume such leadership on the top National League team of the era required not only considerable playing ability but also the right personality.

Campy brought all the necessary attributes at the plate and behind it. A powerful and consistent hitter, as well as an outstanding defensive catcher, Campanella three times won the National League Most Valuable Player Award, in 1951, 1953, and 1955. His greatest season was 1953, when he set major league records for most home runs (41) and runs batted in (142) by a catcher. He also recorded the most putouts (807) by a catcher.

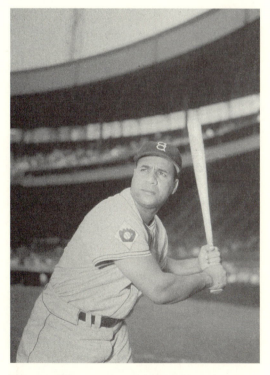

Portrait of baseball player Roy Campanella, Brooklyn Dodgers catcher, standing with bat in an empty stadium, 1950s (Archive Photos)

Campanella was fond of saying, "You gotta have a lot of little boy in you to be a good ballplayer." He never lost that boyish enthusiasm, which contributed to his leadership. His zest for playing and his ease in communicating with other players earned him respect. He would keep up a steady chattering with hitters and generally ignore racial comments. As Jackie Robinson was the right person to integrate the major leagues, Roy Campanella was the right man to integrate the crucial position of catcher. Unfortunately, Campanella did not necessarily gain full recognition for his accomplishments from Robinson.

By 1957, Campanella's skills were eroding. The Dodger great had started playing at 15 in the Negro Leagues and had put in almost a full career there before signing with the Dodgers. Now in his tenth year in the majors, he was 35 and a veteran of two decades of playing professional baseball, sometimes year-round. Limited to 103 games because of injuries in 1957, he hit just .242 with 13 home runs and 62 RBIs. Nonetheless, he was looking forward to joining the Dodgers for their inaugural season in Los Angeles and driving home runs over the short left-field wall in the new stadium. Tragedy, however, intervened on a January 1958 night when he lost control of his car on a slick spot and slammed into a telephone pole. The accident left him a quadriplegic permanently confined to a wheelchair.

Roy Campanella compiled a ten-year record of 242 home runs, 856 RBIs, and a .276 batting average while helping the Dodgers win five National League pennants and the 1956 World Series—the Brooklyn Dodgers' first and only world championship. He also left behind a vast storehouse of goodwill as one of the most popular Dodgers ever to play. His election to the Hall of Fame in 1969 was a tribute to his accomplishments as a player. Not to be overlooked, however, is the role he played in integrating major league baseball. The way that he played the game helped ease the transition of

African Americans into the majors, setting the example for such catchers as Elston Howard, the first African American to play for the Yankees, and Johnny Roseboro, who followed Campanella behind the plate for his Dodgers.

See also: African Americans; Brooklyn Dodgers; Disabilities; Negro Leagues.
Additional Reading:
Campanella, Roy. *It's Good to Be Alive.* Boston: Little, Brown, 1959.
Goodwin, Doris Kearns. *Wait Till Next Year: A Memoir.* New York: Simon and Schuster, 1997.
Kahn, Roger. *The Boys of Summer.* New York: Harper and Row, 1972.

CANADIAN BASEBALL

Although hockey is Canada's own national pastime, Canada has had a significant impact on American baseball and culture. It was in the more racially tolerant atmosphere of Montreal that Branch Rickey launched his effort to integrate major league baseball by assigning Jackie Robinson to the Montreal Royals in 1946. Major league baseball also moved away from its U.S.-only attitude with the addition of the Montreal Expos to the National League in 1969 and the Toronto Blue Jays to the American League in 1977. Both clubs forced American fans to think more globally, a process that continues to advance, although slowly, with increased numbers of players coming from abroad and at least some discussion of adding other teams beyond the 50 states.

Robinson starred for the Royals in 1946, leading the International League in batting (.349), runs scored (113), and stolen bases (40) while playing shortstop. The following year, he moved up to the Dodgers, and baseball was finally integrated. African American teammates of Robinson's would follow from Montreal, including Roy Campanella and Don Newcombe.

Although the Montreal club thereby had an especially important impact on American society, it was far from the only minor league team in Canada. The Toronto Maple Leafs also had a long and distinguished record of success, winning several pennants and Junior World Series. The Maple Leafs were the Triple-A farm club of the Boston Red Sox, sending such players as Reggie Smith, Bob Montgomery, and Sparky Lyle to the Sox. Other minor league teams include four recent Triple-A entries (the Ottawa Lynx in the International League and the Calgary Cannons, Edmonton Trappers, and Vancouver Canadians of the Pacific Coast League) along with other clubs at lower levels.

From organized baseball's earliest days, Canadians have journeyed south to play in the majors. According to writer Neil Munro, 179 Canadians had played in the majors by 1995, with that number obviously continuing to rise. Perhaps the greatest of all was pitcher Ferguson Jenkins, who from 1965 through 1983 won 284 games, posted seven 20-win seasons (six in a row), and won a Cy Young Award. Other noteworthy Canadian major-leaguers include Reggie Cleveland (1969–1981), who pitched in 428 games, almost equally divided between starts and relief appearances; John Hiller (1965–1970, 1972–1980), who overcame a heart attack to become one of the finest relief pitchers of his time; Phil Marchildon (1940–1942, 1945–1950), a tail-gunner with the Royal Canadian Air Force during World War II who was shot down on his twenty-sixth mission and ended up in a German prisoner-of-war camp; George "Twinkletoes" Selkirk (1934–1942), the man who replaced Babe Ruth in right field for the Yankees and had several productive seasons as a hitter; and Larry Walker, one of the finest players in the majors at the end of the twentieth century.

As for the two Canadian major league teams—the Expos and Blue Jays—both have fielded fine teams, with the Expos winning their division in 1981; the Blue Jays finished first in their division five times and captured the World Series in 1992 and 1993. In the recent age of major-market dominance, the Expos found it increasingly difficult to compete financially, losing many top players to free agency; in Toronto, the Blue Jays were rebuilding into a legitimate contender.

See also: Expansion; Major Leagues; Robinson, Jack Roosevelt.

Additional Reading:
Humber, William. *Cheering for the Home Team: The Story of Baseball in Canada.* Erin, Ontario, Canada: Boston Mills, 1983.
———. *Diamonds of the North: A Concise History of Baseball in Canada.* Toronto: Oxford University Press, 1995.
Munro, Neil, and STATS, Inc. *Canadian Players Encyclopedia.* Skokie, IL: STATS, 1996.
Pietrusza, David. *Baseball's Canadian-American League: A History of Its Inception, Franchises, Participants, Locales, Statistics, Demise, and Legacy, 1936–1951.* Jefferson, NC: McFarland, 1990.

CANCER

Cancer remains one of the most feared diseases in society, even as diagnosis, treatment, and recovery rates improve. Although cancer is by no means an automatic sentence of death or even an illness that necessarily impacts either significantly or permanently one's manner of living, the disease retains its ominous presence in the American public.

Cancer, of course, has claimed many former baseball players. Babe Ruth is one of the most prominent former stars to die of the disease. And on rare occasions, active players, such as pitcher Jim Umbricht of Houston in 1964, will succumb to cancer. The disease claimed managers Fred Hutchinson of the Reds (1964) and Dick Howser of the Royals

(1987). On the whole, however, cancer was seen as a rare threat to those actively participating in the game. That changed in the late 1990s.

Brett Butler, star center fielder with the Los Angeles Dodgers, entered a hospital for a tonsillectomy in May 1996 and found that he had cancer that would require surgery. Before the season ended, Butler was back playing for the Dodgers. However, a broken wrist ended his season four days later. He came back to play one more year before retiring.

Eric Davis of Baltimore returned from colon cancer to bat .327 with 28 home runs and 89 RBIs for the Orioles in 1998. While the Yankees were closing in on the world championship that same year, Darryl Strawberry, their slugging left fielder, underwent surgery for colon cancer. As Strawberry attempted to regain his strength and position with the Yankees in spring training 1999, more major-leaguers were diagnosed with cancer: slugging first baseman Andres Galarraga of the Braves, young third baseman Mike Lowell of the Marlins, and manager Joe Torre of the Yankees.

All of these individuals were given favorable prognoses and could look forward to resuming their careers. If they wished to see a promising example of life after cancer, they needed look no farther than outfielder Darrin Jackson, who was diagnosed with cancer in 1987 and recovered to play for more than another decade. As his colleagues were finding that their next adversary was not a pitcher or hitter but cancer, Jackson, at 35, was competing for a position with the Chicago White Sox.

Despite promising futures for these individuals, the sudden prominence of cancer among major-leaguers was a disturbing development for players and fans. Sports figures usually are among the most physically talented and best-conditioned individuals in the country. They seem almost invincible. Add to their physical condition the money that they make, where even fringe players often are millionaires, and the fame that they enjoy, and they seem above the trials and tribulations of ordinary mortals.

In their rational moments, even the most ardent of fans, of course, realize that neither fame, fortune, nor physical conditioning can protect a person from the onslaught of a variety of common problems, including disease. Fans have always known that, but they have not often thought about it. The reality has hit home in recent years. Baseball players may live lives, to quote Shakespeare, of "such stuff as dreams are made on," but they also, again in Shakespeare's eternal phrasing, must endure the same "mortal coil" that afflicts all humans.

See also: New York Yankees; Quisenberry, Daniel Raymond; Ruth, George Herman; Torre, Joseph Paul.

Additional Reading:
Altman, Roberta. *The Cancer Dictionary.* New York: Facts on File, 1992.
Bertino, Joseph R. *Encyclopedia of Cancer.* 3 vols. San Diego: Academic Press, 1997.
Cancer Sourcebook. Detroit: Omnigraphics, 1990.
Nightengale, Bob. "Nothing Keeps This Man Down: Darryl Strawberry Battles Back from Colon Cancer Surgeries." *USA Today Baseball Weekly,* March 3–9, 1999, pp. 8–11.
Overfield, Joseph M. "Tragedies and Shortened Careers." In *Total Baseball.* 5th ed. Ed. John Thorn et al. New York: Viking, 1997, pp. 155–170.

CARAY, HARRY (ca. 1914–1998)

"Holy cow!" There are many ways to measure fame, but certainly one method is for the public to identify a verbal expression with its creator or popularizer. Harry Caray's excited "Holy cow!" punctuated many a moment during his 53 years as a baseball broadcaster, and as a result fans are not likely to forget one of the most popular radio and television broadcasters in the history of all sports.

Harry Caray was born Harry Christopher Carabina in St. Louis somewhere between 1914 and 1920. The Chicago Cubs media guide listed 1920, a date that Caray probably favored. Orphaned at the age of ten, he was reared by an aunt. He auditioned for his first job as a radio announcer at 19 and developed his skills at stations in Joliet, Illinois, and Kalamazoo, Michigan. Before long he was announcing major league games.

The résumé is impressive enough: St. Louis Cardinals, 1944–1969; Oakland A's, 1970; Chicago White Sox, 1971–1981; Chicago Cubs, 1982–1998. Caray, of course, had his faults. With the Cardinals, he seemed to go out of his way to belittle certain players, such as star third baseman Ken Boyer. He lasted only one year with Oakland, as his flamboyant lifestyle and owner Charles Finley's frugality proved oil and water. Caray drank and smoked more than was good for him, and he reveled perhaps too much in his fame.

Nonetheless, Caray became a baseball legend, with a folksy touch that endeared him to fans, perhaps because he enjoyed telling it as he saw it. On the air, he would often identify individuals in attendance who were celebrating an important event like a birthday or anniversary, and he dramatized home runs: "It might be, it could be, it is—a home run!" His style attracted millions of fans and led to many awards. Broadcasting Cardinals games, he was named Baseball Announcer of the Year seven years in a row by *The Sporting News*. In the late 1980s, he was elected to the National Sportscasters and Sportswriters Hall of Fame and enshrined in the broadcasters wing of the Baseball Hall of Fame in Cooperstown.

Because Caray was a throwback in a game that loves its past, his final job, with the Cubs, was a perfect marriage.

The shirt-sleeve crowd and ivy-covered walls of the last major league park to add lights were just what the doctor ordered—not, of course, the doctor who ordered Caray to reduce his drinking to one drink per day, with the patient obeying the letter of the law with about the largest glass he could find. Caray was so popular in the Windy City that he opened a restaurant, Harry Caray's, that became a favorite watering hole for baseball fans and assorted others.

Even a stroke in 1987 could not silence Caray's seventh-inning renditions of "Take Me Out to the Ball Game." He was preparing for another year at the microphone when he took ill at a Valentine's Day dinner in 1998 and died a few days later. His grandson, Chip Caray, followed him into the broadcast booth for the 1998 season. (A son, Skip, has been a longtime announcer for the Atlanta Braves.) At Caray's funeral, the closing hymn was appropriate, although Harry had to let others carry the tune, for this time it was more like the bottom of the ninth.

See also: Brickhouse, John Beasley; Finley, Charles Oscar; Radio Broadcasting; "Take Me Out to the Ball Game"; Television Broadcasting.

Additional Reading:

Caray, Harry, with Bob Verdi. *Holy Cow!* New York: Villard Books, 1989.

McCarver, Tim, with Danny Peary. *The Perfect Season: Why 1998 Was Baseball's Greatest Year.* New York: Villard Books, 1999.

Stone, Steve, with Barry Rozner. *Where's Harry? Steve Stone Remembers His Years with Harry Caray.* Dallas: Taylor, 1999.

Wolfe, Rich, and George Castle. *I Remember Harry Caray.* Champaign, IL: Sports Publishing, 1998.

CARDS, BASEBALL

Few items associated with baseball are more reflective of changes in the game itself, and in American society, than baseball cards. Always essentially commercial,

"Caruthers (P. Brooklyn)" as depicted on an Old Judge and Gypsy Queen cigarette card (Ann Ronan Picture Library)

ice-cream, and (from the 1930s on), bubble-gum companies gradually supplanted tobacco manufacturers as purveyors of baseball cards.

World War II brought production of baseball cards to a halt, but the practice of distributing cards with bubble gum resumed after the war and proceeded full-bore throughout the remainder of the century. At the same time, the cards, formerly trade cards, came to be known as trading cards, reflecting their appeal to America's youth, who collected the cards and often traded them to friends and schoolmates while collecting favorite players.

During the 1950s, Topps Gum Company of Brooklyn bested such competing companies as Leaf and Bowman, dominating the industry throughout the 1970s. That dominance would end, however, as other companies, observing the rising value of baseball cards and the growing practice of collection as investment, broke Topps's hold on the baseball-card business. A major turning point occurred in 1967 when Jefferson Burdick published *The American Card Catalog,* a guide describing cards and listing their value. Before long there were card dealers, buy-and-sell shops, magazines devoted to assessing changing values, and card shows with former and current stars signing autographs for a fee. In September 1996, a Honus Wagner card brought $640,500 at auction, and the world had seen the holy grail of baseball cards and bottom lines.

The final decades of the twentieth century thus witnessed a growing association of baseball cards with the almighty dollar, with baseball itself riding the wave of free agency, escalating salaries, and government funding of new stadiums into the world of megabusiness. Some level of innocence was sacrificed, and the new approach to baseball cards reflects that loss of innocence. The child who buys a complete set of cards and

their degree of commercialism has ebbed and flowed over a century-plus.

The first cards depicting baseball players were produced and distributed in the 1860s as "trade cards," that is, cards promoting specific trades or, more precisely, items sold by companies plying certain trades, such as sporting goods, cigars, and cigarettes. By the 1880s, small cards were inserted into packages of tobacco products. During the first four decades of the twentieth century, the audience for these cards shifted more from adults to children and adolescents, as candy, stores them away unhandled to preserve their mint condition, who devours magazines exclusively devoted to the dollar value of baseball cards, who would never even think about flipping cards toward a wall in a competition with friends, who would be horrified at pink gum sticking to the back of a Mark McGwire, is missing something important about what baseball cards can be.

Yet collecting baseball cards, having started with tobacco-consuming adults, is coming full circle. Even as young people still constituted the primary market, many adults joined the craze, perhaps in an attempt to recapture their youth. Yet most are in it for profit, either as an ongoing business or to build up savings for the future. It may be unfortunate that people are doing for money what earlier they had done for love of the game—but that clearly is a major dimension of baseball at the end of the twentieth century.

See also: Business; Collectibles; Wagner, John Peter.

Additional Reading:

Boyd, Brendan C. *The Great American Baseball Card Flipping, Trading, and Bubble Gum Book*. Boston: Little, Brown, 1973.

Clark, Steve. *The Complete Book of Baseball Cards*. New York: Grosset and Dunlap, 1976.

Halper, Barry, and Bill Madden. "Baseball Collecting." In *Total Baseball: The Official Encyclopedia of Major League Baseball*. 5th ed. Ed. John Thorn et al. New York: Viking, 1997, pp. 549–553.

Lemke, Bob. *1999 Standard Catalog of Baseball Cards*. 8th ed. Iola, WI: Krause, 1998.

Thorn, John, and the National Baseball Hall of Fame and Museum. *Treasures of the Baseball Hall of Fame: The Official Companion to the Collection at Cooperstown*. New York: Villard, 1998.

CARTWRIGHT, ALEXANDER JOY (1820–1892)

No single person invented baseball, but the one who came closest to designing the modern game was Alexander Joy Cartwright. A bank teller in Manhattan, Cartwright regularly joined a group of friends in recreational play in a vacant lot. The men were primarily professionals, including a physician, merchants, brokers, and a U.S. marshal. On September 23, 1845, at Cartwright's instigation, they created the New York Knickerbocker Base Ball Club, named after a volunteer fire company to which Cartwright and some of the others belonged.

The rules for this version of baseball included a number of changes that would become permanent fixtures of the game: a diamond-shaped infield, three swinging strikes (completely missing the ball) to make an "out," foul lines, three outs to an "inning," and requiring a base runner to be tagged or "forced" rather than hit with the thrown ball. This type of ball became the so-called New York game.

Before long, the Knickerbockers began journeying to Hoboken, New Jersey, to play their games in a spacious picnic area called the Elysian Fields, named after the site in Greek mythology where the blessed reposed in complete happiness after death among green groves, softly glowing sunlight, and sweet-tasting air. The name seems especially appropriate in light of the heavy mythological weight that the game now carries, including the story about Abner Doubleday supposedly inventing baseball at Cooperstown, New York, in 1839.

The Knickerbockers' first official contest against another team occurred on June 19, 1846, when they lost 23-1 to the New York Base Ball Club, with their star player, Alexander Cartwright, umpiring rather than playing. The fact that neither side saw anything wrong with one team's player umpiring demonstrates the gentlemanly nature of early baseball. Participants usually were gentlemen, and the Knickerbockers' club was precisely that—

a sporting club. After a game, the players would relax with wine and a good meal, often accompanied by their wives and sweethearts. During the game, all participants were to act in a manner befitting their class: no arguing with umpires, and certainly no profanity. Any slipups automatically drew fines.

The type of game played by this inaugural "modern" baseball team proved immensely popular and quickly spawned many other teams. Although the basic rules established by Cartwright and his fellows would continue, their view of baseball as a gentleman's game quickly dissipated as men from all walks of life turned to baseball for pleasure and, before long, profit.

Gold was discovered in California in 1849, and Alexander Cartwright soon headed West. His journey to the goldfields was slow, however, for he kept stopping to teach his favorite game to miners, wagon-train pioneers, and Native Americans. He found California not to his liking and soon set sail for China and then Hawaii. Cartwright remained in Hawaii for the rest of his life, teaching baseball to schoolchildren and becoming a prosperous businessman. Among other enterprises, he started a trading company, a bank, a hospital, and, returning to an early interest, a fire department. Even before his death in 1892, Cartwright had been largely forgotten by the American baseball world; but as major league baseball set about celebrating what it believed was the one-hundredth anniversary of the game, in 1939, the story of Alexander Cartwright came to light through his grandson Bruce. The Hall of Fame, created in the "centennial" year, was slow to acknowledge Cartwright's role, but acknowledge it they finally did—making Cartwright a member of the Hall of Fame for "meritorious service."

See also: Hall of Fame and Museum; Major Leagues.
Additional Reading:
Alexander, Charles C. *Our Game: An American Baseball History.* New York: MJF Books, 1991.
Seymour, Harold. *Baseball: The Early Years.* 1960. Reprint, New York: Oxford University Press, 1989.
Ward, Geoffrey C., and Ken Burns. *Baseball: An Illustrated History.* New York: Alfred A. Knopf, 1994.

"CASEY AT THE BAT"

"Casey at the Bat" is the most famous baseball poem of all time. Ernest Thayer, a contributor of humorous pieces and light verse to the *San Francisco Examiner* under the pen name "Phin," wrote the poem and contributed it to the paper as his column for June 3, 1888. A clipping of the poem turned up in New York in August 1889 as the New York Giants and Chicago White Stockings, after playing an exhibition game, were about to attend a vaudeville show at Wallack's Theater. The actor William DeWolf Hopper, given the poem by friend and novelist Archibald Clavering Gunter, recited it before his special audience. The event was a great success, and Hopper went on to recite the poem, by his own reckoning, some 10,000 times. His recordings of the poem also enjoyed great popularity. Other renditions of the Mighty Casey abound, including innumerable parodies, several film versions, William Schuman's opera *The Mighty Casey* (1953), and Frank Deford's novel *Casey on the Loose: What Really Might Have Happened* (1989).

The outlook wasn't brilliant for the Mudville nine that day;
The score stood four to two with but one inning more to play.
And then when Cooney died at first, and Barrows did the same,
A sickly silence fell upon the patrons of the game.

A straggling few got up to go in deep despair.
The rest
Clung to that hope which springs eternal in
the human breast;
They thought if only Casey could but get a
whack at that—
We'd put up even money now with Casey at
the bat.

But Flynn preceded Casey, as did also Jimmy
Blake,
And the former was a lulu and the latter was
a cake;
So upon that stricken multitude grim
melancholy sat,
For there seemed but little chance of Casey's
getting to the bat.

But Flynn let drive a single, to the wonder-
ment of all,
And Blake, the much despis-ed, tore the
cover off the ball;
And when the dust had lifted, and the men
saw what had occured,
There was Johnnie safe at second and Flynn
a-hugging third.

Then from 5,000 throats and more there rose
a lusty yell;
It rumbled through the valley, it rattled in the
dell;
It knocked upon the mountain and recoiled
upon the flat,
For Casey, mighty Casey, was advancing to
the bat.

There was ease in Casey's manner as he
stepped into his place;
There was pride in Casey's bearing and a
smile on Casey's face.
And when, responding to the cheers, he
lightly doffed his hat,
No stranger in the crowd could doubt 'twas
Casey at the bat.

Ten thousand eyes were on him as he rubbed
his hands with dirt;
Five thousand tongues applauded when he
wiped them on his shirt.

Then while the writhing pitcher ground the
ball into his hip,
Defiance gleamed in Casey's eye, a sneer
curled Casey's lip.

And now the leather-covered sphere came
hurtling through the air,
And Casey stood a-watching it in haughty
grandeur there.
Close by the sturdy batsman the ball
unheeded sped—
"That ain't my style," said Casey. "Strike one,"
the umpire said.

From the benches black with people, there
went up a muffled roar,
Like the beating of the storm-waves on a
stern and distant shore.
"Kill him! Kill the umpire!" shouted some one
on the stand;
And it's likely they'd have killed him had not
Casey raised his hand.

With a smile of Christian charity great Casey's
visage shone;
He stilled the rising tumult; he bade the game
go on;
He signaled to the pitcher, and once more the
spheroid flew;
But Casey still ignored it, and the umpire said,
"Strike two."

"Fraud!" cried the maddened thousands, and
echo answered fraud;
But one scornful look from Casey and the
audience was awed.
They saw his face grow stern and cold, they
saw his muscles strain,
And they knew that Casey wouldn't let that
ball go by again.

The sneer is gone from Casey's lip, his teeth
are clenched in hate;
He pounds with cruel violence his bat upon
the plate.
And now the pitcher holds the ball, and now
he lets it go,
And now the air is shattered by the force of
Casey's blow.

Oh, somewhere in this favored land the sun is
    shining bright;
The band is playing somewhere, and
    somewhere hearts are light,
And somewhere men are laughing, and
    somewhere children shout;
But there is no joy in Mudville—mighty Casey
    has struck out.

So Mighty Casey joined the ranks of American folk heroes, despite his ultimate failure. Even the mighty fall, which may be a consolation to most people and help to explain the enduring popularity of Thayer's poem. Because several years passed before Thayer acknowledged his authorship, mystery surrounded the poem's author and the identities of Casey and the town of Mudville. Claimants abounded, but only the original poet achieved recognition for creating one of the most famous losers of all time.

See also: Poetry.

Additional Reading:

Gardner, Martin, ed. *The Annotated Casey at the Bat.* 2d ed. Chicago: University of Chicago Press, 1984 (history, bibliography, versions, parodies).

Moore, Jim, and Natalie Vermilyea. *Ernest Thayer's "Casey at the Bat": Background and Characters of Baseball's Most Famous Poem.* Jefferson, NC: McFarland, 1994.

Murdock, Eugene C. *Mighty Casey: All American.* Westport, CT: Greenwood Press, 1984.

Poem's text based on version located at the following URL: http://members.xoom.com/cba2001/catb_1.html.

Regan, F. Scott. "The Mighty Casey: Enduring Folk Hero of Failure." *Journal of Popular Culture* 31(1) (1997): 91–109.

CASTRO, FIDEL (1927–)

Fidel Castro led a revolutionary movement that overthrew Cuban dictator Fulgencio Batista in 1959 and has ruled the island country ever since. It is widely believed that he was a talented pitcher who aspired to play in the major leagues. The common account is that young Fidel was scouted by the Washington Senators, whose Joe Cambria nearly signed him to a contract—only a slight deficiency in Fidel's fastball preventing the deal. Had the Senators signed Castro, so the story goes, there would have been no Cuban revolution, no Bay of Pigs fiasco, no U.S. nuclear standoff with the Russians during the 1960s.

The truth about Castro is less exciting than the myth, but it does involve an even greater impact on baseball than the more fanciful and dramatic accounts popularized for decades. Much of the true story comes from the careful research of baseball historian Peter C. Bjarkman. Castro did play baseball as a boy, organizing a team in his hometown of Birán and later pitching on his Belén high school team as a senior. He appears to have visited two tryout camps run by the Senators, but he neither was offered nor desired a contract. Already by this time, Castro, born into a wealthy family, was set on a career in politics or the law.

Castro's involvement with baseball resumed after he seized power. He played in exhibition games at several sites around Cuba and participated in pickup contests with political associates. In 1962, two years after Cuba's Havana Sugar Kings had been expelled from the International League, Castro established amateur baseball in his country, more for political and propaganda reasons than for love of the game. Cuban baseball teams, strongly supported by Castro, would dominate international amateur competition for the rest of the century.

See also: Cuban Baseball; Latin American Baseball.

Additional Reading:

Bjarkman, Peter C. "Baseball and Fidel Castro." *The National Pastime: A Review of Baseball History* 18 (1998): 64–68.

Bourne, Peter G. *Fidel: A Biography of Fidel Castro.* New York: Dodd, Mead, 1988.

Lockwood, Lee. *Castro's Cuba, Cuba's Fidel: An American Journalist's Inside Look at*

Today's Cuba in Text and Picture. New York: Vintage, 1969.

Quirk, Robert. *Fidel Castro*. New York: Norton, 1993.

Wendel, Tim. *Castro's Curveball*. New York: Ballantine, 1999.

CHADWICK, HENRY (1824–1908)

Henry Chadwick was the first great sports journalist, an early champion of the integrity of the game, and the inventor of the modern box score. His accomplishments are legion: a sometime player for the New York Knickerbockers; for decades the baseball editor of the *Clipper* (New York) and writer for the *Eagle* (Brooklyn); a skilled statistician who developed a scoring system for games and invented the box score, thus providing for future millions the joys of arguing baseball statistics; an early opponent of gambling in baseball; a debunker of the myth of Cooperstown as the birthplace of baseball (knowledge certainly consistent with his British birth and knowledge of rounders and cricket); editor of such baseball guides as the annual *Spalding Baseball Guide;* author of several baseball books, including *Beedle's Dime Base Ball Book* (1880); and chairman of the Rules Committee of the National Association of Base Ball Players.

Chadwick's integrity, journalistic fame, and love of the game earned him the nickname "Father Chadwick" and a reputation as the conscience of baseball. Theodore Roosevelt went so far as to call him the "father of baseball." And when Chadwick died, the baseball pioneer and sporting-goods tycoon A. G. Spalding erected at his gravesite an impressive monument, to which Dodgers president Charles Ebbets led annual pilgrimages.

Henry Chadwick was selected for membership in the Hall of Fame in 1938, but unlike other writers who have been so honored his plaque hangs in the main hall along with the players of the ages. Today, his legacy lives whenever a fan reads the box scores or baseball news in a newspaper or argues the banishment of Shoeless Joe Jackson or Pete Rose. Chadwick even appears in Darryl Brock's 1989 novel *If I Never Get Back*.

See also: Fiction; Journalism (Print); Spalding, Albert Goodwill; Statistics.

Additional Reading:

Chadwick, Henry. Scrapbooks. In the Spalding Collection, New York Public Library.

Seymour, Harold. *Baseball: The Early Years*. 1960. Reprint, New York: Oxford University Press, 1989.

Spalding, Albert G. *Base Ball: America's National Game*. 1911. Reprint, revised and edited by Samm Coombs and Bob West, San Francisco: Halo Books, 1991.

CHANDLER, ALBERT BENJAMIN (HAPPY) (1898–1991)

The election of Happy Chandler as commissioner of baseball on April 24, 1945, formalized the implicit connection between government and baseball. Owners were concerned about retaining their favored status, exemplified by the sport's exemption from the Sherman Antitrust Act; choosing the two-term Kentucky governor and current U.S. senator to replace the deceased Judge Kenesaw Landis seemed prudent. Although many owners would come to regret their decision, players, the baseball public, and American society would be enriched by the folksy commissioner who saw himself as a man of the people.

Happy Chandler's most important accomplishment was helping to integrate baseball. Branch Rickey, who hoped to introduce Jackie Robinson to the majors, came to the commissioner in January 1947 after a 15-1 vote by owners against integration. Unsure whether he could proceed in the face of such opposition, he was reassured by Chandler, who told

Rickey that his was the only approval he needed and that he should go ahead. Chandler used the argument then and with others that if black men could fight and die for their country, they could play major league baseball.

Chandler opposed a unionization effort by players in 1946 but later endeared himself to players by helping to inaugurate a pension plan with health- and life-insurance benefits, partly funded by a new deal with Gillette Safety Razor Company for television sponsorship rights to the World Series and All-Star Games. In that same year, Chandler earned owners' respect by quickly ending efforts by the Mexican League to lure American players away from their teams. Later actions, though, began to alienate owners, who refused to reappoint Chandler, prompting him to resign in July 1951.

See also: Commissioner; Landis, Kenesaw Mountain; Rickey, Wesley Branch; Robinson, Jack Roosevelt.

Additional Reading:

Chandler, Happy, with Vance H. Trimble. *Heroes, Plain Folks, and Skunks: The Life and Times of Happy Chandler.* Chicago: Bonus Books, 1989.

Holtzman, Jerome. *The Commissioners: Baseball's Midlife Crisis.* New York: Total Sports, 1998.

Mann, Arthur William. *Baseball Confidential: Secret History of the War among Chandler, Durocher, MacPhail, and Rickey.* David McKay, 1951.

Marshall, William Leonard. *Baseball's Pivotal Era: 1945–1951.* Lexington: University Press of Kentucky, 1999.

CHAPMAN, RAYMOND JOHNSON (RAY) (1891–1920)

Ray Chapman, a talented shortstop for the Cleveland Indians who batted at least .300 four times during a nine-year career, is the only player confirmed to have died as the direct result of a major league game. Chapman's tragic place in history was fixed by a high and tight pitch from New York Yankees' submariner Carl Mays on August 16, 1920. Mays, notorious for a short temper and the high brushback, apparently attempted to drive Chapman off the plate, not an unusual occurrence in baseball games, especially for hitters, like Chapman, who leaned over home plate. Unfortunately, the pitch hit Chapman in the head. Chapman revived and attempted to walk off the field, only to collapse and be carried to the clubhouse. He was taken to St. Lawrence Hospital and underwent surgery, dying the following morning.

Many people called for Carl Mays's banishment from the game, and he was investigated by the local district attorney. However, he was cleared legally and was permitted to continue pitching. Mays played for almost another decade, finishing his 15-year career in 1929 with 208 victories and five 20-win seasons.

Although the *New York Times* called for use of batting helmets, that protective device would be another 30-plus years in coming. No other player has been killed in a major league game, but at least seven minor-leaguers have died as a result of being struck by pitches, the most recent being Otis Johnson of the Dothan (Alabama) Browns on June 2, 1951.

Additional Reading:

Sowell, Mike. *The Pitch That Killed.* New York: Macmillan, 1989.

CHEATING

In American society, cheating tends to fall within two categories: the serious and the not-so-serious. So it is in baseball. Shoeless Joe Jackson, one of baseball's most notorious cheaters, has been eternally damned to baseball purgatory. Yet lesser cheating is sometimes condoned and even encouraged, as it demonstrates one's competitiveness and will to win. Thus the everybody-does-it theme so common in society also permeates baseball. In this lesser category of cheating sins, a runner gets an edge by leaving base a fraction of a second early, a fielder touches only the shadow of the base when turning a double play, and an outfielder feigns a legitimate catch when he has merely trapped a sinking liner.

Although parents teach children to be honest, honesty goes only so far on the ball field. When was the last time that a runner urged the umpire to reverse a safe call because he knew he truly was beaten to the base by the fielder? When did a pitcher thank the umpire for a strike call but ask him to give the batter credit for a ball because the pitch actually was a smidgen outside?

Pitchers are perhaps the most egregious deceivers. They scuff the baseball, spit on it, apply various foreign substances, rub it with sandpaper—and often get away with such shenanigans. There are exceptions, of course. Detroit Tigers pitcher Brian Moehler, caught using sandpaper on a baseball early in the 1999 season, was suspended for 10 days. Moehler was the first pitcher in 12 years—and only the sixth in 20 years—to be suspended for altering a baseball. Slugger Albert Belle received the same penalty (reduced to seven days after an appeal) for using a corked bat in 1994.

Former baseball commissioner A. Bartlett Giamatti was intolerant of all degrees of cheating. Kevin Gross of the Philadelphia Phillies was suspended for 10 days in 1987 for having a piece of sandpaper in his glove. Gross appealed, but Giamatti rejected the appeal, explaining in his ruling that "acts of cheating . . . strike at the essence of a contest. They destroy faith in the games' integrity and fairness" (*A Great and Glorious Game,* 73).

Giamatti's determination to prevent even the perception of cheating led him

to ban Pete Rose from baseball for life after accusations that Rose had bet on baseball games. Here one moves from the acceptable, even praiseworthy, cheating to "mortal" cheating. The greatest baseball sins traditionally have been throwing games and betting on games, whether played by one's own team or not.

Accepting money from gamblers to lose games has been a potential problem throughout the history of baseball. Attempts were made to fix the 1903 and 1905 World Series. Jim Devlin, an outstanding pitcher with the Louisville Grays, threw games in 1877, leading to his banishment, along with three teammates, for life. Hal Chase, perhaps the most notorious of all players for allegedly throwing games, strangely enough was not banished by Judge Kenesaw Mountain Landis, although Landis banned 14 major league players, including the eight members of the White Sox accused of throwing the 1919 World Series, plus several minor-leaguers. Connie Mack complained that his Athletics players seemed to be following gamblers' orders while losing the 1914 World Series. Thus cheating has dogged baseball virtually since its inception, and it remains a concern even today, sometimes seriously harming the game but usually just being part of the contest.

See also: Black Sox Scandal; Gambling; Giamatti, Angelo Bartlett; Jackson, Joseph Jefferson; Landis, Kenesaw Mountain; Rose, Peter Edward.

Additional Reading:
Asinof, Eliot. *Eight Men Out: The Black Sox and the 1919 World Series.* New York: Holt, 1963.
Giamatti, A. Bartlett. "Decision in the Appeal of Kevin Gross" and "Statement Released to the Press on the Pete Rose Matter." In *A Great and Glorious Game: Baseball Writings of A. Bartlett Giamatti.* Ed. Kenneth S. Robson. Chapel Hill: Algonquin Books, 1998, pp. 67–79, 117–121.
Gutman, Dan. *It Ain't Cheatin' If You Don't Get Caught: Scuffing, Corking, Spitting, Gunking, Razzing, and Other Fundamentals of Our National Pastime.* New York: Penguin, 1990.

Seymour, Harold. *Baseball: The Early Years*. 1960. Reprint, New York: Oxford University Press, 1989.

———. *Baseball: The Golden Age*. 1971. Reprint, New York: Oxford University Press, 1989.

CINCINNATI RED STOCKINGS

The Cincinnati Red Stockings, first formed in 1866, suffered a humiliating 53-10 defeat at the hands of the Washington Nationals in 1867. Leading citizens of Cincinnati decided that their city's honor required a firm response, so they charged Harry Wright with assembling a team that would win—even if players had to be paid. Thus was born the first truly professional baseball club: the Red Stockings of 1869.

Wright managed the team and played center field, paying himself a salary of $1,200 for the season that ran from March to November. As skilled as Harry was, his brother, George, the shortstop, was even better. George accordingly received the highest salary on the squad—$1,400. The other principal players earned $600–1,100: Asa Brainard, pitcher, $1,100; Fred Waterman, third baseman, $1,000; Charles Sweasy, second baseman, $800; Charles H. Gould, first baseman, $800; Douglas Allison, catcher, $800; Andrew J. Leonard, left fielder, $800; Calvin A. McVey, right fielder, $800. The top substitute, Richard Hurley, was paid $600. Three additional substitutes named Fowler, Bradford, and Taylor played occasionally, but neither their exploits nor salaries are known. Fowler would be developed by Darryl Brock as the main character in his novel about the 1869 Red Stockings, *If I Never Get Back*.

Along with being the first all-professional team and playing before audiences that paid up to 50 cents each to watch their performances, the team also manifested a higher degree of specialization, and therefore more of a true team

concept, than previous teams (which followed a "generalist" approach to player contributions). Professionalism, specialization, and baseball-as-business were new developments that took firm root in the rich earth of American society and would forever define baseball at its highest levels.

That these trends would become permanent was assured by the unprecedented success of the Cincinnati Red Stockings. The team rolled past its generally amateur opposition during the 1869 season, perhaps the most seminal season in the history of baseball. Only one tie marred the Red Stockings' record as they accumulated as many as 65 victories (the exact number of games played remains uncertain), when the Troy Haymakers left the field with the score tied to avoid a defeat that would have seriously inconvenienced the New York gamblers who had bet on them.

The Cincinnati Red Stockings toured all the way to both coasts, establishing a national as well as rabid local following. Well into the 1870 season, they had added 27 victories to their consecutive string that had reached as far as 92 (or close to that figure) when they encountered the Brooklyn Atlantics on June 14. In an epic, seesaw battle that stretched to 11 innings, the host Atlantics prevailed by a score of 8-7. The city of Cincinnati was shocked. The schedule continued, but with the team now having lost its mantle of invincibility, followers dwindled. Fortune followed fame, with gate receipts likewise dropping. By the end of the year, the Cincinnati Red Stockings were no more.

Yet baseball had been changed for all time. Henry Chadwick, the first great baseball journalist, declared Red Stockings manager Harry Wright was the "father of professional ball playing." Wright, meanwhile, took several of his top players, including brother George and pitcher Asa Brainard, along with the name of the team, to Boston. The Boston Red Stockings opened the 1871 season as one of the charter members of the new National Association of Professional Base Ball Players (thereby splitting from teams that maintained the traditional amateur and gentlemanly approaches established by the New York Knickerbockers). Wright and crew went on to win four championships in the next five years, and both brothers were selected to the Baseball Hall of Fame. When George died at the age of 90 in 1937, he left behind a game that had changed much from the days when he played, but those changes were very much along the playing and paying paths pioneered by baseball's very own Wright brothers.

See also: Business; Fiction; Major Leagues.
Additional Reading:
Brock, Darryl. If I Never Get Back. New York: Crown, 1990.
Frommer, Harvey. Primitive Baseball: The First Quarter-Century of the National Pastime. New York: Atheneum, 1988.
Goldstein, Warren. Playing for Keeps: A History of Early Baseball. Ithaca: Cornell University Press, 1989.
Guschov, Stephen D. The Red Stockings of Cincinnati. Jefferson, NC: McFarland, 1998.
Seymour, Harold. Baseball: The Early Years. 1960. Reprint, New York: Oxford University Press, 1989.

CLEMENTE, ROBERTO WALKER (1934–1972)

Roberto Clemente achieved in death what he had sought in life—full acceptance of his accomplishments. His death occurred on New Year's Eve at the conclusion of 1972. Clemente and several companions were flying clothing, food, and medical supplies to survivors of a devastating earthquake in Nicaragua when their plane went down at sea. Clemente's body was never recovered, but the death stamped Clemente as a genuine hero in addition to a great baseball player, completing the transformation that had begun belatedly during the 1971 World Series.

Clemente grew up in Puerto Rico and signed with the Brooklyn Dodgers. After an inauspicious season with Montreal in 1954, the young outfielder batting just .257, Branch Rickey, one of baseball's keenest and most imaginative evaluators of talent, drafted him for the Pittsburgh Pirates. Clemente made the Pirates in 1955 and went on to achieve a Hall of Fame career from then through the 1972 season, when the plane crash cut short his career.

Roberto Clemente hit safely an even 3,000 times while batting .317 with 240 home runs. Primarily a line-drive hitter, Clemente hit over .300 12 times in his final 13 years, won four batting titles, and hit over .350 three times. He also was a great defensive right fielder with a magnificent throwing arm. Twelve consecutive Gold Gloves testify to his defensive ability, and five times he led National League outfielders in assists, in three years throwing out 20 or more runners. He played in 11 All-Star Games and won the Most Valuable Player Award in 1966. In two World Series, Clemente batted .362, hitting .414 in the 1971 Series when he was chosen Series Most Valuable Player. The Pirates won both of those Series, defeating the New York Yankees in 1960 and the Baltimore Orioles in 1971.

Yet Clemente did not receive the acclaim he felt he deserved, playing second fiddle in the press to Willie Mays. Clemente was accused by some reporters and fans of being a hypochondriac because of his repeated complaints of injuries. It was later discovered that he in fact had played his career with back problems caused by a 1956 automobile accident. He also grated on some people because he was outspoken regarding

racism, believing that his Latin background explained why he was short-
changed by the media. Although that
may have been the case, playing in Pittsburgh rather than in media centers such
as New York or Los Angeles also contributed to keeping his achievements in
the shadows. Not reluctant to oppose
bias when he saw it, Clemente was in the
forefront demanding postponement of
opening-day games to honor Martin
Luther King Jr. after the Civil Rights leader
was assassinated in 1968.

The 1971 World Series saw Clemente
finally earning the public raves that he
deserved as one of the great all-around
players of the twentieth century. The Pirates were given little chance against the
powerful Orioles, but Clemente spearheaded the Series victory. Finally, he had
his place in the sun.

Roberto Clemente had little time to
enjoy his well-earned fame. He played
one more year, collecting hit number
3,000 at the end of the season. Then he
flew off on a humanitarian trip and into
eternity. The world was shocked at the
news of his death, and baseball quickly
waived the five-year waiting period for
election to the Hall of Fame. Clemente
became the first Latin player to be inducted, and his face appeared on a U.S.
stamp, only the second baseball player
so honored. In an especially fitting memorial, the commissioner's office established an annual award in Clemente's
name to the player who exhibits an outstanding record as an athlete and citizen.

See also: Latin American Baseball.
Additional Reading:
Musick, Phil. *Who Was Roberto? A Biography of Roberto Clemente.* Garden City, NY: Dou-
bleday, 1974.
Regalado, Samuel O. *Viva Baseball! Latin Major Leaguers and Their Special Hunger.* Urbana: University of Illinois Press, 1998.
Wagenheim, Kal. *Clemente!* New York: Praeger, 1973.
Walker, Paul Robert. *Pride of Puerto Rico: The Life of Roberto Clemente.* San Diego: Har-
court, 1991.

COBB, TYRUS RAYMOND (THE GEORGIA PEACH) (1886–1961)

Ty Cobb was an early superstar, someone fans came to see, either to love or to
hate. He did much to popularize baseball
during the early decades of the twentieth
century and became one of the greatest
(some would say the greatest) of all
major league players—certainly the best
of the first two decades of the century.
When the first Hall of Fame inductees
were chosen in 1936, Cobb garnered
more votes than even Babe Ruth. Yet at
Cobb's funeral in 1961, only three men
who played with or against him were in
attendance, most attendees being Little
League players for whom Ty Cobb was
just a name and a set of awesome statistics. Cobb died without many friends,
which is how he lived and played the
game. Winning was everything for Cobb,
and he generated a ferocious passion
that led to his remarkable on-field accomplishments. Yet his passions were
also antisocial, bigoted, and violent.

Some of Cobb's most remarkable
records have been broken in recent
decades, yet he retains an almost mythic
stature in baseball. A star outfielder (and
player-manager for six seasons) with the
Detroit Tigers from 1905 to 1926, Cobb
played his final two seasons with Connie
Mack's Philadelphia Athletics. He is best
known for his total-hits and stolen-base
records (4,189 hits and 892 steals, with a
single-season record of 96 stolen bases in
1915). In the 1980s the hits record finally
fell to Pete Rose, who had to hang on
well past his prime to surpass Cobb.
Rose hit a struggling .264 and .219 in his
final seasons, whereas Cobb, finishing
his career with the Athletics, batted .357

Detroit outfielder Ty Cobb touches a base while running, 1910s. (Archive Photos)

and .323. The stolen-base marks had been surpassed earlier. Maury Wills stole 104 bases for the Dodgers in 1962, and Lou Brock swiped 118 for the Cardinals in 1974. The record was shattered in 1982 when Rickey Henderson of the Oakland Athletics stole 130 bases. Brock and Henderson also set new career records, the former retiring after the 1979 season with 938 steals; Henderson began 2000 with 1,334 steals. The new records, however, have done more to establish the greatness of the record-holders than to diminish Cobb.

No modern player has come close to Cobb's career .366 batting average. Lest moderns dismiss that figure as inflated by a different brand of baseball, it is important to remember that Cobb also consis-

tently outhit his contemporaries. He led his league in hitting 12 times, including nine years in a row. He surpassed .400 three times and hit over .380 in nine different years. Between 1910 and 1913, he compiled averages of .383, .420, .409, and .390. In addition to batting for average, he retains the major league record of 2,245 runs scored. Although he hit just 117 home runs, he played most of his career prior to the home-run era. Yet he had plenty of power, leading his league in slugging average eight times, and he remains among the all-time leaders in doubles (724, fourth all-time) and triples (295, second all-time).

Ty Cobb was one of the most aggressive players of any era, and that will to win served him well on the field, even as it alienated many opposing players. Cobb would practice sliding into base until his legs were badly skinned. Opposing fielders were apt to hurt even more, as Cobb often slid into base with spikes high. He spiked many a fielder, and he was consistently combative, which led to many fights. Not even the spectators were safe. During a 1912 game, a man apparently referred to Cobb as a "half-nigger," whereupon Cobb leaped into the stands and battered the spectator mercilessly, knocking him down and kicking him. Cobb's racism was just one of several disagreeable traits and may explain his extreme reaction to the taunt.

A betting scandal involving Cobb came to light in 1926. Dutch Leonard, a former pitcher for the Tigers, charged that Cobb, along with Tris Speaker and Smokey Joe Wood, had bet on games that he knew to be fixed in 1919, the year of the Black Sox scandal. Speaker and Wood had been teammates with Cleveland that year. By 1926, Wood, once a great fastball pitcher for the Red Sox before developing a sore arm, was out of baseball; Speaker was still one of the game's greats.

Ban Johnson, president of the American League, reportedly paid Leonard $20,000 not to publicize letters documenting the charge and permitted Cobb and Speaker to resign from their positions as player-managers. Each would surface the following year with other clubs, Cobb with the Athletics, Speaker with the Washington Senators. Commissioner Kenesaw Mountain Landis made the cases public in an effort to embarrass Johnson. Eventually, however, Landis exonerated Cobb and Speaker, perhaps bowing to public pressure and not wanting to impose the same lifetime bans on these superstars as he had on Shoeless Joe Jackson and the rest of the Black Sox.

Cobb retired after the 1928 season. His remaining years included considerable drinking, gambling, opposition to integrating baseball, belittling modern players, and failed marriages. He regularly traveled with a loaded Luger pistol. What demons drove Ty Cobb are hard to identify, but they may have had their origins in his family. His father, William Herschel Cobb, was a prominent citizen, a teacher and state senator. He initially opposed his son's choice of career but later came around—with clear directives to be successful. In 1905, with Ty away playing, the father, amid rumors, decided to determine whether his wife, Amanda, was cheating on him. William said that he would be out of town but then returned home at night and climbed to the balcony on the second floor of their house. Amanda, claiming to fear an unknown intruder, shot her husband to death with a shotgun. Although brought to trial for manslaughter, she was acquitted.

Ty Cobb continued with the game that his father reluctantly accepted and more than fulfilled his father's command to achieve success. He became one of the game's greats but spent much of his life alone. In his later years, he expressed regret for the way he had led his life, wishing that he would have sought more friends. In an autobiography, *My Life in Baseball,* Cobb attempted some revisionism in his life and career (with the book also including a foreword by General Douglas MacArthur drawing analogies between baseball and war and championing an aggressive offensive, rather than defensive, approach to each). But the essential Ty Cobb, for better and worse, lives on in the world of baseball lore—hits spraying the field, spikes still drawing opponents' blood.

See also: African Americans; Gambling; Johnson, Byron Bancroft; Landis, Kenesaw Mountain.

Additional Reading:

Alexander, Charles C. *Ty Cobb*. New York: Oxford University Press, 1984.

Cobb, Ty, with Al Stump. *My Life in Baseball: The True Record*. Garden City, NY: Doubleday, 1961.

McCallum, John Dennis. *The Tiger Wore Spikes: An Informal Biography of Ty Cobb*. New York: Barnes, 1956.

————. *Ty Cobb*. New York: Praeger, 1975.

Stump, Al. *Cobb: A Biography*. Chapel Hill: Algonquin Books, 1994.

COLLECTIBLES

Popular culture is a matter not just of attitude and activity but also of artifact. The proliferation of shops lining highways, especially in tourist areas, with signs proclaiming Collectibles (or Collectables), is vivid testimony to the popularity of collecting items of all sorts. The *Oxford English Dictionary* notes the word "collectible" as far back as the seventeenth century, but always as an adjective. The word as noun is a recent phenomenon, signifying the growing importance of collecting items as more people have money to buy beyond basic necessities.

Collecting baseball items serves a number of purposes. The items may be reminders of enjoyable hours at the ballpark, expressions of loyalty to one's favorite team, methods of establishing unity with other like-minded individuals. They also may serve utilitarian or artistic purposes, or perhaps function as a financial investment. Posters, caps, T-shirts, bumper stickers, plates, baseball cards, autographs, statues, and coins are common collectibles. Perhaps the item most suggestive of the impact of baseball is the baseball cap. It functions as a reminder and unifier and is worn within the ballpark and elsewhere, even in schools and homes. Some people almost never remove their caps. In fact, the baseball cap as a style has transcended baseball, to be worn by untold numbers of people who care nothing for the sport.

Selling collectibles has become big business. A typical issue of *USA Today Baseball Weekly* (May 12–18, 1999), under its Collectibles heading, lists for sale arm patches, an autographed Yankee jersey, copies of wills (for Joe DiMaggio, Cy Young, Jackie Robinson, and Satchel Paige), autographs, baseballs, replica gloves, signed caps, and other items, along with invitations to request catalogs from companies that specialize in collectibles. Collecting seems to have staying power among fans and nonfans alike.

See also: Business; Cards, Baseball; Souvenirs.
Additional Reading:

Aldridge, Gwen. *Baseball Archaeology: Artifacts from the Great American Pastime*. San Francisco: Chronicle Books, 1993.

Mote, James. *Everything Baseball*. New York: Prentice Hall, 1989.

Pietrusza, David, Lloyd Johnson, and Bob Carroll. *The Total Baseball Catalog*. New York: Total Sports, 1998.

Plus any number of catalogs; to list them here would, in effect, be to endorse particular companies and be inappropriate.

COLLEGE BASEBALL

Baseball once reigned supreme among college sports in the United States. Decades before the Civil War, college students played games that were precursors of modern baseball, and by the middle of the nineteenth century colleges were an important reason why baseball was becoming a permanent part of American society. In institutions of higher learning, the sport spread in popularity throughout the remaining decades of the nineteenth century and into the twentieth. By the 1920s, however, football had usurped the special place of baseball in college sports, to be joined by basketball as the twentieth century progressed. Today baseball is at best third and, in many institutions, even farther down the scale. Despite its relative decline, college baseball remains too important to ignore.

What may have been the first intercollegiate baseball contest, in 1859, was actually part of a doubleheader of sorts between Amherst College and Williams College on July 1 (a baseball game) and 4 (a chess match). Amherst won both. College baseball spread during the 1860s throughout the Northeast and moved into the Midwest. The games were usually organized by student-athletes, with students also functioning as coaches. Sometimes young, athletic professors joined the competitions.

Colleges in the West added baseball in the 1870s, but southern institutions, suffering the effects of the Civil War, were somewhat slower to embrace the new sport. By 1880, as Harold Seymour has pointed out in *Baseball: The People's Game,* baseball was the principal college sport. College officials looked favorably on baseball, viewing it as conducive to health, character, and school spirit. Professional baseball, though, was a different story. School officials did their best to prevent students from playing professionally (which was easy enough during the summer using false names) and attempted to stem the growing tide of professionalism that crept into the college game (former professionals served as coaches, and school teams were scheduled against professional teams).

Despite these efforts, the college game quickly grew to resemble the professional game. Many colleges, recognizing the potential financial rewards, contributed to that growth with improved facilities, serious recruiting efforts, and athletic scholarships. College men such as Eddie Collins, Christy Mathewson, and Jack Coombs turned professional. Ungentlemanly tactics—taunting, tripping,

and throwing at batters—were adopted. Coaches earned higher salaries than professors—as true today as it was back then.

The decline in college baseball was caused by several factors: the growing popularity of football, with its nonstop action and acceptable violence; criticism of baseball by the Carnegie Foundation and the National Collegiate Athletic Association; and the Great Depression, which limited financial investments to the sport (i.e., football) that promised to attract larger crowds and gate receipts.

College baseball, however, maintains its importance even with its somewhat reduced role. Many of today's top stars—Mark McGwire and Roger Clemens, to name just two—honed their skills at the college level. Approximately half of the number-one picks in the annual amateur draft since 1965 have been college players. College games receive modest media attention in the newspapers and on television, with the College World Series being telecast nationally. Even rules changes receive public attention. The burgeoning offensive statistics ushered in by aluminum bats in the 1970s led to regulations regarding bat construction and performance to be implemented during the 2000 season. Henceforth, aluminum bats will be thinner, heavier, and designed to perform more like wooden bats. Perhaps professional baseball will follow the lead of the college game and attempt to curb the offensive explosion at that level as well. If so, college baseball may start to wield influence as in earlier days.

See also: Equipment; Mathewson, Christopher; McGwire, Mark David.

Additional Reading:

Chu, Donald, Jeffrey Segrave, and Beverly J. Becker. *Sport and Higher Education.* Champaign, IL: Human Kinetics, 1985.
Lapchick, Richard Edward. *The Rules of the Game: Ethics in College Sport.* American Council on Education/Macmillan Series in

Higher Education. New York: Macmillan, 1989.

Rooney, John F. *The Recruiting Game: Toward a New System of Intercollegiate Sports.* 2d ed. Lincoln: University of Nebraska Press, 1987.

Seymour, Harold. *Baseball: The People's Game.* 1990. Reprint, New York: Oxford University Press, 1991.

Smith, Ronald A. *Sports and Freedom: The Rise of Big-Time College Athletics.* New York: Oxford University Press, 1988.

COLORADO SILVER BULLETS

The Colorado Silver Bullets, a women's baseball team created to play against men, was the product of several phenomena within American society, including the impact of mass media (in this case a film), the desire to sell beer, and the so-called battle between the sexes. The fact that the Colorado Silver Bullets ultimately were permitted to fail also reflects an important aspect of society: its refusal to believe that women playing baseball can be anything more than a novelty act.

The film was *A League of Their Own* (1992), which starred Tom Hanks as the manager of the Rockford Peaches in the All-American Girls Professional Baseball League, the World War II–era women's league. Also starring Madonna and Geena Davis, the film excited great interest in the subject of women and baseball. Capitalizing on this film-generated interest and hoping to sell more beer, Coors Brewing Company of Colorado joined with Whittle Communications to create an all-women's team, adopting the nickname for Coors Light beer. Whittle Communications was led by a man with a keen sense of entertainment, Bob Hope (not the famous comedian), who in the 1980s had attempted to add a women's team to the Class-A Florida State League. Hope also had spent time with the Atlanta Braves as their public-relations and marketing director. A former Braves pitcher, Hall of Famer Phil Niekro, was hired to manage the club.

The Silver Bullets began play on Mother's Day, May 8, 1994. They lost 19-0 to the Northern League All-Stars. Some quick rescheduling occurred to substitute opposing teams with more modest talent, but the Silver Bullets concluded the year with only six victories against 38 losses. With women largely excluded from both organized baseball and college teams, the talent source for the Silver Bullets was limited. However, some excellent players did join the team, including first baseman Julie Croteau, who had played Division III baseball for St. Mary's College in Maryland, and pitcher Pamela Davis.

The Silver Bullets played for four years, improving their record each season. By the end of 1997, they had fashioned their first winning season—23 victories against 22 defeats. Pam Davis went 7-5 as their top pitcher. Attendance, however, declined, and Coors withdrew its sponsorship. According to an article by Gai Berlage, Coors had become concerned that its light beer was being perceived as a "chick beer," which would alienate male drinkers.

Without Coors sponsorship, Hope-Beckham, which had bought the team from Whittle, decided not to continue. The demise of the Silver Bullets, in Berlage's opinion, signaled an end to interest in the battle of the sexes. The primary reason for the death of the Silver Bullets is that society remains unwilling to accept baseball as a serious activity for women. Creating a team whose modus operandi required playing against male teams was certainly not new. The Bloomer Girls teams had done the same thing earlier in the century. The beer and media underpinning for the club, however, guaranteed a novel sex-appeal, battle-of-the-sexes approach.

The only way in which women probably will be accepted in baseball is if they play against other women or play on teams truly open to talented players regardless of gender. The latter option would seem to fit a democratic society committed to equality of opportunity.

See also: All-American Girls Professional Baseball League; Women in Baseball.

Additional Reading:

Berlage, Gai Ingham. "The Colorado Bullets." *The Baseball Research Journal* 27 (1998): 40–42.

Shattuck, Debra A. "Women in Baseball." In *Total Baseball.* 6th ed. Ed. John Thorn et al. New York: Total Sports, 1999, pp. 574–577.

COMISKEY, CHARLES ALBERT (CHARLIE, THE OLD ROMAN, COMMY) (1859–1931)

Charles Comiskey contributed much to the history of major league baseball; he also embodied the contrast in some of baseball's most famous characters: saint and sinner. Depending on one's perspective, Comiskey can be viewed as the Noble Roman—innovative, compassionate, committed to the highest ideals of integrity; or as a deceitful tightwad—keeping players in virtual servitude, trying to cover up the 1919 World Series fix, authorizing theft of court documents to cover himself, and scapegoating his players for a gambling problem that went far beyond eight White Sox.

Comiskey started his career as a first baseman, playing for the St. Louis Browns of the American Association from 1882 to 1889. His leadership qualities were quickly noticed, and he became also the Browns' manager in 1883, continuing to be a player-manager throughout his playing career, which ended in 1894 after one year with the Chicago Pirates of the Players League, a brief return to the Browns, and three seasons with the Cincinnati Reds of the National League. The fact that he jumped to the Players League has

A depiction of Charles Comiskey on an Allen and Ginter's cigarette card, part of the World Champions collection (Ann Ronan Picture Library)

been viewed by some as hypocritical given his later disdain for players' rights as owner of the Chicago White Sox.

Comiskey was a mediocre hitter, batting just .264 in his career, but he excelled defensively in both his personal skills and his tactics. As manager and captain, he proved especially creative on defense, playing off first base and requiring the pitcher to cover first on balls hit between first and second. He also pioneered infield shifts in response to the hitter's tendencies. As a manager, he won 839 games and lost just 542 for a lofty winning percentage of .608. His Browns won their pennant four years in a row starting in 1885.

Comiskey's next major achievement was in helping to create the new American League in 1901. Comiskey added the Chicago club, initially naming it the White

Stockings after the National League team but renaming it the White Sox in 1902. Comiskey imported Clark Griffith to be manager and ace pitcher on his first team, and the future owner of the Washington Senators went 24-7 on the mound as the White Sox won the pennant of the new league. The White Sox continued to be one of the league's top teams through the first two decades of the century, winning the World Series in 1906 against the powerful crosstown Cubs despite hitting just .228 for the year, an accomplishment that earned them the title the Hitless Wonders. The Sox won another World Series in 1917, defeating the New York Giants, and, of course, won the pennant in 1919.

Comiskey was known by many people for his generosity. He often hosted large numbers of people at his summer home in Eagle River, Wisconsin, and he even paid tuition for the sons of some of his early Sox players to attend the University of Notre Dame. During World War I, he contributed large sums of money to the American Red Cross.

Yet the White Sox owner also was known as a tightwad, underpaying his players, except for star second baseman Eddie Collins, who as a college man seemed to impress Comiskey more than did other players, or who merely had more options and therefore more bargaining power. He even required his players to pay to clean their own uniforms, a practice that led the 1918 White Sox to wear the same uniforms for weeks in protest and to call themselves, ironically, the Black Sox.

Considerable suspicion still surrounds Comiskey regarding the fixing of the World Series in 1919. He apparently did not suspect beforehand that his team would throw the Series, although Joe Jackson asked him for permission not to play, which should have made him wonder. After the first game, though, manager Kid Gleason was sure that not everything

was on the up-and-up, and Comiskey went to see Ban Johnson, president of the American League. Comiskey later lamented that Johnson should have stopped the Series after two games, but Johnson, a former ally but by then an adversary of Comiskey, was not about to bail the owner out of a tight situation. Even after the Series, Jackson pleaded for a chance to talk with Comiskey, and his wife wrote to the owner, but Comiskey seemed to want to avoid knowing definitively what had happened.

During the court proceedings of 1921, transcripts, including a record of Jackson's statements about trying to warn Comiskey and make amends, disappeared; in 1924, they mysteriously showed up in the hands of Comiskey's lawyer when Jackson sued the Sox for nonpayment of salary. It is hard to escape the conclusion that Comiskey was convinced either during or immediately after the Series that the fix was in and thus tried to sweep the matter under the rug in order not to harm his team in the future Once the fix came to light, he willingly let the eight banished players bear the brunt of the public's criticism.

At the time, the pubic did not blame Comiskey for helping to precipitate the situation by nickel-and-diming his players, keeping their salaries low, and even manipulating events to avoid paying players what he owed them. Star pitcher Eddie Cicotte, for example, had been promised a bonus of $10,000 if he won 30 games. After he reached 29 victories in 1919, Comiskey ordered him benched to avoid having to pay the bonus. So cheap (and ungrateful) could Comiskey be that even after Dickie Kerr won two games in the Series as the only honest starting pitcher on the Sox, and followed with 21 and 19 wins the next two years, the owner would not give him a raise. When Kerr then left the White Sox to play semipro ball and competed against a team for which Jackson was playing, Comiskey reported the supposed infraction to commissioner Kenesaw Mountain Landis, who suspended Kerr for one year.

Comiskey's less desirable traits made him the model for the owner who employs Roy Hobbs in the novel and film versions of *The Natural*. In addition, the growing sympathy for Shoeless Joe Jackson, also supported by fiction and film, inevitably places the wronged player in opposition to Comiskey. The owner has become the villain in the minds of millions of people who know at least a little about the Black Sox. It is important, however, to retain a balanced view of Charles Comiskey, who earned the nickname the "Old Roman" because of his handsome, chiseled, John Barrymore–like profile and wavy, silver hair. His positive contributions to the game merit the continued naming of White Sox stadiums after him. Visitors to Comiskey Park (the second park bearing his name) can enjoy a snack at Old Roman Pizza, which hardly seems appropriate for saint or sinner. Perhaps Comiskey, after all, paid a price for his failures. After 1920, Comiskey never again saw his White Sox finish in the first division. He faded into declining health, dying in 1931.

See also: Black Sox Scandal; Jackson, Joseph Jefferson; Johnson, Byron Bancroft; Landis, Kenesaw Mountain; Major Leagues.

Additional Reading:

Asinof, Eliot. *Eight Men Out: The Black Sox and the 1919 World Series*. New York: Holt, 1963.

Axelson, Gustaf W. *"Commy": The Life Story of Charles A. Comiskey*. Chicago: Reilly and Lee, 1919.

Gropman, Donald. *Say It Ain't So, Joe: The True Story of Shoeless Joe Jackson and the 1919 World Series*. 1979. Reprint, New York: Lynx, 1988.

Lindberg, Richard. *Sox: The Complete Record of Chicago White Sox Baseball*. New York: Macmillan, 1984.

———. *Stealing First in a Two-Team Town: The White Sox from Comiskey to Reinsdorf*. Champaign, IL: Sagamore, 1994.

COMMISSIONER

The office of Commissioner of Baseball was created in 1920 in response to the loss of public credibility after the Black Sox scandal of 1919. Desperate for leadership that would restore confidence and ensure the financial well-being of teams, owners settled on a federal judge, Kenesaw Mountain Landis, and gave him virtual dictatorial power. The owners swore loyalty to Landis, pledging to obey him even when they thought he was wrong and vowing never publicly to disagree with his rulings. Although no subsequent commissioner would wield the same power, the office remained potentially strong and reasonably independent until the 1990s, when the governance structure of baseball was overhauled.

In some ways, the commissioner's office was sharply at odds with American society. Certainly the lack of democracy and due process involved in the total power granted Landis invited abuse of power and unfairness. Fans still argue over the lifetime ban from baseball he imposed on members of the 1919 White Sox, especially Shoeless Joe Jackson. In addition, Landis's powerful hold on baseball helped to keep African Americans out of the majors until after his death.

From 1903 until 1920, organized baseball was ruled by a three-person commission that included the two league presidents. In reality, the dominant figure was Ban Johnson, creator and president of the American League. The ascendancy of Landis meant an enormous loss of power by Johnson, as well as by league presidents and team owners. When Judge Landis died in 1944, his successor, Happy Chandler, enjoyed considerably less power, partly because Landis's imperial demeanor had intimidated owners, partly because the precipitating crisis had long since faded into memory. When Chandler took over, baseball was in relatively good health.

After Landis, owners seldom were thrilled with the men who served as commissioners, tending to see commissioners—who had the impossible task of trying to unify a disparate group of individuals with strong egos and personal agendas—as getting in the way of their own plans. Sometimes, as in the case of Chandler, they were able to get rid of a commissioner, but they always found it impossible not to hire a replacement. As labor issues heated up in the 1970s, the commissioner was seen increasingly as more of an impediment than an aid when it came to trying to impose ownership positions on the players.

A. Bartlett Giamatti was a popular commissioner with owners. Yet because he died only a few months into his tenure, he did not have enough time to antagonize them. He also devoted much of his time (except for the Pete Rose case) to speaking eloquently about the mythic meaning and poetic beauty of baseball, leaving resolution of labor issues primarily to the owners. His successor, Fay Vincent, reverted to the traditional role of commissioner.

In September 1992, Vincent resigned after a vote of no confidence. Despite a very public search for a successor, baseball continued for most of that decade with Bud Selig, owner of the Milwaukee Brewers, as acting commissioner. There are many people who believe that most owners really did not want another independent commissioner, preferring one of their own in order to present a united front in labor negotiations. Finally, in July 1998 Selig was unanimously selected as baseball's ninth commissioner. In the fol-

lowing year, consolidation of power in the commissioner's office continued with the abolition of the league presidencies.

As the role of commissioner initially departed from the all-American principles of democracy and due process, the owners' recent power grab reflects the rising corporatization of business in America, as national and international corporations squeeze out or swallow up smaller companies. If a golden age of commissioners ever existed, it may have been located not in the corporate world of Bud Selig or the dictatorship of Judge Landis or the myth-making of Giamatti but in the ongoing struggles—from Chandler through Peter Ueberroth (who served until 1989)—to mediate among the various owners and between owners and players to achieve a balance that would serve fans well.

See also: Black Sox Scandal; Chandler, Albert Benjamin; Comiskey, Charles Albert; Finley, Charles Oscar; Giamatti, Angelo Bartlett; Kuhn, Bowie K.; Labor-Management Relations; Landis, Kenesaw Mountain; Law; Steinbrenner, George Michael, III.

Additional Reading:

Chandler, Happy, with Vance H. Trimble. *Heroes, Plain Folks, and Skunks: The Life and Times of Happy Chandler.* Chicago: Bonus Books, 1989.

Holtzman, Jerome. *The Commissioners: Baseball's Midlife Crisis.* New York: Total Sports, 1998.

Kuhn, Bowie, and Martin Appel. *Hardball: The Education of a Baseball Commissioner.* New York: Times Books, 1987.

Pietrusza, David. *Judge and Jury: The Life and Times of Judge Kenesaw Mountain Landis.* South Bend, IN: Diamond Communications, 1998.

Valerio, Anthony. *Bart: A Life of A. Bartlett Giamatti.* New York: Harcourt Brace Jovanovich, 1991.

CONNORS, KEVIN JOSEPH ALOYSIUS (CHUCK) (1921–1992)

Chuck Connors is best known to Americans as star of the television series *The*

Rifleman, but before becoming a successful actor in film and television Westerns he was a first baseman in the minors and briefly with the Dodgers and Cubs. At the end of his professional baseball career, he demonstrated considerable independence by rejecting the chance to be drafted by a major league team for the sake of family and future job opportunities.

The Brooklyn-born Connors had worked his way up the Dodger farm system to their top minor league club, the Montreal Royals, by 1948, playing with such future stars as Roy Campanella, Don Newcombe, and Duke Snider. The following year, he got into one game for the Dodgers, with one at-bat. The 1951 season saw Connors playing in 66 games for the Chicago Cubs, where he hit .239 with two home runs and 18 RBIs.

By late 1951, Connors was living in California, under contract to the Los Angeles Angels of the Pacific Coast League while entertaining hopes of becoming an actor. Not wishing to subject his wife and children to another move following the elusive dream of a major league career, and not wanting to leave California, Connors declined to make himself eligible for the major league draft, believing that any organization would draft him merely to provide insurance at a Triple-A affiliate. Western roles started to come his way, with 1958 being his breakthrough year as he played a memorable role in the film *The Big Country* and began *The Rifleman*. In the latter, which ran until 1963, Connors played the widower Lucas McCain, caring for his son Mark (Johnny Crawford) while defeating bad guys with his trick Winchester.

See also: Autry, Orvon Gene; Brooklyn Dodgers; Films; Grey, Pearl Zane.
Additional Reading:
Buscombe, Edward, ed. *The BFI Companion to the Western.* New York: Da Capo, 1988.
Salin, Tony. *Baseball's Forgotten Heroes: One Fan's Search for the Game's Most Interesting Overlooked Players.* Chicago: Masters, 1999.
Sullivan, Neil J. *The Minors: The Struggles and the Triumph of Baseball's Poor Relation from 1876 to the Present.* New York: St. Martin's Press, 1990.
Yoggy, Gary A. "Prime-Time Bonanza! The Western on Television." In *Wanted Dead or Alive: The American West in Popular Culture.* Ed. Richard Aquila. Urbana: University of Illinois Press, 1996, pp. 160–187.
———. *Riding the Video Range: The Rise and Fall of the Western on Television.* Jefferson, NC: McFarland, 1995.

CREIGHTON, JAMES (1841–1862)

Few baseball careers have involved more lasting innovations or ended so tragically as that of James Creighton, a pitcher and slugger who began his short career with the Brooklyn Niagaras in 1859. Pitchers in those early years were required to throw underhand, with a stiff-armed delivery. Creighton decided to alter that delivery, serving up the ball with a slight twist of the wrist, causing the ball to rise at a sharper angle and with such speed that opposing hitters likened it to a ball being shot from a cannon. Thus was born the art of deception, which later would yield the curveball and many other trick pitches.

Creighton's unusual pitching brought him such success that he jumped from the Niagaras to the Brooklyn Excelsiors in 1860, apparently by way of the Brooklyn Stars, helped along by an under-the-table payoff that violated the amateur National Association's rule against paying players; he thus became the first professional ballplayer.

The Excelsiors embarked on the first great baseball tour in 1860, which also marked the first significant use of the railroad by a baseball team. Everywhere the Excelsiors went, they were warmly greeted, and their success and fame caused new teams to spring up in their wake.

James Creighton was as great a hitter as he was pitcher, which, according to reports, occasioned his untimely death. On October 14, 1862, Creighton swung mightily, hit the ball for a home run, and struggled around the bases before collapsing. James Creighton died four days later, his mighty swing supposedly having ruptured his bladder. Fearing that news of his death might deter other young men from playing baseball, the president of the Excelsiors claimed that Creighton had been competing in cricket when he was injured. Grieving teammates erected a granite obelisk topped by a marble baseball over his grave in Brooklyn's Greenwood Cemetery. More universal, if not more durable, memorials to Creighton are the professionalism, the art of pitching, and the use of the latest modes of transportation that characterize modern baseball.

See also: Cricket.

Additional Reading:

Seymour, Harold. *Baseball: The Early Years.* 1960. Reprint, New York: Oxford University Press, 1989.

Spalding, Albert G. *Base Ball: America's National Game.* 1911. Reprint, revised and edited by Samm Coombs and Bob West, San Francisco: Halo Books, 1991.

Thorn, John. "Jim Creighton: To a Ballplayer Dying Young." *Elysian Fields Quarterly* 11(3) (1992): 59–63.

CRICKET

As a sport, cricket had a major influence on American society and then was rejected for its British heritage by a nation anxious to demonstrate its independence. Popular in England from the eighteenth century on, cricket also was widely played in this country, often by individuals (e.g., Harry and George Wright of the 1869 Cincinnati Red Stockings, and before them some of the original New York Knickerbockers) who participated in both cricket and baseball, the game that grew out of cricket and the earlier game known as rounders.

Some aspects of cricket are familiar to modern baseball fans. A bowler (pitcher) throws the ball (on a bounce) to a batter; there are umpires and innings. But the bat is paddle-shaped, the use of wooden wickets bears no obvious visual relationship to baseball, and the rules are so complex that casual participation in the game is far more difficult than in baseball. Perhaps because of the complexity of the game, its length (often taking two days to complete a match), and its association with the British, Americans tend to see cricket as a gentleman's game. In fact, both here and abroad, the game was hailed as a democratic sport, with victory dependent more on skill than on higher-class prerogatives. It was especially popular with blue-collar workers in the United States in the first half of the nineteenth century.

By the 1870s, cricket had largely disappeared in the United States, replaced by versions of townball and the emerging sport that became modern baseball. Cricket remains popular in England, where rules established by the Marylebone Cricket Club of London in 1744 (somewhat revised in later years) are still followed.

See also: Rounders; Townball.

Additional Reading:

Kirsch, George B. *The Creation of American Team Sports: Baseball and Cricket.* Urbana: University of Illinois Press, 1989.

Melville, Tom. *Cricket for Americans: Playing and Understanding the Game.* Bowling Green, OH: Bowling Green State University Popular Press, 1993.

———. *The Tented Field: A History of Cricket in America.* Bowling Green, OH: Bowling Green State University Popular Press, 1998.

Seymour, Harold. *Baseball: The Early Years.* 1960. Reprint, New York: Oxford University Press, 1989.

Zoss, Joel, and John Bowman. *Diamonds in the Rough: The Untold History of Baseball*. 1989. Reprint, Chicago: Contemporary Books, 1996.

CUBAN BASEBALL

Cuba has a long history of baseball, stretching back well into the nineteenth century. Steve Bellan, the first Cuban to play in an American major league, played third base for the Troy Haymakers in 1871. Cincinnati proved especially hospitable to Cuban players, featuring Rafael Almeida and Armando Marsans from 1911 to 1913, the latter continuing his career with other clubs through 1918; and Dolf Luque, who went 27-8 for the Reds in 1923 on his way to amassing 193 victories over a 20-year career.

Washington established consistent scouting efforts in Cuba during the 1940s and 1950s, and other teams followed suit. The period after World War II saw Cubans such as Gil Torres, Minnie Minoso, and Camilo Pascual become major league regulars. Luis Tiant established himself as a potential Hall of Fame pitcher in the 1960s and 1970s, and Tony Oliva won three batting titles with the Minnesota Twins between 1964 and 1971.

Cubans were passionate baseball fans and had occasion to see some of their favorite players in person beginning in the 1920s thanks to winter league ball. When they could not observe their baseball heroes in person, they followed the box scores in the papers, as Santiago does in

Major Ramiro Valdes, vice prime minister of the Revolutionary Armed Forces of Cuba and member of the Central Committee of the Cuban Communist Party, swings at the first ball in the opening game of the Cuban annual Amateur Baseball Championship, which was attended by leaders of Cuba's Revolutionary Government. (Hulton Getty)

Hemingway's *The Old Man and the Sea* to keep track of his idol, Joe DiMaggio. The International League even placed a team in Cuba—the Havana Sugar Kings.

Connections between Cuba and U.S. baseball began to dry up shortly after Fidel Castro came to power in 1959. The International League dropped its Cuban club, and Cuban players found it increasingly difficult to leave the country to join U.S. teams. Castro, however, began an amateur baseball program and continued to support it throughout the subsequent decades of his rule. The result was a strong Cuban League that produced teams for the Olympics and other international games. Cuba, for example, compiled an 80-1 record in international competition between 1987 and 1996, winning gold medals in the 1992 and 1996 Olympics, the first two times baseball was an official Olympic event.

Cuban defections to the United States have increased in recent years. The most prominent case may be that of pitcher Orlando Hernandez, who helped pitch the New York Yankees to a World Series championship in October 1998, just 10 months after fleeing Cuba on a raft. His half-brother, Livan, had defected in 1995, quickly establishing himself as a successful big league pitcher with the Florida Marlins and being named 1997 World Series Most Valuable Player.

Negotiations began in early 1999 between Peter Angelos, owner of the Baltimore Orioles, and the Cuban government for the Orioles to play exhibitions against a national team. The initiative followed an announcement by President Bill Clinton permitting such events so long as proceeds go to nongovernment charities rather than to the Cuban government. The two teams did meet, playing one game each in Cuba and the United States. It appears likely that the major leagues will feature many more Cuban players in the years ahead, almost surely to the detriment of Cuban amateur baseball. Yet as baseball has long served Fidel Castro's political purposes, it may now serve a higher purpose—improved relations between two countries that share more than a love for baseball.

> See also: Castro, Fidel; Hemingway, Ernest Miller; Latin American Baseball.
>
> *Additional Reading:*
>
> Bjarkman, Peter C. *Baseball with a Latin Beat: A History of the Latin American Game.* Jefferson, NC: McFarland, 1994.
>
> ———. "Lifting the Iron Curtain of Cuban Baseball." *The National Pastime: A Review of Baseball History* 17 (1997): 30–34.
>
> Oliva, Tony, with Bob Fowler. *Tono O! The Trials and Triumphs of Tony Oliva.* New York: Hawthorn, 1973.
>
> Regalado, Samuel O. *Viva Baseball: Latin Major Leaguers and Their Special Hunger.* Urbana: University of Illinois Press, 1998.
>
> Torres, Angel. *La historia del beisbol cubano, 1878–1976.* Los Angeles: Angel Torres, 1976.

CUMMINGS, WILLIAM ARTHUR (CANDY) (1848–1924)

Candy Cummings was one of the great pitchers of the early decades of organized baseball, achieving his success and lasting fame with an innovative pitch called the curveball. When Cummings played, pitchers threw a straight-arm underhand pitch and were not to do anything deceitful. Candy apparently was as honest as the next person—just a little more creative.

As a teenager, Candy noticed how a clamshell would curve as it skipped over the water when thrown. So why not a baseball? Cummings worked on his new pitch for a few years and tried it out against Harvard's baseball club while pitching for the Brooklyn Excelsiors. The pitch bedeviled hitters, but only when the wind was blowing into the pitcher's face.

After four years with the Stars of Brook-lyn, Cummings received his big chance when the National Association of Professional Base Ball Players changed its rules in 1872 to permit a pitcher to snap his wrist when pitching. With the curveball delivery now legal, the New York Mutuals signed Cummings. He pitched for four years with four different teams in the league, earning acclaim by famous baseball journalist and lawkeeper Henry Chadwick as the best pitcher of his time. Chadwick also credited Cummings with inventing the curveball, but not all historians agree. The reality is that the curveball probably was invented by various people independently during the 1850s and 1860s.

Cummings then pitched in the National League (1876–1877) before wearing out, served briefly as president of the rival International Association of Professional Baseball Players (now considered the first minor league), and returned to his native Massachusetts to run a paint and wallpaper store.

See also: Chadwick, Henry.

Additional Reading:

Nemec, David. *The Great Encyclopedia of 19th-Century Major League Baseball.* New York: Donald I. Fine, 1997.

Reidenbaugh, Lowell. *Baseball's Hall of Fame: Cooperstown, Where the Legends Live Forever.* Rev. by editors of *The Sporting News.* New York: Crescent Books, 1997.

Seymour, Harold. *Baseball: The Early Years.* 1960. Reprint, New York: Oxford University Press, 1989.

Sullivan, Neil J. *The Minors: The Struggles and the Triumph of Baseball's Poor Relation from 1876 to the Present.* New York: St. Martin's Press, 1990.

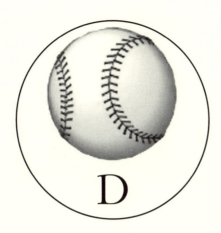

DAMN YANKEES

The New York Yankees are the greatest dynasty in the history of baseball, an opinion seconded in a *Sports Illustrated* special publication entitled *Greatest Teams: The Most Dominant Powerhouses in Sports,* where author Tim Crothers ranks the Yankees first among all professional sports dynasties.

Technically, the Yankee dynasty endured from 1925 to 1964, with two World Series championships in the 1970s keeping alive memories of the glory years and three more titles in the 1990s suggesting a dynastic sequel. With the advent of free agency, however, the dynasty may be a thing of the past, with teams unable to retain stars who tend to follow the money to the highest bidder. But during the golden years of Yankee dominance, the Bronx Bombers rode such greats as Babe Ruth, Lou Gehrig, Joe DiMaggio, and Mickey Mantle to three World Series triumphs in the 1920s, five in the 1930s, four in the 1940s, six in the 1950s, and two in the 1960s. The dominance led to calls of "Break up the Yankees!" and even a musical, *Damn Yankees,* which premiered in the Forty-Sixth Street Theater in New York on May 5, 1955.

Damn Yankees was written by George Abbott and Douglass Wallop, with music and lyrics by Richard Adler and Jerry Ross. Based on the 1954 Wallop novel *The Year the Yankees Lost the Pennant,* the musical has endured despite the fluctuating fortunes of the Yankees in subsequent decades. Its initial run of 1,019 performances starred Stephen Douglass as Joe Hardy, the aging fan who sells his soul to the devil to become a star with the lowly Washington Senators; Gwen Verdon as the sexy Lola, the temptress utilized by the devil to prevent Joe from returning to his wife prior to the deadline for turning over his soul; and Ray Walston as Applegate—the devil himself. Hardy's superhuman feats lead the Senators to a remarkable run to overcome the hated Yankees, but he ultimately thwarts Applegate, resists Lola, and returns to his wife and his previous existence—an aging but wiser and more contented man.

The continuing success of the musical is testimony to its rousing (and sometimes touching) songs, among them "Heart," "Whatever Lola Wants," and "A Man Doesn't Know"; its combination of humor, suspense, and pathos; and its transformation of a pennant race into a morality play by way of the ancient bargain-with-the-devil motif. *Damn Yankees* also continues to transform playgoers who have never witnessed a major league game into diehard Yankee haters.

See also: Fiction; New York Yankees; Theater.
Additional Reading:

Crothers, Tim. *Greatest Teams: The Most Dominant Powerhouses in Sports.* New York: *Sports Illustrated,* 1998.

Henrich, Tommy, with Bill Gilbert. *Five O'Clock Lightning: Ruth, Gehrig, DiMaggio, and the Glory Days of the New York Yankees.* Carol, 1992.

Ross, Jerry. *Damn Yankees: A New Musical Based on the Novel* The Year the Yankees Lost the Pennant. New York: Random House, 1956.

———. *Damn Yankees: Original Broadway Cast.* RCA Victor, 1988.

Wallop, Douglass. *The Year the Yankees Lost the Pennant.* New York: Norton, 1954.

DEAN, JAY HANNA (DIZZY) (1910–1974)

Fans in the 1940s and 1950s knew Dizzy Dean as a colorful radio and television broadcaster who spiced his accounts of the games with entertaining anecdotes, renditions of the song "Wabash Cannonball" (which he recorded for Colonial Records), and consistent fracturing of the English language (for example, "slud" instead of "slid" and "statics" for "statistics"). Dean's popularity and unique style even precipitated a parody recording by Cactus Pryor called "What's the Score, Podner?"

It was not Dean's broadcasting, though, that led to the making of the film *The Pride of St. Louis* in 1952, with Dan Dailey playing Dizzy and Richard Crenna as brother Paul Dean. Dizzy Dean, in fact, was one of baseball's all-time great pitchers, winner of 30 games in 1934; he was inducted into the Hall of Fame in 1953. He also was one of the most popular players on one of the most famous teams ever—the Cardinals' Gashouse Gang. Dizzy was almost as famous as Babe Ruth. Even as a youngster fresh from the cotton fields of Arkansas, he asserted that he was the greatest pitcher in the world and that he would draw more fans than Ruth himself. He was wrong, but not by a great margin.

Dean won 18, 20, 30, 28, and 24 games from 1932 to 1936, striking out at least 190 batters and pitching between 286 and 325 innings each year. After predicting prior to the 1934 season that he and brother Paul (known as "Daffy") would win 45 games, the brothers did even better, Dizzy winning 30 and Daffy 19. Each added two victories in the World Series triumph over the Detroit Tigers. Dean, who struck out 17 Cubs in a 1933 game, supplemented his fastball with good fielding ability, speed on the bases, and even some hitting talent. In the 1934 World Series, he stepped into the Tigers' batting cage during their batting practice prior to the first game and slugged the ball over the fence. In the fourth game, Dean was inserted as a pinch-runner. In a scene appropriate to Dean, a Tiger infielder, apparently inadvertently, hit him in the head with a throw. Dean was knocked unconscious. After cautionary tests, he announced enthusiastically, "They X-rayed my head and found nothing."

A line drive by Earl Averill struck Dean in the 1937 All-Star Game, fracturing a toe. Trying to alter his pitching motion to compensate for the injured toe led to a dead arm. Dean was traded to the Chicago Cubs after the season and continued to pitch until 1941, with minimal success. As a promotional ploy, Dean, broadcasting St. Louis Browns games in 1947, returned to the pitcher's mound for the final game of the season. He completed his career with 150 wins against just 83 losses.

Brother Paul faired even worse. After winning 19 games in 1934 and 1935, he managed only 12 additional victories, although he continued pitching until 1945. Nothing, though, would diminish the legend of the Dean brothers. Other brothers have pitched in the majors since then, some with considerable success, but none with the bravado and general outrageousness of Dizzy and Daffy.

See also: Films; Gashouse Gang; Language, Baseball; Television Broadcasting.

Additional Reading:

Gregory, Robert. *Diz: Dizzy Dean and Baseball During the Great Depression.* New York: Viking, 1992.

Smith, Curt. *America's Dizzy Dean.* St. Louis: Bethany, 1978.

Staten, Vince. *Ol' Diz: A Biography of Dizzy Dean.* New York: HarperCollins, 1992.

DEMOCRACY

Baseball became and remained America's national pastime for a variety of reasons, one of the most important being its natural relationship to democracy. As democracy was being woven ever more securely into the thought processes and actions of the public, baseball was also solidifying its position within that same American public. However, it was not always so.

Baseball's origins were more aristocratic than democratic. The first organized team was the Knickerbocker Base Ball Club of New York. A group of young men who had been playing baseball decided to form what amounted to a social club in 1845. The organizing was led by Alexander Joy Cartwright, variously described as a bank teller or shipping clerk, and a physician named Daniel Lucius "Doc" Adams, the latter serving as president of the club. They found a permanent playing field, the Elysian Fields in Hoboken, New Jersey, and rented the field as well as dressing rooms; they also rented a room at a hotel for business meetings.

There was little democratic about this first organized team. Most of the members, limited to 40 in number, were professionals; in fact, social standing was required for membership, as was the financial wherewithal to pay membership dues and purchase uniforms. The practice of blackballing, whereby individual members could reject applicants out of hand, was utilized to keep membership relatively homogeneous. Various rules were strictly enforced to maintain decorum, backed up by fines for violations. A member, for example, was not allowed to use profane language or dispute an umpire's decision. As historian Harold Seymour has written in *Baseball: The Early Years,* the first volume of his monumental three-volume history of the game:

> To the Knickerbockers a ball game was a vehicle for genteel amateur recreation and polite social intercourse rather than a hard-fought contest for victory. They were more expert with the knife and fork at postgame banquets than with bat and ball on the diamond. Their rules and regulations emphasized proper conduct, and the entire tone of their organization was more akin to the atmosphere surrounding cricket—a far cry from the ethic of modern professional baseball. (15)

This exclusiveness, however, could not withstand the growing popularity of baseball among all levels of society. The game was inexpensive to play, requiring only a bat and ball, and there were plenty of open spaces available. In addition, the vast majority of children, both girls and boys, could (and still can) play the game (or its more modern softball version) at an enjoyable level. Baseball became a common recess game at schools, and large numbers of adults continued to play the game.

As democracy championed the rights of all citizens and preached equality of opportunity, as well as equality before the law, so was baseball available to almost everyone. In addition, the game, like democracy, offered laws that were to be obeyed because, within those laws, all participants had an equal chance. Laws enforced freedoms for all rather than claimed freedom for a special few— at least ideally. The game also fostered a brotherhood (years later a sisterhood) among the participants. If baseball is widely perceived as conducive to such virtues as teamwork, fair play, healthy competition, and even patriotism, Albert G. Spalding, writing in 1911 in his *Base Ball: America's National Game,* opined, in a burst of alliteration:

> Base Ball owes its prestige as our National Game to the fact that as no other form of sport it is the exponent of American Courage, Confidence, Combativeness; American Dash, Discipline, Determination; American Energy, Eagerness, Enthusiasm; American Pluck, Persistency, Performance; American Spirit, Sagacity, Success; American Vim, Vigor, Virility. (2)

For Spalding, "The genius of our institutions is democratic; Base Ball is a democratic game" (3).

A consistent symbol of the democratic spirit in baseball is the tradition of U.S. presidents throwing out the first pitch in a season opener. It is a game for the powerful and wealthy as well as for the ranks of citizens who live content in their knowledge that to be common citizens is to comprise the heart and soul of democratic society. The wealthy, it is true, may today be found in a luxury box rather than in the general-admission seats, but

they nonetheless share the same love of the game.

A look at the Brooklyn Atlantics, the most powerful team of the early 1860s, demonstrates the democratic changes in the game that followed within a few years of the creation of the Knickerbockers. Comprising working-class men, whose fans were mainly longshoremen and generally tough types, the team captured the Brooklyn championship in 1860 from the Excelsiors, a club more in the Knickerbocker mold. Some members of the Atlantics became popular heroes, especially Joe "Old Reliable" Start, so named for his ability to catch everything hit to him; and Jack Chapman, another fielding whiz, who inspired the nickname "Death to flying things."

Baseball spread rapidly from the 1860s. Both sides played baseball in peaceful moments during the Civil War. The rise of sportswriting in the 1880s both responded to and helped expand the popularity of the game. By this time, the expression "America's national pastime," which in varied forms had been used since the 1850s, really fit. No other game in the country came close to equaling baseball in popularity, both as a participatory and spectator sport.

Nonetheless, the title fit imperfectly, for society had not achieved (in politics or baseball) a true democratic system for all. Although black Americans played baseball—in fact, the game became enormously popular within the black community, which gave enthusiastic support to the Negro Leagues—they were kept firmly locked out of the major leagues. Similarly, although slavery ended with the Thirteenth Amendment to the U.S. Constitution, ratified on December 6, 1865, Jim Crow laws in the South and discrimination in the North kept African Americans out of full enjoyment of the democratic process until the civil rights movement of the 1950s and 1960s.

In reality, major league baseball, although closed to blacks until Jackie Robinson broke the color barrier in 1947, proved more progressive than most of American society. As Jackie Robinson traveled with his Brooklyn Dodgers teammates, baseball became the first major American institution to achieve integration. This democratizing function of baseball had earlier brought opportunity to many other, albeit white, groups. Sons of immigrants turned to baseball to find an avenue into mainstream America—and a way to make a good living. Young men like Italian American Joe DiMaggio and Jewish American Hank Greenberg became heroes to their ethnic groups as they excelled on the diamond. In more recent years, baseball has welcomed players from throughout the world, from South America, from Asia, from Cuba. The Statue of Liberty still beckons, and talented athletes continue to follow her guiding light to a land of opportunity and democracy—a land of baseball.

See also: African Americans; Cartwright, Alexander Joy; Jewish Americans; Law; Robinson, Jack Roosevelt; Rural America; Spalding, Albert Goodwill; "The Star-Spangled Banner"; Women in Baseball.

Additional Reading:

Gelber, Steven M. "Working at Playing: The Culture of the Workplace and the Rise of Baseball." *Journal of Social History* 16 (1983): 3–22.

Riess, Steven A. *City Games: The Evolution of American Urban Society and the Rise of Sports.* Urbana: University of Illinois Press, 1989.

Seymour, Harold. *Baseball: The Early Years.* 1960. Reprint, New York: Oxford University Press, 1989.

Spalding, Albert G. *Base Ball: America's National Game.* 1911. Reprint, revised and edited by Samm Coombs and Bob West, San Francisco: Halo Books, 1991.

Voigt, David Quentin. *American Baseball.* 3 vols. (1966–1983). University Park: Pennsylvania State University Press, 1983.

DIMAGGIO, JOSEPH PAUL (JOLTIN' JOE, THE YANKEE CLIPPER) (1914–1999)

Joltin' Joe DiMaggio, the Yankee Clipper, became a superstar, then a hero, and finally a cultural icon. His extraordinary baseball accomplishments were indispensable to, but not the only reason for, this progression. Just as important was the way in which he achieved, and the combination of substance and form made him one of the most recognizable individuals in the United States and abroad.

Joe DiMaggio's most famous achievement was his remarkable hitting streak in 1941, when he set a new major league record by hitting safely in 56 consecutive games. As the streak progressed—with DiMaggio first surpassing Rogers Hornsby's National League record of 33 consecutive games, then George Sisler's modern American League mark of 41—the nation followed in rapt attention. Most Americans wanted the streak to go on forever, and in fact it endured for close to half a season. As DiMaggio neared Sisler's total, a reporter unearthed the fact that Wee Willie Keeler, in 1892, had hit safely in 44 straight games.

DiMaggio tied Sisler in the first game of a doubleheader on June 29, 1941, but between games someone stole his bat. Using a backup, DiMaggio failed to hit safely in his first three attempts. Finally, he borrowed teammate Tommy Henrich's bat, the same model DiMaggio had been using, and stroked a single into left field. Keeler's mark also fell, and DiMaggio kept going until the steak had reached 56 games. Then, against the Indians in

Baseball star Joe DiMaggio, ca. 1940s (Hulton Getty)

Cleveland, three outstanding fielding plays, two by third baseman Ken Keltner and one by shortstop Lou Boudreau, ended the streak. However, the Yankee great immediately set off on another streak of 17 games. Had one of DiMaggio's hot smashes fielded so well by Cleveland's infielders gone through, his record would stand at 74, almost half of the 154 games played that season.

DiMaggio was named Most Valuable Player in the American League in 1941, an award he also received in 1939 and 1947. During his 13 years with the Yankees (1936–1942, 1946–1951), he batted .325 (with a high of .381 in 1939), connected for 361 home runs among his 2,214 total hits, drove in over 100 runs nine times, and struck out on just 369 occasions, as few as 13 times in his 1941 season. The world will likely never again see a power hitter record almost as many home runs as strikeouts, perhaps an even more remarkable feat than DiMaggio's hitting streak.

DiMaggio's teammates often referred to him, especially in later years, not only as their leader but as their hero. Fans, of course, also saw him as heroic, but that was to be expected. Baseball players live with a teammate and see his weaknesses as well as his strengths, but to a man they viewed DiMaggio as a heroic figure: talented, moral, dignified, giving of himself, and, especially in his last few seasons, playing through sometimes excruciating pain.

Joe DiMaggio, as all heroes should, exuded class. He was tall, quiet, and always dignified. Acutely aware of his importance to fans and of his responsibility to them, he never let down his guard. He did not clown in public or, for that matter, much in private. He made sure that his uniform was impeccable on the field, and off the field he dressed consistently in dark suits and blue ties (with shoes always polished), attire that earned him, after his rookie season, inclusion on a list of best-dressed men in America.

The Yankee Clipper usually said little in the clubhouse or away from it. He let his skills speak for him, and they spoke loudly enough to be heard around the globe. Most observers of America's national pastime considered him the best all-around player of his time, even if some might give the nod to Ted Williams

strictly for hitting. DiMaggio could indeed do it all. At bat he was in control, and even the greatest pitchers had their hands full with him. He almost always made good contact and handled the curveball with apparent ease. In the field, he was a smart player who knew how to play individual hitters. The great center fielder played shallow, sometimes too shallow for his pitcher's comfort, but easily caught up with balls that would have dropped over another fielder's head. Also an intelligent base runner, he routinely stretched singles into doubles or went from first to third on hits that would have left a lesser runner resting on second. Although he stole only 30 bases in his career, his early manager, Joe McCarthy, called him the best base runner he ever saw and stated that he easily could have stolen 50 or more bases per season if McCarthy had given him the green light.

Joe DiMaggio also was the team leader, even down to determining World Series shares. His Yankee teams won nine World Series in his 13 years with the club, and, as Hemingway's Santiago says in *The Old Man and the Sea,* DiMaggio was the difference.

Yet DiMaggio was never more heroic than in 1949. A painful bone spur in his right heel led to two operations and kept DiMaggio out of action until almost midseason. Then, after pneumonia sidelined him again, he came back, barely able to stand, for the final two games of the season and led the Yankees, trailing the Red Sox by one game on his return, to a sweep of the final two games and the pennant. DiMaggio's injury that year was to his heel, and also like the Greek mythological hero Achilles, DiMaggio went to war. Although not placed in harm's way during World War II, he did sacrifice three seasons when he was in his prime.

Finally, a long line of shoulder, elbow, and knee injuries caught up with Joltin' Joe, and when he could no longer pull the fastball into left field, he decided to hang up his spikes. The 1951 season was his last, but it was not the end of Joe DiMaggio, not at all.

Part of the story of Joe DiMaggio is that of the poor boy who made good. Son of a Sicilian immigrant who earned his living as a San Francisco fisherman, Joe, growing up, shared a four-room apartment with his parents and eight siblings. Two brothers, Vince and Dom, would become major league ballplayers themselves. He was a symbol of the American dream, the belief that anyone, no matter the person's origins, can become successful with hard work. No wonder fans idolized this son of a fisherman who overcame poverty and injuries to become the greatest player of his day and break supposedly unbreakable records, who always maintained his dignity and never forgot his obligation to the public.

Joe DiMaggio was well on his way to becoming a cultural icon even before he set his consecutive-game streak. During the 1941 season, Alan Courtney and Ben Homer composed a song, "Joltin' Joe DiMaggio," that Les Brown and his orchestra made famous. Yet much earlier, after the 1937 season, Joe's second with the Yankees, he had been persuaded to appear in a movie entitled *Manhattan Merry-Go-Round*. In the film, he met actress Dorothy Arnold, who would become his first wife. After retirement, DiMaggio met, wooed, and wed an even more famous actress, the screen goddess Marilyn Monroe, in one of the most famous marriages in history. Although the marriage lasted less than a year, the love affair endured. After Marilyn's death in 1962, her former husband, for decades, made sure that six roses were placed on her grave three times per week. Not even Shakespeare wrote a more compelling love story.

In later years, the public watched Joe DiMaggio lend instant credibility to commercial products, most notably Mr. Coffee, but no one would label him a pitchman. He made commercials but was careful not to endorse anything that he found offensive or inappropriate. Tommy Henrich, a former teammate, once said that Joe DiMaggio was the most moral man he had ever known. And even old heroes have to earn a living.

The public's view of Joe DiMaggio as a hero in a world short on genuine heroes continued as the decades passed. In some ways, songwriter-singers Paul Simon and Art Garfunkel put it best when they lamented in their song "Mrs. Robinson": "Where have you gone, Joe DiMaggio?" Joe DiMaggio always claimed not to understand the meaning of those lyrics, but the public knew. Joe DiMaggio remained a hero, an icon of America at its dependable, hardworking, striving-for-excellence best, and there are not many of those around any more. Not surprisingly, the American public closely followed DiMaggio's final illness, a combination of cancer and pneumonia, which he fought with his usual dignity and determination. He died on March 8, 1999.

See also: Cancer; Hemingway, Ernest Miller; Heroes; Music; New York Yankees;
Additional Reading:
Allen, Maury. *Where Have You Gone, Joe DiMaggio?* New York: Dutton, 1975.
DiMaggio, Joe. *Lucky to Be a Yankee.* New York: R. Field (publ.), Greenberg (dist.), 1946.
Durso, Joseph. *DiMaggio: The Last American Knight.* Boston: Little, Brown, 1995.
New York Daily News Staff. *Joe DiMaggio: An American Icon.* New York: Sports Publishing, 1999.
Seidel, Michael. *Streak: Joe DiMaggio and the Summer of '41.* New York: McGraw-Hill, 1988.

DISABILITIES

Americans with disabilities often are their own best heroes, and a number of players have performed in the major leagues despite serious disabilities. Pete Gray, for example, dreamed as a boy of playing major league baseball. That dream seemed lost when his right arm was crushed under a truck's wheel. Gray, only six years old at the time of the accident, persevered. The son of a coal miner, Gray made it to the minors, and in 1944 he batted .333 and stole 68 bases in winning the Most Valuable Player for Memphis in the Southern Association. By that time, many players were fighting in World War II, and the St. Louis Browns promoted Gray to the majors. He played the 1945 season with the Browns, appearing in 77 games and batting .218 while striking out only 11 times in 234 at-bats. However, he had little home-run power, and with many major-leaguers returning from the war, Gray found himself back in the minors the following year. Nonetheless, he had reached his goal.

Another player who received an opportunity to play during the war was pitcher Bert Shepard. A veteran himself, Shepard lost a leg when he was shot down over Germany. He returned to pitch one game in relief with Washington in 1945. He pitched five innings, allowing just three hits, one run, and one walk while striking out two batters. Despite that impressive performance, he also was out of a job after the war.

One of the most famous players to strive against a serious physical disability was Monte Stratton. An outstanding pitcher with the White Sox in the late 1930s, he twice won 15 games. After the 1938 season, while hunting rabbits in Greenville, Texas, near his mother's home, he accidentally discharged his pistol; the bullet lodged in his right knee,

Pitcher Jim Abbott, No. 25 of the Milwaukee Brewers, poses for a studio portrait on Photo Day during spring training at the Maryville Baseball Park in Phoenix, Arizona. (Tom Hauck/Allsport)

severing the main artery. His leg was amputated. Although Stratton never returned to a major league mound, he did resume pitching in the minors, winning 18 games with Sherman in the Class-C East Texas League. His story became widely known when Jimmy Stewart played him in the 1949 film *The Stratton Story*. Then there was Bud Daley, a right-hander, whose right arm was badly damaged by polio. He learned to throw with the left hand and became a successful major league pitcher, making the All-Star team in 1959 and 1960 with the Kansas City Athletics.

The most famous recent example of major league determination in the face of disability is Jim Abbott. Abbott was born with an imperfectly developed right arm, which ended about where the wrist should be. Instead of a hand, there was a loose flap of skin. Abbott, however, came to an early love of baseball and played the game throughout childhood and high school. He had become such an effective pitcher that he was drafted by the Toronto Blue Jays in 1985 but opted instead to join the University of Michigan baseball team. Other players and spectators alike marveled at how efficiently he could catch and throw the ball with just one hand. Abbott would pitch with the glove on his right arm. Then he quickly stuck his left hand into the glove and was ready to field the ball if it were hit. He would catch the ball, drop the glove, retrieve the ball, and fire it to first base— all with extraordinary speed.

At Michigan, Abbott became a top-notch pitcher. In the fall of 1987 he received the Golden Spikes Award as the nation's best amateur baseball player. The following year he was the ace on the U.S. Olympic team and pitched the final game that sealed the championship for the United States.

Major league scouts had been following Abbott for years. He was drafted by the Angels in 1988 and this time decided to turn professional rather than return to Michigan for his senior year. His impressive pitching in spring training earned him a spot in the Angels rotation without having pitched a game in the minors. He won 12 games that rookie year, reached 18 victories in 1991; after being traded to the Yankees, he hurled a no-hitter in 1993. Abbott's career went into a tailspin in 1996 when, back with California, he won only two games and lost 18. After sitting out the following season, Abbott worked his way back up through the minors in 1998 to win all five of his decisions with the White Sox. Abbott joined the Milwaukee Brewers in 1999, and

while his future success at the major league level may be uncertain, he continues to inspire Americans, young and old alike.

Jim Abbott, although uncomfortable with being a role model, is exactly that. Countless people, especially children, continue to reach out to him, and Abbott, in turn, responds with unusual patience and a sincere desire to help. He is especially supportive of children with disabilities. Sportswriter Helene Elliott, who covered Abbott when he was with the Angels, was once asked whom she had as heroes. She mentioned her father, but the questioner wanted her to choose among professional athletes. She responded by saying that she knew athletes too well to see them as heroes, except for one: Jim Abbott.

Baseball heroes, of course, are not alone in inspiring others to overcome problems that they face. Society is filled with such role models: Ray Charles, who cannot see, is one of the greatest singers in the history of American music; Stephen Hawking, from his wheelchair, continues to search the most distant reaches of time and space; and countless others who live lives of less fame but no less courage and success. The most famous American to overcome physical disability is Franklin D. Roosevelt, who was stricken with polio and later became U.S. president. As a public figure, he felt it necessary to camouflage his inability to walk. Yet American society may now be ready to accept the reality that disabilities do not make a person less able to achieve great things. If so, public figures—including baseball players—have helped shatter old perceptions.

See also: Films; War.
Additional Reading:
Achieving Physical and Communication Accessibility. Washington, DC: National Center for Access Unlimited, 1991.

Bernotas, Bob. *Nothing to Prove: The Jim Abbott Story*. New York: Kodansha International, 1995.

Brightman, Alan. *Ordinary Moments: The Disabled Experience*. Baltimore: University Park, 1984.

Kashatus, William C. *One-Armed Wonder: Pete Gray, Wartime Baseball, and the American Dream*. Jefferson, NC: McFarland, 1995.

Macht, Norman L. *Jim Abbott: Major League Pitcher*. Great Achievers: Lives of the Physically Challenged Series. New York: Chelsea House, 1994.

DOBY, LAWRENCE EUGENE (LARRY) (1923–)

Larry Doby's fate has been to live somewhat in the shadow of Jackie Robinson. An outstanding Negro League player for the Newark Eagles when his contract was purchased by Bill Veeck, owner of the Cleveland Indians, Doby debuted in the major leagues in July 1947, becoming the first African American to play in the American League. Arriving about two months after Robinson broke the color barrier in the National League with Brooklyn, Doby was given less credit for his contributions to American society and for the courage he exhibited. With his election to the Hall of Fame in 1998, Larry Doby perhaps finally received his due.

Doby was a second baseman with the Eagles, whose owner, Effa Manley, agreed to Veeck's offer to purchase Doby's services, but not until getting Veeck to up his offer of $10,000 by another $5,000 if Doby stuck with Cleveland for at least 30 days. In truth, Manley had little bargaining power, and Veeck's willingness to pay anything testified to his sense of justice.

Doby's baseball career had been interrupted by three years in the U.S. Navy during World War II. When he returned, he was ready to take his place among the Negro League stars. Doby batted .341 in 1946 while helping the Eagles win the Negro League World Series. Also chosen as a Negro League All-Star, he partnered with shortstop Monte Irvin to give the Eagles a memorable double-play combination. Doby was hitting a robust .414 in 1947 when he joined the Indians.

Cleveland decided to switch Doby to center field and had Hall of Famer Tris Speaker, one of the all-time great defensive outfielders, tutor him. Doby made the switch in 1948, helping the Indians win the American League pennant and defeat the Braves in the World Series. He was joined during that championship season by Negro League legend Satchel Paige. Doby hit .301 for Cleveland and was on his way to becoming one of the best all-around players in the game, excelling in the field as well as at the plate.

Larry Doby hit 20 or more home runs every year from 1949 through 1956, becoming, in 1952, the first African American player to win a home-run title. He would add another home-run crown to his record, be selected to seven All-Star Games (and play in six), help the Indians win another pennant in 1954, and conclude his 13-year major league career (which included three seasons split between the Chicago White Sox and Detroit Tigers) with 253 home runs, 970 RBIs, and a .283 batting average. He was one of only four players (along with Paige, Irvin, and Willie Mays) to participate in both Negro League and major league World Series.

The Cleveland Indians apparently were considering Doby to be their manager in 1974 but hired Frank Robinson instead as the first African American manager in major league history. Doby had a brief opportunity to manage the Chicago White Sox during part of the 1978 season and later became special assistant to American League president Gene Budig. A modest man, he never seemed to resent the lack of attention and spoke little about harsh treatment from other players. At his inauguration into the Hall of Fame, he said, "When I look back and think about things that were probably negative, you put those things on the back burner. . . . You're proud and happy that you've been a part of integrating baseball to show people that we can live together, work together, play together, and we can be successful together."

See also: African Americans; Manley, Effa; Negro Leagues; Robinson, Frank; Veeck, William L., Jr.

Additional Reading:

Moore, Joseph Thomas. *Pride against Prejudice: The Biography of Larry Doby*. Westport, CT: Greenwood Press, 1988.

Riley, James. *The Biographical Encyclopedia of the Negro Baseball Leagues*. New York: Carroll and Graf, 1994.

Veeck, Bill, with Ed Linn. *Veeck—As in Wreck: The Autobiography of Bill Veeck*. New York: Putnam's, 1962.

DOUBLEDAY, ABNER (1819–1893)

Baseball, befitting its long history and importance in American society, has produced legends (as well as myths) over the years. One of the most prominent and widely believed legends has Abner Doubleday inventing baseball in 1839 in the grassy, idyllic setting of Cooperstown, New York, where 100 years later the Major League Baseball Hall of Fame would become a fixture of America's cultural landscape.

Doubleday indeed has a place in history, but it has nothing to do with baseball. Born in Ballston Spa, New York, the young Abner Doubleday grew up especially fond of poetry, art, and mathematics. When a bit bored by his surroundings, he would draw maps for recreation. Doubleday later attended West Point, where he diligently prepared to become a soldier just when legend has him creating the rules for baseball.

Doubleday served bravely in the Mexican-American War (1846–1848) and later became a genuine hero as a Union officer in the Civil War. Doubleday fought at several of the most important battles of the Civil War, including Fort Sumter, the second Bull Run, Antietam, and Gettysburg. He rose to the rank of major-general and, with the rank of colonel, continued his military service after the war until his retirement in 1873. The general wrote about his exploits in *Reminiscences of Forts Sumter and Moultrie in 1860–61* (1876) and *Chancellorsville and Gettysburg* (1882).

General Doubleday could not have avoided being at least acquainted with baseball, for soldiers on both sides played the game throughout the Civil War. Yet there is no evidence that Doubleday himself had any personal involvement with the game.

How Doubleday came to be credited with creating baseball remains somewhat perplexing, although part of the story is known. Albert Spalding, former player and baseball owner and, in the early twentieth century, famous and prosperous owner of a sporting-goods company, was determined that baseball was a uniquely American invention. To validate his claim, he set up a commission to pursue the matter. A letter arrived from a man named Abner Graves claiming that Doubleday, in his presence, had devised and written down on a piece of paper the rules for baseball at Cooperstown in 1839. Spalding bought the story, more out of wish fulfillment than logical persuasion, and the commission followed suit. It released its report on December 30, 1907, affirming that baseball was an American game created by Abner Doubleday as described by Graves.

This conclusion was greeted with considerable joy, as it fed Americans' pride and once again established America's independence from Great Britain and such British games as cricket and rounders, the latter being a game primarily played by children and long considered a forerunner of American baseball.

The truth, however, is that baseball was not created by Doubleday or anyone else. It had evolved gradually out of the British games. As America was about to commemorate the centennial of America's pastime, a librarian named Robert W. Henderson, after exhaustive research, demonstrated convincingly that rounders was identical to American baseball as played in the 1820s and 1830s. He had documentary proof in such books as *The Boy's Own Book* (1829) and Robin Carver's *The Book of Sports* (1834), both published in the United States. The former includes the rules for rounders, which are identical to the way that baseball was played at the time; the latter reinforces the identification by printing the rules for the British game but changing its name to "Base, or Goal Ball."

This discovery, now widely accepted by baseball historians, did not interfere significantly with the centennial celebrations. The Hall of Fame, once established, only gradually and grudgingly came to acknowledge the historical truth of baseball's "founding." Within the larger American society, however, the legend lives on, testifying forcefully to the power and self-perpetuating life that legends possess.

> *See also:* Cricket; Hall of Fame and Museum; Rounders; Spalding, Albert Goodwill; Townball; War.
>
> *Additional Reading:*
> Alexander, Charles C. *Our Game: An American Baseball History*. New York: MJF Books, 1991.
> Goldstein, Warren. *Playing for Keeps: A History of Early Baseball*. Ithaca: Cornell University Press, 1989.
> Seymour, Harold. *Baseball: The Early Years*. 1960. Reprint, New York: Oxford University Press, 1989.

DUROCHER, LEO ERNEST (THE LIP) (1905–1991)

"Nice guys finish last"—a famous baseball maxim and one of the best-known quotations among the American public. Millions who know nothing else about Leo Durocher recognize him as the author of this cynical comment on the merits of being nice. Success means being combative, putting winning above playing by the rules, and doing anything (or almost anything) for the sake of victory; that was Durocher's philosophy of competition. Yet millions of people who see themselves as nice people and certainly not as losers detect a thread of truth in Durocher's maxim.

Leo Durocher was enough of a success to be voted into the Hall of Fame in 1994, more for his managing than his playing. A veteran of 17 years as a shortstop with the Yankees, Reds, Cardinals, and Dodgers, Durocher was a slick-fielding shortstop who three times posted the highest fielding average among National League shortstops. At the plate, however, he was mediocre, hitting just .247 for his career and, in one of his more famous at-bats, making the final out that sealed Johnny Vander Meer's second consecutive no-hitter in 1938. Still, he was a contributing member of one of the most famous teams of all times—the St. Louis Cardinals' 1934 Gashouse Gang.

Durocher earned his Hall of Fame stripes while managing the Dodgers, Giants, Cubs, and Astros for 24 years between 1939 and 1973. He won the 1941 pennant with the Dodgers, a team created in the image of the rough-and-tumble Gashouse Gang. With the Dodgers, the volatile Durocher worked for an equally unpredictable chief executive, Larry MacPhail, who before his own firing reportedly fired and rehired his manager about 60 times. Twice with the Giants—1951, when Bobby Thomson won the playoff against the Dodgers with his game-ending home run, and 1954—Durocher won pennants. In 1954, the Willie Mays–led club gave him his only World Series championship as a manager.

Durocher's final managing stints, with the Cubs and Astros, pushed his win total to 2,008, among the top 10 for major league managers. By then, the Lip had become an elder statesman of the game and had somewhat mellowed. Even earlier, however, the fiery Durocher was capable, against his own philosophy, of occasionally being a nice guy. When some members of the Dodgers started passing around a petition in 1947 against the promotion of Jackie Robinson to the majors, their manager quashed the effort, telling them where they could put the petition. A few years later, a youthful Willie Mays, off to a rough start as a big league hitter, sat crying in the Giants' dugout. Leo the Lip sat down beside his future star, put his arm around him, and asked what was the matter. When Willie said that he

was not sure he belonged, the result of a 1-for-26 start as a hitter, Durocher reassured him, "As long as I'm manager of the Giants, you're my center fielder."

Still, Durocher could be menacing, as when he ordered Dodger pitcher Les Webber to hit every player in the Cardinals' lineup. And shortly after his support for Jackie Robinson in spring 1947, he was suspended for the year by commissioner Happy Chandler for associating with known gamblers. Nice guy or not, Leo Durocher led a colorful life—and enjoyed a successful and memorable major league career.

See also: Brooklyn Dodgers; Gambling; Gashouse Gang; MacPhail, Leland Stanford, Sr. and Leland Stanford, Jr.; Mays, Willie Howard; Robinson, Jack Roosevelt.

Additional Reading:
Day, Laraine (Durocher's wife). *Day with the Giants*. Garden City, NY: Doubleday, 1952.
Durocher, Leo, with Ed Linn. *Nice Guys Finish Last*. New York: Simon and Schuster, 1975.
Eskenazi, Gerald. *The Lip: A Biography of Leo Durocher*. New York: William Morrow, 1993.

EQUIPMENT

Early baseball featured no equipment except homemade bats and balls. As the years passed and the nineteenth century approached the twentieth, these essential tools started to be manufactured professionally, and other equipment came into widespread use. Baseball paralleled other endeavors such as cooking and farming, with the homemade giving way to mass-produced goods; even simple equipment became increasingly sophisticated. At the same time, greater attention was given to safety. But it all came at a price, that is, a greater separation of people from the natural way of doing things and a declining sense of heroism. The game was leaving its rural origins for the urban lifestyle—and professionalism.

Bats originally were carved from ax handles, fence posts, wagon tongues, and other pieces of wood. There was no uniformity, as players made bats to fit their own preferences. Thick bats were the rule throughout the nineteenth century. With little emphasis placed on hitting home runs, and with the no-glove and primitive-glove eras producing many errors, the batter wanted generous bat surface in order to make sure that he could put the ball in play. Even flat bats were tried in the 1880s, without success, as a fast pitch would tend to turn the bat in the hitter's hands, leading to a feeble grounder in the infield. The slim-handled bat was far in the future, when striving for home runs placed a premium on bat speed.

The modern era of bat construction is traced to a visit from Peter Browning to J. F. Hillerich in Louisville after a game in 1884. Having broken his bat, Browning needed a replacement for the next game. Hillerich had his son work throughout the night to comply, and the first Louisville Slugger was created.

Baseballs also were made by hand in the early years of baseball, often from whatever material was available. Youngsters would use woolen socks wrapped around something hard, sometimes a bullet or strips of rubber, the surface then sewed with needle and thread to hold it all together. These early baseballs did not have a great deal of bounce and tended not to handle wet weather very well; they gave a great deal of pleasure nonetheless. Even after baseballs were made professionally, they demonstrated great variety

Workers continually check the dimensions of the official baseballs manufactured at the Spalding Plant in Chicopee, Massachusetts. (Hulton Getty)

in size, color, and weight. Some early baseballs had a "lemon peel" construction, with four panels of leather enclosing an interior of string and rubber strips.

Ben Shibe, later co-owner (with Connie Mack) of the Philadelphia Athletics, devised machines to make baseballs of uniform size and weight, although stitched by hand, and exhibited his product at the Centennial Exhibition in Philadelphia in 1876. Albert Spalding, who found that a sporting-goods empire was more lucrative than playing baseball,

gained the exclusive right to manufacture baseballs for the National League in 1877. Paying $1 per baseball to the National League was well worth it for Spalding, who then used that seal of approval to sell large quantities of baseballs to others. In those days, stitches were low, making it difficult to throw a good curveball. In later years, the seams were raised farther from the surface of the ball.

The first controversial piece of equipment was the baseball glove, which, like the catcher's mask and chest protector, called into question the wearer's masculinity. Ultimately, the desire to avoid pain and the desire to make money joined forces to popularize these items as well as future pieces of equipment, such as the batting helmet and the batting glove.

Credit (or blame) for wearing the first glove in a baseball game is usually given to first baseman Charlie Waitt of St. Louis in the National Association. In 1875, Waitt, who had tired of a left hand smarting from his infielders' throws but apparently ashamed of giving in to weakness, attempted to camouflage his glove by wearing one that was flesh-colored. The subterfuge did not work, and both fans and players taunted him for being, in their opinion, less than a man. The following year, however, Spalding began his sporting-goods enterprise, and when Spalding moved from pitching to playing first base he started wearing a glove, one that was padded but not flesh-colored. In short, he was a living advertisement for gloves—a staple of his business.

Infielder's gloves for several decades were padded, and therefore protective, but not particularly suited to improved defensive performance. By the 1920s, the infielder's glove came with a definite pocket that helped trap the ball. The person who developed the pocketed glove was a pitcher, Bill Doak, who perhaps grew tired of his infielders muffing groundballs behind him.

The catcher's mitt also was initially for protection rather than defense. Henry Fabian of New Orleans in 1880 devised a catcher's mitt for himself that had a sheet of lead between two gloves. Many a ball must have bounced off that configuration, but Fabian probably went home after the game with a left hand a bit less red than it might have been.

Catchers, however, were more concerned about their mouths than their hands. A painful palm would ease, and even a broken finger would heal, but broken teeth would not grow back. So the first protective item that players used was a rubber band around the mouth to protect their teeth. That gave way to the mouth protector worn, manufactured, and sold by George Wright in the 1860s, the great shortstop of the Cincinnati Red Stockings also operating a sporting-goods company.

The mouth protector then yielded to the catcher's mask, perhaps the most controversial piece of safety equipment because of its strange appearance, which caused it to be dubbed a "bird cage." Supposedly a Harvard University player named Fred Thayer developed the first catcher's mask for his catcher. It was used by professionals as early as 1877. The mask became more popular with a rule change in 1879 that required the catcher to catch the third strike on the fly rather than on the bounce in order to make an out. That forced the catcher to move up right behind the batter rather than stand some 50 feet back as he had before, a dangerous move because the catcher could easily take a throw or foul tip in the face. Another change in 1884 permitted the pitcher complete freedom in delivery. With the overhand delivery now legal, the pitcher could get even more speed on the pitch, which meant that the catcher's hands, as well as other parts of the anatomy, were at greater risk for injury. So in the 1880s, the chest protector joined the mask and mitt for the catcher's protection. At first, the protector was worn underneath the uniform, producing a boo-inciting visual absurdity; shin guards also became popular. The catcher's protective equipment was dubbed the "tools of ignorance," presumably because anyone would have to be stupid to play a position that posed such dangers.

Today players are protected at the plate (and on the base paths) by a batting helmet. A rule introduced in 1971 made the helmet mandatory; later the earflap was also required. Even hitting gloves are employed, although for many people there remains something undignified about a player carefully pulling his tight glove on, gradually working each finger into position.

Few fans, and perhaps no player, would want to go back to the days before gloves, masks, helmets, and the like. Yet one wonders, in watching the game today, how a Junior Griffey or a Derek Jeter would fare trying to haul in a long fly or snare a hot grounder without a glove. It is hard not to feel that baseball required a much higher degree of courage in the nineteenth century—and perhaps more skill. It seems more natural and certainly more heroic (perhaps foolhardy) to play with bare hands, totally unprotected by the artificial devices that adorn modern players. Still, one major injury proves that the change is for the better. True, there is much money to be made in selling baseball equipment, and historically that motive was as strong as any in pushing players to put gloves and masks between them and the natural state of things. Like so much in modern society, baseball equipment tends to be a mixed blessing—but a blessing nonetheless. We may long for the good old days when men were men, but few of us, when push comes to shove, would choose to return there.

See also: Business; Heroes; Louisville Slugger; Spalding, Albert Goodwill; Uniforms.

Additional Reading:

Frommer, Harvey. Primitive Baseball: The First Quarter-Century of the National Pastime. New York: Atheneum, 1988.

Goldstein, Warren. Playing for Keeps: A History of Early Baseball. Ithaca: Cornell University Press, 1989.

Pietrusza, David, Lloyd Johnson, and Bob Carroll. The Total Baseball Catalog. New York: Total Sports, 1998.

Seymour, Harold. Baseball: The Early Years. 1960. Reprint, New York: Oxford University Press, 1989.

Thorn, John, and the National Baseball Hall of Fame and Museum. Treasures of the Baseball Hall of Fame: The Official Companion to the Collection at Cooperstown. New York: Villard, 1998.

EXPANSION

Major league baseball assumed its modern shape in 1901 with the addition of the American League to the much older National League, which had existed since 1876. The same two major leagues have thus coexisted ever since, overcoming an initial competition to forge the so-called National Agreement in 1903 that has lasted for some 100 years. The teams and cities were set in stone, or so it seemed, by 1903, continuing unchanged (except for occasional name changes early in the twentieth century) until 1953. Originally located in the East and Midwest, baseball stayed put until population changes and the advent of reliable and inexpensive air travel precipitated expansion into new areas of the country, first by relocating existing teams, then by adding new clubs.

The National League comprised 12 teams as late as 1899; four team-cities were dropped after that season: Baltimore, Washington, Cleveland, and Louisville. Of those, only Louisville would never again see another major league club, as owners favored "old" new franchises, that is, they placed teams in cities that had once been part of the system. By 1901, the American League was thus operating franchises in Baltimore, Washington, and Cleveland, in three National League cities (Boston, Philadelphia, and Chicago), as well as Detroit (an American League city to this day) and Milwaukee (which would lose and regain major league status several times after 1901).

The location of National League teams remained unchanged from 1900 until 1953. The American League, though, did a small amount of adjusting its franchises in its first two years of existence, replacing the Milwaukee Brewers with the St. Louis Browns for the 1902 season and transferring Baltimore, which had a distinguished earlier career as a National League club, to New York for 1903; these New York Highlanders would later change their name to the Yankees. By 1903, the American League was firmly rooted in eight cities and remained unchanged until 1954. This consistency (16 teams and two leagues for half a century) was truly remarkable for a business as large as major league baseball, with its two leagues and sixteen teams. Just how remarkable it was becomes clear when one considers the likelihood of a large company with sixteen branch offices neither moving, deleting, nor adding any branch offices over a period of fifty years, a period marked by great growth and change in the United States.

Some of the resistance to change was because of baseball's dependency on the railroad system and the resulting need not only to keep teams located near railroad tracks but also within reasonable train trips from city to city. To take the train from New York to San Francisco in 1920, for example, while possible, would have taken so much time as to stretch out the baseball season beyond feasible limits. The other factor retarding change was the conservatism inherent in baseball, especially during the first fifty years of the century but even today, despite the great changes that have occurred in the game.

Even the changes that began in the 1950s were conservative in their nature. The first move—for the 1953 season—was the Boston Braves of the National League to Milwaukee, returning the major league game to an original American League city. When the St. Louis Browns moved to Baltimore and became the Orioles the following year, that team also was returning to a former major league city, the home of the fabled National League Orioles (briefly in the American League). In 1955, the Philadelphia Athletics relocated to Kansas City, which, though farther west, was still considered the Midwest.

Far-flung geographical expansion did not occur until two East Coast teams moved to the West Coast—the Brooklyn Dodgers to Los Angeles, the New York Giants to San Francisco—for the 1958 season. These moves reflected Western population growth and the ascendancy of air travel, which made coast-to-coast trips feasible. (The first air travel by a major league club took place in 1936, when the Red Sox flew between St. Louis and Chicago; by the 1950s the airplane had permanently replaced the train for major league road trips.)

The 1961 season was the first with new teams beyond the original 16: the Washington Senators (the previous Senators having moved that same year to Minneapolis–St. Paul to become the Minnesota Twins) and the Los Angeles (later California and Anaheim) Angels. The 1962 season saw the first movement southward, with the addition of the Houston Colt .45s (later the Astros) in the National League; that same year, New York welcomed a new National League team—the Mets.

The South continued to attract teams, as the Milwaukee Braves moved to Atlanta for 1966; the new Senators became the Texas Rangers in 1972; Florida acquired the Marlins franchise in 1993 and the Devil Rays in 1998. Western cities also gained franchises, including Seattle, with the short-lived Pilots (later the Milwaukee

Brewers) and then the Mariners, Denver (Rockies), and Phoenix (Diamondbacks); in California, the Athletics relocated to Oakland, and the Padres were added to San Diego.

The future of baseball may be international. Canada already boasts two major league franchises, the Montreal Expos and Toronto Blue Jays. Yet the United States—and hence baseball rosters—are increasingly multiethnic, reflecting growing numbers of players from Latin America, Asia, and Australia. Thus it seems only a matter of time until the World Series will be truly a global championship. Already, clubs have played regular-season or exhibition games in Mexico, Japan, and Cuba. Given the long history of and passion for baseball in Latin America, adding major league clubs south of the U.S.-Mexico border seems inevitable. Yet one city in

the United States seems desperate for a baseball franchise: Washington, D.C. Former home to two American League franchises—which usually lost more than they won—the nation's capital has a long row to hoe before it is awarded another franchise. Nonetheless, it seems appropriate that the country's national pastime should be represented in the center of American government.

See also: Australian Baseball; Canadian Baseball; Cuban Baseball; Japanese Baseball; Korean Baseball; Latin American Baseball; Major Leagues; Railroads; Taiwanese Baseball.

Additional Reading:

Alexander, Charles C. *Our Game: An American Baseball History.* New York: MJF Books, 1991.

Sullivan, Neil J. *The Dodgers Move West.* New York: Oxford University Press, 1987.

Wright, Russell O. *The Evolution of Baseball: A History of the Major Leagues in Graphs, 1903–1989.* Jefferson, NC: McFarland, 1992.

F

FAMILY RELATIONSHIPS

Baseball reflects an all-important element in American society: family relationships. Although any sport may help parents and children build solid relationships, no other sport is so rich in family tradition as baseball.

The parent-child connection has received the most attention. A universal image of growing up in the United States is father and son playing catch in the backyard, perhaps in a park. Fathers often buy infants a baseball glove before the child can even walk. Then there is the first ball game, a moment that people relive well into their later years. One of the greatest collections of writing on this theme is a volume of essays by poet Donald Hall, *Fathers Playing Catch with Sons*.

It is important to recognize that mothers and daughters capture the spirit just as well. Doris Kearns Goodwin, a biographer and political chronicler, writes extensively about her youth with the Brooklyn Dodgers and her father, how her father taught her to keep a scorecard so that when he came home from work they could go over the day's game together. "Wait 'til next year" became a declaration

of faith and hope that she later passed on to her children, as their own trips to Fenway Park in Boston recalled her earlier games at old Ebbets Field.

Among other works of literature on baseball and family is the moving autobiographical account by Ralph Schoenstein, recounting the story of daughter Lori and the incomparable thrill he felt as she belted out "Take Me Out to the Ball Game" with her father and thousands of other fans at Shea Stadium. Fictional narratives like W. P. Kinsella's *Shoeless Joe* and Philip Goldberg's *This Is Next Year* tell of Shoeless Joe Jackson, the father's favorite player, as instruments of reconciliation between father and son; and a fictional Brooklyn family, their love for the Dodgers, and the long-awaited 1955 world championship season.

There are various explanations for why baseball has this hold on the imaginative and emotional lives of parents and children. It seems the right kind of sport, one that goes back into the early days of our country so that it is part of the passing of generation into generation. It also is something of a peaceful sport, lacking the violence of football and hockey, the brutality of boxing. It is a universal sport in American society. Horseracing does not occur everywhere; tennis, bowling, and even golf have had certain class associations that prevent their attaining the universality of baseball as a shared experience. Basketball remains too recent, perhaps too far removed from what normal people can imagine themselves doing. But almost everyone, at some level, can play baseball, and has done so (or the softball variant) in childhood if not later.

Baseball is universal and symbolic: of a primitive America still alive in the modern urban world; of efforts to return home; of our nation's best moments. Baseball itself is something of an extended family, transcending class, race, and religion.

See also: Brooklyn Dodgers; Fiction; Films; Kinsella, William Patrick; Poetry; Ritual; Rural America.
Additional Reading:
Goldberg, Philip. *This Is Next Year.* 1991. Reprint, New York: Ballantine, 1992.
Goodwin, Doris Kearns. *Wait till Next Year: A Memoir.* New York: Simon and Schuster, 1997.
Hall, Donald. *Fathers Playing Catch with Sons: Essays on Sport (Mostly Baseball).* San Francisco: North Point, 1985.
Kinsella, W. P. *Shoeless Joe.* 1982. Reprint, New York: Ballantine, 1996.
Schoenstein, Ralph. *Diamonds for Lori and Me: A Father, a Daughter, and Baseball.* New York: William Morrow, 1988.

FANTASY CAMPS

The rigor and demands of American society require many people to abandon personal dreams, settling for vicarious experiences as spectators or observing through the media. Thus the nourishing dreams of childhood give way to the real world. Yet sometimes adults return to those long-abandoned dreams: getting a college degree, moving into a dream house; opening a bed and breakfast in

Maine; trading Wall Street for the great American novel. So it is with playing baseball in the major leagues.

Fantasy baseball camps make it possible. Originated in the 1980s by former Cubs catcher Randy Hundley, they have proliferated, with some major league organizations even operating their own camps. Typically, a man (some camps now accept women), sometimes required to be at least 30 years old, pays a few thousand dollars for a week of major league–type spring training. With 60–120 other campers, he receives instruction from former major league stars, plays in games, engages in a variety of other activities (films, baseball talk, an awards banquet), and goes home with a uniform (sporting his name and number), an autographed baseball, a team photograph, and a memory he carries for the rest of his life—or until the next fantasy camp.

See also: Men's Senior Baseball League/Men's Adult Baseball League.
Additional Reading:
McCroskey, Dennis. "Fantasy Camps." http://www.HiHard1.com/basfnpg1.html-ssi
Pietrusza, David, Lloyd Johnson, and Bob Carroll. *The Total Baseball Catalog.* New York: Total Sports, 1998.

FAVORITE BASEBALL PLAYER

Virtually every boy and girl who falls in love with baseball adopts a favorite player. A favorite player personalizes the experience of being a big league fan, permits the fan to enter vicariously into the action of the game, and helps satisfy an inherent need for heroes.

Once chosen, the player usually remains the favorite for life. Long after he has thrown his last strikeout, hit his final home run, or turned his last double play, the player continues to live in the fan's memory, binding past and future and keeping alive the dreams, idealism, and joy of youth in mind and heart.

Thus the once and always fan lives again in that age of innocence and freedom known as childhood, merely by recalling the favorite player. An office, a workshop, or a classroom becomes the outdoors; the mundane tools of the trade transform into a baseball and the side of an old red barn. Pitch after pitch against the barn door, childhood leaps from the adult grind, the future reverting to ballparks and victories. A favorite player keeps the fan forever young.

Occasionally, however, trauma breaks the bond between aging fan and favorite player. A favorite player may take every legal advantage in order to win, but he does not bet on baseball games, he does not go to prison, he does not betray the dreams of children. Once having lost a favorite player, the fan most likely goes through life without another. For others, the dreams never die, and the individual is forever young.

See also: Heroes; Rose, Peter Edward.

Additional Reading:

Freedman, William. *More than a Pastime: An Oral History of Baseball Fans.* Jefferson, NC: McFarland, 1998.

Goodwin, Doris Kearns. *Wait till Next Year: A Memoir.* New York: Simon and Schuster, 1997.

Sheed, Wilfrid. *My Life as a Fan.* New York: Simon and Schuster, 1993.

FELLER, ROBERT WILLIAM (RAPID ROBERT) (1918–)

Bob Feller is the quintessential farm-boy fireballer, a young pitcher who brought his prodigious talent from the fields to the major leagues to earn instant success and fame. Feller was the prototype of the "natural," depicted in the opening scenes of the Robert Redford film *The Natural*. Rapid Robert, from Van Meter, Iowa, was a living myth, and he added to his stature by giving up several prime years to serve heroically in World War II.

An autographed portrait of the Cleveland Indians' Bob Feller, 1930s (Archive Photos)

Bob Feller was only 17 when he pitched his first game for the Cleveland Indians in 1936. In his first start, he struck out 15 batters, later whiffed 17 in a game, and finished the season with 76 strikeouts in 62 innings. Two years later, he set a new strikeout record for one game with 18. By 1939, he was firmly entrenched as the game's greatest pitcher. From 1939 through 1941, he compiled won-loss/strikeout totals of 24-9/246; 27-11/261; and 25-13/260. On opening day 1940, he threw a no-hitter. World War II would beckon before long.

Feller was at the top of his game and still only in his early twenties when he entered the U.S. Navy. He served as a gun-crew chief, earning eight battle stars. By the time he returned to Cleveland, with the 1945 season nearing its end, Feller had missed three full seasons and most of a fourth, costing him roughly 100 wins and 1,000 strikeouts.

Despite his absence, Feller picked up where he had left off, winning five of eight decisions in nine games. The next year, aided by a slider he developed while pitching in the service to go with his devastating fastball and curveball, he had his greatest season. Feller led the league with 26 wins, 348 strikeouts, 371 innings pitched, 48 games pitched (including 42 starts), 36 complete games, and 10 shutouts; counting six relief appearances between starts, he fashioned a 2.18 ERA.

Feller was never quite that good again, the heavy workload, and perhaps the pitching during the war, taking a toll on his fastball. Still, he had two more 20-win seasons, and by the time he retired after the 1956 season, he had compiled more than a Hall of Fame career: 266 wins, six 20-win seasons, 2,581 strikeouts, three no-hitters, and 12 one-hitters. He led his league in wins six times, strikeouts seven times, games pitched three times, complete games three times, innings pitched five times, and shutouts four times. All of this was accomplished despite missing close to four prime seasons. *The Sporting News* named Feller Player of the Year in 1940.

Bob Feller retained his stature for many years after he retired, undiminished by his last few seasons, when he was but a shadow of his former self. Feller's last winning season was 1954, when he went 13-3 as the Indians' fifth starter; the following season, he was 4-4; he dropped to 0-4 in 1956. In more recent years, other strikeout artists—Sandy Koufax, Nolan Ryan, Randy Johnson—took over the headlines. Yet Bob Feller remains a baseball legend. Many who saw him pitch will still argue that he was the best there ever was.

See also: Films; Rural America; Strikeouts; War.
Additional Reading:
Feller, Bob. *Now Pitching, Bob Feller.* New York: Carol, 1990.

———. *Strikeout Story.* New York: A. S. Barnes, 1947.
Reeder, Red. *On the Mound: Three Great Pitchers.* Champaign, IL: Garrard, 1966.

FICTION

Baseball has inspired great literature in most every genre—poetry, drama, song, film, and memoir. Of all baseball literature, however, none has risen to higher levels of accomplishment than fiction. In doing so, it has overcome certain prejudices against baseball as a proper subject for serious (i.e., "literary") fiction.

One of those prejudices arose early in the history of baseball: the assumption that baseball fiction was for children, even though baseball from its earliest days was played by serious professional gentlemen, quickly spreading to Civil War soldiers and then all classes. However, as millwrights, farmers, and other members of the working classes took a liking to baseball, some Americans began viewing professional baseball as a sport enjoyable to watch. Yet it was a game they did not want their sons to play for a living when they could become lawyers, bankers, and businessmen. So as the actual performing of baseball came to be associated more with children and the less educated, so did the sport fail initially to catch on with self-conscious creators of literature, except for writers, like poet Walt Whitman, who saw themselves as writing for all Americans.

Accordingly, much of the early baseball fiction was written explicitly for children. Perhaps the first work of baseball fiction, according to James Mote in his invaluable *Everything Baseball,* was William Everett's *Changing Base* (1868), written for a juvenile audience. Two years later he produced *Double Play* (1870). Another early writer of juvenile baseball fiction was Noah Brooks, with such works as *The Fairport Nine* (1880) and *Our*

Baseball Club: And How It Won the Championship (1884). The latter is credited by Mote as being the first novel completely built around baseball in plot and characterization.

Some authors established a steady source of income from juvenile baseball fiction in the late nineteenth and early twentieth centuries. Burt Standish, whose real name was Gilbert Patten, published *Frank Merriwell's Baseball Victory* in 1889, the first of several baseball books he wrote. William Heyliger established his baseball-fiction credentials with his first of many baseball books, *Bartley, Freshman Pitcher,* in 1911. Lester Chadwick wrote the popular Baseball Joe series, starting with *Baseball Joe on the School Nine* in 1912.

Another direction for baseball fiction for children, primarily for boys in those days, was the ghostwritten book published over the name of a famous player. Christy Mathewson gave his name to several books (written by John Wheeler) with such catchy alliterative titles as *Pitcher Pollack* (1914), *Catcher Craig* (1915), *First Base Faulkner* (1916), and *Second Base Sloan* (1917). *The Bride and the Pennant* (1910) was ostensibly written by first baseman Frank Chance. And what youngster would not want a book about a slugger, *The Home Run King: Or How Pep Pindar Won His Title* (1920), from the ultimate, and first true, slugger—Babe Ruth himself?

Two of the more interesting authors of fiction for young readers were Hugh Fullerton and Zane Grey. Fullerton, one of the great sportswriters of his time and one of the first to suspect the 1919 World Series was being thrown, published *Jimmy Kirkland of the Shasta Boys' Team* in 1925, the first of his three juvenile baseball books. Grey, more famous in later years for his Western fiction, used his experience as a baseball player to write books like *The Short-Stop* (1909), *The Young*

Pitcher (1911), and a collection of stories entitled *The Red-Headed Outfield, and Other Baseball Stories* (1915).

In almost all of the juvenile fiction dealing with baseball, the intention was not only to entertain but also to inculcate strong moral values. Teamwork, honor, truth, the value of hard work, and the ultimate triumph of virtue permeate these works.

There was, of course, some baseball fiction being produced for adults, the most enduring being the Ring Lardner stories; the finest of them are in *You Know Me Al* (1916), a collection widely read even today. It would remain for two fictional heavyweights, Ernest Hemingway and Bernard Malamud, to make baseball thoroughly respectable for serious fiction, thereby overcoming the second major literary prejudice against baseball—the view that it was appropriate only for lighter fare—and inspiring many outstanding baseball novels that deserve to be called fine literature.

Hemingway by the 1950s was the most famous writer in the United States, although some critics thought that he was past his prime. That probably was true, but he had at least one outstanding book still to come: *The Old Man and the Sea* (1951). The book won the Pulitzer Prize and clinched the Nobel Prize for its author. Not strictly speaking a baseball book (really more about fishing), it nonetheless gives serious attention to the game through the protagonist, Santiago, who, while battling with the giant marlin, derives inspiration from his hero, Joe DiMaggio, especially from the Yankee Clipper's struggles to overcome his pain.

In the same year that *The Old Man and the Sea* appeared, a young Bernard Malamud published his novel about Roy Hobbs, who aspired to be the greatest player ever. *The Natural* is a fascinating mixture of realism, symbolism, and allegory, with a dark undercurrent in its presentation of the universal struggle between evil and good.

Douglass Wallop's *The Year the Yankees Lost the Pennant* (1954) was quickly adapted for the enduring stage musical *Damn Yankees*. Mark Harris in 1956 published an emotionally engaging baseball novel, *Bang the Drum Slowly* (1956), about the friendship between a star pitcher and a dying catcher. Harris would publish several other excellent baseball novels.

Philip Roth and William Kennedy, two novelists who belong in any all-star list of twentieth-century fiction writers, enjoyed great success with baseball themes. Roth published the immodestly titled *The Great American Novel* in 1973, a funny and satiric work that also shows a real love for the game. Kennedy's *Ironweed* (1983) takes as its protagonist a former third baseman named Francis Phelan whose career and, for all practical purposes, life ended when he dropped not a grounder but his son, who died from the accident.

Gambling lies at the heart of the plot in several outstanding baseball novels. Eric Rolfe Greenberg's *The Celebrant* (1983) concerns the two Kapinski brothers (one of whom becomes heavily involved in gambling), the great pitcher Christy Mathewson, and the 1919 World Series. Other fine novels built around the Black Sox scandal are Harry Stein's *Hoopla* (1983) and Brendan Boyd's *Blue Ruin* (1991). Above them all, however, looms *Shoeless Joe* (1982), by W. P. Kinsella, undoubtedly the fictional laureate of baseball. The novel is about reconciliation of father and son through baseball long after the father's death. Using magic realism with its blend of realistic description, symbolism, and allegory, and intermingling past and present while probing into the psychological depths of characters, the book becomes a powerful tribute

to love and forgiveness between parents and children.

The variety in baseball fiction is indeed rich. William Brashler's *The Bingo Long Traveling All-Stars and Motor Kings* is at once enormously funny and deeply moving, even tragic, in its depiction of African Americans attempting to make a living in baseball while still excluded from the major leagues. Michael Shaara, author of the Pulitzer Prize–winning *The Killer Angels,* about the Civil War, wrote a thin but highly effective baseball story, *For Love of the Game,* about a veteran pitcher's last hurrah and attempt to find meaning outside a game that is passing him by.

Failed dreams supply much of the power of David Small's *Almost Famous* (1982), about a man who seemed to have the world in his grasp, only to lose it. *If I Never Get Back* (1990), by Darryl Brock, gives the protagonist another chance to set his life in order when he is somehow transported back into time with the mighty Cincinnati Red Stockings of 1869.

This modest catalog of outstanding baseball fiction could be much larger. Indeed, outstanding baseball fiction keeps coming out—and surely will continue to do so. Writers have the whole world in which to find material, and baseball reflects so much of that world, at least within the United States, that the confluence of baseball and good writers is inevitable—for which millions of readers give thanks.

See also: Black Sox Scandal; *Damn Yankees;* DiMaggio, Joseph Paul; Field of Dreams; Films; Grey, Pearl Zane; Hemingway, Ernest Miller; Jackson, Joseph Jefferson; Kinsella, William Patrick; Lardner, Ringgold Wilmer; Malamud, Bernard; Mathewson, Christopher; Myth; Twain, Mark; Whitman, Walter.
Additional Reading:
Candelaria, Cordelia. *Seeking the Perfect Game: Baseball in American Literature.* New York: Greenwood Press, 1989.

Morris, Timothy. *Making the Team: The Cultural Work of Baseball Fiction*. Urbana: University of Illinois Press, 1997.

Rielly, Edward J. "Green on Green: Baseball Fiction, Myth, and Money." In *Cooperstown Symposium on Baseball and the American Culture* (1990). Ed. Alvin L. Hall. Westport, CT: Meckler, 1991, pp. 400–417.

Shannon, Mike. *Diamond Classics: Essays on 100 of the Best Baseball Books Ever Published*. Jefferson, NC: McFarland, 1989.

Westbrook, Deeanne. *Ground Rules: Baseball and Myth*. Urbana: University of Illinois Press, 1996.

FIELD OF DREAMS

Outside a small town called Dyersville, Iowa, in the heart of America's heartland, where corn grows taller than mountains and more beautiful than the sea, there is a small baseball field. In that place, scenes were shot for the film *Field of Dreams,* based on W. P. Kinsella's novel *Shoeless Joe.* The story is about fathers and sons, about longing to get back the past, about playing one more game, and living one more dream, with someone you love.

"If you build it, he will come," the mysterious voice announces to Ray Kinsella at the beginning of the story. Ray builds the ball field, and they came: Shoeless Joe Jackson; Ray's father, John (the father and son being estranged before the father's death); and, finally, long lines of car-filled dreamers wanting to play on a field where their dreams, too, can come true. That happens in the novel and in the film. And for car-filled dreamers, it happens in real life because the ball field remains, surrounded by cornfields, open to the public free of charge. Every summer, thousands of people—parents with their sons and daughters, college students, young people in love, whole families—arrive to see, many to participate in the games that arise, the way games used to arise, by people choosing up sides or just joining

in. Middle-aged men in dress shoes join teenagers in T-shirts and sneakers. Embarrassment dies as people cross the lines. All people are equal, all dreams are one, all time melts into the eternal flow of wind through sharp green leaves in center field. It is a place where life imitates art because art captures our dreams. Baseball is about both living and dreaming—and about parents and children and others coming together in a common act that speaks of love.

See also: Black Sox Scandal; Fiction; Films; Jackson, Joseph Jefferson; Kinsella, William Patrick; Myth; Ritual; Rural America.

Additional Reading/Viewing:
Altherr, Thomas L. "W. P. Kinsella's Baseball Fiction, *Field of Dreams,* and the New Mythopoeism of Baseball." In *Cooperstown Symposium on Baseball and the American Culture.* Ed. Alvin L. Hall. Westport, CT: Meckler, 1990, pp. 97–108.

Anthony, Ted. "A Gem, Pure and Simple." *Portland (Maine) Press Herald,* September 21, 1998, pp. C1–2.

Field of Dreams. Dir. Phil Alden Robinson. Universal, 1989.

Kinsella, W. P. *Shoeless Joe.* 1982. Reprint, New York: Ballantine, 1996.

FILMS

Baseball has been a subject for movies since the earliest days of cinema. It is true, as some critics have asserted, that most baseball films have been unrealistic and aesthetically unsatisfying, at least by modern standards. That, however, has also been true of films dealing with almost every other subject. Only a few of the many films produced in Hollywood and elsewhere have been top-flight, and baseball films have fared the same. Still, entertaining and interesting baseball films have appeared throughout the twentieth century, with some of the best coming to the big screen more recently.

The earliest baseball films were Thomas Edison's *The Ball Game* (1898), a series of scenes depicting two amateur teams; and *Casey at the Bat* (1899), a comedy having no special connection to the famous poem of the same title. Apparently the first feature film with a baseball focus was *His Last Game* (1909), a movie that bears remembering for three reasons. First, it unites baseball with Native Americans about 10 years after the first Native American man to play in the majors, Louis Sockalexis, had departed the scene. Second, at a time when films were regularly depicting Native Americans in stereotypical and demeaning ways, this film's protagonist, Bill Going, a Choctaw pitcher for his all-Choctaw team, is a courageous and noble hero. Third is attempted bribery and the fixing of a game, a common theme in early baseball films, anticipating the 1919 Black Sox scandal.

Many of the early silent films dealing with baseball were designed to showcase major league stars, such as Home Run Baker, Hal Chase, Frank Chance, Ty Cobb, Christy Mathewson, John McGraw, and Babe Ruth. Among these, *Babe Comes Home* (1927), starring Babe Ruth as Babe Dugan, retains interest, partly because of the continuing fascination Americans have with Babe Ruth, partly because the film, by current criteria, is totally lacking in political correctness. Dugan is so enamored of his chewing tobacco that, when he promises his bride to give up the habit, he finds it impossible to concentrate on the playing field. Finally, Anna Q. Nilsson, playing Mrs. Dugan, comes through for her man and tosses a plug of tobacco onto the field just as Babe is at bat. Fortified by his tobacco, Babe Dugan hits a game-winning home run.

The Babe acted in several films, usually in small roles, perhaps most memorably in *The Pride of the Yankees* (1942).

The film, which is about Lou Gehrig, was released the year after the Iron Horse's death from amyotrophic lateral sclerosis, with the nation still in mourning. Ruth, playing himself, did not distinguish himself for his acting ability in the film but was at his best with his controlled performance in the final scene where Gehrig, played by Gary Cooper, gives his emotionally wrenching farewell speech at Yankee Stadium during the team's tribute to him. The film itself is overly sentimental, perhaps inevitable given the subject, timing, and filmmaking tendencies of the time. Nonetheless, Cooper, despite lacking natural athleticism and having to learn to bat left-handed, received an Academy Award nomination for best actor.

Babe Ruth himself was the subject of an ambitious biographical film starring William Bendix. *The Babe Ruth Story* (1948) was released shortly before Ruth's death and deserves its reputation as one of the all-time worst baseball films. Bendix, an otherwise capable performer, was miscast, and the plot is not only melodramatic but also ludicrously false. Babe Ruth is depicted as a miracle-working saint, which both falsifies who he really was while actually demeaning a person who, despite his weaknesses, at his best was a sensitive and generous man.

Subsequent decades added an impressive list of worthwhile baseball films, a few of which will be mentioned here. *The Jackie Robinson Story* (1950) starred Robinson as himself, which helped add realism to the film made just three years after Robinson broke the color barrier in the major leagues. *Fear Strikes Out* (1957) depicts Red Sox outfielder Jimmy Piersall's struggle with mental illness and his relationship with his father. It was released at a time when Piersall, an outstanding defensive player and good hitter, was still playing center field for the

Red Sox, forming with Ted Williams and Jackie Jensen one of the great outfields of all time. *Bang the Drum Slowly* (1973), based on Mark Harris's novel, skillfully depicts the friendship between pitcher Henry Wiggen and a dying catcher named Bruce Pearson, with the batterymates played by Michael Moriarty and Robert DeNiro, two talented young actors embarking on distinguished acting careers.

The Bingo Long Traveling All-Stars and Motor Kings (1976) is an entertaining film that, along with William Brashler's excellent novel on which it is based, helped usher in a period of great interest in the Negro Leagues. What *Bingo Long* did for the study of the Negro Leagues, *A League of Their Own* (1992), directed by Penny Marshall, did for women in baseball, specifically the history of the All-American Girls Professional Baseball League. A film combining comedy and drama, romance and real history, and starring Tom Hanks, Madonna, and Geena Davis, it inspired several books on the all-women's league.

Bull Durham (1988) is a much-acclaimed film spiced with a lot of sex, an often-quoted introductory monologue by actress Susan Sarandon's character on the "church of baseball," and an interesting depiction of the relationship between a young pitcher, Nuke LaLoosh (played by Tim Robbins), and a veteran catcher, Crash Davis (Kevin Costner). *Eight Men Out* (1988) is the story of the 1919 White Sox, based on Eliot Asinof's book by the same title. The film is one of the best baseball movies, featuring an effective ensemble of actors, including D. B. Sweeney as Shoeless Joe, John Cusack as Buck Weaver, Charlie Sheen as Happy Felsch, and David Strathairn as Eddie Cicotte.

Two of the most interesting baseball films, and two of the best, are also connected with the Black Sox: *The Natural* (1984) and *Field of Dreams* (1989). Both films are based on highly successful novels, Bernard Malamud's *The Natural* (1952) and W. P. Kinsella's *Shoeless Joe* (1982). Malamud drew from such sources as Babe Ruth (for the Whammer), the nearly fatal shooting of Philadelphia Phillies first baseman Eddie Waitkus by a woman in a hotel room, and the story of Shoeless Joe and the fixing of the 1919 World Series. The protagonist of *Shoeless Joe* is Ray Kinsella, whose father's favorite player was Joe Jackson, with much of the story concerned with the father-son relationship, which necessarily involves Jackson as well. Both novels deal heavily in myth, ritual, and fantasy, although Malamud's book is much darker and antiheroic. The film version of *The Natural* is transformed into a heroic, happy-ending film with a climax that is one of the most visually stunning scenes in any baseball movie. Protagonist Roy Hobbs resists bribery, avoids gluttony, is more respectful of women, and triumphs in the end—the way viewers would expect Robert Redford to behave.

Field of Dreams, starring Kevin Costner, makes some major changes in characters, dropping Ray's twin brother and sister-in-law, along with Eddie Scissons, apparently to focus the story more sharply for the film. J. D. Salinger yields to Terrance Mann, played by James Earl Jones, a change that works well within the time frame, which is moved forward about 10 years from the setting of the novel and which may also have avoided a lawsuit or two. Despite these changes, the film remains faithful to the mood of the novel and to its depiction of the father-son relationship. Ray, having insulted his father and left home—the father dying before the son could apologize—longs to set things right. He builds a baseball field where his cornfield once stood, welcomes Shoeless Joe and the rest of the Black Sox, then watches in amazement as his former minor-leaguer father joins the team. The scene at the end with Ray and his father playing catch is certain to bring tears to the eyes of any man who ever played baseball with his father or simply misses a lost and beloved parent. In addition, Burt Lancaster turns in a remarkable performance as Moonlight Graham, based on an actual player who got into one game with the Giants but never had a chance to bat.

Many other important baseball films have been made, including documentaries such as Ken Burns's *Baseball* (1994) and *The Glory of Their Times* (1977), the latter based on Lawrence Ritter's book; made-for-TV movies include *Don't Look Back: The Story of Leroy "Satchel" Paige* (1981), with Lou Gossett Jr. in the title role, and *A Love Affair: The Eleanor and Lou Gehrig Story* (1978), starring Edward Herrmann and Blythe Danner. Going to the movies remains one of America's favorite pastimes, and baseball has given movie fans the opportunity to combine two important pastimes at once.

See also: Autry, Orvon Gene; Black Sox Scandal; Connors, Kevin Joseph Aloysius; Fiction; Field of Dreams; Gehrig, Henry Louis; Kinsella, William Patrick; Malamud, Bernard; Native Americans; Negro Leagues; Robinson, Jack Roosevelt; Ruth, George Herman.

Additional Reading:

Carroll, Bob, and Rob Edelman. "Reel Baseball." In *Total Baseball.* 6th ed. Ed. John Thorn et al. New York: Total Sports, 1999, pp. 598–609.

Erickson, Hal. *Baseball in the Movies: A Comprehensive Reference, 1915–1991.* Jefferson, NC: McFarland, 1992.

Good, Howard. *Diamonds in the Dark: America, Baseball, and the Movies.* Lanham, MD: Scarecrow, 1996.

Mote, James. *Everything Baseball.* New York: Prentice Hall, 1989.

Zucker, Harvey Marc, and Lawrence J. Babich. *Sports Films: A Complete Reference.* Jefferson, NC: McFarland, 1987.

FINLEY, CHARLES OSCAR (1918–1997)

Charles Finley was one of the most innovative owners in the history of major league baseball. He purchased the Kansas City (later Oakland) Athletics in 1960, bringing his background as a self-made millionaire and an abiding concern for the common workingmen and -women who made up a large portion of his baseball public. The hard work and creativity that brought Finley from laborer to foreman at U.S. Steel in Gary, Indiana, to successful and wealthy owner of a Chicago insurance company stayed with him during his years with the Athletics, through the team's move to Oakland in 1968, and three consecutive World Series championships (1972–1974), until he sold the club in 1980. However, his actions were not always to his players' or fellow owners' liking.

Finley's ideas, some accepted, others rejected—even ridiculed—changed the game forever. He was the prime mover behind the adoption of the designated-hitter rule in the American League in 1973 and the introduction of weeknight World Series games. In fact, the now common schedule for major league contests—7:00 P.M. weekday games, 6:00 P.M. Saturday games, 2:00 P.M. Sunday games—was originally Finley's idea and grew out of his sensitivity toward workingmen and -women. He also was an early proponent of interleague play. In his early years with the Kansas City Athletics, when showmanship often had to substitute for a quality team, he introduced such entertaining (if sometimes bizarre) additions as a mule mascot named "Charlie O," a mechanical rabbit that arose from underground to supply the umpire with baseballs, a zoo and picnic area behind the bleachers, and sheep grazing beyond the outfield wall.

Other innovations did not catch on, such as use of orange baseballs that could be seen better at night, walking hitters on three balls rather than four to increase offense, a pitch clock to guarantee that pitchers followed the 20-second rule for pitching after receiving the ball back from the catcher, and use of a designated runner. However, he was not deterred by criticism. Finley added an exploding scoreboard in right field in the Oakland Coliseum and a huge, computer-activated message board in left field. Special attractions, such as "Hot-Pants Night," pulled in spectators. The players were not immune from Finley's innovations. Finley insisted on colorful nicknames for players, personally inventing such monikers as John "Blue Moon" Odom and Jim "Catfish" Hunter. The story goes that Finley turned down a chance to sign pitcher Don Sutton, later an outstanding hurler for the Dodgers who won over 300 games in his career, because the young pitcher did not have an appropriate nickname. Finley also encouraged his players to wear mustaches and long hair, which, along with their colorful green-and-gold uniforms, made the A's especially striking on color television.

By the mid-1970s, Finley had just about worn out his welcome in the major leagues. Along with alienating other owners, he angered many of his star players, usually over financial dealings. Failure to comply with a provision of Catfish Hunter's contract led to Hunter's free agency after the 1974 season; during the 1976 season, he attempted to sell off some of his top players—Joe Rudi and

Rollie Fingers to the Red Sox, Vida Blue to the Yankees. Commissioner Bowie Kuhn voided both deals, and Finley sued in federal court in Chicago. Both the trial and appellate decisions went against Finley, and he finally sold the A's in 1980 after the once-dominant team had become a shadow of its former self. Finley became something of a nonperson, especially for the baseball powers, but he left a lasting legacy—a changed game. In more recent years, as conflicts between owners and players have often made the fans the forgotten figures in baseball, a few more Charles Finleys might have effected an important corrective to that shortsightedness.

See also: Commissioner; Free Agency; Hunter, James Augustus; Jackson, Reginald Martinez; Kuhn, Bowie K.; Law; Reserve Clause.

Additional Reading:

Clark, Tom. *Champagne and Baloney: The Rise and Fall of Finley's A's.* New York: Harper and Row, 1976.

Markusen, Bruce. *Baseball's Last Dynasty: Charles Finley's Oakland A's.* Indianapolis: Masters, 1998.

FLOOD, CURTIS CHARLES (CURT) (1938–1997)

Curt Flood, an excellent defensive center fielder and a fine hitter and base runner, spent most of his career with the St. Louis Cardinals (1958–1969) between short stints at the beginning and conclusion of his career with the Cincinnati Reds (1956–1957) and Washington Senators (1971). His most lasting achievement, however, was in management-labor relations, especially the reserve clause, a longtime player barrier he helped to destroy.

With the Cardinals, Flood won three National League pennants and two World Series championships in the 1960s. However, his importance to baseball and to society's view toward the game and its players took a quantum leap after the 1969 season, when the Cardinals did what teams had done since the beginning of professional baseball. Management looked at Curt Flood and saw a player whose productivity had started to decline after 12 seasons as a regular starter. The logic had always been clear: Trade the player while he is still performing well enough to bring something of value in return.

The Cardinals did just that, trading Flood to the Philadelphia Phillies in October 1969. Flood refused to report to his new team and filed a lawsuit against Major League Baseball in an attempt to free himself from the reserve clause, which tied a player to his club until he was traded or released. The reserve clause, in various shapes, had existed since 1879. Flood lost the case as well as his appeals all the way to the Supreme Court. Nonetheless, he had set in motion a process that would soon lead to free agency—and the high salaries that accompanied players' new freedom to shop their talents to the highest bidder. On October 27, 1998, President Bill Clinton signed into law the Curt Flood Act of 1998, finally bringing major league players under the jurisdiction of the Clayton Antitrust Act and ending the antitrust exemption long enjoyed by major league owners.

> *See also:* Antitrust Exemption; Commissioner; Free Agency; Kuhn, Bowie K.; Labor-Management Relations; Law; Miller, Marvin James; Reserve Clause.
>
> *Additional Reading:*
>
> Abrams, Roger I. *Legal Bases: Baseball and the Law*. Philadelphia: Temple University Press, 1998.
>
> Flood, Curt, with Richard Carter. *The Way It Is*. New York: Trident, 1971.
>
> Lowenfish, Lee. *The Imperfect Diamond: A History of Baseball's Labor Wars*. Rev. ed. New York: Da Capo, 1991.

> Scully, Gerald W. *The Business of Major League Baseball*. Chicago: University of Chicago Press, 1989.

FOOD VENDORS

If an entertainment event is worth attending, then American spectators expect good eats. At movies, we buy popcorn and candy. Shopping might include a stop at the food court. Baseball is no different. For millions of fans, it hardly seems like a real game without a hot dog—and menus have specialized in recent years at stadiums. Without a Fenway Frank during a Red Sox game, one might as well tear down the Green Monster in left field.

Spectators' culinary cravings have existed since the earliest days of organized baseball. Fans could watch a game at Brooklyn's Union Grounds in the early 1860s and dine on a three-course meal. The famous baseball anthem "Take Me Out to the Ball Game" forever has linked baseball with peanuts and Cracker Jack.

And though spectators today can visit concession booths, the most authentic approach is to buy from vendors making their way up and down the aisles. Exchanging money and food across the rows is a ritual that builds community, making fans part of the family. In fact, many families especially enjoy minor league contests, where modest admission prices leave enough for the hot dogs, sodas, beer (for the grown-ups), popcorn, ice cream, and French fries. Vendors might not rake it in at such contests, but they keep busy, contributing to the great experience of attending a baseball game.

> *See also:* Ballparks; Business; Family Relationships; Ritual; "Take Me Out to the Ball Game."
>
> *Additional Reading:*
>
> Gmelch, George, and J. J. Weiner. *In the Ballpark: The Working Lives of Baseball People.*

Washington, DC: Smithsonian Institution, 1998.

FOSTER, ANDREW (RUBE, JOCK) (1879–1930)

Rube Foster may have been the most important figure in black baseball, which itself was an important part of African American culture from the middle of the nineteenth century through the first six or so decades of the twentieth. Foster not only achieved considerable renown as the best pitcher of his era in black baseball but also was a chief architect of the success of the Negro Leagues during the second and third decades of the twentieth century, when the Negro Leagues achieved a massive following in the black community. He received, and richly deserved, the title "father of black baseball."

Rube Foster skyrocketed to fame with the Chicago Union Giants during the 1902 season when he won 51 games. It probably was in that season that he outdueled the great white pitcher Rube Waddell of the Athletics to earn for himself the nickname "Rube." In 1903, Foster joined the Cuban X-Giants and went 54-1. The story goes that, in the same year, New York Giants manager John McGraw induced Foster to be something of a pitching coach out of uniform for his club and teach future Hall of Fame hurler Christy Mathewson the fadeaway, a type of screwball, that made Mathewson one of the great pitchers in major league history.

For the next three years, Foster starred with the Philadelphia Giants. Such was his reputation as a pitcher and leader that Frank Leland, who ran the Chicago Giants, persuaded him to become player-manager in 1907. Although a tough manager who required discipline from players, Foster was also an imaginative field boss, emphasizing good pitching, sound defense, and speed. His players were required to master the art of bunting and the hit-and-run. In 1909, Foster led the team into the Park Owners Association, which required all teams to own their home stadiums.

Rube Foster formed his own team in 1910, the Chicago American Giants. The team won something like 123 games against just six losses that year. Foster, although past his peak as a pitcher, still won 13 of 15 decisions. The 1910 Chicago American Giants are usually considered to be one of the greatest teams in black baseball history. Always the complete leader, Foster cut a deal with John Schorling, an in-law of Charles Comiskey, to play in the old White Sox stadium that the major league club had vacated. From 1910 through 1922, Foster's Giants won every championship available except in the 1916 season.

Rube Foster's next major contribution to black baseball was to organize a new league, the Negro National League, in 1920. In doing so, he helped make black baseball the largest black-owned industry in the country. Foster served as president of the league and also continued to run the Giants until 1926.

Foster was exhibiting signs of mental illness by 1925. He might suddenly start running for no obvious reason or chase imaginary fly balls. Once, he locked himself in a bathroom and would not leave until a player climbed over the roof and through the bathroom window to retrieve him. Foster was forced to relinquish leadership of the Giants in 1926 and was hospitalized in an asylum in Kankakee, Illinois, where he died in 1930. He left behind an unequaled record as player, manager, organizer, and executive. His impact on the African American community was immense, as he took the sport and made it more popular—and transformed it into big business. He was the father of black baseball as much for being an entrepreneur as a great pitcher and manager.

See also: African Americans; McGraw, John Joseph; Negro Leagues.

Additional Reading:

Ashe, Arthur R., Jr. *A Hard Road to Glory— Baseball: The African-American Athlete in Baseball.* 1988. Reprint, New York: Amistad, 1993.

Holway, John B. *Blackball Stars: Negro League Pioneers.* Westport, CT: Meckler, 1988.

Peterson, Robert. *Only the Ball Was White.* 2d ed. New York: McGraw-Hill, 1984.

Riley, James A. *The Biographical Encyclopedia of the Negro Baseball Leagues.* New York: Carroll and Graf, 1994.

FREE AGENCY

Free agency in baseball means player freedom to change employers. A basic right exercised by most Americans, it was historically denied major league ballplayers from the 1870s until the mid-1970s (this history is detailed in other entries in this book). The reserve clause in the basic agreement between owners and players— imposed and maintained by owners with the threat of permanent blacklisting— bound a player to the team that originally signed him until he was traded, released, or sold. If he did not wish to play for his team, he was free to retire from baseball. That was his only option.

In American society, most any employee is free (and has always been) to seek work with a similar, even competing, organization. Baseball players naturally longed for the same freedom, especially since lack of free agency—and thus lack of competition—kept salaries depressed. On the whole, however, fans cared little that players lacked this freedom. In fact, if they thought of it at all, fans probably appreciated the fact that favorite players were bound to the home team. Today, with the advent of free agency, players move from team to team, signing with franchises that offer better pay or benefits (like the right to use the owner's private jet). The downside of free agency is that there is much less continuity of rosters. As the saying goes, fans often cannot tell who the players are without a scorecard. Fan loyalty declines as a result, perhaps jeopardizing the financial state of some teams.

A major impact of free agency is reflected by the limited longevity of players with a single franchise. As of January 2000, the player with the longest tenure with the Kansas City Royals was Johnny Damon, who joined the team on August 12, 1995. Bobby Higginson was with the Detroit Tigers since April 26, 1995. The most senior member of the Oakland Athletics was Jason Giambi, on the roster since May 8, 1995. Only the Braves, Orioles, Cubs, Reds, Astros, Padres, and Mariners could boast that one of their players had been on the roster at least 10 years.

The powerful Yankees, with three World Series championships in the 1990s, had no player of longer duration than Bernie Williams (1991). By contrast, many of the past Yankee greats played more than a decade with the team, including Babe Ruth (15 years), Lou Gehrig (17), Joe DiMaggio (13), Mickey Mantle (18), Yogi Berra (18), Whitey Ford (16), and Thurman Munson (11). To take another telling example, the Cy Young Award winners in 1999, Pedro Martinez and Randy Johnson, had played for three and four teams, respectively. It's clear that when a player is about to qualify for free agency, teams will often trade him to get something in return. After the 1999 season, with free agency on the horizon for their star players, Texas traded two-time Most Valuable Player Juan Gonzalez to

Detroit, and Houston sent ace pitcher Mike Hampton to the New York Mets.

Free agency has changed major league baseball by increasing player mobility, boosting salaries, and eroding team continuity, thereby making it harder to stay on top and easier to buy a playoff spot, pennant, or championship. None of this is particularly desirable to most fans, but it is the reality, as ballplayers are now treated like any other American employee—as free citizens with the opportunity to choose where and for whom they work.

See also: Antitrust Exemption; Commissioner; Finley, Charles Oscar; Flood, Curtis Charles; Hunter, James Augustus; Kuhn, Bowie K.; Labor-Management Relations; Law; Miller, Marvin James; Reserve Clause; Ward, John Montgomery.

Additional Reading:

Abrams, Roger I. *Legal Bases: Baseball and the Law*. Philadelphia: Temple University Press, 1998.

Lowenfish, Lee. *The Imperfect Diamond: A History of Baseball's Labor Wars*. Rev. ed. New York: Da Capo, 1991.

Sobel, Lionel S. *Professional Sports and the Law*. New York: Law-Arts, 1977.

G

GAEDEL, EDWARD CARL (EDDIE) (1925–1961)

Eddie Gaedel—all of 43 inches tall in his stocking feet—made history on August 19, 1951, when he pinch-hit for St. Louis Browns outfielder Frank Saucier against the Detroit Tigers. He was hired by Browns owner Bill Veeck as a gimmick to generate interest in the woeful team— an insensitive move that probably would not be tolerated today. Gaedel faced pitcher Bob Cain, who walked him on four straight pitches.

The stratagem may have been a crowd-pleaser, but home plate umpire Ed Hurley was not amused, refusing to let Gaedel bat until he had seen the player's contract. Two days later, the commissioner's office ruled that henceforth all player contracts must be approved by that office. Gaedel's brief playing stint earned him fame but little financial gain or long-term happiness. He appeared on TV shows hosted by Ed Sullivan and Bing Crosby, worked as a Buster Brown shoe pitchman, and performed with the Ringling Brothers Circus.

Veeck briefly hired Gaedel again in 1961, along with seven other midgets, to serve food after customers had complained of vendors blocking their view of White Sox games. Within two months, Gaedel was dead. On June 18, he was mugged on a Chicago street for $11. He struggled home but died of a heart attack. Only one baseball person attended his funeral—Bob Cain, the pitcher who had faced him back in 1951. Later, someone posing as a Hall of Fame representative conned Gaedel's mother out of his Browns uniform and bats.

See also: Veeck, William L., Jr.
Additional Reading:
Veeck, Bill, with Ed Linn. *Veeck—As in Wreck: The Autobiography of Bill Veeck.* New York: Putnam's, 1962.
Zoss, Joel, and John Bowman. *Diamonds in the Rough: The Untold History of Baseball.* 1989. Reprint, Chicago: Contemporary Books, 1996.

GAMBLING

Gambling, especially betting on ball games, has long been the mortal sin of baseball. Although the deliberate loss of the 1919 World Series by the White Sox in return for money from gamblers (much of which never materialized) shocked the baseball world and has come down to modern times within the myth of baseball innocence as the baseball counterpart to Adam and Eve's original sin in the Garden of Eden, no one should have been shocked. In Genesis, the serpent had been in the Garden all of the time, although not inhabited by Satan, and in baseball gambling had been around since the early days of organized baseball.

As soon as the New York Knickerbockers organized in 1845 and started competing against other teams, spectators were betting on the outcome. Although the origins of baseball gambling are shrouded in the mist of history, betting quickly became a problem, as the chance to win a wager fostered a desire to limit one's risk by predetermining the outcome. Commissioners Kenesaw Mountain Landis in 1920 and A. Bartlett Giamatti in 1989 would later recognize what had been a nineteenth-century reality: Betting could lead to fixing games; even the perception that the game was fixed would undermine public confidence in the integrity of the game.

Already by 1865, news of fixed games was surfacing. In that year, three members of the New York Mutuals were banned from baseball for taking $100 each to throw a game to the Brooklyn Eckfords. Not surprisingly, the Mutuals were run by the notorious Boss William Tweed of Tammany Hall. Within a few years, the three were readmitted back into baseball. A dozen years later, the Louisville Grays lost seven straight games, much to everyone's amazement—except for the four Louisville players throwing the games. One of those players, pitcher Jim Devlin, became the prototype for Shoeless Joe Jackson. Devlin, one of the best pitchers of his time, pleaded with William Hulbert, creator of the National League, for reinstatement. Devlin's plight and poverty earned tears and $50 from

Hulbert—but not reinstatement. He never played again, continuing his efforts for forgiveness until his early death.

Hulbert's get-tough strategy seemed to work. The next few decades were only occasionally marred by gambling scandals. Umpire Richard Higham was fired in 1881 for betting on games he officiated, and there were rumored attempts to fix the World Series of 1903 and 1905. By the second decade of the twentieth century, though, gambling was increasing its pull on baseball players. After the powerful Philadelphia Athletics were upset by the Boston Braves in the 1914 World Series, Connie Mack smelled something rotten and dismantled his team.

This was the era of Hal Chase, who between 1905 and 1919 proved himself an outstanding first baseman while being widely perceived as being in cahoots with gamblers. Three teams—the Yankees, Reds, and Giants—dumped Prince Hal—so named because of his good looks and graceful play—for questionable activities. Later, Chase would be banned by the Mission and Pacific Coast Leagues. Gambling at the time was widespread in both baseball and society. Individuals openly engaged in betting at many baseball games, and baseball pools were common. Bookmakers offered their services to fans of baseball and other sports.

Although baseball did not have the reputation of horse-racing and prizefighting for crooked contests, owners and other officials hardly were role models. Several former or current owners were close to gamblers, including Charles Stoneham of the Giants, who was a pal of Arnold Rothstein, the man commonly believed to have been behind the 1919 World Series fix; and Charles Weeghman of the Cubs, who was a friend of Mont Tennes, a leading figure in Chicago's gambling world. Stoneham, John McGraw, and Francis McQuade bought a racetrack and casino in Havana, although Landis made them sell the gambling and sporting complex. Owners Stoneham, Jacob Rupert of the Yankees, and Julius Fleischmann of the Reds all owned racing stables.

So the Black Sox scandal of 1919 did not strike an innocent sports world. The eight members of the White Sox (including Shoeless Joe Jackson, Eddie Cicotte, and Buck Weaver), banned from baseball for life by Judge Landis after a trial had found them not guilty, had been traveling a path others had blazed. Also in 1919, two baseball greats, Ty Cobb and Tris Speaker, along with pitcher Smokey Joe Wood, may have bet on games they knew were fixed. Such was the charge brought forward by former pitcher Dutch Leonard in 1926. Landis ultimately exonerated the still-active Cobb and Speaker, although the player-managers had previously resigned from their positions, apparently as part of an earlier arrangement with American League president Ban Johnson. Both men then signed on with other teams strictly as players.

The next blockbuster gambling scandal centered on alleged actions by Pete Rose, who was disqualified from further association with organized baseball (and thereby rendered ineligible for the Hall of Fame) by commissioner Giamatti in 1989. Although Rose never admitted to betting on baseball games, it is widely believed that he did so. However, no evidence indicates that he ever attempted to lose a game. Keeping the man who broke Ty Cobb's all-time record for most career hits out of the Hall of Fame remains a controversial decision, and Rose continues to hope for reconciliation.

Gambling on baseball games still retains its position as the most evil action in the game, threatening the very fabric of the sport. Yet gambling is widespread in U.S. society and is sanctioned by state governments through lotteries and gaming licenses that boost state revenue. Players are told, in effect, that it is okay to buy lottery tickets—even to bet on horse races and gamble in legal venues—but not to bet on baseball. That fine line requires considerable discipline and faith given the place of gambling in American society. And commissioners are unlikely to be swayed from wielding a heavy hand when faced with gambling infractions—even if one were to argue "the devil made me do it."

See also: Black Sox Scandal; Cheating; Cobb, Tyrus Raymond; Commissioner; Giamatti, Angelo Bartlett; Jackson, Joseph Jefferson; Landis, Kenesaw Mountain; Law; Myth; Rose, Peter Edward.

Additional Reading:

Chafetz, Henry. *Play the Devil: A History of Gambling in the United States from 1492 to 1955.* New York: Bonanza, 1960.

Ginsburg, Daniel E. *The Fix Is In: A History of Baseball Gambling and Game Fixing Scandals.* Jefferson, NC: McFarland, 1995.

Pietrusza, David. *Judge and Jury: The Life and Times of Judge Kenesaw Mountain Landis.* South Bend, IN: Diamond Communications, 1998.

Reston, James, Jr. *Collision at Home Plate: The Lives of Pete Rose and Bart Giamatti.* New York: HarperCollins 1991; New York: HarperPerennial, 1992.

Riess, Steven A. *Touching Base: Professional Baseball and American Culture in the Progressive Era.* Rev. ed. Urbana: University of Illinois Press, 1999.

GAMES

Games have been consistently popular in American society. The culture of the United States was built partly on competition, often courageous, not always noble (against nature, against Native Americans, against the unknown, to name a few conflicts that lie at the heart of the founding and expansion of our nation). Even in moments of recreation, competition has seldom been far from American consciousness. Games as simple as checkers, as complex as chess, as common as cards still permeate popular culture and evoke anger and conflict, relaxation and camaraderie. Given the importance of baseball within American society, it should not be surprising to find popular table games, as well as video and computer games, that seek to re-create the game of baseball.

Credit for creating the first baseball table game is usually assigned to Francis C. Sebring, who invented Parlour Baseball. The game was patented in 1868 and advertised even earlier, in an 1866 edition of *Frank Leslie's Illustrated Newspaper*. No copies of the game have been discovered, leading to the conclusion that it may never have gone into production. In any case, a diagram with the patent indicates that the game involved a player projecting a coin forward by means of a spring, while another player swiveled a miniature bat. The result would be a hit or an out depending on the slot in which the coin landed. Similar devices would appear in later games, although cards, dice, and spinners would be more popular, used in perhaps as many as thousands of baseball games over the decades.

The problem with such games was that when participants tried to re-create baseball games involving actual players, there was no way to weight the results in favor of the great pitcher or hitter, whose chances of success were no greater than those of average players. When a participant, for example, threw dice for Lou Gehrig, he was no more likely to hit a home run than any of Gehrig's light-hitting contemporaries. Since one of the objects of table games is to duplicate as much as possible the actual experience of baseball games, this shortcoming was a serious one.

Apparently the first game that factored in baseball players' actual abilities was National Pastime, developed by Clifford A. Van Beek and patented in 1925.

Unfortunately, the Depression had hit prior to the advertising of the game in *Baseball Magazine* in 1931, and the game went nowhere. A similar game, APBA, imitating National Pastime, was fashioned by Richard Seitz and marketed in 1951. Among Seitz's new wrinkles was a ranking for pitchers, which made APBA more representational of actual player performances. Both versions utilized dice, cards depicting players' statistics, and sheets listing various game situations. Other statistical table games followed, among them Strat-O-Matic and Pursue the Pennant.

Advances in technology, including the spread of computers into many homes, made electronic games possible, and they became popular with Americans. Starting in the 1970s, fans found themselves able to simulate baseball contests through a wide range of increasingly realistic video and home-computer games. The most important entrepreneur here was Don Daglow, who created the first computer-simulated baseball game while a student at Claremont College in 1971. In the early 1980s, Daglow, with Eddie Dombrower, created the first video game, World Series Baseball, that simulated actual players' individual performances. Mattell, however, decided to substitute fictional players for real players to save licensing fees. Daglow, with Electronic Arts in the mid-1980s, helped to merge detailed statistics, flashy graphics, and a manager's actual strategy to produce, again with Dombrower, Earl Weaver Baseball. Another Daglow product, from his own Stormfront Studios, was Tony LaRussa Baseball in 1990. Creation of these managerial games included close participation by the managers themselves. By the 1990s, home games had clearly grown up, achieving a level of sophistication that someone like Francis Sebring could never have imagined.

See also: Rotisserie Baseball.
Additional Reading:
Daglow, Don L., Jack Kavanagh, and Garth Chouteau. "Fantasy Baseball Games." In *Total Baseball.* 6th ed. Ed. John Thorn et al. New York: Total Sports, 1999, pp. 592–597.
Zoss, Joel, and John Bowman. *Diamonds in the Rough: The Untold History of Baseball.* 1989. Reprint, Chicago: Contemporary Books, 1996.

GASHOUSE GANG

The St. Louis Cardinals of the mid-1930s, known as the Gashouse Gang, were one of the most famous teams in major league history. Their fame rested not just, or even primarily, on talent (including their 1934 World Series triumph over the Detroit Tigers) but on how they played the game: rough, colorful, disorderly. The Gashouse Gang was a down-and-dirty ballclub. Even their nickname—courtesy of shortstop Leo Durocher—evoked the image of a disreputable, uniform-stained, scratched-and-bruised group of brawlers.

This team, however, was among the greatest ever. Manager Frankie Frisch, who also played second base, never saw an umpire's call that should have gone against him. His special mode of discourse with umpires was to fire his glove into the sky and then leap on it when it descended. Shortstop Durocher brought fielding skill and a fighter's temperament to the diamond. Ducky Medwick, who ran like a duck but also won the Triple Crown in 1937 (leading the league in home runs, runs batted in, and batting average), played left field. Pepper Martin, the third baseman, was known as the "Wild Horse of the Osage" because of his legendary speed and reputed talent back home in Oklahoma for running down rabbits.

Then there were the Dean brothers, Jay Hanna and Paul, better known as Dizzy and Daffy, on the mound. Together they won 49 games in 1934 (30 by Dizzy) plus four more in the World Series. It was a team for the ages; and surely no generation could handle more than one.

See also: Dean, Jay Hanna; Durocher, Leo Ernest.
Additional Reading:
Hood, Robert E. *The Gashouse Gang.* New York: Morrow, 1976.
Martin, Mollie. *St. Louis Cardinals.* Mankato, MN: Creative Education, 1982.
Stockton, J. Roy. *The Gashouse Gang and a Couple of Other Guys.* New York: A. S. Barnes, 1945.
Ward, Geoffrey C., and Ken Burns. *Baseball: An Illustrated History.* New York: Alfred A. Knopf, 1994.

GEHRIG, HENRY LOUIS (LOU, THE IRON HORSE) (1903–1941)

Lou Gehrig became one of the most admired players in the history of baseball. His father was a German American caretaker, and he revered his mother so much that she sometimes traveled with him early in his playing career. To fan and nonfan alike, Gehrig came to symbolize determination and unceasing effort. Like the train from which he derived his nickname, Gehrig kept going forward, without frills and flash, steady, hardworking, and productive. Gehrig demonstrated those attributes during his record streak of 2,130 consecutive games played, and he added the quality of courage during his final years as he carried on in his thirties without complaint while facing death from amyotrophic lateral sclerosis (ALS), a disease forever after known to the public as Lou Gehrig's disease.

Gehrig was still in high school when he demonstrated unusual baseball ability. Playing for Commerce High School of New York in 1920, he hit a grand slam in the ninth inning against Chicago's Lane

Baseball star Lou Gehrig at the moment of his home-run hit at a game between Major League All-Stars and All Japan, circa 1930 (Hulton Getty)

Tech in a game played at Wrigley Field. After high school, Gehrig moved on to Columbia University, but his baseball exploits attracted considerable interest from the New York Yankees. When scout Paul Krichell offered a signing bonus of $1,500, Gehrig set aside his college plans and signed, to his mother's disappointment. But like a loving mother she supported him.

Gehrig made his first Yankee appearance in 1923, but the real beginning of his storied career occurred in late May 1925, when he was called up to pinch-hit. He made an out, and no one imagined that this appearance would mark the first of 2,130 straight games in which he would play. The next day, starting first baseman Wally Pipp developed a headache after being struck with a ball during batting practice. The young player was inserted into the starting lineup and remained there until 1939.

Hitting seemed effortless for Gehrig. His accomplishments are legion, including four home runs in one game during 1932, an American League record 184 RBIs during 1931, a lifetime batting average of .340 for 17 seasons, with 493 home runs and 2,721 total hits. In 1936, his .354 average, 49 home runs, and 152 RBIs earned him his second Most Valuable Player Award. An extraordinary RBI man, he drove in more than 100 in 13 straight seasons, leading the American League five times; on seven occasions he surpassed 150.

Throughout most of Gehrig's career, he played with Babe Ruth. Despite Gehrig's greatness, he consistently came off as second fiddle to the Sultan of Swat. A great home-run hitter in his own right and a superior RBI producer to Ruth, Gehrig was very different from the flamboyant Bambino, who courted public attention. Gehrig was quiet and reserved, letting his on-field achievements speak for themselves. He usually batted after Ruth in the lineup and did not hit the towering home runs with which Ruth awed spectators. Nor did Gehrig make as much money as Ruth. Symbolic of the relationship was the famous World Series game of 1932, when Ruth supposedly called a home run. Gehrig followed with another homer, but it was Ruth's that earned the headlines.

On a personal level, the Gehrig-Ruth relationship was an uneasy one. The two men had a falling-out when Gehrig concluded that Ruth had made an insulting comment about his beloved mother. Even after Ruth's departure from the Yankees, Gehrig kept coming in second in headlines, as a young outfielder named Joe DiMaggio grabbed the public's attention.

Nonetheless, Gehrig was deeply respected by other players and the public. That public esteem was never more evident after Gehrig reported that he had been diagnosed with ALS. The symptoms most likely began to appear during the 1938 season, when he had a good but not Gehrig-quality season, dropping from .351 with 37 home runs and 159 RBIs the previous year to .295, 29, and 114. Usually a great World Series hitter (he batted .361 with 10 homers and 35 RBIs in 34 Series games), he collected just four singles in 14 attempts during the 1938 sweep of the Cubs. By spring training of 1939, the Iron Horse's skills and stamina had badly deteriorated. He had great trouble hitting, running the bases, and fielding. He missed pop-ups that he should have handled easily and once failed to connect on 19 consecutive pitches during batting practice. When he fell in the locker room trying to put on his pants, his Yankee teammates looked on in embarrassment, unsure of what to do.

The 1939 regular season brought more of the same. In eight games, Gehrig managed just four hits in 28 at-bats, a .143

average. All four of his hits were singles, and he had only one RBI. After being congratulated on a routine play at first base, Gehrig took himself out of the lineup. When the Yankees began play on May 2, someone else was at first base.

A stint at the Mayo Clinic in Rochester, Minnesota, during June discovered the truth. Gehrig had ALS. Unable to play baseball, he accepted a position as a parole commissioner with the New York Police Commission, continuing to work with youths until shortly before his death on June 2, 1941.

About 61,000 admirers, along with the 1927 and 1939 Yankee teams, gathered at Yankee Stadium on July 4, 1939, to honor the greatest first baseman ever to play the game. After getting his emotions under control, Gehrig gave a speech free of self-pity. In words immortalized in newspapers as well as the film *Pride of the Yankees,* released in 1942 and starring Gary Cooper, Gehrig stated that he considered himself the "luckiest man on the face of the earth." He went on to praise the fans, his teammates, Yankee owners, managers, and his parents and wife. Ending his speech on an upbeat note, he said, "So I close in saying that I might have had a bad break, but I have an awful lot to live for." As he finished speaking, Babe Ruth rushed forward to embrace his estranged former teammate. In addition, the Yankees retired Gehrig's uniform number 4, and baseball waived the waiting period for his induction into the Hall of Fame.

The story of Lou Gehrig continues, and his place in American culture remains undimmed. A film remake of his story, with a focus on his marriage, was televised in 1978 (*A Love Affair: The Eleanor and Lou Gehrig Story*). As Cal Ripken neared and then broke the consecutive-games streak in the mid-1990s, the world renewed its interest in Lou Gehrig. And every time that a man or woman is diagnosed with Lou Gehrig's disease, many others are reminded of a man whose extraordinary baseball exploits were surpassed only by his love for family and courage in the face of death.

See also: Amyotrophic Lateral Sclerosis; Films; Heroes; Hunter, James Augustus; New York Yankees; Records Set; Ripken, Calvin Edwin, Jr.; Ruth, George Herman.

Additional Reading:
Gehrig, Eleanor. *My Luke and I.* New York: Crowell, 1976.
Graham, Frank. *Lou Gehrig: A Quiet Hero.* New York: Putnam's, 1942.
Henrich, Tommy. *Five O'Clock Lightning: Ruth, Gehrig, DiMaggio, Mantle, and the Glory Years of the New York Yankees.* New York: Carol, 1992.
Robinson, Ray. *Iron Horse: Lou Gehrig in His Time.* New York: Norton, 1990.

GIAMATTI, ANGELO BARTLETT (1938–1989)

Few worlds seem more separate to many people than baseball and higher education (especially the Ivy League). One is common, outdoors, physical; the other elitist, situated in classrooms and libraries, intellectual. Yet A. Bartlett Giamatti moved from president of Yale University, one of the most prestigious universities in the world, to president of the National League and commissioner of Major League Baseball, and he found in baseball a nexus of history, conventions, and myth that firmly positions the sport as a major ingredient within the nation's popular culture. Unfortunately, his tenure as commissioner is also linked to the lifetime banishment of Pete Rose, the man who broke Ty Cobb's all-time hits record, from organized baseball.

Giamatti's father, Valentine, was a Mount Holyoke College professor and Dante scholar. From his father, Bart learned the significance of symbolism and allegory, which he later would apply

Portrait of Baseball Commissioner A. Bartlett Giamatti (Jim Commentucci/Allsport)

to baseball. He grew up in Massachusetts as an avid Red Sox fan and attended Yale, his father's alma mater. Chosen to give the class oration at graduation, he chose as his topic the apathy of his generation, occasioned, he argued, by a lack of myth. He later would find considerable myth not only in Renaissance literature but also in the grand old game of baseball. Giamatti continued at Yale for his doctorate, examining in his dissertation the garden in Renaissance literature—another topic he later related to the game that he loved and would come to lead.

A distinguished academic career, briefly at Princeton, then at his beloved Yale, led to the presidency of the university in 1978. His years as Yale president were less satisfying and more frustrating than he had hoped. There was the loss of his

teaching and scholarship, abandonment by faculty friends, and lengthy labor-management conflict. It was with a great sense of relief and anticipation that he became president of the National League in 1986. In fact, Giamatti had turned down the opportunity to become commissioner in 1983 because he felt obliged to complete his term as president of Yale and settle a difficult labor strike at the university. When he finally moved from Yale to the National League, it was with an understanding that he would succeed Peter Ueberroth as commissioner.

Giamatti saw in baseball the embodiment of much of what it meant to be an American. Baseball, he argued, was the quintessential American game, a game whose history paralleled the history of the nation (an early version having been played by Revolutionary War soldiers); and baseball offered immigrants an opportunity to belong, urbanites a chance to return to their rural roots, the working class cheap entertainment, and both boys and girls a relatively safe game to play. Baseball also manifested, Giamatti believed, that union of the individual and the group, personal initiative and respect for law, that reflects the nation's most valued political principles. Finally, he saw the game itself as an allegory of the human condition: our desire to return home regardless of how far we have journeyed, and our eternal search for an ideal state—that green garden called paradise that many have located somewhere in the West, perhaps on an island, but that may exist only in the human mind. No wonder baseball owners revered Giamatti, for his vision of baseball ennobled the sport while he refrained from interfering in what the owners considered their proper business.

Giamatti became commissioner of Major League Baseball in 1989, much to the delight of the owners, who had tired of what they saw as Ueberroth's tendency to be a one-man show. Unfortunately, Giamatti inherited a problem that had been growing for years: Pete Rose's love of gambling.

Amid concerns that Rose may have bet on baseball, Giamatti hired an outside attorney, John Dowd, to investigate Rose, who by this time had retired as a player but was managing the Cincinnati Reds. Dowd's investigation led to a 225-page report concluding that strong evidence existed that Rose had bet on baseball and on his own team. Rose strongly denied the charges but ultimately, while continuing his denials, agreed to a conclusion of the matter that both banished him from baseball for life (although with the opportunity to request reinstatement) and acknowledged "that the Commissioner has a factual basis to impose the penalty provided herein."

The basis for Giamatti's concern with Rose's betting was his determination to protect the integrity of the game, which Giamatti earlier enunciated in a decision upholding a ten-day suspension of Kevin Gross for allegedly having a piece of sandpaper attached to his glove. Giamatti, in his written decision, affirms the necessity of a "level playing field" in which all participants play by the same rules in order for the public to have confidence in the game. Violating Baseball Rule 21(d), which states that "any player, umpire or club or league official or employee, who shall bet any sum whatsoever on any baseball game in which the bettor has a duty to perform shall be declared permanently ineligible," which Dowd's report indicated that Rose probably had violated, was perceived by Giamatti as seriously undermining the integrity of the sport. Giamatti feared that betting on one's own team, even to win (and there was no evidence that Rose had ever bet against his team), might

bring the bettor into association with disreputable individuals, place the bettor in danger of incurring gambling debts, therefore creating an environment in which the bettor might be induced into jeopardizing his team's chances for victory, and thus call into question the integrity of the game. Although there was no formal declaration that Rose had violated Rule 21(d), and Rose's settlement was predicated on a broader rule, Rule 21(f) (referring to behavior not in the best interest of the game), Giamatti responded to a direct question during his press conference after announcing the Rose decision by stating, "I have concluded he bet on baseball."

On September 1, 1989, nine days after issuing his decision, A. Bartlett Giamatti, the seventh baseball commissioner, died of a heart attack. He served only five months in office, but he influenced permanently the way that society views baseball. If he was the commissioner who banished Rose, he also was the commissioner who found in baseball a rich trove of metaphors, symbols, and allegories that speak to human aspirations and to the history and values of the nation.

See also: Cheating; Commissioner; Gambling; Landis, Kenesaw Mountain; Myth; Rose, Peter Edward.

Additional Reading:

Giamatti, A. Bartlett. *A Great and Glorious Game: Baseball Writings of A. Bartlett Giamatti.* Ed. Kenneth S. Robson. Chapel Hill: Algonquin Books, 1998.

———. *Take Time for Paradise: Americans and Their Games.* New York: Summit Books, 1989.

Holtzman, Jerome. *The Commissioners: Baseball's Midlife Crisis.* New York: Total Sports, 1998.

Reston, James, Jr. *Collision at Home Plate: The Lives of Pete Rose and Bart Giamatti.* New York: HarperCollins, 1991; New York: HarperPerennial, 1992.

Valerio, Anthony. *Bart: A Life of A. Bartlett Giamatti.* New York: Harcourt Brace Jovanovich, 1991.

GIBSON, JOSHUA (JOSH)
(1911–1947)

Josh Gibson was as revered in the African American community as Babe Ruth was in white America. A powerful slugger who also hit for power, Gibson often has been referred to as the "black Babe Ruth." However, as many people have noted, given Gibson's prodigious tape-measure home runs and ability to amass both huge home-run totals and high batting averages wherever he played, it would be just as accurate to call Babe Ruth the "white Josh Gibson." The most popular player in the black community next to pitcher Satchel Paige, Gibson died young, his health gone along with his dream of playing in the major leagues.

Gibson moved north from his Georgia home to Pittsburgh at the age of 12 when his father acquired a job in a steel mill. While still in his teens, he joined the Homestead Grays and quickly established himself as a powerful right-handed hitter and a steadily improving catcher. Behind the plate he was quick and possessed a strong throwing arm. It was at the plate, though, that he earned his fame and brought fans to cheer his every at-bat.

The batting statistics for Gibson, most accessible in James Riley's *Biographical Encyclopedia of the Negro Baseball Leagues,* are overwhelming: 75 home runs in 1931, 69 in 1934, 84 in 1936; and high batting averages at every stop, including .354 in the Negro Leagues, .373 in two Mexican League seasons, .353 in two Cuban winter seasons, .412 against major-leaguers during barnstorming tours, .479 in the Puerto Rican winter league, and .483 in nine All-Star Games.

After Gibson's first tour with the Grays (1929–1931), he joined the Pittsburgh Crawfords. There he was paired with pitcher Satchel Paige, perhaps the greatest battery in the history of any baseball league. After the Crawfords disbanded following the 1936 season, Gibson and Paige went their separate ways, Gibson back to the Grays, Paige to the Kansas City Monarchs. That set up memorable contests that attracted large numbers of excited fans. Paige especially looked forward to the encounters. Reports indicate that occasionally Paige would even walk batters to reach Gibson. If that did not make for smart baseball, it made for great showmanship and contributed to the popularity of Negro League baseball.

Such was Gibson's ability that Hall of Fame pitcher Walter Johnson, watching him play in the 1930s, called him better than the great Yankee backstop Bill Dickey. Monte Irvin, who played in the Negro Leagues and major leagues, considered Gibson the best hitter he ever saw. The acclaim and success that Gibson enjoyed, however, did not prevent his heavy drinking and use of drugs. All the while, Gibson longed to play in the major leagues.

By 1943, Gibson's lifestyle had caught up with him, although it was not yet evident on the baseball field. He suffered a nervous breakdown in January of that year and was hospitalized. At bat, the home runs kept coming. As the 1946 season ended, however, Gibson knew that his days were numbered and his major league dream was dead. Jackie Robinson had played for the Dodgers' Montreal farm team during the 1946 season and was ready to move up in 1947, the first African American player in the majors since the nineteenth century. In looking for the player to integrate the major leagues, Rickey had bypassed the two greatest Negro League stars, Josh Gibson and Satchel Paige.

Gibson suffered from an assortment of ailments by that time, including hypertension, kidney and liver problems, and bronchitis. He was feeling the physical and mental effects of years of heavy drinking, and his once burly body had deteriorated to 180 pounds. Shortly after his thirty-fifth birthday, on January 19, 1947, Gibson suffered a stroke while in a theater. Carried home, he died the next morning, not, as many have written, of a broken heart from being excluded from the majors, but because of declining health caused at least partly by alcohol. Yet the sad and untimely end of Gibson's life did not remove his mammoth accomplishments. In 1972, one year after Satchel Paige, he was inducted into the Hall of Fame at Cooperstown.

See also: African Americans; Negro Leagues; Paige, Leroy Robert; Substance Abuse.
Additional Reading:
Brashler, William. Josh Gibson: A Life in the Negro Leagues. New York: Harper and Row, 1978.
Gilbert, Tom. Baseball and the Color Line. New York: Franklin Watts, 1995.
Holway, John B. Josh and Satch. New York: Meckler, 1991.
Peterson, Robert. Only the Ball Was White. 2d ed. New York: McGraw-Hill, 1984.
Ribowsky, Mark. The Power and the Darkness: the Life of Josh Gibson in the Shadows of the Game. New York: Simon and Schuster, 1996.

GIBSON, PACK ROBERT (BOB, HOOT) (1935–)

Few pitchers in modern times have left a more lasting impression on the public than Bob Gibson. For 17 years, from 1959 to 1975, Gibson intimidated hitters with a powerful fastball, pride that refused to lose, a stern glare, and a take-no-prisoners approach to the game. A hitter who dug in at the plate would be apt to be digging himself out of a hole in the dirt he had made trying to elude a pitch high and tight.

Gibson was a throwback in more than just his approach to the game. He also compiled statistics reminiscent of a Three-Finger Brown or Walter Johnson.

In fact, when Gibson posted an almost unbelievable 1.12 ERA in 1968, it was the National League's lowest mark since Brown's 1.04 in 1906. That same year, Gibson had one of the greatest seasons ever by a pitcher. He threw 13 shutouts (second highest in National League history), pitched 28 complete games, and won 22 while losing nine. Given the way he pitched, it was remarkable that he ever lost.

Gibson, however, was far from a one-season wonder. He had been a top pitcher for several years prior to 1968, and the previous fall he had pitched as well as anyone ever in a World Series: three wins in three starts and 27 innings pitched, allowing 14 hits and five walks with a 1.00 ERA and 26 strikeouts. In three World Series for the Cardinals (victorious in 1964 and 1967, losers to the Tigers in 1968), Gibson won seven, lost two, pitched eight complete games in nine starts, struck out 92 hitters while walking just 17, and gave up only 55 hits in 81 innings, achieving an earned-run average of 1.89. He was the ultimate clutch pitcher.

Gibson was also red-hot in the regular season: 251 wins, 255 complete games, 56 shutouts, 3,117 strikeouts, a 2.91 ERA, five 20-win seasons, one no-hitter, two Cy Young Awards, and a Most Valuable Player Award. In addition, he was a fine hitter for a pitcher, losing little opportunity to help win the game. Gibson was voted into the Hall of Fame in 1981.

All of this Gibson accomplished despite a youth marred by rickets, asthma, and a heart murmur. He overcame these ailments plus much more (as indicated by the title of his book From Ghetto to Glory), to star in baseball and basketball at Creighton University and play for the Harlem Globetrotters. The latter opportunity Gibson quickly dropped, not wanting to clown on the basketball

A general view of the Bob Gibson statue in front of Busch Stadium, taken during a game between the St. Louis Cardinals and the Houston Astros in St. Louis, Missouri, July 12, 1998. The Cardinals defeated the Astros 6-4. (Stephen Dunn/Allsport)

court. Bob Gibson, as major league hitters would quickly come to realize, was anything but a clown.

Gibson is the type of pitcher many people would pay to see perform today. He surely would refuse to be the seven-inning starter so common even among the game's elite pitchers, and he would not brook the avalanche of home runs currently being hit. Neither his talent nor his personal pride would allow it.

See also: African Americans; Strikeouts.

Additional Reading:
Broeg, Bob. *Bob Broeg's Redbirds: A Century of Cardinals' Baseball*. Rev. ed. Marceline, MO: Walsworth, 1992.
Gibson, Bob. *From Ghetto to Glory: The Story of Bob Gibson*. Englewood Cliffs, NJ: Prentice-Hall, 1968.
———. *Stranger to the Game*. New York: Viking, 1994.
Lipman, David, and Ed Wilks. *Bob Gibson: Pitching Ace*. New York: Putnam's, 1975.
Martin, Mollie. *St. Louis Cardinals*. Mankato, MN: Creative Education, 1982.

GREENBERG, HENRY BENJAMIN (HANK) (1911–1986)

Hank Greenberg was the first great Jewish American ballplayer as well as one of the most selfless of the players who left their careers behind to join in the U.S. effort during World War II.

Greenberg grew up in the Bronx, on Crotona Park North, now known as East 174th Street, and spent countless hours honing his baseball skills on the diamond at Crotona Park. After graduating from high school in 1928, he briefly attended New York University before pursuing a baseball career. The Giants showed no interest in him despite his stellar high school career in New York, where he made all-city first baseman;

and when the Yankees offered a contract, Greenberg turned them down rather than spend years behind Lou Gehrig waiting for a chance to play. He ended up with the Detroit Tigers, played in his first Tigers game in 1930, and reached the big time to stay in 1933. By 1934, he was a star, hitting .339 with 26 home runs, 139 RBIs, and a league-leading 63 doubles. It was during that season that his Jewish heritage became the talk of Detroit.

Neither fans nor sportswriters lost sight of Greenberg's religion. Writers routinely referred to him as the "Jewish slugger" and the "Hebrew star." That practice, however, did not single out Jewish players, for many players were regularly identified by ethnic designations, whether Irish, French, German, or some other. Viewing an individual as a representative of his group was encouraged by the teams, because it gave each ethnic group a reason to come to the ballpark. It was, we would say today, a marketing strategy.

Sometimes, of course, offensive epithets were used by fans as well as players, a practice much ignored by the press. Greenberg later acknowledged that he had faced considerable anti-Semitism, but he noted that it only made him play harder. In fact, he drew a sharp distinction between ethnic insults hurled by fans and players, viewing the latter largely within the acceptable context of attempts to distract an opposing player and make him lose concentration.

As the 1934 pennant race progressed, Tiger fans, seeing their first baseman as a major reason for the team's success, wondered if Greenberg would play on Rosh Hashanah, the Jewish new year. Greenberg himself apparently agonized over the decision, and sportswriters spilled much ink wondering about the outcome and considering the choices. Much to their credit, they took the issue seriously,

viewing it as a matter of conscience. The issue was complex, for it placed loyalty to the team against personal convictions; but other matters loomed in the background, such as the theme of America and its national pastime as melting pots that fostered assimilation of immigrant groups and their descendants into the mainstream. The basic question ultimately was the relationship of personal beliefs versus public life. That issue remains current today and continues to provoke debate, growing from the efforts of religious groups to influence public policy.

The holy day came, and Greenberg opted to play. He hit two home runs as the Tigers defeated the rival Red Sox 2-1. Much to Greenberg's relief, the public at large, including the Jewish community, on the whole applauded his decision. Later in the season, with the Tigers safely ahead in the pennant race, his decision not to play during Yom Kippur, the Jewish Day of Atonement, drew far less attention.

Greenberg became one of the greatest home-run hitters of all time. He came close to Babe Ruth's record in 1939 with 58 home runs, but the record he most wanted was the RBI mark—190 set by Hack Wilson of the Cubs in 1930. Greenberg came within seven of the record in 1937. Greenberg took special pride in driving in runs, viewing that as most crucial to winning games.

Greenberg was drafted for military duty after playing in just 19 games in 1941. Discharged two days before Pearl Harbor, he immediately reenlisted after the December 7 Japanese attack. Greenberg spent most of his war years in India and China with the Air Force Twentieth Bomber command, a B-29 unit in the China-Burma-India Theater. In all, he missed about four and a half prime seasons. He returned in 1945 for the second half of the season and helped Detroit to a World Series win over the Cubs with two home runs. After hitting a league-leading 44 home runs in 1946, Greenberg was sold to the Pittsburgh Pirates, for whom he played one year and then retired. When he closed out his major league career, he stood fifth on the all-time home-run list with 331. Were it not for his years of military service, he surely would have surpassed 500 home runs.

Greenberg later worked the front offices for Bill Veeck with the Cleveland Indians and the Chicago White Sox. After the war, Greenberg had become "Captain Henry" rather than the "Jewish first baseman," the result of his war service and the declining emphasis on ethnicity as the major league focus shifted to racial integration. Greenberg was a strong supporter of Jackie Robinson when he broke in with the Dodgers during Greenberg's final season. Greenberg, after all, knew discrimination, although he later said that he had never undergone the level of bigotry that Robinson experienced. In fact, Greenberg felt hampered by anti-Semitism only after he moved into the owner's office. When Veeck chose to sell out because of declining health, Greenberg considered purchasing a majority share of the White Sox but decided that prejudice on the part of co-owners would undermine his success.

Hank Greenberg was an outstanding hitter and first baseman, deserving membership in the Hall of Fame. Perhaps more importantly, however, his career spanned major social developments in the history of baseball, and he did what he could to make that history as positive as possible.

See also: Jewish Americans; Koufax, Sanford; Religion; War.
Additional Reading/Viewing:
Greenberg, Hank. Hank Greenberg: The Story of My Life. Ed. Ira Berkow. New York: Times Books, 1989.
The Life and Times of Hank Greenberg (documentary). Dir. Aviva Kempner. Ciesla Foundation, 1999.

Ritter, Lawrence S. The Glory of Their Times: The Story of the Early Days of Baseball by the Men Who Played It. 1984. Reprint, New York: Vintage Books, 1985.
Simons, William M. "Hank Greenberg: The Jewish American Sports Hero." In Sports and the American Jew. Ed. Steven A. Riess. Syracuse: Syracuse University Press, 1998, pp. 185–207.

GREY, PEARL ZANE (1875–1939)

Zane Grey, one of the nation's most successful authors of Western stories, also had a long association with baseball, thereby combining two of the most American forms of entertainment. Grey starred as an outfielder for the University of Pennsylvania, enabling his college team to defeat the New York Giants in an 1896 exhibition game with an outstanding catch. He later played several years in the minors; brother Reddy actually made it to the majors for two games with Pittsburgh in 1903 (collecting two hits in six at-bats).

Zane Grey became a dentist but soon tired of that and turned to writing, producing about 80 books. Three of his volumes were about baseball: The Short-Stop (1909), The Young Pitcher (1915), and The Red-Headed Outfield and Other Baseball Stories (1915). He is best known, however, for Westerns. In such books as Riders of the Purple Sage (1913), The Light of the Western Stars (1914), and The Rainbow Trail (1915), Grey combined realistic descriptions based on firsthand observations with dramatic action and conflicts between heroes and villains that were as much moral as physical confrontations.

The good guy in Zane Grey's Westerns is the man who can respond to the spiritual presence in nature, as well as to love. His novels are passionate and romantic without abandoning the shootouts readers expected in stories of the Old West. The sentimentality of his fiction, its idealism and clear appreciation for the land, and the sustained action of the narratives offer a mixture of ingredients not unlike those that constitute the allure of baseball.

See also: Autry, Orvon Gene; Connors, Kevin Joseph Aloysius; Fiction.
Additional Reading:

Bloodworth, William. "Writers of the Purple Sage: Novelists and the American West." In *Wanted Dead or Alive: The American West in Popular Culture.* Ed. Richard Aquila. Urbana; Chicago: University of Illinois Press, 1996, pp. 43–68.

Jackson, Carlton. *Zane Grey.* Rev. ed. New York: Twayne, 1989.

Kimball, Arthur G. *Ace of Hearts: The Westerns of Zane Grey.* Fort Worth: Texas Christian University Press, 1993.

May, Stephen. *Zane Grey: Romancing the West.* Athens: Ohio University Press, 1997.

Overfield, Joseph M. "Zane Grey's Redheaded Outfield." In *The National Pastime.* Ed. John Thorn. New York: Warner, 1987, pp. 285–293.

GRIFFEY, GEORGE KENNETH, JR. (JUNIOR, KEN) (1969–)

Ken Griffey Jr. is considered to be the greatest all-around major league player of the 1990s. The son of a former outfielder with the Cincinnati Reds, he reached the majors with the Seattle Mariners in 1989. By his second year, he was a .300 hitter, and in 1993 he stroked 45 home runs. By the end of the decade he had hit 40 or more home runs six times, over 50 twice. His defensive skill in the outfield and accomplishments on the bases (routinely in double figures in stolen bases) contributed to his value.

By the end of 1999, however, Junior's future in Seattle was cloudy. Griffey wanted to join his father, by then a coach with the Reds, and he wanted to play closer to his Florida home (where the Reds, but not the Mariners, did their spring training). In the last year of his contract and with control over where he could be traded, Griffey gave the Mariners little choice but to trade him to the

Reds. In February 2000, Seattle made the historic trade.

Strangely enough, the move earned Griffey widespread plaudits when it was learned that he had made the deal possible by agreeing to a multiyear contract ($116.5 million over nine years) that was close to $40 million less than the Mariners' offer. Griffey made the decision in an era when athletes often seem to care about little except the highest salary they can earn; he apparently did it for family and the opportunity to work with his father. In a sport so long associated with parents and children, the reunion of Ken Sr. and Junior struck an especially responsive chord among a large segment of society.

See also: Family Relationships.
Additional Reading:

Christopher, Matt. *At the Plate with Ken Griffey, Jr.* Boston: Little, Brown, 1997.

Griffey, Ken, Jr. *Junior: Griffey on Griffey.* Ed. Mark Vancil. New York: Collins, 1997.

Gutman, Bill. *Ken Griffey, Jr.: Baseball's Best.* Brookfield, CT: Millbrook, 1998.

Kramer, Barbara. *Ken Griffey, Junior: All-Around All-Star.* Minneapolis: Lerner, 1996.

Nicholson, Lois. *Ken Griffey, Jr.* Philadelphia: Chelsea House, 1999.

GRIFFITH, CLARK CALVIN (THE OLD FOX) (1869–1955)

Clark Griffith was a baseball pioneer whose life stretched from the year of the legendary unbeaten Cincinnati Red Stockings into the Eisenhower years, including roles as pitcher, manager, and owner. Along the way, he helped to bring the American League into being and became friend to a succession of U.S. presidents. His determined effort to keep the often lowly Senators in Washington became, more than anything, a continuing act of American patriotism.

Griffith was born in a log cabin in frontier Missouri. His father died of an accidental gunshot when Clark was just two, and the boy grew up to become a trapper, cowboy, and saloon singer. He once found himself holding Jesse James's horse for the outlaw. Then he discovered baseball, learning to pitch from Old Hoss Radbourn. Throughout the 1890s until 1906 (with an occasional appearance until 1914), Griffith fashioned an impressive pitching career, notching seven seasons of 20 or more victories. His best years were with the Chicago ballclubs in the National and American Leagues. He finished with 237 wins against just 146 defeats.

As Ban Johnson attempted to bring the American League into existence as a major league, he recruited Clark Griffith to assist. Griffith took on the dual role of manager-pitcher for the Chicago White Sox (initially known, after the National League team, as the White Stockings), winning 20 games in 1901 as the staff ace and leading them to the new league's inaugural pennant. Griffith managed 20 years but never won another pennant.

A stint as manager of the Yankees ended with Griffith's firing in 1908, making him the original Yankee-hater for life. In 1912, he moved to the Washington Senators, buying part interest in the club and becoming majority owner in 1920. Griffith had some good seasons in Washington, winning pennants in 1924, 1925, and 1933, capturing the 1924 World Series as the aging but still great Walter Johnson finally won a world championship.

Financial problems hindered the Senators during Griffith's final decades as owner. In the most famous of his attempts to make ends meet, he sold player-manager (and son-in-law) Joe Cronin to the Boston Red Sox in 1934. Griffith continued to contribute to the success of major league baseball. He helped open up Latin America as a source of players, and his friendship with U.S. presidents, several of whom threw out the first pitch at opening day for the Senators, helped to keep baseball going during two world wars. The Old Fox was elected to the Hall of Fame in 1946 and continued as owner of the original Washington Senators until his death in 1955. By 1961, that team was in Minnesota, and an expansion Senators team was in Washington (but not for long; it headed to Texas after the 1971 season). The nation's capital awaits another Clark Griffith to return the city to the big time.

See also: Expansion; Major Leagues; Presidents of the United States.
Additional Reading
Povich, Shirley. *The Washington Senators.* New York: Putnam's, 1954.

H

HALL OF FAME AND MUSEUM

Museums are an important part of American society, preserving history and culture. Some museums, like the Smithsonian in Washington, D.C., or the Metropolitan Museum of Art in New York, enjoy international reputations and are visited by hundreds of thousands every year. Others are small and local in focus but still vitally important in keeping alive our heritage. Baseball museums are part of this cultural treasure that enriches young and old alike.

Baseball fans, cultural historians, scholars of the world of sport, and casual sight-seers spend many profitable and enjoyable hours at such places as The Babe Ruth Birthplace and Orioles Museum in Baltimore, the Louisville Slugger Museum in Louisville, and the Negro Leagues Baseball Museum in Kansas City. As good as these establishments are, the ultimate repository of baseball's past is the National Baseball Hall of Fame and Museum in Cooperstown, New York.

Cooperstown was chosen as the site for the Hall of Fame and Museum partly because of the erroneous conclusion of the Mills Commission, established by Albert Spalding and chaired by former National League president Abraham Mills. The commission, seeking to determine the origins of baseball, declared at the end of 1907 that Abner Doubleday had created the rules for baseball at Cooperstown in 1839. Before long, the people of Cooperstown were pushing to celebrate the supposed onc-hundredth anniversary of baseball. Naturally, they believed that the celebration should be held at Cooperstown. Stephen C. Clark, president of the Otsego County Historical Society, came up with the idea of creating a baseball museum. Then National League president Ford Frick suggested adding a hall of fame.

Almost everyone today agrees that baseball actually evolved from the British game of rounders and that Doubleday had nothing to do with the game's invention (in fact, he was at West Point preparing to become a Civil War hero in 1839). Yet that does not detract from the beautiful setting that is Cooperstown, named after the father of novelist James Fenimore Cooper. Early versions of baseball were played in the small towns of America, and the value of Cooperstown, apart from its aesthetic setting, is symbolic. It stands for all of those places throughout the land that have contributed to and gained from America's national pastime.

The first election to the Hall of Fame, in 1936, included five baseball immortals: Ty Cobb, Walter Johnson, Christy Mathewson, Babe Ruth, and Honus Wagner. By the time the building was dedicated in 1939, three additional elections had occurred, yielding 25 inductees. Players and managers selected to the Hall of Fame are honored with a plaque detailing their accomplishments. The number of inductees, of course, continues to grow and includes former umpires, executives, and, since 1971, Negro League stars. Recipients of the J. Taylor Spink Award for sportswriting and the Ford C. Frick Award for broadcasting have plaques in the National Baseball Library.

The complex grew considerably after 1939. Especially important was a separate building for the National Baseball Library and Archive in 1968, enlarged in 1993 and connected to the Hall of Fame building. The most recent expansion was the Barry Halper Gallery in 1999 to house items from Halper's personal collection. The complex also includes a ball field.

The National Baseball Hall of Fame and Museum has different meanings to different people. Aside from a world championship, achieving induction is the ultimate goal for major league players. Being denied eligibility, as with Pete Rose, means an eternal banishment from baseball paradise. The library houses mountains of information for baseball historians. Yet the most important person is the average visitor. For that person, the museum, the plaques, the ancient baseballs and early cards, the films, the bats and photographs, all of the artifacts and interactive experiences, bring the past alive. The visitor is in a sort of time machine traveling back into baseball's past. At the Baseball Hall of Fame, everyone is a child again; there is only the joy and innocence of a timeless game passed on from generation to generation.

See also: Doubleday, Abner; Myth; Rural America; Spalding, Albert Goodwill.

Additional Reading:

Astor, Gerald. *The Baseball Hall of Fame 50th Anniversary Book.* New York: Prentice Hall, 1988.

Baseball Hall of Fame website: www.baseballhalloffame.org

James, Bill. *Whatever Happened to the Hall of Fame: Baseball, Cooperstown, and the Politics of Glory.* 1994. Reprint, New York: Simon and Schuster, 1995.

Reidenbaugh, Lowell. *Baseball's Hall of Fame: Cooperstown, Where the Legends Live Forever.* Rev. by editors of *The Sporting News.* New York: Crescent Books, 1997.

Thorn, John, and the National Baseball Hall of Fame and Museum. *Treasures of the Baseball Hall of Fame: The Official Companion to the Collection at Cooperstown.* New York: Villard, 1998.

Vlasich, James A. *A Legend for the Legendary: The Origin of the Baseball Hall of Fame.* Bowling Green, OH: Bowling Green University Popular Press, 1990.

HEMINGWAY, ERNEST MILLER (1899–1961)

Ernest Hemingway is renowned as one of the giants of American literature, author of such classics as *The Sun Also Rises* (1926), *A Farewell to Arms* (1929), *For Whom the Bell Tolls* (1940), and *The Old Man and the Sea* (1952). Awarded the Pulitzer Prize for fiction in 1953 for *The Old Man and the Sea* and the Nobel Prize for Literature in 1954, Hemingway probably has influenced more writers than any other American author. That influence extends beyond his innovative prose style to include his macho image; popularizing of such subjects as war, bullfighting, and fishing; his philosophy of life, including the famous definition of courage as "grace under pressure"; and legitimizing writing about baseball in serious literature. This final accomplishment opened the door for a wealth of outstanding literature about America's national pastime.

Baseball was important to Hemingway, who followed the exploits of the Cubs and White Sox as he grew up in the Chicago suburb of Oak Park. In the aftermath of the Black Sox scandal of 1919, Hemingway shared the disillusionment felt by legions of fans, a reaction expressed in the story "The Three-Day Blow," written during the early 1920s. Bill suggests to Nick Adams, the protagonist of a famous series of stories, that they drink to fishing. Nick agrees with the suggestion and with Bill's comment that fishing is better than baseball, wondering "How did we ever get talking about baseball?" The disillusionment, however, is only temporary; in fact, earlier in the story the two young men discuss a number of baseball issues, including the current National League pennant race and Giants manager John McGraw's ability to buy whatever players he needs.

That Hemingway had been following baseball closely is conveyed by references to Heinie Zimmerman, a 1916 McGraw acquisition, and how "that bonehead will do him a lot of good," an allusion to Zimmerman's horrid performance in the fourth inning of the deciding sixth game of the 1917 World Series against the victorious Chicago White Sox. After Zimmerman committed a throwing error earlier in the inning, he concluded the inning's mishaps by taking a throw from pitcher Rube Benton picking Eddie Collins off third base. Unable to throw home when neither the catcher, Bill Rariden, nor the first baseman, Walter Holke, covered the plate, Zimmerman was reduced to chasing Collins in a futile race for home plate. Unfortunately, the image

that remained in the public consciousness was not Holke and Rariden's failure but the sight of Zimmerman chasing unsuccessfully after the future White Sox Hall of Famer.

Nick's (and Hemingway's) understanding of the subtleties of the game is reflected as well in Nick's response to Bill's statement about how Zimmerman is a good fielder but he still loses games. "Maybe that's what McGraw wants him for," Nick says, an allusion that would perplex readers unaware of McGraw's betting on games and rumors that he might have thrown a game now and then. Nick, despite the disgust for baseball he expresses later in the story, ends this exchange by saying that he would like to attend the World Series.

Hemingway refers to baseball in a number of his stories. About half of an unpublished Nick Adams sketch (now known as "Crossing the Mississippi") describes Nick wondering about how the 1917 World Series is going and remembering in detail a Happy Felsch home run for the White Sox in the first game (although Hemingway misspells the Giants pitcher Slim Sallee's name as Solee). When the magazine vendor comes down the aisle, Nick asks about the Series and is told that the White Sox have prevailed. The news gives the Chicago-area Nick a nice feeling. Frederic Henry, protagonist of *A Farewell to Arms,* reads in a newspaper about the Sox winning their pennant and the Giants leading in the National League. Lieutenant Henry expresses a lack of interest in baseball, but that hardly conveys Hemingway's actual attitude. The 1917 season clearly was an important one for Hemingway, as his hometown team claimed the world championship.

The most famous baseball association for Hemingway, though, involves Joe DiMaggio and *The Old Man and the Sea.*

The old fisherman, Santiago, prepares to embark on another day of fishing, hoping to break his string of 84 days without a catch. Early in the book, Santiago talks baseball with his young friend Manolin. Manolin, like Santiago, is a Yankee fan but worries about the pennant race. Although the text does not supply the year, they are talking about 1950, DiMaggio's next-to-last season and the year after his return from missing almost half of the season due to a bone spur in his right heel.

Manolin worries about the Indians and Tigers, but Santiago tells him to "have faith in the Yankees" and "think of the great DiMaggio." Later in the day, Manolin returns with food for the old man and reports that the Yankees have lost. That does not deter Santiago, who assures the boy that "DiMaggio is himself again" and that "he makes the difference." The Yankees, of course, will go on to win the pennant and defeat the Phillies in the World Series, something that Hemingway knows, for he finishes the book well after the 1950 Series.

Santiago also comments on other baseball figures, again demonstrating Hemingway's close following of the game. Santiago talks of Dick Sisler (son of Hall of Famer George Sisler) and "those great drives in the old park." Santiago also talks about several managers: Leo Durocher, manager of the Giants in the 1951 World Series won by the Yankees; John McGraw, the former Giants manager who often visited Cuba in his role as part owner of the Havana Oriental Park racetrack; and two Cubans, Mike Gonzalez and Adolpho Luque, both of whom had distinguished major league playing careers and coached in the majors. Gonzalez and Luque were unable to gain managing jobs in the majors, held back by their ethnic identity, but they were both successful and famous managing in Cuban winter ball.

It is Joe DiMaggio, however, who dominates Santiago's thoughts, especially as he finds himself alone at sea struggling to land the giant marlin and then desperately and unsuccessfully trying to keep sharks from devouring the marlin's flesh. DiMaggio, as the son of a fisherman, has a natural attraction for Santiago, but it becomes increasingly clear that DiMaggio is also Santiago's hero and inspiration. The Yankee great, who had struggled to overcome the painful bone spur, inspires Santiago to continue with his struggles despite exhaustion and severe pain in his back and hands. He wonders if DiMaggio would be proud of him. He wonders if his sore and bleeding hands are as great a handicap as DiMaggio's bone spur. Only at the end of the novel does Santiago, physically and emotionally spent from his struggle, no longer think about Joe DiMaggio.

The Yankee great was the type of person Hemingway liked: strong, inclined to let his performance do his talking, bearing up with dignity under his growing physical handicaps (certainly an exemplar of Hemingway's grace under pressure). Hemingway did not enjoy a close personal relationship with DiMaggio, although the two men attended a Sugar Ray Robinson–Carmen Basilio fight together during DiMaggio's first return to Yankee Stadium after his retirement as a player. The excursion, described by Maury Allen, provided an interesting vignette regarding fan reaction to the famous men. The fans went wild as DiMaggio tried to reach his seat, ignoring Hemingway. One boy, after getting an autograph from DiMaggio, noticed Hemingway and asked him who he was. Hemingway never hesitated: "I'm his doctor," he said.

Hemingway's use of baseball perplexed many critics, who did not think baseball worthy of serious literary attention. That view would soon start on a steady, if slow, decline as many excellent writers placed baseball at the center of their novels. Hemingway had made baseball artistically legitimate in fiction and deserves credit for laying the groundwork for acceptance of baseball fiction from such authors as Mark Harris, Michael Shaara, Eric Rolfe Greenberg, W. P. Kinsella, William Kennedy, and many others.

See also: Black Sox Scandal; Castro, Fidel; Cuban Baseball; DiMaggio, Joseph Paul; Fiction; McGraw, John Joseph.

Additional Reading:

Allen, Maury. *Where Have You Gone, Joe DiMaggio?* New York: Dutton, 1975.

Hemingway, Ernest. *The Nick Adams Stories.* Ed. Philip Young. New York: Scribner's, 1972.

————. *The Old Man and the Sea.* New York: Scribner's, 1952.

Hurley, C. Harold. *Hemingway's Debt to Baseball in* The Old Man and the Sea: *A Collection of Critical Readings.* Lewiston, NY: Edwin Mellen, 1992.

Lynn, Kenneth S. *Hemingway.* New York: Simon and Schuster, 1987.

HEROES

A common lament in contemporary America is that society lacks heroes, that the age of heroes is gone. Certainly it is difficult to view individuals as heroes when every detail of their lives is subjected to microscopic examination by the media. Such scrutiny of sports figures exposes their warts as well as virtues. The more that fans know about their favorite players, the more likely players will be seen in terms of their failings and imperfections. Familiarity breeds contempt.

In days past, many ballplayers were viewed as heroes, figures who succeeded far beyond the normal run of men, who were seen as role models by fans who knew only what sportswriters wrote about them. Until recent decades, though, sportswriters, like other reporters, would not report on a player's private misbehavior—drinking, gambling, philandering. Babe Ruth was a hero to millions of Americans, who never knew the extent of his appetites. Ty Cobb benefited from lack of reporting about his racist views (though one wonders whether that would have disqualified him from hero status during his era). Youngsters in the 1950s had no idea about Mickey Mantle's carousing, or how many times he arrived at the ballpark hung over.

There is more to the issue of heroism, however. To be heroic implies being larger than life, if not physically, at least in human accomplishments. A utility infielder who bats .220 may indeed be heroic in his personal life because of impediments he overcomes just to do his daily job—as countless people behave heroically in carrying out their personal responsibilities in the face of huge challenges. But the public seldom sees people as heroic unless their accomplishments are clearly monumental.

When people think of heroes today, they like to think in terms of gigantic achievements. So as fans look back to baseball's past, they see extraordinary things: Old Hoss Radbourn winning 59 games, pitching 73 complete games, and striking out 441 batters in 678 innings in 1884, figures that would take a contemporary pitcher three years to equal (and, in the case of the complete games, probably never reach); Big Ed Walsh winning 40 games, pitching 42 complete games, and hurling 464 innings in 1908; Iron Man Joe McGinnity winning both ends of three doubleheaders in August of 1903; Cy Young totaling 511 victories from 1890 to 1911; Rogers Hornsby compiling batting averages of .397, .401, .384, .424, and .403 from 1921 to 1925; Babe Ruth hitting 54 home runs in 1920, almost doubling the previous all-time record of 29, which he had set the year before.

Lou Gehrig was widely recognized as a hero, partly for playing in 2,130 consecutive games while hitting a lifetime .340, but even more so for his courage in the face of a deadly disease. Only a true hero could look at a particularly frightening form of early death and say, "I consider myself the luckiest man on the face of the earth."

Joe DiMaggio may have been a loner and not an especially easy person to get along with, but fans saw the graceful star who could do everything well and who overcame serious injury to continue winning. When he could no longer play at a heroic level, he walked away from the game. During his record string of 56 consecutive games hitting safely, society honored him with one of the most famous baseball songs ever, "Joltin' Joe DiMaggio," recorded during that memorable 1941 season by Les Brown and His Orchestra, with Betty Bonney singing. Such was his heroic stature that Santiago, the old fisherman of Hemingway's *The Old Man and the Sea,* gains inspiration from thinking about his hero's battle with the painful bone spur in his heel. Decades later, Simon and Garfunkel would wonder in "Mrs. Robinson" where DiMaggio had gone, as a lonely nation yearns for its old hero in its hour of need.

Songs are a sign of heroism. In earlier centuries, poets composed epics and sagas about heroes. In the nineteenth and twentieth centuries, songwriters filled in. The first baseball song to make the charts was "Slide, Kelly, Slide," recorded on wax cylinders by George Gaskin, in 1892, about the versatile Mike "King" Kelly. Teresa Brewer did most of the singing of "I Love Mickey" in 1956, with Mickey Mantle, the most popular player of his time, assisting.

Whether sports figures merit hero worship is debatable, but Jackie Robinson, most people today recognize, was truly heroic. The first African American player in the major leagues in modern times, Robinson broke the color barrier in 1947 in the face of racial hatred, including taunts and on-field and off-field threats. Robinson was a hero not just for his own race but for all of America. Many other African American players also qualified as heroes, continuing to live their baseball dream in the segregated towns across America that paid witness to their Negro League contests.

Recently, players do not seem to ignite the same type of hero worship. Fans know too much about their faults—and about their enormous contracts. Of course, their statistics also tend to be more modest, except for home runs and strikeouts. Players no longer bat .400 or win 40 games (few manage to reach even 20). Yet an occasional player still manages to scale that elusive heroic mountain. Cal Ripken is a clear example.

After the strike season of 1994, Ripken showed the baseball world that despite high salaries and work stoppages a man could go about his business day after day, year after year, and keep producing. Ripken broke Lou Gehrig's consecutive-games record and still continued to play every day until he ended his magnificent string at 2,632 games. There may be a lesson there, for Ripken became a hero less for superhuman feats than for doing his job day in and day out. That, after all, may be the most realistic and accurate view of heroism.

See also: DiMaggio, Joseph Paul; Equipment; Gehrig, Henry Louis; Hornsby, Rogers; Kelly, Michael Joseph; Music; Myth; Radbourn, Charles Gardner; Ripken, Calvin Edwin, Jr.; Robinson, Jack Roosevelt; Ruth, George Herman; Wagner, John Peter; Walsh, Edward Augustine; Young, Denton True.

Additional Reading:

Browne, Ray. *Heroes of Popular Culture.* Bowling Green, OH: Bowling Green University Popular Press, 1972.

Davis, Mac. *100 Greatest Sports Heroes*. New York: Grosset and Dunlap, 1958.

Smith, Robert. *Heroes of Baseball*. Cleveland: World, 1953.

Additional Reading:

Lindberg, Richard. *Sox: The Complete Record of Chicago White Sox Baseball*. New York: Macmillan, 1984.

HITLESS WONDERS

The Hitless Wonders were the 1906 Chicago White Sox, famed for overcoming their dismal performance at the plate to upset the mighty Chicago Cubs in the World Series. The Sox had batted just .230 that year with a total of seven home runs for the season. Facing the Cubs, who had won 116 games (still the record) with pitcher Three Finger Brown and the double-play combination of Tinker to Evers to Chance, the Sox seemed not to have a prayer. Yet they won and in doing so established a phrase that continues to be used today, both within and outside the game of baseball.

The White Sox, though, were not as pathetic offensively as the two statistics might indicate. Their playing manager, Fielder Jones, and outfielder Ed Hahn finished second and third in their league in drawing walks; second baseman Frank Isbell and first baseman Jiggs Donahue were among the top five in stolen bases. As a result, the White Sox were able to score 570 runs, third highest in the American League.

The term "hitless wonders" remains current today, although it is usually employed as a derogative wisecrack. The White Sox were wonders—that is, winners—despite their deficiencies. Most hitless wonders today wallow in defeat as a result of their weakness, and the term heaps scorn on top of losses, like adding insult to injury. And not only in baseball does one find modern hitless wonders. Anyone who strikes out a lot or fails consistently to make a hit, let alone a home run, in any endeavor is likely to become known as a hitless wonder.

See also: Brown, Mordecai Peter Centennial; Tinker to Evers to Chance.

HOME RUN

The home run has become the most important positive baseball metaphor in American society. People talk about hitting a home run at work, on a special project, on a test in school. No one wants to get just part way to a goal. The individual heading up a capital campaign is not likely to say to the employer, "Well, I hit a double on that effort." Not often does someone come home from a day at work calling out, "Honey, I made this big presentation to the partners. I think I hit a single!" The options usually are hitting a homer or striking out. It's all or nothing.

The popularity of the home-run metaphor comes from the importance of the big hit in baseball, especially since the 1920s. Perhaps no scene in baseball films is more visually striking than the climactic home run hit by Roy Hobbs in *The Natural*—the ball smashing into the stadium lights, setting off a spectacular fireworks display. No play in baseball grabs spectators like the home run.

Throughout the nineteenth century and the first two decades of the twentieth century, the home run was not emphasized in the game. A player like Ty Cobb, who had plenty of power, did not step up to the plate swinging for the fences. That was not the way the game was played, yet when John Franklin Baker homered off Rube Marquard and Christy Mathewson in the 1911 World Series, he forever earned the nickname "Home Run" Baker.

Home-run records became significant when Babe Ruth came along. Prior to Ruth, the season records had been held by men named George Hall, Charley Jones, Harry Stovey, and Ned Williamson.

Chicago Cubs slugger Sammy Sosa hugs St. Louis Cardinals slugger Mark McGwire after McGwire hit his sixty-second home run of the season, Tuesday, September 8, 1998, in St. Louis. (AP Photo/Chicago Tribune, Nuccio DiNuzzo)

Hall hit five home runs in 1876 for Philadelphia in the first season for the National League. He earned more fame (or infamy) after the following year, when he had played for Louisville, banned for life from baseball (with star pitcher Jim Devlin). Jones upped the record to nine with Boston in 1879. In 1880, he set another record by hitting two home runs in an inning. Stovey hit 14 for Philadelphia of the American Association in 1883, one of five times that he led his league in home runs. A complete player, Stovey also was an outstanding defensive first baseman and an accomplished base stealer. Then came Ned Williamson, with 27 home runs in 1884 for Cap Anson's Chicago White Stockings. This Williamson record deserves an asterisk, for he played home games in a bandbox. Lakefront Park was so tiny that balls hit over its fences were ruled doubles, except for the year when Williamson stroked his 27 homers. The following season, the doubles rule was restored, and Williamson hit three home runs. He finished with 64 in his 13-year career.

The year 1919 changed the game of baseball permanently. Two monumental events occurred: the Black Sox scandal, and Babe Ruth's coming of age as an everyday hitter. Ruth, then with the Red Sox, converted from great pitcher to even greater slugger, hitting 29 home runs. After the season, Ruth was traded to the Yankees, for whom he hit 54 home runs in 1920, almost doubling his record of the previous year. Runner-up George

Sisler hit just 19. In fact, Ruth outhomered every major league team except the Phillies, who hit 64.

The records kept coming. In 1921, Ruth hit 59, also surpassing the previous career record of 138 held by Roger Connor. In 1927, Ruth hit the magic number of 60, and his final home runs in 1935 gave him 714. The Babe, however, did not compile his extraordinary feats in a sterile laboratory. He was the most popular player of his time, probably of all time. He was a giant among mortals, and anyone who considers his towering status in relation to the rest of the baseball world in 1920 would have a hard time arguing with that assessment. The Babe was loved beyond compare, which helps to explain some of the fan animosity later exhibited toward Roger Maris and Hank Aaron.

Babe Ruth also started his record-setting slugging (and exuberant public life) at a time when the United States was swinging into the Roaring Twenties. It was a time of exuberance, of indulgence, of mighty dreams and often mighty accomplishments. F. Scott Fitzgerald, the great chronicler of the Jazz Age (he even gave the period that title), wrote, after the 1920s had given way to the Great Depression, that "in those days life was like the race in *Alice in Wonderland,* there was a prize for every one" ("Echoes of the Jazz Age," p. 21). For millions, the prize was another Babe Ruth home run.

Home runs have carried strong emotional content ever since. When Roger Maris, one of baseball's good guys, broke the Babe's record in 1961 with 61 home runs, neither fans nor sportswriters, on the whole, applauded. In the minds and memories of many, Maris just was not worthy. Ford Frick, then serving as commissioner of baseball (and, earlier, a ghostwriter for Babe Ruth), ruled that there should be a notation with the figure indicating that the record was set in a 162-game schedule (the origin of the famous "asterisk"). Not until the 1990s (long after Maris had died) was the qualification removed, giving Maris his due for setting the home-run record.

Some of the same feelings surfaced in reaction to Hank Aaron's successful assault on the career mark. There also was considerable racism involved, with Aaron receiving hate mail, including threats against him and his family. Many Americans did not want to see a black man break Ruth's record, but break it Aaron did in 1974, although without commissioner Bowie Kuhn in attendance. When Aaron retired after the 1976 season, he had hit 755 home runs, which stands as the career home-run record.

Though Aaron's career record remains, Maris's single-season mark fell in 1998, this time to widespread feelings of excitement and goodwill. Mark McGwire and Sammy Sosa engaged in a home-run duel throughout the season. With television audiences rapt, McGwire hit number 62 on September 8. More than a few tears of joy fell as McGwire, caught up in the thrill of the moment, made his way around the bases. He almost missed first base, having to be grabbed by coach Dave McKay, who pulled him back to touch the bag. Then McGwire continued his exuberant dash, receiving congratulations from Cubs players, hugging third baseman Gary Gaetti and catcher Scott Servais. Sammy Sosa dashed in from right field to hug the man who had beaten him to the record.

After crossing home plate, McGwire hoisted son Matthew high in the air as the chests of all fathers tightened just a little. Then McGwire jumped over a railing to go up into the stands and embrace the children of Roger Maris—and suddenly people had a better understanding of what reconciliation means (McGuire also thanked his former wife). It was a time for joy among all. Any lingering anger from the baseball strike of 1994 evaporated.

Yet Mark McGwire was not through, and neither was Sammy Sosa. The sluggers continued to battle for the final record. Sosa finished with 66, while McGwire pushed the record into the stratosphere, finishing with 70. After the season, Sosa, who consistently had demonstrated how competition and good fellowship can flow together, and how desire can exist without jealousy, was named Most Valuable Player in the National League, as if the baseball gods had found a way to dispense justice with unusual clarity. The world was happy, but soon enough people began questioning whether the deluge of home runs was ultimately good or bad for baseball.

See also: Aaron, Henry Louis; Bauman, Joe Willis; Films; Heroes; Jackson, Reginald Martinez; Kiner, Ralph McPherran; Mantle, Mickey Charles; Maris, Roger Eugene; McGwire, Mark David; Records Set; Ruth, George Herman; Sosa, Samuel Peralta; Strikeouts; Williams, Theodore Samuel.

Additional Reading:

Daley, Arthur. All the Home Run Kings. New York: Putnam's, 1972.

Fitzgerald, F. Scott. "Echoes of the Jazz Age." In The Crack-Up. Ed. Edmund Wilson. 1945. Reprint, New York: New Directions, 1956, pp. 13–22.

McCarver, Tim, with Danny Peary. The Perfect Season: Why 1998 Was Baseball's Greatest Year. New York: Villard Books, 1999.

Robertson, John G. The Babe Chases 60: That Fabulous 1927 Season, Home Run by Home Run. Jefferson, NC: McFarland, 1999.

Sullivan, George. Home Run! New York: Dodd, Mead, 1977.

HORNSBY, ROGERS (RAJAH) (1896–1963)

Rogers Hornsby earned lasting fame as a great hitter. Usually considered the finest right-handed hitter of all time, Hornsby set a still unmatched major league record when he batted .424 in 1924, surely a record that never will be broken. It was one of three .400 seasons that he enjoyed; in fact, over a five-year span (1921–1925), he averaged better than .400. Hornsby's lifetime average of .358 ranks second only to Ty Cobb's .366. After his glory years, he tutored a minor-leaguer named Ted Williams with the Minneapolis Millers in 1938. Williams would hit .344 for his career but failed to win recognition from his old hitting coach as a great hitter because he refused to hit to the opposite field, which surely would have raised Williams's average even higher.

Rogers Hornsby earned the nickname "Rajah," a title given to a prince or chief in India, by being completely devoted to being the best. Hornsby, by his own admission, had no interests beyond baseball. Once asked what he did in the off-season, he replied, "I stare out the window and wait for spring." He neither drank nor smoked and refused to read books or go to the movies for fear of harming his vision. When his mother died during the 1926 World Series, Hornsby, the Cardinals' player-manager, postponed the funeral until after the Series. St. Louis won in seven games over the favored Yankees.

Having quarreled with owner Sam Breadon, Hornsby was traded to the Giants after the championship season. His final great season was with the Cubs in 1929 when he batted .380. Ironically, Hornsby, who so zealously protected his eyesight, was in a hospital for cataract surgery when he died in 1963.

See also: Heroes; Records Set; Williams, Theodore Samuel.

Additional Reading:

Alexander, Charles C. Rogers Hornsby: A Biography. New York: Holt, 1995.

Eisenbath, Mike. The Cardinals Encyclopedia. Philadelphia: Temple University Press, 1999.

Finlayson, Ann. *Champions at Bat: Three Power Hitters*. Champaign, IL: Garrard, 1970.

Lieb, Frederick G. *The St. Louis Cardinals: The Story of a Great Baseball Club*. New York: Putnam's, 1944.

HOUSE OF DAVID

The House of David was an unusual semipro baseball team. Most of its players wore long hair and beards. More significantly, the team represented a cross-section of America, boasting religious, cultural, racial, and gender diversity among its players.

Benjamin Purnell started the House of David colony at Benton Harbor, Michigan, after a 1903 dream in which a white dove had named Purnell as the Sixth Son of the House of David and charged him with uniting the Lost Tribes of Israel. Purnell established a strict code of behavior: no smoking, sex, or drinking, but cultivation of long hair and beards. When tourists increasingly found the colony an interesting place to visit, Purnell started a baseball team in 1910. His wife managed the squad, which became a famous barnstorming troupe over the next few decades, competing against Negro League teams and various local squads.

In the 1930s, the House of David established close ties with the Kansas City Monarchs, one of the great Negro League teams. The Monarchs, pioneers of night baseball, leased their portable lighting system to the House of David club and altered their own schedule to accommodate the bearded nine. The two teams had the same booking agent and sometimes traveled together, competing against each other and opposition. The House of David welcomed noncolony players regardless of race, creed, or sex, including, for example, Negro League star Satchel Paige, major-leaguer Grover

Cleveland Alexander, and two-time 1932 Olympic gold medalist Babe Didrikson Zaharias. The rest of American baseball still has not caught up.

See also: Jewish Americans; Negro Leagues; Religion; Women in Baseball.
Additional Reading:
Ward, Geoffrey C., and Ken Burns. *Baseball: An Illustrated History*. New York: Alfred A. Knopf, 1994.

White, G. Edward. *Creating the National Pastime: Baseball Transforms Itself, 1903–1953*. Princeton: Princeton University Press, 1996.

HUNTER, JAMES AUGUSTUS (CATFISH) (1946–1999)

Catfish Hunter's importance to society is threefold: athletic, legal, and medical. A Hall of Fame pitcher who five times won 20 or more games, pitched a perfect game, and captured the Cy Young Award in 1974, Hunter also played a significant role in fighting the reserve clause. In 1998, his playing days over, he was diagnosed with Lou Gehrig's disease.

Hunter was signed out of high school by Charles Finley, owner of the Athletics. Finley created the nickname "Catfish" for the young hurler, who moved into the Athletics starting rotation without ever having pitched a game in the minors. He helped his team to three consecutive World Series championships (1972–1974), but financial disagreements gradually disrupted the player's relationship with the owner. After Finley apparently failed to comply with a provision of Hunter's 1974 contract, the pitcher successfully sought and gained free agency, although the arbitrator's decision did not address the broader issue of the reserve clause. Hunter's victory nonetheless gave hope to other players that the system might be changed, as it was the following year. Hunter signed with the Yankees and remained with them from 1975 through 1979.

Hunter was diagnosed with amyotrophic lateral sclerosis (ALS, or Lou Gehrig's disease) in 1998. Never one to turn away from a challenge, Hunter established a foundation to aid people with ALS. In June 1999, he returned to Oakland, scene of his greatest pitching triumphs, to raise money for the battle against the disease. In August, he fell at his home, hitting his head on concrete steps. After several weeks in a hospital, Hunter returned home, but he passed away on September 9.

See also: Amyotrophic Lateral Sclerosis; Finley, Charles Oscar; Free Agency; Gehrig, Henry Louis; Labor-Management Relations; Law; Miller, Marvin James; Reserve Clause.

Additional Reading:

Clark, Tom. *Champagne and Baloney: The Rise and Fall of Finley's A's*. New York: Harper and Row, 1976.

Hunter, Jim. *Catfish: My Life in Baseball*. New York: McGraw-Hill, 1988.

Libby, Bill. *Catfish: The Three Million Dollar Pitcher*. New York: Coward, McCann, and Geoghegan, 1976.

Stambler, Irwin. *Catfish Hunter: The Three Million Dollar Arm*. New York: Putnam's, 1976.

I

INDUSTRIAL LEAGUES

Baseball, even from its early days in the middle of the nineteenth century, proved popular with people of all stripes. There was little sense of play for its own sake, however, as baseball, although entertaining for spectators, was usually associated with values like health, teamwork, and discipline. Baseball also was associated with work, and the vocabulary of work was often applied to the game by reporters and participants alike. Hard work and practice were seen as vital to success on the field of play as much as in the working world.

Many of the early teams were drawn from workplaces. The Eckford Club of Brooklyn drew its players from among the shipwrights and mechanics employed at the Henry Eckford shipyards. Several teams, including the Atlantics, consisted of players from the food trades. This alliance between the workplace and the diamond accelerated as ballplayers increasingly came from blue-collar occupations. By the early decades of the twentieth century, industrial leagues had become common, consisting of teams from companies involved in such industries as the railroad, electricity, meatpacking, and textiles.

Teams sponsored by, for example, textile companies would play each other. Companies took the games seriously, as management believed that baseball competition promoted good health, kept their workers' minds off labor issues, and helped to integrate immigrants into the American culture. Winning was sufficiently important that teams would recruit nonemployee ringers to gain an edge, such as the Parisian Cloak Company, which paid the teenage Casey Stengel $3 per game to pitch. Women's leagues also developed, featuring such teams as the Goodyear Girls and Westinghouse Maids. Even prisons featured teams, which would play against visiting clubs.

These sorts of teams became generically known as the industrial leagues, which remained popular even during the Depression. Their popularity remains potent even today, as the legions of workplace softball teams attest.

See also: Business; Jackson, Joseph Jefferson; Women in Baseball.

Additional Reading:
Goldstein, Warren. *Playing for Keeps: A History of Early Baseball.* Ithaca: Cornell University Press, 1989.
Perry, Thomas K. *Textile League Baseball: South Carolina's Mill Teams, 1880–1955.* Jefferson, NC: McFarland, 1993.
Seymour, Harold. *Baseball: The People's Game.* 1990. Reprint, New York: Oxford University Press, 1991.
Ward, Geoffrey C., and Ken Burns. *Baseball: An Illustrated History.* New York: Alfred A. Knopf, 1994.

INTERNET

Baseball is typically slow to embrace advances in technology and other innovations in society, including night games, radio broadcasting, and airplane travel. The Internet, however, has spread throughout baseball as in much of the world. Indeed, major league clubs rushed to utilize the Internet, perhaps because it does not alter the game but rather helps market baseball by supplying information about the organization, its players, and its history. Similarly, sports publications and broadcasting networks quickly moved to establish often richly informative websites. Even individual players, like their nonathletic contemporaries, established their own websites. And, of course, online fantasy leagues and discussion groups are common.

All major league clubs developed their own websites, varying in depth of information, quality of graphics, ease in moving within the site, multimedia experiences, and links to other sites. The best websites offered appealing features, such as colorful graphics, chat rooms, material for children, opportunities for visitors to express their views (e.g., on the best team first basemen ever) and vote for the All-Star Game, art galleries, press archives, and baseball culture. Even the simplest team websites offered useful information in a straightforward, season-by-season format.

Of special interest is the Baseball Hall of Fame and Museum website, which includes online exhibits like Women in Baseball, the Single Season Home Run Record, and History of the World Series. Of special importance is the Hall of Fame Gallery, which lists all members, with links to individual websites.

Media websites keep fans up-to-date with scores, stories, helpful search options, and many other content elements. There are also resources aimed especially at fantasy-leaguers, offering the latest statistics and player transactions. Other helpful websites for fans include baseball-only media, sites listing individual players, and those offering visually striking scenes of current and former ballparks. No student of baseball will want to ignore treasures from the past that are available. Discussion groups are also available online.

The huge number of online resources for fans demonstrates that baseball is intent on keeping up with this technology, especially if it enhances fans' enjoyment and involvement in the game.

See also: Hall of Fame and Museum; Home Run; Periodicals; Women in Baseball.

Additional Reading:
Coleman, Pat. "Dodgers Still the Best of the 30 Official Sites." *USA Today Baseball Weekly,* April 14–20, 1999, p. 47.
Edelman, Rob. *Baseball on the Web.* New York: MIS, 1998.
Singer, Tom. "The Wide World of Web Sports." *Sport* 90, no. 3 (March 1999): 54–57.

IRVIN, MONFORD (MONTE) (1919–)

Monte Irvin helped to secure integration of the major leagues and, after retirement, continued to work for recognition of Negro League players. And though he was not the only one to play in the Negro Leagues and the major leagues, he excelled in both—more so than anyone else (including Satchel Paige, who arrived in the majors long past his prime, and Larry Doby, whose tenure in the Negro Leagues was relatively short). For a time he thought he might never make the majors; his first opportunity was dashed when Effa Manley, perhaps out of resentment against Branch Rickey, resisted the Dodgers' attempt to sign him.

Monte Irvin was one of the great hitters in the Negro Leagues, playing for the Newark Eagles from 1938 to 1948 (except for wartime service, 1943–1945, and part of the 1942 season, spent in the Mexican League after a salary dispute with Manley). Twice he won Negro League batting titles, hitting .395 in 1941 and .404 in 1946. Roy Campanella called Irvin the best all-around player he ever saw. Irvin reportedly was the Negro Leagues' choice to break the color barrier but was in the service when Rickey chose Jackie Robinson.

Manley, after thwarting Rickey's attempt to sign Irvin, arranged an opportunity for him with the New York Giants, for whom he played from 1949 to 1955 before a final season with the Cubs. He hit .293 during his eight years in the majors, with his best seasons in 1951 and 1953 (24 home runs, 121 RBIs, a .312 batting average; followed by figures of 21, 97, and .329).

After retiring as a player, he served as an assistant to the commissioner from 1968 until 1984 and was a member of both the Hall of Fame's Special Committee on the Negro Leagues and Veterans Committee, helping to select Negro League players for induction into the Hall. Irvin himself was selected for enshrinement in 1973.

See also: African Americans; Manley, Effa; Negro Leagues.

Additional Reading:

Overmyer, James. *Queen of the Negro Leagues: Effa Manley and the Newark Eagles.* Rev. ed. Lanham, MD: Scarecrow, 1998.

Riley, James A. *The Biographical Encyclopedia of the Negro Baseball Leagues.* New York: Carroll and Graf, 1994 (includes a foreword by Monte Irvin).

JACKSON, JOSEPH JEFFERSON (SHOELESS JOE) (1889–1951)

"Say it ain't so, Joe!" That lament, from a boy to his big league hero, is among America's most recognizable quotations. And one of the most famous nicknames is "Shoeless Joe," the ballplayer who broke the little fan's heart. How he achieved that nickname is often misunderstood. Joe Jackson was a country boy from South Carolina who got his baseball start playing for textile league teams. He did not regularly play barefoot as a young man but did once play in his stocking feet because a pair of baseball shoes was too tight and causing blisters. Once was enough, because the nickname seemed to fit Jackson's background.

Jackson loved baseball but was not keen on playing in the major leagues because he did not want to leave the South to play in a large and strange Northern city. So when Connie Mack signed Jackson while he was playing minor league ball in 1908, Jackson was a reluctant call-up at the end of the season. Jackson's reluctance to play in Philadelphia led Mack, despite his recognition of the player's potential, to trade him to Cleveland in July 1910.

Finally persuaded to play in Cleveland, Jackson achieved stardom in 1911, hitting .408. The sportswriters loved writing about his exploits, at times even mocking him. There was plenty of material for the writers in addition to Jackson's astounding hitting ability and powerful throwing arm. He used a special bat named "Black Betsy," a 48-ounce piece of lumber especially made for him and colored with layers of tobacco juice. The lefty-hitting Jackson had used the bat in the mill leagues and disdained choking up on the huge bat, usually holding it at the very bottom, with the little finger of his right hand curled around the knob. Jackson could neither read nor write, spoke with a distinctive Southern accent, and was noticeably naive about many aspects of urban life.

Jackson, however, knew how to crush enemy pitchers. He starred with Cleveland until traded to the Chicago White Sox before the 1915 season. His lifetime batting average, .356, remains the third best in baseball history. Such was Jackson's ability, and the beauty of his swing, that Ty Cobb and Babe Ruth both considered him to be the best natural hitter they ever saw; a future slugger, Ted Williams, at least partly modeled himself after Jackson.

Unfortunately, Jackson's fame owes more to the Black Sox scandal of 1919 than to his on-field accomplishments. He was one of eight players charged with conspiring to throw the World Series to the Cincinnati Reds. Jackson was not a willing conspirator, twice turning down a chance to participate in the fix before finally agreeing when it appeared that the fix would occur with or without him. Jackson received $5,000 but always claimed that he did his best to win. His outstanding hitting in the World Series, when he established a Series-record 12 hits, seems to bear out his claim. Jackson's knowledge of the plot, even if he did not participate in throwing the games, weighed heavily on him. Just before the first Series game, he begged not to play, and immediately after the Series he attempted to see Charles Comiskey, who would not receive him, probably so the owner could continue to plead ignorance regarding the fixed Series.

Banned from baseball for life, along with the seven others, Jackson played for years on semipro teams under assumed names and later ran a dry cleaner and a liquor store. In 1951, efforts to clear his name accelerated, as the South Carolina legislature passed a resolution urging baseball to reinstate him, and the Cleveland Baseball Hall of Fame elected Jackson a member. He was scheduled to appear on television on *The Ed Sullivan Show* but died on December 5, 1951, 10 days before the show was to air. Efforts to remove Jackson from the disqualified list, and thus make him eligible for the Hall of Fame, continue, supported by the growing body of literature and films depicting his plight. His defenders include such luminaries as Ted Williams and U.S.

Senators Strom Thurmond of South Carolina and Tom Harkin of Iowa.

> *See also:* Black Sox Scandal; Cheating; Comiskey, Charles Albert; Commissioner; Fiction; Field of Dreams; Films; Gambling; Industrial Leagues; Kinsella, William Patrick; Landis, Kenesaw Mountain; Williams, Theodore Samuel.

Additional Reading:
Asinof, Eliot. *Eight Men Out: The Black Sox and the 1919 World Series.* New York: Holt, 1963.
Frommer, Harvey. *Shoeless Joe and Ragtime Baseball.* Dallas: Taylor, 1992.
Gropman, Donald. *Say It Ain't So, Joe: The True Story of Shoeless Joe Jackson and the 1919 World Series.* 1979. Reprint, New York: Lynx, 1988.
Kinsella, W. P. *Shoeless Joe.* 1982. Reprint, New York: Ballantine, 1996.
Lurs, Victor. *The Great Baseball Mystery: The 1919 World Series.* New York: A. S. Barnes, 1966.

JACKSON, REGINALD MARTINEZ (REGGIE) (1946–)

Just about every baseball fan, indeed any American with a passing interest in the World Series, is familiar with Reggie Jackson's nickname: "Mr. October," a timeless homage to his clutch performances under pressure. Reggie Jackson had another nickname, which he modestly gave himself: "The straw that stirs the drink." Indeed, he was a great slugger, finishing his career with 563 home runs (as well as 2,597 strikeouts, the most ever), but he was at his best when it counted most. Everybody in the United States loves a winner, and Jackson was one of the biggest, playing on teams that won 11 division titles, six pennants, and five World Series. More often than not, he was the man who made the difference when everyone was watching.

October truly became Jackson's month in 1977. On three consecutive pitches from three different Dodger pitchers in Game 6 of the World Series, Jackson hit

Reggie Jackson of the Oakland Athletics, swinging the bat in uniform, on the field of an empty baseball stadium, 1969 (Archive Photos)

three home runs. The Bronx Bombers went on to win their first world championship since 1962. Altogether, Jackson hit 10 home runs in Series play, a record five in that remarkable 1977 classic, and batted .357 in 27 Series games.

There was more to Jackson, of course, than end-of-season heroics. He played in 12 All-Star Games, was American League Most Valuable Player in 1973, won four home-run titles, helped Charles Finley's A's win three consecutive championships from 1972 to 1974, became one of the early free-agent millionaires when he signed with the Yankees prior to 1977, feuded with Yankee manager Billy Martin and owner George Steinbrenner, continued accumulating headlines and home runs for 21 seasons, and was elected to the Hall of Fame in 1993.

Every October, it seems that fans throughout the nation can still hear chants of "Reg-gie!" "Reg-gie!" "Reg-gie!" as Jackson swings for the fences. His were among the most electrifying moments in baseball history.

See also: Finley, Charles Oscar; Free Agency; Home Run; New York Yankees; Steinbrenner, George Michael, III.

Additional Reading:

Allen, Maury. *Mr. October: The Reggie Jackson Story*. New York: Times Books, 1981.

Jackson, Reggie, with Mike Lupica. *Reggie: The Autobiography of Reggie Jackson*. New York: Villard Books, 1984.

Madden, Bill. *Damned Yankees: A No-Holds-Barred Account of Life with "Boss" Steinbrenner*. New York: Warner, 1990.

JAPANESE BASEBALL

Japan imported baseball from the United States during the nineteenth century, and by 1911 the sport had become so popular that Albert Spalding devoted a chapter of his early history of the sport, *Base Ball: America's National Game,* to baseball in the Orient. Spalding noted that baseball was especially popular in Japanese universities and discussed visits of the Waseda University team to the United States and of the University of Wisconsin club to Japan. In those early years of international competition, Japanese teams held their own. According to Spalding, the Japanese were "first-class" in fielding but second-rate in hitting and pitching.

The early twentieth century witnessed many visits by U.S. all-star teams and individual clubs to Japan. The White Sox and Giants toured Japan in 1913; riding the wave of popularity, the first professional Japanese team was formed in 1920. The most famous visit by an American team occurred in 1934, when a group of All-Stars, including the aging but still powerful Babe Ruth, played 18 games, winning all but one. The Babe hit

The Keio team warms up before its match with Waneda at the Meiji Shrine Diamond stadium, Japan's classic baseball match circa 1950. (Hulton Getty)

13 home runs and so endeared himself to Japanese fans that 15 years later, on his death, Japanese games came to a brief halt to pay tribute to "Beibu Rusu," as they called him. In the wake of Babe Ruth's historic trip, the first Japanese professional league was established in 1936.

In one game during Ruth's tour, the great Japanese pitcher Eiji Sawamura, still just a teenager, consecutively struck out Charley Gehringer of the Detroit Tigers, Ruth, Lou Gehrig of the Yankees, and Jimmy Foxx of the Philadelphia Athletics. Sawamura would later die in World War II; his heritage remains in the award named after him, given annually to the best pitcher in the Japanese major leagues. After the war American teams resumed their trips, mingling sportsmanship with diplomacy. Joe DiMaggio, in fact, followed his final season with the

Yankees in 1951 with a tour of Japan. It was there that DiMaggio stroked his final home run.

Subsequent years saw continued growth in quality as well as popularity. The Tokyo Giants became the premier Japanese team, winning nine consecutive Japanese championships from 1965 to 1973. Their great slugger, Sadaharu Oh, surpassed Babe Ruth's career home-run record by hitting 868 and leading his league for 13 straight years (1962–1974). No American player has surpassed that record, although Cal Ripken of the Baltimore Orioles finally broke not only Lou Gehrig's American record but the mark established by Sachio Kinugasa of 2,215 consecutive games played.

Later Japanese stars include the powerful home-run hitter Hideki Matsui of the Tokyo Giants and Ichiro Suzuki, the

Kobe Blue Wave star who won a fifth consecutive batting title in 1998. Japanese clubs have proved competitive against American teams, winning a slim majority of the games that they played against the Los Angeles Dodgers in 1989 (9-8) and an all-star team the following year (4-3).

The Japanese leagues have opened their teams not only to Americans but to Koreans, Taiwanese, and Latin Americans. Rivaling the U.S. majors in internationalism, Japanese baseball also continues to prove a strong rival in quality. At the amateur level, Japan has outplayed the United States in recent Olympics, winning one gold and two silver medals from 1984 through 1996, compared with one gold and one silver for the United States. In addition, U.S. teams have started heavily recruiting Japanese players, especially pitchers. Hideo Nomo, Hideki Irabu, and Masato Yoshii were among several talented Japanese players that were recruited and signed by U.S. teams, and more are on the way.

A day may come when the world championship is played between teams from the United States and Japan, the best of the West against the best of the East.

See also: Australian Baseball; DiMaggio, Joseph Paul; Expansion; Korean Baseball; Ruth, George Herman; Spalding, Albert Goodwill; Taiwanese Baseball.

Additional Reading:

Cromartie, Warren. *Slugging It Out in Japan: An American Major Leaguer in the Tokyo Outfield*. New York: Kodansha International, 1991.

Johnson, Daniel E. *Japanese Baseball: A Statistical Handbook*. Jefferson, NC: McFarland, 1999.

Nagata, Yoichi, and John B. Holway. "Baseball in Japan." In *Total Baseball*. 5th ed. Ed. John Thorn et al. New York: Viking, 1997, pp. 465–472.

Spalding, Albert G. *Base Ball: America's National Game*. 1911. Reprint, revised and edited by Samm Coombs and Bob West, San Francisco: Halo Books, 1991.

Whiting, Robert. *You Gotta Have WA*. New York: Macmillan, 1989.

JEWISH AMERICANS

Jewish Americans have played important roles in baseball since the sport's beginning, but not always in large numbers on the playing field. In the nineteenth century, an observer was perhaps more likely to see a Jewish owner than a Jewish player. Especially in the National League, several Jewish businessmen exercised at least partial ownership of ballclubs. Beginning with Nathan Menderson, several Jewish businessmen owned the club in Cincinnati, a city that had a prominent and influential Jewish population. One of Menderson's successors in Cincinnati was Julius Fleischmann, a major stockholder with the club and mayor of the city in the early 1900s.

One of the most famous (or perhaps infamous) of the Jewish American owners was Andrew Freedman (New York Giants, 1895–1902). A disagreeable individual, he regularly insulted fans, players, sportswriters, and other owners; he exercised considerable clout with owner colleagues thanks to his Tammany Hall connections. His approach to managers would make George Steinbrenner seem like a paragon of patience, as Freedman sped through 16 managers in eight seasons.

Other Jewish contributions include an impressive tradition of Jewish sportswriters, who have enriched the fans' enjoyment and understanding of baseball. Reporters Shirley Povich, Roger Kahn, Dick Young, and Jerome Holtzman, among others, have written themselves a place in the history of the sport they have chronicled so effectively. In the broadcast booth, Mel Allen, another Jewish American, long enhanced the drama of New York Yankees games. And in the bookstores, libraries, and classrooms, novels by some of the nation's finest writers of fiction have enriched the cultural life of the nation. To cite a few: Bernard Malamud's *The Natural* (1952), Mark Harris's *Bang the Drum Slowly* (1956), Philip Roth's *The Great American Novel* (1973), and Eric Rolfe Greenberg's *The Celebrant* (1983).

Jewish players, at least in small numbers, were involved in baseball from its earliest days. Lipman Pike was a player with the Philadelphia Athletics in 1866 and managed and played for Troy in the National Association of Professional Base Ball Players, the first professional league, in 1871. In 1876, Pike continued his involvement with the history of baseball by playing in the National League during its inaugural season.

On the field, however, Jews struggled to establish themselves in the face of anti-Semitism and often encountered active discouragement from within their own community. About 2 million Jewish immigrants arrived in the United States from Eastern Europe between 1882 and 1914. They came hoping, like all immigrants to the American shores, for a better life. That meant getting a good job and making sure their children received an education to permit entry into the professions, where they could earn a steady living. They came, in most cases, with no experience in sports and tended to view baseball and other athletics as a dangerous diversion from their children's all-important studies and career preparation.

The immigrants' children, though, had different ideas. They seldom had the money to attend baseball games, but they watched from a distance, following the exploits of their new sports heroes. They did not have access to baseball diamonds, a condition endemic to life in the inner cities at the turn of the century and years thereafter. Like African Americans in subsequent decades, they relied on the streets, improvising with sticks and makeshift balls, transforming baseball into stickball and similar versions of the game. Given parents' understandable opposition, the limited resources, and the inaccessibility of diamonds—not to mention severe anti-Semitism within organized baseball—it is not surprising that Jewish youths could look up to few professional Jewish ballplayers as role models.

Between 1900 and 1909, according to David Spaner, only five Jewish ballplayers performed in the major leagues. The next decade was a little better, with 13 Jewish players. Between 1920 and 1960, only about 76 Jewish players were active in the majors. These numbers, of course, probably are somewhat low, because of the difficulty in identifying early Jewish players just from their names. Nonetheless, the number of Jewish players was quite small, again according to Spaner, a total of 134 from 1871 to 1996, just 1 percent of the total number of major league ballplayers. The number, in fact, declined after World War II, despite an easing of anti-Semitism as the race issue replaced ethnic preoccupations. In the 1990s, however, Jewish players reached the majors in increasing numbers (13 in 1995).

Jewish American youths who tried to make a career in baseball saw the sport as a means of assimilation into the American mainstream. At the same time, organized baseball saw itself as a major embodiment of the melting-pot metaphor at work, despite the constant identification of players by ethnic background. Sportswriters and broadcasters routinely referred to players' Irish or Italian or German or French or Jewish backgrounds, a practice encouraged by management to attract fans to the stadiums to root for their ethnic heroes. Players thus became representatives of ethnic groups, despite the melting-pot concept, which forbade reporting of anti-Semitism because that would undermine the belief that on the field of play there were only Americans.

This schizophrenic response to ethnicity was not only dutifully followed by broadcasters and sportswriters but also by fans and players. Jews, for example, saw baseball as a way to become a real American and make a real living, but they also saw Jewish players as Jewish players rather than just players. Andy Cohen, for example, who replaced Rogers Hornsby as the second baseman of the Giants in 1928, was the darling of Jewish American fans. Faced with on-field discrimination, however, many players, including several named Cohen, played under pseudonyms.

The first great Jewish American player, Hank Greenberg, tended to dismiss anti-Semitic jibes by players as typical (and legitimate) efforts to distract him from concentrating on the game. He drew a line, though, between ethnic insults from players and fans, condemning the latter. When Greenberg was faced with the question of whether to play on Rosh Hashanah during the pennant race of 1934, he agonized over the decision, finally opting to play. This decision was supported strongly by Jews and non-Jews alike as a choice of the team over the individual and, by extension, the melting pot and cultural assimilation over ethnic separation.

Since Greenberg, baseball has witnessed other Jewish American stars, including Al Rosen, the slugging third baseman for the Cleveland Indians in the 1950s who won the Most Valuable Player Award in 1953; and Sandy Koufax, three-time Cy Young Award winner with the Los Angeles Dodgers in the 1960s and a Hall of Famer. With Jewish Americans facing less discrimination and enjoying greater material wealth, they face no special impediments to playing in the major leagues today, which explains the rise in the number of Jewish ballplayers. The road they traveled, though, was difficult, yet despite those obstacles Jewish Americans have helped make baseball what it is today. Not least among their accomplishments was their support of racial integration. Hank Greenberg, for example, was one of the first white players to support Jackie Robinson in 1947, as Jewish Americans in the following decade would contribute significantly to the civil rights movement.

See also: Democracy; Fiction; Greenberg, Henry Benjamin; Koufax, Sanford; Malamud, Bernard; Povich, Shirley; Religion.

Additional Reading:
Bjarkman, Peter C. "Six-Pointed Diamonds and the Ultimate Shiksa: Baseball and the Jewish-American Immigrant Experience." In *Cooperstown Symposium on Baseball and the American Culture.* Ed. Alvin L. Hall. Westport, CT: Meckler, 1990, pp. 306–347.
Riess, Steven A. *City Games: The Evolution of American Urban Society and the Rise of Sports.* Urbana: University of Illinois Press, 1989.
Riess, Steven A., ed. *Sports and the American Jew.* Syracuse: Syracuse University Press, 1998.
———. *Touching Base: Professional Baseball and America in the Progressive Era.* Westport, CT: Greenwood Press, 1980.
Spaner, David. "Greenberg to Green: Jewish Ball Players." In *Total Baseball.* 5th ed. Ed. John Thorn et al. New York: Penguin, 1997, pp. 171–180.

JOHNSON, BYRON BANCROFT (BAN) (1864–1931)

Ban Johnson was a physically imposing man, weighing close to 300 pounds and, like many baseball leaders of his day, highly autocratic. He also was a brilliant organizer who spearheaded the creation of the American League, which would endure unchanged for about 50 years and continues today as one of the two major leagues. Ultimately, his growing hostility toward Charles Comiskey, a former friend and partner in establishing the American League, would lead to hiring Judge Kenesaw Mountain Landis as baseball's first commissioner and end Johnson's own reign as the "czar of baseball."

Johnson graduated from the University of Cincinnati's law school and, after practicing law for a time, became a reporter (later city editor and sports editor) for the Cincinnati *Commercial-Gazette*. It was then that he developed a friendship with Charles Comiskey, who was managing the Cincinnati Reds. The two men became business associates, taking over leadership of the Western League in 1893. Johnson was the leading figure in this enterprise, changing the league's name to the American League in 1900 and declaring the organization a major league for the 1901 season. Many National League players, including such stars as Cy Young, Joe McGinnity, and Willie Keeler, jumped to better-paying jobs in the new league. The quality of the American League was so high that its champion, the Boston Pilgrims, defeated the National League's Pittsburgh Pirates in the first modern World Series in 1903.

By 1903, the American League had achieved such success with Johnson's philosophy—moderately priced tickets, no gambling or profanity, absolute power invested in umpires to keep the game decorous—that the older National League reached an accommodation with the upstart in the so-called National Agreement. Both sides agreed to respect the reserve clause and not raid the other league's clubs. The two leagues would be ruled jointly by the National Commission comprising the two league presidents and a third party functioning as permanent chairman of the commission. That individual turned out to be Garry Herrmann, president of the Reds, but

Johnson became the real power. The agreement also made possible the annual World Series, won by the American League 14 times in the first 24 championship meetings.

After some shuffling of American League cities in the first two years, the league enjoyed extraordinary stability, consisting of the same eight teams in the same eight cities from 1903 until 1953.

By 1919, however, events were beginning to go beyond Johnson. His detestation for Comiskey blinded him to what was happening in the World Series, and even when the White Sox owner informed him after the first game of his fear that the Sox were throwing the Series, Johnson ridiculed his former friend's concerns as the "whelp of a beaten cur." Had Johnson listened more sympathetically to Comiskey, he might have been able to intervene and save the day from the gambling and baseball conspirators, with the result that a commissioner might not have been hired. Johnson thus would have retained more power himself. That, however, did not happen, and the Black Sox scandal hastened the end of Johnson's exalted position. He continued as president of the American League, increasingly at odds with Landis and other owners and in declining health, until 1927, when he resigned. The Hall of Fame beckoned in 1937, six years after Johnson's death.

See also: Black Sox Scandal; Comiskey, Charles Albert; Commissioner; Landis, Kenesaw Mountain; Major Leagues.

Additional Reading:

Allen, Lee. *The American League Story*. Rev. ed. New York: Hill and Wang, 1965.

Asinof, Eliot. *Eight Men Out: The Black Sox and the 1919 World Series*. New York: Holt, 1963.

Dickey, Glenn. *The History of American League Baseball Since 1901*. New York: Stein and Day, 1980.

Honig, Donald. *The American League: An Illustrated History*. New York: Crown, 1983.

Seymour, Harold. *Baseball: The Golden Age.* 1971. Reprint, New York: Oxford University Press, 1989.

JOHNSON, WALTER PERRY (THE BIG TRAIN) (1887–1946)

Walter Johnson was a fan favorite during his career, and he has retained a position in the minds of fans befitting his nickname. Like a big train that just keeps coming, Johnson was no trickster on the pitching mound. He kept to his fastball, delivered with a smooth, sidearm motion—and he almost always threw it exactly where he aimed. Yet despite his considerable ability and legendary accomplishments, he remained modest and polite; he did not drink or smoke. These personal attributes he developed growing up in rural Kansas before coming to Washington by way of an Idaho semipro league. To support himself while he pitched in Idaho, he dug postholes for a telephone company.

Even after many decades, Walter Johnson's statistics seem almost superhuman. From 1907 to 1927, with the Washington Senators, he won 417 games, completed 531 of 666 starts, threw 110 shutouts (still the major league record), and struck out 3,509 hitters. He led his league in wins six times, complete games six times, shutouts seven times, innings pitched five times, strikeouts 12 times (twice fanning more than 300), and earned-run average five times. He pitched almost 56 consecutive scoreless innings in 1913, a record that stood until broken by Don Drysdale in 1968. The year before, he won 16 straight decisions.

Finally, in 1924, the popular Johnson was a member of a World Series champion, and the Senators honored their ace pitcher by having him lead the championship parade to the White House to meet President Calvin Coolidge. It ultimately took a broken leg in 1927 to do what hitters could not accomplish. Struck by a line drive that shattered one of his legs, Johnson donned a brace and continued to pitch, going 5-6. His performance, however, was far below his normal level, and he retired. Nine years later Walter Johnson was among the original five players elected to the Hall of Fame.

See also: Griffith, Clark Calvin; Strikeouts.

Additional Reading:

Kavanagh, Jack. *Walter Johnson: A Life.* 1995. Reprint, South Bend, IN: Diamond Communications, 1996.

Povich, Shirley. *The Washington Senators.* New York: Putnam's, 1954.

Thomas, Henry W. *Walter Johnson: Baseball's Big Train.* 1995. Reprint, Lincoln: University of Nebraska Press, 1998.

Treat, Roger L. *Walter Johnson: King of the Pitchers.* New York: J. Messner, 1948.

JOURNALISM (PRINT)

No development in American society has contributed more to the continuing popularity of baseball than the newspaper. The printed word became increasingly important as literacy spread throughout the United States and as the principles of democracy in an expanding and increasingly complex nation required an informed electorate. Newspapers helped to meet those needs. And as newspapers grew in number and scope in the middle of the nineteenth century, they also turned toward an increasingly popular sport—baseball.

Even today, as the world enters a new millennium and as radio, television, and the Internet supply cascades of information and opportunities to enjoy games, the printed word—next to physical attendance at stadiums—remains the most important vehicle for engaging the fan. President Ronald Reagan, a former radio broadcaster of baseball games, admitted to reading the sports section first in the morning. He was not alone in doing so, joined by millions of fans from common people to international shakers and movers. Television sports report scores and perhaps a few highlights, usually for local or regional teams, but the newspaper prints full box scores, enabling readers to re-create all games through imagination. Narrative accounts report highlights from games throughout the land, columns offer in-depth discussions, and many Sunday papers supply comprehensive accounts of the actions and issues associated with the sport. How did this baseball journalism come about?

It began in the 1850s, with people like William Trotter Porter, who started including baseball in his sports journal *Spirit of the Times,* apparently becoming the first to label baseball the "national game"; William Cauldwell, who combined editing the *New York Mercury* with reporting on baseball; and the man whom Cauldwell hired to relieve him of the baseball-writing duties on the *Mercury,* Henry Chadwick. Chadwick's enormous contributions to the success of the game led to his Hall of Fame plaque being placed in the main hall along with the great players of the game; other writers are honored in the Hall of Fame Library.

Most major daily newspapers had established sports sections before the end of the century, written by full-time sports reporters. The plum assignment was baseball, especially before the advent of night games. The reporter would attend the game, which usually commenced at 3:00 P.M., and have ample time to write his account of the game (often two or three columns long) before the deadline for the morning paper. This leisurely approach encouraged flights of imagination and attracted reporters who had a keen interest in the written word.

Such writers as Grantland Rice and Franklin Pierce Adams often began their accounts with verse, cementing a relationship between poetry and baseball that began with no less a poetic giant than Walt Whitman and continues today. Baseball is the poet's game, and if much of the verse written by baseball reporters does not rise to the level of Keats and Milton, it nonetheless had great impact. Perhaps no example more clearly shows the effect of the reporter-poet than Adams's lines forever enshrining the great Cubs double-play combination in the minds of future fans—and playing no small part in the infielders' enshrinement in the Hall of Fame:

> Ruthlessly pricking our gonfalon bubble,
> Making a Giant hit into a double,
> Words that are weighty with nothing but
>   trouble,
> Tinker to Evers to Chance.

Along with poetry, baseball reporting in the early years of the twentieth century produced great baseball stylists in prose and even regional styles. Once a reader left the East Coast, he or she was apt to encounter prose renditions of games that combined a clear love for the game with wit, humor, and a flair for a baseball dialect that included deliberate use of jargon, mispronunciations (with their representational misspellings), and exaggeration. Chicago was the capital city of this brand of baseball writing, and its great practitioners included Hugh Fullerton and Ring Lardner. Fuller to later generations is more famous for having been instrumental in bringing the Black Sox scandal to light. Lardner eventually shifted his primary emphasis from journalism to fiction and produced some of the most entertaining baseball fiction ever written, including the still widely read *You Know Me Al* letters. Paul Gallico and Damon Runyon, like Lardner, left sportswriting for the world of fiction; but plenty of great sportswriters, among them Red Smith and Shirley Povich, chose to stay with sports journalism.

During this time organized baseball, like much of American society, was segregated. African Americans were not allowed to play in the major leagues until Jackie Robinson broke the color barrier in 1947. As there were Negro League clubs, so there were African American newspapers to cover the baseball accomplishments of those denied access to the majors. Such papers as the *Baltimore Afro-American,* the *People's Voice* of Harlem, the *Pittsburgh Courier,* and the *Chicago Defender* featured outstanding sports journalists like Sam Lacy, Joe Bostic, Wendell Smith, and Frank Young.

Baseball reporting began to change after the Depression and the introduction of night baseball in the 1930s. Working night games was not popular with baseball journalists, who found their leisurely pace greatly altered. Instead of having little to do after turning in their accounts of games in the evening until the middle of the following afternoon, they found themselves working until the wee hours to file their reports on games that may have run until midnight and preparing follow-up stories for afternoon editions.

The Depression seriously hurt baseball attendance; consequently, the number of newspapers and baseball reporting jobs also declined. With the advent of popular radio in the 1930s, the broadcaster began to challenge the sportswriter as the most glamorous popularizer of the game. Nonetheless, the baseball journalist remained an important figure, even as his role changed. The best of the baseball writers, such as Dick Young, used their own initiative and creativity to respond to the changing times as well as to transform the role of baseball journalist even more. Young, for example, regularly visited the clubhouse to gather not only information

but also quotations. His method helped establish virtually an absolute requirement in later years that every article must include quotes from players and managers. What Young was doing, of course, paralleled the growing practice among so-called hard news journalists.

Another change involved the longstanding conflict between the journalist as objective reporter and the journalist as publicist for the hometown team. Before the advent of air travel, the reporter usually traveled by train with the team and spent considerable time hobnobbing with the players. Reporters could easily lose any sense of journalistic distance. As G. Edward White describes in his book *Creating the National Pastime,* Marshall Hunt of the *New York Daily News* became so close to Babe Ruth that he resisted an assignment to get the facts about Babe Ruth's alleged illegitimate child.

Baseball reporters, like other journalists, tended to view a celebrity's private life as off-limits, thereby helping to create the myth of baseball players as model citizens. This approach, of course, was what the public wanted. The fans wanted heroes that were heroic, and those who were in the business of writing for, and therefore helping to sell, newspapers gave the public what it wanted. That approach also made life easier for the reporter, who was able to maintain friendships with players and his access to them. Not until the 1970s would this approach change significantly; ironically, one of the leading figures in whetting the public's appetite for more realistic accounts (including salacious details) was a former player, Jim Bouton, whose 1970 book *Ball Four* made him a baseball outcast for almost 30 years.

Players obviously were not always pleased with this journalistic change. Yet players, whose salaries at least partly depended on the popularity of the game, as

well as team owners needed sportswriters. The relationship between reporters
and baseball professionals became more
adversarial. Again, baseball was not alone
in this phenomenon, as those in print and
other media came to be viewed suspi-
ciously by most anyone in the public eye,
from politicians to Hollywood stars.

The enduring importance of the baseball writer is evident within the duties of
the members of the Baseball Writers Association of America, an organization
founded by baseball writers in 1908 to
secure more dignified and consistent
working conditions at major league
parks. Association members annually
elect recipients of the most prestigious
baseball awards: Most Valuable Player,
Cy Young Award, Rookie of the Year,
and Manager of the Year. Even more important, they have been charged by organized baseball with electing members
to the Hall of Fame since it opened in
1939. Since 1962, baseball writers also
have been eligible for membership in
the Hall of Fame. The honoree is granted

the J. G. Taylor Spink Award, named for
the founder of *The Sporting News,* and is
honored with a scroll on a wall in the
Hall of Fame Library.

See also: African Americans; Bouton, James
Alan; Chadwick, Henry; Hall of Fame and
Museum; Lacy, Samuel H.; Language, Base-
ball; Lardner, Ringgold Wilmer; Periodicals;
Poetry; Povich, Shirley; Rice, Grantland;
Smith, Walter Wellesley; Smith, Wendell; *The
Sporting News;* Tinker to Evers to Chance;
Whitman, Walter.

Additional Reading:

Holtzman, Jerome. *No Cheering in the Press
Box.* New York: Holt, 1974.
Lang, Jack. "Baseball Reporting." In *Total Base-
ball.* 6th ed. Ed. John Thorn et al. New
York: Total Sports, 1999, pp. 586–591.
Orodenker, Richard. *The Writers' Game: Base-
ball Writing in America.* New York:
Twayne, 1996.
Reisler, Jim, ed. *Black Writers/Black Baseball:
An Anthology of Articles from Black Sports-
writers Who Covered the Negro Leagues.* Jef-
ferson, NC: McFarland, 1994.
White, G. Edward. *Creating the National Pas-
time: Baseball Transforms Itself, 1903–
1953.* Princeton: Princeton University Press,
1996.

K

KELLY, MICHAEL JOSEPH (KING) (1857–1894)

King Kelly is usually credited with being the first true baseball superstar. He was also the subject of "Slide, Kelly, Slide," the first baseball song to become a hit. An outstanding catcher and outfielder, Kelly combined great hitting and throwing with a certain flamboyance on and off the field. Fans loved him so much that when he was traded from Cap Anson's Chicago White Stockings to Boston, the fans in his new city gave him a carriage and two white horses to pull it.

Kelly, son of Irish immigrants, was strikingly handsome and often appeared decked out in silk hat, ascot, patent-leather shoes, and cane. Once the game started, he delighted fans with such tricks as cutting directly from first base to third if the umpire was not looking, dropping his catcher's mask in front of a runner, or (one of his most famous ploys when taking a game off) calling out "Kelly now catching for Boston" and grabbing a pop foul. This last trick quickly led to a rules change regarding player substitutions.

Kelly played from 1878 to 1893, helped the White Stockings win five

"Kelly (C. Boston)" depicted on an Old Judge and Gypsy Queen cigarette card, part of the Champions collection (Ann Ronan Picture Library)

championships in the 1880s, and pioneered such practices as backing up the infield while playing the outfield and doing the same for the first baseman when catching. He also developed the hit-and-run play and the hook, or "fadeaway," slide, precipitating the comic song fans loved to sing when he was on base. In the off-season he appeared on the stage, telling stories and reciting "Casey at the Bat." Alcoholic excess finally robbed him of some of his skills, and he became ill in 1894 while traveling to Boston for a stage appearance. While being carried into a hospital, he is reported to have said, "Boys, I think I've just made me last slide."

Also see Anson, Adrian Constantine; Heroes; Music; Substance Abuse.
Additional Reading:
Appel, Marty. Slide, Kelly, Slide: The Wild Life and Times of Mike "King" Kelly, Baseball's First Superstar. Lanham, MD: Scarecrow, 1999.
Nemec, David. The Great Encyclopedia of 19th-Century Major League Baseball. New York: Donald I. Fine, 1997.

KINER, RALPH MCPHERRAN (1922–)

"Home-run hitters drive Cadillacs" became a popular expression shortly after World War II. It represented a reality that existed much earlier thanks to Babe Ruth, but by the postwar period this truth had become part of America's popular conversation. The subject was Ralph Kiner more than any other.

Kiner enjoyed his greatest years with the Pittsburgh Pirates, the brightest star on an otherwise lusterless team. He joined the Pirates in 1946, and every year through 1952 he either led the National League in home runs or tied for the lead. In his second season, with the assistance of tutoring by the great Hank Greenberg, who played his final season with Pittsburgh in 1947,

Kiner slugged 51 home runs, raising that total to 54 in 1949. By 1951, he was the highest-paid player in the league.

Kiner finished his career with the Chicago Cubs (1953–1954) and the Cleveland Indians (1955). In 10 seasons, he hit 369 home runs and drove in 1,015 runners despite a modest .279 batting average. With little protection in the batting order, Kiner walked 1,011 times, drawing over 100 walks in six seasons and three times leading the league. A long broadcasting career followed his playing days, mainly with the New York Mets, as well as enshrinement in the Hall of Fame in 1975.

See also: Home Run.
Additional Reading:
Kiner, Ralph McPherran. Kiner's Korner: My Quarter Century with the New York Mets. New York: Arbor House, 1987.
McCollister, John. The Bucs: The Story of the Pittsburgh Pirates. Lenexa, KS: Addax, 1998.
Smizik, Bob. The Pittsburgh Pirates: An Illustrated History. New York: Walker, 1990.

KINSELLA, WILLIAM PATRICK (W. P.) (1935–)

W. P. Kinsella helped to popularize baseball fiction among the public as well as critics. A highly successful author of novels and short stories, Kinsella established his reputation with the novel Shoeless Joe (1982), later made into one of the most popular baseball films of all time, Field of Dreams (1989). A later novel, The Iowa Baseball Confederacy (1986), and collections of baseball stories, Go the Distance (1988) and Box Socials (1991), secured his position as the most important writer of baseball fiction in the final 20 years of the twentieth century.

Kinsella was born in Edmonton, Alberta, Canada, and remains a Canadian citizen despite his widespread association with the United States in general and with Iowa in particular. His two most important novels are set in that state, and he attended the University of Iowa, earning a master's degree in fine arts in 1978. Vast numbers of people who have neither read the book nor seen the film are familiar with the famous question-and-answer sequence when Shoeless Joe returns from the great beyond to play on Ray's field. "This must be heaven," he says. Ray answers, "No. It's Iowa."

Kinsella's first published stories were about a set of fictional Cree Indians living on a reservation. These stories, generally praised by critics for their realistic portraits and understanding of human nature, Kinsella has continued to write; many of them have been collected in such volumes as *Dance Me Outside* (1977), *Scars* (1978), *Born Indian* (1981), and *The Moccasin Telegraph* (1983).

The turning point in Kinsella's career occurred in 1980, when he published a collection of stories set in Iowa entitled *Shoeless Joe Jackson Comes to Iowa* (1980). An editor at Houghton Mifflin was impressed with the title story and suggested to Kinsella that he expand it into a novel. Kinsella used the existing story as the first chapter and developed the narrative from that point. The result was an example of what has been called "magic realism," a combination of realistic detail and a transcendent reality that blends myth, history, legend, and universal human longings.

At the heart of the novel *Shoeless Joe* is the relationship between Ray Kinsella and his father, a minor league catcher in his youth; Ray had become estranged from his father, who died before Ray could reconcile with him. When Ray, attempting to make a go of a farm in Iowa, starts hearing voices in his cornfield, he develops a compulsive need to find the answers to the strange directives that he receives. This quest leads to involvements with the famous author J. D. Salinger and an old-time player-turned-doctor, Moonlight

Graham; to the return of Shoeless Joe Jackson (the father's favorite player) and the other Black Sox, who come to play on the baseball field Ray built out of his cornfield; and finally to what all of the strange voices were really about—reconciliation with the young catcher who joins the mystical games. In the film version, hardly a father can sit dry-eyed through the ending, when Ray plays catch with his youthful and future father.

The other stories that Kinsella has written and continues to write form an impressive body of literature. Where baseball fans are concerned, however, their favorite Kinsella story almost surely will remain *Shoeless Joe*. That book and the film version probably should be shared by every parent and child who seek to experience or recover treasured moments of love and respect.

See also: Black Sox Scandal; Family Relationships; Fiction; Field of Dreams; Films; Jackson, Joseph Jefferson; Myth; Native Americans.

Additional Reading:
Altherr, Thomas L. "W. P. Kinsella's Baseball Fiction, *Field of Dreams,* and the New Mythopoeism of Baseball." In *Cooperstown Symposium on Baseball and the American Culture* (1990). Ed. Alvin L. Hall. Westport, CT: Meckler, 1991, pp. 97–108.
"Kinsella, W(illiam) P(atrick) 1935–." In *Contemporary Authors*. New Revision Series. Detroit: Gale Research, 1981–. 21: 217–223.
Kinsella, W. P. *Shoeless Joe*. 1982. Reprint, New York: Ballantine, 1996.
Rielly, Edward J. "Green on Green: Baseball Fiction, Myth, and Money." In *Cooperstown Symposium on Baseball and the American Culture* (1990). Ed. Alvin L. Hall. Westport, CT: Meckler, 1991, pp. 400–417.
Westbrook, Deeanne. *Ground Rules: Baseball and Myth*. Urbana: University of Illinois Press, 1996.

KOREAN BASEBALL

Korea has been a vital component of U.S. geopolitics for over half a century, with the Korean War (1950–1953) exercising a lasting impact on the strategic planning of U.S. foreign policy. In recent years, there has been some promise of a greater openness in North Korea while the United States remains a strong ally of South Korea. Only within the past few years, however, has baseball become part of the American-Korean exchange.

American players were first accepted into the Korean Baseball Organization (KBO) in 1998, the most successful of which has been Tyrone Woods. The former Red Sox farmhand hit 42 home runs that first year, breaking the Korean home-run record. The record-setting performance earned Woods the Most Valuable Player Award in the KBO.

A trickle of Korean players into the United States has increased into a stream and may yet swell into a river. Chan Ho Park joined the Los Angeles Dodgers in 1994 and won 14, 15, and 13 games in 1997, 1998, and 1999. Byung-Hyun Kim joined the Arizona Diamondbacks in 1999 at the age of 20 with a hard sinker and an unsettling sidearm delivery. Jin Ho Cho excelled in the Red Sox system and made his major league debut in 1998. Other prospects include pitcher Sun-Woo Kim (Red Sox), pitcher Jung Bong (Braves), and first baseman Hee Seop Choi (Cubs).

See also: Expansion; Japanese Baseball; Taiwanese Baseball.

Additional Reading:

Cho, Kwang Min. "Attitudes of Korean National Athletes and Coaches toward Athletics Participation." Ph.D. diss., University of Iowa, 1990.

Oliver, Robert Tarbell. *A History of the Korean People in Modern Times: 1800 to the Present.* Newark, NJ: University of Delaware Press, 1993.

St. John, Thomas. "History of the Korean Baseball Organization." In *Total Baseball.* 6th ed. Ed. John Thorn et al. New York: Total Sports, 1999, pp. 559–562.

KOUFAX, SANFORD (SANDY) (1935–)

Sandy Koufax, the most dominant pitcher of his era and one of the great pitchers of all time, also was the finest Jewish American pitcher ever to play in the major leagues. A Brooklyn kid who possessed a blazing fastball and considerable difficulty throwing it to a particular spot, Koufax never played a day in the minor leagues.

Coincidentally, his signing paralleled that of another Jewish American star, Hank Greenberg. Like Greenberg, Koufax was ignored by the Giants, turned down an opportunity to sign with the Yankees, and ultimately inked a contract with another team (Greenberg with the Tigers and Koufax with the Brooklyn Dodgers).

Koufax put in six mediocre years after joining the Dodgers in 1955 before he harnessed his fastball to the strike zone, also making his curveball more effective. For the next six years, he threw largely unhittable fastballs and curves past great and weak hitters alike, establishing himself as a Hall of Famer in waiting.

Koufax won five earned-run-average titles in a row from 1962 through 1966, three times registering a 2.00 or less ERA. Three times he struck out more than 300 batters, setting a major league record in 1965 (later broken by Nolan Ryan) of 382. He went 25-5 in 1963, followed by marks of 26-8 in 1965 and 27-9 in 1966; in all of those three years he won the Cy Young Award, given to the greatest pitcher in the majors (before the award was given in each league). In his first Cy Young season, he also captured the National League Most Valuable Player Award. The 27 victories that Koufax recorded in 1966 were the most by a National League left-hander in the twentieth century (although Steve Carlton would equal that figure in 1972). He also pitched four no-hitters, including a perfect game against the Chicago Cubs in 1965.

Sandy Koufax teamed with fearsome right-hander Don Drysdale to pitch the Los Angeles Dodgers (the team having moved west after the 1957 season) into four World Series (in 1959, 1963, 1965, and 1966), with the Dodgers prevailing in the first three. Then, at the peak of his career, having won 27 games and still only 30 years old, Koufax retired. His arthritic left elbow had pained him for years, and Koufax decided that he would not risk further injury to it.

In addition to being one of baseball's greatest pitchers and earning selection to the Hall of Fame in 1971, Koufax wrote his name into the culture of his country in two important ways. First, Koufax's Jewish heritage earned him considerable respect from members of his own faith as well as from others. Although Hank Greenberg, at a time when discrimination against Jews was more widespread, was more consistently viewed as a representative of his faith, Koufax went against the grain of American sports by putting his religion first. He consistently refused to pitch on Rosh Hashanah and Yom Kippur. A man of firm principles, he demonstrated his integrity as a teenager by turning down an offer from the Pittsburgh Pirates of $10,000 more than the Dodgers were offering him because, although he had not yet signed a contract, he had given his word to the Brooklyn club.

Koufax also drew considerable attention prior to the 1966 season when he and Drysdale held out for more money. They demanded a sum of $1 million to be split between them over the next three years and that the Dodgers negotiate through their agent. Walter O'Malley vowed never to bargain with agents, and in the end the star pitchers did not get

everything they sought. However, they became the highest-paid players in the majors, earning individual one-year salaries of $125,000 (Koufax) and $110,000 (Drysdale). Both men prefigured the near future, as players were coming to see themselves, as Koufax put it, as "coequal partners to a contract." Developments such as binding arbitration and free agency were just around the corner, developments that would forever change the baseball world and affect the way that fans came to view ballplayers.

See also: Greenberg, Henry Benjamin; Jewish Americans; Labor-Management Relations; Religion; Strikeouts.

Additional Reading:

Gruver, Edward. *Koufax.* Dallas: Taylor Publishing Company, 2000.

Reidenbaugh, Lowell. *Baseball's Hall of Fame: Cooperstown Where the Legends Live Forever.* Rev. by editors of *The Sporting News.* New York: Crescent Books, 1997.

Verducci, Tom. "The Left Arm of God." *Sports Illustrated,* July 12, 1999, pp. 82–100.

Ward, Geoffrey C., and Ken Burns. *Baseball: An Illustrated History.* New York: Alfred A. Knopf, 1994.

KUHN, BOWIE K. (1926–)

Bowie Kuhn was commissioner of Major League Baseball from 1969 until 1984. An imposing figure, six and a half feet tall, Kuhn, a descendant of Alamo hero Jim Bowie and holder of a law degree from the University of Virginia, was deeply involved, for better or worse, in some of the most important events in the history of the major leagues. Many of these events brought political, social, and financial dimensions of baseball into the American consciousness.

Kuhn had a baptism of fire in his first year as commissioner. With baseball embarking on a new alignment of 12 teams and two divisions in each league, the sport was hit by a spring holdout over issues that included demands for increased contributions to the players' pension fund and improved retirement benefits. Kuhn persuaded owners to settle these issues in order to ensure that the season start on time. During the year, he was caught in the middle of a large antiwar effort in New York by the New Mobilization Committee to End the War, including Mayor John Lindsay's order to support the effort by flying flags at half-staff at city facilities. Kuhn, however, responded to the outrage of military veterans by ordering the flags at Shea Stadium returned to full-mast.

Greater problems for Kuhn came later: Curt Flood's refusal to accept a trade to the Phillies and subsequent appeal for free-agent status; the Denny McLain suspensions; the loss of major league baseball in the nation's capital; struggles with players' union leader Marvin Miller, leading to free agency for players and rising salaries; conflicts with owner Charles Finley, including the commissioner's refusal to approve the sale of some of Oakland's top players to the Yankees and Red Sox, and Finley's lawsuit against Kuhn; suspension of Atlanta owner Ted Turner for alleged tampering with a player under contract to another team; a perceived snub of Henry Aaron when Kuhn did not attend Braves games after Aaron tied Babe Ruth's record of 714 career home runs; suspensions of superstars Willie Mays and Mickey Mantle from working for baseball clubs because of their public-relations positions with gambling casinos; and the 1981 players' strike, which wiped out approximately the middle third of the season.

Despite these many difficult moments, and regardless of how well Kuhn did or did not handle them, baseball made significant advances in a number of ways on his watch. Attendance records were set nine times, and annual network-television revenues jumped from $15.5 million to $183 million. Kuhn introduced World Series night games and steered the sport through the troubled waters of management-labor disputes with minimal inconvenience to fans. He saw himself, as have most commissioners, as working for the owners and sought to ally himself with the most powerful members of that group. Gradually, however, he alienated enough other owners to prevent his continuing as commissioner. By 1982, he did not have the votes to be reappointed and accepted the inevitable, though agreeing to complete his term. He continued for several additional months on an interim basis until a new commissioner was installed.

See also: Antitrust Exemption; Bouton, James Alan; Commissioner; Finley, Charles Oscar; Flood, Curtis Charles; Free Agency; Hunter, James Augustus; Labor-Management Relations; Law; Mantle, Mickey Charles; Mays, Willie Howard; McLain, Dennis Dale; Miller, Marvin James; Reserve Clause; Steinbrenner, George Michael, III; Turner, Robert Edward.

Additional Reading:

Flood, Curt, with Richard Carter. *Curt Flood: The Way It Is.* New York: Trident, 1971.

Holtzman, Jerome. *The Commissioners: Baseball's Midlife Crisis.* New York: Total Sports, 1998.

Kuhn, Bowie, and Martin Appel. *Hardball: The Education of a Baseball Commissioner.* New York: Times Books, 1987.

L

LABOR-MANAGEMENT RELATIONS

The key concepts in labor-management relations during the history of baseball have been the reserve clause, exemption from antitrust laws, and unionization. Working within the parameters of these concepts, baseball has been at various times in line with, behind, and ahead of the labor movement in the rest of American society. Players, as workers, have moved from a position of being almost indentured servants (albeit well paid ones at times) to members of perhaps the most powerful trade union in the United States. That progression has had enormous ramifications within baseball and society, leading to such varied results as huge leaps in salary, work stoppages, and fan animosity toward both players and owners. A challenge of labor-management relations continues to be whether fan loyalty can be retained as attending a baseball game becomes increasingly expensive and star players individually make in one year many times the amount of money that a fan will earn in a lifetime.

The reserve clause was the owners' primary tool to control player salaries. The reserve clause was embedded in the basic contract between owner and player and was backed up by the threat of permanent blacklisting. It secured a player to the team that originally signed him for the duration of his career or until the team sold, traded, or released him. The clause was in force within the National League by the late 1870s, binding five players of the owner's choice to each team, and was extended to 11 players per team by the National League and the new American Association in 1883, when team rosters usually numbered only about 14. The major leagues extended the reserve system during the 1888 off-season to cover all players. The system remained in place until the 1970s despite several legal attacks.

Workers were beginning to organize to secure better working conditions and wages in American society by about the middle of the nineteenth century. In 1869, the year when the Cincinnati Red Stockings, usually considered the first professional team, demonstrated their superiority with an unbeaten season, the Knights of Labor were formed. By 1886, the Knights, profiting from their success against the railroad industry, numbered

Donald Fehr, head of the Baseball Players Association, 1988 (Rick Stewart/Allsport)

about 700,000 members. With workers flexing their muscles in skilled trades, ballplayers sought to achieve liberation from the reserve clause by forming the National Brotherhood of Professional Baseball Players in 1885. Chief organizer of this first baseball union was star player John Montgomery Ward. The brotherhood established chapters in each National League city.

With Ward leading the way, baseball players organized their own league, the Players League, for the 1890 season. The new league rejected the reserve clause, decided to utilize three-year contracts, and promised profit-sharing between financial backers (called "contributors") and players. Each team was run by a group of eight individuals (four contributors and four players). The New York Giants, Ward's previous team, sued in the New York Supreme Court to seek an injunction against Ward. The court declared

the reserve clause too vague to be enforced in a victory for the players. Nonetheless, financial pressure from the National League brought down the Players League after just one season.

The National League had learned in the 1880s to abandon competition for cooperation with rival leagues, at that time with the American Association, in order to maintain a monopoly on major league baseball and thus limit the ability of players to move from team to team and thereby increase salary scales. Shortly after the American League became a major league in 1901, the two leagues repeated the earlier approach. They formulated the so-called National Agreement in 1903, setting up the National Commission (three people, including the two league presidents) to govern baseball and reaffirming the reserve clause. Teams as well as leagues thus continued to refrain from going after players owned by other clubs.

Players attempted to form associations to further their interests, but three successors to the National Brotherhood of Professional Baseball Players all proved short-lived and ineffective: the League Protective Players Association (1900–1902), the Baseball Players' Fraternity (1912–1918), and the American Baseball Guild (1946).

In the meantime, American society was reacting against monopolies in many spheres of economic life. As fuel, railroad, sugar, and beef trusts were established to control markets, eliminate competition, and increase profits, Congress acted in 1890 to pass the Sherman Antitrust Act, forbidding "every contract, combination in the form of trust or otherwise, or conspiracy in restraint of trade or commerce among the several States, or with foreign nations." This act was strengthened by creation of the Federal Trade Commission in 1914 and passage of the Clayton Antitrust Act in the same year.

As Congress was passing the Clayton Antitrust Act in 1914, the rival Federal League began play. The Federal League guaranteed players a 5 percent annual salary increase and free agency after 10 years. It attracted over 80 major-leaguers, including such stars as Three Finger Brown, Joe Tinker, and Hal Chase. The new league sued the major leagues under the antitrust laws. The presiding judge, Kenesaw Mountain Landis, later to become baseball commissioner, delayed action while the major league owners succeeded in buying out most of the Federal League owners. The failure of the Federal League ended a chance to break the monopoly formed by the National and American Leagues. The fact that even during its short life the Federal League had led to a doubling of salaries among prominent major-leaguers was evidence of what could happen with real competition.

Ned Hanlon, owner of the Baltimore franchise in the Federal League, decided to fight. He brought a suit against the major leagues that ultimately made it to the U.S. Supreme Court. There, Chief Justice William Howard Taft (a former U.S. president) and the other justices unanimously found against Hanlon by declaring that major league baseball was not involved in interstate commerce and therefore did not come under antitrust legislation. Thus was established, in essence, the antitrust exemption for baseball.

The antitrust exemption effectively prevented players from breaking the owners' hold over them through the reserve clause. The tide began to turn in 1969 when the St. Louis Cardinals traded star center fielder Curt Flood to the Philadelphia Phillies. Flood refused to report to Philadelphia and filed a lawsuit against baseball in order to overturn the reserve clause. Flood's case reached the U.S. Supreme Court, which ruled in 1972 in another, but temporary, defeat for players' freedom to choose their employer. The majority opinion, however, acknowledged that baseball was a matter of interstate commerce but left the reserve clause in force, claiming that the intent of Congress, evident through its refusal to remove the antitrust exemption, was to leave the exemption in effect.

While the Flood case was moving through the courts, the major leagues recognized the Major League Baseball Players Association (MLBPA) as the bargaining agent for players and accepted arbitration to settle policy disputes. The MLBPA had begun as a fraternal organization in the 1950s. The turning point occurred in 1966 when Marvin Miller was hired as the MLBPA's executive director, a position he held through 1982. Miller immediately set about raising revenue with which to make the organization viable. He earned $66,000 from Coca-Cola in exchange for putting players' pictures inside bottle caps, the first step toward the huge licensing fees that would be earned in later years for players. Miller also established a permanent MLBPA office in New York City.

Miller's victories came not easily but with great effect. After the 1973 season, owners accepted salary arbitration, which had the effect of pushing up player salaries because owners wanted to make sure that their offers were sufficiently high to be accepted by the arbitrator rather than the players' even higher demands.

Then came the Andy Messersmith and Dave McNally decision in 1975, as Messersmith (and the retired McNally) gained free agency (thus defeating the reserve clause) by arguing successfully that the one-year renewal right of the owners applied to just one year in all rather than to a series of one-year renewals in perpetuity. This decision, rendered by baseball arbitrator Peter Seitz, overturned what previous legal actions, rival leagues, and player organizations had been unable to accomplish. Freedom through free agency had come to players, and owners had lost their most valuable tool of control—the reserve clause. The owners, of course, did not accept defeat well. They filed suit in federal court in Kansas City and lost as Donald Fehr, who would later succeed Miller as MLBPA executive director, ably represented the players. Under Miller's leadership, the association then accepted a limited reserve system under which players would not be eligible for free agency until they had six years of major league service. Miller wisely recognized that unlimited free agency would create an oversupply of free agents, depressing salaries. Under the compromise system, the number of free agents in any one year would be limited, increasing demand and elevating salaries, which is precisely what happened.

The battles between management and labor continued. A strike in 1972 eliminated the first two weeks of the season. A much longer stoppage in 1981 over the issue of compensation for players lost to free agency wiped out about 10 weeks of competition. Another strike, this one for only two days in August, briefly interrupted the 1985 season. The owners tried to find ways around free agency. One of these approaches involved agreements by owners not to hire free agents unless their previous owners no longer wanted them. This tactic went down to defeat in 1987 when arbitrator Tom Roberts ruled that clubs had violated the anticollusion clause in the basic agreement between owners and players. Seven members of the 1985 class of free agents, including catcher Carlton Fisk, were declared free agents and awarded back pay. Subsequent decisions found that owners also had colluded in regard to the 1986 and 1987 free agents. Finally, in December 1990, owners and the MLBPA agreed to a settlement of $280 million. The impact of the anticollusion rulings on salaries is evident from the rise in average salaries, from $430,000 in 1988 to over $1 million in 1992.

MLBPA victories and the continued strength of the union through the 1980s and 1990s were at odds with union scorecards throughout American society in those decades. During the administration of President Ronald Reagan, unions declined in political influence, membership, and victories, partly in response to a growing management bias on the part of the political establishment, partly because many of the manufacturing industries that had spawned powerful unions were in decline in a changing, more technologically oriented economy.

Baseball owners may have been moving with the flow that characterized the broader society, but they had more than their hands full with the players association. Owners, attempting to impose a wage scale and a salary cap (the latter was used in the National Basketball Association and the National Football League), locked the players out of training camp as the 1990 season approached. The issue was temporarily settled in time for the season to begin two and one-half weeks late.

Owners plotted future strategy, part of which apparently involved firing commissioner Fay Vincent and replacing him with Milwaukee Brewers' owner Bud Selig as acting commissioner. The conventional interpretation is that the owners wanted to make sure that a commissioner would not get in the way of a new get-tough approach as the collective-bargaining agreement neared its concluding date of December 31, 1993. Owners devised a plan to fund continued sharing among clubs of revenue from teams televising both home and away games, with the financial hit on large-market teams moderated through savings gained from a salary cap. Owners also proposed to end salary arbitration while offering to lower the free-agency requirement from six to four years. However, players with four to five years of service would be restricted free agents, which meant that their current teams could match other contract proposals.

Players responded by planning a 1994 strike that would take effect during the peak attendance months of August and September and include the World Series in order to place maximum pressure on owners to modify their proposal. Acting commissioner Selig countered by canceling the rest of the season on September 14.

The two sides jockeyed for position. President Bill Clinton appointed William Usery, a former labor secretary, to attempt to mediate a settlement, but owners declared an impasse in the negotiations on December 23, 1994, and moved to implement a salary cap. They also started to set up replacement teams, except for Baltimore owner Peter Angelos, a labor lawyer. In February 1995, President Clinton made another attempt to settle the dispute as fans wondered whether the next season would occur at all, or with minor-leaguers and former major-leaguers substituting for the real thing. The president summoned both sides to the White House and asked them to accept binding arbitration as a means of settling their differences. Owners refused, apparently thinking that they held the winning hand.

Then the National Labor Relations Board filed for an injunction to restore the status quo. The presiding judge, Sonia Maria Sotomayor, ruled that the reserve and free-agency system (including such matters as anticollusion and salary arbitration) was a mandatory subject for bargaining between the two parties and issued an injunction. Surprisingly, both sides agreed to resume playing, and the 1995 season began only a few days late.

An agreement was hammered out by negotiators on October 24, 1996. It called for revenue-sharing among clubs, a luxury tax on clubs' total salaries (a device for depressing salaries in a more limited way than through a salary cap), and a payroll tax on players. In addition, both parties would ask Congress to repeal the antitrust exemption.

Although their negotiators had agreed to the plan, owners rejected it by a vote of 18-12. One of the strongest opponents of the compromise was White Sox owner Jerry Reinsdorf. Shortly after the rejection, though, Reinsdorf lost his credibility on maintaining a hard line with players by signing slugger Albert Belle to a five-year, $55 million contract. Angered by Reinsdorf's actions and facing public accusations of hypocrisy, owners voted again on November 26, this time accepting the agreement by a vote of 26-4. The new contract was signed on March 14, 1997, with an end date of October 31, 2000, plus a players association option for one additional year. On October 27, 1998, President Clinton signed the appropriately named Curt Flood Act of 1998, bringing baseball under the antitrust laws.

Baseball had taken a considerable hit from the 1994 strike and the protracted disagreements. Fans stayed away in droves once play resumed in 1995, and in some areas minor league baseball was a beneficiary of antagonism toward the major league game. A pox-on-both-your-houses attitude was common, and many observers wondered if the game could recover. It did recover, thanks as much to a single player—Cal Ripken—as to any other factor. Fans followed Ripken's iron-man effort to break Lou Gehrig's record for most consecutive games played. When Ripken set the record in 1995, fans applauded especially because the Oriole great did not seem much like the apparently money-hungry owners and players who had precipitated the strike. Ripken looked instead like a normal, hard-working laborer who got up every morning, went to work, and did his job.

If fans are to continue supporting baseball as they have in the past, there must be more Cal Ripkens and fewer strikes. But the high cost of attending games, astronomical player salaries, and a feeling that owners are ripping off taxpayers to make fortunes buying and selling franchises and stadiums pose great challenges. Never has it been more important for labor and management to work together in a moderate and common-sense way.

See also: Antitrust Exemption; Commissioner; Finley, Charles Oscar; Flood, Curtis Charles; Free Agency; Hunter, James Augustus; Koufax, Sanford; Kuhn, Bowie K.; Law; Major Leagues; Miller, Marvin James; Reserve Clause; Ward, John Montgomery.

Additional Reading:

Abrams, Roger I. *Legal Bases: Baseball and the Law.* Philadelphia: Temple University Press, 1998.

Dworkin, James B. *Owners versus Players: Baseball and Collective Bargaining.* Boston: Auburn House, 1981.

Jennings, Kenneth M. *Swings and Misses: Moribund Labor Relations in Professional Baseball.* Westport, CT: Praeger, 1997.

Lowenfish, Lee. *The Imperfect Diamond: A History of Baseball's Labor Wars.* Rev. ed. New York: Da Capo, 1991.

Staudohar, Paul. *The Sports Industry and Collective Bargaining.* 2d ed. Ithaca: ILR, 1989.

LACY, SAMUEL H. (SAM) (1903–)

Sam Lacy has enjoyed one of the longest careers of any sportswriter, extending from his teenage years covering high school baseball for the *Washington Tribune* to the end of the twentieth century as sports editor for the *Baltimore Afro-American.* He was an eloquent and consistent voice for justice and opportunity for African American baseball players at a time when they were excluded from the major leagues. Lacy's efforts, along with those of journalist Wendell Smith and other writers for African American newspapers, helped to bring about the integration of baseball.

Lacy, then with the *Washington Tribune,* embarked upon his campaign for equal opportunity with a series of letters to the commissioner of baseball, Judge Landis, and major league owners. Neither Landis nor the owners were moved. Lacy accepted a position with the *Chicago Defender* in 1940 to be closer to the center of baseball activity. After repeated tries, Lacy finally was given an opportunity in 1943 to speak personally with baseball owners. The *Defender,* however, sent singer Paul Robeson instead. Lacy resented that decision because he believed that Robeson, accused of being sympathetic to communism, would alienate the owners.

Lacy returned east and in 1944 became sports editor for the *Afro-American*. With Judge Landis now dead, Lacy was able to meet with owners, encouraging them to make the Negro Leagues a minor league from which they would draw players to the majors. Although this particular effort did not succeed, Lacy's support of Branch Rickey's choice of Jackie Robinson as the best candidate to integrate the majors helped bring the journalist's long quest to a successful conclusion. Sam Lacy was selected for admission to the Hall of Fame in 1998.

See also: African Americans; Journalism (Print); Landis, Kenesaw Mountain; Negro Leagues; Robinson, Jack Roosevelt.

Additional Reading:

Lacy, Sam, with Moses J. Newson. *Fighting for Fairness: The Life Story of Hall of Fame Sportswriter Sam Lacy*. Centreville, MD: Tidewater, 1998.

Reisler, Jim, ed. *Black Writers/Black Baseball: An Anthology of Articles from Black Sportswriters Who Covered the Negro Leagues*. Jefferson, NC: McFarland, 1994.

LANDIS, KENESAW MOUNTAIN (1866–1944)

Judge Kenesaw Mountain Landis was hired as the first commissioner of baseball in 1920, more with the public than the internal workings of baseball in mind. His role was ostensibly to clean up baseball, but in the minds of the businessmen who ran the teams it was more to convince the public of the unquestioned integrity of the game and thus induce it to continue supporting the sport with dollars. He did what he was supposed to do, and his plaque in the Hall of Fame speaks truly the following words regarding his accomplishments: "Baseball's First Commissioner, Elected 1920—Died in Office, 1944. His Integrity and Leadership Established Baseball in the Respect, Esteem and Affection of the American People." The plaque, however,

does not convey the commissioner's failings in character and personality.

Landis was a small man in physical stature at five-foot six and 130 pounds, but his demeanor was intimidating. By 1919, he was one of the more famous (and infamous) judges in the United States, having been appointed to the federal bench in Chicago by President Theodore Roosevelt in 1905. Skilled in dramatics, he affected an old, floppy hat and a cane and used considerable profanity. Extremely arbitrary, he courted publicity and received plenty of it.

Landis received his unusual name from the mountain in Georgia (spelled Kennesaw Mountain) where his father had been wounded and lost a leg while serving as a Union surgeon during General William Tecumseh Sherman's drive to Atlanta. The son earned a law degree from Union Law School but gave little indication of great accomplishments until his appointment by Roosevelt. Landis developed his dramatic persona on the bench and viewed himself as a man of the people, willing to make the law yield to his own personal sense of justice. His reputation for questionable decisions was reinforced by the high rate at which they were overturned on appeal, including the fine of approximately $29 million he leveled against John D. Rockefeller's Standard Oil Company.

Another of Judge Landis's famous trials involved his jailing of 94 members of the International Workers of the World during World War I, leading to his office being bombed (he was absent at the time). A public patriot, Landis wanted to indict the German Kaiser after World War I on the grounds that he was responsible for the sinking of the *Lusitania* with a Chicago resident aboard. That effort did not fly legally, but it added to his public esteem. Although the public was much taken with the judge, the Congress and the American Bar Association were not impressed. The former began impeachment proceedings against Landis after he became baseball commissioner (partly on grounds that a federal judge was not to receive compensation from other sources), and the latter had serious problems with Landis's mode of judicial conduct. Landis avoided continuing problems with both by resigning his judgeship, claiming that the commissioner's job left insufficient time for other professional pursuits.

None of these problems mattered much to the titans of baseball, who were grateful to Landis for assisting them in 1915 when the Federal League sued the major leagues, claiming violations of antitrust legislation. Landis, a longtime baseball fan, was the presiding judge and delayed a decision until major league owners had time to come to an accommodation with most of the Federal League owners.

Thus during the turmoil of the Black Sox scandal following the 1919 World Series, the owners hired Landis to become the first baseball commissioner. Gone was the tripartite National Commission. Landis had a good bargaining position and a high intimidation factor, which led him to get what he wanted: absolute power. When the owners offered an annual salary of $50,000, he graciously offered to reduce the salary by an amount equal to his judicial compensation, an accommodation that proved quite comforting to the money-conscious owners.

Landis continued as commissioner until his death in 1944. He wasted no time seeking to clean up the game and demonstrating his authority. He expelled the eight White Sox conspirators from baseball for life the day after a jury found them not guilty—a strange rejection of judicial process for a man who had served so long in the legal system. Other players followed the eight into baseball oblivion over the next few years until the

total reached 19. Landis was not shy about suspending players, including Babe Ruth, who had violated the commissioner's policy against World Series participants barnstorming during the following off-season. Landis felt that such behavior detracted from the dignity of the World Series.

Landis, holding most of the cards when he became commissioner, forced the owners to sign a loyalty pledge, promising not to disagree publicly with Landis even when they believed him wrong. One of his final acts was to kick Phillies owner Bill Cox out of baseball in 1944 for betting on his own team. Few people went up against Landis and came away winners. Branch Rickey was a rare exception, and even then his victories were only partial. Landis, who occasionally exhibited real concern for the rights of players, objected to the farm system and especially believed that Rickey was squirreling away players who might have been able to play for other major league clubs. Rickey succeeded in building his farm system with the Cardinals, but over the years Landis freed large numbers of Cardinals players (and later Detroit Tigers farmhands).

On another major issue, Rickey had to wait for the commissioner's death to succeed. Landis was a staunch opponent of integrating baseball and would have remained a bulwark against it as long as he was commissioner. Within two years of his death, Jackie Robinson was playing minor league ball, and within three years integration had come to the majors.

To many, it appeared as if Judge Landis would rule baseball forever. He served 24 years, and the owners had agreed to renew his contract yet again, to run through 1953. When death came, it was shocking to the baseball world. Landis had indeed helped to clean up the game and restore public confidence in it, yet he had denied access to African Americans and acted with an arbitrariness that may have denied justice in individual cases as often as it granted it. Whether all eight of the Black Sox, for example, should have been painted with the same brush remains a matter of great controversy. Owners recognized their debt to Landis but also had come to appreciate the dangers in absolute power. They had been willing to have Landis continue in office, but they were not willing to confer the same degree of authority to subsequent commissioners. The era of the absolute monarch in baseball was over.

See also: Black Sox Scandal; Cheating; Comiskey, Charles Albert; Commissioner; Gambling; Jackson, Joseph Jefferson; Johnson, Byron Bancroft; Law; Rickey, Wesley Branch.

Additional Reading:

Holtzman, Jerome. *The Commissioners: Baseball's Midlife Crisis*. New York: Total Sports, 1998.

Landis, D. B. *The Landis Family of Lancaster County, Pa*. Lancaster: Privately printed, 1888.

Pietrusza, David. *Judge and Jury: The Life and Times of Judge Kenesaw Mountain Landis*. South Bend, IN: Diamond Communications, 1998.

Spink, J. G. Taylor. *Judge Landis and Twenty-five Years of Baseball*. 1947. Reprint, St. Louis: Sporting News, 1974.

Voigt, David Quentin. *American Baseball: From Gentleman's Sport to the Commissioner System*. Norman: University of Oklahoma Press, 1966.

LANGUAGE, BASEBALL

To speak of a "single" English language is misleading. Even to speak of "American" English is insufficient. Although the United States has been, and to some extent remains, a melting pot of cultures, it never has completely eradicated differences. Cultural differences remain especially visible in language. Linguists speak of "Standard" American English, an idealization that carries with it certain prestige and that exists more as an abstract ideal to which many people aspire rather than as a practiced reality. Standard American English actually is just one among many dialects of American English, dialects that include baseball English. Among dialects that have contributed substantially to the use of English throughout popular culture, baseball deserves high marks. The language would be much poorer without baseball's contributions.

To explain terms a bit: A "dialect" is a form of the language spoken by a certain regional or social group. Each individual within a dialect speaks an individualistic version of the dialect known as an "ideolect." When the public thinks of dialects, it usually has regional dialects in mind, dialects spoken in a certain region (e.g., Boston, Downeast Maine, southern Indiana, Brooklyn, and so forth). However, there are other ways to categorize dialects. African American English, or black English, also is a dialect, or perhaps more properly a group of closely related dialects spoken by many African Americans. Another group of similar dialects is Latino, or Hispanic, English, spoken by Spanish-speakers or their descendants. Chicano English is spoken by some descendants of Mexican Americans.

Members of speech groups or communities may speak more than one dialect. A man or woman may attempt to speak Standard American English in the workplace but revert to another dialect, regional or cultural, at home. Then there are specific speech groups associated with certain professions and activities. Computer technicians utilize enough specialized terminology that one may consider their at-work language a type of dialect. The same is true of some other professions and activities. Then there is baseball language.

Baseball language, actually a dialect of American English, started to evolve with the rise of baseball around the middle of the nineteenth century. The basic terminology of the game (e.g., "bat," "hit," "play," "strike," "team") came from the English game of rounders. As baseball spread, and its popularity demanded extensive coverage by the newspapers and then radio, baseball language also grew, as living languages inevitably do. Sportswriters, beginning around the 1880s, increasingly attempted to enliven their accounts with vivid description and turned to expressive phrasing to help achieve their goals. Writers like Lennie Washburn of the *Chicago Herald,* Charles Dryden with the *Chicago Examiner,* Ring Lardner of the *Chicago Tribune,* and such radio and television broadcasters as Red Barber helped to popularize baseball language. Dryden, for example, delighted in spicing his prose with nicknames that became part of history and still are used today in any number of applications: the Hitless Wonders for the Chicago White Sox of the early twentieth century, the Peerless Leader for Sox manager Frank Chance. How many employees have referred to their boss, usually sarcastically, as their "peerless leader"? Dryden also invented the expression about the dismal Washington Senators: "First in war, first in peace, and last in the American League." Red Barber's "Barberisms" are discussed elsewhere in this book.

In the midst of this burst of linguistic creativity, which stretched from the 1880s through the early decades of the twentieth century (to some extent continuing today, though in more moderate forms befitting the millionaire status of current ballplayers), a great debate developed over using what was referred to as "baseball slang" in newspapers. This debate reached its zenith in the years leading up to World War I and was set-tled on the side of Standard American English. Newspaper writers began to moderate their prose, with the result that increasing numbers of sportswriters came to exhibit few stylistic differences. On-the-air broadcasters, however, became the new linguistic adventurers as baseball English remained alive and well.

Baseball language is filled with memorable examples of language use. Most any person can identify the great Yankee catcher Yogi Berra as the creator of such classics as "It's déjà vu all over again"; "It ain't over 'til it's over"; "I really didn't say everything I said"; and "Baseball is 90 percent mental; the other half is physical." Such expressions have moved, lock, stock, and barrel into the broader language. Berra, of course, learned at the feet (or mouth) of the master—manager Casey Stengel. Once, when discussing his choice of one alternative over the other, Stengel explained, apparently keeping his options open, "I made up my mind, but I made it up both ways." One wonders how his players reacted to Casey's order, "All right, everybody line up alphabetically according to your height."

Perhaps no baseball figure deviated more consistently from Standard American English, though much to the delight of his listeners (except perhaps for some teachers of grammar), than pitcher-turned-broadcaster Dizzy Dean. Examples of Dizzy's statements: "The runners return to their respectable bases"; "He slud into third." Most likely Dizzy deliberately cultivated his colorful language to be more entertaining, which puts him in the same ballpark with those who created fictional characters that derived at least part of their humor through departures from the language norm. Ring Lardner's Jack Keefe of the *You Know Me Al* series of letters is one of the most famous fictional speakers of baseball English, his misuse of Standard American English standing in ironic contrast to his over-blown sense of himself. Other areas of popular culture have seen countless examples of characters distorting the language with comic effects. To cite just two of them, both from television: Archie Bunker from the groundbreaking series *All in the Family,* and Festus Haggen from the long-running Western series *Gunsmoke.*

The most significant aspect of baseball English within popular culture is the rich trove of expressions that has migrated from the sport into common, nonbaseball usage. A person asking for an approximate cost of an item may request a "ballpark" figure. Anyone who does extremely well has "hit a home run"; conversely, a failure may be acknowledged as having "struck out." Perhaps the person failed because someone unexpectedly threw him a "curveball." An individual may call a friend or business associate on the telephone, explaining, "I just wanted to touch base with you." People engaged in a strident dispute are involved in a "rhubarb." Having just attained a favorable position, the person finds herself in the "catbird seat." Anyone who denies the importance of baseball terminology in general English usage is clearly off base, perhaps even so intellectually disjointed as to be out in left field.

See also: Barber, Walter Lanier; Berra, Lawrence Peter; Dean, Jay Hanna; Lardner, Ringgold Wilmer; Nicknames; Periodicals; Stengel, Charles Dillon.

Additional Reading:

Berra, Yogi. *The Yogi Book: I Really Didn't Say Everything I Said!* New York: Workman, 1998.

McBride, Joseph. *High and Inside: An A-to-Z Guide to the Language of Baseball.* Lincolnwood (Chicago): Contemporary Books, 1997.

Mencken, H. L. *The American Language: An Inquiry into the Development of English in the United States.* 4th ed. New York: Knopf, 1936.

Whiteford, Mike. *How to Talk Baseball.* 1983. Reprint, New York: Galahad Books, 1996.

Williamson, Juanita V., and Virginia M. Burke. *A Various Language: Perspectives on American Dialects.* New York: Holt, 1971.

LARDNER, RINGGOLD WILMER (RING) (1885–1933)

Ring Lardner was the first person to achieve both popular and critical recognition for baseball fiction. He did so in a vernacular prose that attracted the admiration even of the British novelist Virginia Woolf, who, despite her lack of familiarity with American baseball, discerned in Lardner's stories his use of baseball as the focal point, a type of enclosed society, within which he brings his characters alive. Lardner's fictional success was within the short-story genre, many of the stories built around a particular character.

Lardner's professional beginnings did not promise a notable career as a writer or in any other field. Although born into a prosperous Niles, Michigan, family with a poet-mother who provided home schooling for Ring during his childhood, he achieved little in the years immediately following graduation from high school in 1901. He worked for the railroad for a time, flunked out of the Armour Institute of Technology while supposedly studying mechanical engineering, and got a job with the Niles Gas Company, where he contended with rats while reading gas meters.

The future began to open for Lardner, however, when he got a job with the *South Bend Times.* Positions followed at the *Chicago Inter-Ocean* (thanks to famous sportswriter Hugh Fullerton, who recommended him for the job), the *Chicago Examiner,* the *Chicago Tribune, The Sporting News* (as managing editor), the *Boston American,* the *Chicago American,* and the *Examiner* again. By 1913, the peripatetic journalist had returned to the *Tribune,* where he would start his transition from journalist to fiction writer.

That transition actually had begun during Lardner's three months with *The Sporting News*, when he wrote a series of club-car dialogues involving baseball players. These "Pullman Pastimes" anticipated the sketches that Lardner incorporated into his "In the Wake of the News" column for the *Tribune*—a series of fictional letters from Bill to Steve that ran for about two years. By this time, Lardner had the colloquial dialogue mastered as well as the form—letters to a friend—that would produce the first of 26 stories about Jack Keefe, a pitcher attempting to make it with the Chicago White Sox.

The Jack Keefe stories were published in *The Saturday Evening Post*, beginning with "A Busher's Letters Home" on March 7, 1914. The first six of these stories, published in book form in 1916 as *You Know Me Al,* are usually considered his best. Letters from Keefe to his friend Al Blanchard in Bedford, Indiana, allow the writer to expose his dreams but also his many shortcomings through his own words. The surrounding cast consists of actual members of the White Sox and other teams. The stories are masterful not only in duplicating the dialect of a not-very-educated protagonist but also in character development and in showing players as actual people.

Jack Keefe is a talented pitcher who manages at times to outpitch such luminaries as Walter Johnson and Smokey Joe Wood, but he is never as good as he thinks. Keefe cannot conceive of losing a game because he did not pitch well. In fact, nothing is ever his fault, whether the situation is a baseball game or a romantic relationship gone sour. Along with his vanity, and more striking because of it, Keefe is also quite naive. He fails, for example, to recognize the practitioners of the world's oldest profession when they approach him on a street, instead imagining himself irresistible to women. Nor

does he recognize insults, such as the time when he has a brief encounter with a man scalping tickets to the Follies: "I says You must take me for some boob. He says No I wouldn't insult no boob. So I walks on but if he had insulted me I would of busted him" (*Baseball Stories*, p. 84). Although Keefe is greedy and talks endlessly about money, he is easily taken advantage of by White Sox owner Charles Comiskey. These and other attributes make Jack Keefe a thoroughly realized character and the stories remarkably entertaining.

Lardner's subsequent stories would take Jack Keefe through 1919, including his war service, stopping just short of the World Series. Other Keefe stories were published in the collections *Treat 'Em Rough* (1918) and *The Real Dope* (1919). In addition to these and other baseball stories, Lardner also utilized other storylines and character types. Lardner has Gullible, another memorable protagonist, whose exploits were collected in *Gullible's Travels, Etc.* (1917), relate his stories orally rather than convey them in letters. Later stories, some of them Lardner's best, appear in *How to Write Short Stories (with Samples)* (1924), collected at the urging of F. Scott Fitzgerald, and *The Love Nest and Other Stories* (1926). In these later stories, humor often gives way to a darker satire.

A man much loved, and apparently disliked by almost no one, Lardner especially enjoyed a large roster of friends during his seven years at Great Neck, Long Island, in the 1920s. He and Fitzgerald spent much time together talking and drinking, giving each other pleasure but hastening their serious encounters with alcoholism and other illnesses. Heart problems and tuberculosis affected Lardner in his final years. When he died in 1933, Fitzgerald responded with a moving portrait of his friend.

Although Fitzgerald denigrates baseball in this essay, many of his comments about Lardner mark well his achievements and merit consideration here. Fitzgerald recognizes that Lardner "existed in the literary world as well as with the public," and that he, even then, had become much imitated—"only Hemingway has been so thoroughly frisked." Lardner's former neighbor and drinking buddy notes personal characteristics, such as "the impenetrable despair that dogged him for a dozen years to his death," but also that "he was a faithful and conscientious workman to the end."

Fitzgerald shares with Virginia Woolf the observation that Lardner found in baseball an "enclosure" within which "the result was magnificent: within it he heard and recorded the voice of a continent." Fitzgerald theorizes that this enclosure held Lardner back from achieving even more than he did, "that Ring got less percentage of himself on paper than any other American of the first flight." Yet Fitzgerald, who knew writing as well as anyone, does place Lardner in that "first flight" of writers, enumerating among his greatest accomplishments *You Know Me Al* and "about a dozen wonderful short stories." Certainly Fitzgerald's assessment, if not always completely accurate, is close. Lardner is still read with pleasure and admiration, especially the stories that Fitzgerald listed, and later generations of writers plying their fictional trade within the world of baseball follow a trail that he blazed.

See also: Comiskey, Charles Albert; Fiction; Journalism (Print); Language, Baseball; *The Sporting News;* Substance Abuse.

Additional Reading:

Fitzgerald, F. Scott. "Ring. " In *The Crack-Up.* Ed. Edmund Wilson. 1945. Reprint, New York: New Directions, 1956, pp. 34–40.

Lardner, Ring, Jr. *The Lardners: My Family Remembered.* New York: Harper and Row, 1976.

Lardner, Ring W. *The Annotated Baseball Stories of Ring W. Lardner, 1914–1919.* Ed. George W. Hilton. Stanford: Stanford University Press, 1995.

Patrick, Walton R. *Ring Lardner.* New York: Twayne, 1963.

Yardley, Jonathan. *Ring: A Biography of Ring Lardner.* New York: Random House, 1977.

LARSEN, DONALD JAMES (DON) (1929–)

Don Larsen would seem an unlikely person to reach perfection. He had, after all, compiled one of the worst records in the history of the major leagues just two years before, winning three games and losing 21 for the Baltimore Orioles.

As a Yankee Larsen went 11-5 in 1956, still a modest record. Drawing the pitching assignment in Game 2 of the World Series against the Brooklyn Dodgers, Larsen was hit hard and shelled from the game in the second inning of a 13-8 defeat. Yet on October 8, 1956, Don Larsen pitched the greatest game in World Series history—the first, and still today only, Series perfect game. It took Larsen just 97 pitches to complete the game, although the contest was not without drama. The score remained close, ending 2-0, and several balls were hit hard. Yet when Yogi Berra caught Larsen's third strike, sending pinch-hitter Dale Mitchell down for the twenty-seventh consecutive out, Don Larsen had earned immortality.

One year later, Larsen lost the decisive seventh game of the Series to the Milwaukee Braves, and after the 1959 season he was traded in a package of players to Kansas City for Roger Maris. He finished his career with the Chicago Cubs in 1967, ending with an 81-91 career mark. Perhaps Don Larsen's ultimate legacy is not the World Series perfect game, as remarkable as that effort was, but the realization for fans and participants that the greatest mountains sometimes are scaled by climbers of modest talents. Don Larsen's story is a matter of dreams, the stuff of baseball, really coming true.

See also: New York Yankees; Perfection; World Series.

Additional Reading:

Allen, Lee. *The World Series: The Story of Baseball's Annual Championship.* New York: Putnam's, 1969.

Schoor, Gene. *The History of the World Series: 85 Years of America's Greatest Sports Tradition.* New York: Morrow, 1990.

Silverman, Al. *Heroes of the World Series.* New York: Putnam's, 1964.

Smith, Robert. *World Series: The Games and the Players.* Garden City, NY: Doubleday, 1967.

LASORDA, THOMAS CHARLES (TOMMY) (1927–)

Most people bleed red blood; Tommy Lasorda bled Dodger blue. In a world in which so many hate their jobs, Tommy Lasorda loved being a Dodger and spent most of his professional career being one. His enthusiasm, loyalty to team and players, and gregariousness made him one of baseball's most popular figures. Working in Los Angeles made everything even more perfect for Lasorda, as it led to friendships with a wide cast of celebrities, including Frank Sinatra.

Lasorda also produced as a manager, a job for which he spent many years in preparation. Signed out of a Pennsylvania high school by the Phillies in 1944, Lasorda was sold to the Dodgers. He spent most of his pitching career in the minors, making it to Brooklyn for cups of coffee in 1954 and 1955 (eight games, no decisions). He made 18 appearances with Kansas City in 1956, losing four, winning none.

Soon Lasorda was back in the Dodgers' system as a scout and later a minor league manager (winning five pennants in eight years). He returned to the major league club in 1973 as a coach under Walter Alston and became manager in 1977. Lasorda guided the Dodgers until 1996, winning eight division titles, four pennants, and two World Series. He won 1,599 games while losing 1,439 as manager of the Dodgers, becoming one of only four men to manage a major league club for 20 or more years (along with Connie Mack, John McGraw, and Alston). His 61 postseason games managed to rank second only to Casey Stengel's 63. A heart attack and angioplasty in the summer of 1996 led to his resignation, and the Hall of Fame opened its doors to him the next year.

Additional Reading:

Lasorda, Tommy, and David Fisher. *The Artful Dodger.* New York: Avon, 1985.

LATIN AMERICAN BASEBALL

President Theodore Roosevelt urged the United States in the early twentieth century to "speak softly and carry a big stick" as he extended the Monroe Doctrine to include both resisting European influence in the Americas and expanding U.S. influence over Latin American nations. That big stick might, in retrospect, have applied to the baseball bat, and the influence has increasingly moved northward as well as southward. In recent decades, increasing numbers of Latin Americans have joined the major leagues, until by the end of the millennium the combined totals of Latin Americans and Hispanic Americans born in the United States outnumber African American players in the majors. Indeed, almost 10 percent of major-leaguers come from the Dominican Republic alone. These Latin American players include such luminaries as Sammy Sosa from the Dominican Republic, breaker (along with Mark McGwire) of the single-season home-run record; Pedro Martinez from the Dominican Republic, winner of the Cy Young Award in each league; Ivan Rodriguez from Puerto Rico, winner of the Most Valuable Player Award in the American

Sammy Sosa, No. 21 of the Chicago Cubs, takes a swing against the St. Louis Cardinals at Busch Stadium in St. Louis, Missouri, April 6, 2000. (Elsa/Allsport)

League in 1999; and Mariano Rivera from Panama, star relief pitcher with the World Champion Yankees of 1998 and 1999.

This influx of Latin American stars into the major leagues, however, was slow in developing, hindered by the same color line that precluded African Americans. Until Jackie Robinson broke the color barrier in 1947, the only Latin Americans in the majors were those who were light-skinned enough to be accepted as white. Most of them were from Cuba, including the highly successful pitcher Adolfo Luque and catcher Mike Gonzalez. Once the color barrier was broken, the number of Cuban players increased, reflecting the importance of baseball in Cuba since the nineteenth century. Until the Cuban revolution in 1959 and the subsequent U.S. blockade and embargo, when virtually all baseball ties between the two countries were severed, Cuba was the dominant Latin American provider of major league talent. So important has Cuba been to baseball in the United States that Cuban baseball receives an individual entry in this volume and therefore will not be discussed in detail here.

With the Cuban connection broken, major league clubs increasingly turned to other nations for prospects, especially the Dominican Republic, Mexico, Nicaragua, Panama, Puerto Rico, and Venezuela. Among the great stars of the 1950s and 1960s were Luis Aparicio (Venezuela), Orlando Cepeda (Puerto Rico), Juan Marichal (Dominican Republic), and Roberto Clemente (Puerto Rico). They paved the way for other Latin American players, fostering a more diverse culture in the dugout and an increasing acceptance of Spanish-speaking players.

Mexico, despite the size of its population, has played a smaller role than several other Latin American countries in major league baseball, with regulations supporting the right of Mexican professional teams to sign amateur players and retain the rights to those players. Nonetheless, some players do move from Mexico to the United States, including pitcher Fernando Valenzuela, who captured the Cy Young Award in his first full season with the Los Angeles Dodgers in 1981. Such was the excitement engendered by Valenzuela that a name was coined to describe the frenzy—"Fernandomania."

In addition to the emigration of Latin American players into the U.S. major leagues, there have been other significant chapters in the story of baseball relationships north and south of the border. The history of the Negro Leagues is closely bound up with Latin America, a tie forged especially by color of skin. African American players denied access to the major leagues in their own country could supplement their income by playing in Latin America. Negro League stars, in fact, could play almost year-round by heading south for the winter. Many also were wooed and won away from their U.S. teams by Latin American clubs that offered more money and less discriminatory living conditions. Josh Gibson was only one of several Negro League stars to make that move.

At the same time, Latin American players moved north, competing against and with Negro League teams. Perhaps the greatest Cuban player of all time was Martin Dihigo, who excelled as a second baseman, outfielder, hitter, and pitcher in Cuba, in Mexico, and with the Negro Leagues in the United States. He is a member of the respective halls of fame in all three countries. After his playing days, Dihigo served as minister of sports in Castro's Cuba until his death in 1971.

Dihigo finished his career as a player with the Mexican League in the 1940s, a league that inserted itself into major league consciousness during that decade by raiding the northern leagues for players. The most talented player who jumped was pitcher Sal "the Barber"

Maglie, who left behind a promising career with the New York Giants. He later was permitted back into the National League and won 18 games for the Giants in 1950 and 23 in 1951. Maglie helped the Giants defeat the Indians in the 1954 World Series and contributed to the Dodgers' pennant in 1956.

White players from the United States also traveled south to earn more money and sharpen their skills. Prominent players barnstormed in Latin America during the winter or played in the winter leagues. Since the 1970s, primarily younger players trying to develop their talents in hopes of making a major league roster have participated in winter league ball. The leagues now exist in the Dominican Republic, Mexico, Puerto Rico, and Venezuela. In recent years, however, many of the top U.S. prospects have played instead in the Arizona Fall League.

The major leagues have long seen in Latin America a rich source of young men, often still boys, from such poverty that they jump at the chance to get an opportunity to make it to the major leagues. With little education and no legal representation, these youngsters, who under major league rules must be at least 16 years old to be signed, are cheap investments, willing to sign in most cases for only a few thousand dollars. In fact, that sum sounds like a fortune to many of the youngsters approached by major league scouts. Sports agents finally are becoming involved with some of these young players, and Scott Boras, representing third baseman Adrian Beltre from the Dominican Republic, charged that the Dodgers had signed Beltre while he was just 15. This case and the publicity arising from it may help young players in Latin America to cash in on their talent like players from the United States, Canada, and Puerto Rico, all of whom are subject to the baseball draft. Major league clubs probably will sign players more selectively in the future if they find themselves making greater financial investments in individual Latin American players. That will result in fewer Latin Americans having an opportunity to start their journey toward the major leagues but will give those who do begin the journey much more financial security.

See also: African Americans; Castro, Fidel; Clemente, Roberto Walker; Cuban Baseball; Expansion; Marichal, Juan Antonio; Negro Leagues; Sosa, Samuel Peralta.

Additional Reading:

Bjarkman, Peter C. *Baseball with a Latin Beat: A History of the Latin American Game.* Jefferson, NC: McFarland, 1994.

Oleksak, Michael M., and Mary Adams Oleksak. *Beisbol: Latin Americans and the Grand Old Game.* Grand Rapids, MI: Masters, 1991.

Regalado, Samuel O. *Viva Baseball! Latin Major Leaguers and Their Special Hunger.* Urbana: University of Illinois Press, 1998.

Ruck, Rob. "Baseball in the Caribbean." In *Total Baseball.* 6th ed. Ed. John Thorn et al. New York: Total Sports, 1999, pp. 536–543.

Van Hyning, Thomas E. *Puerto Rico's Winter League: A History of Major League Baseball's Launching Pad.* Jefferson, NC: McFarland, 1995.

LAW

Like any other societal institution, baseball has been closely tied to the law of the land since its early days as an organized business. That relationship, however, has been neither simple nor always fair—perhaps even less so than many business-law relationships. At times, baseball has operated very much within the normal legal processes, involving both public and private law. Yet at other times, baseball has existed outside the normal legal parameters. In addition, baseball has found itself on occasion, most notably regarding integration, ahead of the law in American society.

So many instances of baseball's utilization of the law exist that a comprehensive account here would not be possible. A few examples will have to suffice instead.

Although sports often stand to some extent by themselves, exercising internal governance to resolve conflicts, baseball players and owners, like all citizens, retain the right to file lawsuits. Indeed, if baseball were not the national pastime, suing might qualify. A famous baseball case involved the great second baseman Napoleon Lajoie and the formation of the American League.

Ban Johnson, president of the Western League, renamed the league in 1900, and the following year declared the American League a major league. That, of course, opened some interesting financial opportunities for National League players. Lajoie, a star for the Philadelphia Phillies, decided to switch to the American League entry in the new league—the Athletics, owned by Connie Mack. The Phillies sought help in the Pennsylvania trial court, requesting an injunction requiring Lajoie to fulfill his Phillies contract. National League teams then had, and the majors would continue throughout most of the twentieth century to exercise, a reserve clause in the basic player contract binding the player to his current team until released, traded, or sold—or until the player retired. The National League therefore argued that Lajoie had no right to switch to another team or league. The court denied the Phillies' claim, finding that damages would be appropriate in lieu of an injunction because someone else could be found to play second base, and that the contract between the National League and players was unfair, lacking mutuality. That is, the provisions were not mutually protective but heavily weighted toward one party. The Phillies, for instance, could terminate the contract with 10 days' notice, but Lajoie was bound to the club for life.

The Phillies then appealed the case to the Pennsylvania Supreme Court, which declared, in opposition to the lower court, that a player of Lajoie's caliber was not readily replaceable. Regarding the important issue of mutuality, the state high court ruled that both parties did not have to possess approximately equal protection under the terms of a contract so long as both had the right to seek legal enforcement, and that the team had compensated Lajoie for the right to terminate his contract with a 10-day notice by paying him a large salary. The court, however, did not order Lajoie to play for the Phillies, an order that would have been impossible to enforce without seriously harming the club itself; instead, it ordered him not to play for any other team.

Other state courts found differently for other players who jumped to the American League, but the prominence of Lajoie gave special and lasting significance to the Pennsylvania decision. As it turned out, Lajoie continued his career, which would lead to the Hall of Fame, without returning to the Phillies. Connie Mack traded him to Cleveland, and the Ohio courts refused to enforce the Pennsylvania injunction. Lajoie personally avoided the injunction by temporarily taking a vacation when the Cleveland team traveled to Philadelphia to play the Athletics. The American and National Leagues soon came to an agreement that brought the new league into harmony with its brief rival, simply enlarging the monopolistic nature of major league baseball. A side-effect of the agreement, though, permitted Lajoie to remain with Cleveland.

Organized baseball generally has relied on private law rather than public law (as in the Lajoie case) to enforce its agreements and dictates. Operating through a National Commission consisting of the two league presidents and a third individual chosen by the two presidents, and since 1921 by a commissioner, the major leagues have tried to resolve issues internally. The commissioner has traditionally received from the owners great freedom to make decisions himself, even without following precedence, for the good of the game. Similarly, courts have usually upheld that role and been disinclined to overturn decisions made by the commissioner.

A case five decades after the institution of the office of commissioner was one in a long line of reaffirmations of the commissioner's power. Charles Finley, owner of the Oakland Athletics, attempted to sell three of his star players during the 1976 season, Joe Rudi and Rollie Fingers to the Red Sox, Vida Blue to the Yankees. Commissioner Bowie Kuhn voided the sales in the "best interests of baseball," and Finley sued. A federal court in Chicago and the U.S. Court of Appeals for the Seventh Circuit ruled against Finley, finding that the commissioner had the authority to decide as he did. However, the record is not 100 percent for the commissioner. An important exception occurred in 1989 when Pete Rose successfully sued in his hometown of Cincinnati to halt commissioner Bart Giamatti's action against him for allegedly betting on baseball games. Judge Norbert Nadel issued a temporary restraining order on the basis of Giamatti's having prejudged the question of Rose's guilt or innocence.

The Pete Rose matter, as writer Roger Abrams has pointed out, combined a cross section of American law—private and public, civil and criminal. Giamatti attempted to handle the question of whether Rose bet on baseball games internally within the usual baseball framework of private law. Rose sought help by moving the matter into the public-law sector with a civil case seeking an injunction against the commissioner. While this was occurring, prosecutors were investigating the possibility of Rose's having committed tax evasion, thus adding public criminal law to the legal mix. Finally,

in August, Rose accepted permanent suspension from organized baseball. Giamatti banned Rose from baseball for life (a ban supplemented by the Hall of Fame declaring Rose ineligible for induction), but the criminal case continued. Rose pleaded guilty to tax evasion and was sentenced in July 1990 to five months in prison. Criminal cases in recent years have especially focused on substance-abuse crimes involving such baseball stars as Vida Blue, Steve Howe, and Darryl Strawberry.

Baseball's interfacing with the law has involved many other important issues, including antitrust law, where the longstanding baseball exemption from antitrust legislation placed the sport outside the normal reach of law in ways that have had profound effects on the game, especially on opportunities for players to change teams and improve their compensation. The antitrust issue, along with collective bargaining, arbitration, and the National Labor Relations Board, are looked at elsewhere in this book. Similarly, other entries consider additional examples of baseball's use of both private and public law.

A final look here at baseball and law shows that baseball was also capable of being much more progressive compared to the rest of the United States. Although baseball shared society's practices of racial discrimination and segregation for about a century, it moved ahead of most of society in the 1940s. The law of the land did not guarantee African Americans the right to play major league ball or to play in the minor leagues. Nor did the law prevent massive segregation throughout much of the country. Branch Rickey and Jackie Robinson, with help from many other people (including writers like Wendell Smith and Sam Lacy and supportive players such as Robinson teammate Pee Wee Reese), relied not on the law in 1947 when Robinson played his first game for the Brooklyn Dodgers but on courage, a commitment to justice, and sound business sense. Baseball, as wrong as it was for a century, suddenly became right and helped propel the country toward racial justice. The civil rights movement of the 1950s and 1960s would transform the law and, to some extent, the heart and soul of America, but baseball was there earlier. To be ahead of the curve where the law is concerned can be dangerous, but it also can be very good. In this case, it was indeed very good.

See also: African Americans; Antitrust Exemption; Black Sox Scandal; Chandler, Albert Benjamin; Commissioner; Finley, Charles Oscar; Flood, Curtis Charles; Free Agency; Gambling; Jackson, Joseph Jefferson; Kuhn, Bowie K.; Labor-Management Relations; Landis, Kenesaw Mountain; McLain, Dennis Dale; Miller, Marvin James; Reserve Clause; Robinson, Jack Roosevelt; Rose, Peter Edward; Steinbrenner, George Michael, III; Substance Abuse; Ward, John Montgomery.

Additional Reading:

Abrams, Roger I. *Legal Bases: Baseball and the Law.* Philadelphia: Temple University Press, 1998.

Waller, Spencer Weber, Neil B. Cohen, and Paul Finkelman. *Baseball and the American Legal Mind.* New York: Garland, 1995.

Weiler, Paul, and Gary Roberts. *Sports and the Law.* Westbury, NY: Foundation, 1993.

Weistart, John, and Cym Lowell. *The Law of Sports.* Charlottesville, VA: Michie, 1979.

LITTLE LEAGUE

Little League was the brainchild of Carl Stotz, who got the idea for organized baseball for young boys while playing ball with his six- and eight-year-old nephews in Williamsport, Pennsylvania. The year was 1938, and while sitting down for a few minutes after incurring a minor ankle injury, Stotz, listening to the boys, remembered his own childhood dream of having a baseball team for boys, with uniforms, and playing on a real field. The rest, as the saying goes, is history, al-though that history has been one of enormous growth and change, with Little League achieving a major presence in society while following a path of increasing size and complexity that parallels the history of many other types of organizations in American society, including many businesses.

Stotz started the first league (with three teams) in 1939 and recruited George and Bert Bebble to coach the other two teams. A second league was added in 1940, Little League spread beyond its home state in 1947, and 10 years later there were 307 leagues. A national championship, which came to be called the Little League World Series, originated in 1947. Little Leagues outside the United States were formed, starting with one in British Columbia, Canada, in 1951, ultimately spreading to 15 other nations by 1955 and more than 60 by the 1990s.

Stotz turned toward sponsors early on in order to purchase uniforms and equipment, gaining, in 1939, his first official sponsor, Lycoming Dairy Farms, after 56 others had turned Stotz down. As Little League grew, Stotz gained increasing financial support. By late 1947, he was actively soliciting national sponsorship, successfully gaining support from U.S. Rubber. At the same time, Stotz entered into agreements with Spalding to make an official Little League baseball and with Hillerich and Bradsby, maker of Louisville Slugger bats, to manufacture bats for the program.

The decade of the 1950s was a turning point for Little League. Now incorporated—with a board of directors (initially including Ford C. Frick, president of the National League, and Paul Kerr, vice president of the Baseball Hall of Fame), national headquarters in Williamsport, with J. Walter Kennedy, formerly of the University of Notre Dame, as business manager, and an organization expanding around the world—Little League began to attract

"Never Mind"—the coach of a Massachusetts Little League team consoles a hitter who has been called out on strikes. (Hulton Getty)

increasing media coverage. The Little League World Series was televised for the first time, by CBS, in 1953, with Howard Cosell doing radio play-by-play for ABC. Such baseball immortals as Connie Mack and Cy Young also were attracted to Little League, attending various World Series competitions during the 1950s.

Meanwhile, Peter J. McGovern, an executive with U.S. Rubber, replaced Stotz as president of Little League, with Stotz serving as commissioner and traveling widely as a sort of ambassador. Stotz came increasingly to feel, apparently correctly, that much of his previous authority had been pulled away, and he objected to philosophical changes in the direction of Little League competition. He feared that too much emphasis was being placed on winning and was concerned that coaches were aiming for the World Series rather than focusing on the goals that had driven Stotz: fun for the boys, a sense of belonging, sportsmanship. A case in point involved the decision to increase roster sizes from 12 boys to 15. Stotz wanted each boy to have ample opportunity to play, with no one spending most of his time on the bench. The more players, the more likely that the less-talented youngsters would spend most of their time sitting and watching. In 1955, the founder and guiding spirit of Little League left the organization.

How much of Stotz's fears have been realized is hard to say. Certainly Little League has continued to grow. Additional levels have been added for younger and older children. Legal action finally forced the admission of girls in the mid-1970s. Foreign teams have won many World Series. Regional and international offices make Little League clearly an international concern, and a Little League Baseball International Congress is held every three years. The second week of June annually, by direction of President Dwight Eisenhower in 1959, continues to be celebrated as National Little League Baseball Week.

The popularity of Little League demonstrates that vast numbers of parents and children view it as a good experience for youngsters. Many others express concern that too much emphasis is placed on winning and that many coaches, however committed and well-intentioned, are insufficiently sensitive to the emotional development of young children. Almost anyone who has attended Little League games can testify to abusive language by parents or coaches and coach-umpire arguments that would seem to run counter to the ideals of sportsmanship that Little League seeks to inculcate.

The development of Little League into an organizationally complex entity probably was inevitable once it began to grow. Stotz's idea was too good to keep small or to himself. Like any number of successful businesses that began with one creator and then grew, to be transformed into a large corporation or bought out by a national or international enterprise, Little League has followed a common path. Still, much depends on what happens locally. The individual coach and the parents who encourage their children to play Little League can make the experience succeed or fail. Little League can offer children an opportunity to achieve the goals that Carl Stotz established and thereby enable parents to grow closer to their children through shared experiences and dinner-table conversations about the games. Little League can help children to play together in ways that benefit them physically and emotionally—or it can teach them to win at all costs.

Students of sports sometimes draw useful distinctions among such concepts as sports, games, and play, with the three concepts on a continuum from extensive organization and direction to largely spontaneous, self-directed enjoyment. Critics of Little League argue that it has moved too far along this spectrum away from play. Others will argue that winning is what is really fun. The reality, however, is that much of life is spent not exactly winning. To learn that one can have fun, feel fulfilled, and gain a sense of satisfaction, even when not coming in first, is an important lesson. Perhaps Little League succeeds best when it teaches that lesson.

See also: American Legion Baseball; Babe Ruth League; Pony Baseball and Softball; Women in Baseball.

Additional Reading:

Fine, Gary Alan. *With the Boys: Little League Baseball and Preadolescent Culture.* Chicago: University of Chicago Press, 1987.

Ralbovsky, Marty. *Destiny's Darlings: A World Championship Little League Team Twenty Years Later.* New York: Hawthorn, 1974.

Robinson, Jackie. *Jackie Robinson's Little League Baseball Book.* Englewood Cliffs, NJ: Prentice-Hall, 1972.

Stotz, Carl E., as told to Kenneth D. Loss. *A Promise Kept: The Story of the Founding of*

Little League Baseball. Jersey Shore, PA: Zebrowski Historical Services, 1992.

Yablonsky, Lewis, and Jonathan Brower. *The Little League Game: How Kids, Coaches, and Parents Really Play It*. New York: Times Books, 1979.

LOUISVILLE SLUGGER

The name "Louisville Slugger" is synonymous with the baseball bat in the minds of many. In reality, it refers to bats made by Hillerich and Bradsby, and the fact is that a number of other companies have made fine bats as well. Nonetheless, the Louisville Slugger has a mystique all its own. Part of that is the history of the product, going back to 1884 (which has given rise to one of the nation's best baseball museums), part is the number of baseball greats who have endorsed bats made by Hillerich and Bradsby, and part is the genuine quality that the term "Louisville Slugger" reflects.

It all began when Pete "the Old Gladiator" Browning of the Louisville Eclipse in the American Association broke a bat in 1884. Already mired in a slump, Browning was beside himself at losing his favorite bat. A young man named John Andrew "Bud" Hillerich, who worked for his father, J. Frederick Hillerich, in a woodworking shop came to the rescue. He offered to make a new bat for Browning. Bud Hillerich worked all night, and when Browning collected three hits the next day, a new industry was born.

The father did not care for the new product line, but the son kept the bats coming. In 1894, Hillerich changed the name of the bat from the "Falls City Slugger" to "Louisville Slugger." The batmaker created his bats to fit individual specifications requested by players, including stars like Willie Keeler, Hugh Jennings, and John McGraw. Honus Wagner helped to usher in the practice of player endorsements by agreeing to have his name used on Louisville Sluggers. More recent users of Louisville Sluggers include Ted Williams, Mickey Mantle, Hank Aaron, and George Brett.

Frank Bradsby took over sales for the company in 1912, and the name of the company was changed to Hillerich and Bradsby four years later. Bud Hillerich continued with the company until he died in 1946, at which time his son, Ward, became CEO, followed by another son, John. John Hillerich III became president in 1969.

The company makes a lot of other items. Long gone are the bedposts and swinging churns crafted by Bud's father; instead, hockey sticks, baseball and softball gloves, golf clubs (manufactured by the company since 1916), batting gloves, and even aluminum bats flow forth from Hillerich and Bradsby. Yet the Louisville Slugger remains the hallmark, the name of the bat far more recognizable than the name of the company itself.

Visitors to Louisville, Kentucky, can drop in to the Louisville Slugger Museum and find a treasure trove of baseball artifacts second only to the collection in the Baseball Hall of Fame Museum at Cooperstown. Then they can receive a guided tour through the plant, watching skilled craftsmen turn out Louisville Sluggers. Each visitor receives a miniature bat as a souvenir, and outside a giant bat towers over the building. The name branded into the barrel of this huge "Genuine Louisville Slugger" is, appropriately, that of the man who first created the world's most famous bat—J. A. "Bud" Hillerich.

See also: Equipment; Spalding, Albert Goodwill.
Additional Reading:

Hill, Bob. *The Louisville Slugger Story*. Santa Monica, CA: General Publishing Group, 1999.

Louisville Slugger Museum Website. http://www.slugger.com/museum

MACK, CORNELIUS ALEXANDER (THE TALL TACTICIAN) (1862–1956)

Connie Mack was born Cornelius Alexander McGillicuddy but changed his name so that it would fit in a box score. The public during most of Mack's long tenure as manager and owner of the Philadelphia Athletics (1901–1950) saw the conservative and dignified gentleman, later elderly gentleman, attired in suit, high collar, and straw hat motioning players into their correct positions with a scorecard seemingly forever in his hand. Mack, when other managers wore the same uniform as their players, was always somewhat apart, almost a stranger in the modern world, a throwback to the early days of baseball when gentlemen played the game, the most conservative of baseball symbols.

It was not always so. As a young man, Connie Mack was far from conservative. A light-hitting catcher from 1886 to 1896, Mack used his defensive ability and quick wit to help his team defeat the opposition. He was not averse to bending the rules a bit. His specialty was imitating the sound of ball against bat by flicking his tongue against the roof of his mouth to get a strike call. When John Montgomery Ward led the creation of the Players League in 1890, the young catcher was one of the jumpers. A decade later, as manager of the Athletics in the new American League, he stood ready to raid the older league and hired away crosstown hero Napoleon Lajoie from the Phillies. When the Phillies succeeded in getting an injunction against Lajoie, Mack traded him to Cleveland.

As the decades passed, however, Mack assumed the persona by which he is still remembered. Along the way, he built and demolished two dynasties and continued to lead the Athletics into his late eighties. Altogether, he won nine pennants and five World Series, accumulating 3,731 wins in 53 years of managing, including three earlier years heading Pittsburgh in the National League. His first great Athletics team dominated in the second decade of the twentieth century. They won their fourth pennant in five years in 1914 with an All-Star cast: pitchers Eddie Plank, Chief Bender, and Jack Coombs; and the $100,000 infield of Stuffy McInnis, Eddie Collins, "Black Jack" Barry, and Home Run Baker.

The Athletics lost the 1914 World Series to the Boston Braves in a stunning upset all the more incredible for being a sweep. Mack then started auctioning off his stars in a foreshadowing of what another A's owner, Charles Finley, would attempt some 60 years later. Although finances certainly played a part in Mack's decision, as he faced increased salary demands made possible by the Federal League of 1914–1915 (in an ironic parallel to Mack's earlier involvements with the Players League and early American League), rumors circulated then, and have continued down to the present, that Mack had gotten wind of his players putting less than their best efforts into the championship series.

Mack rebuilt the Athletics in the late 1920s and early 1930s with a collection of stars that included outfielder Al Simmons, slugging first baseman Jimmie Foxx, catcher Mickey Cochrane, and pitcher Lefty Grove. His second version of the mighty A's finished first three times and captured two World Series. Then Mack tore down his championship house once again. This time, the motivation clearly was money. The Great Depression had hit, and Mack had to pay off bank loans. With attendance low, he was forced to cut costs, which he did by removing high-priced players. There would not be another return to greatness.

Never again would the Philadelphia Athletics win or even come close. They finished above fifth only once from 1934 through 1950, when Mack stepped down, apparently not very willingly. He had divided his shares of team stock among his three sons in 1946. Roy and Earle bought out Connie Jr. and persuaded their father to retire after the 1950 season. That final year witnessed many well-deserved expressions of affection, including a ticker-tape parade through the streets of New York. The team was sold after the 1954 campaign, and it was moved by the new owner, Arnold Johnson, to Kansas City. Connie Mack died two years after the move.

See also: Baker, John Franklin; Ballparks; Finley, Charles Oscar; Major Leagues.

Additional Reading:

Jordan, David M. The Athletics of Philadelphia: Connie Mack's White Elephants, 1901–1954. Jefferson, NC: McFarland, 1999.
Kashatus, William C. Connie Mack's '29 Triumph: The Rise and Fall of the Philadelphia Athletics Dynasty. Jefferson, NC: McFarland, 1999.
Lieb, Fred. Connie Mack: Grand Old Man of Baseball. New York: Putnam's, 1945.
Mack, Connie. From Sandlot to Big League: Connie Mack's Baseball Book. Rev. ed. New York: Knopf, 1960.
———. My 66 Years in the Big Leagues: The Great Story of America's National Game. Philadelphia: Winston, 1950.

MACPHAIL, LELAND STANFORD, SR. (LARRY) (1890–1975); and LELAND STANFORD, JR. (LEE) (1917–)

The MacPhails have been prominent in baseball throughout most of the twentieth century and into the twenty-first, finding ways to make baseball more exciting and accessible, thus positioning the sport securely within American society as a popular pastime. The first of the MacPhails was the most innovative of the generations but also the most controversial. Deeply flawed, he nonetheless was one of the giants of the game.

Larry MacPhail first looked to the law as a career, graduating from law school at George Washington University in 1910. When war broke out, he entered a field artillery unit and ended up being wounded and gassed. After the war, the already flamboyant MacPhail participated in a plan to kidnap the German Kaiser. The plot proved more imaginative than practical, but MacPhail would soon find ways to combine both qualities to bring baseball to the masses.

MacPhail took over the Columbus, Ohio, farm team of the St. Louis Cardinals in 1930. By 1933, he was summoned to Cincinnati to resurrect the moribund Reds. MacPhail joined with Powel Crosley, who owned two radio stations, and hired Red Barber to announce games. Despite fears by many that putting baseball games on the radio would dissuade fans from attending in person, the opposite occurred. The fan base grew, and so did attendance. The next step was to introduce night baseball, which MacPhail did in 1935, again in the face of considerable skepticism. The common-sense realization that more people were free to attend games at night when they were not tied to their jobs led to an attendance explosion and more revenue with which to build the team. By 1939, the Reds were National League champions, and in the following year they won the World Series.

MacPhail moved to the Brooklyn Dodgers in 1938 to work his magic with another ailing club. He brought Red Barber over from Cincinnati and hired the mercurial Leo Durocher as manager. Night baseball followed as well, and by 1941 the Dodgers were champions of their league. Unfortunately, MacPhail's hard drinking and unpredictable behavior were causing problems. MacPhail repeatedly fired and rehired his manager, and shortly after a drunken episode following the 1941 World Series loss he himself was fired.

The New York Yankees were the next team to benefit from his ideas and to grow tired of his increasingly erratic behavior. With co-owners Dan Topping and Del Webb, he helped to forge another generation of championship Yankee teams. Yet his feuding with Joe McCarthy led the great manager to quit, and a public brawl at the 1947 Series celebration led to MacPhail's ouster. Nor will history

judge favorably his opposition to integrating the Yankees.

Despite his shortcomings, Larry MacPhail showed major league organizations how to create winning teams. He also inaugurated night games, established the importance of radio broadcasts, and popularized such developments as the batting helmet, old-timers' games, pension plans for players and other club employees, and air travel. His legacy of leadership was passed along to his son, Lee.

Lee MacPhail was perhaps less innovative than his father, certainly less volatile, but steadier. His consistent leadership showed forth in a succession of important positions: director of player personnel for the Yankees (helping to produce seven World Series winners in 10 years), general manager of the Baltimore Orioles (culminating in a World Series victory in 1966), a return to the Yankees as general manager, more than a decade as president of the American League (a position he left in 1983), and president of the Players Relations Committee.

Lee was elected to the Hall of Fame in 1998, joining his father as the first father-son combination ever elected. Their legacy remains alive still today, not only in the effects of their contributions to baseball but also in the third generation of MacPhail baseball leaders. Andrew B. MacPhail has served as president and chief executive officer of the Chicago Cubs—a team and a family both rich in baseball tradition.

See also: Barber, Walter Lanier; Brooklyn Dodgers; Durocher, Leo Ernest; New York Yankees; Night Baseball; Substance Abuse; War.

Additional Reading:

MacPhail, Lee. *My 9 Innings: An Autobiography of 50 Years in Baseball.* Westport, CT: Meckler, 1989.

Warfield, Don. *The Roaring Redhead: Larry MacPhail, Baseball's Great Innovator.* South Bend, IN: Diamond Communications, 1987.

White, G. Edward. *Creating the National Pastime: Baseball Transforms Itself, 1903–1953.* Princeton: Princeton University Press, 1996.

MAJOR LEAGUES

Americans like to be first. It was of George Washington that Henry Lee spoke in 1799 when he uttered the declaration, "First in war, first in peace, and first in the hearts of his countrymen." That concept of being first has solidified the nation over some 200 years. We want to be first in the world, and we wish to be first ourselves. "Everybody loves a winner," goes the cliché, and so people strive to rise to the top. In baseball, rising to the top means the major leagues. Fame and fortune await the individual who climbs the baseball ladder to the pinnacle. Initially, though, it was not quite that way.

Baseball historians generally agree that the first major league was founded in 1871; the National Association of Professional Base Ball Players (NAPBBP) was formed by nine teams splitting off from an earlier organization called the National Association of Base Ball Players. The concept of a major league, however, was not much in people's minds in those early days, and the primary difference between the two leagues is that the latter planned from the first to be professional, whereas the earlier league had seen itself as amateur, although some teams, led by the powerful Cincinnati Red Stockings of 1869, had, in fact, become professional. Harry Wright, manager of the Red Stockings, led a number of his top players to Boston to form the Boston Red Stockings and dominated the new league, which lasted through the 1875 season, when various problems, including gambling, declining attendance, and organizational difficulties, led to its replacement by another league.

The earlier league, despite its amateur status, should not be neglected in any discussion of major leagues. Baseball came of age in the National Association of Base Ball Players, formed in 1857 by 16 teams, including the pioneering New York Knickerbockers. Doc Adams, a physician and one of the organizers of the Knickerbockers, served as president of the new league and brought about changes that transformed the game essentially into what is played today. Among Adams's contributions was a new baseball. The ball in use at the time was so light that it could not readily be thrown from the outfield to the infield, requiring a fielder to play between infield and outfield to relay the throw. Adams devised a new, harder baseball covered with horsehide, stuffed with rubber cuttings, and wound with yarn. With the new ball, a relay throw was usually not necessary, permitting the fielder to move forward into what became known as the shortstop position. The famous sportswriter Henry Chadwick served as chairman of the league's Rules Committee. Among the rules changes were solidification of the number of players per side at nine, placement of bases 90 feet apart, and empowerment of the umpire to call strikes. Innovations such as the stolen base, bunt, and curveball came into the game at this time, and the Brooklyn Atlantics, recruiting heavily from the working class, was a powerhouse for much of the league's history.

Gradually, however, professionalism and gambling crept in, and by 1869 baseball had its first clearly professional team—the Red Stockings. Cincinnati's success assured the continuation of professional baseball, a development not to everyone's liking, which led to a split between teams that wished to continue on an amateur basis and the professional teams that formed the new NAPBBP. Two of the NAPBBP teams exist today, the Boston Red Stockings (as the Atlanta

Braves, descendants of the Boston and later Milwaukee Braves) and the Chicago White Stockings (not as the White Sox but as the Cubs).

Next came the National League of Professional Base Ball Clubs, which is still in existence. William A. Hulbert, owner of the Chicago White Stockings, decided that what baseball needed was rule by owners rather than by players (who had exercised considerable power in the NAPBBP). Having built his own team by signing such stars as Cap Anson and Al Spalding, Hulbert was principal organizer of a replacement league, the National League. The league consisted of eight teams, in Boston, Chicago, Cincinnati, St. Louis, Hartford, New York, Philadelphia, and Louisville. Two of the original teams, the Philadelphia Phillies and New York (now San Francisco) Giants, are still in the National League, as are the Chicago and Boston clubs that moved into the National League from the NAPBBP. The league's most exciting team during the nineteenth century, however, was the Baltimore Orioles, an aggressive championship club featuring Ned Hanlon as manager and standout players Hughie Jennings, Willie "Hit 'Em Where They Ain't" Keeler, and John McGraw. The Orioles had begun in the American Association before switching to the National League in 1892. Unfortunately, the club was dropped from its new home when the National League reduced its number to eight teams after the 1899 season.

Hulbert and the other owners consolidated their power by introducing a reserve clause into the standard player contract, retaining exclusive control of the player until he was sold or traded. The National League was the first league to see itself as the exclusive major league. In fact, it strenuously sought to exert a monopoly through the reserve clause. Also during the early decades of the

National League, minor leagues began to form, giving added significance to the concept of the major league.

The National League, however, left many major cities without teams, thereby inadvertently inviting formation of a rival league. The American Base Ball Association rose to fill the vacuum, establishing itself in 1882 in cities excluded by the National League. It also sought success by giving fans an alternative in a variety of ways. The National League envisioned itself as something of a gentlemen's league, abstaining from Sunday games, prohibiting alcoholic beverages from being sold at games, and setting ticket prices at 50 cents. The new American Association tried to undercut its more established competitor by selling tickets for 25 cents and offering fans the chance to see games on Sundays, when people had more free time. At the same time, fans were able to slake their thirst for more than just baseball, giving rise to the nickname "Beer and Whiskey League" for the American Association. As one might expect, the games did not always attract the best audiences, and rowdyism became a problem at some of the contests.

The National League made peace with the upstart in the so-called National Agreement of 1883, with the American Association agreeing to adopt the reserve clause and refrain from raiding National League teams. Three of the American Association clubs continue to this day, although in the National League: Cincinnati, St. Louis, and Allegheny (now Pittsburgh); Brooklyn (now the Los Angeles Dodgers) entered play in 1884.

The nineteenth century was witness to two new rival major leagues, the Union Association and the Players League. Neither league lasted beyond one season (1884 and 1890, respectively), and both were brave but failed attempts by players to assert their freedom against the major leagues' reserve clause. The only Union team to survive beyond 1884 was the St. Louis Maroons, for the following two years in the National League.

The guiding spirit behind the Players League was John Montgomery Ward, attorney, union organizer, and star player. Leading the charge against the reserve clause and a classification plan to keep player salaries low, Ward arranged financial backing for teams that were to be primarily player-run. Many stars deserted to the Players League, including future club owners Connie Mack and Charles Comiskey. Unfortunately, only one of the clubs, the new Boston Red Stockings team with Dan Brouthers, Old Hoss Radbourn, and manager King Kelly, turned a profit. Competition and considerable pressure from the National League persuaded most of the financial backers to withdraw their support, and several of the teams merged with National League clubs.

The presence of three leagues in competition—the National League, American Association, and Players League—tended to glut the market, and the American Association suffered. Adding to its difficulties was a conflict with the National League over reassignment of players returning from the defunct Players League. The American Association withdrew from the National Agreement, leading to a major struggle between the now rival leagues during 1891 and the American Association's demise after the season. For the rest of the decade, the National League had a complete monopoly on major league ball, limiting player salaries and imposing a salary cap of $2,400 for individual players, although occasional under-the-table deals were made with top stars.

The grand isolation of the National League, however, would last only until 1901, and the key person in ending it was Ban Johnson. Johnson had transformed the Western League, which he

led as president, into a financially thriving organization and decided to upgrade the league to major league status. He renamed it the American League, thus adopting a name parallel to the existing major league, and recruited over 100 National League players, including Willie Keeler, Joe "Iron Man" McGinnity, and Cy Young. Emphasizing proper, more gentlemanly behavior over the sometimes violent National League contests with their brawls and umpire-baiting, Johnson succeeded. The old league, which had learned to compromise with the American Association, did the same with the American League. The two leagues, rather than continuing to compete, came to an agreement in 1903 to share in a monopoly, both sides enforcing the reserve clause to prevent a third league from intruding. They also established the National Baseball Commission to provide leadership, consisting of the two league presidents and a third individual chosen by the presidents. The American League, after adding a New York club in 1903, would remain unchanged until the 1950s. In addition, the agreement between the National and American Leagues would establish a stable organization that remains in place today.

That stability, however, would face additional challenges. The Federal League had started in 1913 as a minor league (named the Western League), successor to the predecessor of the American League. The Western League owners decided to declare themselves a major league for the 1914 season. Once again players were tempted to jump from the established leagues to the new. Hal Chase gave the Chicago White Sox 10 days' notice, reversing the 10-day clause in players' contracts whereby the major league team owned a player's rights for the duration of his career but needed to give the player only 10-days' notice before releasing him.

Chase joined the Buffalo Blues of the Federal League. Joe Tinker of the Chicago Cubs did not have to leave the city to join the Federal League, becoming player-manager of the Chicago Whales. Chicago finished a close second in the 1914 pennant race and came in first in 1915. Tinker's ace pitcher in that championship season was an aging former teammate, Three Finger Brown. Walter Johnson, the great Washington pitcher, briefly jumped to the Federal League but returned to Washington when his salary was increased.

National League owners, targeted by the Federal League with an antitrust suit, bought out most of the Federal League owners. Charles Weeghman, owner of the Whales, was given the opportunity to purchase the Chicago Cubs. Ned Hanlon, owner of the Baltimore Terrapins, was largely ignored in these settlements and sued the major leagues. He won in the District of Columbia but lost both in an appeals court and in the U.S. Supreme Court, which ruled that antitrust legislation did not apply to baseball.

No other major league would actually take the field in competition against the National and American Leagues, but Branch Rickey, after his remarkable transformations of baseball by establishing the farm-system structure and integrating the major leagues, planned the Continental League. Rickey announced the league in 1959, with teams planned for New York, Atlanta, Houston, Dallas, Denver, Minneapolis–St. Paul, Buffalo, and Toronto. His league therefore would be based in cities and regions ignored by the major leagues while adding a team in New York to replace the Dodgers and Giants, gone to California. The established leagues cut Rickey off at the pass by moving quickly to expansion. Today, of course, most of those cities have major league clubs, thanks at least in part to Rickey's progressive thinking.

When fans, serious and casual alike, think of the major leagues, two organizations come to mind: the American League and the National League. The reality, however, is that the organizations and teams constituting the majors have changed considerably over the years. At first, participants and fans did not think of what they were playing or watching as "major league baseball"; that came later, as minor leagues developed in the latter decades of the nineteenth century.

For players and fans, what really matters is the major leagues play the best baseball. Common to all is love for the game, even though some also may be in it to make a buck. Young players can dream of "making it to the big leagues." Fans share that dream, and through the players they can know the pleasure of having made it—of being number one.

See also: All-Star Games; Business; Labor-Management Relations; Minor Leagues; World Series.

Additional Reading:

Bjarkman, Peter C. *Encyclopedia of Major League Baseball Team Histories*. Westport, CT: Meckler, 1991.

Ivor-Campbell, Frederick, and Matthew Silverman. "Team Histories." In *Total Baseball*. 6th ed. Ed. John Thorn et al. New York: Total Sports, 1999, pp. 13–71.

Seymour, Harold. *Baseball: The Early Years*. 1960. Reprint, New York: Oxford University Press, 1989.

Voigt, David Quentin. *American Baseball*. 3 vols. 1966–1983. University Park: Pennsylvania State University Press, 1983.

———. "America's Game: A Brief History." In *The Baseball Encyclopedia*. 10th ed. Editorial Director, Jeanine Bucek. New York: Macmillan, 1996, pp. 3–13.

MALAMUD, BERNARD (1914–1986)

Bernard Malamud, one of the most respected writers of the twentieth century, produced books that will remain firmly entrenched as American classics. Among his greatest achievements are the novels *The Assistant* (1957) and *The Fixer* (1966, winner of the National Book Award and the Pulitzer Prize for fiction in 1967), and the collection of short stories *The Magic Barrel* (1958, winner of the National Book Award in 1959). Malamud also spent many years as a teacher in New York City high schools and at Oregon State University and Bennington College in Vermont.

Malamud's *The Natural* (1952) helped to establish the artistic credibility of the baseball novel. It later was made into a popular film released in 1984 and starring Robert Redford as Roy Hobbs. In the novel, Hobbs is determined to become the greatest baseball player ever. Loosely based on Shoeless Joe Jackson of the 1919 Black Sox, Hobbs sees his career end before it begins when a woman shoots him in her hotel room. Hobbs resurfaces at 34 when the struggling New York Knights sign him. His second opportunity, however, is marred by personal failings, illness, and attempts to fix the league playoff game.

Malamud's novel rises above the realistic and comic approach of Ring Lardner's earlier baseball fiction and anticipates the later work of W. P. Kinsella by combining realism, fantasy, and moral choices that must be made. *The Natural* also includes considerable symbolism, as the story develops within the context of the knight and holy grail legends.

The novel and film offer interesting contrasts, with the film depicting a more heroic protagonist who inevitably makes the correct moral choices. The moral ambiguity of Malamud's Roy Hobbs gives way to the moral rectitude of Redford's portrayal. In the film, the good triumphs, whereas in the novel it is not always clear just who is good. Certainly, Hobbs is far from morally perfect in the book as he yields to lust, greed, and even gluttony, making his way through a number of the seven deadly sins. There is far more depth to Malamud's vision, but the changes made in transferring the story from page to screen yield a popular and exciting film experience.

Although Malamud continued to utilize both realism and fantasy in many of his later works, he turned to other subjects. One can say, however, that he found the baseball story in its immaturity and helped mature it into a strong, complex, diverse, sometimes provocative, and often entertaining adult genre.

See also: Fiction; Films; Jackson, Joseph Jefferson; Myth.

Additional Reading:

Abramson, Edward A. *Bernard Malamud Revisited*. New York: Twayne, 1993.

Candelaria, Cordelia. *Seeking the Perfect Game: Baseball in American Literature*. New York: Greenwood Press, 1989.

Malamud, Bernard. *The Natural*. 1952. Reprint, New York: Noonday, 1990.

———. *Talking Horse: Bernard Malamud on Life and Work*. Ed. Alan Cheuse and Nicholas Delhanco. New York: Columbia University Press, 1996.

O'Connor, Gerry. "Bernard Malamud's *The Natural:* 'The Worst There Ever Was in the Game.'" *Arete* 3(2) (1986): 37–42.

MANLEY, EFFA (1900–1981)

Effa Manley, co-owner and business manager of the Brooklyn Eagles in 1935 and the Newark Eagles from 1936 until 1948, both in the Negro National League, crossed a number of lines in American society. A white woman who passed for black, a woman owner in a male-dominated industry, and a flamboyant, aggressive fun-seeker who championed civil rights, Effa Manley was a woman far ahead of her time.

Manley was born to a white seamstress mother, Bertha Ford Brooks, and her white lover, a wealthy and prominent financier, John M. Bishop. The liaison destroyed Bertha's wedding to her black husband, Benjamin Brooks, and she later married another black man, B. A. Cole. Effa officially claimed Brooks as her father and was reared by Bertha, spending her life passing as a light-skinned black woman. After moving from her native Philadelphia to New York City, she married a well-to-do former numbers banker, Abe Manley, who had a passion for baseball as well as for Effa. The 1933 marriage was her second. Effa easily adopted a rich lifestyle, fancying especially the mink coats that her husband bought for her. She also became involved in charity work and took up the cause of fairness in hiring, helping to pressure Harlem businesses run by whites into agreements to hire black employees for other than menial jobs.

The Manleys purchased the Brooklyn Eagles in 1935 and added the Newark Dodgers in 1936, when they merged the two teams into the Newark Eagles. The Eagles would remain one of the Negro National League powers through the 1948 season, when dwindling attendance following integration of major league baseball led to the league's demise. Effa Manley essentially ran the club, sometimes giving orders to her manager on game strategy. Effa sometimes took more than a passing interest in a number of players. In one instance, she and pitcher Terris McDuffie had an argument that led to the pitcher knocking her down and kicking her. Abe found out about the altercation (and their relationship) and shipped him off to the New York Black Yankees for two bats and a pair of sliding pads.

By 1947, Jackie Robinson was playing for Branch Rickey and the Dodgers, the Negro Leagues were dying, and Manley was involved in trying to reconcile her distaste for Rickey's hiring away Negro League players without paying compensation with her wish to see the majors integrated. Her hope was that the majors would work out arrangements whereby the Negro Leagues could function essentially as minor leagues. When Bill Veeck came calling for Larry Doby in 1947, Manley did the only thing she could do, which was to let Doby go—but not for free. Veeck offered $10,000, but Manley succeeded in getting him to add another $5,000 if Doby remained with the Indians for at least 30 days. Manley also offered Veeck Monte Irvin for an additional $1,000, but Veeck unwisely turned down that addition to the deal.

Effa and Abe sold their club after the league folded, and the new owners moved the team to Houston as a member of the Negro American League. Abe died in 1952, and Effa later moved to California, devoting much of her time until her death persuading the Hall of Fame to welcome Negro League veterans. Her efforts succeeded, as the Hall of Fame instituted a Special Committee on the Negro Leagues in 1971 to select former Negro League players. Among the committee members was one of Manley's former stars, Monte Irvin, who himself would be chosen for induction. The Veterans Committee later was given continuing responsibility for Negro League selections. Manley died in 1981, before two more of her greatest players, Doby and pitcher Leon Day, were chosen. Effa Manley may have worn mink coats and taken a flamboyant approach to player relations, but she was a real leader, both in the substantial black business of Negro League baseball and in the quest for justice for black Americans.

See also: African Americans; Business; Doby, Lawrence Eugene; Negro Leagues; Women in Baseball.

Additional Reading:
Holway, John B. *Voices from the Great Black Baseball Leagues.* Rev. ed. New York: Da Capo, 1992.
Manley, Effa, and Leon Herbert. *Negro Baseball . . . Before Integration.* Chicago: Adams, 1976.

Newark Eagle Files. Newark Public Library. New Jersey Collection. Newark, NJ.

Overmyer, James. *Queen of the Negro Leagues: Effa Manley and the Newark Eagles.* Rev. ed. Lanham, MD: Scarecrow, 1998.

Rogosin, William Donn. *Invisible Men: Life in the Negro Baseball Leagues.* New York: Athenaeum, 1987.

MANTLE, MICKEY CHARLES (MICK, THE COMMERCE COMET) (1931–1995)

Mickey Mantle came to the New York Yankees with talent seldom equaled in major league history and became perhaps the most popular player of his day. Millions of Americans adopted Mantle as a hero, a status he never lost even through later revelations of excessive drinking and partying. Bob Costas, the baseball broadcaster and commentator, routinely carries a 1958 Topps All-Star card of Mantle in his billfold; many other men, advancing into middle age, carry memories of the Mick in their hearts and minds as they keep alive those moments of youth when they followed enthusiastically the exploits of the great Yankee center fielder.

Part of Mantle's appeal was that the boyishly handsome player came from the hinterlands—Commerce, Oklahoma— where both his father, Elvin "Mutt" Mantle, and grandfather, Charley Mantle, worked in the mines and pitched for mining teams. The two older men pitched hour after hour to the child, the grandfather left-handed, the father right-handed, to develop Mickey into a switch-hitter. Mutt had named his son after the great catcher Mickey Cochrane, planning a big league career for him from the start.

Mantle played shortstop in high school in Commerce and began at that position in the minors. Called up to the big time in 1951, Mantle played right field in Joe DiMaggio's final season as the Yankees' center fielder. A batting slump, though,

Portrait of New York Yankees outfielder Mickey Mantle at a baseball stadium, readying to swing a bat, 1960s (Archive Photos)

sent Mantle back down to the minors, and it took a visit from his father, dying from Hodgkin's disease, to keep the dejected youngster from quitting. Injuries already were laying their trap for Mantle. In high school, he had suffered a football injury that led to osteomyelitis in his legs. In the 1951 World Series, Mantle, back in the Yankee outfield, was called off a fly ball at the last minute by DiMaggio. Trying to hold up, he caught his spikes on a drainage outlet and injured his right knee. Other injuries—foot, knee, and shoulder— would follow, keeping Mantle from even greater achievements. Also hindering Mantle was his partying habit with teammates like Billy Martin and Whitey Ford, the result of his knowledge that none of the Mantle men had lived past the age of 40. Why not, then, live just for the present? In later years, Mantle regretted that he had not taken better care of himself, feeling that he should have accomplished even more, especially for his father's sake.

Nonetheless, Mantle had awesome ability, and what he did accomplish has earned him a position as one of the greatest center fielders of all time—many would say the best ever. By 1952, DiMaggio was retired and Mantle was in center field, where he would stay until shifting his aching legs to first base for the final two years of his career. From 1951 through 1968, Mantle hit 536 home runs, drove in 1,509 runners, accumulated 2,415 hits, and batted .298. He was a member of 20 All-Star squads, and in World Series play he hit more home runs (18) and drove in more runners (40) than anyone.

Mantle's greatest season may have been 1956, when he won the Triple Crown, leading the American League in batting (.353), home runs (52), and runs batted in (130). He also received his first of three Most Valuable Player Awards. In addition to winning the award in 1956, 1957, and 1962, he finished a close second to roommate Roger Maris twice, losing out by three and four votes in Maris's greatest seasons (1960 and 1961). Mantle led the league in home runs four times, but not during his second season of hitting over 50. In 1961, he challenged Babe Ruth's record, but an injury late in the season kept him at 54 while Maris finally hit number 61 in the last game of the season.

The Triple Crown season was followed by Mantle's greatest year in batting average (.365), only to be bested by the aging Ted Williams, who hit a remarkable .388. Mantle was limited by injury to just 123 games in 1962, but he still hit .321 with 30 home runs. The following year, he played in only 65 games, but when he could play the talent was still there: 15 home runs and a .314 average. He had his final great year in 1964, batting .303 in 143

games, with 35 home runs and 111 RBIs. He was again second in balloting for Most Valuable Player and led the Yankees to another pennant; although the Yankees lost in seven games to the Cardinals, Mantle hit three home runs.

Mickey Mantle was a complete player. Virtually no one was faster. Early in his career, he could go from home to first in 3.1 seconds. It was not an era for stealing bases, so Mantle never stole more than 21 in a season, but every base that he did steal risked injuring his legs even more. An outstanding fielder, Mantle could cover a wide expanse of ground, and his arm was one of the best. What awed spectators most, however, was his power from either side. The tape-measure home run became a part of baseball because of Mantle's powerful shots.

Mantle went to spring training in 1969, but his legs had finally given out, and so he retired. Subsequent years were not always kind to Mantle, although he surprised himself by living past 40. He lost a son, Billy, to Hodgkin's disease, drank heavily, and was banished from baseball by commissioner Bowie Kuhn in 1983 for taking jobs with Atlantic City casinos. Commissioner Peter Ueberroth reinstated him two years later.

By 1995, Mantle's health had deteriorated badly. He received a liver transplant on June 8 but lived little more than two months. In his final trip around the bases, Mantle did good once again, as he had for so many people during his heroic days as a baseball superstar. He talked openly about his drinking, attempting to prevent others from following his example. In fact, many people did follow him at the end, as organ donations sharply increased. After it all, Mickey Mantle perhaps was not a good role model, but he remained a hero—especially to men who still remembered when both he and they were young and strong.

See also: Bouton, James Alan; Heroes; Home Run; Maris, Roger Eugene; Music; New York Yankees; Rural America; Substance Abuse.
Additional Reading:
Falkner, David. *The Last Hero: The Life of Mickey Mantle.* New York: Simon and Schuster, 1995.
Mantle, Merlyn. *A Hero All His Life.* New York: HarperCollins, 1996.
Mantle, Mickey. *All My Octobers: My Memories of Twelve World Series When the Yankees Ruled Baseball.* New York: HarperCollins, 1994.
———. *The Mick.* Garden City, NY: Doubleday, 1985.

MARICHAL, JUAN ANTONIO (MANITO) (1937–)

Juan Marichal was not the first Latin American player in the major leagues, but he was one of the best. From humble origins in the Dominican Republic, where as a youngster he made his own baseballs, he rose to become one of the most dominant pitchers of his time. His 243 career victories remained the record for Latin American pitchers until Dennis Martinez surpassed that total in 1998.

Marichal is remembered for his high-kick delivery of a repertoire of pitches from various angles (overhand, three-quarters, sidearm). He is also remembered for having won 20 or more games six times, twice reaching 25 victories, and once 26. He completed 244 of his 457 career starts while fashioning a fine 2.89 ERA. His greatest seasons were with the San Francisco Giants from 1960 until 1973 before finishing his career with the Red Sox and Dodgers.

An unfortunate Marichal memory is his attack on Dodger catcher Johnny Roseboro in 1965. The Giants and Dodgers were heated rivals, and when Marichal was brushed back with a pitch, and then felt Roseboro's return throw sailing just inches from his ear, he retaliated by striking the catcher on his head with the bat. Marichal was suspended for nine days and fined the then high figure of $1,750.

It was Marichal's fate to have his greatest seasons in 1963, 1966, and 1968. In the first two, Sandy Koufax had two of his greatest seasons, and in the third, Bob Gibson posted his astonishing 1.12 ERA. In retrospect, it is difficult to rank Marichal beneath either of his contemporaries. His election to the Hall of Fame in 1983 added more luster to a very bright, if slightly underappreciated, star.

See also: Gibson, Pack Robert; Koufax, Sanford; Latin American Baseball.
Additional Reading:
Devaney, John. *Juan Marichal: Mister Strike.* New York: Putnam's, 1970.
Marichal, Juan. *A Pitcher's Story.* Garden City, NY: Doubleday, 1967.

MARIS, ROGER EUGENE (1934–1985)

Roger Maris was a good player who had a great season in 1961 and for the rest of his life regretted it. He hit 61 home runs that year, breaking Babe Ruth's record. The public and sportswriters, however, largely resented Maris's accomplishment, finding him unworthy of the record. Commissioner Ford Frick, once a ghostwriter for Ruth, declared that the record must include "some distinctive mark" to indicate that it had been broken in a 162-game schedule, eight more games than were played in Ruth's time.

Maris and friend and roommate Mickey Mantle were locked in a home-run duel for much of the season, before injuries stopped Mantle six home runs short of Ruth. The public much preferred that Mantle, perhaps the most popular player of his time, break the record if someone had to do it. Maris, however, had trouble handling media pressure and the inconstancy of fans. He took to chain-smoking, clumps of his hair fell out as the season progressed, and he became increasingly withdrawn.

Injuries hampered Maris in later years, and he never again approached his statistics of the 1961 season, although he played for Yankee pennant winners from 1960 to 1964 and finished his career helping the St. Louis Cardinals win the National League pennant in 1967 and 1968. Maris died in his fifties, still resentful of his treatment. In later years, the public and media became more sympathetic to Maris, believing that he had not been given his due. Millions of fans therefore were deeply moved and grateful when Mark McGwire, after hitting home run number 62 in 1998, went up into the stands to embrace Maris's children. It was as if Roger Maris was finally receiving the applause and respect he had long deserved.

See also: Cancer; Home Run; Mantle, Mickey Charles; McGwire, Mark David; New York Yankees; Records Set; Ruth, George Herman.
Additional Reading:
Allen, Maury. Roger Maris: A Man for All Seasons. New York: D. I. Fine, 1986.
Houk, Ralph. Season of Glory: The Amazing Saga of the 1961 New York Yankees. New York: Putnam's, 1988.
Maris, Roger. Roger Maris at Bat. New York: Duell, Sloan, and Pearce, 1962.

MATHEWSON, CHRISTOPHER (MATTY, BIG SIX) (1880–1925)

Christy Mathewson, star pitcher for the New York Giants from 1900 to 1916, was known as the "Christian gentleman" because of his impeccable behavior and high moral values. Matinee handsome with blond hair and blue eyes, a college man from Bucknell who was class president and a member of the school's literary society, and a consistently upright individual who married his school sweetheart and taught Sunday school, Mathewson became one of the most popular players ever to step onto a baseball field. Even the hard-bitten manager of the Giants, John McGraw, loved him like a son and insisted on protecting him from the bad influence of other players.

Mathewson wasted little time in establishing himself as one of baseball's greatest pitchers. By his first full season, he was a 20-game winner. He went on to win 373 games while losing just 188, pitch 434 complete games in 551 starts, post a career 2.13 ERA, strike out 2,502 batters, notch 13 20-win seasons (including four 30-win seasons, with 37 victories in 1908), and fashion 79 shutouts. He led the National League in wins four times, strikeouts five times, and earned-run average five times. In the 1905 World Series, he hurled three shutouts in six days.

Mathewson was a thinking man's pitcher, combining pinpoint control with a wide assortment of pitches, including his famous "fadeaway" pitch, actually a screwball. His book Pitching in a Pinch: Or, Baseball from the Inside (1912) attracted readers from both inside and outside baseball, including poet Marianne Moore. His ability to move readily through the opposing lineup earned him the nickname "Big Six" after New York's most famous fire engine.

Mathewson lent his fame and name to a series of uplifting baseball books for boys written by John Wheeler. There was a book for each position: Catcher Craig (1915), First Base Faulkner (1916), Pitcher Pollack (1914), Second Base Sloan (1917), and so forth. Such was the esteem in which the public held Mathewson that the pitcher has long been seen (erroneously) as the model for Burt Standish's series of books about the supermoral Yale athlete Frank Merriwell. Actually, Standish, whose real name was Gilbert Patten, published his first Merriwell book, Frank Merriwell's Baseball Victory, in 1889, long before the world came to know and love their Matty. At one point, Mathewson's wife felt she had to refute the notion that her husband was perfect, explaining that he had his faults, such as occasionally playing checkers for money.

Christy Mathewson's life took a tragic turn when he entered the service during World War I. Accidentally gassed, he returned home with his lungs ruined. Ever the epitome of rectitude, he accepted a request from sportswriter Hugh Fullerton to leave his sanitarium to watch the first game of the 1919 World Series in order to test the rumors that the Series was fixed. After a number of unusual plays, Matty and Fullerton agreed that the White Sox were not playing honestly.

Mathewson's death came in 1925, when he was just in his mid-forties. His old manager, fighting back tears, helped to carry Mathewson's coffin to his final resting place. The nation mourned the loss of one of its genuine heroes, and at the World Series the following day flags flew at half-staff, players wore black armbands, and a band played "Nearer My God to Thee."

See also: College Baseball; Disabilities; Fiction; Heroes; McGraw, John Joseph; War.

Additional Reading:

Mathewson, Christy. *Pitching in a Pinch: Or, Baseball from the Inside*. New York: Grosset and Dunlap, 1912.

Robinson, Ray. *Matty: An American Hero*. New York: Oxford University Press, 1993.

Schoor, Gene. *Christy Mathewson: Baseball's Greatest Pitcher*. New York: J. Messner, 1953.

MAYS, WILLIE HOWARD (SAY-HEY KID) (1931–)

Few people did more to demolish racial barriers than Willie Mays. He began in the Negro Leagues the year after Jackie Robinson first played for the Dodgers, arriving in New York with the Giants in 1951. A horrible start at bat threatened to destroy his confidence, but manager Leo Durocher assured him that he was in center field to stay. Mays came out of the slump and went on to be named Rookie

of the Year and help the Giants to a pennant. Fans sat up and took notice, not just at the ability—the power, the speed, the constant threat to steal a base or hit the ball over the fence—but at the joie de vivre that manifested itself both on and off the field. He loved to play baseball, and he made others love to watch him play—the basket catches on the run in center field, the cap flying off, the stolen bases, the home runs, the power and the glory of the game being played as perhaps no one had ever played it.

When Willie was not at the Polo Grounds, he was apt to be playing stickball in the streets of Harlem. New York took to him as the city had taken to few. A tour of military duty removed most of 1952 and all of 1953, but he returned with a bang, winning the Most Valuable Player Award. Mays led the National League in hitting in 1954 with a .345 average. He also hit 41 home runs, drove in 110 runners, and led the league with 13 triples as the Giants took the pennant and faced the Cleveland Indians, winners of an American League record 111 games, in the World Series. The Indians were expected to ride their great pitching staff to victory, but Mays turned things around in the eighth inning of the first game. With the score tied and two runners on base, Vic Wertz drove the ball deep to the outfield. Mays turned and raced backward, grabbing the drive with an over-the-shoulder catch, whirling, and firing the ball to the infield. That catch still stands as a contender for the best defensive play ever in World Series competition.

The years rolled on for Willie Mays, his accomplishments accumulating. He moved with the Giants to San Francisco in 1958 and remained with the club until 1972, when he returned to New York to conclude his career with the Mets in 1973. He finished with 660 home runs (third behind Aaron and Ruth), 1,903 RBIs, 3,283 hits, 338 stolen bases, and a .302 batting average. Four times Mays led his league in home runs and stolen bases, and three times he had the most triples. He hit 40 or more home runs in six seasons, twice going over 50, and drove in 100 or more runners 10 times. In 1961, he smashed four home runs in a single game. A second Most Valuable Player Award came along in 1965, and *The Sporting News* named Mays the greatest player of the 1960s.

Willie Mays remains enormously popular. He was a pioneer, one of the first African American superstars. He helped to demonstrate that baseball belongs to everyone, regardless of race, and he did so not just with statistics but by playing the game with enthusiasm and joy.

See also: African Americans; Durocher, Leo Ernest; Negro Leagues; Polo Grounds; World Series.

Additional Reading:

Einstein, Charles. *Willie's Time: A Memoir.* Philadelphia: Lippincott, 1979.

Epstein, Samuel. *Willie Mays: Baseball Superstar.* Champaign, IL: Garrard, 1975.

Hano, Arnold. *Willie Mays.* New York: Grosset and Dunlap, 1966.

Mays, Willie. *Born to Play Ball.* New York: Putnam's, 1955.

———. *Say Hey: The Autobiography of Willie Mays.* New York: Simon and Schuster, 1988.

MCGRAW, JOHN JOSEPH (MUGSY, LITTLE NAPOLEON) (1873–1934)

John McGraw was one of the most entertaining, competitive, feisty, complex, and contradictory managers to guide a major league team. He also may have been the best manager ever as he helped to make baseball a big part of modern New York.

McGraw played in the major leagues from 1891 until 1906, the last several as a player-manager. His greatest years as a player were as a shortstop and third baseman for the Baltimore Orioles. He hit .334 for his career and stole 436 bases. Determined to win no matter what it took, McGraw would bump runners to throw them off their stride, even grab the runner's belt. A fight that he got into during a 1894 game in Boston led to a general brawl that resulted in the ballpark and about 170 neighboring buildings burning to the ground. Umpires were seldom safe around McGraw, who would demonstrate his disdain for decisions that went against his team by spiking the umpire with accompanying language so offensive that he and his almost equally aggressive Oriole teammates caused the National League to approve the "Measure for the Suppression of Obscene, Indecent, and Vulgar Language upon the Ball Field."

Perhaps McGraw's aggressiveness resulted from his short stature—just five-foot seven. Or it may have had its roots in McGraw's difficult youth. John was the oldest of eight children. When his mother and four siblings died of diphtheria in 1884, his Irish immigrant father, who worked for the railroad, transferred his anger to John. Tired of being beaten, 16-year-old John ran away and joined the Olean, New York, baseball team.

When McGraw assumed the managerial role with the American League Orioles in 1901, his behavior did not change, and Ban Johnson, creator of the new league, suspended McGraw for his continued depredations on umpires. Johnson wanted a respectable league, with players and managers comporting themselves like gentlemen. McGraw clearly did not fit the mold, and he departed the league in midseason 1902 to become manager of the New York Giants. So thorough was his dislike for Johnson that McGraw, after winning the 1904 pennant, refused to let the Giants play the American League champion Boston Pilgrims.

With the Giants, McGraw came into his own as a manager. He guided the team for 30 years, winning 10 pennants (four pennants in a row, 1921–1924) and three World Series. He ruled his players with total power, referring to himself as an "absolute czar," yet he was consistently generous to his former players with money and jobs. Although he had no time for Ban Johnson's gentlemanly approach to baseball, his favorite player was pitcher Christy Mathewson, known as the "Christian gentleman" for his conduct on and off the field. Mathewson fought in World War I and inhaled poison gas, which permanently affected him. When Mathewson died of tuberculosis in 1925, a weeping McGraw was a pallbearer. As dedicated to winning as anyone who ever participated in a baseball contest, he also bet on games, winning $400 on his own victorious team in the 1905 World Series; at one time he owned a pool hall with Arnold Rothstein, often identified as the person responsible for fixing the 1919 World Series.

McGraw played and managed long before Jackie Robinson made his first major league appearance in 1947, but McGraw would have liked little better than to recruit an interracial team. He once tried to pass off a black player, Charlie Grant, as a Cherokee named Charlie Tokahoma in 1901, but his stratagem failed. After McGraw's death, his widow found a list he had made of black players he wanted to hire. His health deteriorating, McGraw retired in June 1932 and died two years later. His widow, attending the final game ever played in the Polo Grounds by the Giants in 1957, was asked what her husband would have thought of the team's imminent relocation to the West Coast. She replied that it "would have broken John's heart." The Giants' departure closed an era for the citizens of New

York that John McGraw had helped to open.

See also: Johnson, Byron Bancroft; Mathewson, Christopher; Native Americans; Polo Grounds.

Additional Reading:

Alexander, Charles C. *John McGraw.* New York: Viking, 1988.
Durso, Joseph. *The Days of Mr. McGraw.* Englewood Cliffs, NJ: Prentice-Hall, 1969.
McGraw, Blanche Sindall. *The Real McGraw.* New York: D. McKay, 1953.
McGraw, John Joseph. *My Thirty Years in Baseball.* New York: Boni and Liveright, 1923.
Pope, Edwin. *Baseball's Greatest Managers.* Garden City, NY: Doubleday, 1960.

MCGWIRE, MARK DAVID (1963–)

Baseball was still recovering from the 1994 player strike when the 1998 season began. One of the questions on fans' minds was whether Mark McGwire, who had hit 58 home runs the previous season (remarkable in that he split the season between Oakland and St. Louis), would break the home-run record of 61 held by Roger Maris. The slugger seemed primed to accomplish that feat after coming so close the year before. McGwire did not disappoint as both he and Sammy Sosa achieved baseball immortality and the adulation of the American public.

Slugging his way past Babe Ruth and Roger Maris would not be easy. McGwire reached the majors with the Oakland Athletics near the end of the 1986 season and remained there until July 31, 1997, when he was traded to the St. Louis Cardinals. McGwire early on seemed destined for greatness, winning the Rookie of the Year Award in 1987, when he slugged 49 home runs. He teamed with Jose Canseco to form one of the most feared slugging duos in the game, and the "Bash Brothers" helped Oakland win three pennants and one World Series between 1988 and 1990. Yet McGwire's performance at the plate after his rookie

Mark McGwire, No. 25 of the St. Louis Cardinals, hits his thirty-eighth home run of the season during the eleventh inning of a game against the Houston Astros at Busch Stadium in St. Louis, Missouri, July 11, 1998. The Cardinals defeated the Astros 4-3. (Stephen Dunn/Allsport)

season was not as stellar, reflected in declining batting averages; McGwire hit bottom in 1991 with a .201 average and only 22 home runs. It looked as if McGwire would not pay off on his promising rookie season.

But the 1991 off-season became a turning point for the Oakland first baseman. He embarked upon a regimen of weight lifting and began counseling sessions, efforts that ultimately would produce a healthy body and a healthy mind. It would take time, though, as McGwire fought a series of injuries that limited him to 27, 47, 104, and 130 games from 1993 through 1996. Despite the lengthy stints on the disabled list, McGwire had truly blossomed as a power hitter. He connected for 52 home runs with 113 RBIs and a .312 batting average in 1996. Long a fine defensive first baseman and an intelligent student of the game, McGwire was becoming a complete player.

McGwire made the transition to the National League during the 1997 season, hitting a combined total of 58 home runs for two teams. For the first time in years, he was able to play almost every day, appearing in 156 games. And he had won over the hearts of the St. Louis fans by signing a three-year contract, rejecting the opportunity to become a free agent and cash in. His contract even included a provision whereby he would donate $1 million per year to his new charitable foundation to assist children who had been physically or sexually abused. The stage was set for his record performance.

McGwire began the 1998 season by hitting home runs at a furious pace, and he never slowed up. He left many home-run hitters, including Ken Griffey Jr., far behind; and as the season rolled along, only Sammy Sosa could keep pace. The two men developed true mutual admiration, inspiring the nation with their displays of sportsmanship.

The Cardinals were at home against the Cubs for the Cardinals' 145th game. Sosa was in right field, McGwire was at bat, and fans at the ballpark and the millions watching on television were ready. McGwire swung and golfed the ball toward left field. The ball barely made it over the fence; the home run, ironically, was the shortest one that McGwire had hit all year—just 341 feet. But it was number 62, breaking the record set by Roger Maris in 1961.

Fans loved it. McGwire was jubilant, almost forgetting to touch first base in his excitement. He seemed to hug everyone as he made his way around the bases. After touching home plate, he waved and blew kisses. Sammy Sosa raced in from right field to embrace him. McGwire hoisted his son, Matt, into the air. He jumped into the stands to embrace the children of the late Roger Maris—a move that left countless onlookers with tears. It was as if Roger Maris, so resented by the Babe Ruth–loving baseball world when he was gunning for the record, was finally receiving the love and admiration he had long deserved. In his comments, McGwire also thanked his former wife and her husband. This muscular, truly Ruthian figure, this baseball giant, cried and thanked and hugged and virtually burst with excitement. The public, so tired of the downbeat, the sullen, the ungrateful, readily accepted him as a national hero.

McGwire and Sosa made the 1998 baseball season one for the ages, McGwire finishing with the extraordinary total of 70 home runs, Sosa with 66—but they did not stop there. The following year saw another home-run contest between the two. It lacked much of the suspense of the previous season, but it clearly demonstrated that both men were there to stay. Again both sluggers surpassed 60 home runs: McGwire finished with 65, Sosa with 63.

As the 1999 season neared its end, McGwire was first among any major league player in history in frequency of home runs, that is, he slammed one out of the park in just over 9 percent of his at-bats. Babe Ruth is second on that list, homering in approximately 8.5 percent of his trips to the plate; Ralph Kiner is a distant third at 7.1 percent.

Prior to the 1999 All-Star Game, the top 30 players of the century were introduced; Mark McGwire was among them. He had overcome years of injuries and on-field and off-field struggles to reach the highest level of baseball greatness. He did so while becoming one of the most loved and respected men ever to play the game. He helped make it fashionable to talk once again about heroes.

See also: College Baseball; Heroes; Home Run; Maris, Roger Eugene; Sosa, Samuel Peralta.
Additional Reading:
Hall, Jonathan. *Mark McGwire: A Biography*. New York: Pocket Books, 1998.
Miklasz, Bernie, et al. *Celebrating 70: Mark McGwire's Historic Season*. St. Louis: Sporting News, 1998.
Noden, Merrell. *Home Run Heroes: Mark McGwire, Sammy Sosa, and a Season for the Ages*. New York: Simon and Schuster, 1998.
Rains, Rob. *Mark McGwire: Home Run Hero*. New York: St. Martin's, 1998.
Schreiber, Lee R. *Race for the Record: The Great Home Run Chase of 1998*. New York: HarperCollins, 1998.

MCLAIN, DENNIS DALE (DENNY) (1944–)

Denny McLain achieved international fame by reaching a goal that many thought unattainable—30 victories in a season. Not since Dizzy Dean won 30 for the St. Louis Cardinals in 1934 had a pitcher reached that mark, and no one has done it since McLain. Yet in 1968, the 24-year-old McLain won 31 games for the World Series–champion Detroit Tigers, earning the Cy Young and Most Valuable Player Awards. Capitalizing on his fame, McLain took to performing on the organ in Hollywood and Las Vegas, recording the albums *Denny McLain at the Organ* (1968) and *Denny McLain in Las Vegas* (1969).

McLain followed that extraordinary season with a 24-9 record in 1969 and shared the Cy Young Award with Baltimore's Mike Cuellar. At the age of 25, McLain had won 114 games, 108 in the past five years. Baseball immortality and the Hall of Fame loomed on the horizon—but troubles with the law would cut those dreams short.

McLain was suspended for much of 1970 for allegedly drenching sportswriters with water, threatening a parking-lot attendant, carrying a gun onto a plane, and becoming involved in bookmaking operations. Passing quickly through Washington, Oakland, and Atlanta, he was out of baseball within three years, posting only 17 additional victories after receiving his second Cy Young Award. McLain was convicted of bookmaking, extortion, loan-sharking, and possession of cocaine in 1985, serving 29 months before the verdict was overturned. In 1996, he was convicted, with co-owner Roger Smigiel of the Peet Packing Company, of stealing $2.5 million from pension funds. A later and separate charge—of participating in phone-card fraud—finally was dropped. Denny McLain had transformed himself from baseball's brightest star into a morality play, with erstwhile fans hoping for a happy ending.

See also: Dean, Jay Hanna; Law; Music.
Additional Reading:
Anderson, William M. *The Detroit Tigers: A Pictorial Celebration of the Greatest Players and Moments in Tigers' History*. South Bend, IN: Diamond, 1991.
Cantor, George. *The Tigers of '68: Baseball's Last Real Champions*. Dallas: Taylor, 1997.
Falls, Joe. *The Detroit Tigers: An Illustrated History*. New York: Walker, 1989.

McLain, Denny, with Dave Diles. *Nobody's Perfect*. New York: Dial, 1975.

Sullivan, George. *Detroit Tigers: The Complete Record of Detroit Tigers Baseball*. New York: Collier, 1985.

MEN'S SENIOR BASEBALL LEAGUE/ MEN'S ADULT BASEBALL LEAGUE

The dream of eternal youth remains alive in the United States, especially in baseball thanks in part to the Men's Senior Baseball League (MSBL). Men aged 30 and up are welcome, regardless of skill level, to join the MSBL for organized competition (usually one game per week), including regional tournaments and a World Series.

Steve Sigler founded MSBL, which started play in 1986. Sigler was managing his sons' Little League team when he decided to recruit other fathers who would like to play baseball. He began with four teams; a newspaper notice led to 17 teams in 1987. An article the following year in *Sports Illustrated* swamped Sigler with expressions of interest. By 1999, the numbers had risen to about 3,000 teams and 40,000 members throughout the country.

The MSBL now includes three divisions: 30 and over, 40 and over, and 50 and over. In addition, there is a parallel organization for younger men 18 and over, the Men's Adult Baseball League. Participants may find themselves playing with or against former major-leaguers. Current or past MSBL players include Jim Barr, Orlando Cepeda, Bert Campaneris, Bill Lee, and Jim Willoughby. These adult leagues, along with fantasy camps and visits to the Field of Dreams in Iowa, demonstrate that dreams can stay with people past their youth.

See also: Fantasy Camps.

Additional Reading:

Men's Senior Baseball League [also Men's Adult Baseball League] official website: http://www.msbl.com/msbl

MSBL/MABL website: http://www.msblnational.com

Wortman, Marc. "Diamonds Are Forever: Once a Game Only for the Boys of Summer, Amateur Baseball Leagues Are Now Filled with Thousands of Men Over 30." September/October 1998. *Cigar Aficionado* website: http://www.cigaraficionado.com/Cigar/Aficionado/Archives/199810/fh1098.html

MERKLE BONER

Virtually everyone wishes to be remembered for their accomplishments rather than failures. Fred Merkle had a different fate.

Near the end of the 1908 season, John McGraw's New York Giants and the Chicago Cubs were locked in a fierce pennant race. Merkle, a mere 19 years old, was playing instead of the Giants' regular first baseman. It was the bottom of the ninth at the Polo Grounds, with the game tied 2-2; the Giants threatened with Moose McCormick on third and Merkle on first. Al Bridwell stroked a single, McCormick scoring what appeared to be the winning run. Jubilant fans rushed onto the field, and the young Merkle, halfway to second, seeing McCormick scoring and fans racing toward him, turned and sprinted for the clubhouse. The Cubs' great second baseman, Johnny Evers, however, had kept his wits about him and pursued the ball to force Merkle at second, a task not easily accomplished because third-base coach Joe McGinnity grabbed the ball and heaved it into the stands. Two Cubs caught up with the fan who had captured the baseball, retrieved it, and threw it to Evers, who tagged second.

The game was declared a tie, and the two teams finished in a dead heat, setting up a one-game playoff, which the Cubs won. McGraw never blamed Merkle, but the public did. Merkle played 16 seasons, hitting a respectable .273, but what the public forever remembered was his "bonehead" play that cost the Giants the 1908 pennant.

See also: McGraw, John Joseph; Tinker to Evers to Chance.

Additional Reading:

Anderson, David W. More than Merkle: A History of the Best and Most Exciting Baseball Season in Human History. Lincoln: University of Nebraska Press, 2000.

McGraw, John Joseph. My Thirty Years in Baseball. New York: Boni and Liveright, 1923.

Seymour, Harold. Baseball: The Golden Age. 1971. Reprint, New York: Oxford University Press, 1989.

Ward, Geoffrey C., and Ken Burns. Baseball: An Illustrated History. New York: Alfred A. Knopf, 1994.

MILLER, MARVIN JAMES (1917–)

Marvin Miller was executive director of the Major League Baseball Players Association (MLBPA) from 1966 through 1982. Under his leadership, the MLBPA went from a fraternal organization to one of the strongest unions in the United States, the first time that major league players had succeeded in unionizing. Under Miller's leadership, the MLBPA succeeded in ending the reserve system as it had existed, elevating the average salary of players from $19,000 to $240,000, and earning players large opportunities in licensing fees.

Miller came to baseball from the Steelworkers Union, where he was chief economist. He wasted no time in attempting to achieve for major league players what unions had earned for workers in many other American industries, and negotiating victories came regularly if not always easily. Major league owners agreed in 1968 to engage in collective bargaining and in 1970 accepted arbitration for contract grievances. A 1972 strike led to 86 games being canceled, and a 50-day strike occurred in 1981. The price was worth it for players, who had received only one increase in their minimum salary during the 20 years preceding Miller's arrival—from $5,000 to $6,000.

Miller's greatest achievement was defeat of the reserve clause in 1975 as Andy Messersmith and Dave McNally used previously agreed to binding arbitration to gain free agency. Also important, however, was the MLBPA's acceptance of a compromise reserve system whereby major league clubs could reserve players for six years, the result of Miller's astute observation that unlimited free agency would create an oversupply of free agents, depressing salaries. Instead, Miller agreed to a system that would control the number of free agents in any one year, thereby increasing demand and elevating salaries. Many wealthy players are much indebted to Marvin Miller.

See also: Antitrust Exemption; Business; Commissioner; Flood, Curtis Charles; Free Agency; Hunter, James Augustus; Kuhn, Bowie K.; Labor-Management Relations; Law; Reserve Clause.

Additional Reading:

Abrams, Roger I. Legal Bases: Baseball and the Law. Philadelphia: Temple University Press, 1998.

Dworkin, James B. Owners Versus Players: Baseball and Collective Bargaining. Dover: Auburn House, 1981.

Lowenfish, Lee. The Imperfect Diamond: A History of Baseball's Labor Wars. Rev. ed. New York: Da Capo, 1991.

Miller, Marvin. A Whole Different Ball Game: The Sport and Business of Baseball. Secaucus, NJ: Carol, 1991.

MINOR LEAGUES

The minor leagues play an interesting role in American society despite a perceived second-class status. Most players in the minors aspire to be elsewhere, namely, in the major leagues. The media, except for local television stations and newspapers, largely ignore the minors. Yet minor league attendance exceeded 35 million in 1998. Attending a local game is a delightful outing for families—inexpensive entertainment in the sunshine with enjoyable food and a variety of special events, often utilizing local amateur talent. Many minor league games are interactive: costumed mascots drawing children into comedy routines; fans, often young ones, brought onto the field to participate in a race around the bases or to throw a baseball at a target; and the players readily available to sign autographs and have their pictures taken.

Minor league baseball historically is as American as drive-in movies and Fourth of July parades. It is still small-town U.S.A., in feel if not in fact. And like those small towns scattered around the country, it also is patriotic America. The person leading the singing of "The Star-Spangled Banner" is apt to be someone a lot of people in the stands know, and a Fourth of July game is likely to be followed by a grand fireworks display. Going to a minor league game is like stepping into the past, to a time of simplicity and innocence.

The minor leagues originally established teams far distant from major league clubs, which were located in the Northeast and Midwest until the late 1950s. But even in those areas, major league clubs by necessity were confined to large urban areas well beyond the reach of most communities. Before television, most people who wanted to see a professional ball game had only one avenue open to them: minor league contests.

Organized, professional minor leagues began to develop around 1880 in the Northeast but spread geographically far faster than did the major leagues. By 1890, minor leagues had spread throughout most of the country, including the Midwest, South, Northwest, and California. Presidents of seven minor leagues formed a National Association of Professional Baseball Leagues in 1901 to bring order and direction in such areas as classifications, salaries, and a draft system. In 1903, the National Association entered into the so-called National Agreement with the two major leagues to formalize relationships between the majors and minors, especially regarding ownership of player rights.

The concept of the farm team originated in the 1880s, although most minor league teams remained independent of major league clubs for several decades. By 1912, an occasional minor league team was owned by a major league club, but the modern farm system was unknown until 1921, when Branch Rickey started building one with the St. Louis Cardinals. Rickey saw a system of minor league teams (either owned or under contract to a major league club and operating at different classification levels) as a way to sign and develop prospects. Those players who were not needed could be sold to other organizations. By 1936, the Cardinals had a system of 28 minor league teams; the Reds had 16, but only two other organizations had more than nine. The wealth of talent developed in Rickey's farm system produced five pennants from 1926 to 1934.

Many other big league organizations later followed the Cardinals' example and built elaborate farm networks. After a downturn during World War II when most young men were fighting the war and were unavailable for baseball, the farm systems came back strong. However, the majors started to reduce the number of farm teams in the late 1940s to cut expenses, resulting in increased numbers of teams not affiliated with major league clubs. By 1950, that unaffiliated category included 232 teams. Many teams therefore were largely outside the player-development process, although they offered fans the chance to see talented veteran players considered too old or too one-dimensional to be considered major league prospects.

Unfortunately, the era of the independent team virtually vanished by 1960. For the next few decades, minor league ball was primarily developmental, with no room for nonprospects who in earlier years had entertained fans with talented play. By 1969, some major league organizations operated as few as four farm teams; the standard had risen to at least six in each organization by the end of the 1990s.

A sudden explosion of interest in minor league ball occurred in the 1980s. Attendance, which had been below 11 million through most of the 1970s, jumped to 20 million in 1987 and reached 35 million 10 years later. Independent leagues also staged a comeback. The Northern League began operation in 1994 and benefited from both the general upsurge of interest in minor league ball and the 1994 big league strike. The Northern League featured teams in the upper Midwest and Canada, including the St. Paul Saints. Mike Veeck, before moving to Tampa Bay in the American League (later resigning because of his daughter's health problems), ran the St. Paul club. Learning the art of promotion from his father, Bill Veeck, who had owned three major league clubs during his career, the son put on special events, including Irish Night, with green players' caps and bases; Kitchen Appliance Night; and Mary Tyler Moore Appreciation Night. It was the Duluth-Superior Dukes, though, that featured the first woman to start a game in professional baseball (Ila Borders, in 1998). Veterans, hoping to continue playing the game they loved and longing for one last shot at the big time, played next to youngsters otherwise overlooked by organized baseball. One of the more famous players in the league was J. D. Drew; drafted but

unsigned by the Philadelphia Phillies, he continued to stay sharp with St. Paul until signing with the St. Louis Cardinals. After the 1998 season, the Northern League merged with the Northeast League.

Several other independent leagues have surfaced in recent years. Their success varies, but the independent league movement seems healthy overall. In 1998, for example, a new Atlantic League began play. Its approach involved hiring former major league stars (Sparky Lyle, Willie Upshaw) as managers and attracting a lot of former major-leaguers by paying high salaries. Bridgeport won the first pennant playing against teams like Nashua, Newark, and Atlantic City. Eleven Atlantic League players were signed by the majors after that inaugural season. Although the independent leagues by definition are not part of the major leagues' developmental system, the majors keep a close eye out for players who might help at the big league level. At the same time, these leagues, along with the rest of minor league baseball, continue to help fans stay in touch with the professional game and with a flavor of the small-town past that is an important part of the history and psyche of America.

See also: Brooklyn Dodgers; Expansion; Major Leagues; Rickey, Wesley Branch; Rural America; Women in Baseball.

Additional Reading:

Fatsis, Stefan. *Wild and Outside: How a Renegade Minor League Revived the Spirit of Baseball in America's Heartland.* 1995. Reprint, New York: Walker, 1996.

French, Robert. *50 Golden Years in the American Association of Professional Baseball Clubs, 1902–1951.* Minneapolis: Syndicate Printing, 1951.

Hoie, Bob. "The Minor Leagues." In *Total Baseball.* 6th ed. Ed. John Thorn et al. New York: Total Sports, 1999, pp. 510–526.

Obojski, Robert. *Bush League.* New York: Macmillan, 1975.

Sullivan, Neil J. *The Minors: The Struggles and the Triumph of Baseball's Poor Relation from*

1876 to the Present. New York: St. Martin's Press, 1990.

MURDERER'S ROW

The name "Murderer's Row" conjures up images of the St. Valentine's Day Massacre, shootouts between gangsters and police, and most-wanted posters. It actually refers, however, to a group of five men wearing Yankee pinstripes, not the stripes of prison garb.

In 1927, Babe Ruth hit 60 home runs, the fourth time in five years he had set a new mark for homers. He also batted .356 and drove in 164 runs. First baseman Lou Gehrig hit .373, drove in 175 runs, and hit 47 home runs, the most ever by anyone other than the Babe. Left fielder Bob Meusel batted a career-high .337, drove in 103 runs, and collected 47 doubles and nine triples to go with his eight home runs. Center fielder Earle Combs batted .356; he had only six home runs and 64 RBIs but led the league with 23 triples. Second baseman Tony Lazzeri hit .309, connected for 18 home runs, and batted in 102 runs.

This squad of outstanding hitters, along with a strong pitching corps featuring Waite Hoyt, Herb Pennock, Wilcy Moore, and Urban Shocker, carried the Yankees to 110 regular-season wins and a four-game sweep of the Pirates in the World Series. In the many years since then, no team (including the 1998 Yankees, who won a total of 125 games) has convincingly shoved aside these 1927 Yankees, featuring Murderer's Row, as the greatest team in the history of major league baseball.

See also: Gehrig, Henry Louis; New York Yankees; Ruth, George Herman.
Additional Reading:
Anderson, Dave. *The Yankees: The Four Fabulous Eras of Baseball's Most Famous Team.* New York: Random House, 1979.
Henrich, Tommy. *Five O'Clock Lightning: Ruth, Gehrig, DiMaggio, Mantle, and the Glory Years of the New York Yankees.* New York: Carol, 1992.
Honig, Donald. *Baseball America: The Heroes of the Game and the Times of Their Glory.* New York: Barnes and Noble, 1997.
Meany, Thomas. *The Yankee Story.* New York: Dutton, 1960.
Robertson, John G. *The Babe Chases 60: That Fabulous 1927 Season, Home Run by Home Run.* Jefferson, NC: McFarland, 1999.

MUSIAL, STANLEY FRANK (STAN THE MAN) (1920–)

"The Man," for some 50 years, has been Stan Musial. The nickname reflects Musial's position as probably the finest hitter of his era in the National League and an individual almost universally respected and admired. Musial achieved this stature through his accomplishments both on and off the field. That he retains his popularity long after the last of his 3,630 hits is evidenced by two awards in 1999: the SABR Hero of Baseball Award, given to Musial by the Society for American Baseball Research for excellence as a player and as a person; and the Missouri Sports Legends Award, from the Missouri Sports Hall of Fame in Springfield, located, appropriately enough, on Stan Musial Drive.

Stan Musial began his professional career as a pitcher and, after going 18-5 in 1940, appeared headed for a long career on the mound. An injury to his pitching arm, though, led to his conversion to full-time outfielder, and it was in that role that he donned a Cardinals' uniform in 1941. He wore it with skill and grace through the 1963 season (except for 1945, when he traded it for a U.S. Navy uniform), finishing with 475 home runs, 1,951 RBIs, a .331 batting average, 725 doubles, 177 triples, and 3,630 total hits. A model of consistency, Musial accumulated the exact same number of hits at home as away—1,815.

Musial's dominance is reflected in the many times that he led the National

Stan Musial of the St. Louis Cardinals swinging the bat during a baseball game, 1950s. Musial was inducted into the Baseball Hall of Fame in 1969. (Archive Photos)

League in a variety of categories: seven times in batting, five times in runs scored, six times in total hits, eight times in doubles, five times in triples, twice in runs batted in. He never won a home-run title, hitting a career-high 39 in 1948, his greatest season. That year he topped the league with 135 runs, 230 hits, 46 doubles, 18 triples, 131 RBIs, and a .376 batting average. Early in his career, he was primarily a line-drive hitter, collecting large numbers of doubles and triples, before developing home-run power.

Musial accumulated three Most Valuable Player Awards. A perennial All-Star, he won the 1955 game with a home run in the twelfth inning, one of the most dramatic moments in All-Star history. At the age of 41, in 1962, he was still able to hit .330. When he retired, he held about 50 major league or National League records, although many have since been broken. The Hall of Fame at Cooperstown extended its invitation in 1969, shortly after a statue of Musial was erected outside Busch Stadium in St. Louis.

The memory that many have of Stan Musial is the famous Musial crouch as he waited at the plate for a pitch. He would curl his body like a spring ready to be released, his bat back and straight up, his face seeming to peek around a corner. Then he would uncurl as the pitch approached. A unique stance that almost no one could imitate successfully, it worked remarkably well for The Man. But fans, especially those who met Musial in person, also remember him as consistently affable, friendly to virtually everyone; he was willing to help where he could, such as serving on the President's Council on Physical Fitness and Sports. Stan Musial came far for the son of a Polish immigrant miner, achieving much, and he gave back a great deal.

Additional Reading:

Broeg, Bob. *Bob Broeg's Redbirds: A Century of Cardinals' Baseball*. Rev. ed. Marceline, MO: Walsworth, 1992.

Musial, Stan. *Stan Musial: "The Man's" Own Story, as Told to Bob Broeg*. Garden City, NY: Doubleday, 1964.

Musial, Stan, Jack Buck, and Bob Broeg. *We Saw Stars*. St. Louis: Bethany, 1976.

Robinson, Ray. *Stan Musial: Baseball's Durable "Man."* New York: Putnam's, 1963.

MUSIC

Music has been part of baseball since the sport's earliest days of organized recreation. When people like something, they compose songs about it. The most famous songs that relate to baseball, of course, are the national anthem, "The Star-Spangled Banner," now sung at each game, and the sport's unofficial anthem, "Take Me Out to the Ball Game." Both of these songs are discussed in separate entries elsewhere in this book, so attention here will be given to other baseball music.

The first piece of baseball music published may have been "The Base Ball Polka" in 1858 (this was before the advent of sound recording, when music was published in sheet form). The song was composed by J. Randolph Blodgett, a member of the Niagara Base Ball Club. By 1869, music was sufficiently part of baseball that the unbeaten Cincinnati Red Stockings would line up and sing their theme song prior to each game. As strange as that may seem today, until the advent of radio and television, people routinely sang for entertainment, and a gathering around the piano in the evening was a popular family activity.

In the African American community, baseball and jazz went hand in glove, both important parts of black culture; and players and musicians, especially in Kansas City, an important center for jazz in the 1920s and 1930s, frequented each other's places of entertainment. In addition, bands often performed at ballparks prior to World War II, yielding in the 1940s to individual, and cheaper, organists. Gradually, electronic music over the public-address system came to replace live music, although having an individual sing "The Star-Spangled Banner" remains popular to this day, often one of many family-oriented attractions featuring local talent at minor league contests.

Baseball stars have inspired many songs, a connection between song and heroism going back far into tradition. As music technology evolved from sheet music to cylinders, 78-rpm records, albums, 45s, tapes, and compact discs, the heroic subjects also progressed: King Kelly (for whom the first baseball hit, "Slide, Kelly, Slide," was repeatedly sung), Ty Cobb, Babe Ruth, Joe DiMaggio (most famously "Joltin' Joe DiMaggio," about the 1941 hitting streak), Jackie Robinson, Mickey Mantle, Willie Mays, Fernando Valenzuela, and many more.

Baseball players themselves have not been shy about offering to the public their all-too-often limited vocal and instrumental talents. In earlier decades, players often went on the vaudeville stage to earn some off-season money and applause. In more recent years, they have resorted to issuing recordings of their performances. The list of such players is almost endless, but a few have demonstrated genuine talent. Lee Maye, an outfielder with the Milwaukee Braves and several other clubs between 1959 and 1971, has had a long and successful career as a singer. Jack McDowell, winner of the Cy Young Award with the Chicago White Sox in 1993, is lead singer and guitarist of an accomplished rock band, Stick Figure. Denny McLain was a reasonably talented organist in the late 1960s, capitalizing on his 31-win performance in 1968 by playing in Hollywood and Las Vegas and releasing albums of nonbaseball songs. Willie Stargell probably deserves a prize for song selection, repeatedly playing another nonbaseball song, "We Are Family," by Sister Sledge, which became a motivating force for the Pittsburgh Pirates as they drove to the 1979 world championship.

Other musical highlights relating to baseball include the very successful musical *Damn Yankees* (discussed elsewhere in this book), and the top recording stars who occasionally have ventured into the world of baseball. Frank Sinatra, for example, recorded the ballad "There Used to be a Ballpark," a nostalgic reminder of lost innocence; Peter, Paul, and Mary offered the story of a not-very-talented youngster consigned to "Right Field"; and John Fogarty gave the world one of the finest baseball songs ever recorded, "Centerfield," which universalizes the desire to enter a game into the broader willingness to reenter life after hiding from it.

See also: Damn Yankees; DiMaggio, Joseph Paul; Heroes; Kelly, Michael Joseph; Mantle, Mickey Charles; McLain, Dennis Dale; Robinson, Jack Roosevelt; "The Star-Spangled Banner"; "Take Me Out to the Ball Game."
Additional Reading/Listening:
Baseball's Greatest Hits. Compact Disc. Rhino, 1989.

Baseball's Greatest Hits: Let's Play II. Compact Disc. Rhino, 1990.
Mote, James. *Everything Baseball.* New York: Prentice Hall, 1989.
Pietrusza, David, Lloyd Johnson, and Bob Carroll. *The Total Baseball Catalog.* New York: Total Sports, 1998.
Play Ball! Compact Disc. Telarc, 1998.

MYTH

Myth admits many definitions, some positive, some pejorative. Myth, for example, may be synonymous with lies or false beliefs, drawing an opposition between myth and truth. Yet even those who occasionally use the term in negative ways are likely to accept that myth also has important meanings that tell us much about ourselves as well as about other cultures.

Myth usually exists in the form of a narrative, a story. It tends to exist in partnership with other related stories, sometimes grouped around a particular portion of the world and time, as in Greek mythology. Myths often relate the actions of supernatural beings and seek to explain how certain phenomena relating to the natural world and humankind originated, as in the Old English epic *Beowulf*. Myth is viewed by most people in the modern world as essentially fictional, contrasted with history, science, and (for believers) theology. Myth often is viewed as other people's religions, especially the religions of primitive peoples. Within a religious framework especially, but not exclusively, myth is acted out in repetitive actions known as rituals. However, anthropologists, cultural historians, psychologists, and students of literature, among others, are likely to find, even in the fictive nature of myth, much that is "real" or "true," much that helps to explain who we are and why we are as we are.

Baseball has long been viewed as the national pastime, and even as it gradually yields some of its primacy in popularity to other sports such as football and basketball, it remains the most American of sports. This unique position of baseball owes a great deal to its long history within the United States, but baseball also encapsulates certain myths that are at the heart of who Americans are. Indeed, certain myths inherent within baseball transcend national and temporal boundaries to reflect universal narratives of self, that is, myths reflecting human values and aspirations throughout time.

The late Bart Giamatti, former baseball commissioner, deserves considerable credit for popularizing (although not inventing) the mythic nature of the sport. In various speeches and writings, especially in his posthumously published book *Take Time for Paradise,* Giamatti explored certain myths, calling upon both his knowledge of the game and his background as a Renaissance scholar whose academic research had involved myths reflecting such archetypal themes as the existence of a Golden Age and the attempt to return home.

What are some of these myths that Giamatti and others have discovered within baseball? Certainly one is the search for a Golden Age, or paradise, or heaven, or an earthly Utopia. It is the search for a perfect, or nearly perfect, society, or the belief that such a perfect state once existed or may exist sometime in the future. Giamatti points out in *The Earthly Paradise and the Renaissance Epic* that this perfect place has always been imagined as a garden—as a rural setting—never urban.

The baseball field is essentially rural; even within large cities it is a rural oasis in the middle of a concrete-and-steel stadium. But since paradise is perhaps even more a state of mind than a physical locale, the baseball field also is the locus for a psychic return to an earlier time, which helps to explain why change is so difficult for many fans. Baseball calls to mind earlier times, including one's youth, when paradise seemed quite possible, for example, lands to the West, a future where dreams come true.

Baseball, like all efforts to capture a Golden Age, is the search for perfection. There is, of course, a perfect symmetry, a geometric perfection, in the interrelationships among squares (or diamonds) and circles (long a symbol of perfection) that one needs only to gaze at in order to appreciate. Then there is the exalted status given the perfect game, when the pitcher retires each of the 27 batters that he faces; or hitting for the cycle—a single, double, triple, and home run in the same game—a complete, perfect performance that transcends numbers.

Another eternal myth is the return home, that which Odysseus struggled so hard to do, and which the novelist Thomas Wolfe averred cannot be done. Nonetheless, in every game, the goal is to do just that—to return home, again and again. Certainly, calling that goal "home plate" is not an inconsequential act of naming but part of the archetypal truth that baseball captures, that humans desire to return to their roots, to their home, to their parents. Seeking the father is part of this mythology, and part of the experience of baseball. How thoroughly the parent-child relationship is part of the game can be attested to by those millions of fans throughout the years who have sought to repeat with their children their own experiences of attending games (and playing catch) with their fathers (and, in some cases, with their mothers). Seeking one's parent and home transcends the earthly family and home and helps to explain why baseball shares with religion such a heavy reliance on ritual and myth. Baseball also reflects many additional myths, but space does not permit examining them here. Readers, however, can find at least some of those myths by visiting their favorite ballpark and gazing carefully both at the game and themselves.

Baseball is inextricably bound up with the past, and all of the talk by baseball owners and executives about progress cannot erase that condition. Baseball, embodying the mythic attempt to regain certain things (one's home, a perfect state, one's parent) and permeated by a philosophy of primitivism (the belief that people and society were morally better in an earlier state) is at heart antithetical to the idea of progress. In fact, progress itself is another myth, a narrative projected into the future, outlining continued improvement. The contrast between primitivism and progress is one of the great moral and intellectual contrasts of history: an ongoing engine of change and reaction to change affecting religion, society, technology, and virtually every other dimension of human life. One of the great challenges to the lords of baseball is to find a way to prevent baseball from being squeezed to death within that opposition. Myth versus myth can be as damaging as any battle between the gods of antiquity. Baseball, if it is to remain America's national pastime, must be able to face a changing world while safeguarding its timeless myths.

See also: Black Sox Scandal; Fiction; Films; Giamatti, Angelo Bartlett; Religion; Ritual; Rural America.
Additional Reading:
Candelaria, Cordelia. *Seeking the Perfect Game: Baseball in American Literature.* New York: Greenwood Press, 1989.
Doty, William. G. *Mythography: The Study of Myths and Rituals.* 2d ed. Tuscaloosa: University of Alabama Press, 2000.
Giamatti, A. Bartlett. *The Earthly Paradise and the Renaissance Epic.* Princeton: Princeton University Press, 1966.
———. *Take Time for Paradise: Americans and Their Games.* New York: Summit Books, 1989.
Westbrook, Deeanne. *Ground Rules: Baseball and Myth.* Urbana: University of Illinois Press, 1996.

NATIVE AMERICANS

Native Americans have contributed greatly to baseball, popular culture, and American society. The ban on African Americans in organized baseball did not extend to Native Americans—but racism did. The difference in treatment is reflected in John McGraw's attempt to get a black player, Charlie Grant, onto his team by passing him off as a Native American; at the same time, the general attitude toward Native Americans, essentially condescending and demeaning, is reflected in McGraw's choice of a fictitious name for Grant—Charlie Tokahoma, a play on "stroke a homer."

Stereotyping was as much the rule in depicting the Native American in baseball as in the Western dime novel and later Hollywood films. The Native American ballplayer was usually billed as a tribal chief, betraying a woeful lack of sensitivity and understanding. Charles Albert Bender, the Hall of Fame Chippewa pitcher for Connie Mack's Athletics, was "Chief" Bender; John Meyers, a Cahuilla and catcher for McGraw's Giants, was "Chief" Meyers; George Johnson, a Winnebago who pitched in both the National and Federal Leagues, was "Chief" Johnson; Allie Reynolds, a clutch hurler with the Yankees in the 1940s and 1950s, was Allie "Big Chief" Reynolds; and Louis Sockalexis, the enormously talented and tragic outfielder with the Cleveland Spiders at the end of the nineteenth century, was publicized as a descendant of Sitting Bull, although Sitting Bull was a Hunkpapa Sioux who lived half a nation away from Sockalexis's Penobscots in Maine.

Of all Native Americans who played baseball, Bender had the greatest career. Although he was a 20-game winner only twice, he recorded 212 victories against just 127 defeats, three times posting the best winning percentage in the American League. His lifetime earned-run average was an outstanding 2.46. Meyers was McGraw's regular catcher for half a dozen years, hitting .332, .358, and .312 from 1911 through 1913. His lifetime average for nine seasons was .291. Meyers was interviewed by Lawrence Ritter for the classic book on early stars, *The Glory of Their Times,* where he expressed great admiration for McGraw, who, despite the insensitive choice of a fictitious name for Grant, was far ahead of his time in his attitude toward Native Americans and African Americans. George Johnson already was 27 when he joined Cincinnati in 1913, winning 14 games that first season. He then jumped to the Federal League and won 17 games for Kansas City in 1915, the final year of that league's existence. Allie Reynolds joined New York from Cleveland in 1947 and helped the Yankees continue their run of championships. He retired with a bad back after the 1954 season, having won 182 games and lost just 107, including a 20-8 mark in 1952 with a league-low 2.06 ERA.

Many other men of complete or partial Native American heritage have played in the major leagues, but the most famous of all Native American baseball players, although far from the best, was Jim Thorpe, son of Sauk and Fox parents. Considered by many people as the world's best athlete, Thorpe won All-America football honors twice in college while performing skillfully in baseball, basketball, hockey, lacrosse, boxing, tennis, archery, swimming, and track and field. He excelled in the 1912 Olympics, winning both the pentathlon and decathlon as a member of the U.S. track-and-field team. However, his having played semipro baseball came to light in 1913 and led to confiscation of his gold medals. Thorpe then played professional baseball, primarily with the Giants, but had trouble hitting the curveball and compiled a lifetime batting average of just .252. He was more successful as a professional football player, organizing the Bulldogs of Canton, Ohio, and starring with the club. A poll conducted in 1950 of about 400 sportswriters and broadcasters named Jim Thorpe the best all-around athlete of the first half of the twentieth century.

The most tragic story of Native American ballplayers concerns Louis Sockalexis. Blessed with great athletic ability, including speed, a powerful throwing arm, and considerable hitting ability, Sockalexis departed his reservation near Old Town, Maine, to attend Holy Cross College and later the University of Notre Dame. Already in his college days, he had a serious drinking problem and was expelled from school in 1897. Patsy Tebeau, manager of the Cleveland Spiders, came to his assistance with the offer of a position with Cleveland, thus making Sockalexis apparently the first Native American to play in the major leagues. He quickly demonstrated his ability, hitting .338 in 66 games with 42 RBIs and 16 stolen bases in 1897. By the following year, however, his drinking and suspensions were derailing his career and his life. He hit just .224 in 21 games, and after seven games in 1899 his major league career was over. Sockalexis returned to Maine, leaving sportswriters to use him as an exemplum on the evils of drinking. The once-great player died in 1913 at the age of 42, his press clippings inside his shirt. The larger lesson that should have been learned from Sockalexis's tragic personal story was how the nation treated Native Americans. That lesson remains largely unlearned at the beginning of the twenty-first century.

Legend has it that the Cleveland team changed its name to "Indians" after Sockalexis, although recent scholarship tends to refute that thesis. Even so, the team mascot, Chief Wahoo, does no credit to anyone, much less to team management and fans who persist in failing to understand the demeaning nature of the characterization. Also contributing to the perpetuation of stereotypes is the "tomahawk chop" popular with Atlanta Braves fans, unwittingly mimicking the common depiction of Native Americans in print and film as savages. Baseball has come a long way toward justice, greater opportunity, and sensitivity toward diverse ethnic backgrounds. It still has far to go.

See also: Fiction; Films; Kinsella, William Patrick; McGraw, John Joseph; Nicknames; Sockalexis, Louis Francis.

Additional Reading:

Ritter, Lawrence S. *The Glory of Their Times: The Story of the Early Days of Baseball by the Men Who Played It.* 1984. Reprint, New York: Vintage Books, 1985.

Seymour, Harold. *Baseball: The Golden Age.* 1971. Reprint, New York: Oxford University Press, 1989.

Wellman, Trina. *Louis Francis Sockalexis: The Life-Story of a Penobscot Indian.* Augusta, ME: Department of Indian Affairs, 1975.

Wheeler, Robert W. *Jim Thorpe: World's Greatest Athlete.* Rev. ed. Norman: University of Oklahoma, 1979.

Zoss, Joel, and John Bowman. *Diamonds in the Rough: The Untold History of Baseball.* 1989. Reprint, Chicago: Contemporary Books, 1996.

NEGRO LEAGUES

Black Americans have been playing baseball since the early days of the game. Initially, African Americans played on entirely black teams as well as mostly white clubs. On the whole, however, the racism that marked American society at large affected baseball from the start. Baseball has always been something of a social barometer within American society; perhaps in no area has it been more so than in race relations.

Blacks were largely excluded from professional baseball during the nineteenth century, sometimes by written rule, more commonly by informal "gentlemen's agreements." One of the most obvious examples of racial exclusion in the early decades of baseball involved the African American Pythian Base Ball Club of Philadelphia, composed of middle-class players who belonged to a fraternal organization called the Knights of Pythias. The Pythians requested admission into the National Association of Base Ball Players in 1867 but were rejected. From then on, black players focused primarily on developing their own teams, although, like the Pythians, from time to time they would compete against white clubs in exhibition contests.

Some black individuals played for white clubs in the nineteenth century. Bud Fowler, born and reared in Cooperstown, home of the future Hall of Fame, played for several white teams; and Moses Fleetwood Walker became the first African American to rise to the majors, catching for Toledo of the American Association in 1884—later becoming a newspaper editor and publishing a pamphlet entitled *Our Home Colony—A Treatise on the Past, Present, and Future of the Negro Race in America,* in which he urged blacks to move to Africa to escape the injustices of American society. As the 1880s came to an end, however, the door that had been slightly ajar slammed shut. Most members of the St. Louis Browns refused to play even an exhibition against an all-black team in 1887, and the influential star of the Chicago White Stockings, Cap Anson, asserted that he and his teammates would never play against a black team. Major league owners entered into another gentlemen's agreement to exclude black players, and the door remained shut until Jackie Robinson kicked it open in 1947.

African American teams almost died out completely in the early 1890s, but the first two decades of the twentieth century witnessed a steady growth of interest in baseball within the black community. The most important figure in the rise of organized black baseball was Rube Foster, who became playing manager of the Chicago Leland Giants and led the team into the Park Owners Association in 1909. The league was so named because all teams were required to own their own ballparks. The Chicago Giants stadium included 3,000 grandstand seats and 400 box seats, at the time the most impressive black-owned stadium in baseball. Foster, who received the nickname "Rube" after outpitching Hall of Famer Rube Waddell in 1902, later started his own club, the Chicago American Giants, and was the principal architect of the Negro National League, which began play in 1920. Foster added the role of president of the league to his previous efforts as player, manager, and organizer, earning the honorary title "father of black baseball." What Foster achieved, however, transcended baseball. He had created the largest black-run business in the United States.

The Depression of the 1930s hit black baseball hard, as it did the rest of the country. The Negro National League folded in 1931, but a new Negro National League (funded in large part by underworld figures) arose two years later to replace it. Black baseball continued its rise throughout the rest of the decade with inauguration of annual East-West All-Star Games, barnstorming tours against major league teams, baseball tournaments in Denver and Wichita, and creation of a new Negro American League in 1937. The latter league was free of the criminal influence of the Negro National League.

The Negro Leagues remained popular throughout the 1940s. The East-West Game in 1944, for example, drew 46,247 fans, some 15,000 more than the major league All-Star contest. A great deal of Negro League popularity was engendered by the style of play (which emphasized speed with many bunts, hit-and-run plays, and stolen bases), excellent pitching, and some of the greatest baseball talent in any league at any time in the history of baseball.

The Negro Leagues in the 1920s to 1940s featured such legendary players as pitcher Satchel Paige, third baseman William "Judy" Johnson, catcher and slugger Josh Gibson, center fielder Cool Papa Bell, and shortstop Willie Wells. Future major league greats such as Monte Irvin, Jackie Robinson, and Hank Aaron began their playing careers in the Negro Leagues. From the early days of black baseball, the black community enjoyed watching their favorite stars, not only against Negro League competition but also in exhibition games against white teams. Few memories were more cherished by black fans than when a Satchel Paige outdueled a Dizzy Dean. Dean, in fact, called Paige the best pitcher he had ever seen. John Holway's extensive research in game records indicates that Negro League players were 268-168 head-to-head against major-leaguers.

Holway's records almost certainly are not definitive, but they help to establish what does appear certain: The best players in the Negro Leagues were easily of major league caliber. African American players knew they were good, and throughout baseball history integration into the majors was beckoning, although even that was a mixed blessing. Certainly many black players longed to play where greater fame and fortune lay, and fans hoped to see them succeed, as Joe Louis did in boxing. The black press took up the cause and, in 1942, supported establishment of a citizens committee to promote black players into the big leagues. Among the black sportswriters writing eloquently on behalf of integrating baseball were Sam Lacy and Wendell Smith. Integrating baseball became an important part of the civil rights movement. One option given serious consideration by Negro League leaders was to encourage acceptance of entire black teams into the major leagues, or at least into the minors.

The major league color barrier was finally broken in 1947, when Jackie Robinson took the field for the Brooklyn

Dodgers. Integration, though, also had its downside. Even on the playing field, integration was slow in coming. It took 12 years before the final major league team would have at least one black player (in 1959, when Pumpsie Green joined the Boston Red Sox). Even today, few blacks are to be found in managerial and executive positions.

Some members of organized baseball had argued in the 1940s that integrating the majors would mean the end of the Negro Leagues. That often was used as an argument against opening the majors to African Americans. That prophecy proved true. The Negro National League disbanded the year after Jackie Robinson made the majors as the best young players from the Negro Leagues began to play their way into the majors. The Negro American League continued through 1960, but then, with dwindling fan support, also came to an end.

James Weldon Johnson, the great African American poet, described Negro League baseball as one of the cultural expressions of black America. The price for being accepted into white baseball was the loss of much of that expressiveness. Today, anyone attending a major league game will see many African Americans on the field but few in the stands. Baseball has been separated to a great extent from black culture. In addition, the African American community has lost its largest black-owned business enterprise. Baseball offers great financial and fame opportunities for players but remains, for a large segment of the black community, just another white-owned and white-managed industry.

See also: Aaron, Henry Louis; African Americans; Banks, Ernest; Bell, James Thomas; Campanella, Roy; Democracy; Doby, Lawrence Eugene; Fiction; Foster, Andrew; Gibson, Joshua; Irvin, Monford; Journalism (Print); Lacy, Samuel H.; Landis, Kenesaw Mountain; Law; Major Leagues; Manley, Effa; Minor Leagues; Night Baseball; Paige, Leroy Robert; Rickey, Wesley Branch; Robinson, Jack Roosevelt; Smith, Wendell; Wilson, August.

Additional Reading:

Ashe, Arthur R., Jr. *A Hard Road to Glory—Baseball: The African-American Athlete in Baseball.* 1988. Reprint, New York: Amistad, 1993.

Brashler, William. *The Bingo Long Traveling All-Stars and Motor Kings.* 1973. Reprint, Urbana: University of Illinois Press, 1993.

Holway, John B. *Blackball Stars: Negro League Pioneers.* Westport, CT: Meckler, 1988.

Peterson, Robert. *Only the Ball Was White.* 2d ed. New York: McGraw-Hill, 1984.

Riley, James A. *The Biographical Encyclopedia of the Negro Baseball Leagues.* New York: Carroll and Graf, 1994.

NEW YORK YANKEES

Most people prefer to be loved rather than hated. The choice, however, may not be clear-cut when success is added to the equation. Is it better to be successful and hated or be a failure and loved? The Yankees became the greatest success story in the history of major league baseball, and while they had millions of loyal fans who loved them, they also became the most hated team because it seemed as if they always won. In fact, for many decades, they won almost every year; and along the way, they also became the best-known ballclub in the world.

However, it was not always so. The Yankees had humble beginnings befitting the history of many of the fans who followed their exploits. Migrating from Baltimore, where the latest version of the Orioles had become a member of the new American League in 1901, the team, then known as the Highlanders, settled into New York in 1903. The team performed in Hilltop Park, atop the highest elevation on Manhattan Island, symbolic of the club's future success.

The team occasionally challenged but never came in first in those early years.

Members of the New York Yankees congratulate one another after defeating the Atlanta Braves during Game 1 of the Major League Baseball World Series at Turner Field in Atlanta, Georgia, October 23, 1999. (Jamie Squire/Allsport)

The Highlanders lost 103 times in 1908, and the 1912 season saw them finishing 55 games behind the Boston Red Sox, a team that would become their lifelong rival. Renamed the Yankees in 1913, they moved from Hilltop Park to the Polo Grounds, home of the National League Giants, and played their home games there through 1922.

The turning point for the Yankees came during the off-season between 1919 and 1920 when Colonel Jake Ruppert, the Yankees' owner, took the recommendation of his manager, Miller Huggins, and acquired the pitcher-turned-slugger Babe Ruth from the Red Sox. Ruth had been a World Series pitching ace for Boston before his Red Sox manager, Ed Barrow, converted him into an everyday outfielder. Ruth had hit 29 home runs in 1919, the highest total ever in the major

leagues. The new Yankee slugger almost doubled that total in his first season in New York, hitting 54 home runs. The Yankees contended for the pennant, finishing third, and Ruppert brought over from Boston the perceptive Barrow to become general manager.

Ruth hit 59 home runs in 1921, and the Yankees won the first pennant in their history. The Yankees won another pennant the following year and, in 1923, playing in their own ballpark, Yankee Stadium, posted their first World Series championship by beating the Giants.

The Yankees continued to dominate baseball throughout the 1920s, 1930s, 1940, 1950s, and part of the 1960s. There were occasional brief downturns, like the seventh-place finish in 1925, but the mighty Yankees came right back. With Lou Gehrig aboard as the second Yankee immortal, and with outfielder Earle Combs, outfielder Bob Meusel, and second baseman Tony Lazzeri joining Ruth and Gehrig as the famous "Murderer's Row," the 1927 Yankees rolled to 110 victories, winning the pennant by 19 games and sweeping the Pirates in the World Series. Many students of the game still consider the 1927 Yankees the greatest team in baseball history.

A dying Miller Huggins resigned as manager in September 1929. The next great Yankee manager, Joe McCarthy, brought the team back to the top in 1932 (the World Series featuring Babe Ruth's "called shot") and led the team to eight pennants and seven world championships in his 15 years with the club.

The stars, owners, and managers continued to change, but the effect remained the same. Lou Gehrig left, victim of a disease that would take his life and name; Joe DiMaggio assumed the mantle of the next Yankee superstar; Mickey Mantle followed in the early 1950s; Roger Maris hit 61 home runs in 1961 to break the Babe's record. Dan Topping and Del Webb bought the Yankees in 1945; Larry MacPhail, who had resurrected the Reds and Dodgers, joined the owners as president. After MacPhail self-destructed through public brawling, he was replaced by Topping as president, and George Weiss was promoted from minor league director to general manager. Casey Stengel was hired to manage the Yankees in 1948, and the championships continued, as Stengel won 10 pennants and seven World Series in 12 years.

The 1960s would be the end of this dynasty for a while, although no one saw it coming at first. With Ralph Houk at the helm, the Yankees added more world championships in 1961 and 1962. In the World Series of 1963, however, the Yankees were swept by the Los Angeles Dodgers, and with former catching great

Yogi Berra managing in 1964, the Yankees again won the pennant but were defeated in the World Series. That year had seen Topping sell the club to CBS, and in 1965 the Yankees suffered their first losing season in 40 years. The following year they slid to last place.

George Steinbrenner headed a syndicate that purchased the Yankees in 1973 and set about restoring the winning tradition. With former second baseman Billy Martin managing, the Yankees won the pennant in 1976. Newly acquired stars like Catfish Hunter and Reggie Jackson joined Thurmon Munson, Chris Chambliss, and Graig Nettles to bring world championships back to New York in 1977 and 1978. Reggie Jackson's five home runs in the 1977 World Series and two more in 1978 earned him the title "Mr. October." Martin, who had been a buddy of Mickey Mantle and star pitcher Whitey Ford in the 1950s, was almost constantly at odds with Steinbrenner and was hired and fired five times by the owner during the 1970s and 1980s, once during the 1978 season.

Yankee success proved more elusive during the 1980s and early 1990s, with Steinbrenner himself running into legal trouble and being suspended from running the team in the early 1990s. By the middle of the decade, both Steinbrenner and the Yankees were back. The team was leading the league when a strike cut short the 1994 season; the following year the Yankees earned a wild-card berth in the playoffs.

Joe Torre became skipper of the Yankees in 1996 and led the team to its first world championship since 1978, defeating the highly regarded Atlanta Braves. As a wild-card team the following year, the Yankees were eliminated by the Cleveland Indians. The century concluded, however, with the Yankees adding World Series triumphs number 24 and number 25. The 1998 team even invited comparisons with the 1927 Yankees by winning 114 regular-season games and increasing the total to 125 by the conclusion of the World Series, which they swept from the San Diego Padres. Throughout 1999, the Yankees struggled to overcome high expectations set by their record season, a spring-training discovery that Joe Torre had prostate cancer, and a series of deaths within players' families. Without superstars like Ruth and Mantle, but with many outstanding players and strong team spirit, the Yankees overcame all obstacles to win the World Series.

The New York Yankees concluded the twentieth century where they had spent much of it: as the finest team in the majors. Since Babe Ruth had joined the Yankees, the New York club had averaged almost one World Series championship every three years. And along the way to their latest run of championships, something new had happened. Those "damn Yankees" had turned into lovable heroes. They had achieved enormous popularity with that portion of the United States outside New York City. They had become, in a new way, America's team.

See also: Allen, Mel; Berra, Lawrence Peter; Bouton, James Alan; *Damn Yankees;* DiMaggio, Joseph Paul; Fiction; Films; Free Agency; Gehrig, Henry Louis; Hemingway, Ernest Miller; Home Run; Hunter, James Augustus; Jackson, Reginald Martinez; Language, Baseball; Larsen, Donald James; MacPhail, Leland Stanford, Sr.; and Leland Stanford, Jr.; Mantle, Mickey Charles; Maris, Roger Eugene; Murderer's Row; Music; Nicknames; Perfection; Polo Grounds; Records Set; Ruth, George Herman; Steinbrenner, George Michael, III; Stengel, Charles Dillon; Theater; Torre, Joseph Paul; War; World Series; Yankee Stadium.

Additional Reading:

Anderson, Dave. *The Yankees: The Four Fabulous Eras of Baseball's Most Famous Team.* New York: Random House, 1979.

Golenbock, Peter. *Dynasty: The New York Yankees, 1949–1964.* Englewood Cliffs, NJ: Prentice-Hall, 1975.

Henrich, Tommy. *Five O'Clock Lightning: Ruth, Gehrig, DiMaggio, Mantle, and the Glory Years of the New York Yankees.* New York: Carol, 1992.

Madden, Bill. *Damned Yankees: A No-Holds-Barred Account of Life with "Boss" Steinbrenner.* New York: Warner, 1990.

Meany, Thomas. *The Yankee Story.* New York: Dutton, 1960.

NICKNAMES

Nicknames have been common in baseball throughout its history, both to the players themselves and to their fans. Nicknames encourage camaraderie within the ranks, and they serve fans who want to establish a bond with their favorite players. Americans traditionally have loved familiarity, reflected in the tendency to get on a first-name basis with even casual acquaintances, and nicknames serve that desire.

Some nicknames were coined by players for teammates, others were brought along from childhood, and still others leaped from the imaginations of sportswriters and broadcasters. Whatever their origins, nicknames fall into certain categories.

Some nicknames denote the player's background, such as "Shoeless Joe" for a player from the country, "Dixie" for someone from the South, and "Arky" for a native of Arkansas. Such names have become far less common in recent years as regionalism has yielded to national homogenization and an increasingly mobile society engulfed baseball players along with everyone else.

Certain nicknames convey a particular skill: "Scooter" for a fleet-of-foot shortstop, "Rapid" Robert for a great fastball pitcher, "The Man" for one who stands above others of his generation in ability and dignity, "Joltin'" Joe for a powerful hitter, "The Big Hurt" for a slugger capable of lasting damage to almost any pitcher, "The Barber" for a pitcher inclined to pitch close to the batter's head, and "Mr. October" for a performer who regularly comes through in the World Series.

Racial nicknames as well as especially pejorative or insensitive names are now generally avoided, at least in public, testimony to greater civility in baseball and society in recent decades. Even such a choice as "Pee Wee" would likely be viewed as offensive today in light of society's distaste for classifying people on the basis of physical or mental characteristics. "Big Mac," however, gained wide popularity as the Bunyanesque Mark McGwire closed in on the all-time home-run record in 1998.

Although nicknames remain in use, their popularity has declined considerably in the face of rising player salaries, increased free agency, and higher educational levels for players and fans. It is less easy to refer to a multimillionaire as "Doc" or "Lefty," and increased intellectual and social sophistication tends to foster greater formality. There is an increased seriousness of purpose among players, for whom baseball is big business rather than just a way to earn a living wage. Less cohesion with teams as a result of free agency also lessens fans' and players' identification with specific players and teams.

Also contributing to the decline of nicknames, especially colorful ones, is the modern style of broadcasting and sportswriting. Current broadcasters and writers are better educated and more professional than most of their predecessors, and while they love the game, they tend to be far less flamboyant than their earlier counterparts.

Nicknames, though, are unlikely to become extinct. There will always be a "Big Mac" or a "Rocket." and within the team players will continue to show their affinity for teammates by using nicknames. Increasingly, however, the nationally known, creative nickname will be reserved for a select few, primarily those on their way to home-run records and Cooperstown.

See also: Journalism (Print); Language, Baseball; Lardner, Ringgold Wilmer; Radio Broadcasting; Television Broadcasting.
Additional Reading:
Martinez, David H. *The Book of Baseball Literacy.* New York: Plume, 1996.
McBride, Joseph. *High and Inside: An A-to-Z Guide to the Language of Baseball.* Lincolnwood (Chicago): Contemporary Books, 1997.
Phillips, Louis, and Burnham Holmes. *Yogi, Babe, and Magic: The Complete Book of Sports Nicknames.* New York: Prentice-Hall, 1994.

NIGHT BASEBALL

Night baseball was slow in coming as traditional attitudes held back technology. The reluctance of baseball owners to institute night baseball was rooted in the widespread belief, still common among fans and students of the game, that baseball is essentially a natural sport that requires a natural setting. As the game had originated on outdoor fields under the sunshine, so the game should remain faithful to its nature. Gradually, however, other forces led to a change that in retrospect appears as logical and natural as the game itself.

The world of the 1930s was still a daytime world for most Americans, especially in rural areas. As electricity spread, however, nighttime possibilities proliferated, from simply staying up late to read without eyestrain to going out. And while cityfolk had long become accustomed to going out, the rest of the world began to change its mentality from the old "early to bed, early to rise" adage.

Playing baseball games at night made sense. Night games would be easier for working people to attend. As it was, owners had long compromised with the game-under-the-sunshine tradition by starting games at 3:00 P.M., reasoning that people might be able to get off work early to attend. Also, summer days in the Midwest could be unbearably hot and humid, while by late afternoon more shadows and less overhead sun meant a slightly more comfortable setting for fan and player alike. The evening obviously offered an even cooler setting. Thus modern fans find it difficult to understand why owners would refuse the positives night baseball had to offer.

Baseball and society were sufficiently different then to justify the owners' reluctance. First, additional revenue was not extremely important to some owners in the 1920s; many were sportsmen first and businessmen later. The reserve clause bound players to their teams and kept down salaries, thus limiting overall costs of running a team and requiring less revenue. Owners could keep firm control over costs and therefore felt little financial pressure to change a good thing. If attendance seems minuscule by today's standards—5,000 at a game was normal—it was sufficient to satisfy owners.

When first steps were taken toward night games in the early decades of the twentieth century—occasional exhibition games and, in the late 1920s and early 1930s, installation of lights at some Negro League and minor league stadiums—players, owners, and the baseball establishment generally disapproved. Players were concerned that they would be injured on slippery grass, hurt arms in the damp air, and not be able to see the ball. Owners and the most prominent printed expression of baseball tradition, *The Sporting News,* raised high the banner of tradition.

Fans, however, living in a world increasingly charged with electricity, were ready to embrace night baseball, but it took the developing effects of the Depression, along with an unusually creative general manager, to push owners toward night games. The 1934 season

ended with the third straight year of declining attendance in the major leagues. Some teams, such as the Cincinnati Reds, were on the verge of disaster. Fortunately for the Reds, the Cincinnati Central Trust bank forced Reds management to hire a new general manager, Larry MacPhail, who in 1931 had introduced night games for the Louisville Colonels and had outdrawn the St. Louis Cardinals. MacPhail persuaded Powel Crosley, owner of broadcasting stations and manufacturer of radios, to purchase a controlling interest in the team. The National League voted in December 1934 to allow each team to play seven night games per season, and the Reds went ahead with their plan to install lights for the 1935 season.

President Franklin D. Roosevelt threw a switch from the White House to illuminate the lights at Crosley Field for the first night game—May 24, 1935. The lighting system cost $50,000 to build and $250 per night to run. After the seven night games of 1935, the lights had paid for themselves: In those seven night games, the Reds drew 130,337; the attendance for the remaining 69 daylight home games was 324,256. Overall, the Reds more than doubled home attendance from the previous season.

Despite the obvious success of night baseball in Cincinnati, progress in adding night games elsewhere was slow. Not until 1938 did another team add night games. That team was the Brooklyn Dodgers, and the architect of those night games was the same Larry MacPhail, who had left the Reds to serve as Brooklyn's general manager. Again fans responded in droves, with night games attracting crowds seven times larger than those at day games. Another effect of night baseball was that the increased revenue for the Reds and Dodgers permitted both teams to acquire the players necessary to turn those teams, for years also-rans, into regular pennant contenders. Further contributing to the success of night games for Brooklyn was the result of their first night game, on June 15, which drew the second largest crowd in Dodger history, a crowd that witnessed Johnny Vander Meer's second consecutive no-hitter.

Finally, most major league owners had been convinced. The Athletics, White Sox, and Indians added lights in 1939; the Browns, Cardinals, Pirates, and Giants followed suit in 1940. The Washington Senators installed lights for the 1941 season, but then World War II temporarily halted the spread of night games. It was feared that lighted stadiums would endanger cities and port facilities in case of bombing or submarine attacks.

All of the other teams, with the exception of the Chicago Cubs, added lights after the war, concluding with the Detroit Tigers in 1948. Teams came to appreciate that night baseball was not just a novelty but a way to generate much larger attendance figures and therefore more revenue. In subsequent decades, night baseball became the norm except for weekend games. Even the Cubs finally added lights, although not until 1988, as Wrigley Field maintained its traditional ambiance.

Today, baseball, at both the major and minor league levels, has become part of nocturnal America. It vies for crowds with other evening entertainment, such as films, plays, and concerts. Night games have increased the opportunity for individual fans as well as families to attend. The expanded revenue, of course, has been a mixed blessing for owners, for it increased pressure to raise salaries, which in turn created a stronger impetus toward unionization and free agency, which have transformed some elements of major league baseball. These changes, however, in ways unforeseen by most observers of the game in the middle third of the century, have helped to maintain the position of baseball as America's pastime. The movement toward higher salaries and greater job mobility parallels similar movements in many other areas of American life and work.

See also: Ballparks; Business; MacPhail, Leland Stanford, Sr.; and Leland Stanford, Jr.; Minor Leagues; Negro Leagues; Presidents of the United States; *The Sporting News;* War.

Additional Reading:
Gershman, Michael. *Diamonds: The Evolution of the Ballpark.* Boston: Houghton Mifflin, 1993.
Pietrusza, David. *Lights On! The Wild Century-Long Saga of Night Baseball.* Lanham, MD: Scarecrow, 1997.
White, G. Edward. *Creating the National Pastime: Baseball Transforms Itself, 1903–1953.* Princeton: Princeton University Press, 1996.

O

OTT, MELVIN THOMAS (MASTER MELVIN) (1909–1958)

One of the most famous hitting stances in baseball was developed by Mel Ott: right leg raised as the left-handed hitter started his forward motion to swing. It was a batting style copied by many, including the Japanese home-run king Sadaharu Oh. The swing helped the diminutive Ott compensate for his five-foot nine frame as he accumulated 511 home runs in his 22-year career with the New York Giants (1926–1947). When he retired, he held the National League record for most homers, as well as league records for runs batted in (1,860), runs scored (1,859), and walks (1,708). Ott's walk total was about twice the number of his strikeouts (896).

Ott's records have since been broken, and he did achieve his home-run totals playing in the Polo Grounds, with its short distance to the right-field wall. Nonetheless, he remains one of the great hitters during the early decades of the home-run era. He also was a strong defensive right fielder with an excellent arm. In 1951, he was selected for membership in the Hall of Fame. Unfortunately, Ott's managerial career with the Giants (1942–1948) never yielded a finish higher than third, which was reached in his first year as manager. An unfailingly pleasant individual, Ott was the subject of Leo Durocher's famous declaration that "nice guys finish last."

See also: Durocher, Leo Ernest; Home Run; McGraw, John Joseph; Polo Grounds.
Additional Reading:
Hano, Arnold. Greatest Giants of Them All. New York: Putnam's, 1967.
Hynd, Noel. The Giants of the Polo Grounds: The Glorious Times of Baseball's New York Giants. New York: Doubleday, 1988.
Stein, Fred. Mel Ott: The Little Giant of Baseball. Jefferson, NC: McFarland, 1999.

P

PAIGE, LEROY ROBERT (SATCHEL) (ca. 1906–1982)

Satchel Paige was one of the greatest stars of the Negro Leagues and, by most accounts, one of the greatest pitchers ever to play the game in any league. He also became famous, perhaps even more famous to the broader public, as one of baseball's all-time great philosophers. "Don't look back," his most famous truism went. "Something might be gaining on you."

Not many batters gained on Satchel Paige, who got his nickname, as Paige told the story, carrying satchels for passengers at the railroad depot in Mobile, Alabama, where he was born sometime around 1906. Telling the story of Satchel Paige inevitably comes back to stories he himself told and retold; it is hard to discern fact from what may have been just a good story. When Paige was first brought up to the majors by Bill Veeck to pitch for the Cleveland Indians in 1948, a rookie well past 40, he was asked whether he still had his world-famous control. As Paige told this story, he gave his catcher, Jim Hegan, a gum wrapper and directed him to lay it on the plate.

Old Satch then proceeded to fire his fastball right across the wrapper.

Satchel Paige was an effective pitcher for Cleveland and the St. Louis Browns through 1953. In 1965, when Paige was almost 60 by his own (perhaps optimistic) reckoning, he returned to the majors with the Kansas City Athletics. He worked just one game, pitching three innings, but he allowed only one hit and no runs or walks while striking out a batter. A few years later, in 1971, he was inducted into the Hall of Fame. The image of Satchel Paige that many fans carry is that of the ancient pitcher rocking in his rocking chair in the bullpen while waiting to be summoned to the mound.

Those who saw Satchel Paige in his prime, though, saw something far different. Paige had a blazing fastball and could pitch almost every day. He played his first professional season in 1924 and kept striking out batters for decades, often pitching during the summer in the United States and then in the Caribbean leagues during the winter. He played for some of the finest teams in Negro League history, including the Pittsburgh Crawfords of the 1930s. That team included

Josh Gibson, Oscar Charleston, Cool Papa Bell, and Judy Johnson—all future Hall of Famers.

The ban on African American players kept Paige out of the majors until he was well past his prime. The Negro League teams often barnstormed against white all-star teams, though, and the competition pitted Paige against some of the greatest major league hitters of all time. Joe DiMaggio considered Paige the "best and the fastest pitcher" he ever faced and was so thrilled as a young player when he got an infield hit off Paige that he was sure he was ready for the big leagues. Satchel once outpitched Dizzy Dean 1-0 and struck out Rogers Hornsby five times in a single game. Like the Negro League players who regularly competed against Paige, they were faced with the tall, thin right-hander winding up, the extraordinarily high kick, his size-12 shoe seemingly headed right for the batter's face, his unusually long arm whipping his fastball across the plate at will.

Satchel Paige was disappointed not to be the first African American to play in the major leagues, but he harbored no resentment against Jackie Robinson. When he was selected for the Hall of Fame, the intent was to honor former Negro League players in a part of the building separate from where major league stars were honored. Massive protest altered that plan, but Satchel, always ready with a retort, responded at his induction by thanking the Hall of Fame for converting him from a "second-class citizen" into a "second-class immortal."

See also: African Americans; Bell, James Thomas; Gibson, Joshua; Hall of Fame and Museum; Negro Leagues; Veeck, William L., Jr.

Additional Reading:
Gilbert, Tom. *Baseball and the Color Line.* New York: Franklin Watts, 1995.
Paige, Leroy. *Maybe I'll Pitch Forever: A Great Baseball Player Tells the Hilarious Story Behind the Legend.* 1962. Reprint, Lincoln: University of Nebraska Press, 1993.

PEANUTS

In early 2000, the United States mourned the loss of Charles M. Schulz and the final *Peanuts* cartoon. Thus drew to a close one of America's favorite comic strips as well as its longest-running baseball series.

Charlie Brown, hat sideways, pitched, giving his best, but his supporting cast was less than stellar. Lucy, in center field, was a constant source of complaints—about how Charlie was pitching, that he did not have a nickname (as all real pitchers do, so Lucy gave him one—"Cementhead"), or that the weather was too bad for baseball. Snoopy had some punch in his bat but tended to fall asleep in the field. And the rest—Linus, Schroeder, and crew—provided little offense or defense. The defeats kept piling up, 63-0, 123-0, 184-0, and on and on.

Charlie finally got a win in 1993 after over 40 years of losing, slugging a ninth-inning home run, but his team later reverted to form. In the little book *It's Baseball Season, Again!* the *Peanuts* team lost 207-0. Afterward, Charlie lamented how he would like to talk with the person who invented baseball. Asked why, he responded, "To apologize!" In reality, there was no need to apologize. No team ever brought so much pleasure to so many, even while losing, as Charlie Brown's squad.

Suffering from ill health, Schulz decided to retire Charlie Brown and the gang. A few hours before the final original *Peanuts* strip ran (Sunday, February 13, 2000), Charles Schulz passed away—and into baseball immortality.

See also: Art.

Additional Reading:
Kindred, Dave. "A Good Man, That Charlie Brown." *The Sporting News,* January 10, 2000, p. 70.

Schulz, Charles M. *The Charlie Brown Dictionary.* New York: Random House, 1973.

———. *Charlie Brown, Snoopy and Me, and All the Other Peanuts Characters.* Garden City, NY: Doubleday, 1980.

———. *It's Baseball Season, Again!* New York: HarperCollins, 1999.

———. *Peanuts Jubilee: My Life and Art with Charlie Brown and Others.* New York: Holt, Rinehart, and Winston, 1975.

PERFECTION

Much of American society is about the quest for perfection. Although perfection is unattainable in this life, people seek it as a goal that promotes productivity or, from the spiritual side, sound moral behavior. Baseball shares this quest.

The perfect game is the most obvious example of perfection pursued. In a perfect game, the pitcher retires all 27 hitters without anyone reaching base. It is one of the few times when perfection is possible in a game where hitting safely three times out of 10 qualifies the player for stardom.

How important the lack of perfection is—not only as a reality but also as an ideal—was demonstrated during the 1999 season when umpire Frank Pulli, working a Cardinals-Marlins game, used a dugout camera's viewfinder to review a long fly ball. He correctly changed the call from a home run to a double but was chastised by the National League president, Len Coleman, who reaffirmed that instant replay is not to be used in baseball. "Part of the beauty of baseball," Coleman explained, "is that it is imperfect. Players make errors. Managers are constantly second-guessed." To some extent, that is the same traditional mind-set that balked at night baseball, air travel, and broadcasting as violations of the nature of the game.

Perhaps some day instant replay will take its place in baseball. Until then, however, many if not most fans, like Len Coleman, will embrace the imperfection of baseball while applauding the rare achievement of perfection.

See also: Larsen, Donald James; Myth.

PERIODICALS

Periodicals permeate the American lifestyle and enrich the world of baseball. There are untold thousands—too many to count. A recent edition of the annual *Writer's Market* devotes about 400 pages to entries for consumer magazines and about 125 additional pages to trade, technical, and professional journals. Even then, most professional journals are not included; nor are literary magazines, newspapers, and countless other magazines, to say nothing about newsletters. All of this, of course, is happy news for readers, writers, and editors.

Where sports is concerned, and in particular baseball, fans can find quality periodicals to interest, inform, and entertain them, including publications that have been around for a very long time. *The Sporting News,* the most respected of sports papers, was founded in 1886 and still retains its popularity. *Sport Magazine* was begun in 1946, and sports enthusiasts for over half a century have looked forward to its regular appearance. *Sports Illustrated* came upon the scene in 1954 and has developed almost a mythic aura. It has long been believed that to grace the cover of *SI* is a curse. In recent years, *SI* has tended toward more investigative reporting than most of its competitors; it also has spawned separate editions for women and children.

Baseball fans can turn to periodicals that specialize. The small-format *Baseball Digest,* started in 1942, makes up in content and durability what it lacks in size. *USA Today Baseball Weekly* is like a good fastball, coming at readers hard and straight. Those who like baseball history mixed with poetry and fiction can try *Elysian Fields Quarterly;* travelers and others who want their news short, if not sweet, grab the newspaper *USA Today;* and baseball scholars who belong to the Society for American Baseball Research eagerly await *The National Pastime: A Review of Baseball History* and *The Baseball Research Journal.* Bookstores and newsstands are flooded during winter and spring months with annual publications heralding the coming season. Two old friends are *Street & Smith's Baseball* and *Who's Who in Baseball* (the latter dating to 1912). The issues of *Who's Who* offer an extraordinary history of most of the century, and its constants (statistics and a bright-red cover), modified with the introduction of photographs in the 1960s and, in the 1970s, a team photo of the World Series champs on the back cover, reflect the way many people like to see baseball: slowly evolving, but in ways that do not alter the timelessness of the sport.

Fans also enjoy the yearbooks put out by their favorite teams, magazines devoted to collectibles and Rotisserie ball, and a multitude of newsletters relating to almost any aspect of baseball. In a nation that often bemoans illiteracy among its citizens, huge numbers are reading and writing about baseball. And much of the writing, as those who are familiar with a sampling of these periodicals certainly know, is well worth the reading.

> *See also:* Cards, Baseball; Collectibles; Internet; Journalism (Print); Rotisserie Baseball; *The Sporting News.*
> *Additional Reading:*
> Pietrusza, David, Lloyd Johnson, and Bob Carroll. *The Total Baseball Catalog.* New York: Total Sports, 1998.
> Periodicals, including those mentioned above and countless others.

POETRY

Baseball is the poet's game. The reason is difficult to determine, but it surely comes from the nature of the sport—its fusion of past and present in a kind of cosmic timelessness, its relatively slow pace, allowing opportunities to focus on details of the contest and reflect on them, the family associations, especially between parent and child, the pastoral character of the game, and the enormous wealth of ritual and myth that has grown up around baseball. No other sport offers such rich poetic sources and influences, and poets have responded to baseball with a rather distinguished body of work.

That connection between baseball and poetry goes back to the nineteenth century. Walt Whitman practiced his wordsmithing as a sports reporter and followed baseball all his life. When he wrote "Song of Myself," published in *Leaves of Grass* in 1855, he included in Section 33 "a good game of base-ball" among the fine, manly sports he encountered. After suffering a stroke in the 1870s and no longer able to attend games, he continued to enjoy talking baseball. Something of an honorable traditionalist, Whitman lamented the growing use of the deceitful curveball.

The only person who rivals Whitman as America's poet is Robert Frost. In 1956, a few years before reading a poem at John F. Kennedy's inauguration, Frost wrote an essay on baseball for *Sports Illustrated,* wherein he notes, "I never feel more at home in America than at a ball game be it in park or sandlot." Frost was not a Johnny-come-lately to the sport, having written in the poem "Birches," published 40 years earlier, of birches bent by a boy "too far from town to learn baseball."

Whitman and Frost are good company indeed, and fine poets have entered the ranks. An all-star team might include William Carlos Williams, Richard Hugo, Robert Creeley, Carl Sandburg, David Bottoms, Gail Mazur, Fred Chappell, Lillian Morrison, and William Heyen. The captain of the team, though, must be Marianne Moore, so established as a baseball fan that she was invited to throw out the ceremonial first pitch at the Yankees' home opener in 1968. A famous story goes that the writer Alfred Kreymborg took Moore to a baseball game in 1915 in order to demonstrate that he could find a subject about which Moore knew nothing. Much to his amazement, his companion, who never before had seen the Giants' pitcher, correctly identified him as Christy Mathewson, based upon her having read Mathewson's book about pitching.

Some of the most immortal of baseball poems have not been written by great poets and probably do not qualify as great art on strictly aesthetic grounds. Yet they continue to entertain down through the years. "Casey at the Bat," by Ernest L. Thayer, first published in 1888, remains the most famous and most quoted baseball poem, even though it recounts the depressing story of a hero's failure. About 20 years later, though, Casey achieved redemption in C. F. McDonald's "The Volunteer," coming out of the stands to replace an injured player and hitting a home run to win the game. Tears streaming down his face, he identifies himself to the ecstatic crowd. Everyone should have a second chance.

Other memorable, if less than brilliant, baseball poems include Franklin P. Adams's "Baseball's Sad Lexicon," which helped to immortalize the double-play combination of Tinker to Evers to Chance; and famous sportswriter Grantland Rice's poem on the death of Babe Ruth, "Game Called" ("Game called by darkness").

Much good poetry is to be found in recent periodicals. One of the finest baseball magazines publishing poetry has long been *Spitball: The Literary Baseball Magazine,* edited by Mike Shannon. The magazine began as primarily a poetry publication but broadened to include fiction and nonfiction. (*Spitball* celebrated the centennial of Babe Ruth's birth by conducting a national poetry contest and publishing the winners in issue number 50; one of the three winners, for his poem "Refiguring the Babe's Home Runs," was yours truly.) *Elysian Fields Quarterly,* edited by Stephen Lehman, publishes several poems per issue along with other selections.

Fan Magazine, edited by artist Mike Schacht, includes a medley of poetry, artwork, first-person narratives, and short pieces published under the heading "Mudville Diary." In 1998, Schacht produced an issue devoted exclusively to baseball haiku. The innovative issue recognized the growing interest in haiku on the part of American poets and the appropriateness of baseball as a haiku subject. After all, baseball was transported to Japan from the United States, while haiku crossed the Pacific in the opposite direction.

If there were a baseball laureate at the beginning of the twenty-first century, it would have to be Donald Hall. In addition to writing beautiful prose about baseball (including the essay "The Poet's Game"), he has written some of the finest baseball poetry. Perhaps most significant is his epic poem "Baseball," composed in nine "innings," each inning consisting of nine stanzas, and each stanza written in nine lines, all of it an attempt to explain baseball. In a sense, that is what all baseball poetry attempts to do.

See also: "Casey at the Bat"; Periodicals; Quisenberry, Daniel Raymond; Rice, Grantland; Tinker to Evers to Chance; Whitman, Walter.

Additional Reading:

Hall, Donald. "Baseball." *The Museum of Clear Ideas: New Poems.* New York: Ticknor and Fields, 1993, pp. 11–39.

———. "The Poet's Game." *Fathers Playing Catch with Sons: Essays on Sport (Mostly Baseball).* San Francisco: North Point, 1985, pp. 57–63.

Johnson, Don, ed. *Hummers, Knucklers, and Slow Curves: Contemporary Baseball Poems*. Urbana: University of Illinois Press, 1991.

Kerrane, Kevin, and Richard Grossinger, eds. *Baseball Diamonds*. Garden City, NY: Doubleday, 1980.

Issues of such magazines as *Spitball: The Literary Baseball Magazine, Elysian Fields Quarterly,* and *Fan Magazine.*

POLO GROUNDS

The Polo Grounds in New York City hosted many historic moments. Actually, there were four baseball parks by that name; the first one, constructed on a former polo field, was located on 5th Avenue between 110th and 112th Streets outside Central Park. The Giants (originally called the Gothams) played there from 1883 until they moved to new quarters at 155th Street and 8th Avenue in 1889.

By 1891, the Giants had moved a bit north to Coogan's Bluff, the site that would forever be associated with them. The bluff overlooked the field, and New Yorkers liked to congregate there to observe the action below. A fire destroyed much of the stadium on April 14, 1911, but the wooden edifice was replaced quickly, this time primarily in concrete and steel. The fourth Polo Grounds retained its previous bathtub shape, with short distances down the right- and left-field lines. The highly ornate ballpark could seat 34,000 by the end of 1911, the largest stadium in the country.

The Polo Grounds was home to a long line of great moments: Christy Mathewson's third shutout of the 1905 World Series; Fred Merkle's baserunning blunder during the 1908 pennant race; the tragic death of Cleveland's Ray Chapman, beaned in a game against the Yankees (who also called the Polo Grounds home from 1913 to 1922); John McGraw's Giants defeating those same Yankees in all–New York World Series in 1921 and 1922; Mel Ott's home runs; Bobby Thomson's "shot heard 'round the world" in the 1951 playoffs; and Willie Mays's remarkable Series catch in 1954. Three years later, the Giants played their last game in the Polo Grounds before moving to San Francisco. A great era in baseball history had come to a close.

See also: Ballparks; Chapman, Raymond Johnson; Mathewson, Christopher; Mays, Willie Howard; McGraw, John Joseph; Merkle Boner; World Series.

Additional Reading:

Gershman, Michael. *Diamonds: The Evolution of the Ballpark*. Boston: Houghton Mifflin, 1993.

Hynd, Noel. *The Giants of the Polo Grounds: The Glorious Times of Baseball's New York Giants*. New York: Doubleday, 1988.

Ritter, Lawrence S. *Lost Ballparks: A Celebration of Baseball's Legendary Fields*. 1992. Reprint, New York: Penguin, 1994.

Stein, Fred. *Giants Diary: A Century of Giants Baseball in New York and San Francisco*. Berkeley: North Atlantic Books, 1987.

PONY BASEBALL AND SOFTBALL

PONY Baseball and Softball is an organization that demonstrates commitment to the youth of the United States as well as the ability to find a theme and stay with it—in this case, horses. PONY stood for "Protect Our Neighborhood Youth" when the first league was started in Washington, Pennsylvania, in 1951. As new leagues were created and spread across the land, the slogan shifted to "Protect Our Nation's Youth." By 1999, about 500,000 boys and girls were participating annually in PONY baseball or softball.

Initially, PONY was for 13- and 14-year-old players who had graduated from Little League. Before the end of the second year of PONY's existence, the number of teams had grown from the original six in one league to over 500 in 106 leagues across the United States, and the first PONY World Series was held. Gradually, other leagues were formed: the Palomino League (for players ages 17 to 18), Colt League (for players 15 and 16 years of age), Bronco League (11 to 12), Mustang League (9 to 10), Pinto League (7 to 8), and Shetland League (5 to 6). There are similar levels for PONY softball for girls, although girls also are eligible to play in the baseball leagues.

Though PONY officials deserve congratulations for coming up with enough equine names for all of these leagues, they have seriously contributed to the impressive array of baseball and softball opportunities for American youngsters, keeping kids off the streets and helping them have fun while learning the value of teamwork.

See also: American Legion Baseball; Babe Ruth League; Little League; Softball; Women in Baseball.

Additional Reading:
PONY Baseball and Softball Website. http://www.pony.org

POSTEMA, PAMELA (1954–)

Pam Postema's career in baseball was within the context of a wide range of efforts in American society to break down barriers to women in previously all-male domains. The twentieth century saw male exclusivity overcome in military schools, Little League baseball, social clubs, military combat, and countless companies and industries that previously featured at best token representation by women. So far, two especially visible jobs have not had a female occupant: president of the United States and major league umpire.

Pam Postema blazed a largely unmarked trail into organized baseball, following a path only slightly, if bravely, marked by Bernice Gera and Christine

Wren, the first two women to become minor league umpires (both in the 1970s). Postema grew up in Ohio and after high school and a few years of largely unsatisfying jobs decided to pursue her interest in umpiring. She succeeded in gaining admission into Al Somers's highly respected school for umpires in Daytona Beach, Florida. After graduating in 1977, she was offered an umpiring job in the Gulf Coast League.

Postema advanced steadily up the minor league ladder during 13 years of umpiring, including seven years at the Triple-A level. She also worked major league spring training games, the Hall of Fame game between the Yankees and Braves at Cooperstown in 1988, and a Triple-A All-Star Game. Like many other women, she found that glass ceilings can be difficult to break through. After the 1989 season, Postema was released, the official reason being that she was no longer considered a major league prospect. She later sued the major leagues, charging sex discrimination, but settled out of court. Over 40 years after Jackie Robinson smashed the color barrier, women still were not permitted on the baseball field.

Additional Reading:
Postema, Pam, and Gene Wojciechowski. *You've Got to Have Balls to Make It in This League.* New York: Simon and Schuster, 1992.

POVICH, SHIRLEY (1905–1998)

Shirley Povich's death on June 4, 1998, was greeted with a sense of loss that transcended his journalistic accomplishments, as impressive as they were. Povich, who wrote sports columns for the *Washington Post* for 75 years, earned numerous awards during his long career and, in November 1997, became the first sportswriter ever to receive the Fourth

Estate Award from the National Press Club. One of his more unusual awards came when his accomplishments and unusual first name (for a man) mistakenly brought him inclusion in the 1962 edition of *Who's Who of American Women*. His friend Walter Cronkite quickly dashed off a telegram proposing marriage.

Povich's career began when he was a teen caddie at the Kebo Valley Golf Club in his native Bar Harbor, Maine. Ned McLean, publisher of the *Washington Post,* who summered at Bar Harbor, was so impressed with the youngster that McLean invited him to come to Washington and work as a copyboy. Povich joined the paper in 1922 and never left, earning his first byline two years later and becoming sports editor in 1926 when he was only 21. Also in 1926, Povich, whose favorite sport always remained baseball, began his "This Morning with Shirley Povich" column. Povich retired from his regular column in 1974 but continued to write for the paper, filing his final column one day before his death. Among the thousands of columns that Povich wrote was a 15-part series supporting integration of major league baseball in 1947, the year that Jackie Robinson became the first African American major league player in modern times.

In his later years, Shirley Povich meant much more than his columns to baseball fans. Having covered every World Series since 1924, and having conversed with such baseball greats as Walter Johnson and Babe Ruth, he connected late-twentieth-century fans with an earlier, almost mythical time.

See also: Jewish Americans; Journalism (Print).
Additional Reading:
Povich, Shirley. *All These Mornings*. Englewood Cliffs, NJ: Prentice-Hall, 1969.
———. *The Washington Senators*. New York: Putnam's, 1954.

PRESIDENTS OF THE UNITED STATES

U.S. presidents have been associated with baseball since the earliest days of the game. William Howard Taft may have been the biggest baseball fan of all presidents, and it is fitting that he was the first president to throw out the first pitch on opening day, a practice that all subsequent presidents except Jimmy Carter have followed at least once during their terms in office.

Earlier presidents, however, had demonstrated an affinity for the young game. Abraham Lincoln played before and during his years as president; Andrew Johnson, like Lincoln, enjoyed watching games being played on the White Lot in back of the White House; Benjamin Harrison became the first president to attend a major league game; and William McKinley worked his way up through the minors, throwing the first pitch for Columbus in the Western League. Teddy Roosevelt, unfortunately, viewed baseball as a "mollycoddle" game, preferring rugged endeavors like football, hunting, and boxing.

Taft's gesture, however, set a pattern that future occupants of the White House could not ignore (a legacy that almost died at birth; during that first game, Home Run Baker cracked a foul ball off the head of Secretary of State Charles Bennett). Taft, despite his love for the game, declined to attend the 1912 opener, which followed the sinking of the *Titanic* by just four days, claiming among its victims Archie Butt, the presidential aide who had convinced Taft of the appropriateness of his attending his first opening day.

Some presidents brought their own experience as ballplayers to Washington. Woodrow Wilson had played for Davidson College, which may help to account

President Franklin Delano Roosevelt (1882–1945) throws the ball into play at a baseball match, circa 1943. (Hulton Getty)

for his decision to support keeping baseball going during World War I, the same decision Franklin Roosevelt made during the next world war. Dwight Eisenhower played on the junior-varsity team at the U.S. Military Academy and also moonlighted as a sometime professional to earn money for college. George Bush may have been the best player of them all, starting at first base for the Yale varsity squad and distinguishing himself as a sure-handed gloveman.

Other presidents were equally supportive of America's national pastime, even if they had not played the game in any official capacity. John Kennedy was a sports enthusiast whose personal preference may have been touch football, but as a Bostonian, he was a devoted fan of the Red Sox and Ted Williams. Harry Truman set the record for games attended—16—and demonstrated the unique ability to make his opening-day pitches with either the right or left hand.

Perhaps the two most interesting fans, however, were Richard Nixon and Ronald Reagan. Nixon was a scholar of the game who delighted in making lists of all-star teams. Out of work after losing bids for the presidency and the California governorship, he was wooed by players to head the Major League Baseball Players Association. He was tempted but declined, leaving the players to choose Marvin Miller. The owners, not to be outdone, offered Nixon the position of commissioner. Again, Nixon was interested but did not accept. Ronald Reagan earned some renown as a young Cubs broadcaster before going into acting. He worked from telegraph reports, adding color for his radio audience. During one game, the line went dead, and Ronald Reagan had to improvise. For almost seven minutes he had Billy Jurges of the Cubs foul off pitch after pitch from the Cardinals' Dizzy Dean until contact was restored, and the anxious and tired broadcaster could catch up with the real game. Ronald Reagan also is known for a strange three-way relationship with another president and one of the great baseball pitchers. Grover Cleveland Alexander was a Hall of Fame hurler named after President Grover Cleveland. President Reagan, in his acting days, once played the pitcher, which led to a moment of confusion when Speaker of the House Tip O'Neill told the president about his speaker's desk, which was once owned by Grover Cleveland. "I played him in the movies," the president offered. The Speaker had to clear up the matter.

Most of those ceremonial pitches, of course, were made for the Washington Senators, both the original club (before it moved to Minnesota and became the Twins), and the expansion team that moved to Texas to become the Rangers. In more recent years, without a hometown team, presidents have gone further afield to make that first pitch, but the tradition lives on. It surely will continue as long as baseball and the United States exist.

See also: Ballparks; Democracy; Films; War.
Additional Reading:
Durant, John. *The Sports of Our Presidents.* New York: Hastings, 1964.
Hollander, Zander. *Presidents in Sport.* New York: Associated Features, 1962.
Mead, William B. *Baseball Goes to War.* Washington, DC: Farragut, 1985.
Mead, William B., and Paul Dickson. *Baseball: The Presidents' Game.* New York: Walker, 1997.

QUISENBERRY, DANIEL RAYMOND (1953–1998)

Dan Quisenberry was atypical in just about everything he did. One of the all-time great relief pitchers, he temporarily set the single-season saves record with 45 in 1983 with the Kansas City Royals, five times led the league in saves, and helped the Royals win their first World Series in 1985. A submariner, throwing underhanded with a devastating sinker-ball, who seldom threw faster than 85 miles per hour and preferred grounders to strikeouts, Quisenberry was far from the typical reliever.

Neither was Quisenberry typical after he retired in 1990 with 244 career saves and five Fireman of the Year awards from *The Sporting News*. He turned to social action and poetry. Quisenberry ran an annual charity golf tournament in Kansas City and put great effort into helping the hungry and homeless. He wrote poetry, often about baseball, giving readings and publishing in such magazines as *Fan* and *Spitball*.

Quisenberry wrote in his poem "A Career," published in *Spitball*, about his former manager Dick Howser succumbing to brain cancer ("He died that summer/we froze and played like statues"). On May 30, 1998, Quisenberry was honored at Kauffman Stadium by about 30,000 fans saddened by the news that he suffered from the same illness. On September 30, death came to the worker for social justice, poet, former great pitcher, and one of the most loved players both during and after his playing days.

See also: Cancer; Periodicals; Poetry.
Additional Reading:
McCarver, Tim, with Danny Peary. *The Perfect Season: Why 1998 was Baseball's Greatest Year.* New York: Villard Books, 1999.
Quisenberry, Dan. Poems in *Spitball: The Literary Baseball Magazine,* No. 51 (1997): 33–40.

R

RADBOURN, CHARLES GARDNER (OLD HOSS) (1854–1897)

Old Hoss Radbourn is the quintessential old-time player, what many think of when they let their imaginations return to yesteryear: An almost superhuman player who never sat out a game; who played through injuries, sore arms, and inclement weather; whose only goal was to beat the opponent.

The figure that most stands out is 60—the number of games that Charley Radbourn was credited with winning in 1884, in the era when the batter could call for a high or low pitch. Actually, *Total Baseball* has lowered that total to 59, but the reduction does not alter the fact that Old Hoss in 1884 had one of the greatest seasons ever for a pitcher. He won 59 while losing just 12, pitched 678 innings, struck out 441 batters, appeared in 75 games, starting 73, and completed every start. He also compiled a microscopic 1.38 ERA. As the season progressed, Radbourn found himself the only pitcher remaining on his Providence Grays and did not hesitate to start every game for much of the season. When his right arm started to hurt, as it must have

under those conditions, he simply applied wet towels and went out to pitch again.

It took Radbourn only 11 seasons to win 309 games. After retirement in 1891, he ran a combination saloon–pool hall. Always a man's man, he loved hunting, but one day in 1894 he accidentally shot himself, losing an eye and a portion of his face. Not wanting people to see him that way, he spent much of his time during his few remaining years in the pool hall's back room.

See also: Heroes; Records Set; Statistics.

Additional Reading:

Frommer, Harvey. *Primitive Baseball: The First Quarter-Century of the National Pastime.* New York: Atheneum, 1988.

Holst, David L. "Charles G. Radbourne [sic]: The Greatest Pitcher of the Nineteenth Century." *Illinois Historical Journal* 81(4) (1988): 255–268.

Ivor-Campbell, Frederick. "1884: Old Hoss Radbourne [sic] and the Providence Grays." In *The National Pastime.* Ed. John Thorn. New York: Warner, 1987, pp. 156–169.

Kull, Andrew. "Baseball's Greatest Pitcher." *American Heritage* (April-May 1985): 102–106.

Nemec, David. *The Great Encyclopedia of 19th-Century Major League Baseball.* New York: Donald I. Fine, 1997.

RADIO BROADCASTING

The first radio station, KDKA in Pittsburgh, was established in 1920, and throughout the decade radios spread to approximately half of all U.S. homes. The first network radio broadcast of a symphony orchestra occurred in 1926, the Metropolitan Opera went on the air in 1937, and by 1938 the Music Appreciation Hour was reaching 7 million children in 70,000 schools. Radios had become such an integral part of American life by the 1930s that shortly after taking office, during the depths of the Great Depression, President Franklin D. Roosevelt began his evening radio addresses to the people, his famous fireside chats. Baseball, however, was slow to follow suit.

Organized baseball, as with night games, resisted broadcasting games. This opposition to radio was partly idealistic and partly financial. Traditionalists in baseball, which is to say almost all of the leaders of the sport, found something unnatural in listening to games, as they felt that games experienced away from the natural sunshine under which they were played violated the essence of the sport. Baseball, they believed, was meant to be participated in and, when that was not possible, at least seen. Baseball was a spectator sport to be viewed, not mere listening entertainment.

Owners also feared that broadcasting games would discourage attendance. Fans would be satisfied to follow the games in the comfort of their homes rather than journey to the ballparks. This fear was not unlike the reaction that producers of phonograph records felt as radio listeners chose to listen virtually for free (once they had purchased a radio) rather than hand over cash to keep buying records. What happened, however, was that radio broadcasts soon increased interest in music, and, as music lovers wanted their music available at all times,

Leo Durocher, manager of the Brooklyn Dodgers, during a broadcast of a weekly sports question-and-answer program on ABC (Hulton Getty)

the record industry boomed. So it was with baseball attendance.

Yet only the most insightful baseball leaders foresaw the positive impact of radio broadcasting on the turnstiles. The first baseball game was broadcast in 1921 (between Pittsburgh and Philadelphia, on KDKA), and World Series games were broadcast regularly from 1922 (with Grantland Rice as the first announcer), but during the 1920s only Chicago, Cleveland, Boston, Philadelphia, Detroit, and St. Louis broadcast games, and then only home contests. Not until 1939 did the final holdouts—the Yankees, Giants, and Dodgers—put their games on the air. The final push came from the innovator Larry MacPhail, who, along with inaugurating night baseball with the Reds, hired Red Barber to broadcast Reds games on the radio. MacPhail, having moved to the

Dodgers for the 1938 season (during which he offered night games), brought Barber over to the Dodgers and moved forward with plans to broadcast Dodgers games in 1939, thereby forcing the other New York teams to compete on the airwaves.

Most of the teams by the mid-1930s had come to recognize the financial gains of radio broadcasting due to broadcast and sponsorship fees. The pace of baseball games permitted many lulls in action, during which commercials could be aired, a reality that such sponsors as General Mills readily understood. In addition, it became clear that broadcasting helped to create additional interest in baseball and thereby boost attendance. These new sources of revenue were especially helpful to teams trying to fight their way through the Depression.

Nonetheless, it was not until after World War II that live broadcasts of away games became the custom. Until then, away games usually were re-created. One of the practitioners of this type of broadcasting later became president of the United States. The young Dutch Reagan worked for WHO in Des Moines, Iowa, during the 1930s, where he re-created Cubs and White Sox games. He would work out of a studio in Des Moines, with a Western Union reporter who received transmissions from the ballpark. President Reagan fondly recalled one time when the wire went dead during a Cubs game. Reagan, not missing a beat, had Billy Jurges of the Cubs keep fouling pitches off until transmission resumed, long after Jurges had popped out.

Radio broadcasters faced the same conflict that confronted sportswriters: whether to be objective or root for the home team. The eastern broadcasters tended to favor objectivity, while Midwestern announcers like Jack Brickhouse, Bob Prince, and Harry Caray clearly supported their own teams. There were, of course, exceptions to the rule. Red Barber practiced the objective approach with Cincinnati, and Mel Allen later would champion his Yankees. Despite their different styles, these men and many others enjoyed considerable success at the microphone, spreading enthusiasm for baseball throughout the land.

Listening to the same team, and hence the same announcer, on a daily basis led fans to associate the team with the broadcaster. The broadcaster became a familiar and comfortable presence for fans and was likely to achieve a level of fame that equaled or surpassed that of top players. Tim McCarver in his book *The Perfect Season* recalls a conversation with Mark Grace of the Cubs during which the Cubs first baseman told of an incident in the late 1980s. Grace and fellow Cubs stars Ryne Sandberg and Andre Dawson were signing autographs when Harry Caray stepped out of the dugout. Suddenly some 100 fans hurried from the Cubs players to Caray. Caray, of course, had radio and television broadcasting duties, but he had made his fame first on radio and remained, in tradition-bound Wrigley Field, primarily an old radio man.

As networks grew and revenue increased, broadcasting, like night baseball, became a double-edged sword, bolstering baseball revenue while creating a desire on the part of players to share in the bounty. The financial rewards would become even greater as television joined, but never eliminated, radio.

Radio broadcasts shared time and often announcers with television stations and networks from the 1950s on, and although there was fear that television would destroy radio, that proved not to be the case. The automobile helped to save radio, as drivers and passengers enjoyed listening to their favorite game while traveling. Newer generations of Americans have grown up listening to the radio, and so there is little reason to think that radio broadcasts will become obsolete. Radio remains an important component in the daily lifestyle of many Americans today.

See also: Allen, Mel; Barber, Walter Lanier; Brickhouse, John Beasley; Caray, Harry; MacPhail, Leland Stanford, Sr.; and Leland Stanford, Jr.; Presidents of the United States.
Additional Reading:
Barnouw, Erik. *A History of Broadcasting in the United States.* 3 vols. New York: Oxford University Press, 1966–1970.
Douglas, George H. *The Early Days of Radio Broadcasting.* Jefferson, NC: McFarland, 1987.
Smith, Curt. *The Storytellers: From Mel Allen to Bob Costas—Sixty Years of Baseball Tales from the Broadcast Booth.* New York: Macmillan, 1995.
———. *Voices of the Game.* South Bend, IN: Diamond Communications, 1987.
White, G. Edward. *Creating the National Pastime: Baseball Transforms Itself, 1903–1953.* Princeton: Princeton University Press, 1996.

RAILROADS

The rise of railroads in the nineteenth century paralleled and facilitated the rise of professional baseball. As the public traded stagecoach and horseback for the comfort and safety of railcars, they might well have rubbed shoulders with athletic young men traveling from town to town in the new profession of baseball. So closely was baseball identified with the railroad industry that nicknames for some of the greatest of baseball stars were borrowed from trains, most famously Walter "Big Train" Johnson and the "Iron Horse"—Yankee first baseman Lou Gehrig.

Passenger travel by railroad began in the early 1830s, and the first sleeping car was introduced in 1836 to heighten comfort on long trips. By 1848, about 6,000 miles of railroad routes served the eastern United States. From there, tracks reached toward the Mississippi River and its river-towns. At this time, railroads were serving fans and teams. By the late 1850s, special trains were transporting fans to the Fashion Race Course on Long Island to witness the Brooklyn and New York all-stars face off in this exciting new game.

Pressure from merchants and from citizens anxious to make their fortunes during the 1849 Gold Rush pushed the railroads across the continent. (Among those heading west in pursuit of gold in 1849 was Alexander Joy Cartwright, an important figure in the creation of the New York Knickerbockers.) President Abraham Lincoln signed the first Pacific Railway Bill on July 1, 1862, authorizing construction of a rail line that would unite the nation, even as the Civil War was ripping the nation apart. The Union Pacific headed west from Omaha, while the Central Pacific moved east from Sacramento. The two met at Promontory, Utah, in May 1869 to drive the famous golden spike.

Two years after that meeting, the National Association of Base Ball Players split between two groups: those who wished to maintain the earlier gentleman's game played by the Knickerbockers, and those who wanted to pursue professional baseball. The latter formed the National Association of Professional Base Ball Players, which included nine teams located in Boston, Chicago, Cleveland, Fort Wayne, New York, Philadelphia, Rockford, Troy, and Washington. It is not a coincidence that the cities composing this early league were limited by the scope of the railroad system.

Even as the railroad network spread through the country, major league baseball limited itself to cities inside the earlier railroad network. Teams would travel by train for road trips that lasted, at most, a few weeks. Rail travel to California obviously would not be feasible, and therefore major league teams were not allowed beyond roughly the northeast quarter of the country, even though great population shifts affecting the West and South were well under way. Owners opposed airplane travel for fear of accidents, because airplanes did not fit the "natural" way that the game was conducted and because the status quo both was more comfortable and protected owners who did not want others to gain a great advantage from expansion that might come at a cost to their own success.

Thus, when expansion did occur in the 1950s, it tabbed cities on or close to the railroad network already in use: Baltimore, Kansas City, Milwaukee. Not until the Dodgers and Giants decided to move their franchises to Los Angeles and San Francisco for the 1958 season did major league baseball escape static thinking about transportation. Once airplane travel was accepted, major league baseball could become geographically what it had long claimed to be—the national pastime.

See also: Cartwright, Alexander Joy; Expansion; Gehrig, Henry Louis; Johnson, Walter Perry; Major Leagues.
Additional Reading:
Bryant, Keith L. *Railroads in the Age of Regulation, 1900–1980,* New York: Facts on File, 1988.
Douglas, George H. *All Aboard: The Railroad in American Life.* New York: Paragon House, 1992.
Hubbard, Freeman H. *Encyclopedia of North American Railroading.* New York: McGraw-Hill, 1981.
Stover, John F. *American Railroads.* Chicago: University of Chicago Press, 1961.

RECORDS SET

At one point in Mark Harris's novel *Bang the Drum Slowly,* several characters engage in a humorous mocking of baseball's preoccupation with setting records. It is

Sid's pursuit of Babe Ruth's home-run record that triggers the exchange:

"You set a record," said Ugly. "Up to yesterday you probably only switched the radio off 15,738 times. Now you switched it off 15,739."
"Officially or unofficially?" said I.
. . .
"I talked 3,112 official words today," said Jonath. "That puts me 3,112 official words up on yesterday."
"Today is the first time I ever officially hung this jock on this particular nail at 4:02 P.M. in the afternoon of July 9, 1955," said Perry. (160)

Followers of baseball at the dawn of the twenty-first century find ever increasing attention given to records—and not only to the most obvious standards, such as home runs, victories, and strikeouts. In an age of specialization in American society, it is perhaps natural that specialized, minute records be recorded, analyzed, and preserved for posterity (or for the next person or team to set the record anew).

The 1998 season was particularly notable for new records, and even a partial catalogue of the marks established during that campaign imparts the importance of setting records. Foremost is the record for home runs in a single season, the old record (Roger Maris's 61 in 1961) being broken by two players: Mark McGwire (70) and Sammy Sosa (66).

Although the home-run derby riveted America during the season, many other records fell. Dennis Martinez retired at the conclusion of the season with 245 career victories, exceeding by two the previous high by a Latin American pitcher, Juan Marichal. Sammy Sosa drove in 158 runners, the most ever by a Hispanic player; the previous record was just two years old, set by Andres Galarraga in 1996. Dennis Eckersley took the mound 1,071 times, most of them in relief, before retiring, leaving Hoyt Wilhelm behind by just one appearance. Prior to 1998, no team had ever featured 10 players who hit 10 or more home runs in the same season; in this year of records, both the Yankees and Orioles set the new standard. The Yankees, winner of the World Series, established new highs for most victories by an American League club (114) and most total victories including playoffs and World Series (125). The Atlanta Braves had five pitchers win at least 15 games, another first. Barry Bonds became the first player to reach 400 in both career home runs and stolen bases. Cal Ripken, who had broken Lou Gehrig's apparently unbreakable record of 2,130 consecutive games played, stretched his string to 2,632 before deciding to sit out a game. Jim Leyland used 27 different rookies during the season in an exercise in record-breaking futility. And these are just a few of the new marks set that historic season.

Americans never seem to tire of records, even when acknowledging the absurdity of many. The United States has long been a nation of firsts, which is to say a nation of records. "Records were made to be broken," the old saying goes. That is an American truism in sports and in society. It has never been more true. It may, of course, account for a considerable portion of the greatness of the United States, as well as the quest for greatness in America's national pastime.

See also: Fiction; Home Run; Statistics; Strikeouts.

Additional Reading:

Debs, Victor, Jr. *Still Standing after All These Years: Twelve of Baseball's Longest Standing Records.* Jefferson, NC: McFarland, 1997.

Dittmar, Joseph J. *Baseball Records Registry.* Jefferson, NC: McFarland, 1997.

Harris, Mark. *Bang the Drum Slowly.* 1956. Reprint, Lincoln: University of Nebraska Press, 1984.

Lewis, Allen. *Baseball's Greatest Streaks: The Highs and Lows of Teams, Pitchers, and Hitters in the Modern Major Leagues.* Jefferson, NC: McFarland, 1992.

RELIGION

There has been a strong relationship between religion and baseball since the beginning. Throughout the latter part of the nineteenth century and until the mid-1930s, the question of whether professional baseball should be permitted on Sundays was passionately debated. Different positions on that issue grew out of different perceptions of baseball, as either a force for moral good or as a dangerous subversion of religious values. Final acceptance of Sunday baseball did not completely end conflicts between religion and baseball, as the greatest Jewish American hitter and pitcher respectively faced choices regarding team loyalty and observance of Judaism's most sacred holy days. While these debates were occurring, various religious organizations were both supporting baseball and using the sport as a way to attract additional sheep into the fold. More recently, deeply emotional connections between spirituality and baseball have been presented in interviews, fiction, films, newspaper articles, and essays. Although the specific terms of the baseball-religion connection have changed over the years, that there is a connection remains widely accepted.

So-called blue laws prohibiting certain types of recreational and business activity on the Sabbath originated in Virginia as early as 1610. Anything that would detract from a reverential observance of Sunday as a day dedicated to God was opposed in many regions well into the twentieth century. Some prohibitions, selling liquor, for example, remain in force. So it is not surprising that baseball also was affected by blue laws.

The National League, from its inception in 1876, banned games on Sunday. Teams that violated this ban did so under threat of expulsion. When the American Association began play in 1882, it permitted Sunday games, but teams sometimes were fined for playing on the Sabbath. St. Louis owner Chris Von der Ahe had to appear before the Court of Criminal Correction, where he got a favorable ruling that Sunday baseball in St. Louis was legal.

The issue of Sunday ball was a religious and a financial matter. Many workers were free to attend games only on Sundays, which made games on that day potentially lucrative. At least in part because of financial concerns, the National League shifted to a more flexible approach in 1890, permitting member teams to make their own decisions about playing on Sunday, subject to local laws. Sometimes, teams played even when it was not legal, actions that did not always go unpunished. In 1897, the entire Cleveland and Washington clubs were arrested for violating the Sabbath. Finally, by 1934, all major league teams were able to play legally on Sunday, Pennsylvania (home to the Phillies, Pirates, and Athletics) being the last state with major league clubs to permit Sunday play.

There always were some participants who chose personal religious principle above the wishes of the team. Branch Rickey, from a devout Methodist family, promised his mother that he would not play on Sundays, a vow that he kept, even when it led to his being fired by Cincinnati in 1904.

Some of the most famous cases of individual players facing the decision to play or not to play involved the Jewish American stars Hank Greenberg, the great Detroit Tigers slugging first baseman, and Sandy Koufax, the fireballing left-hander of the Los Angeles Dodgers. As Greenberg achieved stardom in the 1930s in the face of considerable anti-Semitism from both fans and players,

Jews came to see him as a heroic representative of their faith. Initially, Greenberg had not played on the holy days of Rosh Hashanah and Yom Kippur. In 1934, however, with the Tigers locked in a pennant race with the Yankees, Greenberg debated whether to play on Rosh Hashanah, the Jewish new year. With the general blessing of the Detroit Jewish community, Greenberg chose to play, and newspapers applauded his decision. Sandy Koufax in the 1960s came to a different decision. With considerably less public controversy, and with anti-Semitism far less overt, Koufax decided not to pitch on the holy days.

The question of whether baseball is conducive to or destructive of moral virtues continued to be debated for several decades in the twentieth century. To some extent, the question remains alive today, although usually in different terms, involving greed and materialism. Many strong churchgoers, though, including clergymen, believed that baseball was beneficial for a variety of reasons. It made boys and young men physically stronger, encouraged teamwork, strengthened moral character, bred patriotism, at worst was better than many other forms of entertainment, and when sponsored by churches encouraged church attendance.

Consequently, many religious organizations and churches sponsored baseball teams and leagues. The Young Men's Christian Association (YMCA) added baseball to their athletic programs in the 1880s, encouraging a kind of "muscular Christianity." The devout Christy Mathewson was among those boys who played on YMCA teams. By 1889, the New York City YMCA ran a 30-team league. Catholic Bishop Bernard Sheil of Chicago founded the Catholic Youth Organization in 1930, which included baseball competition.

By 1930, a variety of religions (including Lutheran, Baptist, Catholic, and

Presbyterian) were running church leagues, featuring future baseball greats such as Babe Herman and Pee Wee Reese. Sunday-school attendance was often required for participation in the games. Other religious-affiliated institutions of various kinds offered baseball opportunities for children. The most famous example may be St. Mary's Industrial School, a combination orphanage–reform school operated by the Xaverian Brothers in Baltimore, which numbered Babe Ruth among its residents. Ruth later gave much credit to the school, especially to Brother Gilbert, for teaching him how to play baseball.

Baseball often was the primary sport at church-operated colleges early in the twentieth century and remains important at many of them today. African American youngsters, shut out of so many baseball opportunities, were able to play in some localities on teams sponsored by black churches. However, many black churches, especially in rural areas and in the South, saw sports as injurious to the spirit and urged instead a serious commitment to hard work.

Today, there continues to be much discussion of baseball and religion. Pamela Schaeffer, writing in the *National Catholic Reporter* on September 18, 1998, saw Mark McGwire's sixty-second home run very much in religious terms, as "liturgy erupting into euphoria." Annie, a leading character in the film *Bull Durham,* talks of the "church of baseball" and compares a baseball to the Catholic rosary, a baseball having 108 stitches, the number of beads in the rosary. In W. P. Kinsella's novel *Shoeless Joe,* Ray Kinsella, J. D. Salinger, and the hitchhiking Archie "Moonlight" Graham stop off to sneak into the Twins' stadium in Minneapolis. Playing ball in the moonlight, they feel a religious sense to what they are doing, with the stadium like a great church.

It is not uncommon for a baseball player to utter religious expressions when being interviewed or make the sign of the cross before going to bat, although it is hard to imagine God actually taking sides in baseball contests. Mark McGwire is quoted in the *National Catholic Reporter* article referred to above as likening his record-setting 1998 season to "a great script written by the man upstairs."

Thus baseball and religion are closely intertwined. They have been since the inception of organized baseball, and they surely will continue to travel into the future together. That pairing should strike many people as appropriate, especially those individuals who see baseball as relating to most things, and religion as relating to all things.

See also: Fiction; Films; Greenberg, Henry Benjamin; Jewish Americans; Koufax, Sanford; Myth; Ritual; Substance Abuse; Sunday, William Ashley.

Additional Reading:

Gilbert, Brother. *Young Babe Ruth: His Early Life and Baseball Career, from the Memoirs of a Xaverian Brother.* Ed. Harry Rothgerber. Jefferson, NC: McFarland, 1999.

Seymour, Harold. *Baseball: The Early Years.* 1960. Reprint, New York: Oxford University Press, 1989.

———. *Baseball: The Golden Age.* 1971. Reprint, New York: Oxford University Press, 1989.

———. *Baseball: The People's Game.* 1990. Reprint, New York: Oxford University Press, 1991.

Williams, Peter W. *America's Religions: Traditions and Cultures.* Urbana: University of Illinois Press, 1998.

RESERVE CLAUSE

Baseball, from its earliest days, has been both an important part of popular culture and, occasionally, a law largely unto itself. Baseball simultaneously has relied on the American legal system, using the law to cement such aspects of the game as its contractual relationships, and sought to remove itself from the normal application of law. The reserve clause is a prime example of the latter.

Unlike most American professions, where an employee is free to seek employment with another company within the same industry, the major league baseball player remained the property of the team that originally signed him for the duration of his career or until the team sold, traded, or released him. This reserve clause was embedded in the basic contract between owner and player and was backed up by the threat of permanent blacklisting. Its rationale was that the reserve system was necessary to ensure competitive balance among teams. Without the reserve system, players would be gobbled up by teams that could pay the most. The system also was vital, owners argued, to protect their investment in players, including the money put into signing players and developing them through the minor leagues.

The clause was in force within the National League by the late 1870s, binding five players of the owner's choice to each team, and was extended to 11 players per team by the National League and the new American Association in 1883 when team rosters usually numbered only about 14. In reaction to John Montgomery Ward's attack on the reserve clause, the major leagues extended the reserve system during the 1888 off-season to cover all players. The system remained in place through several legal attacks until the 1970s, when an arbitration decision freeing pitchers Andy Messersmith and Dave McNally also triggered the end of the reserve system as it had been enforced for a century.

See also: Antitrust Exemption; Commissioner; Finley, Charles Oscar; Flood, Curtis Charles; Free Agency; Hunter, James Augustus; Kuhn, Bowie K.; Labor-Management Relations; Law; Miller, Marvin James; Ward, John Montgomery.

Additional Reading:

Abrams, Roger I. *Legal Bases: Baseball and the Law.* Philadelphia: Temple University Press, 1998.

Lowenfish, Lee. *The Imperfect Diamond: A History of Baseball's Labor Wars.* Rev. ed. New York: Da Capo, 1991.

Sobel, Lionel S. *Professional Sports and the Law.* New York: Law-Arts, 1977.

Weiler, Paul, and Gary Roberts. *Sports and the Law.* Westbury, NY: Foundation, 1993.

Weistart, John, and Cym Lowell. *The Law of Sports.* Charlottesville, VA: Michie, 1979.

RICE, GRANTLAND (1880–1954)

Grantland Rice was one of the most popular and erudite of all sportswriters. A member of what Rice biographer Charles Fountain has called the "Gee Whiz!" school of journalism, Rice brought his love for baseball (and for many other sports) to his reporting. He also brought to his reporting his literary learning, often beginning accounts of games with a piece of verse and leavening the pieces with literary allusions.

Rice was born in Murfreesboro, Tennessee, and attended Vanderbilt University, where he captained the baseball team. After college, he worked on a variety of newspapers, including the Atlanta *Constitution,* the Cleveland *News,* and the New York *Evening Mail, Tribune,* and *Sun.* While writing for the Atlanta paper, he received a number of letters written by Ty Cobb under other names praising the still unknown Cobb's baseball ability. That the future baseball great in the first decade of the twentieth century saw in Rice a baseball writer with the journalistic clout to get Cobb his break demonstrated how quickly Rice, still in his twenties, had scaled the sportswriting ladder. Rice finally responded to the letters and reported on the young player who was stirring up such fan interest.

Rice's accomplishments bridged the gap between baseball and the broader public in a variety of ways. As a poet, Rice could entertain with parodies of "Casey at the Bat" or delight with more serious poetry. He published several books of poetry and served as the president of a company that produced documentaries about sports, while at the same time helping to elevate the position of sportswriter to celebrity status. Rice also helped to establish sports figures as almost mythic heroes and consistently pushed his belief that good sportsmanship could morally ennoble societies as well as individuals.

See also: "Casey at the Bat"; Cobb, Tyrus Raymond; Heroes; Journalism (Print); Myth; Poetry.

Additional Reading:

Fountain, Charles. *Sportswriter: The Life and Times of Grantland Rice*. New York: Oxford University Press, 1993.

Harper, William. *How You Played the Game: The Life of Grantland Rice*. Columbia: University of Missouri Press, 1999.

Rice, Grantland. *The Omnibus of Sport*. New York: Harper, 1932.

———. *Only the Brave and Other Poems*. New York: Barnes, 1941.

———. *The Tumult and the Shouting: My Life in Sport*. New York: Barnes, 1954.

RICKEY, WESLEY BRANCH (THE MAHATMA) (1881–1965)

Few people have had as profound an effect on baseball and popular culture as Branch Rickey. A brilliant student of the game and evaluator of baseball talent, Rickey also combined a lawyer's acumen with a deep moral sense of justice. As a result, he deliberately and successfully introduced two enormous changes into baseball: the farm system, and integration. With the latter, he anticipated the civil rights movement of the 1950s and 1960s and offered African Americans a model to follow in Jackie Robinson and hope that a discriminatory society might finally be transformed. Jackie Robinson and Branch Rickey blazed a path that others would follow.

Rickey grew up as a farm boy in Ohio, son of Methodist parents who not only taught him right from wrong but also imposed stern discipline. Rickey learned to avoid cursing and smoking and promised his mother that he would not attend baseball games on Sunday—a promise that he kept. The religious training of his youth established the moral bedrock upon which Rickey would make the momentous decisions of his life—decisions that would have consequences far beyond himself.

Rickey turned to baseball young and experienced a range of roles within the game. While a young coach of the Ohio Wesleyan College team, Rickey brought his club to South Bend, Indiana, in 1904 to play the University of Notre Dame. Rickey signed his team into a South Bend hotel but was told that the single black player on his club could not stay with the rest of the players. Rickey refused to accept that dictate and finally persuaded the hotel to let Charles Thomas share a room with him. That moment and the emotional impact on the young black player stayed with Rickey for the rest of his life.

Rickey caught for the St. Louis Browns and New York Highlanders from 1905 to 1907 and later managed the Browns (1913–1915) and St. Louis Cardinals (1919–1925). Neither as a player nor manager did Rickey enjoy great success. He hit just .239 in a total of 120 games and had an overall losing record as a manager. Nonetheless, his knowledge of baseball was recognized, and he was hired to run the Cardinals, trading the manager's role for a position in which he could make a greater difference.

Under Rickey's direction, the Cardinals moved from their own stadium into the Browns' Sportsman's Park; with the saved money, Rickey had the capital to purchase part ownership of the Fort Smith and Syracuse minor league clubs. Thus began the first farm system in major league history. Although major league teams had reached into the minors for players long before 1926, Rickey created the first unified system of minor league teams stretching from the lowest levels of organized baseball to the highest minors (in those days Class D to Double-A). The Cardinals owned these clubs, and Rickey supplemented the more than 20 owned teams through agreements with other teams and leagues. Commissioner Kenesaw Mountain Landis strongly opposed Rickey's plan, believing that it would fail financially, but Rickey had the courage to follow his convictions. The farm system permitted the Cardinals to develop such players as Stan Musial, as well as to make money by selling superfluous players to other major league teams. When other organizations witnessed the Cardinals' success (pennants in 1926, 1928, 1930, 1931, 1934, and 1942), they followed suit. Today, farm systems remain an essential part of each major league team's development plan, although with far fewer teams.

Rickey and Cardinals owner Sam Breadon had a falling-out, which resulted in Rickey's contract not being renewed after the 1942 season. He had no trouble finding another job, joining the Brooklyn Dodgers, then a consistent also-ran, as president and general manager. Rickey now had another important idea to implement: integration of baseball. With Landis, a forceful opponent of integration, dead, and a new commissioner, Happy Chandler, in place, Rickey believed that the time was right. Critics have argued that Rickey sought to add black players just to improve the Dodgers, not for altruistic reasons. The reality is certainly a combination of both, for Rickey knew the talent that existed in the Negro Leagues.

Rickey wanted the perfect player for an enormously difficult position. He would have to be talented but able to endure taunts and insults and physical threats as well as confrontations on the field without retaliating. The role required courage and the ability to maintain personal dignity without fighting back. Rickey believed Jackie Robinson to be that man, and he was proved right as Robinson survived unceasing racism without responding or losing his sense of personal worth. Robinson went on to enjoy a Hall of Fame career and helped make the Bums of Brooklyn one of baseball's finest teams.

Rickey sold his interest in the Dodgers in October 1950 and joined the Pittsburgh Pirates as chairman. When the majors resisted expanding the number of teams, depriving many thriving cities of major league clubs, Rickey left the Pirates to become president of a new Continental League in 1959. The league planned to operate teams in non–major league cities and, in the case of New York, a city that had lost teams: New York, Houston, Denver, Toronto, and Minneapolis–St. Paul. The majors met this challenge by rushing into expansion. The National League voted to add two new clubs, and the New York Mets and Houston Colt .45s (later the Astros) were added for the 1962 season. The American League moved even faster, with the Washington Senators and Los Angeles Angels (both of which would later move) joining in 1961. These were the first structural alterations in the major leagues since 1900. Once again Branch Rickey had brought profound change, if less directly.

Rickey's final role in baseball was as a senior consultant to the Cardinals from 1962 until his death in 1965. His life was more than a success story. It was a story of how a society, given the right leadership, can grow morally and prosper financially. He also is one of the most striking examples in the history of the United States of an old adage: "One person can make a difference."

See also: African Americans; Brooklyn Dodgers; Canadian Baseball; Chandler, Albert Benjamin; College Baseball; Landis, Kenesaw Mountain; Minor Leagues; Robinson, Jack Roosevelt;

Additional Reading:

Anderson, Donald Ray. *Branch Rickey and the St. Louis Cardinal Farm System: The Growth of an Idea*. Diss. University of Wisconsin-Madison, 1975.

Frommer, Harvey. *Rickey and Robinson: The Men Who Broke Baseball's Color Barrier*. New York: Macmillan, 1982.

Mann, Arthur William. *Branch Rickey: American in Action*. Boston: Houghton Mifflin, 1957.

Polner, Murray. *Branch Rickey: A Biography*. New York: Atheneum, 1982.

Rickey, Branch. *The American Diamond: A Documentary of the Game of Baseball*. New York: Simon and Schuster, 1965.

RIPKEN, CALVIN EDWIN, JR. (CAL) (1960–)

Cal Ripken, shortstop and later third baseman for the Baltimore Orioles, broke one of baseball's most unbreakable records: Lou Gehrig's string of 2,130 consecutive games played. The fact that Ripken broke the record to almost universal acclaim was remarkable, given the continuing devotion accorded the Yankees' Iron Horse, whose streak was ended in 1939 by amyotrophic lateral sclerosis, known ever after as Lou Gehrig's disease. Ripken, however, became a national hero in his successful pursuit of the record, which he broke on September 6, 1995; in doing so he almost single-handedly redeemed major league baseball from the stigma of the strike that had wiped out the World Series the previous season.

What won the hearts of fans, and led them back to baseball after the disenchantment of the strike, was the way in which Ripken went about his job. Every day Cal Ripken showed up for work. He arrived on time, played quietly but efficiently, signed autographs, and went home—another solid day's work done.

Cal Ripken, No. 8 of the Baltimore Orioles, stands ready at bat during a game against the Detroit Tigers at Camden Yards in Baltimore, Maryland, April 9, 2000. The Orioles defeated the Tigers 2-1. (Doug Pensinger/Allsport)

He was like the person who packs his lunchbox and heads to the factory, works hard, and never complains. Through a variety of injuries, some of them serious enough to cause almost anyone else to sit out—a severe ankle sprain in 1985, a twisted ankle in 1992, a right knee injury in 1993, serious back pain in 1997—Ripken kept working. The record fell, and he still did not stop. Fans who had dragged themselves out of bed through aches and pains to keep showing up for work identified with this workingman's ballplayer. There was little about Cal Ripken that was glamorous; he just kept going to work and doing his job.

Ripken, of course, was no run-of-the-mill player in talent. Although he may never have been the best at any one thing, he did almost everything well, and he was the consummate team player. Thus when Ripken had played in 2,632 consecutive games and finally informed his manager, Ray Miller, that he would take a day off—September 20, 1998, some 16 years after the streak began— the lunchbox player did it for the team. He knew that the streak was taking the focus away from the club and was limiting his manager's flexibility.

The steak was over, but Cal Ripken's career was not. As Ripken prepared for his poststreak season, he could look back over a career that had already produced 2,878 hits, leaving him within ready striking distance of his next great milestone— 3,000 hits. He had hit 384 home runs, driven in 1,514 runs, and played steady, sure-handed defense. Twice Cal Ripken had been named Most Valuable Player in the American League (1983, 1991), and he deserved a special Saving Baseball Award for bringing millions of fans back to the game in 1995. In an era of high-priced baseball players who ride free agency from team to team, and in a society in which "me" comes so often before "team," Cal Ripken demonstrated a work ethic and an old-fashioned set of values that would have been recognized as such throughout America's factories and farms. In a sport that is constantly looking to its past and to a simpler, more basic world, Cal Ripken proved to be a modern man who represents the best values of the past.

See also: Gehrig, Henry Louis; Heroes; Records Set.

Additional Reading:
Ripken, Cal. *The Only Way I Know.* New York: Viking, 1997.
Rosenfeld, Harvey. *Iron Man: The Cal Ripken, Jr. Story.* New York: St. Martin's, 1995.
Strazzabosco, Jeanne. *Learning about the Work Ethic from the Life of Cal Ripken, Jr.* New York: PowerKids, 1996.

RITUAL

Ritual is the repetition of actions that, in their repetition, take on ceremonial, and often religious, significance. Ritual is comforting and often transcendent. It carries the performer beyond the transitory moment into the timeless, linking present with past and, when performed in a communal setting, binding the individual to fellow practitioners. Ritual helps to answer humankind's need for belief that is lasting, experience that is constant, existence that leads the individual into communion with others in the temporal sphere and toward a reality beyond the here and now.

Ritual is as endemic to baseball as leather and wood, which helps to explain the enduring popularity of the sport. In ritual, baseball also approximates something of the religious experience. Most religious ceremonies or liturgies contain shared, repetitive actions. Any regular participant in religious ceremonies quickly comes to know these rituals and to share in their observance.

The baseball stadium itself is much like a cathedral, where domed roof or open air parallels the vaulted roof of a medieval cathedral built to approximate the eternal vault of the heavens. Within this cathedral, or—in the case of a minor league stadium—within something more akin to a country church, participants, whether on the field or in the stands, share rituals. Some rituals are performed by the players or other on-field personnel. The catcher crouches behind the plate and gives the signal; individual batters straighten a cap or follow a certain sequence of practice swings; infielders throw the ball around the infield (in a set pattern) after each first and second out (unless, of course, there are runners on base who might profit from an errant throw).

For many players, rituals reflect an attempt to exercise control over actions that can easily go awry. For all his talent, even an ace pitcher is at the whim of fate. The best-positioned pitch, thrown with all the velocity or movement of which the pitcher is capable, can be blooped over infielders' heads for a game-winning hit. Even the best hitter connects safely far less than 50 percent of the time, so the odds are always against him. If a certain action has occurred in conjunction with success in the past—perhaps keeping a certain coin in a locker, eating a particular food before games, or wearing the same pair of socks—then the player may continue that action until it no longer accompanies success. Conversely, any action that is associated in the player's mind with past failure is to be avoided at all costs. Most people would call such rituals superstition, but the player who gains confidence from such behavior is unlikely to worry about pejorative tags.

Rituals, however, are just as important, perhaps more important, for the fans. What is a baseball game without a hot-dog? Rituals include the seventh-inning stretch, singing "Take Me Out to the Ball Game," booing the umpires (by otherwise thoroughly courteous human beings), getting an autograph before the game, taking one's son or daughter or grandchild to the game, and on and on.

The religious audience stands, sits, kneels, sings, recites prayers as one. Similarly, fans share in certain rituals, including the aforementioned standing and singing during inning seven. But fans (at least those sharing a particular section) also move as one to follow the flight of a foul ball, rise from their seats to celebrate a home-team home run, express their disdain for a call that goes against them, and applaud the many heroics of their favorites. The "wave" is one of the most visible collective actions of fans, often enveloping the entire stadium. Even failure merits a collective sign of apprecia-

tion when it accompanies a good effort, witness the applause of a starting pitcher who, after seven or eight successful innings, departs having loaded the bases. Fans may want perfection, but they appreciate a decent effort.

Ritual ultimately looks forward. That has been true since people began the practice of ritual. Ritual is essentially hopeful, like baseball. "Wait 'til next year!" sounds the clarion call of all those baseball practitioners and fans whose teams came up a little (or perhaps a lot) short. In the spring, that season of rebirth, all teams are equal, at least until they start playing. The holy grail of baseball victory—the championships—is once again the object of pursuit by adventurous knights of the round ball and the strong wooden bat. Ritual is as old as civilization, and its presence within baseball reminds us that something in human nature seeks unity of belief and community throughout the diverse realms that make up the days and ways of human life, including such realms as religion, myth, and the game we call baseball.

See also: Family Relationships; Fiction; Films; Myth; Religion; "Take Me Out to the Ball Game."

Additional Reading:

Doty, William G. *Mythography: The Study of Myths and Rituals.* 2d ed. Tuscaloosa: University of Alabama Press, 2000.

Driver, Tom Faw. *The Magic of Ritual: Our Need for Liberating Rites That Transform Our Lives and Our Communities.* San Francisco: HarperSanFrancisco, 1991.

Gmelch, George. "Superstition and Ritual in American Baseball." *Elysian Fields Quarterly* 11(3) (1992): 25–36.

Guttmann, Allen. *From Ritual to Record: The Nature of Modern Sports.* New York: Columbia University Press, 1978.

ROBINSON, FRANK (1935–)

Frank Robinson, like the great Brooklyn Dodger star with the same last name, was a pioneer in breaking the color barrier in the major leagues. When Frank Robinson was appointed manager of the Cleveland Indians in 1975, he became the first African American ever to manage in the majors. He had a keen sense of the historical importance of the moment. At the press conference announcing his selection as manager, he expressed his disappointment that Jackie Robinson, who had died three years earlier, could not be with him. Frank Robinson was a smart choice, for he brought with him a long and distinguished career as one of the great players of his time.

Frank Robinson was born in Beaumont, Texas, one of 10 children. It was while playing baseball for the Bill Erwin Legion Post team in Oakland, California, however, that he was discovered by scouts. At the time, he was something of a second prize for the Cincinnati Reds, who were more interested in Legion Post catcher J. W. Porter. Porter signed instead with the Detroit Tigers and went on to have modest success in the major leagues. The Reds settled for Robinson and got a future Hall of Famer.

Robinson came up to the Reds in 1956 and hit 38 home runs as a rookie. The Reds won the pennant in 1961, Robinson picking up the Most Valuable Player Award. A complete player, respected as much for his drive and determination as his skills, Robinson routinely crashed into walls trying to catch fly balls and dared pitchers to hit him. He overcame a severe beaning early in his career to play 21 years, 10 with the Reds before being traded to the Baltimore Orioles prior to the 1966 season in a controversial deal.

With the Orioles, Robinson immediately proved Reds management wrong for thinking that he was over the hill. He won the Triple Crown in 1966 with 49 home runs, 122 RBIs, and a .316 batting average. More important, he helped lead his team to a World Series championship over Sandy Koufax and the Los Angeles Dodgers. By the time Robinson completed his playing career, he had accumulated 586 home runs, 1,812 RBIs, 204 stolen bases, a .294 career batting average, the National League Rookie of the Year Award, a Most Valuable Player Award in each league (the only player ever to achieve that feat), a Triple Crown, a World Series Most Valuable Player Award, and, despite the early beaning, led his league in being hit by pitched balls six times. He retired as an active player just 57 hits shy of 3,000. In addition to the 1966 title, he helped the Orioles win three pennants in 1969, 1970, and 1971 and another World Series in 1970.

Robinson played for the Dodgers in 1972, the California Angels in 1973 and part of 1974, and the Indians from 1974 to 1976 (the final two seasons as player-manager). Robinson had trouble getting the weak Cleveland club into contention during his tenure there, and he was let go in June 1977. Robinson later managed the San Francisco Giants and the Orioles. United Press International named him National League Manager of the Year with the Giants in 1982, the same year he was inducted into the Hall of Fame.

By accepting the managerial position with San Francisco, Frank Robinson became the first African American to manage in the National League (as he had been the first in the American League), a fact that brings great credit to Robinson but does not speak well of the major leagues' commitment to hiring minority managers. It also demonstrates the double standard employed in hiring African Americans in the major leagues. White managers with modest playing and managing credentials were hired (and rehired) in huge numbers, but to be an African American manager required Hall of Fame credentials. That double standard would only slowly change. Robinson's talents continue to be recognized. He recently was appointed vice president of on-field operations for the major leagues.

See also: African Americans; Robinson, Jack Roosevelt.

Additional Reading:

Ashe, Arthur R., Jr. *A Hard Road to Glory— Baseball: The African-American Athlete in Baseball*. 1988. Reprint, New York: Amistad, 1993.

Robinson, Frank. *My Life in Baseball*. Garden City, NY: Doubleday, 1968.

Schneider, Russell, Jr. *Frank Robinson: The Making of a Manager*. New York: Coward, McCann, and Geoghegan, 1976.

ROBINSON, JACK ROOSEVELT (JACKIE) (1919–1972)

Anyone who doubts the importance of baseball in American society should look more closely at the life and impact of Jackie Robinson. Robinson became the first African American in modern times to play in the major leagues. The fact that he integrated baseball (as opposed to a lesser institution) is as significant as it was difficult. He played the game in the open, before tens of thousands, where any failure in talent, courage, or self-control would have been immediately visible. When he came to bat, fielded a grounder, or started his dash for second base on an attempted steal, it wasn't only the Dodgers' fortunes that rode on his shoulders. He carried also the future of his race and the cause of racial justice in American society.

Jackie Robinson succeeded magnificently, demonstrating that he was more than a Hall of Fame player; he was a hero, larger than most any in American history. In the long and difficult civil rights struggle by African Americans to make true the promise of America, no leader save Martin Luther King Jr. stands taller than Jackie Robinson. But it was Robinson who blazed the path that King would follow.

Branch Rickey, general manager and co-owner of the Brooklyn Dodgers, was determined to integrate the major leagues, and he looked for the ideal player to achieve that most challenging goal. He could not have chosen better. Seldom has anyone had a more diverse and appropriate background for any position than did Jackie Robinson. Born in Georgia, Robinson, along with three brothers and a sister, was reared in Pasadena, California, by his mother, Mallie. The father, Jerry, left the family the year that Jackie, youngest of the children, was born. Brother Mack preceded Jackie into athletic success, finishing second in the 200-meter dash at the 1936 Olympics in Berlin, where, in Hitler's domain, the great African American athlete Jesse Owens won four gold medals.

Jackie Robinson attended Pasadena Junior College and later UCLA, where he earned letters in basketball, football, track, and baseball. He led his league in scoring in basketball, set a record in the broad jump, and achieved fame as a running back on the football team. Baseball was of less interest to Robinson at the time.

World War II beckoned after college, and Robinson became a second lieutenant in the U.S. Army. On a July 1944 day in Texas, Robinson boarded a bus on his military base and was ordered to the back. Vehicles on military bases had been officially desegregated by then, the result of embarrassing incidents involving boxing greats Joe Louis and Ray Robinson, and Robinson refused. He was taken to a guardhouse for questioning and later put on trial for insubordination but subsequently acquitted. Robinson's refusal to accommodate a racist order was consistent with his behavior earlier at UCLA, where he had earned the reputation of what then was called a "race man," an individual proud of his race. That was one of the qualities that attracted Robinson's future wife, Rachel, when they were students.

King Feisal II of Iraq (center) with Brooklyn Dodgers baseball star Jackie Robinson (right) and Dodgers manager Charles Dressen in New York, August 18, 1952 (Hulton Getty)

After leaving the military, Robinson looked for work and found it with the Negro League Kansas City Monarchs. In 1945, his only season with the Monarchs, Robinson played shortstop, hit .387, and excelled on the bases. Sportswriter Wendell Smith arranged a tryout with the Boston Red Sox for Robinson and two other players from the Negro Leagues. They were not signed, and the Red Sox would not have an African American player until 1959, being the last major league team to integrate.

By that time, Branch Rickey was engaged in his search for the right player to break the color barrier. He sent scout and former catcher Clyde Sukeforth to scout Robinson. Near the end of August, Robinson was invited to meet with Rickey and Sukeforth, ostensibly about a job with a new all-black team, the Brown Dodgers, that Rickey was planning. Once Robinson arrived, Rickey informed him that his real interest was in having the Monarch star play for the Dodgers. Rickey put Robinson through an exhaustive interview process, testing his character, courage, and self-control. At one point, Robinson asked whether Rickey wanted someone afraid to fight back against insults and threats. As Robinson reports in his autobiography, Rickey's response was, "I'm looking for a ballplayer with guts enough not to fight back." Before the session ended, Robinson had a job with the Montreal Royals, the Dodgers' top minor league team.

Robinson starred with Montreal in 1946, leading the league in batting and helping Montreal win the Little World Series. Meanwhile, major league owners, with the exception of Rickey, were expressing their opposition to integrating the majors by a 15-1 vote. A worried Rickey met with commissioner Happy Chandler in January 1947 and received strong support from the former Kentucky governor and senator. A far cry from Judge Kenesaw Mountain Landis, who opposed allowing blacks to play in the majors, Chandler believed that if African American men could fight for their country in war, they were quite capable of playing baseball in the majors.

Jackie Robinson went to spring training with the Dodgers in 1947, where his entrance into the majors was far from easy. St. Louis Cardinal players threatened to strike if they were forced to play a Dodger club that included Robinson. Ford Frick, National League president, not previously a strong supporter of integrating the majors, reacted forcefully, threatening any players who refused to play with suspension. Even players on his own team, such as outfielder Dixie Walker and backup catcher Bobby Bragan, started a petition to keep Robinson off the team. Shortstop Pee Wee Reese, like Chandler a Kentuckian, refused to sign and proved to be a consistently strong supporter of Robinson; while manager Leo Durocher, who a few years before had been disciplined by Landis for saying that he would like to sign black players, came down hard on those opposing Robinson.

As Robinson's first season in the majors progressed, he faced continued taunts from opposing players, was spiked and thrown at, faced the indignities of Jim Crow laws regarding accommodations during road trips, and saw his wife and young son threatened. Fans, however, including large numbers of African Americans, turned out to see the new Dodger star, setting attendance records in several cities. And Robinson gave them a lot to see. He batted .297 with 42 bunt hits and stole a league-leading 29 bases while winning the Rookie of the Year Award. Brooklyn won the first of six pennants it would capture during Robinson's 10 years with the team, along with the World Series in 1955, the first-ever world championship for the Dodgers.

Jackie Robinson followed his extraordinary rookie season with even greater years. He won the batting title in 1949 with a .342 average and was named Most Valuable Player in the National League. That year he also drove in 124 runs and won another stolen-base title, with 37. The 1949 season was the first of six consecutive years that Robinson batted over .300. As the 1956 season ended, Robinson had a lifetime batting average of .311 with 1,518 hits and 197 stolen bases. Having not reached the majors until he was 28 because of military service and the ban on African American players, Robinson was now 38, old for a major league player, and his last two seasons had been below his standard, with batting averages of .256 and .275 in 105 and 117 games. The Dodgers traded him to the archrival New York Giants, and Robinson retired.

Jackie Robinson had brought a new style of play to the National League, the type that fans were accustomed to watching in Negro League competition: speed, stolen bases (including stealing home, which became a Robinson trademark), bunts, and the hit-and-run play. He also, of course, had opened a door for African American players. He had reminded Americans that equal opportunity belonged in all areas of life, and that lesson would be repeated over and over throughout the 1950s and 1960s as Americans, black and white, worked, and sometimes died, for the cause of equal rights.

Jackie Robinson continued the battle after retiring from baseball. He became a successful businessman and encouraged other African Americans to do likewise. He traveled South during the 1960s to lend his support to the civil rights movement, and when Curt Flood fought the reserve clause, Robinson, when most of Flood's fellow players remained silent, stood up in federal court to testify on behalf of individual freedom. Suffering from heart disease and diabetes, Jackie Robinson, only 53 years of age, died just 10 days after throwing out the first ball at the 1972 World Series. As long as there is a United States, citizens, both on and off the baseball field, will continue to enjoy the fruits of Robinson's labors. He is among the most important athletes in American history.

See also: African Americans; Brooklyn Dodgers; Canadian Baseball; Chandler, Albert Benjamin; Films; Heroes; Landis, Kenesaw Mountain; Music; Negro Leagues; Rickey, Wesley Branch; War.

Additional Reading:
Mann, Arthur William. *The Jackie Robinson Story*. New York: Grosset and Dunlap, 1956.
Robinson, Jackie. *I Never Had It Made: The Autobiography of Jackie Robinson*. 1972. Reprint, Hopewell, NJ: Ecco, 1995.
Robinson, Sharon. *Stealing Home: An Intimate Family Portrait by the Daughter of Jackie Robinson*. 1996. Reprint, New York: Harper-Perennial, 1997.
Tygiel, Jules. *Baseball's Great Experiment: Jackie Robinson and His Legacy*. New York: Oxford University Press, 1983.
Tygiel, Jules, ed. *The Jackie Robinson Reader: Perspectives on an American Hero*. New York: Dutton, 1997.

ROSE, PETER EDWARD (PETE, CHARLIE HUSTLE) (1941–)

Pete Rose, who spent most of his career with the Cincinnati Reds, was one of the great major league players in history. As every fan knows, he broke one of the

supposedly unbreakable records, Ty Cobb's career mark of 4,191 hits. Rose, a switch-hitter, surpassed Cobb in 1985 and concluded his remarkable playing career the following year with a total of 4,256 hits over 24 seasons. He also played in more games (3,562), went to bat more times (14,053), and collected more singles (3,510) than anyone who ever played in the majors. He finished second all-time in doubles with 746 and fourth in runs scored with 2,165. He made the All-Star team at five different positions (first, second, and third base; right and left field). Rose hit over .300 15 times, leading the National league in hitting on three occasions. He collected over 200 hits 10 times and led the league in hits seven times. He was National League Rookie of the Year in 1963 and Most Valuable Player in 1973. Rose was a vital member of three World Series winners: the Big Red Machine of 1975–1976, and the Philadelphia Phillies in 1980. He was player-manager for the Reds from 1984 until 1986 and, after retiring as a player, continued to manage the team until his removal from baseball during the 1989 season.

Such impressive statistics, however, do not tell the full Pete Rose story. Pete was a hometown boy who reached the pinnacle of baseball success despite inferior talent. Little was heroic about Rose's five-foot eleven appearance, but the average fan could relate to him all the better. He was the underdog who overachieved, the boy who beat the big guys. And he achieved his remarkable feats by compensating for his modest talent through hard work, hustle, and taking advantage of any slip-up by the other team. His trademark play was the head-first slide into third base when the opposing team assumed he would stop at second. He earned the nickname "Charlie Hustle" because of this style of play, an ironic name after his betting habits came to light. Rose was generous with the fans and always had a good story, usually a funny one, for the press, all of which added to his regular-guy persona.

Rose grew up in Cincinnati and personified the city and its small-town, rough-around-the-edges character. His departure for Philadelphia as a free agent after the 1978 season was blamed on Reds management, and when he was traded back to the Reds during the 1984 season (by Montreal, for whom he had played part of the year), his homecoming was greeted with great joy in Cincinnati. Rose assumed the role of player-manager, and the public and media alike followed with intense interest his pursuit of Cobb's record.

The Reds had fallen on hard times in recent years, with two sixth-place finishes and one fifth-place finish in the Western Division from 1982 to 1984. In 1985, as Rose pursued Cobb's record, he also managed the team to a second-place finish. Although Cincinnati won no titles under Rose's direction, they challenged each year, finishing second each season through 1988. With rumors swirling about the team during the 1989 campaign, the Reds struggled to fifth place.

Few players captured public attention as did Pete Rose during his pursuit of the hits record in 1985, and few athletes have been so identified with their hometown. Rose could have been just about anything he wanted to be in Cincinnati inside or outside baseball. However, as stories gradually emerged about his betting, his downfall looked increasingly certain.

Rose had enjoyed betting from his childhood days when he accompanied his father, Harry, an accountant and local amateur sports hero, to the River Downs racetrack, where Harry enjoyed betting modestly on the horses. In later years, as Rose tried to fill the void left by the end of his record-setting playing career, he apparently turned increasingly to gambling for excitement. This gambling allegedly included extensive betting on baseball teams, including the Reds. Although there is no evidence to indicate that Rose ever bet against his own team, baseball Rule 21(d) forbids betting on any team in which the bettor "has a duty to perform" and provides a penalty of permanent ineligibility for anyone who violates the rule.

Amid concerns that Rose may have bet on baseball, commissioner Bart Giamatti hired an outside attorney, John Dowd, to investigate Rose. Dowd's investigation led to a 225-page report concluding that strong evidence existed that Rose had bet on baseball and on his own team. Rose strongly denied the charges but ultimately, while continuing his denials, agreed to a conclusion of the matter that both banished him from baseball for life (although with the opportunity to request reinstatement) and acknowledged "that the Commissioner has a factual basis to impose the penalty provided herein."

If Rose in fact violated baseball Rule 21(d), why did he do it? Despite his heroic accomplishments, Rose possessed serious flaws, including a love for gambling, which seemed to be embedded in his very nature. This led to his consorting with unsavory types from the world of gambling. That combination would destroy his career. Gambling addiction has come to be recognized as an illness that must be treated, but Rose refused to admit that he had a problem. If he had admitted such a flaw and thrown himself on the mercy of a forgiving public, he might well have escaped the ultimate baseball penalty, or at least established a firm basis for lifting the penalty after a reasonable wait. Pete Rose would have likely been welcomed back into the fold as a prodigal son, but not as a sinner refusing to admit that he had a problem or bet on baseball games. In addition, Rose seemed to view himself as above the rules, reflecting an excessive pride that occasioned his downfall. Rose apparently saw himself as untouchable, especially after he broke Cobb's record.

It was a dangerous combination: a compulsion for gambling; a sense of immunity; no mountains left to climb. As a result, Rose was driven into exile. But more was to come. Rose pleaded guilty in April 1990 to tax evasion and served five months in prison. In February 1991, shortly before Rose would have been eligible for Hall of Fame balloting, the directors of the Hall of Fame altered the selection rules to prohibit any player on the baseball ineligible list from being considered. Disqualification from the Hall of Fame may have been the most severe blow for Rose. The decision remains controversial, considering the moral shortcomings of some players already enshrined there. Nonetheless, Pete Rose's fall from greatness was complete.

The plot remains unresolved. There may still be an opportunity for Pete Rose to reclaim a measure of what he lost. Certainly many fans feel betrayed by him; others hope for some type of reconciliation between major league baseball and one of its great stars. When Rose joined the other living members of the top 100 players of the century at the 1999 All-Star Game, his ovation was one of the loudest. At that same game, interviewer Jim Gray kept urging Pete Rose to admit that he had bet on baseball, a decision that would backfire on Gray, who appeared as hostile and spoiling the memorable occasion.

Rose has yet to regain the spot in the sun for which he longs, but that may yet occur.

See also: Cheating; Favorite Baseball Player; Gambling; Giamatti, Angelo Bartlett; Hall of Fame and Museum; Heroes; Jackson, Joseph Jefferson; Records Set.

Additional Reading:
Ginsburg, Daniel E. *The Fix Is In: A History of Baseball Gambling and Game Fixing Scandals*. Jefferson, NC: McFarland, 1995.
Reston, James, Jr. *Collision at Home Plate: The Lives of Pete Rose and Bart Giamatti*. New York: HarperCollins, 1991; New York: HarperPerennial, 1992.
Rose, Pete, and Roger Kahn. *Pete Rose: My Story*. New York: Macmillan, 1989.
Wheeler, Lonnie, and John Baskin. *The Cincinnati Game*. Wilmington, OH: Orange Fraser, 1988.

ROTISSERIE BASEBALL (FANTASY LEAGUES)

Rotisserie baseball, also known as fantasy baseball or fantasy leagues, originated in 1980 with a group of fans in New York City. It since has grown into a popular and widespread pastime for fans who imagine themselves not as players but as owners and general managers. It is a descendant of the so-called hot-stove league, which goes back at least through the early decades of the twentieth century: a gathering of men sitting around the stove in a general store or barber shop discussing baseball (sometimes with boys in attendance, but usually a bit apart, listening rather than participating). The hot-stove league especially functioned during the off-season and centered around the possible fortunes of the interlocutors' favorite teams the following spring. Trades, of course, were a popular topic of conversation.

The New York originators of Rotisserie, named after the restaurant where they often met to carry on their discussions, created dream teams of active players and constructed a league for their competition. Performances of players were tracked, with team standings based on how the team members performed in eight statistical areas: home runs, runs batted in, batting average, and stolen bases (for hitters); wins, saves, earned-run average, and ratio of walks plus hits over innings (for pitchers).

The number of teams now in existence is impossible to determine, especially as other varieties of fantasy baseball have arisen, but there probably are somewhere between 100,000 and 200,000. The "managers" often put considerable time into their hobby, following the daily accomplishments of players in actual major league games and steadily updating the relevant statistics. If a player is disabled or sent to the minors, the Rotisserie manager activates another player from a "farm club." Within the Rotisserie league, managers may trade and waive players. Managers initially construct their teams by bidding for desired players, usually with a maximum amount of money permitted per team. The invested money, usually a modest sum of perhaps $200–300 per participant, may be divided at season's end among the managers of the top-ranked teams.

Those players of Rotisserie ball who want to save time may utilize computer software or even pay a firm (there are several available) to compile statistics and provide standings on a regular basis. Players also may find many sources of information and enjoyable supplements to their game in magazines devoted to fantasy baseball, the name that seems to be catching on in the media. *USA Today Baseball Weekly* includes a section called "Fantasy Insider." Many Internet sites are devoted to fantasy ball, providing information, inviting discussion, and selling products. Periodicals such as *Baseball Weekly* and *The Sporting News,* as well as TV network sports sites, offer fantasy baseball links.

Fantasy baseball may seem far removed from the game itself as played on sandlots, in baseball parks, or in school playgrounds. Certainly, many fans scoff at fantasy devotees. If baseball, as many once felt, should not be played at night or in an enclosed stadium, but outside under the bright light of day on real grass, playing baseball around a table or via an online chat room must seem especially unnatural. Yet something of the same spirit drives both groups. And certainly the game as played physically has had, almost from its start, its imaginative counterparts for later replay. The box score is one such example, though somewhat primitive by modern standards. In any case, there is more than one way to play the game. Rotisserie baseball fills a niche for fans looking for excitement.

See also: Games; Periodicals; Statistics.
Additional Reading:
Zoss, Joel, and John Bowman. *Diamonds in the Rough: The Untold History of Baseball.* 1989. Reprint, Chicago: Contemporary Books, 1996.
Assorted magazines and websites.

ROUNDERS

Recreation is an important part of American culture, as it is in many other cultures. Rounders is one form of play (cricket is another) that Americans inherited from England, where it was popular as early as the sixteenth century. In the United States, rounders was an enjoyable pastime into the nineteenth century, yielding townball and, finally, modern baseball.

In rounders, a feeder tosses the ball to a striker, who, using a flat piece of wood, hits the ball and attempts to circle the sanctuaries (usually four stakes driven into the ground) before making an out (by having his hit caught in the air or on one bounce, or by being hit with the ball). If the player makes it home (the castle) in one run, without having to stop at a sanctuary, he has completed a rounder (an early version of the home run). Unlike base runners in modern baseball, the player runs clockwise. One team hits until all members have made an out. Both sides must be in ("inning") an equal number of times, and the team with the higher tally (number of runs) wins.

The fiction that Abner Doubleday invented baseball in 1839 was a nationalistic attempt to demonstrate that America owed nothing to England for this great game. However, Henry Chadwick, America's first major sportswriter, disputed the Doubleday story, recalling how, as a boy in his native England, he had played rounders and that the game was similar to early American baseball. An American scholar, Robert Henderson, discovered rules for rounders in William Clarke's *The Boy's Own Book* (1829) and Robin Carver's *The Book of Sports* (1834), the latter a Boston-published book that copied the rules for rounders from Clarke and changed the name of the game from rounders to base (or goal) ball.

See also: Chadwick, Henry; Cricket; Doubleday, Abner; Townball.

Additional Reading:

Henderson, Robert William. *Ball, Bat, and Bishop: The Origin of Ball Games.* New York: Rockport, 1947.

———. *Early American Sport: A Check-List of Books by American and Foreign Authors Published in America Prior to 1860, Including Sporting Songs.* 2d ed. New York: A. S. Barnes, 1953.

Seymour, Harold. *Baseball: The Early Years.* 1960. Reprint, New York: Oxford University Press, 1989.

RURAL AMERICA

Baseball is usually viewed as essentially a rural sport, part of the early heritage of the United States. Today, in modern concrete-and-steel ballparks, some with retractable roofs and the atmosphere of a shopping mall, the field is an urban refuge, a green moment from the past. To attend a baseball game, even at the major league level, is to seek lost innocence. It is an attempt to return home, even if that home is centuries and many thousands of miles away.

There is some truth to this mythic portrayal of baseball. The reality is that earlier versions of baseball were widely played by boys and men in colonial America, which, of course, was primarily rural. When organized baseball began with the New York Knickerbockers in the 1840s, the players were adults, mainly professional urbanites who had leisure time to play. As organized ball and then the professional game developed over the next few decades, they too were largely urban; the professional game was dependent on population centers to make it financially worthwhile.

Nonetheless, youngsters, including rural youths, easily picked up the rules of the new game. In addition, baseball was relatively easy to play. It required little in the way of equipment—just a bat and ball, both of which could be made by inventive youngsters; a field or lot where there was sufficient room for the game; anything such as rocks, pieces of wood, clumps of weeds, or circles of dirt to serve as bases; and not much in the way of natural ability. Almost any child could play the game at a rudimentary level.

Many rural boys, like their urban counterparts who worked in factories and mills, had limited time to play, spending most of their hours when not in school at fieldwork, milking, and other farm chores. Nonetheless, most boys in the nineteenth century surely played when they could, including at recess on school days.

The method of getting up a game remained much the same throughout the nineteenth and early twentieth centuries before yielding to Little League and other adult-organized efforts. Youngsters chose up sides, with the two best players heading the respective teams. One boy would toss the bat vertically, handle up, to the other, who would grab the bat with one hand encircling it. The previous captain would encircle the bat with one of his hands directly above the other captain's hand. They would move up the bat that way, hand shifting above hand, to the knob at the end of the bat. The last boy whose hand could go around the bat and hold it without letting it drop, would get the first pick. Choosing friends was fine, but usually choices were based on an ability to play the game. The two captains then alternated choices; ideally until everyone was chosen, leaving the youngest, slowest, and weakest until the end.

The options in the country were usually to play in the schoolyard or in a cow pasture, as crop fields were out of bounds for fear of damage. Rural players sometimes had to share the pasture with cows but made certain that no bull was in the vicinity, and players were always on the lookout for bovine calling cards.

A popular but now fading image of baseball as it was played at least through the first half of the twentieth century is that of youngsters competing with a one-room school in the background, the sort of site where the author of this book played many games. The one-room school also is receding into the past, where boys and girls forever will continue their exuberant games in a world beyond time. All of this is part of both the history and myth of baseball, a memory colored a deeper green than the city lots but not necessarily the parks where urban youngsters learned to play the game.

See also: Family Relationships; Little League; Myth.

Additional Reading:

Danbom, David B. *Born in the Country: A History of Rural America*. Baltimore: Johns Hopkins University Press, 1995.

Gulliford, Andrew. *America's Country Schools*. 3d ed. Niwot: University Press of Colorado, 1996.

Hathaway, Dale E. *People of Rural America*. Washington, DC: U.S. Department of Commerce, 1968.

Seymour, Harold. *Baseball: The People's Game*. 1990. Reprint, New York: Oxford University Press, 1991.

RUTH, GEORGE HERMAN (BABE, THE BAMBINO, THE SULTAN OF SWAT) (1895–1948)

Babe Ruth—the Sultan of Swat—is the great mythic figure of baseball. His impact on the game was enormous, affecting the very nature of baseball and the way that the public viewed the game. He was a larger-than-life giant of a man who so dominated the public consciousness that his visage remains among the most recognizable in the world.

Born in Baltimore to a saloonkeeper father and a mother who bore eight children, only two of whom survived, Ruth was unwanted and unloved. Often in trouble, he was branded "incorrigible" by the age of seven and exiled to St. Mary's Industrial School for Boys. There he was befriended by Brother Matthias, who encouraged Ruth to play baseball and, when Ruth was 19, introduced him to Jack Dunn of the Baltimore Orioles, who signed him.

Ruth was in the majors with the Boston Red Sox by 1914, where he established himself as a dominant pitcher. He won 18, 23, and 24 games from 1915 through 1917, but by 1919 he was splitting time between the mound and the outfield, as Boston tried to take advantage of his hitting ability. A Hall of Fame–quality pitcher, Ruth starred in the 1916 and 1918 World Series, fashioning a record $29^2/_3$ consecutive scoreless innings and helping the Red Sox win both Series.

After the 1919 season, Babe Ruth was sold to the New York Yankees for

George Herman "Babe" Ruth (1895–1948), circa 1930 (Hulton Getty)

$125,000 and a $300,000 loan so that Boston owner H. Harrison Frazee, also a theatrical producer, could finance a production of *No, No Nanette*. It was a hit but no home run.

Fans had become disillusioned with baseball after the 1919 Black Sox scandal and perhaps a bit tired of the pitcher-dominated baseball then being played. The country had just emerged from World War I, and prosperity and the Jazz Age were around the corner. The rule-makers of baseball may have sensed what lay ahead, for they moved in 1920 to give hitters a better chance, outlawing the spitball and other pitches that involved defacing the ball. Umpires were ordered to remove blackened baseballs so that batters had a more visible white target at which to swing. Even the ball itself was altered, making it more lively.

None of these changes, though, lessens the accomplishments of Babe Ruth. In his final season in Boston, Ruth had hit 29 home runs, a new record. In the following year, his first with the Yankees, Ruth pounded out 54 home runs. Yet the rule changes had at best a modest effect on other players. With 54 home runs, Ruth outhomered not only every player but every team except one. The next year, he broke his record again, hitting 59.

Babe Ruth took New York and the nation by storm. But Ruth's fame and success seemed to induce in him a feeling that he was above the rules established for others; perhaps he simply had become incapable of controlling his vast appetites. In either case, 1922 was a disaster. Several suspensions caused him to miss approximately one-third of the season. His home-run output dropped to 35, and he hit a minuscule .118 in the World Series loss to the Giants.

Ruth rebounded the next year, helping to inaugurate Yankee Stadium with a home run in the first game played there and thereby supplied a nickname for the stadium: "The House That Ruth Built." Endorsement requests poured in during these glory days. Wheaties, Quaker Puffed Wheat, Ruth's Home Run Candy Bar, underwear, cigars, cigarettes; whatever the product, Ruth endorsed it, and he had to hire accountants and a business manager to look after his earnings. Although not the first sports figure to endorse a product for money, Babe Ruth was the first to do it in a big way—which is how he did most everything.

In 1925, Ruth relapsed into excess. Notorious for his excessive eating and drinking, as well as his fondness for women, he reported to training camp 30 pounds overweight. On April 9, he collapsed, supposedly from an especially gluttonous episode. His manager, Miller Huggins, later suspended Ruth after he stayed out two nights in a row. Meanwhile, his wife suffered a nervous breakdown. Even these excesses, however, added to Ruth's reputation as a colossus among mortals; Ruth had come to epitomize the self-indulgence, as well as the glamour, of the Roaring Twenties.

Once again, however, Ruth rebounded, and the home runs kept coming, including a new record of 60 in 1927. Ruth's flame burned ever brighter. He even gave his name to a book for boys (ghostwritten, of course): *Babe Ruth's Own Book of Baseball*. If his authorship of the book was spurious, his love for children was thoroughly genuine, perhaps stemming from his own unhappy childhood. Ruth readily signed autographs for the myriad children who hovered about him. Michael Gibbons, of the Babe Ruth Birthplace Museum in Baltimore, estimates that he signed as many as 600,000 balls during his lifetime. As much as the home run and the commercial endorsement, Babe Ruth established the autograph as an essential part of baseball.

One of the most memorable events of Babe Ruth's career occurred in the 1932 World Series between the Yankees and the Chicago Cubs. In Game 3, Ruth stroked a three-run homer off Cubs' pitcher Charlie Root. Then, in the third inning, the Babe faced Root again. Ruth took two balls and two strikes. Before the fifth pitch, he took off his cap and held up two fingers of his right hand, gesturing, perhaps, toward center field. Ruth then drove the next pitch over the center-field wall, the home run that would always be known as the "called shot." Root always denied that Ruth had actually called the home run, but his disclaimers had little effect on the public.

Ruth barnstormed Japan with other American players during a 1934 tour. The Japanese were so affected by the magic of Ruth that they formed Japan's first professional baseball league within two years of the visit. Ruth was so much an American icon that during World War II Japanese soldiers would mock American soldiers by yelling, "To Hell with Babe Ruth!" Japan's genuine admiration for Ruth, however, came out clearly when, upon his death, Japanese players paused during play to honor him. Also during the war, Americans would use Babe Ruth as a touchstone to identify spies trying to pass themselves off as Americans. If the suspected spy could not answer questions about the Babe, he was liable to be shot, spy or not.

Released by the Yankees after the 1934 season, Ruth joined the Boston Braves. He had one final great moment left in him. On May 25, he shocked everyone in attendance at Forbes Field by hitting three home runs. The final one cleared the roof; it was number 714, Ruth's last.

With his pleas to manage the Yankees consistently rejected, and now largely an outcast from the game he loved so much, Ruth fell ill in 1946. Surgery the following year discovered cancer along the left wall of his neck. On April 27, 1947, the Yankees honored the Babe at Yankee Stadium. Now frail and thin, Ruth could barely speak above a whisper. On June 13 of the following year, he made his last appearance at a Yankee ceremony, a celebration of the twenty-fifth anniversary of the house that he built. Ruth needed to use a bat as a cane to walk onto the field. His number 3 was retired, just the second number, following Lou Gehrig's number 4, to be reserved always for its most famous wearer. About two months later, on August 16, Babe Ruth was dead.

Babe Ruth left behind a .341 career batting average, records for home runs in a season and a career, and the distinction of having been one of the original players inducted into the Hall of Fame in 1939. His home-run records ultimately would fall, but the name "Babe Ruth" would remain synonymous with the home run, and his impact would continue. "Ruthian" remains an adjective denoting a monumental accomplishment, much like the folktales of Paul Bunyan. Actor Jack Webb, who played Joe Friday in the TV series *Dragnet,* wore the number 714 on his badge in honor of his hero, Babe Ruth. At the end of the millennium, Ruth still remained the number-one sports personality in marketing, his image continuing to be used to sell a variety of products; and a baseball signed by Ruth sold in August 1998 for $35,500. Babe Ruth's appeal remains as strong as ever, his fame as enduring as his effect on the game of baseball.

See also: Business; Cancer; Fiction; Films; Gehrig, Henry Louis; Heroes; Home Run; Japanese Baseball; Maris, Roger Eugene; New York Yankees; Records Set; World Series; Yankee Stadium.

Additional Reading:

Creamer, Robert W. *Babe: The Legend Comes to Life*. New York: Simon and Schuster, 1974.
Robertson, John G. *The Babe Chases 60: That Fabulous 1927 Season, Home Run by Home Run*. Jefferson, NC: McFarland, 1999.
Ruth, Claire Merritt. *The Babe and I*. Englewood Cliffs, NJ: Prentice-Hall, 1959.
Smelser, Marshall. *The Life That Ruth Built: A Biography*. New York: Quadrangle/New York Times Book, 1975.
Wagenheim, Kal. *Babe Ruth: His Life and Legend*. New York: Holt, 1992.

RYAN, LYNN NOLAN (1947–)

Nolan Ryan is the rare genuine hero in American society. Anyone doubting that should go to Texas and look around. There, in the state where the self-styled "country boy" grew up, and where the state legislature declared Ryan an official Texas hero in 1989, one can find the Nolan Ryan Expressway south of Houston and the Nolan Ryan Center for Continuing Education, built by the Nolan Ryan Historical Foundation at Alvin Junior College in Ryan's hometown.

The reasons for Ryan's enshrinement in Texas and in the hearts of fans and other Americans, long before his 1999 enshrinement in the Baseball Hall of Fame, are many. Some of his stature depends, of course, on his pitching. Ryan threw the glamour pitch, the fastball (certainly one of the best ever, although helped along by an outstanding curveball); he was especially adept at the glamour play for pitchers—the strikeout; and he kept recording those no-hitters.

Just a sampling of Nolan Ryan's records: most no-hitters (7), most strikeouts in a career (5,714), most strikeouts in a season (383), most seasons with 200 or more strikeouts (15), and most seasons with 300 or more strikeouts (6). True, he also set records for most walks

Nolan Ryan of the Texas Rangers signs autographs for fans at the team's spring training camp, March 6, 1992. (Reuters/Jeff Christensen/Archive Photos)

in a career (2,795) and most times leading the majors in walks (8), but no one is perfect. In fact, the wildness, especially earlier in his career, added to the mystique of the pitcher and certainly contributed to the intimidation factor for batters attempting to stand in against him. Ryan also won 324 games in his career, most of those victories coming with weak or mediocre clubs.

But there is more to Nolan Ryan the hero. He really was a country boy, and he never forgot his roots. When he could have made a lot more money going somewhere else to pitch, he chose Texas teams for the final 14 years of his career—the Houston Astros and Texas Rangers. After retirement, he stayed in his home state ranching, engaging in various business ventures, and investing in a minor league team, the double-A Round

Rock Express. One of Ryan's guests at the Hall of Fame induction ceremony was his high school coach, Jim Watson.

The general manager of Nolan Ryan's new minor league team is a young man named Robert Reid Ryan—and that also explains a lot about why Nolan Ryan is so revered. He is a genuine family man. He married his wife, Ruth, in 1967, and they have two sons and a daughter. The family has always been close, with Ryan keeping his children around him as much as possible during the baseball season when he was playing.

The longer Ryan pitched, the more popular he became, especially with the older crowd. Ryan pitched 27 years, and was still striking out batters at a steady clip at the age of 46. He threw his seventh no-hitter when he was 44, setting a record that he had earlier established for being the oldest player ever to pitch a no-hitter. At the age of 42, he became the oldest pitcher ever to win an All-Star Game.

When Rickey Henderson fanned against Ryan on August 22, 1989, strikeout number 5,000, he said, "If you haven't been struck out by Nolan Ryan, you're nobody." It does seem as if Ryan pitched long enough and fanned enough batters that he must have struck out half of the players who ever played the game. That may be just an impression, but Ryan certainly occupies a prominent place in baseball history. His place in American culture seems equally secure, as evidenced by the national attention he received during a hospital stay in 2000. The outpouring of support from fans and nonfans alike illustrated the deep feeling this hero-pitcher engenders among the American public.

See also: Heroes; Records Set; Rural America; Strikeouts.

Additional Reading:

Cheung, Ming. *Nolan Ryan Tribute Page.* http://www.ghgcorp.com/mingster/

Ryan, Nolan. *Kings of the Hill: An Irreverent Look at the Men on the Mound.* New York: HarperCollins, 1992.

———. *Miracle Man: Nolan Ryan, the Autobiography.* Dallas: Word, 1992.

———. *Throwing Heat: The Autobiography of Nolan Ryan.* New York: Doubleday, 1988.

Trujillo, Nick. *The Meaning of Nolan Ryan.* College Station: Texas A&M University Press, 1994.

S

SCHACHT, ALEXANDER (AL) (1892–1984)

Baseball is many things, but funny is usually not among them. All experiences, of course, can be turned to humor with the right humorist and situation. Al Schacht was perhaps the greatest humorist to practice his trade primarily within (and with) the sport. The title "Clown Prince of Baseball" was his own invention, but the public quickly acclaimed him as such.

Comedy was not Al Schacht's first career. He began as a ballplayer. In his professional debut with Cleveland of the United States League, Schacht struck out 11 of the first 15 batters. After a Giants' contract, a sore arm, and World War I service, he finally received a break from the Washington Senators after he repeatedly sent letters to owner Clark Griffith about himself, signed "Just a Fan." He pitched for the Senators from 1919 to 1921, winning 14 games and losing 10 while relying, appropriately, on a screwball. The highlight of his career came on July 5, 1920, when, subbing for the injured Walter Johnson, he beat the Yankees 4-3.

Schacht later coached in the minors and majors, but by the late 1930s he had turned to clowning, achieving his greatest fame in that venue. He performed at 27 World Series, affecting such props as a four-foot-wide catcher's mitt and a bullfighter's costume in which he did battle with goats. He would single out players, managers, and especially umpires for mock arguments. During World War II, the Clown Prince took his act abroad to entertain the troops at more than 300 performances, earning not only increased fame but the lasting gratitude of his audiences. His legacy endures in the antics of myriad mascots trotted out by today's clubs to entertain fans at the ballpark.

See also: Griffith, Clark Calvin; War; "Who's on First?"

Additional Reading:

Kavanagh, Jack. *The Heights of Ridiculousness: The Feats of Baseball's Merrymakers*. South Bend, IN: Diamond Communications, 1999.

Schacht, Alexander. *My Own Particular Screwball: An Informal Autobiography*. Garden City, NY: Doubleday, 1955.

SCOUTS

The farm boy with a blazing fastball joins his favorite major league team; the city kid playing stickball moves into the fast lane of major league stardom. Such stories are a real part of the myth and history of baseball. It is one of the universal dreams for countless boys and girls, but myth can and does transform into concrete fact.

For most aspiring players who are discovered, there must be one who does the discovering: the scout, an often solitary (and low-paid) wanderer, a sort of Ancient Mariner traveling back roads and databases until he finds that talented future star hypnotized by the vision of future fame and riches.

So much depends on personal observation that the scout is unlikely to leave anytime soon, even with computer printouts and the Major League Scouting Bureau conducting camps and reporting its findings to the major league organizations that subscribe to the service (currently all of them). Major league clubs typically have some 25 scouts, most being assigned to a region wherein they observe hundreds of high school, college, American Legion, and semipro games each year, in addition to a generous sampling of minor league contests. The scout's job is to evaluate a player's OFP, or Overall Future Potential, and his judgment is likely to be the deciding factor in whether the young man is drafted, signed as a free agent, or left to find another career. The future of every major league team—along with the dreams of many young players—thus rests to a great extent on the success of its scouts.

See also: Minor Leagues; Myth; Rural America.
Additional Reading:

Gmelch, George, and J. J. Weiner. In the Ballpark: The Working Lives of Baseball People. Washington, DC: Smithsonian Institution, 1998.

Kerrane, Kevin. Dollar Sign on the Muscle: The World of Baseball Scouting. 1984. Reprint, Lincoln: University of Nebraska Press, 1999.

Winegardner, Mark. Prophet of the Sandlots: Journeys with a Major League Scout. New York: Atlantic Monthly, 1990.

SEAVER, GEORGE THOMAS (TOM TERRIFIC) (1944–)

"Tom Terrific" was an appropriate nickname for Tom Seaver. He was a great pitcher, clean-cut, handsome, articulate, popular, completely dedicated to self-discipline and being the best. More than any other player, he was responsible for leading the previously hapless Mets to a World Series championship in 1969. He played in New York, the media capital of the world; to top it off, he was all that he appeared to be.

Seaver joined the expansion Mets, the losers and clowns of the baseball world, in 1967 and immediately won 16 games. By 1969, Seaver had increased his win total to 25, had captured the Cy Young Award, and was the ace pitcher for a world champion. With a fastball that topped out at 98 miles per hour, a dominating slider, and excellent control, Seaver went on to pitch 20 years, winning 311 games with 61 shutouts, 3,640 strikeouts, and a 2.86 career ERA.

Seaver's accomplishments included the Rookie of the Year Award, three Cy Young Awards, and 19 strikeouts (10 in a row) during a game in 1970. He won 20 or more games five times and in 10 seasons struck out over 200 batters. Much to the dismay of Mets fans, he twice left them, once in a trade to the Reds in 1977, and later for the White Sox, for whom he won game number 300 in 1985. Although he helped the Mets win the National League pennant in 1973, he was fated to toil primarily for mediocre clubs. Sixteen times his personal winning percentage bested that of his team. In 1992, Tom Terrific was elected to the Hall of Fame.

Additional Reading:

Schoor, Gene. Seaver: A Biography. Chicago: Contemporary Books, 1986.

Seaver, Tom, with Lee Lowenfish. The Art of Pitching. New York: Hearst Books, 1984.

Seaver, Tom, with Herb Resnicow. Beanball. New York: Morrow, 1989.

Seaver, Tom, with Norman Lewis Smith. *How I Would Pitch to Babe Ruth: Seaver versus the Sluggers*. Chicago: Playboy, 1974.

Sullivan, George. *Tom Seaver of the Mets*. New York: Putnam's, 1971.

SEYMOUR, HAROLD (1910–1992)

Harold Seymour made baseball respectable for the historian and contributed enormously to our understanding of the history of the game. Each person who studies baseball as an important dimension of American society owes an extraordinary debt to this pioneer. Seymour was uniquely qualified for his role, for he was a professionally trained historian as well as a lifelong devotee of baseball.

Harold Seymour earned his doctorate from Cornell University, preparing the first doctoral dissertation ever on baseball. He later revised his dissertation as volume one of his monumental three-volume work on the history of baseball. Entitled *Baseball: The Early Years* and published in 1960, it demonstrated a depth of historical research previously unknown in books about baseball. Making exhaustive use of source materials, Seymour wrote the first truly detailed, accurate, and substantiated history of the origins and rise of the game. As Seymour states in the preface to the volume, "The book is the product of a lifetime love of baseball that began as a boyhood enthusiasm and developed into the mature interest of the professional historian."

Supplementing the professional historian and university professor in Seymour was the baseball participant. At various times, he was a batboy, high school and college player, coach, umpire, and scout. His love of the game never left him, and the fan remained always within the scholar. Five years after Harold Seymour died, scholars, fans, and his widow, Dorothy, gathered on Doubleday Field in Cooperstown for a memorial and funeral service. Seymour had helped to debunk the myth of Abner Doubleday's invention of baseball, but he nonetheless chose that site for his final resting place. After readings and songs, the historian's ashes were scattered near first base—the position he had played in college.

See also: Doubleday, Abner; Hall of Fame and Museum.

Additional Reading:

Grella, George. "Harold Seymour (1910–1992)." *The National Pastime: A Review of Baseball History* 17 (1997): 128–130.

Seymour, Harold. *Baseball: The Early Years*. 1960. Reprint, New York: Oxford University Press, 1989.

———. *Baseball: The Golden Age*. 1971. Reprint, New York: Oxford University Press, 1989.

———. *Baseball: The People's Game*. 1990. Reprint, New York: Oxford University Press, 1991.

SMITH, WALTER WELLESLEY (RED) (1905–1982)

Sportswriting at its best has always been as much about journalism as sports. Red Smith typified this approach, cautioning would-be sportswriters to choose the profession because of their love for journalism rather than their love for sports. That caution reflected Smith's own professionalism.

Smith moved into sportswriting with a solid academic background, having graduated cum laude from the University of Notre Dame in 1927. His first jobs, with the *Milwaukee Sentinel* and *St. Louis Star*, involved general-assignment reporting, copyreading, and rewriting. Not until he was with the *Star* did he gravitate to the sports department. Smith later moved to the *Philadelphia Record*, where he was given a full-time column, and the *New York Herald Tribune*, where he again had his own column. With the *Herald Tribune*, Smith earned national fame as he covered not only sports but also national political conventions. He was even referred to in Hemingway's novel *Across the River and into the Trees.* Colonel Cantwell, the protagonist, "went on reading the *New York Herald.* He was reading Red Smith, and he liked him very much" (166).

After the demise of the *Tribune,* Smith joined the *New York Times* in 1971, winning a Pulitzer Prize in 1976. He became particularly interested in the subject of baseball as business. He continued to write until the end of his life, his final column appearing four days before his death. His columns typically were entertaining, creative, and illustrative of a point of view that took writing seriously without taking sports too seriously.

> *See also:* Hemingway, Ernest Miller; Journalism (Print).
> *Additional Reading:*
> Berkow, Ira. *Red: A Biography of Red Smith.* 1986. Reprint, Boston: Hall, 1988.
> Holtzman, Jerome. *No Cheering in the Press Box.* New York: Holt, 1974.
> Smith, Red. *The Red Smith Reader.* New York: Random House, 1982.
> ———. *To Absent Friends.* New York: Atheneum, 1982.
> ———. *Views of Sport.* New York: Knopf, 1954.

SMITH, WENDELL (1914–1972)

Wendell Smith may have been the most influential African American sportswriter and broadcaster of the twentieth century. He also was a consistent and effective opponent of racial discrimination. A strong supporter of Branch Rickey's choice of Jackie Robinson to integrate the major leagues, Smith moved in his life from being the son of Henry Ford's chef to president of the Chicago Press Club. His papers are housed in the Baseball Hall of Fame, which posthumously honored him with the J. G. Taylor Spink Award in 1993 and inclusion in the so-called writers wing.

Wendell Smith early on learned the difficulty of being a lone black in otherwise white groups. He was the only African American student in his Detroit high school and played on the high school baseball team. Smith later played baseball at West Virginia State College at Charleston and was sports editor for the college newspaper. After graduating, he joined the *Pittsburgh Courier,* the most respected African American weekly paper in the nation, and quickly became sports editor. Part of his job was to cover the Pittsburgh Crawfords and Homestead Grays of the Negro Leagues as well as the Pittsburgh Pirates. He later would work for *Chicago Today* (a largely white paper later called the *Chicago American*), Chicago television stations WBBM and WGN, and the *Chicago Sun-Times.* Only after leaving the *Courier* was he able to gain membership in the Baseball Writers' Association.

Smith's efforts to further integration were many, including a poll of National League players and managers that he conducted in 1938 showing that 75 percent of respondents favored integration of the major leagues. Smith presented these findings to major league owners in a joint appearance with *Courier* publisher Ira Lewis and singer Paul Robeson, with little effect.

Smith later persuaded Boston politician Isadore Muchnick to induce the Red Sox and Braves to offer tryouts to African American players. Among those receiving a tryout with the major league clubs in 1945 was Jackie Robinson (the teams passed). Smith, who had chosen the players to try out for the Boston teams, decided against Satchel Paige and Josh Gibson, decisions he later regretted. Paige, of course, would eventually make it to the majors, although long past his prime. Gibson would be dead within two years. His support for Robinson led to Smith's coauthoring of Robinson's 1948 book *Jackie Robinson: My Own Story.* At the same time, Smith continued to urge support for the Negro Leagues, arguing that they should become part of organized baseball and function as minor leagues.

Throughout his career, and especially in the 1940s, Wendell Smith was at the heart of the push to integrate baseball. His involvement in this historic period is demonstrated by his papers, which are housed at the National Baseball Hall of Fame Library. Donated by his widow, Wyonella, they include correspondence with Jackie Robinson and Branch Rickey. The correspondence involves, among other subjects, spring-training accommodations for Robinson in the segregated South. Smith's articles, including his "Sports Beat" columns for the *Courier* and the *American,* offer important information about a wide range of men and women intimately involved in the history of black baseball, including Newark Eagles owner Effa Manley, Satchel Paige, Roy Campanella, Branch Rickey, Robinson's personal experiences, and the support that the great Jewish American star Hank Greenberg gave Robinson as he broke the color barrier. Smith's accomplishments extend well beyond his journalistic talents and have enriched American culture.

See also: African Americans; Hall of Fame and Museum; Journalism (Print); Negro Leagues; Rickey, Wesley Branch; Robinson, Jack Roosevelt.

Additional Reading:

Reisler, Jim, ed. *Black Writers/Black Baseball: An Anthology of Articles from Black Sportswriters Who Covered the Negro Leagues.* Jefferson, NC: McFarland, 1994.

Robinson, Jackie. *Jackie Robinson: My Own Story, as Told to Wendell Smith.* New York: Greenberg, 1948.

Smith, Wendell. "Wendell Smith Papers." National Baseball Hall of Fame Library.

http://www.baseballhalloffame.org/library/aids/msb1.html

SOCIETY FOR AMERICAN BASEBALL RESEARCH

The Society for American Baseball Research (SABR), a nonprofit organization devoted to gathering and disseminating information about baseball, demonstrates, along with the huge number of baseball books published annually, how seriously the sport is taken by scholars and fans. Baseball, SABR recognizes, is an important part of America, as worthy of serious research as most aspects of American society. To understand the origins, development, and current status of baseball in relation to society is a vital part of understanding the history and current state of the larger society.

SABR, based in Cleveland, was created by 16 individuals meeting at the National Baseball Hall of Fame Library in Cooperstown in 1971. From that modest beginning, the organization has expanded to over 7,000 members, some 40 regional chapters, and several research committees, from the Ballparks Committee to the Women in Baseball Committee. Services include many publications, a SABR lending library, copies of collections of baseball papers available for research, archives that are housed at Western Reserve Historical Society, and a website. Among the awards presented by SABR are the Seymour Medal, named after the great baseball historian Harold Seymour, for the best book of baseball history or biography from the preceding year. For many members, the most appealing aspects of the organization probably are the *SABR Bulletin, National Pastime: A Review of Baseball History,* and *Baseball Research Journal.*

Those who wish to join this organization, which is open to all, may write to

SABR, 812 Huron Road E #719, Cleveland, Ohio 44115.

See also: Seymour, Harold; Statistics.

Additional Reading:

Society for American Baseball Research. *Membership Directory 1999–2000*. Cleveland: SABR, 1999.

Society for American Baseball Research. Website www.sabr.org.

SOCKALEXIS, LOUIS FRANCIS (CHIEF, SOCK) (1871–1913)

Louis Sockalexis is the most famous Native American to play major league baseball. After the 1914 season, the Cleveland club of the American League was renamed the "Indians" by vote of the Cleveland fans, possibly with Sockalexis in mind. Sockalexis may have been the most talented Native American baseball player ever, and he probably also was the most tragic.

Sockalexis was born on a reservation near Old Town, Maine, a member of the Bear clan of the Penobscot tribe and grandson of the Penobscot chief. Athletically gifted, Sockalexis starred in several sports at St. Anne's Convent School (later Old Town High), continuing his schooling and sports at St. Mary's School in Van Buren, Maine, under the direction of a priest who had taken special interest in the youngster's ability to hit baseballs. Louis also was known for his speed and his throwing ability. At area fairs, he would put on exhibitions, throwing baseballs over the grandstand.

The opportunity to attend Holy Cross College and play for its baseball team proved a magnetic attraction for the young athlete, although his father apparently had other plans. The story (possibly legend) has it that Louis's father journeyed, at least partly by canoe, to implore President Grover Cleveland to make Louis chief of the Penobscots in order to keep Louis home. Upon returning to Maine, the father found that his son had already departed for Holy Cross.

Sockalexis pitched and played outfield for Holy Cross, but when his coach, Doc Powers, left for the University of Notre Dame, his star player followed. Things did not go well for Sockalexis in South Bend, where he got into trouble because of his drinking and apparently was expelled. However, he had been scouted by the Cleveland Spiders of the National League, and manager Patsy Tebeau signed him for the team in 1897.

Billed as a descendant of Sitting Bull (as few fans had much knowledge of the different Native American nations), Sockalexis became an instant hit with Cleveland, excelling on the field and becoming a favorite of the fans. Likely the first Native American to play in the majors (at least with notable success), he hit a robust .338 with 42 RBIs and 16 stolen bases in 66 games during his first season, missing time with a broken foot. Fans would cheer his appearances with war whoops.

Tragically, Sockalexis developed a severe drinking problem, quite possibly made worse by his unique situation. A Native American from a distinguished family, Louis Sockalexis must have felt he was treated as something of a talented freak. Fans applauded him but had little sensitivity to his true identity. Alone in a largely alien world, his identity deliberately distorted, war whoops escorting him to the plate, he could not find even his considerable baseball talent sufficient.

The 1898 season saw Sockalexis going downhill sharply, as he played in only 21 games, batting .224. He played in seven more games in 1899 but then drifted among minor league clubs as his life deteriorated. Reporters took to writing about him as an example of the evils of drink.

Returning to Maine, Sockalexis gradually got his life back on track, marrying, earning a living as a woodcutter, playing amateur ball, and coaching. On Christmas Eve 1913, he was missing when the day shift returned to the Burlington lumber camp. A search ensued, and a crew member found him in the woods, dead of an apparent heart attack. Inside a pocket of his flannel shirt were old newspaper clippings about his all-too-few days as one of baseball's greatest stars.

See also: College Baseball; Native Americans; Substance Abuse.

Additional Reading:

Hanchett, Doug. "Welcome to Mudville: A Look at Worcester's Baseball Past." *Worcester Magazine,* April 7–13, 1999, pp. 10–11.

Hatch, Francis W. "Maine's All-Time Great Baseball Player." *Down East* (August 1963): 37–39, 59.

Wellman, Trina. *Louis Francis Sockalexis: The Life-Story of a Penobscot Indian.* Augusta, ME: Department of Indian Affairs, 1975.

SOFTBALL

Softball originated in the United States in the latter part of the nineteenth century, probably in the late 1880s. It is played in various versions, usually categorized as "fast pitch" or "slow pitch." The game has included some consistent differences from baseball, including a larger and softer ball, underhand pitching, and a smaller diamond. The sport is popular among men, but women especially are encouraged to play, which actually works to limit their opportunities to play baseball.

Softball is an easier, safer game than baseball, which also helps to explain its popularity with children. Being struck by a softball is less severe than being struck by a baseball. Pitching also is easier, with the more natural underhand delivery.

Softball in its early days was often an indoor sport played in gymnasiums before migrating to the outdoors as a more clearly recognized version of baseball. Softball grew in importance during the 1920s and 1930s, when companies began to encourage and sponsor industrial softball leagues. The American Softball Association also came into existence and, in 1933, declared the term "softball" the official name of the game. Public-works projects during the Great Depression included construction of ballparks, which increased the opportunities to play softball.

The sport so increased in popularity that national tournaments for women's teams occurred annually. The most successful club, the Raybestos Brakettes of Stratford, Connecticut, won 25 fast-pitch national championships between 1942 and 1973. Passage of Title IX legislation in 1972, mandating equal sports opportunities for females athletes, greatly encouraged organized softball. High schools and colleges added softball teams to comply with the law, thus perpetuating the American view of baseball as a male-only sport. Only rarely would women make the roster of a college baseball team; thanks to Title IX, however, girls were accepted into Little League competition.

The most recent milestone in women's softball occurred in 1996, when the U.S. entry won the gold medal at the Summer Olympics in Atlanta—the first time that softball had been included as a medal sport. The stars of that team included Dot Richardson, a shortstop, and Lisa Fernandez, who excelled as a pitcher and also played third base. Richardson had been a four-time All-America at UCLA and was named the NCAA Softball Player of the Decade for the 1980s. She later became an orthopedic surgeon. Fernandez, the daughter of Cuban immigrants, also starred at UCLA. In the Olympics, she compiled an 0.33 ERA in 21 innings with 31 strikeouts while batting .393. In light of the Olympic victory, and the opportunity

Melanie Travis of Victoria hits during the Victoria–Western Australia match at the 2000 Australian Women's Fastpitch Softball Championships at NSW Softball Center, Sydney, Australia, January 20, 2000. (Scott Barbour/Allsport)

for the United States to gain another medal at the 2000 Summer Olympics in Sydney, Australia, softball continued to grow in popularity. National college tournaments receive increased media attention, and women's semipro teams offer exciting contests to be enjoyed by players and spectators alike.

See also: All-American Girls Professional Baseball League; Pony Baseball and Softball; Women in Baseball.

Additional Reading:

Amateur Softball Association of America. *The Official Rules of Softball: USA Softball.* Chicago: Triumph Books, 1994.

Dickson, Paul. *The Worth Book of Softball: A Celebration of America's True National Pastime.* New York: Facts on File, 1994.

Kneer, Marian E. *Softball: Slow and Fast Pitch.* Dubuque: W. C. Brown, 1987.

Nutt, Amy Ellis. "Baseball and Softball." In *Nike Is a Goddess: The History of Women in Sports.* Ed. Lissa Smith. New York: Atlantic Monthly, 1998, pp. 33–54.

Sullivan, George. *The Complete Guide to Softball.* New York: Fleet, 1965.

SOSA, SAMUEL PERALTA (SAMMY) (1968–)

Sammy Sosa, a fleet-footed, power-hitting outfielder, was born into poverty in the Dominican Republic. Even after making the major leagues, he spent almost a decade playing in obscurity for mediocre Chicago teams. But in 1998 Sosa achieved greatness and earned a lasting place in the hearts of Americans through his record-setting home-run duel with St. Louis Cardinal Mark McGwire. The tandem won over the nation with their heartfelt displays of sportsmanship as they battled one another for baseball's single-season home-run mark.

Sosa was seven years old when his father died. Left with his mother and six siblings in San Pedro de Macoris, Sammy earned money by shining shoes, selling oranges, and washing cars. One of those cars belonged to slugger George Bell, for whom Sosa would later be traded from the White Sox to the Cubs. At 14, he began playing baseball, using a milk carton as a glove. By 1985, Sosa had developed his baseball talents sufficiently to be signed by the Texas Rangers, and he was on his way.

Cubs fans, if few others, were well aware of Sosa's abilities prior to 1998. He hit 36, 40, and 36 home runs from 1995 to 1997, driving in at least 100 runners each year. Yet no one was prepared for the power surge that followed. For much of 1998, Sosa was neck-and-neck with McGwire, pulling even, only to fall back. Ultimately, the St. Louis slugger made it to 62 home runs first and finished with 70. Yet Sosa outdistanced everyone else who had ever played in the big leagues, hitting 66, along with a .308 batting average and a league-leading 158 RBIs. Sosa also set the record for the most home runs in one month, with 20 in June.

Sosa's tremendous season propelled the Cubs to a wild-card berth and earned him the Most Valuable Player Award. He also earned the affection and esteem of fans throughout the United States as well in the Dominican Republic and the rest of Latin America. He unfailingly displayed the highest ideals of sportsmanship, competing with McGwire for the home-run record but never losing respect for his opponent. And seldom, it seemed, did Sosa lose his endearing smile.

On that record-setting night when Roger Maris's record fell, Sosa was in right field and rushed in to hug McGwire after the home run. Seldom have sports fans witnessed two adversaries more appreciative of each other. Sosa, in fact, often referred to McGwire and himself as "brothers." Yet Sosa did not forget his origins, even during the climactic late-season race

for the record. As Hurricane Georges slammed into Sosa's native Dominican Republic, hitting his hometown of San Pedro de Macoris with particular force, he began to collect clothing, food, and water through his previously established Sammy Sosa Charitable Foundation to help relieve the suffering of his fellow citizens. Sammy Sosa may have come in second in the home-run race, but he ended up at least tied for first with the public.

The following year, Sosa demonstrated that his greatness on the baseball field was not a one-year phenomenon. Once again he vied with McGwire for the home-run lead, and once again he finished second. However, Sosa joined McGwire as one of the first two players in major league history to hit over 60 home runs twice, as the two finished with 63 and 65, respectively. Although the Cubs slumped as a team, Sosa batted in 141 runs. It had been a long and brilliant climb from milk cartons to the ivy-covered walls of Wrigley Field and the love and admiration of much of the world.

See also: Heroes; Home Run; Latin American Baseball; McGwire, Mark David; Records Set; Wrigley Field.

Additional Reading:
Duncan, Patricia J. *Sosa! Baseball's Home Run Hero*. New York: Simon and Schuster, 1998.
Gutman, Bill. *Sammy Sosa: A Biography*. New York: Pocket Books, 1998.
Noden, Merrell. *Home Run Heroes: Mark McGwire, Sammy Sosa, and a Season for the Ages*. New York: Simon and Schuster, 1998.
Schreiber, Lee R. *Race for the Record: The Great Home Run Chase of 1998*. New York: HarperCollins, 1998.

SOUVENIRS

Souvenirs are concrete objects that keep a special experience alive. A souvenir may be an autograph or even a collectible, but the term deserves its own category. A true souvenir is kept not to become a part of a collection or as a financial investment but as something that relates primarily to an experience. For this reason, photographs are often the most valued souvenirs, because they visually reflect the original experience and retain a permanence that ticket stubs and other, more easily discardable items may lack.

Within baseball, the game program also is a popular souvenir. Less common, and therefore especially valued, is a foul ball or home-run ball luckily caught on the fly or grabbed on the rebound. Of course, souvenirs such as caps and T-shirts also may be purchased at the game. Some souvenirs may be out of the ordinary: a chunk of turf or a seat from a stadium being renovated or destroyed, or a vial of dirt or ear of corn from the Iowa farm where *Field of Dreams* was filmed (and where a baseball field still awaits those who visit).

Mementos are souvenirs from one's personal life, often keepsakes passed on from generation to generation. They also are important within baseball: a father's antiquated baseball glove, a catcher's mask no longer fitting the owner but the perfect size for a grandchild, a bat too filled with old hits ever to be risked in action again. Baseball is about memories, and souvenirs help to keep memories, like dreams, alive.

See also: Ballparks; Business; Collectibles; Family Relationships.

SPALDING, ALBERT GOODWILL (1850–1915)

Albert Spalding has been called the "father of baseball," not because he invented the game (in fact, he did his best to popularize the fiction that Abner Doubleday invented the game at Cooperstown in 1839) but because as a player, manager, club president, owner of a sporting-goods business, and concerned citizen he did so much to publicize the game both in the United States and abroad. In his time, he was even referred to as the "baseball Messiah" as he sought to spread baseball to the far corners of the earth.

Spalding's association with baseball began as a player in the game's early days. He joined the Boston Red Stockings (forerunners of today's Atlanta Braves) in 1871, starring with them through 1875 as one of the game's great pitchers. From 1872 through 1876 (his first year with the Chicago White Stockings), he won 38, 41, 52, 54, and 47 games. In five years in the National Association of Professional Base Ball Players (1871–1875), he won 204 games (more than 40 per year). The 47 victories in his first year in the National League pushed the total to 251, but he added just one more win in 1877 as he left the mound for first base.

Spalding had joined Chicago as player-manager to help inaugurate the new National League in 1876. Inserting himself as the ace pitcher, he led his team to the pennant that first season. The following year, though, the White Stockings slumped, and Spalding left to run his sporting-goods firm, which he had started in 1876 with a loan from his mother. Spalding quickly tied his sporting-goods firm to the future of the National League, earning the right to publish the official league book, which he entitled *Spalding's Official Baseball Guide*. He manufactured baseballs and paid $1 per dozen that he supplied to the league in order to advertise his product as the official ball. Later items to come from Spalding included bats, gloves, hats, uniforms, golf clubs, tennis rackets, bicycles, basketballs, and various rules books. His biggest flop probably was his attempt to get teams to dress players differently by position. The resulting multiplicity in uniform colors and designs made the players look more like a motley crew of clowns than baseball players, and the experiment mercifully ended.

By 1882, Spalding was officially back in the National League, serving as president of the Chicago franchise until 1891. With Cap Anson managing, the White Stockings consistently were one of the finest teams in the league. It was during this period that Spalding organized a world tour for his White Stockings and an accompanying all-star team. The teams traveled to 14 countries, but with mixed results. In Egypt, the teams played in the shadows of the Sphinx and the great pyramids but had trouble keeping spectators from running off with the baseball. The trip to Rome produced some major disappointments as Spalding could not gain permission for his players to play in the Coliseum and to meet the Pope. Upon their return to the United States, though, the teams were honored at a grand banquet held at Delmonico's restaurant in New York City. Theodore Roosevelt and Mark Twain were among those present to welcome the baseball disciples back home.

Spalding left his position as president of the White Stockings in 1891, but his influence continued to grow. Determined to believe that baseball was a special manifestation of the American spirit, he set up a commission in 1907 headed by Abraham Mills, former president of the National League, to discover the true birthplace of baseball. The commission dutifully returned its report by year's end, asserting that Abner Doubleday had invented the game in rural New York. A few years earlier, Spalding had served, at President William McKinley's request, as a U.S. commissioner to the Summer Olympics in Paris, where he won over his hosts and was made a member of the French Legion of Honor. The *Boston Herald* called him the most famous name in American history next to George Washington and Abraham Lincoln. In 1910, Spalding sought a seat in the U.S. Senate, but for once he was not successful. The Hall of Fame, though, gladly admitted him posthumously in 1939 during baseball's celebration of the fictitious birth of the game that no one really had invented but that Spalding, as much as anyone, had helped to make America's national pastime.

See also: Anson, Adrian Constantine; Business; Chadwick, Henry; Doubleday, Abner; Equipment; Hall of Fame and Museum; Major Leagues; Presidents of the United States; Twain, Mark; Uniforms.

Additional Reading:

Anson, Adrian Constantine. *A Ball Player's Career, Being the Personal Experiences and Reminiscences of Adrian C. Anson.* Chicago: Era, 1900.

Bartlett, Arthur C. *Baseball and Mr. Spalding: The History and Romance of Baseball.* New York: Farrar, Straus, and Young, 1951.

Levine, Peter. *A. G. Spalding and the Rise of Baseball: The Promise of American Sport.* New York: Oxford University Press, 1985.

Spalding, Albert G. *Base Ball: America's National Game.* 1911. Reprint, revised and edited by Samm Coombs and Bob West, San Francisco: Halo Books, 1991.

THE SPORTING NEWS

The Sporting News, long called the "bible of baseball," occupies a special place in American society because of its age, association with the rise of baseball, and continued quality (although many people might quarrel with format and content changes over the years). The family that created the newspaper in 1886 and owned it until 1977—the Spinks—remains a hallowed name within the baseball world. The J. G. Taylor Spink Award, given annually to a sportswriter and earning that person a permanent place in the Baseball Hall of Fame, is named after the family member most responsible for the continued growth of *The Sporting News.*

The creator of *The Sporting News* was Alfred Henry Spink, who had played amateur baseball in Chicago, moved to St. Louis as a sportswriter for the *St. Louis Post-Dispatch,* and helped to create Sportsman's Park and the St. Louis Browns. He later served as secretary for the second version of the Browns, owned by Chris Von der Ahe. The popularity of baseball in St. Louis by the mid-1880s created a climate conducive to starting a sports paper, and Spink's knowledge of the game served him well. For business expertise, he summoned his brother, Charles C. Spink, returned from his homesteading ventures in the Dakotas. While Alfred devoted part of his time to other pursuits, including playwriting, his brother essentially ran the paper until his death in 1914, when he was succeeded by his son, J. G. Taylor Spink.

During these years a variety of men served as editor. The most famous name today is Ring Lardner, although his tenure at *The Sporting News* was brief (about three months in 1911). The most important editor was Joe Flanner, who took over the desk in 1899 and helped the young publication firmly establish itself. Flanner also helped to draft the so-called National Agreement between the National and American Leagues in 1903. J. G. Taylor ran the paper until his death in 1962, followed by his son, Charles C. "Johnson" Spink. With no child to succeed him, and worried about the future of *The Sporting News* should something happen to him, Johnson Spink sold out in 1977 to the Times-Mirror Company, publisher of the *Los Angeles Times.*

Although *The Sporting News* was intimately connected to baseball from its inception, the newspaper featured stories about other sports and even included a column entitled "The Stage," reflecting its founder's interest in theater. J. G. Taylor Spink changed this varied approach, devoting the paper exclusively to baseball,

a concentration that continued until World War II when the paper gradually increased its focus on other sports.

One of the constant aspects of the newspaper is the "Caught on the Fly" column. The first issue of *The Sporting News* included this column as a collection of newsy tidbits, such as the following: "Joe Murphy, it is said, will pitch for the Prickly Ash the coming season"; "Duane and Crawford, Dubuque players, will join Ted Sullivan's St. Paul nine"; and "Charles Boles, the present Chancellor of Excelsior, is a ball crank [that is, fan] from the word go." This final example is about as witty as the early column gets, unlike the entertaining, often irreverent tone of the current column. An item from the August 2, 1999, issue: "Fresh from the Rumorama, where unlike Copper River salmon, it's *always* Junior or A-Rod rumor season: Griffey's already told M's suits not to leave the light on after next season and has four teams on his destination wish list: 1. Atlanta; 2. Atlanta; 3. Atlanta; 4. Atlanta." The clubhouse dialect recalls Ring Lardner's "Pullman Pastimes" column, forerunner of his *You Know Me Al* letters.

The Sporting News is no longer a Spink family enterprise, and in appearance it now looks more like a magazine than a newspaper. Nonetheless, it continues to provide columns, statistics, and insights regarding baseball and a variety of other sports, especially football, basketball, and hockey. Not bad for a publishing graybeard well into its second century.

See also: Journalism (Print); Lardner, Ringgold Wilmer; Periodicals; Statistics.
Additional Reading:
Centennial Issue. *The Sporting News.* 1986.
Reidenbaugh, Lowell, Joe Hoppel, and Mike Nahrstedt. *The Sporting News: First Hundred Years, 1886–1986.* St. Louis: The Sporting News, 1985.
Spink, J. G. Taylor. *Judge Landis and Twenty-five Years of Baseball.* 1947. Reprint, St. Louis: Sporting News, 1974.

The Sporting News Website. http://www.sportingnews.com

"THE STAR-SPANGLED BANNER"

"The Star-Spangled Banner," the national anthem of the United States, is a rousing and patriotic song. Its association with baseball antedates by over a decade its designation by Congress as the national anthem. In fact, the song has a long and lively history.

Francis Scott Key, the creator of the lyrics as well as a lawyer, poet, and ancestor of the famous American novelist F. Scott Fitzgerald, received permission to board a British ship during the War of 1812 to arrange release of a prisoner. When the British began their bombardment of Fort McHenry in Baltimore Harbor, Key was detained aboard the ship and became deeply moved by his view of the U.S. flag still flying over the fort in the morning. He immediately penned the famous words that begin, "O say can you see by the dawn's early light, / What so proudly we hail'd at the twilight's last gleaming."

The melody, however, was not new. Key borrowed a tune that, by most accounts, had been composed around 1770 by John Stafford Smith, with words by Ralph Tomlinson, for a music club called the London Anacreontic Society, named after the ancient Greek poet Anacreon, who was famous for his short poems celebrating love and wine. The popular melody had been borrowed for many other songs, including an earlier song by Key called "When the Warrior Returns" (1805). So when Francis Scott Key witnessed the stirring sight of his national flag still standing after a long night of "the rocket's red glare" and "bombs bursting in air," he naturally thought of the melody that he had already associated with war and heroism.

Key published the lyrics in the *Baltimore American* on September 21, 1814; the song caught on quickly and steadily increased in popularity. On March 31, 1931, by act of Congress, Key's celebration of heroic endurance was declared the national anthem of the United States.

Baseball, however, deserves much credit for elevating the song to this ultimate level. The date was September 5, 1918, and the event the first game of the World Series between the Boston Red Sox and the Chicago Cubs. During the seventh-inning stretch, the band struck up "The Star-Spangled Banner." Fans and players alike stood to face the source of the music and increasingly joined in singing the lyrics. Thunderous applause at the conclusion of the song ensured that the band would replay the song the next day. Indeed, it was performed at each of the following Series games, and from then on the practice of a communal singing of "The Star-Spangled Banner" grew to become a tradition at all ball games as well as at other events. The widespread singing of the song ultimately led to the decision by Congress.

In some respects, "The Star-Spangled Banner" is less appropriate than "America," also known as "My Country 'Tis of Thee," as the national anthem. With heavily militaristic lyrics, Key's song most directly salutes the flag, while "America" praises the United States in a broader and more inclusive manner, as witnessed by its opening lines: "My country 'tis of thee, sweet land of liberty, of thee I sing." Perhaps its history as a song derived from the British national anthem, "God Save the King," discouraged its selection.

"America" also is easier to sing than "The Star-Spangled Banner," whose high notes have led in recent years to the song often being sung by a professional singer, with most fans and players standing in silent respect, facing the flag with their right hand over their heart, cap doffed. This increasingly silent participation of a large percentage of attendees also reflects changes in lifestyles regarding forms of entertainment. In the earlier decades of the twentieth century, family members would gather around the piano to sing in the evening. Now, with more opportunities for entertainment, there are far fewer family songfests, and a great many Americans, especially males, with less experience in song. Nonetheless, "The Star-Spangled Banner" remains a rousing tribute to the heroic past of the United States and to those individuals who have fought and died beneath the Stars and Stripes.

See also: Ballparks; Democracy; Music; War.
Additional Reading:
Lichtenwanger, William. *The Music of the Star-Spangled Banner from Ludgate Hill to Capitol Hill.* Washington, DC: Library of Congress, 1977.
Muller, Joseph. *The Star-Spangled Banner.* New York: Da Capo, 1973 (annotated bibliography of versions and arrangements, with notes on music publishers).
Svejda, George J. *History of the Star-Spangled Banner from 1814 to the Present.* Washington, DC: Division of History, Office of Archeology and Historic Preservation, 1976.
Weybright, Victor. *Spangled Banner: The Story of Francis Scott Key.* New York: Farrar and Rinehart, 1935.

STATISTICS

Baseball fans love statistics. They have for 150 years, and the affair shows no signs of weakening. The numbers represent if not the heart and soul of baseball at least the bones, the skeleton of the game. Statistics permit games to be replayed, seasons to be repeated, careers to be drawn out once again. Statistics keep the past alive and allow ample space for imagination and memory to fill in and flesh out the numbers. Statistics permit every room and yard to become a field of dreams.

Of all baseball statistics, the most important are located within the box score, which recapitulates a game while memorializing the details of each player's performance. The box score was invented sometime in the 1840s, but the modern box score is the creation of Henry Chadwick, who drew upon his cricket background (following his British birth) to devise a way to report a baseball game by recording numbers of such acts as runs, hits, and outs. Chadwick continued improving his box score through the 1850s and 1860s, and led the way to computing averages that permit more accurate comparisons among players. Chadwick devised the batting average in 1865, and statistics were on their way to becoming a growth industry.

The popularity of baseball statistics was facilitated by several developments. *Baseball Magazine* published *Who's Who in Baseball* in 1912, an annual presenting year-by-year statistics for active players that continues to appear each spring. *The Sporting News Baseball Register* began in 1940 and was followed in 1951 by the first real baseball encyclopedia, *The Official Encyclopedia of Baseball* (by the A. S. Barnes Company). Macmillan's *The Baseball Encyclopedia,* a remarkable milestone in applying computer technology to the accumulation and distribution of baseball statistics, first appeared in 1969. More recently, *Total Baseball* debuted in 1989, and by its fifth edition in 1997 had become indispensable for devotees of baseball statistics.

By the end of the twentieth century, baseball fans could read, memorize, and discuss such figures as OBP (on-base percentage), SBA (stolen-base average, that is, stolen bases divided by attempts to steal), PRO+ (production-plus, computed by normalizing on-base percentage plus slugging average to league average, with adjustments for the home-park factor), and TPI (total pitcher index, which measures the sum of a pitcher's pitching, batting, and fielding runs beyond the league average). Fans could also join organizations such as the Society for American Baseball Research (its acronym SABR pronounced as "saber"), where they could interact with other sabermetricians in practicing "sabermetrics," a new term for the statistical analysis of America's national pastime.

See also: *The Baseball Encyclopedia;* Chadwick, Henry; Games; Periodicals; Records Set; Rotisserie Baseball; *The Sporting News; Total Baseball.*

Additional Reading:

Runquist, Willie. *Baseball by the Numbers: How Statistics Are Collected, What They Mean, and How They Reveal the Game.* Jefferson, NC: McFarland, 1995.

Thorn, John, Pete Palmer, and Joseph M. Wayman. "The History of Major League Baseball Statistics." In *Total Baseball.* 5th ed. Ed. John Thorn et al. New York: Viking, 1997, pp. 554–568.

STEINBRENNER, GEORGE MICHAEL, III (1930–)

George Steinbrenner, owner of the most storied franchise in major league history, is one of the most controversial, successful, criticized, and best-known owners in baseball annals. Steinbrenner grew up in a wealthy shipping family, aspired to a career as a football coach, and later gravitated into baseball, becoming the principal owner of the New York Yankees in 1973. The mighty Yankees had fallen on hard times prior to Steinbrenner's entry, but since then he has built two powerful clubs, each in a different way.

Steinbrenner took over the Yankees at a time when the team had not won a pennant since 1964 and a World Series since 1962. Turning to talented and high-priced free agents such as Reggie Jackson, Catfish Hunter, and Goose Gossage, the new owner built a pennant-winning team by 1976 and captured the World Series in 1977 and 1978. The Yankees won their division in 1980 and the pennant in 1981, but then declined again.

The public and the press grew increasingly critical of the Yankees' owner amid steady changing of managers (Billy Martin was hired and fired five times), accusations of ownership meddling in managerial decisions, and public criticisms by Steinbrenner of his players (including a very public feud with Dave Winfield). Legal problems also dealt him some severe blows. He was convicted of a felony involving a financial contribution to President Richard Nixon and was suspended by baseball in 1973 for 15 months. Almost two decades later, he would be forced temporarily to relinquish administration of the Yankees (1990–1993) for alleged involvement with a gambler.

Despite these legal and public-relations difficulties, Steinbrenner succeeded in rebuilding the Yankees by constructing a successful minor league system that produced such stars as Bernie Williams, Derek Jeter, Andy Pettitte, and Mariano Rivera. To help rebuild his team, Steinbrenner hired Bob Watson as general manager, the only African American general manager in the majors. Watson later left, reportedly because working with the owner was too stressful, but he had helped to create a solid team with the ability to compete for years. The manager that Steinbrenner brought in was Joe Torre, who had enjoyed only limited success in earlier managerial positions but whose unflappable temperament, extensive experience, and ability to relate to players justified Steinbrenner's choice.

The Yankees returned to the top, familiar to the club for much of the twentieth century. They won the pennant and World Series in 1996. After making the playoffs as a wild card in 1997 but falling short of the World Series, the Yankees put together one of the greatest seasons in history. The Yankees set an American League record by winning 114 games in 1998, and by the time they were crowned world champions they had increased that total to 125, the most wins ever in a single season. Another pennant followed in 1999, as did another World Series triumph, this one, as in 1996, over the Atlanta Braves.

Although the Atlanta Braves made it into postseason competition more often than the Yankees in the 1990s, they won only one World Series. It is hard, unless one is a Braves fan, not to see the Yankees as the team of the 1990s. For all the criticism that he received, certainly much of it deserved, George Steinbrenner had returned the Yankees to the top. He made them winners again, which is how American society has long viewed the Yankees. Baseball fans came to hate the Yankees for their extensive winning ways (the team that people loved to hate), but a funny thing happened on the way to the latest dynasty: More and more people learned to at least like the Yankees.

> See also: Free Agency; Hunter, James Augustus; Jackson, Reginald Martinez; Kuhn, Bowie K.; Law; New York Yankees; Torre, Joseph Paul; World Series.
>
> Additional Reading:
>
> Ladson, William, ed. The Yankees: Steinbrenner's 25 Years of Triumph and Turmoil. Special Collector's Edition of The Sporting News. 1998.
>
> Linn, Edward. Steinbrenner's Yankees. New York: Holt, 1982.
>
> Madden, Bill. Damned Yankees: A No-Holds-Barred Account of Life with "Boss" Steinbrenner. New York: Warner, 1990.
>
> Schaap, Dick. Steinbrenner! Rev. ed. New York: Avon, 1983.

STENGEL, CHARLES DILLON (CASEY, THE OLD PROFESSOR) (1890–1975)

Casey Stengel achieved fame within and outside the world of baseball—among fans, among people who possessed only a nodding acquaintance with baseball, even with Congress, when he testified on antitrust legislation in 1958. During his six decades in baseball, he was known (sometimes notoriously) as a competent outfielder, failed-turned-genius manager, entertainer, and speaker of a fractured language known as "Stengelese." Viewed for much of his career as something of a clown, he achieved Hall of Fame status as the manager of the New York Yankees from 1949 to 1960, then punctuated his career as folk-hero manager of the expansion and bumbling New York Mets.

Stengel was born in Kansas City, from whence he received his nickname "Casey," for the initials of his home city. He pitched while in high school for the Parisian Cloak Company in a Kansas City industrial league. By 1910, he was playing in the minors and reached the majors in 1912 with the Brooklyn Dodgers. He would also play for the Pirates, Phillies, Giants, and Braves until 1925. He batted .284 in his 14-year career and earned a reputation as a solid defensive outfielder. Nonetheless, he was even better known for his antics on the field. Once, shortly after being traded by the Dodgers to the Pirates, he was playing in Brooklyn and being roundly booed. When he came to the plate, he bowed ostentatiously and doffed his cap. From under his cap flew out a sparrow.

Stengel received his first managing job with Worcester in the Eastern League in 1925 and took with him his penchant for bizarre behavior. One of his favorite acts was to feign fainting when the umpire made a call that Casey did not like. He finally stopped the practice when he fell to the ground one day and finally opened his eyes to find the umpire also on the ground mimicking Stengel's act. Stengel was not only manager of Worcester but also an outfielder and president of the club. He grew unhappy with the job and wanted out but feared that the owner would refuse to let him go. So

Portrait of manager and players for the New York Yankees (l-r): Allie Reynolds, Vic Raschi, Casey Stengel, and Ed Lopat, 1950s (Archive Photos)

Stengel released himself as a player, fired himself as manager, and then, as president of the club, resigned.

Stengel managed the Dodgers and Boston Braves from 1934 to 1943 but never finished higher than fifth. When he was let go, he seemed to be at the end of his major league career. Given that he had accumulated considerable wealth from oil in Texas and land and bank deals in California, he did not need to continue working. Nonetheless, he resumed managing, working with Milwaukee, Kansas City, and Oakland in the minors before, to most everyone's amazement, being hired to manage the New York Yankees for the 1949 season. When George Weiss brought Stengel to the Yankees, the team had been in brief decline following the departure of manager Joe

McCarthy. The new manager brought a reputation for clownish behavior, age (almost 60), a record of managerial futility in the majors, and a five-year absence from the big time. Veteran players, among them Joe DiMaggio, were at best skeptical, especially when he instituted platooning and heavy use of the bullpen. He also upset the Yankee Clipper by briefly experimenting with DiMaggio at first base. In a season when a number of the veteran players, such as DiMaggio and outfielder Tommy Henrich, were injured, Stengel managed to weave young players into the lineup successfully. The Yankees came from behind to edge the Red Sox for the pennant in 1949 and went on to defeat the Dodgers in the World Series.

Casey Stengel's success with the Yankees was extraordinary. In 12 seasons he won 10 pennants, a record he shares with John McGraw among major league managers, but Stengel won a record five in a row (in his first five years with the Yankees). He also won seven World Series, sharing that record with Joe McCarthy as well, but McCarthy could not equal Stengel's accomplishment of five consecutive Series triumphs. An innovative manager who popularized platooning and expanded use of relief pitchers, he also organized coaches and veteran players by specialty, for example, using a catcher or former catcher to work with the catchers on the roster. And he introduced intensive instructional training in the spring of 1951. All of these practices marked Stengel as an innovative manager whose creativity and leadership belied the impression given by his use of the English language, which had earlier in his career won him the sarcastic nickname "Old Professor," often deliberately mispronounced as "perfessor." In later years that nickname would instead convey affection and respect.

Stengel was famous for such statements as "All right, everybody line up alphabetically according to your height." Another time he offered the observation that "good pitching will always stop good hitting, and vice versa." He was even more famous for his rambling monologues that moved through almost endless sequences of fractured syntax and apparent non sequiturs to arrive at a point of insight (or at least entertainment) for the listener. Congress received its introduction to Stengelese when the manager testified at a hearing on antitrust legislation in 1958. Asked by Senator Estes Kefauver of Tennessee for his background and opinion of the legislation under discussion, Stengel responded with rambling comments that elicited from the senators both confusion and laughter. Senator Kefauver finally ended Stengel's testimony and called upon

Mickey Mantle next. The exchange, in light of what had just been offered by Stengel, brought the house down, figuratively if not literally:

> Kefauver: Mr. Mantle, do you have any observations with reference to the applicability of the antitrust laws to baseball?
> Mantle: My views are just about the same as Casey's.

Casey Stengel was fired by the Yankees after losing to the Pirates in the 1960 World Series. After one year away from managing, he was brought back to New York by old friend George Weiss, now with the Mets, to lead the expansion club. Stengel had neither the players nor perhaps the energy to get the Mets out of the cellar, but he brought fans to the ballpark and became even more of a folk hero with his entertaining actions, especially fitting for the hapless Mets. Stengel finally stepped down from managing for good during the 1965 campaign. He left behind a career that, for its success and entertainment value, has never been equaled among major league managers. His prominent position in the popular mind, as well as in baseball history, appears permanent.

See also: Antitrust Exemption; Brooklyn Dodgers; DiMaggio, Joseph Paul; Mantle, Mickey Charles; Language, Baseball; New York Yankees; World Series.

Additional Reading:
Allen, Maury. *Now Wait a Minute, Casey!* Garden City, NY: Doubleday, 1965.
———. *You Could Look It Up: The Life of Casey Stengel.* New York: Times Books, 1979.
Creamer, Robert W. *Stengel: His Life and Times.* New York: Simon and Schuster, 1984.
MacLean, Norman. *Casey Stengel: A Biography.* New York: Drake, 1976.

STRIKEOUTS

The concept of the strikeout has long been part of English phrasing, one of many examples of American society's borrowings from baseball language. In nonbaseball use, the strikeout usually denotes a failure: "I struck out again!" Users of this expression almost always implicitly see themselves as the batter in the baseball parallel. When one succeeds, he or she "hits a home run."

Yet the strikeout is also a very positive development within baseball—if one is a pitcher. In fact, the strikeout is parallel to the home run within baseball, the most dramatic act that a pitcher can perform within the limit of a specific play. It is a dramatic moment of total victory over the adversary, an example of the pitcher's power to dominate. Something of this sense of power and domination is reflected in the expression "to punch out," often used as a synonym for recording a strikeout.

The strikeout has become more common in recent decades. Strikeout totals from baseball's primitive days are extremely high, but that reflects to a great extent the number of innings that pitchers worked. Charley Radbourn, for example, struck out 441 hitters in 1884 but pitched 678 innings. Radbourn still threw underhand in 1884, but that was the year in which pitchers were permitted to deliver the ball with an overhand motion, a rules change that gave pitchers the ability to generate greater velocity on pitches.

There were great strikeout pitchers in the early days of the twentieth century. Walter Johnson, one of the best ever, still ranks seventh in career whiffs with 3,509, but he is the only pre-1960s pitcher in the top 10 as well as the only pitcher prior to then to record 3,000 strikeouts. Nolan Ryan leads with what may be as unbeatable a record as any that exists: 5,714. The next highest early star is Cy Young, whose 2,803 place him fourteenth on the all-time list.

Also indicative of the growing importance of the strikeout are the numbers of pitchers who have struck out 300 or more hitters in a season. *Total Baseball* breaks down the single-season highs by eras. Between 1893 and 1919, four pitchers surpassed that milestone. Between 1920 and 1941, no one did. Bob Feller, with 348 strikeouts in 1946, was the sole pitcher to reach that mark between 1942 and 1960. Then Sandy Koufax matured, fanning over 300 batters three times and setting a new major league record with 382 strikeouts in 1965. Ryan broke that record by one in 1973, one of six times that he fanned over 300. Twelve times from 1961 through 1976, and 12 more times from 1977 to 1999, the 300 mark was equaled or surpassed.

Changes in pitching and hitting philosophies are responsible at least in part for this growth in strikeouts. There is greater emphasis on strikeouts, as opposed to groundouts, for pitchers. But batters today are swinging from the heels much more, so they either hit a home run or strike out. Undisciplined hitters eschew the idea of putting the ball in play and instead go for broke, aiming for the fame and fortune that follow home-run hitters. Mark McGwire, for example, hit 70 home runs in 1998—but he also struck out 155 times. By contrast, Joe DiMaggio struck out only eight more times in his entire career than he hit home runs (369 versus 361); and when Ted Williams batted .406 in 1941, he outhomered his strikeouts 37 to 27. In 1950, major league teams averaged 130 home runs and 598 strikeouts. By 1998, the home-run average had risen to 169 while the strikeout average exploded to 1,063 per team.

One might argue that the undisciplined hitting of the modern era reflects a changing society that places greater emphasis on instant gratification rather than self-discipline, on individual goals rather than teamwork. Perhaps baseball will change back to the days when the hitter wanted to make sure that he made contact with the ball, when the pitcher tried to save his arm and get two outs with one pitch by inducing grounders, especially with a runner on first. Perhaps society will change along with baseball, but neither is likely to happen soon.

See also: Feller, Robert William; Home Run; Johnson, Walter Perry; Koufax, Sanford; Radbourn, Charles Gardner; Records Set; Ryan, Lynn Nolan; Statistics; Young, Denton True.

Additional Reading:

Curran, William. Strikeout: A Celebration of the Art of Pitching. New York: Crown, 1995.
Feller, Bob. Strikeout Story. New York: A. S. Barnes, 1947.
Hano, Arnold. Sandy Koufax: Strikeout King. Rev. ed. New York: G. P. Putnam's, 1967.
Kessler, Leonard. Here Comes the Strikeout. New York: Harper and Row, 1965.
Reiser, Howard. Nolan Ryan: Strikeout King. Chicago: Childrens Press, 1993.

SUBSTANCE ABUSE

Substance abuse, of both legal and illegal substances, is a major problem in American society. It always has been and probably will remain so. Similarly, baseball, representative of both the good and bad in American society, has manifested the same problems since its inception. Alcohol has long been associated with baseball, but over the years the bottle has shared the bill with smokeless tobacco, cigarettes, cocaine, steroids, amphetamines, and various other concoctions. Many relevant factors come into play where baseball players are concerned, some helping, others hurting. Athletes in many ways take good care of their bodies, knowing that success depends on good health. At the same time, they know that the career of an athlete is short, so they often turn to chemical additives to enhance their performance. Self-perceptions, traditional views of the

athlete, and an excess of money contribute to decisions to use certain substances. At the same time, education, testing, and punishments also come into play.

Hard drinking has been associated with baseball players from the earliest days of the sport and continues to be a problem. Steps have been taken to break that association, from the National League's refusal in the nineteenth century to permit liquor sales at games to current recognition of alcoholism as a disease. Yet beer remains readily available in clubhouses after games, and even one of the newest ballparks, Miller Park, home of the Milwaukee Brewers, is named after a beer company that in turn is owned by tobacco company Philip Morris. Mickey Mantle, near the end of his life, admitted to abusing alcohol (and his health) during his years with the Yankees and attempted to dissuade others from following a similar path. Tragically, the former Yankee great had little time to speak out against drinking, dying of cancer in August 1995, about two months after receiving a liver transplant. Bob Welch, an outstanding pitcher for the Dodgers and later the Athletics (for whom he won 27 games in 1990), underwent voluntary rehabilitation in the mid-1980s, later writing a book about his experiences, Five O'Clock Comes Early: A Young Man's Battle with Alcoholism (1982).

Tobacco, like beer, is legal but no less harmful for not being against the law. Also like beer, tobacco has always been a baseball problem. For a century or so, ballplayers chewed tobacco to moisten their mouths, lubricate their gloves, and appear manly. Baseball cards were included with packages of tobacco. By the middle of the twentieth century, baseball, like most of society, had turned to cigarettes. As cigarette smoking was proven to cause serious illnesses, players began to turn back toward smokeless tobacco, unwittingly substituting mouth cancer for lung cancer.

Illegal drugs are another bond between baseball and the broader culture. The naive assumption that there was no serious drug problem in baseball was dispelled in the 1980s when cocaine use among players came to light. Mets ace Dwight Gooden admitted to cocaine use and entered the Smithers Institute in New York for rehabilitation prior to the 1987 season. Four Kansas City players, including Willie Wilson and Vida Blue, were suspended in 1983 for using illegal drugs. A drug trial in 1985 revealed drug use by many players, including major stars Keith Hernandez and Dave Parker. LaMarr Hoyt, a former Cy Young Award winner, was arrested three times on drug charges in 1986. Trying a comeback in 1987, he was arrested late in the year, charged with intent to distribute cocaine and marijuana, convicted, and sentenced to prison. Steve Howe, a relief pitcher for the Dodgers and Yankees, ran into drug problems several times in the 1980s and 1990s. In 1999, Darryl Strawberry was arrested, allegedly for possessing cocaine and soliciting a prostitute, and suspended from baseball for much of the season. Another incident led to his suspension for the entire 2000 season.

Baseball players have long made heavy use of amphetamines, often called "greenies." Although legal with a prescription, and apparently capable of enhancing performance on a short-term basis, these drugs pose serious long-term health problems, especially affecting the heart. More recently, anabolic steroids have come into use. Although more popular in football and bodybuilding than in baseball because steroids build bulk, power, and aggressiveness, they are reportedly used by some players to increase power at the plate. Human growth hormones, derived from the pituitary glands of cadavers,

also can build muscle mass and pose another temptation for athletes.

Even Mark McGwire, one of the most popular players in the game and the first to hit 70 home runs in a single season, admitted to using androstenedione, known as "andro." Andro is not prohibited by the major leagues, and a study of its effects by Harvard scientists, released in early 2000, was inconclusive regarding the long-term impact of its use. Baseball plans to engage in further examination of the effect of andro before deciding whether to prohibit it. And there is no evidence that the additive contributed directly to McGwire's home-run accomplishments. McGwire insisted that he took andro to help prevent injury but has since stopped using the substance in order to serve more effectively as a role model for youngsters.

Then there are the fans. From the beginning of professional baseball, rowdy fans have been a problem at games, and nothing makes fans more rowdy than alcohol. The National League banned the sale of alcoholic beverages at games, although eventually that prohibition fell because of the money that could be made from beer sales. The modern nadir for drunken fans was June 4, 1974, in Cleveland. The Indians were hosting Beer Night, selling all the beer anyone wanted for 10 cents per cup. As the game and the drinking proceeded, two fans accosted Texas right fielder Jeff Burroughs. Players from both teams went to his aid, and some 50 additional spectators joined the fray. Officials were unable to establish order, and the Indians were forced to forfeit the contest. Some 5,000 people were on the field fighting, some with chains and bottles. Major league teams attempt to prevent drunken fans from making life miserable for other fans and players, but it is difficult to ensure that innocent spectators will not be bothered by the language and rudeness of fans who have tipped a few too many. As long as beer is served—in fact, pushed—at games, the problem will continue.

As society wins some battles and loses others in its fight against substance abuse, so does baseball. With huge salaries riding on the athlete's ability to perform, and with considerable stress facing the athlete, there are inducements both to abstain from and to use substances that scientific evidence has shown to be harmful. The evidence of history suggests that the baseball arena will continue to reflect what society thinks and does about these substances. Fans also have an important role to play in making baseball as free of substance abuse as possible—both by expressing clearly their opposition to such usage and by behaving properly at games.

See also: Ballparks; Business; Food Vendors; Kelly, Michael Joseph; Lardner, Ringgold Wilmer; Mantle, Mickey Charles; McGwire, Mark David; Religion; Sockalexis, Louis Francis; Wilson, Lewis Robert.
Additional Reading:
Goldman, Bob. *Death in the Locker Room: Drugs and Sports.* 2d ed. Chicago: Elite Sports Medicine, 1992.
Miller, Roger W. *Athletes and Steroids: Playing a Deadly Game.* Rockville, MD: Department of Health and Human Services, 1988.
National Cancer Institute. *Spitting into the Wind: The Facts about Dip and Chew.* Bethesda, MD: National Cancer Institute, 1999.
Stainback, Robert D. *Alcohol and Sports.* Champaign, IL: Human Kinetics, 1997.
Zoss, Joel, and John Bowman. *Diamonds in the Rough: The Untold History of Baseball.* 1989. Reprint, Chicago: Contemporary Books, 1996.

SUNDAY, WILLIAM ASHLEY (BILLY, PARSON, THE EVANGELIST) (1862–1935)

Baseball often is likened to religion in its emphasis on ritual and myth. These two areas of human activity provided two careers for Billy Sunday, a fleet outfielder noted for his defensive ability who later became the most famous evangelist in the United States.

Sunday was from a poor family in Iowa, his father dying a few weeks after Billy's birth, with Billy and his brother spending several years in orphanages because of their mother's inability to support them. Billy turned to baseball as a teenager and caught the eye of Cap Anson, manager of the Chicago White Stockings. Sunday played eight years with Chicago, Pittsburgh, and Philadelphia in the National League. Although he hit only .248, he stole as many as 71 and 84 bases in a season and fielded brilliantly.

While playing baseball, Sunday started teaching Sunday school. Still in his prime, and earning an impressive $400 per month, he left the game in 1890 to take up preaching. Ordained as a Presbyterian minister, Billy Sunday traveled widely, conducting crusades that often ran two or three weeks. A million people came forth to the altar to answer Sunday's calls to accept the faith. A dramatic preacher, he reached a level of fame he could hardly have imagined in the orphanages of his youth—dining with presidents and even seeking the Republican nomination for president himself in 1920. At his death, he was believed to have preached Christianity to more people than anyone in history.

See also: Anson, Adrian Constantine; Religion.
Additional Reading:
Bruns, Roger. *Preacher: Billy Sunday and Big-Time American Evangelism.* New York: Norton, 1992.
Dorsett, Lyle W. *Billy Sunday and the Redemption of Urban America.* Grand Rapids, MI: W. B. Eerdmans, 1991.
McLoughlin, William Gerald. *Billy Sunday Was His Real Name.* Chicago: University of Chicago Press, 1955.
Sunday, Billy. *"Billy" Sunday, the Man and His Message, with His Own Words which Have Won Thousands for Christ.* Philadelphia: John C. Winston, 1914.

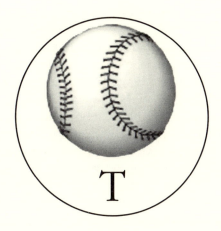

T

TAIWANESE BASEBALL

Although the U.S. major leagues have drawn players from Canada, many Latin American nations, Australia, Japan, and Korea, no player from Taiwan has played in the majors. That condition exists despite the popularity of baseball in Taiwan and Taiwan's extraordinary success in Little League baseball.

Americans, however, have played and coached in Taiwan. Former major league managers Jim Lefebvre, Kevin Kennedy, and Bill Russell have coached there. A limited number of foreign players is permitted per year, with Jay Kirkpatrick probably the most successful American player. Kirkpatrick, a former Dodgers' minor-leaguer, won the 1998 Most Valuable Player Award in the Chinese Professional Baseball League (CPBL) while topping the league in home runs, runs batted in, and batting average.

Baseball in Taiwan suffers from several problems that have slowed movement of players to the United States: Traditionally, Taiwanese players have taken their skills to Japan; players share in the island's requirement of compulsory military service; there is little cooperation between the two Taiwanese major leagues, the CPBL and the Taiwan Major League; and a serious gambling scandal rocked the CPBL in the 1990s. Nonetheless, it seems only a matter of time until Taiwanese players make the increasingly common international journey into professional baseball in the United States.

> *See also:* Australian Baseball; Canadian Baseball; Cuban Baseball; Japanese Baseball; Korean Baseball; Latin American Baseball.
> *Additional Reading:*
> Rubinstein, Murray A. *Taiwan: A New History*. Armonk, NY: M. E. Sharpe, 1999.
> Wilson, Jeffrey. "Baseball in Taiwan." In *Total Baseball*. 6th ed. Ed. John Thorn et al. New York: Total Sports, 1999, pp. 563–569.

"TAKE ME OUT TO THE BALL GAME"

After "Happy Birthday" and "The Star-Spangled Banner" (the latter having its own baseball association), "Take Me Out to the Ball Game" is the song most often sung in the United States, although few people know its complete lyrics.

Songwriter Jack Norworth, best known today (next to "Take Me Out to the Ball Game") for "Shine on Harvest Moon," was riding the New York City subway in 1908 when he noticed a sign advertising a baseball game at the Polo Grounds. Norworth, who had never attended a baseball game, hurriedly scratched out the lyrics to a song on some pieces of paper. By the time he disembarked, he had written what would soon become the unofficial anthem of baseball. Albert Von Tilzer added the music, and, as soon as audiences heard the song, it skyrocketed to popularity.

The song is about a young woman originally named Kitty Casey (later Nelly Kelly) who loves baseball. When her boyfriend, Joe, wants to take her to Coney Island, she puts up a fuss and insists on a ball game instead, where she roots for her favorite players and chides the umpires. Most people today, however, skip those sections, singing just the chorus about "peanuts and Cracker Jack" and expressing their lack of concern about ever leaving the stadium—unless, presumably, it starts to rain, although Nelly Kelly probably would have sat right through a downpour. The song is especially popular during the seventh-inning stretch. The late Harry Caray may be the voice recent fans most associate with the song, which goes to show that a message that adequately taps into the fanaticism of baseball fans can transcend even the worst singing voices.

See also: Ballparks; Caray, Harry; Family Relationships; Food Vendors; Music; "The Star-Spangled Banner."

Additional Reading/Listening:

Levy, Lester S., ed. *Take Me Out to the Ball Game and Other Favorite Song Hits, 1906–1908*. Mineola, NY: Dover, 1984.

"Take Me Out to the Ball Game." *Play Ball!* Compact Disc. Telarc, 1998.

TELEVISION BROADCASTING

Television, almost since its inception, has engendered controversy. Branded a "vast wasteland" by Newton Minow, it has been both praised and decried over the decades. While bringing information and entertainment into American homes, it also has disseminated moral and cultural values at odds with large segments of the population. At the start of the twenty-first century, after more than five decades of popularity, television continues to be blamed for real or imagined effects such as increased insensitivity to violence, declining educational performance by students, and a general "dumbing down" of the culture.

It should not be surprising, then, to find that television has also been controversial in relation to sports, baseball in particular. From its earliest days, television was associated with sports. The first station to offer programming was NBC's New York City station in 1939. On May 17 that year, the first televised sporting event was a college baseball game between Princeton and Columbia. The first major league game was televised by station W2XBS out of the Empire State Building on August 26. In addition to the Dodgers-Reds game, viewers could see Red Barber pouring himself a bowl of Wheaties during a commercial and the broadcaster's famous egg timer, used to remind himself to give the score every few minutes. Viewers of station W2XBS could watch the game from as far away as 50 miles, which amazed the public.

NBC televised the World Series in 1947, although most of the 3.9 million viewers had to watch the game in bars. Televisions still were too expensive for most households, but the telecast began a tradition that quickly turned into a requirement for bars if they wanted to succeed—having a TV set in the corner so that patrons could follow their favorite teams. Stores selling televisions in those days would often leave a set running in the display window to advertise the product, commonly attracting crowds of pedestrians who did not own their own sets to watch a favorite show from the sidewalk.

Television caught on fast. According to NBC, only 9 percent of homes had TV sets during 1949–1950. That percentage grew rapidly, reaching 64.5 percent in 1954–1955 and 87.1 percent by 1959–1960. Later statistics, compiled by Nielsen Media Research, show that over 98 percent of homes had at least one TV set by the mid-1990s. Many of these viewers were watching baseball, and both historic events and technological developments contributed to their interest, including Don Larsen's televised perfect game in the 1956 World Series and the advent of color broadcasts in the 1960s.

Not all fans and team officials, however, were fond of televised games. Baseball was not an easy game to televise because action often would be occurring simultaneously in two locations on the field (e.g., an outfielder was chasing down a hit while a runner circled the bases). Especially in the early days, when only one or two cameras were used, the game appeared very flat on the screen, and, of course, viewers often missed crucial action. Early television did a better job with such events as boxing and wrestling matches, where the action was confined. Even football and basketball were easier to follow because the ball was the focal point.

Over the years, increasing numbers of cameras were used to capture all corners of the stadium. Today seven cameras are common, nine or more not unusual, especially for such games as the playoffs and World Series. The result is a fuller representation of the game, although a related complaint remains important. Radio, it is believed by many fans, encourages an imaginative re-creation of the game in the listener's mind, while

television limits the viewer to what is seen, which necessarily, even with enhanced camera work, excludes many of the sights and sounds of the game itself.

Another controversial issue is whether broadcasting discourages attendance at games, a concern also aimed at radio broadcasting. In the case of radio, broadcasting appeared actually to stimulate greater interest in major league baseball and therefore boosted attendance. The answer is not as clear with television. Certainly television has hurt minor league baseball. Given the choice between watching major league games on television or going out to the minor league ballpark, increasing numbers of fans chose the former. During the early decades of television broadcasting, the number of minor leagues declined from a total of 59 to 20. The number of minor league players dropped from 7,800 to 2,500 in the 1950s. Attendance also proved to be a problem for some major league clubs in the 1950s, and the majors went through another period of attendance problems in the late 1960s and early 1970s. Television was not the sole cause of these difficulties, as baseball vied with other entertainment options and faced competition from the growing popularity of professional football and basketball. Even here, however, television bears some indirect responsibility, as the medium seemed to capture more effectively the excitement of the competing sports than it did baseball, which, as a slower game, may be less naturally suited for television.

Still other issues confronted baseball and television, including the financial ramifications of telecasting. Television revenue amounted to only $3.25 million in 1960; by 1990 that total had risen more than a hundredfold to $365 million. Along the way, Major League Baseball entered an agreement with NBC prior to

296 Television Broadcasting

the 1969 season that would pay baseball $40 million; only $4 million of that total, however, was earmarked for the players' pension fund. The increasing revenues from television, and the limited proportion of that revenue accruing to ballplayers, triggered considerable unhappiness among players. Marvin Miller, executive director of the Major League Baseball Players Association, led the players to strike. The holdout ended three days before spring training, with an agreement increasing the total for the players' pension fund to $6.5 million and lowering from five to four the years of service for players to qualify. The big bucks available from media pushed the game toward free agency and mushrooming player salaries, with concomitant increases in ticket prices and other expenses.

In the following years, the relationship of television broadcasting to baseball would grow even more complex. Cable television brought with it new sports networks, most prominently ESPN (Entertainment and Sports Programming Network), which started in September 1979 and began broadcasting baseball games in April 1990. Superstations arose, such as WTBS in Atlanta, carrying Braves games, and WGN-TV in Chicago for Cubs and White Sox contests. Regional networks, as their name implies, focused on particular areas of the country. One of the most prominent examples is HSE (Home Sports Entertainment), which features games by the Texas Rangers and Houston Astros. Viewers, especially those with cable, were able to watch more games than ever.

Money remained a source of contention between baseball and the networks in the mid-1990s. Facing increased costs, Major League Baseball entered a six-year agreement to establish The Baseball Network with ABC and NBC, beginning with the 1994 season. Rather than work with the old approach of rights fees, each of the three parties agreed to supply $16 million in startup costs and then share revenue, with Major League Baseball receiving about 90 percent of the profits. Baseball also struck a more traditional deal with ESPN.

Local rights were unaffected by these agreements, but since local broadcasting fees bring in almost as much revenue as the network deals, and are not distributed evenly, another problem remained: growing disparity in local broadcast revenue among major league teams. This made it almost impossible for a team like the Minnesota Twins to compete with the New York Yankees and other big-market clubs.

As the 1999 season began, the agreement between Major League Baseball and ESPN broke down over the network's desire to transfer some games from ESPN to ESPN2, a less-watched sister network offering sports that usually draw smaller audiences. Although this dispute was resolved, controversy involving television and baseball continues. As in the public spectrum of television in general, it shows no signs of ending.

See also: Brickhouse, John Beasley; Business; Caray, Harry; Miller, Marvin James; Radio Broadcasting; Turner, Robert Edward.

Additional Reading:

Catsis, John R. *Sports Broadcasting*. Chicago: Nelson-Hall, 1996.

Freeman, Michael. *ESPN: The Uncensored History*. Dallas: Taylor Publishing Company, 2000.

Klatell, David A. *Sports for Sale: Television, Money, and the Fans*. New York: Oxford University Press, 1988.

Sands, Jack. *Coming Apart at the Seams: How Baseball Owners, Players, and Television Executives Have Led Our National Pastime to the Brink of Disaster*. New York: Macmillan, 1993.

Zimbalist, Andrew. *Baseball and Billions: A Probing Look inside the Big Business of Our National Pastime*. Rev. ed. New York: Basic-Books, 1994.

THEATER

Two of the most memorable theatrical productions centering on baseball, the musical *Damn Yankees* and August Wilson's *Fences,* are discussed elsewhere in this book. They were not the only significant occasions, though, for baseball to grace the stage. Charles Hoyt wrote several entertaining comedies, most notably *A Runaway Colt,* which had its Broadway premiere in 1895. The cast included baseball great Cap Anson playing himself, trying to persuade parents to let their son join the Chicago White Stockings, managed by Anson and sometimes referred to as the "Colts" because of the many young players on the team. *A Runaway Colt* was the first baseball play to appear on Broadway and Anson's final Broadway role, although he continued to act in local and vaudeville productions.

Ring Lardner, the author of many immortal baseball stories, including the collection published as *You Know Me Al,* wrote a comedy called *Elmer the Great,* which appeared in New York in 1928 and ran for 40 performances. The still regularly produced *Damn Yankees* first appeared on Broadway in 1955, running for 1,019 performances. An opera, *The Mighty Casey,* based on the poem "Casey at the Bat," appeared in 1953, written by Pulitzer Prize–winner William Schuman with Jeremy Gury.

On the whole, however, baseball drama did not reach its peak until the 1970s. *Bleacher Bums* appeared off-Broadway in 1977, a comedy about loyal and therefore long-suffering Cubs fans. In the following decade theater-goers could enjoy a number of successful plays in addition to *Fences,* among them *The First* (1981), a musical about Jackie Robinson's first year with the Dodgers; *Say It Ain't So, Joe!* (1983) and *Out!* (1986), both dealing with the 1919 Black Sox scandal; a musical revue called *Diamonds* (1984),

featuring such songs as "God Threw Out the First Ball," "Let's Play Ball," and "The Boys of Summer"; and *The Signal Season of Dummy Hoy* (1987), about William "Dummy" Hoy, a talented player who could neither speak nor hear, at least much, but began a 14-year career in 1888 that produced a .287 batting average, 2,044 hits, and 594 stolen bases.

Other dramatic avenues also proved receptive to baseball subjects. Ring Lardner wrote a humorous sketch called *The Bull Pen* for the Ziegfeld Follies of 1922. It features two relief pitchers, one veteran, the other a rookie, whose lack of work yields plenty of time to discuss such topics as women. The world-famous humorist Will Rogers played the veteran, giving audiences, in Lardner and Rogers, an unbeatable combination for creating and delivering authentic and entertaining dialogue.

Many baseball players in the early decades of the twentieth century found financially rewarding off-season jobs in vaudeville. New York Giants pitcher Rube Marquard and his wife, actress Blossom Seeley, starred in two vaudeville musicals in 1912 and 1913. Mike Donlin, an outfielder for the Giants, formed a husband-and-wife team with comedienne Mabel Hite in several vaudeville sketches. Donlin had a serious case of the acting bug, appearing as himself in a movie story of his life, *Right Off the Bat* (1915), and achieving a postbaseball career as a film actor in dozens of supporting roles. The year before release of the film, Donlin had previewed his life story on the vaudeville stage, acting with another baseball player, Marty McHale, a pitcher for the New York American League club. Although New York players had opportunity ready at hand to turn to the stage, players from other cities also made the transition from the baseball field, including Chicago stars Cap Anson, already mentioned, and Joe Tinker, who starred in *A Great Catch* during the 1910 vaudeville season.

Baseball thus took center stage in America in more ways than one.

See also: Anson, Adrian Constantine; Black Sox Scandal; *Damn Yankees;* Fiction; Lardner, Ringgold Wilmer; Music; Wilson, August.

Additional Reading:

Bordman, Gerald. *American Musical Theatre.* New York: Oxford University Press, 1978.

———. *The Oxford Companion to American Theatre.* New York: Oxford University Press, 1984.

Douglas, Gilbert. *American Vaudeville: Its Life and Times.* 1940. Reprint, New York: Dover, 1963.

Mote, James. *Everything Baseball.* New York: Prentice Hall, 1989.

Slide, Anthony. *The Encyclopedia of Vaudeville.* Westport, CT: Greenwood Press, 1994.

TINKER TO EVERS TO CHANCE

Many individual stars and some teams have played their way permanently into the American consciousness, but seldom has a single unit of a team achieved lasting fame. An exception to the rule is the Chicago Cubs double-play combination from the early days of the twentieth century. However, as great as shortstop Joe Tinker, second baseman Johnny Evers, and first baseman Frank Chance were, they probably would not have earned their place in popular culture (and in the Hall of Fame) without a journalist named Franklin P. Adams and a poem, "Baseball's Sad Lexicon," that he wrote for the *New York World* in 1910. The lines echo still over all these years:

These are the saddest of possible words:
"Tinker to Evers to Chance."
Trio of bear cubs and fleeter than birds,
"Tinker to Evers to Chance."
Ruthlessly pricking our gonfalon bubble,
Making a Giant hit into a double—
Words that are heavy with nothing but
　　trouble:
"Tinker to Evers to Chance."

Adams lamented but also admired the way this Cubs trio burst the Giants' gonfalon—that is, pennant—bubble and helped the Cubs win four pennants in five seasons between 1906 and 1910. The Cubs set a major league record of 116 victories in 1906 and, although upset by the crosstown White Sox that year, captured the World Series in 1907 and 1908.

The three played together for 11 seasons (1902–1912). Tinker and Evers had a falling-out in 1905 and did not speak to each other until an emotional reconciliation during a World Series broadcast in 1938. Chance, known as the "Peerless Leader," also managed the Cubs from 1905 to 1912. The three have been long gone, but in America's collective mind's eye, they continue to turn double plays forever.

See also: Brown, Mordecai Peter Centennial; Hitless Wonders; Journalism (Print); Poetry.

Additional Reading:

Brown, Warren. *The Chicago Cubs.* New York: Putnam's, 1946.

Enright, Jim. *Chicago Cubs.* New York: Macmillan, 1975.

Holtzman, Jerome. *The Chicago Cubs Encyclopedia.* Philadelphia: Temple University Press, 1997.

Wilbert, Warren, and William Hageman. *Chicago Cubs: Seasons at the Summit.* Champaign, IL: Sagamore, 1997.

TORRE, JOSEPH PAUL (1940–)

Joe Torre achieved considerable success as a player and manager, although it was as the latter that he became a truly beloved public figure. As a player, Torre had an 18-year career as a catcher and infielder with the Milwaukee and Atlanta Braves, St. Louis Cardinals, and New York Mets from 1960 to 1977. Nine times an All-Star, Torre compiled a lifetime .297 batting average with 252 home runs and a total of 2,342 hits. His best season was in 1971 with St. Louis, when he led the league in batting (.363), hits (230), and runs batted in (137), a performance that

Manager Joe Torre, No. 6 of the New York Yankees, looks on during a spring training game against the Toronto Blue Jays at Legends Field in Tampa, Florida. (Scott Halleran/Allsport)

earned Torre the Most Valuable Player Award.

As a manager with the Mets, Braves, and Cardinals, Torre achieved only modest success, winning one division title (with the 1982 Braves) in 14 seasons. After being let go as the Cardinals' manager after the 1995 season, Torre assumed that his dugout days were over.

George Steinbrenner, however, unexpectedly hired Torre to manage the Yankees in 1996. There Torre found his managing niche, bringing unity and direction to a group of talented players and leading the club to a World Series championship. The victory was especially moving for the manager, whose brother Rocco died during the season; his other brother, Frank, a former first baseman with the Braves, underwent a heart transplant between Games 5 and 6 of the Series. When Joe Torre cried after the Series victory, more than a few fans cried with him.

And millions of former Yankee-haters rooted for Joe Torre and the Yankees as they rolled to a record 114 victories in 1998 and 11 more in the postseason. The two world championships in three years had returned the Yankees to their glory days and established Torre as perhaps baseball's most popular manager. Despite an ominous appearance occasioned by a constant five o'clock shadow, Joe Torre had been accepted as one of baseball's genuine good guys. This expanded popularity occasioned much genuine concern when Torre was diagnosed with prostate cancer during spring training 1999. The ensuing operation was successful, and Torre resumed his managerial duties with the Yankees, leading them to yet another world championship.

See also: Cancer; New York Yankees; Records Set; Steinbrenner, George Michael, III; World Series.

Additional Reading:

McCarver, Tim, with Danny Peary. *The Perfect Season: Why 1998 Was Baseball's Greatest Year.* New York: Villard Books, 1999.

Torre, Joe, with Henry Dreher. *Joe Torre's Ground Rules for Winners.* New York: Hyperion, 1999.

Torre, Joe, with Tom Verducci. *Chasing the Dream: My Lifelong Journey to the World Series.* 1997. Reprint, New York: Bantam, 1998.

TOTAL BASEBALL

Total Baseball has replaced *The Baseball Encyclopedia,* formerly published by Macmillan, as the official encyclopedia of major league baseball. The earlier *Baseball Encyclopedia* served its purpose well and may do so again with a new publisher, and it deserves the soft spot it occupies in the hearts of countless fans who since its arrival in 1969 turned to it repeatedly for the statistics that mean so much to fan and historian alike. But for now, *the* book is *Total Baseball*.

Total Baseball first appeared in 1989 and was endorsed by the major leagues as the official encyclopedia for its fourth edition in 1995. As this is being written, the current edition is the sixth, published in 1999 by Total Sports. Statistics, of course, are at the heart of this work, as they were of the Macmillan book, including certain categories of statistics not found anywhere else. Updating statistics, while important, also carries certain risks, including overturning accomplishments long acknowledged. Even many errors on Hall of Fame plaques have been discovered. In recent editions, *Total Baseball* has adopted a sensitive approach to this matter, agreeing with Major League Baseball that statistics should be updated but that titles and awards are permanent.

Unlike *The Baseball Encyclopedia,* which was almost completely statistical, *Total Baseball* also includes a rich array of essays on the history of the game, players, other leagues, and the game away from the field. These essays are highly informative and reflect the finest in scholarship. Many fans may find more than they want in the range of statistics, but those same fans probably will enjoy the essays, which are much easier to understand than some of the statistics.

See also: *The Baseball Encyclopedia;* Records Set; Statistics.
Additional Reading:
Thorn, John, et al., eds. *Total Baseball.* 6th ed. New York: Total Sports, 1999.

TOWNBALL

Townball grew out of rounders and developed into modern baseball. Actually, townball is not one game but many versions of a game. A thoroughly local and democratic form of recreation, townball followed rules modified according to the wishes of the local populace. Townball, also known by many other names (goal ball, stick ball, base, base ball, and so on), was played throughout the first half of the nineteenth century, being formalized into the "Massachusetts Game" in 1858.

Like the earlier rounders, townball (the Massachusetts Game version of 1858) includes a striker hitting the ball and attempting to run from base to base (sometimes stakes) before making an out. The striker is put out by having his hit caught, by striking out, or by being hit with a thrown ball when not at a base. Some significant changes from rounders include the addition of a catcher, use of a round bat, requiring that the ball be caught on the fly for the striker to be out (rather than on the first bounce), retiring the side when one player makes an out, and declaring victory when 100 tallies (runs) have been recorded.

Townball, in its many versions, was widely popular. College students enthusiastically played the game, although sometimes they were forced to desist by administrators who found the sport unbecoming of gentlemen and scholars. The famous explorers Lewis and Clark played townball with Native Americans as they returned from their expedition. Civil War soldiers turned to townball during lulls in fighting. Today, a team called the Leatherstocking Base Ball Club of Cooperstown, New York, turns the clock back by staging townball games.

See also: College Baseball; Cricket; Democracy; Rounders; Rural America.
Additional Reading:
Henderson, Robert William. *Ball, Bat, and Bishop: The Origin of Ball Games.* New York: Rockport, 1947.
———. *Early American Sports: A Check-List of Books by American and Foreign Authors Published in America Prior to 1860, Including Sporting Songs.* 2d ed. New York: A. S. Barnes, 1953.
Leatherstocking Base Ball Club Website. http://www.freeyellow.com/members2/tbone-tabor

TURNER, ROBERT EDWARD (TED) (1938–)

Ted Turner embodies the modern synthesis of sports and television. Owner of the Atlanta Braves, Turner also founded the Cable News Network (CNN) and pioneered development of superstations with WTBS, which carries the Braves throughout the country. The national exposure, coupled with the team's consistent success in the 1990s, made the Braves, more than any other club, America's team.

Turner started Turner Broadcasting System in 1970 and merged with Time Warner in 1996. He purchased the Atlanta Braves in 1976, but the team experienced inconsistent success until the 1990s, when the Braves boasted one of the finest starting pitching staffs in major league history, featuring Greg Maddux, Tom Glavine, John Smoltz, Steve Avery, Denny Neagle, and Kevin Millwood.

Ted Turner is a man of many talents and interests who also has had his share of controversial moments. A classics major at Brown University, he later won America's Cup in 1977 in his yacht *Courageous*. Four times Turner was named Yachtsman of the Year. One of his most outrageous actions as owner of the Braves was to don a uniform and take the manager's spot in the dugout, an act that drew the ire of baseball officials. His marriage to actress Jane Fonda, also remembered for her opposition to the Vietnam War, further raised his profile among media and fans. Turner remains one of the few baseball owners whose name and face are readily recognized by millions of people in the United States and abroad.

See also: Kuhn, Bowie K.; Television Broadcasting.

Additional Reading:

Bibb, Porter. *It Ain't as Easy as It Looks: Ted Turner's Amazing Story*. New York: Crown, 1993.

Goldberg, Robert. *Citizen Turner: The Wild Rise of an American Tycoon*. New York: Harcourt Brace, 1995.

Vaughan, Roger. *Ted Turner: The Man Behind the Mouth*. Boston: Sail Books, 1978.

Whittemore, Hank. *CNN: The Inside Story*. Boston: Little, Brown, 1990.

TWAIN, MARK (1835–1910)

Samuel Langhorne Clemens, better known by his pen name, Mark Twain, is widely recognized as one of the great American writers, author of such enduring classics as *Tom Sawyer* (1876) and *Huckleberry Finn* (1884). As a humorist and satirist, his fame is secure. His influence on other writers, among them Ernest Hemingway, has been well documented. Mark Twain is also associated with baseball, more so than almost any other nineteenth-century writer.

Twain never wrote strictly baseball stories. He does introduce baseball into *A Connecticut Yankee in King Arthur's Court* (1889), where the visitor induces a medley of royal personages to engage in a baseball game, with armor intact. The Connecticut Yankee utilizes chain mail and plate armor to distinguish the two teams. The account is both humorous and satirical, having much good fun at the expense of umpires while more seriously attacking the authoritarianism, privilege, and lack of equality that so offended Twain. Twain's democratic principles are obvious in much of his writing—his own popularity is often seen as a democratic rejection of the eastern literary elite—and his interest in baseball, very much a democratic sport, may spring from the same source.

When Albert G. Spalding brought his White Sox and an all-star team home in early 1889 from a foreign tour that included, among other nations, Australia, Egypt, Italy, and England, Mark Twain was among those present to welcome the returning heroes at a formal banquet at Delmonico's restaurant in New York City. In his welcoming address, Twain spoke of taking baseball, "the very symbol, the outward and visible expression of the drive and push and rush and struggle of the raging, tearing, booming nineteenth century . . . to places of profound repose and soft indolence," an ironic effort that Twain mirrored in *Connecticut Yankee,* published that same year. Twain went on to praise the players "who ploughed a new equator round the globe stealing bases on their bellies!" (*Mark Twain Speaking,* 244–247).

Darryl Brock names the protagonist of his novel *If I Never Get Back* Samuel Clemens Fowler. When Fowler was a boy, his grandfather repeatedly read to him from Twain's books, especially *Huckleberry Finn, Connecticut Yankee,* and *Life on the Mississippi.* Brock also introduces Twain into the story when Fowler is mysteriously transported back in time to become a substitute player on the famous 1869 Cincinnati Red Stockings. Brock's novel, published in 1990, is one of the more recent expressions of the connection between Mark Twain and baseball, a connection that appears unlikely to be forgotten.

See also: Fiction; Spalding, Albert Goodwill.

Additional Reading:

Brock, Darryl. *If I Never Get Back.* New York: Crown, 1990.

Gerber, John C. *Mark Twain.* Twayne's United States Authors Series. Boston: Twayne, 1988.

Hoffman, Andrew Jay. *Inventing Mark Twain: The Lives of Samuel Langhorne Clemens.* New York: William Morrow, 1997.

Levine, Peter. *A. G. Spalding and the Rise of Baseball: The Promise of American Sport.* New York: Oxford University Press, 1985.

Twain, Mark. *Mark Twain Speaking.* Ed. Paul Fatout. Iowa City: University of Iowa Press, 1976.

U

UMPIRES

"The United States is a nation of laws, not of men," the saying goes. At the same time, the nation needs people to enforce the laws, like peace officers and judges. Baseball is no different from larger society, which is why there are umpires. Umpires do not make the laws, but they exercise considerable power in enforcing them, functioning as police officer, judge, and jury. For carrying out this difficult job, they are ignored, often reviled, even hated. "Kill the umpire!" is the old refrain.

In the beginning, umpires were selected from the crowd or from among the players in keeping with the amateur spirit of the early game. The professional umpire came into being with the National League in the late 1870s, when umpires were paid $5 per game. In 1882, the American Association established a salary of $140 per month; the league also established a uniform of blue caps and coats for umpires. One umpire handled the entire game, stationing himself well behind home plate. Sometimes he would seek the advice of fans to determine difficult calls in the outer reaches of the field. Utilizing two umpires first occurred

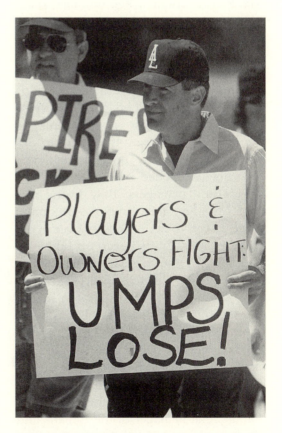

An American League umpire pickets in front of a baseball park during a spring training game in Florida, April 1995. (Andy Lyons/Allsport)

for the postseason series between National League and American Association champions in 1887, but regular use of two officials for games did not start until 1909, a change that greatly improved officiating efficiency. The number per game increased to three for all major league games in 1933 and to four in the 1950s.

Umpires faced great challenges to calling a game well and sometimes were in physical danger. Tim Hurst, for example, was hit in the face by a stein of beer thrown from the stands in an 1897 game. Hurst fired it back, knocking out the spectator. Fortunately, police reached Hurst before a mob of spectators, both saving and arresting him. Fans in Washington once set vicious dogs on an umpire. Players also attacked umpires, using whatever was available, including fists and bats. Some umpires carried a revolver for protection.

Despite the negative attitude toward umpires and owners' refusal to take steps to protect them—Albert Spalding once argued that fans who abused umpires were merely exercising their right to oppose tyranny—many umpires achieved not only excellence but the respect of players and managers. Billy Evans was one of the first great umpires, becoming at age 22 the youngest umpire ever in the major leagues. Evans began his umpiring career when the regular umpire for a semipro team failed to appear. Known as a fair sportswriter, he was chosen by the two managers to substitute. Evans went on to a long career in the American League, briefly interrupted by a few months near death after being hit on the head by a thrown pop bottle. Later, Evans was president of the Southern Association, general manager of the Indians and Tigers, and farm director for the Red Sox.

Bill Klem is still considered by baseball historians to be perhaps the best National League umpire ever. He served on the field for 37 years (1905–1941) and then was chief of the umpiring staff for 10 years. Cal Hubbard was an All-America football player at Geneva College and an all-league lineman with the Green Bay Packers in the National Football League. A masterful student of the rules of football as well as baseball, he was recognized as an outstanding arbiter from his first year in the American League in 1936. Hubbard continued to excel until a hunting accident after the 1951 season affected his vision. He later became supervisor of American League umpires until 1970. Hubbard is unique in having been chosen for the halls of fame for college football, professional football, and major league baseball. These are only a few of the men who have achieved greatness as umpires.

Umpires remain controversial long after the days when they faced real dangers to life and limb. It is largely a male-only club, and to this day no woman has umpired in the majors. The best-known example of a woman attempting to climb to that level is Pamela Postema, who after graduating from Al Somers's highly respected school for umpires in Daytona Beach, Florida, accepted a position umpiring in the Gulf Coast League. Postema advanced steadily up the minor league ladder during 13 years of umpiring but was released after seven years at the Triple-A level. She later sued, charging sex discrimination, settling out of court.

Labor struggles have occurred regularly since major league umpires first unionized successfully in 1969, with umpires scoring major victories while taking some public-relations hits. Richie Phillips became general counsel for the Major Leagues Umpire Association in 1978, when major league umps earned between $17,500 and $40,000 annually. By the time he was ousted as union head in 1999, umpires earned a minimum of $95,000 and as much as $282,000 per year. In between, Phillips led the union through a seven-week strike in 1979 that yielded average salary increases of $7,000 and two weeks of vacation during the baseball season, the first-ever in-season vacation for umpires. The umpires later went on strike during the first four postseason games in 1984, carried out a one-day stoppage in 1991, and were locked our for the first eight days in 1995.

A crisis developed as umpires, looking toward the expiration of their collective-bargaining agreement on December 31, 1999, feared that the owners would lock them out at that time. With a no-strike provision in their contract, Phillips devised a plan to force owners into an agreement. The plan called for umpires to resign effective September 2. Phillips expected minor league umpires to participate as well, leaving baseball with no alternatives short of using college umpires or dealing with the union. His assumption was that owners would not dare to continue without professional umpires.

In the meantime, owners were readying a proposal that would have included a new evaluation system to answer growing concerns among fans and players regarding inconsistency, incompetence, and arrogance on the part of many umpires. Supervision of umpires would be centralized in the commissioner's office under Major League Baseball vice president Sandy Alderson. However, the number of umpires would increase, with 15 crews of five umpires each, rather than 17 teams of four each. One member of each team would be on vacation at any given time. An increase in salary and a standard manual for all umpires were also included in the plan. Phillips, however, apparently misjudged that a substantial number of current umpires would be replaced at the end of the year.

Not all umpires supported Phillips's resignation ploy. Some had tried unsuccessfully to oust Phillips as union head in February. The plan, though, went ahead, with virtually every commentator judging the resignation strategy as dangerous and foolish. An article in *USA Today Baseball Weekly* later called it "the worst strategy in the history of the labor movement" (September 8–14, 1999, 8). Resignations were submitted in July, but minor league umps did not follow, and more than two-thirds of the American League umpires decided not to resign. With a break in ranks, many umps who had resigned rescinded their resignations. Nonetheless, 22 resignations were accepted, and minor league umpires were promoted to fill the slots.

The major league umpires voted 57-35 in early December 1999 to remove Richie Phillips, decertify the union, and create a new union called the Major League Umpires Independent Organizing Committee. Phillips unsuccessfully appealed the action to the National Labor Relations Board. In addition, minor league umpires began forming a union of their own, although in discussing the action they kept their comments decidedly nonconfrontational.

A new, less militant umpires' union that accepts an evaluative and developmental system and clearly recognizes the need to be accountable for game performance may go a long way toward assuaging the negative feelings toward umpires that developed throughout the 1990s. Just as the United States requires competent and fair enforcers of the law throughout society, so does baseball.

See also: Art; Equipment; Labor-Management Relations; Law; Spalding, Albert Goodwill; Women in Baseball.

Additional Reading:

Abrams, Roger I. *Legal Bases: Baseball and the Law.* Philadelphia: Temple University Press, 1998.

Frommer, Harvey. *Primitive Baseball: The First Quarter-Century of the National Pastime.* New York: Atheneum, 1988.

Gerlach, Larry R. *The Men in Blue: Conversations with Umpires.* New York: Viking, 1980.

Postema, Pam, and Gene Wojciechowski. *You've Got to Have Balls to Make It in This League.* New York: Simon and Schuster, 1992.

Skipper, John C. *Umpires: Classic Baseball Stories from the Men Who Made the Calls.* Jefferson, NC: McFarland, 1997.

UNIFORMS

Uniforms have been part of baseball since its early days as an organized sport. The New York Knickerbockers began organized baseball in the 1840s and quickly settled on a standard uniform, although it did not actually include knickerbockers—their name borrowed instead from a term given to descendants of the Dutch who settled New York. Instead they wore long blue trousers (woolen, which remained the cloth of choice for a century or so, summer heat notwithstanding), white flannel shirts, and straw hats ("boaters," as they were called). The Knickerbockers set the tone for the well-dressed young baseball player, and a good-looking uniform would remain a permanent part of the player's preparation to play, even as styles changed considerably.

The Cincinnati Red Stockings introduced knickerbocker pants (knickers) in the late 1860s, finding the shorter, knee-length attire more conducive to effective performance than the long, baggy pants of their predecessors. A cakebox-style cap became popular in the 1870s (the boater long since discarded) and was resurrected a century later by the Pittsburgh Pirates.

Stockings were especially important, with several teams formally or informally being known by the color of their socks: the White Stockings; Red Stockings; Green Stockings (actually the Mutuals); and Blue Stockings (the Washington Olympics). Ties were worn by many teams in the early decades. By the 1880s, low shoes were replacing high-tops, leather footwear was replacing canvas, and spikes added intimidation to better traction.

Over the years, many subtle changes occurred, although some proved especially noteworthy. The famous pinstripes became part of the New York Yankee image in 1915. Some 60 years later, the innovative Bill Veeck clad his White Sox in shorts. That was an abundantly sensible approach given the hot, humid weather of the Midwest summer, but it posed some dangers when sliding. More importantly, shorts did not fit the manly baseball image, and they were quickly discarded.

Perhaps the most bizarre proposal regarding uniforms came in the 1880s, when sporting-goods entrepreneur Albert Spalding offered a different-colored uniform for each position. Spalding must have been seeing dollar signs when he pushed this radical idea, but players saw clowns' costumes instead and strongly resisted.

Uniforms have served various purposes over the years. It is questionable whether uniforms, unlike the catcher's mask, fielder's glove, and batting helmet, actually aid performance or safety. Yet uniforms continue to be seen as an integral part of the game. Initially, organized baseball developed, despite its rural origins, as a gentleman's game. The Knickerbockers and other early teams wanted to distinguish themselves from the rabble, and stylish uniforms added the sense of dignity they sought.

In addition, baseball uniforms respond to a contradictory set of attitudes in American society. Americans have long wanted to see themselves as rugged individualists who settled the West and spread civilization from ocean to ocean through the efforts of heroes. In reality, almost everything important that has been accomplished has been accomplished with help from others.

Baseball combines these two views of how things get done: It is more of an individual game than some team sports, with players separated physically around the diamond and outfield, unlike football, where players tend to bunch up together, the offense even huddling before plays. Yet each player depends on every other teammate. The pitcher can be the best in the game, but if his fielders do not handle the grounders and fly balls, then his pitching will go for naught; the examples could go on and on. Uniforms fit into this fusion of opposites. The uniform sets players visually apart from the fans (without whom, of course, there would be no game) and the other team. Yet the uniform helps to bind players into a cohesive unit. The batter may stand alone as he faces the opposing pitcher, but he is a member of a team, for better

or worse. His uniform is a continuing symbol of that unity in diversity.

See also: Cincinnati Red Stockings; Equipment; New York Yankees; Rural Baseball; Spalding, Albert Goodwill; Veeck, William L., Jr.
Additional Reading:
Frommer, Harvey. *Primitive Baseball: The First Quarter-Century of the National Pastime.* New York: Atheneum, 1988.
Goldstein, Warren. *Playing for Keeps: A History of Early Baseball.* Ithaca: Cornell University Press, 1989.
Okkonen, Marc. *Baseball Uniforms of the 20th Century: The Official Major League Baseball Guide.* New York: Sterling, 1991.
Pietrusza, David, Lloyd Johnson, and Bob Carroll. *The Total Baseball Catalog.* New York: Total Sports, 1998.
Ward, Geoffrey C., and Ken Burns. *Baseball: An Illustrated History.* New York: Alfred A. Knopf, 1994.

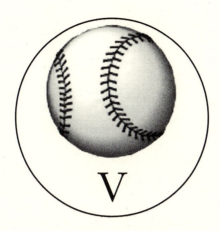

V

VEECK, WILLIAM L., JR. (1914–1986)

Bill Veeck approached baseball the way one might approach running a circus: Try to have capable performers (so no one falls off the high wire or gets eaten by a lion), market the enterprise with a lot of gimmicks that add fun but do not interfere with the basic action, and always keep in mind that the point is to entertain the audience. Baseball, like the circus, is a pastime for "children of all ages," who have the most fun when they are actively engaged. This approach ran counter to the way most owners viewed their business, but Veeck argued that the only really bad word he knew was "conformity."

Bill Veeck grew up around baseball. His father was general manager of the Cubs, and the young Veeck worked at a hot dog stand in the Roaring Twenties and even planted the original ivy that remains a Wrigley Field hallmark. After working in the Cubs ticket office and later serving as treasurer, Veeck moved on in the early 1940s to the minor league Milwaukee Brewers to become a general manager himself.

Serving as a U.S. Marine in the South Pacific during World War II, he had his lower left leg crushed by a recoiling antiaircraft gun. The leg was amputated in 1946, the same year he bought the Cleveland Indians. Veeck won the pennant and World Series in 1948 with such stars as manager-shortstop Lou Boudreau and pitchers Bob Feller, Bob Lemon, and rookie Gene Bearden.

Also on that 1948 Indians team were two players who, along with Veeck, made history. In 1947 Veeck brought in outfielder Larry Doby, the first African American to play in the American League. By 1948, he was a star, on his way to the Hall of Fame, and Veeck was a hero of the effort to integrate the major leagues. In that championship season, famous Negro League pitcher Satchel Paige, although well past his prime, joined the Indians. Veeck's addition of Paige, at least in his early forties, was criticized by some as just a publicity stunt, but Paige proved that he could still pitch. The Negro League immortal won six of seven decisions, compiling a low 2.48 ERA in 21 games. A record 2.6 million fans turned out to see the Indians play that year.

Veeck sold the Indians in 1949 and purchased the feeble St. Louis Browns in 1951. Between then and 1953, when he sold the club, Veeck had to rely on something other than talented teams to draw fans. The most famous attraction occurred in 1951, when Veeck hired Eddie Gaedel—who was 43 inches tall—to pinch-hit. Gaedel walked, much to the delight of the fans, but an angry baseball power structure quickly passed a rule requiring all baseball contracts to be approved by the commissioner's office to head off such shenanigans. Veeck capitalized on the team's own ineptitude by giving spectators signs to determine managerial decisions: "Yes" or "No" cards, for example, would express the fans' judgment whether a pitcher should be removed.

Veeck owned the Chicago White Sox twice, from 1959 to 1961 and then from 1976 until January 1981. The White Sox won the pennant in Veeck's first year, the first Sox pennant since the Black Sox scandal of 1919. Among Veeck's colorful innovations were an exploding scoreboard, short pants, names on players' uniforms, Disco Demolition Night (which so damaged the grounds that the second game of the scheduled doubleheader had to be canceled), Smith Day (everyone named Smith or a version thereof was admitted free), relievers entering the game by car, and a pitch-o-meter to tell whether pitchers were delivering their pitches within the required 20 seconds. The White Sox never won another pennant, but fans had a great time. And the colorful Bill Veeck certainly did not fall prey to conformity, the only dirty word he knew.

See also: African Americans; Business; Doby, Lawrence Eugene; Gaedel, Edward Carl; Paige, Leroy Robert; War; Wrigley Field.

Additional Reading:
Eskanazi, Gerald. *Bill Veeck: A Baseball Legend.* New York: McGraw-Hill, 1988.
Jordan, David M., Larry R. Gerlach, and John P. Rossi. "A Baseball Myth Exploded: Bill Veeck and the 1943 Sale of the Phillies." *The National Pastime: A Review of Baseball History* 17 (1998): 3–13.
Vanderberg, Bob. *'59: Summer of the Sox.* Champaign, IL: Sports Publishing, 1999.
Veeck, Bill, with Ed Linn. *The Hustler's Handbook.* New York: Putnam's, 1965.
———. *Veeck—As in Wreck: The Autobiography of Bill Veeck.* New York: Putnam's, 1962.

WAGNER, JOHN PETER (HONUS, THE FLYING DUTCHMAN) (1874–1955)

Honus Wagner is still mentioned as the finest shortstop ever to play the game. In his time, the debate was whether he or Ty Cobb was the greatest all-around player. Many considered Wagner to be the absolute best because of his outstanding hitting, great defense, and base-stealing skill.

In physical appearance, Wagner did not look like a baseball star. He was bow-legged, with a thick chest and long arms. He always looked awkward at bat and certainly did not convey the image of a speedy runner. Yet Wagner, who spent all of his playing career (1897–1917) virtually with the same club (two years with Louisville, which then merged with the Pittsburgh Pirates), won eight batting titles while accumulating 3,415 hits. He batted .327 for his career, with 640 doubles, 252 triples, 1,732 RBIs, and 722 stolen bases. He also earned the reputation as a peerless fielder at shortstop.

Wagner worked the Pennsylvania coalfields as a youth before embarking on a baseball career. Despite his accomplishments, he remained genuinely humble, patient with teammates, and generous to rookies. Aware of his obligations to the nation's children, he demanded that a tobacco company stop putting his picture in packs of cigarettes. The pictures were removed, giving rise to perhaps the most valuable baseball card in history: An American Tobacco Company 1909 Honus Wagner card sold in 1996 for $640,500. After leading the Pirates to pennants in 1901, 1902, and 1903, and a World Series triumph in 1909, Wagner returned from retirement to coach new generations of Pirates from 1933 until 1951. He was one of the five stars chosen for the original class of the Baseball Hall of Fame in 1936.

See also: Cards, Baseball; Cobb, Tyrus Raymond; Heroes; Records Set.

Additional Reading:
DeValeria, Dennis, and Jeanne Burke DeValeria. *Honus Wagner: A Biography.* 1996. Reprint, Pittsburgh: University of Pittsburgh Press, 1998.
Gutman, Dan. *Honus and Me: A Baseball Card Adventure.* New York: Avon, 1997.
Hageman, William. *Honus: The Life and Times of a Baseball Hero.* Champaign, IL: Sagamore, 1996.
Hittner, Arthur D. *Honus Wagner: The Life of Baseball's "Flying Dutchman."* Jefferson, NC: McFarland, 1996.

WALSH, EDWARD AUGUSTINE (BIG ED) (1881–1959)

Big Ed Walsh was not big physically—six-foot one and some 190 pounds—but he had huge endurance. In five separate seasons he pitched over 360 innings, and he won 40 games in 1908. A great pitcher for the Chicago White Sox, Walsh remains something of a legend for his superhuman achievements, especially during a memorable run at the 1908 pennant.

The White Sox found themselves in a tight race as the season approached its conclusion, so they kept handing the ball to their best pitcher. Walsh hurled seven games in the final nine days, including a doubleheader win. He pitched three complete games in two days. The Sox lost the pennant, but Big Ed wrote his name into baseball history and sports folklore. In that historic 1908 season, Walsh set a modern major league record that still stands: 464 innings pitched; he also led his league with 40 wins, 66 games pitched, 42 complete games, 11 shutouts, 269 strikeouts, and six saves (although saves were not computed then). His earned-run average was 1.42, which contributed to his lifetime mark of 1.82—the lowest ever in the majors. His 40 wins are the second highest total in the twentieth century, one behind Jack Chesbro's 41 in 1904.

Ed Walsh's early work in the Pennsylvania coal mines helped him develop strength and stamina to go with a devastating spitball. Perhaps the highlight of his career may actually have come two years before his 40-win season, when he led the White Sox to victory in the World Series, twice defeating the mighty Cubs, who had won 116 games that year. The triumph was a major upset for the Sox, known as the Hitless Wonders for their season batting average of .230 and team total of seven home runs.

See also: Heroes; Hitless Wonders; Tinker to Evers to Chance.
Additional Reading:
Lindberg, Richard. *Sox: The Complete Record of Chicago White Sox Baseball.* New York: Macmillan, 1984.

WAR

War has both affected and been affected by baseball. The Civil War helped spread baseball throughout the United States, while World War I and, to a much greater degree, World War II drew players away from the game to serve their country. During World War II especially, fans had to be satisfied with an inferior quality of play as major league teams utilized replacements. Later wars had much less impact on baseball; the Vietnam War, while in other ways almost ripping the country apart, barely scratched the national pastime.

Soldiers played early versions of baseball during the Revolutionary War, but the Civil War began just as baseball was spreading across the Northeast and Midwest. Although the game was not unknown in the South, having achieved popularity in New Orleans and being played occasionally by slaves, it was still primarily the North's game when hostilities began. As the war progressed, Union soldiers brought baseball with them into the South, playing between battles, sometimes with the sounds of cannon fire in the distance. Baseball was easy to transport, as it required almost no equipment save for a ball and bat.

Confederate soldiers came most directly into contact with baseball when Union prisoners staged games in some of the prisoner camps. When the war ended, soldiers from both sides returned home, and baseball went with them. Before long, the South would become a major producer of major league players, although much of the twentieth century would pass before major league clubs started joining minor league teams in the Deep South.

By the time the United States entered World War I in 1917, baseball was firmly entrenched. Patriotism was high, although it had its limits where making money was concerned. Ban Johnson, president of the American League, ordered teams to learn military drill, which they did, using bats in place of rifles. National League president John K. Tener announced that "baseball is the very watchword of democracy," but owners also attempted to get baseball declared an "essential industry," thus exempting players from wartime service. That effort failed, and the government issued a "work or fight" order, with many players subsequently departing for war-related industries, where they also played on industrial teams on the side, sometimes for big money.

Owners reduced the 1918 schedule from 154 to 128 games in a show of support; and when "The Star-Spangled Banner" was sung at the first game of the 1918 World Series that autumn, the song was received with so much enthusiasm that it quickly became a staple of baseball games. By 1931, the song officially was the country's national anthem.

Approximately 227 players served in the military during World War I, with three dying, the most prominent being Eddie Grant, former third baseman and captain of the New York Giants. In addition, Robert Troy and Alex Barr, who had played briefly for the Tigers and Yankees, respectively, lost their lives in combat. Many others returned home permanently affected by the war. Christy Mathewson, the great pitcher for the Giants and one of the most loved players in the history of the game, was accidentally gassed and returned with permanently damaged lungs. He died seven years later at the age of 45. Another pitching immortal, Grover Cleveland Alexander, served in an artillery unit and developed shell shock, today known as post-traumatic stress disorder. He pitched for many more years after the war but suffered from damaged hearing, epilepsy, and heavy drinking. Branch Rickey, at 36, became a major, commanding a unit that included Lieutenant George Sisler, who later hit over .400 twice with the St. Louis Browns; Ty Cobb, the Tiger great; and Mathewson.

As in the Civil War, servicemen played baseball among themselves when they could, at the same time introducing the sport to France, Belgium, Italy, and Germany. Service baseball would become even more popular during World War II, when it would be employed as a fundraiser for the war effort as well as a morale booster. Japan had received the American game during the nineteenth century and, both before and after the war, competed against touring American teams.

The game that had helped to bring Japan and the United States together in the early decades of the twentieth century was sometimes used against Americans by the Japanese during World War II. The Japanese had loved Babe Ruth when he visited Japan, and would express that love again after the war when, upon hearing of Ruth's death, Japanese teams stopped play to pay tribute to the man they called "Beibu Rusu." During the war, however, Japanese soldiers tried to antagonize American troops by cursing Ruth, while Americans used knowledge of the Bambino to ferret out spies trying to pass as Americans.

With war spreading across Europe, the United States instituted a military draft in the fall of 1940. One of the first players to be drafted was the great Tiger slugger Hank Greenberg. His time up shortly before Pearl Harbor, Greenberg turned around and reenlisted. By the end of the war, about 340 major league players and several thousand minor-leaguers had answered the nation's call, either in the draft or by enlisting. Many played on service teams, some entertaining and raising money rather than facing the enemy directly. Many, however, did go into combat, and over 50 professional baseball players died during the conflict, including sons of major league managers Billy Southworth, Mickey Cochrane, and Jimmie Wilson.

Many other players were injured in the war. Bert Shepard was shot down over Germany and lost his right leg below the knee. He later made a pitching appearance for the Washington Senators in 1945. Cecil Travis, shortstop of the Senators, suffered frozen feet at the Battle of the Bulge and saw his baseball career curtailed by continuing foot problems. Hugh Mulcahy of the Phillies and Charlie Wagner of the Red Sox survived the Philippines, but extreme dysentery precipitated health problems that ended their baseball careers. Superstars like Ted Williams, Joe DiMaggio, and Bob Feller lost years out of their prime—and a great many additional home runs or pitching wins—but their loss paled in comparison to the price paid by many soldiers.

To help meet Americans' desire for baseball during the absence of so many of the game's stars, the All-American Girls Professional Baseball League was created. Meanwhile, substitute players joined the major league clubs, including veteran players in their forties like Babe Herman and Paul Waner. Fifteen-year-old Joe Nuxhall pitched briefly for the Cincinnati Reds, returning several years later to become an effective major league pitcher. Pete Gray, with only one arm, played for the St. Louis Browns.

One of the positive developments of the war was integration of service teams abroad. Negro League pitcher Leon Day, for example, hurled for a primarily white team in Germany. Back home, service teams remained segregated during the war, but the cause of integration was picking up steam as black soldiers fought and died for their country. Baseball resumed its place in Japan after the war, aided by strong support from General Douglas MacArthur. From the American point of view, the democratizing game of baseball was a helpful instrument for turning Japan from its wartime status back into a peaceful, and freer, country.

Subsequent wars have had less impact on baseball. The Korean War drew far fewer players away from the game, although a number of prominent players were drafted, mainly into the army. Ted Williams, who had served with distinction in World War II, was recalled to active service as a fighter pilot and flew 38 missions, his plane taking antiaircraft fire three times. The Yankees had to play without pitcher Whitey Ford and infielders Bobby Brown and Jerry Coleman but managed to continue winning pennants anyway. The Giants were less fortunate in the absence of Willie Mays, but in 1954, with their young center fielder back in the lineup, they won the world championship. Pitcher Don Newcombe returned from the Korean War to win 27 games with the Dodgers in 1956. The war claimed only one life among the players and former players who fought: Major Bob Neighbors, formerly of the Browns.

The Vietnam War proved little more than an annoyance for major league players, although some minor-leaguers fought in it. With reserve programs in place, most major-leaguers who might have been drafted succeeded in going that route, working their duty assignments around the baseball season. Ironically, baseball, which has had such a major impact on other areas of American life, and which has reflected so much of American society over the years, was one of the few major institutions generally unaffected by the Vietnam War.

See also: African Americans; Alexander, Grover Cleveland; Disabilities; Greenberg, Henry Benjamin; Japanese Baseball; Mathewson, Christopher; Presidents of the United States; Rickey, Wesley Branch; Williams, Theodore Samuel.

Additional Reading:
Crissey, Harrington E., Jr. "Baseball and the Armed Services." In Total Baseball. 6th ed. Ed. John Thorn et al. New York: Total Sports, 1999, pp. 2513–2520.
Gilbert, Bill. They Also Served: Baseball and the Home Front, 1941–1945. New York: Crown, 1992.
Goldstein, Richard. Spartan Seasons: How Baseball Survived the Second World War. New York: Macmillan, 1980.
Ryczek, William J. When Johnny Came Sliding Home: The Post–Civil War Baseball Boom, 1865–1870. Jefferson, NC: McFarland, 1998.
Van Blair, Rick. Dugout to Foxhole: Interviews with Baseball Players Whose Careers Were Affected by World War II. Jefferson, NC: McFarland, 1994.

An illustration of John M. Ward on an Allen and Ginter's cigarette card, part of the World Champions collection (Ann Ronan Picture Library)

WARD, JOHN MONTGOMERY (MONTE) (1860–1925)

Few baseball players have been as multitalented as John Montgomery Ward, and few have more thoroughly mirrored profound changes in American society. Ward finally was unsuccessful in changing the legal and economic face of major league baseball in his own lifetime, but that does not change the fact that he foreshadowed changes in baseball that a century later would alter the relationship between labor and management and make players some of America's richest citizens.

Ward started his baseball career as a pitcher and later shifted to shortstop, becoming the only player ever to win over 100 games and collect over 2,000 hits in the major leagues. As a pitcher, he won 164 games and lost 102, winning 47 and 39 games in 1879 and 1880 while becoming one of the first pitchers to master the curveball. When his arm gave out, he became a solid full-time infielder. In addition, he earned a law degree from Columbia Law School in 1885, spoke five languages, authored a book for children on how to play baseball, and married a famous actress named Helen Dauvray.

Ward fought hard against the reserve clause, which he likened to a "fugitive slave law," by organizing the first players' union, the National Brotherhood of Professional Baseball Players, in 1885, then leading development of the first (and so far only) players' league. Although labor was gaining increased power in American society, including a major victory by the Knights of Labor against the railroad industry, Ward's efforts were defeated by financial pressure exerted by the National League. The Players League lasted for just the 1890 season. Ward continued as a player and manager through the 1894 season before retiring to practice law. A century later, the Major League Baseball Players Association would fulfill Ward's vision, as baseball players were freed from the reserve clause.

See also: Antitrust Exemption; Flood, Curtis Charles; Free Agency; Labor-Management Relations; Law; Reserve Clause.
Additional Reading:
Abrams, Roger I. *Legal Bases: Baseball and the Law.* Philadelphia: Temple University Press, 1998.
Di Salvatore, Bryan. *A Clever Base-Ballist: The Life and Times of John Montgomery Ward.* New York: Pantheon, 1999.
Nemec, David. *The Great Encyclopedia of 19th-Century Major League Baseball.* New York: Donald I. Fine, 1997.
Stevens, David. *Baseball's Radical for All Seasons: A Biography of John Montgomery Ward.* Lanham, MD: Scarecrow, 1998.
Ward, John Montgomery. *Base Ball: How to Become a Player.* Philadelphia: Athletic Publishing Company, 1888.

WHITE, WILLIAM DEKOVA (BILL) (1934–)

Bill White, who reached the major leagues about a decade after Jackie Robinson broke the color barrier, was himself a pioneer. White became president of the National League in 1989, the first African American to head one of baseball's top leagues.

White was an outstanding defensive first baseman and a consistent hitter during his major league career, which stretched from 1956, when he broke in with the New York Giants, to 1969, when he concluded his playing days as a part-timer in his second stint with the St. Louis Cardinals.

Bill White spent his best playing years with the Cardinals from 1959 through the 1965 season. In seven seasons, he batted over .300 four times, hit 20 or more home runs five seasons in a row, drove in over 100 runners three times, and was a five-time National League All-Star. He concluded his playing career with a lifetime batting average of .286, a total of 1,706 hits, 202 home runs, and 870 RBIs. White later spent 18 years as an announcer for the New York Yankees.

More famous players, such as Bob Gibson, Lou Brock, and the aging Stan Musial, overshadowed White during his playing days. White's quiet leadership ability, however, was recognized by those with whom he associated and earned him the highest position in baseball ever reached by an African American. White continued as president of the National League until 1994.

See also: African Americans.
Additional Reading:
Helyar, John. *Lords of the Realm: The Real History of Baseball.* 1994. Reprint, New York: Ballantine Books, 1995.

WHITMAN, WALTER (WALT) (1819–1892)

Walt Whitman, long before A. Bartlett Giamatti's allegorical exegesis of baseball, perceived the sport as a metaphor for America itself. The poet of *Leaves of Grass* wrote that baseball is "America's game: has the snap, go, fling, of the American atmosphere—belongs as much to our institutions, fits into them as significantly, as our constitutions, laws: is just as important in the sum total of our historic life" (Folsom, 29).

Whitman's love affair with baseball began early, when he played with his brother, Thomas Jefferson Whitman, and covered games for Brooklyn newspapers. For Whitman, baseball was a way for workingmen to enjoy life and improve their health while bonding in a spirit of fellowship.

Whitman continued to enjoy the game, if mainly as a spectator, in Washington during the Civil War. After the war, baseball came to be viewed as a unifying force, an effect of the game dear to Whitman's heart. He also admired baseball terminology and utilized such expressions as "home stroke," "hits," and "on the fly" in his conversation. He saw the baseball field as a model of how people could enjoy nature with only slight modifications to the natural habitat. Baseball was, in short, an example of democracy at its healthiest.

Whitman apparently did not focus on commercial changes to the game like salaries and varying costs of admission that in his own time produced both player and spectator elites. Neither did he seem to perceive the racism that the game, by the end of the Civil War, had firmly institutionalized, although he lamented the growing emphasis on the curveball, which he viewed as deceitful. Whitman instead remained fascinated with baseball, establishing an association of poets with baseball that continues to the present day. Baseball remains the poet's game.

See also: Journalism (Print); Poetry; War.

Additional Reading:

Folsom, Ed. "Whitman and Baseball." *Walt Whitman's Native Representations*. New York: Cambridge University Press, 1994, pp. 27–54.

Hall, Donald. "The Poet's Game." *Fathers Playing Catch with Sons: Essays on Sport (Mostly Baseball)*. San Francisco: North Point, 1985, pp. 57–63.

Ryczek, William J. *When Johnny Came Sliding Home: The Post–Civil War Baseball Boom, 1865–1870*. Jefferson, NC: McFarland, 1998.

Traubel, Horace. *With Walt Whitman in Camden*. Ed. Sculley Bradley. Carbondale: Southern Illinois University Press, 1959.

Whitman, Walt. *The Works of Walt Whitman*. New York: Funk and Wagnalls, 1968.

"WHO'S ON FIRST?"

Baseball humor is not a common phenomenon anymore, but there were times when seriousness and humor coexisted within baseball and when laughter, occasioned by baseball skits and jokes, rang throughout the vaudeville audience or on radio and television. Today, in the face of strikes, scandals, huge salaries, and owners pressuring taxpayers to finance new stadiums, humor from the past can still bring relief and pleasure. As baseball is the most nostalgic of all sports, it may be fitting that humor takes a seat in the dugout next to nostalgia.

No baseball skit has entertained more people than Bud Abbott and Lou Costello's "Who's on First?" The story began shortly after Abbott and Costello teamed up in 1936, when they transformed a word-play skit (the type known as "pitter-patter" sketches) that they had performed around the words "watts" and "volts" ("What are volts?" "That's right. Watts are volts.") into what would become their baseball classic. Abbott is the knowledgeable partner in the skit, informing his partner about how "they give ballplayers peculiar names nowadays." Costello plays the increasingly frustrated interlocutor trying to make sense of what his buddy is saying. For those unfortunate enough not to have heard the routine, it goes in part like this:

Costello: "You know the fellows' names?"
  Abbott: "Yes."
Costello: "Well, then, who's playin' first?"
  Abbott: "Yes."
Costello: "I mean the fellow's name on first base."
  Abbott: "Who."

Costello: "The fellow's name on first base for St. Louis."

Abbott: "Who."

Costello: "The guy on first base."

Abbott: "Who is on first base."

Costello: "Well, what are you askin' me for?"

No printed script, of course, can do justice to the two men's impeccable timing; the palpable sense of rising, almost volcanic frustration on Costello's part; and the continuing factual and infuriating responses of Abbott.

The comedic team signed to appear regularly on *The Kate Smith Show* in 1939, and once they performed their baseball skit on the radio show its fame was fixed. Abbott and Costello estimated that they performed the skit 10,000 times on radio and television and in live appearances before their separation as partners in 1957. They entertained the troops during World War II with their "Who's on First?" routine and included the skit in their 1945 film *Naughty Nineties.* The routine also was included in the 1965 film retrospective *The World of Abbott and Costello,* and James L. Seay adapted the skit into a play in 1975. Visitors to the Hall of Fame in Cooperstown are able to see the famous comedy team perform their skit on film, and recordings of Abbott and Costello continue to attract new fans who sympathize with the obfuscating literalism of Bud Abbott, the enormous frustration of Lou Costello, and remembrance of things past, such as the days when baseball could be funny.

See also: Schacht, Alexander.

Additional Reading/Viewing/Listening:

Abbott, Bud, and Lou Costello. "Who's on First?" *Play Ball!* Compact Disc. Telarc, 1998.

Seay, James L. *Who's on First?* Elgin, IL: Performance Publishing, 1975.

Thomas, Bob. *Bud and Lou: The Abbott and Costello Story.* Philadelphia: J. B. Lippincott, 1977.

The World of Abbott and Costello. Narr. by Jack E. Leonard, 1965 (documentary).

WILHELM, JAMES HOYT (1923–)

Hoyt Wilhelm gave hope to millions of middle-aged men that just possibly they might be able to trade couch for diamond, or at least enabled them to dream about it with a little thinner coating of fancy. When Wilhelm threw his last knuckleball, he was just days short of his forty-ninth birthday. And he had made more pitching appearances (1,070) than any player in major league history (a record not broken until 1998), despite his not having made the majors until he was nearly 29.

Primarily a relief pitcher, Wilhelm spent his career (1952–1972) winning more games in relief (123) than anyone at a time when the save was neither documented nor defined as it is today. A manager would use his best relief pitcher whenever the game appeared to be most on the line, so a relief pitcher would win more games and pitch more innings than today but record fewer saves. Nonetheless, Wilhelm still had 227 saves. More importantly, he pitched in 50 or more games 14 times and in six seasons recorded an earned-run average below 2.00. With the White Sox while in his forties, he was below 2.00 five seasons in a row. Wilhelm briefly worked as a starter with the Orioles in midcareer, pitching a no-hitter against the Yankees and recording his second ERA title (having led his league as a reliever during his rookie season with the Giants).

Wilhelm's ascent to the major leagues was delayed by his World War II action, during which he was wounded and earned a Purple Heart at the Battle of the Bulge. He went on to become the first relief pitcher and the first knuckleballer in the Hall of Fame.

See also: War.
Additional Reading:
Lindberg, Richard. *Sox: The Complete Record of Chicago White Sox Baseball.* New York: Macmillan, 1984.

WILLIAMS, THEODORE SAMUEL (THE KID, TEDDY BALL GAME, THE SPLENDID SPLINTER) (1918–)

Ted Williams is a name virtually every American knows. Williams, considered by many to be the greatest hitter ever, truly became a legend in his own time. The last player to surpass .400, Williams was also one of the most controversial players of his era, feuding with fans as well as sportswriters, even drawing the ire of teammates, some of whom, especially in Williams's early years, considered him selfish. Yet by century's end, Williams had become the grand old man of the game, perhaps the most beloved figure associated with baseball.

Williams learned early in his career what became one of his most prized principles of hitting. He was playing with the minor league Minneapolis Millers in 1938, and coach Rogers Hornsby, one of the all-time great hitters, advised Williams always to "get a good ball to hit." Williams became the ultimate scientist of hitting, examining every facet of batting from proper care of bats to methods of strengthening his grip on the bat (constantly squeezing a rubber ball). Williams's goal was to be the best hitter ever, and he may well have achieved that goal.

From 1939 through 1960, Williams played left field and intimidated pitchers for the Boston Red Sox—minus the years he was away for military service. He lost 1943–1945 to World War II when he was a navy pilot. Called back during the Korean War, Williams was away from baseball for most of 1952–1953, during which time he

flew 38 combat missions, once crash-landing with his plane on fire.

The 1941 season was when Williams wrote his name forever into baseball history. With a season-ending doubleheader yet to play, Williams was hitting .3995, a figure that would have been rounded up to .400. Given the chance to sit out the closing games and preserve his .400 average, Williams refused. He played not only the first game, elevating his average well above .400 with a four-for-five performance, but also insisted on playing the final game. He added two more hits to finish the season at .406. In some 60 years since, no other player has batted .400.

Williams twice won the Triple Crown, leading his league in home runs, runs batted in, and batting average. He accomplished that feat in 1942 (36, 137, .356) and 1947 (32, 114, .343). Six times he led the American League in batting, four times in home runs and runs batted in, eight times in walks and slugging average, and 12 times in on-base percentage. At the age of 39, he almost hit .400 again, finishing at .388. The following year, at 40, he won yet another batting crown. He also earned the Most Valuable Player Award in 1946 and 1949. *The Sporting News* named Williams the Player of the Decade for the 1950s.

Williams's career totals are staggering, considering the years he missed during his prime. He hit .344 lifetime, falling below .300 only once, in 1959. His totals include 2,654 hits, 521 home runs, 1,839 RBIs, and 2,019 walks. His lifetime on-base percentage was .483, and his slugging average was .634. In addition to almost five years away for military service, Williams did not get more than 420 official at-bats in any season after 1951, partly due to the number of walks he received because of his remarkable batting eye (as

Ted Williams (left) of the Boston Red Sox and Mickey Mantle of the New York Yankees, in uniform with baseball hats, 1950s (Archive Photos)

well as pitchers' fear and good sense), but partly due to injuries and advancing age. Had Williams not missed those five seasons, he probably would have reached at least 3,500 hits and approached 700 home runs. If the designated hitter had been in

effect during Williams's final years, when he would have been able to play virtually every game, his statistics would have been even greater.

Despite such on-field achievements, Williams labored for most of his career under a deep shadow of criticism. He disliked most sportswriters; resented fans who, in his opinion, did not sufficiently understand the game; and engaged in enough unpleasant incidents, such as spitting toward fans or the press box, to draw considerable negative press. Even at the end of his career, he refused to doff his cap for the fans, not even when he concluded his career with a home run in his final at-bat. A proud man, Williams chose not to change his behavior, explaining that special gestures would not be who he was. That same pride had kept Williams from altering his swing when the Cleveland Indians employed the so-called Williams shift in 1946, moving most of their fielders to the right side of second base. Ty Cobb had offered to show Williams how to slap singles into left field, but that was not Williams's way, not even when the St. Louis Cardinals used the Williams shift in defeating the Red Sox in the World Series later that year.

Williams returned to the majors in 1969 to manage the Washington Senators for four years. Although he was named Manager of the Year in his first season, during which he brought the Senators back to respectability, his later years were less successful, as he finished with a career managerial record of 273 wins and 364 losses. After 1964, he returned to Florida to spend as much time fishing as possible.

Gradually, however, Williams mellowed, and Boston fans came increasingly to focus on his extraordinary hitting feats and recognize Williams as a genuine American original—a man who chose always to pursue excellence, and to pursue it his way. In fact, there had always been other sides to Williams, including efforts to help children with cancer, such as his support for the Jimmy Fund (which provides money for childhood-cancer research) and Boston's Dana-Farber Cancer Institute.

The new level of love and admiration for Ted Williams—baseball great, humanitarian, war hero—was evident to the nation at the 1999 All-Star Game. Williams, 81 years old, physically frail, his legendary eyesight severely diminished, was driven onto the field at Fenway Park as baseball greats past and present lined his approach. He even doffed his cap, repeatedly waving it toward the Fenway faithful in a move that may have been a gesture of reconciliation. Whatever it was, the fans loved it. Introduced as the "greatest hitter who ever lived," Williams was steadied by Tony Gwynn as he threw the ceremonial first pitch to another former Red Sox star, Carlton Fisk. Then the 1999 All-Stars huddled around Williams, many of them in tears, as they shared an unforgettable moment with a person who, even in his advancing years and sitting in a cart, stood tall as only legends do.

See also: All-Star Games; Hornsby, Rogers; Jackson, Joseph Jefferson; War.
Additional Reading:
Linn, Edward. *Hitter: The Life and Turmoils of Ted Williams.* New York: Harcourt, 1993.
Pope, Edwin. *Ted Williams.* Englewood Cliffs, NJ: Prentice-Hall, 1970.
Sampson, Arthur. *Ted Williams: A Biography of the Kid.* New York: Barnes, 1950.
Williams, Ted. *My Turn at Bat: The Story of My Life.* New York: Simon and Schuster, 1969.
———. *The Science of Hitting.* New York: Simon and Schuster, 1971.

WILSON, AUGUST (1945–)

August Wilson's *Fences* may be the finest play ever written about baseball. Good plays, however, like effective novels, seldom are about only one thing.

Wilson, recipient of a National Humanities Medal from the National Endowment for the Humanities in 1999, attempts in his plays to chronicle the history of black Americans within the social and political movements of the twentieth century. Such plays as *Ma Rainey's Black Bottom* (first produced in 1984 and published in 1985), *Fences* (1985, 1986), and *The Piano Lesson* (1987, 1990), firmly established Wilson's popularity and importance as a chronicler of the black experience in the United States.

Baseball, especially within the immensely popular Negro Leagues, has been one of many important manifestations of black culture throughout the nineteenth and twentieth centuries. The Pulitzer Prize–winning *Fences,* set in 1957, a decade after Jackie Robinson integrated the major leagues, features Troy Maxson, 53 years old and still proud of his achievement as a player in the Negro Leagues but resentful of the ban that kept him out of the majors and unable to acknowledge changing times in the world of sports. Convinced that professional sports remains a white man's enterprise, Troy refuses to permit son Cory to accept a scholarship to play college football.

Fences is a perceptive reaction to the complex aspects of integration in big-time sports. Often in subtle ways, the play presents a changing world still rooted in a racist past, an ironic inversion of the common father-son theme of bonding through sports, baseball metaphors that convey the character's views of death and of his own unfulfilled life, and the opportunities for African Americans in baseball that also robbed the black community of an important part of its culture—the Negro Leagues.

See also: African Americans; Negro Leagues; Theater.

Additional Reading:

Moyers, Bill. "August Wilson's America: A Conversation with Bill Moyers." *American Theatre* (June 1989): 13–17, 54.
Nadel, Alan. "Boundaries, Logistics, and Identity: The Property of Metaphor in *Fences* and *Joe Turner's Come and Gone.*" In *May All Your Fences Have Gates: Essays on the Drama of August Wilson*. Ed. Alan Nadel. Iowa City: University of Iowa Press, 1994, pp. 86–104.
Pereira, Kim. *August Wilson and the African-American Odyssey*. Urbana: University of Illinois Press, 1995.
Wilson, August. *Fences*. New York: NAL, 1986.

WILSON, LEWIS ROBERT (HACK) (1900–1948)

Hack Wilson achieved a combination of fame and notoriety that comes to those who join talent with personal excess, accomplishment with irresponsible behavior. Such individuals tend to see success diminish too quickly, as did Wilson, who still holds the major league record for runs batted in during a season—191 (until 1999 incorrectly recorded as 190).

Wilson was said to be a "low-ball hitter and highball drinker." Perhaps his tendency to drink heavily may have resulted from lack of self-confidence. He came from a modest background and had little education, leaving school in the sixth grade to go to work. Neither did he possess the type of physical characteristics usually associated with athletes. Only five-foot six, Wilson had broad shoulders and a heavy chest with short, thick arms and legs. The physique better fit the ironworker and shipyard laborer that he once was than the ballplayer he became.

Wilson achieved fame with the Chicago Cubs in the 1920s, and his brief ascendancy and tragic decline mirrored that decade of excess. For five straight years (1926–1930), he drove in over 100 runs, with consecutive seasons of 159 and 190. After Joe McCarthy resigned as Cubs manager to lead the Yankees, Wilson faded quickly. The new manager, Rogers Hornsby, had limited talent and interest in interpersonal relations, and he expected his players to accept personal responsibility. Subject to Hornsby's criticism, Wilson retreated into whiskey. By 1934, his career

The Barnard College team on the college campus, New York (Hulton Getty)

was over. After a series of often menial jobs, he died broke in 1948. Money to pay for his funeral in Martinsburg, West Virginia, was raised by passing the hat in a saloon. Approximately 30 years later, the Veterans Committee voted Wilson into the Hall of Fame.

See also: Hornsby, Rogers; Substance Abuse.
Additional Reading:
Enright, Jim. *Chicago Cubs*. New York: Macmillan, 1975.
Wilbert, Warren, and William Hageman. *Chicago Cubs: Seasons at the Summit*. Champaign, IL: Sagamore, 1997.

WOMEN IN BASEBALL

Baseball has had a symbiotic relationship with popular culture since the first games during the Revolutionary period and, to a much greater extent, since the rise of organized teams in the 1840s. That relationship has been much like marriage—for better or worse. Much of the time, baseball

has reflected admirable values, as demonstrated throughout this book, including the link between baseball and democracy. The game, however, has also reflected and reinforced failures in American society, such as the exclusion of African Americans from full realization of the great promises of our democratic society—life, liberty, and the pursuit of happiness.

The relationship between women and baseball also has been characterized by limited opportunity. Even today, a glass ceiling remains in place, preventing women from fully participating in major league baseball. Now, with racial and national barriers removed, women remain the only group denied entrance to the major league field of dreams. Nonetheless, despite great obstacles, women have played important roles in baseball through the years.

Women initially were confined to the role of spectator at baseball games. In that role, they were often highly valued, both for the revenue they brought through the price of admission and in the "civilizing" atmosphere that they were believed to extend over a game that could become both rowdy and profane. It was not long before baseball clubs sought to systematize that beneficial contribution by instituting Ladies Day. The New York Knickerbockers, first of the organized ball clubs and much committed in their own rules to proper language and behavior, were apparently the first team to offer women this special day, in 1867. Players were especially encouraged to invite wives or girlfriends to the game. The first professional teams to host Ladies Day were the Athletics and Orioles in 1883. The National League ended such promotions in 1909 but reinstated the practice in 1917. The New York Giants even held a Women Suffrage Day at the Polo Grounds in 1915, financially benefiting suffragists, who resold their tickets, and the Giants, who made an extra $2,500, which they split with the visiting Cubs.

At the same time that women were being welcomed as spectators (or, as one might say today, when baseball was first being marketed to women), some had played baseball informally as children and longed to become participants. Vassar College in 1866 added baseball contests at the urging of a female doctor who considered baseball a healthy exercise. The Laurel Baseball Club and the Abenakis Baseball Club were created to play what essentially were intramural contests. About 10 years later, the Vassar Resolutes, attired in ankle-length dresses and wide-striped caps, were competing against teams from Smith, Mount Holyoke, Wellesley, and Barnard.

Mothers, however, who feared for their daughters' limbs and femininity, opposed baseball competition, and in the face of this opposition Vassar eventually capitulated, disbanding the teams. A similar fate befell women's teams at other colleges. When five women students joined in a men's game at the University of Pennsylvania in 1904, the resulting outcry was so loud from university officials that the school quickly banned baseball-playing for women at the institution. As late as the 1920s, about two dozen women's teams played in intramural competition on college campuses. The National Amateur Athletic Federation proposed in 1923, however, that women's sports should be less competitive. In the aftermath of that declaration, women's baseball teams began to die out, never to recover.

Higher education had in effect ruled that women were not to be competitive, presumably because that would require a level playing field—that is, equality of opportunity. This vision, reflective of a more general view on the part of American society of the supportive, but never competitive, woman, had serious consequences throughout society. It would be several decades before women would achieve general acceptance into, for example, the competitive worlds of elective politics and business—and as the old century yielded to a new one, that acceptance remained far from complete.

As college baseball receded from women, they were turning to other avenues to express their love for the game. Women's teams barnstormed the country, sometimes even abroad. The Springfield Blondes and Brunettes competed in the 1880s, although their games were viewed more as sideshows than serious baseball games. In the same decade, the Red Stockings and Blue Stockings offered the public similar entertainment.

By the 1900s, "Bloomer Girls" teams were barnstorming the nation, even traveling to Japan and Cuba. Some of the teams were very good and competed against men's amateur and semipro teams, even some minor league clubs. The Boston Bloomer Girls in 1903 played 28 games in 26 days and won them all. Bloomer teams often would include one or more male players, including, as teenagers, future Hall of Fame players Rogers Hornsby and Smokey Joe Wood. Such male participants were called "toppers" because they wore wigs (and sometimes skirts). One of the most famous and successful of the Bloomer Girls was Maud Nelson, who, beginning in 1897, starred as a player for several clubs, including the male Cherokee Indian Base Ball Club in Michigan. She also was scout, manager, and owner (with her husband) with the Western Bloomer Girls from 1911 to 1917. Nelson then played and managed for various teams until retiring from baseball in the 1930s. She and her second husband spent their final years living almost within the shadow of Wrigley Field, where, nine months after her death in 1944, tryouts were held for the new All-American Girls Professional Baseball League.

In the meantime, women were scoring a number of firsts. Helen Dauvray, a famous stage actress in New York, established the Dauvray Cup (awarded between 1887 and 1892), given to the winner of a postseason series between the National League and American Association pennant winners. Her interest in baseball coincided with her marriage to shortstop John Montgomery Ward, now in the Hall of Fame. The Dauvray Cup was an important step on the way toward the modern World Series, which began in 1903. Lizzie Arlington became the first woman to play in a minor league game when she pitched several innings for Reading in a Class-A Atlantic League game in 1898. Amanda Clement became the first woman umpire in 1905, umpiring semipro games until

1911. Highly respected for her umpiring skill, she earned $20 per game, enough to help her get through Yankton College in South Dakota.

Helene Robison Britton inherited the St. Louis Cardinals in 1911, becoming the first woman to own a major league team. She would be the first of several women owners, including Joan Whitney Payson, who became majority owner of the New York Mets in 1961; and Marge Schott, the controversial owner of the Cincinnati Reds from 1985 to 1999.

The first woman to play in a major league exhibition game was Lizzie Murphy, a first baseman, who performed for a team of American League and New England All-Stars against the Boston Red Sox. Known as the "queen of baseball," Murphy made her living from the game until retiring in 1935 at the age of 41. She was one of several women who distinguished themselves playing for men's teams early in the century. Virnie Beatrice "Jackie" Mitchell, at 17, signed a minor league contract with the Double-A Chattanooga Lookouts in 1931. In an exhibition that year against the mighty New York Yankees, the left-hander struck out Babe Ruth and Lou Gehrig before walking Tony Lazzeri. Within the week, commissioner Kenesaw Mountain Landis voided Mitchell's contract, explaining that baseball was too strenuous for women. This was the same Landis who also shut the door to African Americans. Three years later, Mildred "Babe" Didrikson, who had won two gold medals at the 1932 Olympics, played in major league exhibitions. After spring training, she barnstormed with the House of David team during the 1934 season. Toni Stone became the first woman to play in the Negro Leagues when she joined the Indianapolis Clowns of the Negro American League in 1953. By that time, the Negro Leagues were in decline, as the most talented young black players gunned for the integrating major leagues, and team officials attempted to boost attendance by employing Stone and a handful of other women players.

College baseball witnessed a small comeback by women starting in 1951. Margaret Dobson played briefly for the men's team at Vanport College in Portland, Oregon. Susan Perabo played in several games for Webster University in 1987, and Julie Croteau became the first woman to make a men's Division III team, playing for St. Mary's College in Maryland in 1988. Croteau, important within baseball in several ways, worked in broadcasting; played for the Colorado Silver Bullets, an all-women's team sponsored by Coors Brewing Company that competed against men's teams for four years starting in 1994; coached, becoming the first female assistant coach with a men's Division I team, at the University of Massachusetts–Amherst in 1995; and joined Major League Baseball in 1997 as associate director of game development. Ila Borders, who previously had pitched for Southern California College (becoming the first woman to record a victory in a men's college baseball game) and Whittier College, signed with the St. Paul Saints of the independent Northern League in 1997. The Saints traded her to the Duluth-Superior Dukes later in the season, and in 1998 she became the first woman to start and win a professional regular-season game.

The most famous women's league was the All-American Girls Professional Baseball League, which operated from 1943 to 1954. The league was created by Cubs owner Philip Wrigley to attract fans during World War II. Originally a cross between softball and baseball, the game evolved into a close approximation of standard baseball. The league proved popular for a number of years and made

some of its players famous, including seven-time All-Star first baseman Dorothy Kamenshek, base-stealing whiz Sophie Kurys (nicknamed "Tina Cobb"), and pitcher Jean Faut. Declining crowds, the lack of a farm system, and competition from television caught up with the league, and it closed down after the 1954 season. The 1992 film *A League of Their Own,* starring Tom Hanks, Madonna, and Geena Davis, renewed interest in the league.

Avenues for young girls to play baseball on organized teams have increased thanks to Title IX, legislation passed in 1972 that mandates equal opportunity for women and girls in athletics. As a result of Title IX, girls can now play Little League. Although girls still make up a small minority of Little League players, significant numbers have participated, and sometimes excelled, given the opportunity. Title IX also generated increased support for high school and college softball for women, as colleges sought—or were forced—to comply by making greater sports opportunities available to women students. In addition, girls have demonstrated their ability in Pitch-Hit-Run competition, with 11-year-old Crystal Fields of Cumberland, Maryland, winning the national championship in 1979.

Despite the many contributions that women have made to baseball and the interest and talent that women brought, and still bring, to the game, Major League Baseball continues to resist full participation by women. When shortstop Eleanor Engle signed a contract with the Harrisburg Senators of the Class-B Interstate League in 1951, commissioner Ford Frick banned women from playing in the minors and the majors. Neither has a woman umpire been promoted to the major leagues. Among those who have officiated at the minor league level, Pam Postema served the longest apprenticeship—13 years. She was let go by the

Triple-A Alliance in 1989, ostensibly because the major leagues were not interested in her. Postema, who had umpired major league exhibition games and the 1987 Hall of Fame game in Cooperstown, sued Major League Baseball, charging sex discrimination, and settled out of court.

The relationship between baseball and women remains, in some ways, a strange one. Women are able to participate at the highest level—ownership of a major league club—but barriers circle the playing field, which remains exclusively a male domain. This phenomenon runs counter to many other areas of life, including the political and business worlds, where women may do the work (paralleling the baseball game) but often have considerable trouble reaching the highest decisionmaking positions. The most important aspect of baseball, for better or worse, is the game itself—not the ownership of it or any other dimensions of the contest—but the actual playing of it. At one level, there is a purity in the maintenance of that traditional focus. Yet because baseball began as a man's game, that same perspective has kept women down—more than mere spectators but less than full participants. Baseball, for all its glory, retains the virtues as well as the sins of its fathers.

> See also: All-American Girls Professional Baseball League; Colorado Silver Bullets; Little League; Manley, Effa; Minor Leagues; Pony Baseball and Softball; Softball.
>
> Additional Reading:
>
> Berlage, Gail Ingham. *Women in Baseball: The Forgotten History*. Westport, CT: Praeger, 1994.
>
> Browne, Lois. *Girls of Summer: In Their Own League*. Toronto: HarperCollins, 1992.
>
> Johnson, Susan E. *When Women Played Hardball*. Seattle: Seal, 1994.
>
> Nutt, Amy Ellis. "Baseball and Softball." In *Nike Is a Goddess: The History of Women in Sports*. Ed. Lissa Smith. New York: Atlantic Monthly, 1998, pp. 33–54.

WORLD SERIES

The World Series pits the American League and National League champions in a best-of-seven competition. Yet the "World" Series is actually an American tournament (with two Canadian teams eligible), excluding many nations where baseball is played.

Postseason play started in the 1870s between National Association teams, but the first real postseason championship playoff began in 1884 when the Providence Grays of the National League defeated the New York Metropolitans of the American Association. Old Hoss Radbourn led the Grays to victory with three consecutive wins. The champions of the two leagues continued to meet through 1890, but the encounters ended with the death of the American Association in 1891. The first- and second-half champions of the National League met in 1892, and the first- and second-place finishers in the regular season (no longer broken into two halves) met at the conclusion of the 1894–1897 campaigns. That format understandably did not ignite great fan interest, although it was brought back for 1900.

The modern World Series began in 1903, after the National League and the new American League had entered into the so-called National Agreement, ending raids on National League players and establishing the National Commission to govern the leagues. The league champions first met in 1903, and much to the embarrassment of the older league, the Boston Pilgrims, led by pitching ace Cy Young, triumphed over the Pittsburgh Pirates. John McGraw's Giants won the National League pennant the following year, but McGraw, still angry with Ban Johnson, president of the American League, from his brief tenure as a manager in the new league, refused to participate in a postseason series. The World Series resumed in 1905 and has continued down

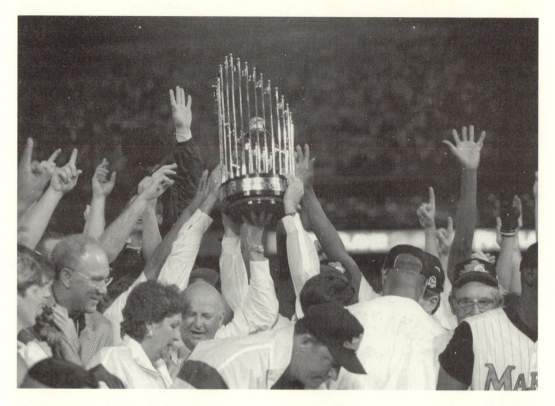

Florida Marlins players hold the trophy after the seventh game of the World Series against the Cleveland Indians at Pro Player Stadium in Miami, Florida, October 26, 1997. The Marlins won the game 3-2 and took the series. (Jed Jacobsohn/Allsport)

to the present day with the exception of 1994, when a strike by players ended the season and wiped out the World Series.

The early Series, from 1905 to 1919 (the year of the Black Sox scandal), saw a handful of teams dominate, including clubs that have had little championship success in recent decades. The Chicago Cubs played in five World Series, winning twice; the Chicago White Sox won two Series before losing in 1919; the Boston Red Sox won four times in as many appearances; the Athletics took three of five Series; while the Giants, under McGraw, and the Tigers, with Ty Cobb, had little luck in the postseason, the Giants losing four of five, the Tigers losing all three times that they participated.

Babe Ruth first achieved fame as a pitcher with the Boston Red Sox, starring in the 1916 and 1918 Series. In the 1916

Series, Ruth hurled a 14-inning victory for the triumphant Red Sox, while two years later he extended his string of consecutive scoreless innings pitched to $29\frac{2}{3}$, a World Series record. In the following decade, he would turn to hitting home runs for the Yankees, finishing his career with a record 15 in Series play, including the famous "called shot" against the Cubs in 1932. Another great Yankee slugger, Mickey Mantle, would break Ruth's Series home-run record in 1964, hitting the final three of his 18.

Ruth, Mantle, Gehrig, DiMaggio, and many other Yankee greats would make the New York club the all-time World Series champion. Series triumphs in 1998 and 1999 gave the Yankees 25 world championships. Other teams, however, contested Yankee dominance from time to time. Connie Mack's Athletics had two impressive runs, winning three Series out of five in the early years, later making three more appearances (1929–1931), winning twice. The Dodgers made plenty of Series appearances during their final years in Brooklyn, the Boys of Summer (Snider, Robinson, Reese, Hodges, Newcombe, Campanella, et al.) going to the postseason in 1947, 1949, 1952, 1953, 1955, and 1956, winning only in 1955. The hero of that Series was a young left-hander named Johnny Podres, who won two games while allowing only two runs in 18 innings. The Oakland Athletics had a great run in the 1970s, winning the World Series in 1972, 1973, and 1974; the Cincinnati Big Red Machine rolled over its opponents in 1975 and 1976; and the Toronto Blue Jays won in 1992 and 1993

One of the most exciting Series was in 1954. The Cleveland Indians (featuring a remarkable pitching staff headed by Early Wynn, Bob Lemon, Mike Garcia, and an aging but still effective Bob Feller) set an American League record by winning 111 games but were swept in four straight by the New York Giants, featuring the young Willie Mays. Again, though, the hero was an unlikely player: pinch-hitter Dusty Rhodes, who contributed four hits in six at-bats with two home runs and seven RBIs. Mays supplied the fielding gem of the Series—indeed one of the finest catches ever in Series play—by hauling down a long drive by Vic Wertz in Game 1.

World Series highlights are numerous and certainly include Don Larsen's perfect game for the Yankees in 1956, the only no-hitter in Series history. They also include Enos Slaughter scoring from first base for the Cardinals on a double by Harry Walker in the bottom of the eighth in Game 7 to give the Cardinals the championship over the Red Sox in 1946; Ruth's called home run in 1932; the twelfth-inning home run by the Red Sox

catcher Carlton Fisk in Game 6 of the 1975 Series; and the tenth-inning ground ball through Red Sox first baseman Bill Buckner's legs that gave Game 6 to the New York Mets in 1986.

As the twenty-first century dawns, the team of the twentieth century—the New York Yankees—continues to challenge annually for the world championship. With the spread of baseball to other nations, and the growing numbers of foreign-born players in the majors (including increasing numbers from Asia), the day may not be far off when it will truly be a "World" Series. The U.S. team, if it indeed prevailed in an international Series, would then have the right to consider itself truly first in the world.

See also: Black Sox Scandal; Brooklyn Dodgers; Expansion; Jackson, Joseph Jefferson; Jackson, Reginald Martinez; Landis, Kenesaw Mountain; Larsen, Donald James; Major Leagues; Mays, Willie Howard; McGraw, John Joseph; New York Yankees; Radbourn, Charles Gardner; Ruth, George Herman; Young, Denton True.

Additional Reading:

Allen, Lee. *The World Series: The Story of Baseball's Annual Championship.* New York: Putnam's, 1969.

Dickey, Glenn. *The History of the World Series Since 1903.* New York: Stein and Day, 1984.

Ivor-Campbell, Frederick, and David Pietrusza. "Postseason Play." In *Total Baseball.* 6th ed. Ed. John Thorn et al. New York: Total Sports, 1999, pp. 306–492.

McKelvey, G. Richard. *Fisk's Homer, Willie's Catch, and the Shot Heard 'Round the World: Classic Moments from Postseason Baseball, 1940–1996.* Jefferson, NC: McFarland, 1998.

Smith, Robert. *World Series: The Games and the Players.* Garden City, NY: Doubleday, 1967.

WRIGLEY FIELD

Wrigley Field, on Chicago's North Side, is the home of the lovable Cubs and continues to express the best aspects of America's national pastime: Tradition, working-class culture, the democratic impulse that lay at the heart of America's love for baseball, natural grass and sunshine, and ivy crawling up outfield walls—these make Wrigley Field a representation of what the sport once was and what it remains today for traditionalists.

Once Fenway Park is replaced in Boston, Wrigley Field will be the oldest major league ballpark in operation. It was built in 1914 as Weeghman Park on former seminary grounds. At that time, the Chicago club was a member of the Federal League. After the league's demise following the 1915 season, Charles Weeghman, a prosperous owner of restaurants, bought the Cubs and moved them into the park. William Wrigley Jr., he of the chewing-gum business, purchased the Cubs in 1920, and the ballpark was renamed Wrigley Field in 1926.

Every ballpark has seen its moments of glory. Perhaps the most famous moment in Wrigley Field occurred during the 1932 World Series, when Babe Ruth supposedly called a home run and then delivered into the center field bleachers. What makes Wrigley Field distinctive, though, are its ties to baseball's past—it is the only Federal League ballpark still in use—and its physical characteristics.

Wrigley Field is famous, among other things, for its outfield wall, which is covered thickly with ivy vines that Bill Veeck planted in 1937. In that same year a new scoreboard was added, which remains intact, although a clock was added four years later. One of baseball's most famous unreachable home-run targets is the scoreboard, which no batted ball has ever struck. In 1941, along with the clock, Wrigley Field received the first organ to appear in a ballpark. That same organ has continued to make music ever since.

The most famous example of Wrigley's commitment to tradition is in the long refusal by team owners to add lights for night baseball. Philip K. Wrigley did acquire lights, but as the United States entered World War II, he donated them to the war effort. Not until 1988 did Wrigley Field offer night games, 40 years after the next-longest holdout—Briggs Stadium in Detroit—added lights.

Wrigley Field also is famous for its characters. Announcer Harry Caray, who died in 1998, exemplified Cubs fans, especially the Bleacher Bums in the outfield stands; he called 'em as he saw 'em and led the singing of "Take Me Out to the Ball Game" during the seventh-inning stretch. Then there was Pat Pieper, who worked for the Cubs from 1904 until 1974. He spent 59 of his 71 seasons with the club as public-address announcer.

Wrigley Field is often buffeted by swirling onshore winds from Lake Michigan, but one seldom hears complaints. Wind, after all, is natural. It is part of the environment of the game in what was wisely coined by Phil Wrigley as the "friendly confines" of "beautiful Wrigley Field." Sometimes the park was known as "Bobby Dorr's House," after the groundskeeper, who lived in a six-room apartment near the left-field gate in the 1920s and 1930s. That small-town, stop-in-to-visit sense conveyed by the Dorr nickname—although few people today would know who he was—remains part of Wrigley Field. Consequently, an important part of American culture remains alive and well in Chicago's North Side ballpark.

See also: Ballparks; Caray, Harry; Ruth, George Herman; "Take Me Out to the Ball Game"; Veeck, William L., Jr.

Additional Reading:

Gershman, Michael. *Diamonds: The Evolution of the Ballpark*. Boston: Houghton Mifflin, 1993.

Golenbock, Peter. *Wrigleyville*. New York: St. Martin's, 1996.

Hartel, William. *A Day at the Park: In Celebration of Wrigley Field*. Rev. ed. Rock Island, IL: Quality Sports, 1994.

Wheeler, Lonnie. *Bleachers: A Summer in Wrigley Field*. Chicago: Contemporary Books, 1988.

YANKEE STADIUM

Yankee Stadium, home of the New York Yankees, is the only stadium built by a player: It is "The House that Ruth Built." Babe Ruth, of course, used his bat and glove—not hammer and saw—to build the historic structure. His popularity drew the fans that provided the financial means whereby a permanent home went up to house the first great home-run hitter in the history of baseball, a stadium that would feature 25 World Series champions by the end of the twentieth century and become the most famous ballpark ever.

The Yankees, fans might be surprised to know, were not an original American League ballclub. They started as the Baltimore Orioles in 1901, and when the team was moved to New York for the 1903 season, they were known as the New York Highlanders. That name became associated with the team's original home, Hilltop Park, located at the highest elevation on Manhattan Island. Known as the Yankees in 1913, the team moved into the Polo Grounds, renting space from the National League Giants through 1922.

The franchise enjoyed little success until Babe Ruth was acquired from the Boston Red Sox prior to the 1920 season. Ruth had set the home-run record in 1919 with 29; in his first season with New York, he almost doubled that total, smashing 54 round-trippers. The fans loved him, even if managers did not always share that feeling, and they turned out in droves to see the next mighty blast fly off his bat. Season attendance soared from 619,164 in 1919 to 1,289,422 in 1920.

Yankee Stadium was built on a 10-acre lot in the Bronx carved out of the William Waldorf Astor estate across the Harlem River from the Polo Grounds. The stadium originally had massive dimensions to center and left-center, measuring 487 feet to dead center and 500 feet at its deepest point in left-center. Right field was much more agreeable, especially to the left-handed Ruth—only about 295 feet at its shortest. Center field became known as "Death Valley" because of the certain fate that met fly balls hit there.

The ballpark sat as many as 70,000 in its early history and struck visitors as enormous. The size and expanse created a sense of quiet dignity that added to the Yankee aura—not that quiet dignity ever described the Babe. In later years, a monument area was established in left-center field, now behind the wall, honoring Yankee greats (Ruth, Lou Gehrig, manager Miller Huggins, Mickey Mantle). Plaques honor additional stars and a few others, including Pope Paul VI and Pope John Paul II.

Renovations have shortened distances to the left-field and center-field walls, reduced seating capacity to below 58,000, taken the monuments out of fair territory, and made seating more comfortable. Yankee Stadium remains, however, the House that Ruth Built many decades after his final home run, and this sense of history continues to permeate the ballpark. That history, and a feeling of belonging to it, helped forge the team spirit of the Yankees during the final years of the twentieth century, as they won three of four world championships before turning their gaze to a new century of greatness.

See also: Ballparks; New York Yankees; Polo Grounds; Ruth, George Herman.

Additional Reading:

Gershman, Michael. *Diamonds: The Evolution of the Ballpark*. Boston: Houghton Mifflin, 1993.

Mark, Stephen. *Double Play: The Economics and Financing of Stadiums for the Yankees and Mets*. New York: Independent Budget Office, 1998.

Robinson, Ray. *Yankee Stadium: 75 Years of Drama, Glamour, and Glory*. New York: Penguin Studio, 1998.

YOUNG, DENTON TRUE (CY) (1867–1955)

Cy Young's name is synonymous with pitching excellence. The man who won more games than any other hurler in major league history—an astonishing total of 511—lends his name to the annual award given to the best pitcher in each major league. Although he was born just two years after the conclusion of the Civil War, he lived long enough to be remembered by many current fans, thus retaining a more human stature than figures like Old Hoss Radbourn.

Cy Young came off an Ohio farm, and his nickname has been interpreted as short for "cyclone," in honor of his fastball, and as a commentary on his naive behavior when he first arrived in the majors ("cy" being a common derogatory term equating to "hayseed"). In either case, he used an array of pitches—including an overhand curve, a sidearm curve, and a "tobacco" ball—to augment his fastball and great control. He pitched from 1890 until 1911 with Cleveland and St. Louis in the National League, Boston and Cleveland in the American League, and, for part of his final season, Boston of the National League. When he finished, he tallied 511 wins against 316 defeats, 906 games pitched, 815 starts, 749 complete games, 7,356 innings pitched, 76 shutouts, a 2.63 ERA, and three no-hitters (including a perfect game).

Cy Young won 20 or more games 15 times, and in five of those seasons he rang up at least 30 victories. He pitched over 300 innings 16 times, five times going over 400 innings. Among his most important highlights were two World Series games for the triumphant Boston Pilgrims (now the Red Sox) against the Pirates in the 1903 World Series. The modern award for pitching excellence is a fitting tribute to his great accomplishments.

See also: Heroes; Records Set; Rural America; Strikeouts; World Series.

Additional Reading:

Browning, Reed. *Cy Young: A Baseball Life*. Amherst: University of Massachusetts Press, 2000.

Macht, Norman L. *Cy Young*. New York: Chelsea House, 1992.

Bibliography

Aaron, Hank. *Aaron*. Rev. ed. New York: Crowell, 1974.

———. *I Had a Hammer: The Hank Aaron Story*. New York: HarperCollins, 1991.

Abbott, Bud, and Lou Costello. "Who's on First?" *Play Ball!* Compact Disc. Telarc, 1998.

Abrams, Roger I. *Legal Bases: Baseball and the Law*. Philadelphia: Temple University Press, 1998.

Abramson, Edward A. *Bernard Malamud Revisited*. New York: Twayne, 1993.

Achieving Physical and Communication Accessibility. Washington, DC: National Center for Access Unlimited, 1991.

Adair, Daryl. *Sport in Australian History*. New York: Oxford University Press, 1997.

Ahrens, Art. *The Cubs: The Complete Record of Chicago Cubs Baseball*. New York: Collier, 1986.

Aldridge, Gwen. *Baseball Archaeology: Artifacts from the Great American Pastime*. San Francisco: Chronicle Books, 1993.

Alexander, Charles C. *John McGraw*. New York: Viking, 1988.

———. *Our Game: An American Baseball History*. New York: MJF Books, 1991.

———. *Rogers Hornsby: A Biography*. New York: Holt, 1995.

———. *Ty Cobb*. New York: Oxford University Press, 1984.

Allen, Lee. *The American League Story*. Rev. ed. New York: Hill and Wang, 1965.

———. *The World Series: The Story of Baseball's Annual Championship*. New York: Putnam's, 1969.

Allen, Maury. *Mr. October: The Reggie Jackson Story*. New York: Times Books, 1981.

———. *Now Wait a Minute, Casey!* Garden City, NY: Doubleday, 1965.

———. *Roger Maris: A Man for All Seasons*. New York: D. I. Fine, 1986.

———. *Where Have You Gone, Joe DiMaggio?* New York: Dutton, 1975.

———. *You Could Look It Up: The Life of Casey Stengel*. New York: Times Books, 1979.

Allen, Mel. *It Takes Heart*. New York: Harper, 1959.

———. *You Can't Beat the Hours: A Long, Loving Look at Big-League Baseball, Including Some Yankees I Have Known*. New York: Harper and Row, 1964.

Altherr, Thomas L. "W. P. Kinsella's Baseball Fiction, *Field of Dreams,* and the New Mythopoeism of Baseball." In *Cooperstown Symposium on Baseball and the American Culture*. Ed. Alvin L. Hall. Westport, CT: Meckler, 1990, pp. 97–108.

Altman, Roberta. *The Cancer Dictionary*. New York: Facts on File, 1992.

Amateur Softball Association of America. *The Official Rules of Softball: USA Softball*. Chicago: Triumph Books, 1994.

American Legion Website (American Legion Baseball features). http://www.legion.org

Amyotrophic Lateral Sclerosis: Lou Gehrig's Disease: Research Strikes Back. Rev. ed. Bethesda, MD: Department of Health, Education, and Welfare, Public Health Service, National Institutes of Health, 1977.

Anderson, Dave. "Bouton's Day Was Long Time in Coming" (syndicated column from *New York Times*). *Portland (Maine) Press Herald*, July 27, 1998, p. D-1.

———. *The Yankees: The Four Fabulous Eras of Baseball's Most Famous Team*. New York: Random House, 1979.

Anderson, David W. *More than Merkle: A History of the Best and Most Exciting Baseball Season in Human History*. Lincoln: University of Nebraska Press, 2000.

Anderson, Donald Ray. *Branch Rickey and the St. Louis Cardinal Farm System: The Growth of an Idea*. Diss. University of Wisconsin–Madison, 1975.

Anderson, William M. *The Detroit Tigers: A Pictorial Celebration of the Greatest Players and Moments in Tigers' History*. South Bend, IN: Diamond, 1991.

Anson, Adrian Constantine. *A Ball Player's Career, Being the Personal Experiences and Reminiscences of Adrian C. Anson*. Chicago: Era, 1900.

Anthony, Ted. "A Gem, Pure and Simple." *Portland (Maine) Press Herald*, September 21, 1998, pp. C1–2.

Appel, Marty. *Slide, Kelly, Slide: The Wild Life and Times of Mike "King" Kelly, Baseball's First Superstar*. Lanham, MD: Scarecrow, 1999.

Aquila, Richard, ed. *Wanted Dead or Alive: The American West in Popular Culture*. Urbana; Chicago: University of Illinois Press, 1996.

Ashe, Arthur R., Jr. *A Hard Road to Glory—Baseball: The African-American Athlete in Baseball*. 1988. Reprint, New York: Amistad, 1993.

Asinof, Eliot. *Eight Men Out: The Black Sox and the 1919 World Series*. New York: Holt, 1963.

Astor, Gerald. *The Baseball Hall of Fame 50th Anniversary Book*. New York: Prentice Hall, 1988.

Autry, Gene. *88 Complete Song Hits*. Chicago: Cole, 1939.

———. *Back in the Saddle Again*. Garden City, NY: Doubleday, 1978.

Axelson, Gustaf W. *"Commy": The Life Story of Charles A. Comiskey*. Chicago: Reilly and Lee, 1919.

Babe Ruth League website: http://www.baberuthleague.org

Baker, Mark Allen. *The Standard Guide to Collecting Autographs: A Reference and Value Guide*. Iola, WI: Krause, 1999.

Banks, Ernie, and Jim Enright. *Mr. Cub*. Chicago: Follett, 1971.

Barber, Red. *The Broadcasters*. New York: Dial, 1970.

———. *Rhubarb in the Catbird Seat*. Garden City, NY: Doubleday, 1968.

Barnouw, Erik. *A History of Broadcasting in the United States*. 3 vols. New York: Oxford University Press, 1966–1970.

Bartlett, Arthur C. *Baseball and Mr. Spalding: The History and Romance of Baseball*. New York: Farrar, Straus, and Young, 1951.

The Baseball Encyclopedia. 10th ed. New York: Macmillan, 1996.

Baseball Hall of Fame website: www.baseballhalloffame.org

Baseball's Greatest Hits. Compact Disc. Rhino, 1989.

Baseball's Greatest Hits: Let's Play II. Compact Disc. Rhino, 1990.

Berkow, Ira. *Red: A Biography of Red Smith*. 1986. Reprint, Boston: Hall, 1988.

Berlage, Gail Ingham. "The Colorado Bullets." *The Baseball Research Journal* 27 (1998): 40–42.

———. *Women in Baseball: The Forgotten History*. Westport, CT: Praeger, 1994.

Bernotas, Bob. *Nothing to Prove: The Jim Abbott Story*. New York: Kodansha International, 1995.

Berra, Yogi. *The Yogi Book: I Really Didn't Say Everything I Said!* New York: Workman, 1998.

———. *Yogi: It Ain't Over*. New York: McGraw-Hill, 1989.

———. *Yogi: The Autobiography of a Professional Baseball Player*. Garden City, NY: Doubleday, 1961.

Bertino, Joseph R. *Encyclopedia of Cancer*. 3 vols. San Diego: Academic Press, 1997.

Bibb, Porter. *It Ain't as Easy as It Looks: Ted Turner's Amazing Story*. New York: Crown, 1993.

Bjarkman, Peter C. "Baseball and Fidel Castro." *The National Pastime: A Review of Baseball History* 18 (1998): 64–68.

———. *Baseball with a Latin Beat: A History of the Latin American Game*. Jefferson, NC: McFarland, 1994.

———. *Encyclopedia of Major League Baseball Team Histories*. Westport, CT: Meckler, 1991.

———. "Lifting the Iron Curtain of Cuban Baseball." *The National Pastime: A Review of Baseball History* 17 (1997): 30–34.

———. "Six-Pointed Diamonds and the Ultimate Shiksa: Baseball and the Jewish-American Immigrant Experience." In *Cooperstown Symposium on Baseball and the American Culture*. Ed. Alvin L. Hall. Westport, CT: Meckler, 1990, pp. 306–347.

Bloodworth, William. "Writers of the Purple Sage: Novelists and the American West." In *Wanted Dead or Alive: The American West in Popular Culture*. Ed. Richard Aquila. Urbana; Chicago: University of Illinois Press, 1996, pp. 43–68.

Bordman, Gerald. *American Musical Theatre*. New York: Oxford University Press, 1978.

———. *The Oxford Companion to American Theatre*. New York: Oxford University Press, 1984.

Bourne, Peter G. *Fidel: A Biography of Fidel Castro*. New York: Dodd, Mead, 1988.

Bouton, Jim. *Ball Four*. 20th anniv. ed. New York: Macmillan, 1990.

———. *I'm Glad You Didn't Take It Personally*. New York: Dell, 1972.

Bouton, Michael. "For Bouton, Let Bygones Be Bygones." *New York Times,* June 21, 1998, sec. 8, p. 13.

Boyd, Brendan C. *The Great American Baseball Card Flipping, Trading, and Bubble Gum Book*. Boston: Little, Brown, 1973.

Brashler, William. *The Bingo Long Traveling All-Stars and Motor Kings*. 1973. Reprint, Urbana: University of Illinois Press, 1993.

———. *Josh Gibson: A Life in the Negro Leagues*. New York: Harper and Row, 1978.

Brickhouse, Jack. *Thanks for Listening*. South Bend, IN: Diamond Communications, 1986.

Brightman, Alan. *Ordinary Moments: The Disabled Experience*. Baltimore: University Park, 1984.

Brock, Darryl. *If I Never Get Back*. New York: Crown, 1990.

Broeg, Bob. *Bob Broeg's Redbirds: A Century of Cardinals' Baseball*. Rev. ed. Marceline, MO: Walsworth, 1992.

Brown, Warren. *The Chicago Cubs*. New York: Putnam's, 1946.

Browne, Lois. *Girls of Summer: In Their Own League*. Toronto: HarperCollins, 1992.

Browne, Ray. *Heroes of Popular Culture*. Bowling Green, OH: Bowling Green University Popular Press, 1972.

Browning, Reed. *Cy Young: A Baseball Life*. Amherst: University of Massachusetts Press, 2000.

Bruns, Roger. *Preacher: Billy Sunday and Big-Time American Evangelism*. New York: Norton, 1992.

Bryant, Keith L. *Railroads in the Age of Regulation, 1900–1980,* New York: Facts on File, 1988.

Buscombe, Edward, ed. *The BFI Companion to the Western*. New York: Da Capo, 1988.

Butler, Hal. *Baseball All Star Game Thrills*. New York: J. Messner, 1968.

Cagan, Joanna, and Neil deMause. *Field of Schemes: How the Great Stadium Swindle Turns Public Money into Private Profit*. Monroe, ME: Common Courage, 1998.

Campanella, Roy. *It's Good to Be Alive*. Boston: Little, Brown, 1959.

Cancer Sourcebook. Detroit: Omnigraphics, 1990.

Candelaria, Cordelia. *Seeking the Perfect Game: Baseball in American Literature*. New York: Greenwood Press, 1989.

Cantor, George. *The Tigers of '68: Baseball's Last Real Champions*. Dallas: Taylor, 1997.

Caray, Harry, with Bob Verdi. *Holy Cow!* New York: Villard Books, 1989.

Carroll, Bob, and Rob Edelman. "Reel Baseball." In *Total Baseball*. 6th ed. Ed. John Thorn et al. New York: Total Sports, 1999, pp. 598–609.

Cashman, Richard I. *Paradise of Sport: The Rise of Organised Sport in Australia*. New York: Oxford University Press, 1995.

Catsis, John R. *Sports Broadcasting*. Chicago: Nelson-Hall, 1996.

Centennial Issue. *The Sporting News*. 1986.

Chadwick, Henry. Scrapbooks. In the Spalding Collection, New York Public Library.

Chafetz, Henry. *Play the Devil: A History of Gambling in the United States from 1492 to 1955*. New York: Bonanza, 1960.

Chandler, Happy, with Vance H. Trimble. *Heroes, Plain Folks, and Skunks: The Life and Times of Happy Chandler*. Chicago: Bonus Books, 1989.

Cheung, Ming. *Nolan Ryan Tribute Page*. http://www.ghgcorp.com/mingster/

Cho, Kwang Min. "Attitudes of Korean National Athletes and Coaches toward Athletics Participation." Ph.D. diss., University of Iowa, 1990.

Christopher, Matt. *At the Plate with Ken Griffey, Jr.* Boston: Little, Brown, 1997.

Chu, Donald, Jeffrey Segrave, and Beverly J. Becker. *Sport and Higher Education*. Champaign, IL: Human Kinetics, 1985.

Clark, Steve. *The Complete Book of Baseball Cards*. New York: Grosset and Dunlap, 1976.

Clark, Tom. *Champagne and Baloney: The Rise and Fall of Finley's A's*. New York: Harper and Row, 1976.

Cobb, Ty, with Al Stump. *My Life in Baseball: The True Record*. Garden City, NY: Doubleday, 1961.

Coleman, Pat. "Dodgers Still the Best of the 30 Official Sites." *USA Today Baseball Weekly*, April 14–20, 1999, p. 47.

Creamer, Robert W. *Babe: The Legend Comes to Life*. New York: Simon and Schuster, 1974.

———. *Stengel: His Life and Times*. New York: Simon and Schuster, 1984.

Crissey, Harrington E., Jr. "Baseball and the Armed Services." In *Total Baseball*. 6th ed. Ed. John Thorn et al. New York: Total Sports, 1999, pp. 2513–2520.

Cromartie, Warren. *Slugging It Out in Japan: An American Major Leaguer in the Tokyo Outfield*. New York: Kodansha International, 1991.

Crothers, Tim. *Greatest Teams: The Most Dominant Powerhouses in Sports*. New York: *Sports Illustrated*, 1998.

Curran, William. *Strikeout: A Celebration of the Art of Pitching*. New York: Crown, 1995.

Daglow, Don L., Jack Kavanagh, and Garth Chouteau. "Fantasy Baseball Games." In *Total Baseball*. 6th ed. Ed. John Thorn et al. New York: Total Sports, 1999, pp. 592–597.

Daley, Arthur. *All the Home Run Kings*. New York: Putnam's, 1972.

Danbom, David B. *Born in the Country: A History of Rural America*. Baltimore: Johns Hopkins University Press, 1995.

Davis, Mac. *100 Greatest Sports Heroes*. New York: Grosset and Dunlap, 1958.

Day, Laraine. *Day with the Giants*. Garden City, NY: Doubleday, 1952.

Debs, Victor, Jr. *Still Standing after All These Years: Twelve of Baseball's Longest Standing Records*. Jefferson, NC: McFarland, 1997.

DeValeria, Dennis, and Jeanne Burke DeValeria. *Honus Wagner: A Biography*. 1996. Reprint, Pittsburgh: University of Pittsburgh Press, 1998.

Devaney, John. *Juan Marichal: Mister Strike*. New York: Putnam's, 1970.

Di Salvatore, Bryan. *A Clever Base-Ballist: The Life and Times of John Montgomery Ward*. New York: Pantheon, 1999.

Dickey, Glenn. *The History of American League Baseball since 1901*. New York: Stein and Day, 1980.

———. *The History of the World Series since 1903*. New York: Stein and Day, 1984.

Dickson, Paul. *The Worth Book of Softball: A Celebration of America's True National Pastime*. New York: Facts on File, 1994.

DiMaggio, Joe. *Lucky to Be a Yankee*. New York: R. Field (publ.), Greenberg (dist.), 1946.

Dittmar, Joseph J. *Baseball Records Registry*. Jefferson, NC: McFarland, 1997.

Dorsett, Lyle W. *Billy Sunday and the Redemption of Urban America*. Grand Rapids, MI: W. B. Eerdmans, 1991.

Doty, William G. *Mythography: The Study of Myths and Rituals*. 2d ed. Tuscaloosa: University of Alabama Press, 2000.

Douglas, George H. *All Aboard: The Railroad in American Life*. New York: Paragon House, 1992.

———. *The Early Days of Radio Broadcasting*. Jefferson, NC: McFarland, 1987.

Douglas, Gilbert. *American Vaudeville: Its Life and Times*. 1940. Reprint, New York: Dover, 1963.

Driver, Tom Faw. *The Magic of Ritual: Our Need for Liberating Rites That Transform Our Lives and Our Communities*. San Francisco: HarperSanFrancisco, 1991.

Duncan, Patricia J. *Sosa! Baseball's Home Run Hero*. New York: Simon and Schuster, 1998.

Durant, John. *The Sports of Our Presidents*. New York: Hastings, 1964.

Durocher, Leo, with Ed Linn. *Nice Guys Finish Last*. New York: Simon and Schuster, 1975.

Durso, Joseph. *The Days of Mr. McGraw*. Englewood Cliffs, NJ: Prentice-Hall, 1969.

———. *DiMaggio: The Last American Knight*. Boston: Little, Brown, 1995.

Dworkin, James B. *Owners versus Players: Baseball and Collective Bargaining*. Boston: Auburn House, 1981.

Edelman, Rob. *Baseball on the Web*. New York: MIS, 1998.

Edwards, Bob. *Fridays with Red: A Radio Friendship*. New York: Simon and Schuster, 1993.

Einstein, Charles. *Willie's Time: A Memoir*. Philadelphia: Lippincott, 1979.

Eisenbath, Mike. *The Cardinals Encyclopedia*. Philadelphia: Temple University Press, 1999.

Enright, Jim. *Chicago Cubs*. New York: Macmillan, 1975.

Epstein, Samuel. *Willie Mays: Baseball Superstar*. Champaign, IL: Garrard, 1975.

Erickson, Hal. *Baseball in the Movies: A Comprehensive Reference, 1915–1991*. Jefferson, NC: McFarland, 1992.

Eskanazi, Gerald. *Bill Veeck: A Baseball Legend*. New York: McGraw-Hill, 1988.

———. *The Lip: A Biography of Leo Durocher*. New York: William Morrow, 1993.

Falkner, David. *The Last Hero: The Life of Mickey Mantle*. New York: Simon and Schuster, 1995.

Falls, Joe. *The Detroit Tigers: An Illustrated History*. New York: Walker, 1989.

Fatsis, Stefan. *Wild and Outside: How a Renegade Minor League Revived the Spirit of Baseball in America's Heartland*. 1995. Reprint, New York: Walker, 1996.

Feller, Bob. *Now Pitching, Bob Feller*. New York: Carol, 1990.

———. *Strikeout Story*. New York: A. S. Barnes, 1947.

Field of Dreams. Dir. Phil Alden Robinson. Universal, 1989.

Fine, Gary Alan. *With the Boys: Little League Baseball and Preadolescent Culture*. Chicago: University of Chicago Press, 1987.

Finlayson, Ann. *Champions at Bat: Three Power Hitters*. Champaign, IL: Garrard, 1970.

Fitzgerald, F. Scott. "Echoes of the Jazz Age." In *The Crack-Up*. Ed. Edmund Wilson. 1945. Reprint, New York: New Directions, 1956, pp. 13–22.

———. "Ring." In *The Crack-Up*. Ed. Edmund Wilson. 1945. Reprint, New York: New Directions, 1956, pp. 34–40.

Flood, Curt, with Richard Carter. *Curt Flood: The Way It Is*. New York: Trident, 1971.

Folsom, Ed. "Whitman and Baseball." *Walt Whitman's Native Representations*. New York: Cambridge University Press, 1994, pp. 27–54.

Fountain, Charles. *Sportswriter: The Life and Times of Grantland Rice*. New York: Oxford University Press, 1993.

Freedman, William. *More Than a Pastime: An Oral History of Baseball Fans*. Jefferson, NC: McFarland, 1998.

Freeman, Michael. *ESPN: The Uncensored History*. Dallas: Taylor Publishing Company, 2000.

French, Robert. *50 Golden Years in the American Association of Professional Baseball Clubs, 1902–1951*. Minneapolis: Syndicate Printing, 1951.

Frommer, Harvey. *Primitive Baseball: The First Quarter-Century of the National Pastime*. New York: Atheneum, 1988.

———. *Rickey and Robinson: The Men Who Broke Baseball's Color Barrier*. New York: Macmillan, 1982.

————. *Shoeless Joe and Ragtime Baseball*. Dallas: Taylor, 1992.

Galt, Margot Fortunato. *Up to the Plate: The All-American Girls Professional Baseball League*. Minneapolis: Lerner, 1995.

Gardner, Martin, ed. *The Annotated Casey at the Bat*. 2d ed. Chicago: University of Chicago Press, 1984.

Gaughran, Richard. "Saying It Ain't So: The Black Sox Scandal in Baseball Fiction." In *Cooperstown Symposium on Baseball and the American Culture* (1990). Ed. Alvin L. Hall. Westport, CT: Meckler, 1991, pp. 38–56.

Gehrig, Eleanor. *My Luke and I*. New York: Crowell, 1976.

Gelber, Steven M. "Working at Playing: The Culture of the Workplace and the Rise of Baseball." *Journal of Social History* 16 (1983): 3–22.

Gerber, John C. *Mark Twain*. Twayne's United States Authors Series. Boston: Twayne, 1988.

Gerlach, Larry R. *The Men in Blue: Conversations with Umpires*. New York: Viking, 1980.

Gershman, Michael. *Diamonds: The Evolution of the Ballpark*. Boston: Houghton Mifflin, 1993.

Giamatti, A. Bartlett. *The Earthly Paradise and the Renaissance Epic*. Princeton: Princeton University Press, 1966.

————. *A Great and Glorious Game: Baseball Writings of A. Bartlett Giamatti*. Ed. Kenneth S. Robson. Chapel Hill: Algonquin Books, 1998

————. *Take Time for Paradise: Americans and Their Games*. New York: Summit Books, 1989.

Gibson, Bob. *From Ghetto to Glory: The Story of Bob Gibson*. Englewood Cliffs, NJ: Prentice-Hall, 1968.

————. *Stranger to the Game*. New York: Viking, 1994.

Gilbert, Bill. *They Also Served: Baseball and the Home Front, 1941–1945*. New York: Crown, 1992.

Gilbert, Brother. *Young Babe Ruth: His Early Life and Baseball Career, from the Memoirs of a Xaverian Brother*. Ed. Harry Rothgerber. Jefferson, NC: McFarland, 1999.

Gilbert, Tom. *Baseball and the Color Line*. New York: Franklin Watts, 1995.

Ginsburg, Daniel E. *The Fix Is In: A History of Baseball Gambling and Game Fixing Scandals*. Jefferson, NC: McFarland, 1995.

Gmelch, George. "Superstition and Ritual in American Baseball." *Elysian Fields Quarterly* 11(3) (1992): 25–36.

Gmelch, George, and J. J. Weiner. *In the Ballpark: The Working Lives of Baseball People*. Washington, DC: Smithsonian Institution, 1998.

Goldberg, Philip. *This Is Next Year*. 1991. Reprint, New York: Ballantine, 1992.

Goldberg, Robert. *Citizen Turner: The Wild Rise of an American Tycoon*. New York: Harcourt Brace, 1995.

Goldman, Bob. *Death in the Locker Room: Drugs and Sports*. 2d ed. Chicago: Elite Sports Medicine, 1992.

Goldstein, Richard. *Spartan Seasons: How Baseball Survived the Second World War*. New York: Macmillan, 1980.

Goldstein, Warren. *Playing for Keeps: A History of Early Baseball*. Ithaca: Cornell University Press, 1989.

Golenbock, Peter. *Dynasty: The New York Yankees, 1949–1964*. Englewood Cliffs, NJ: Prentice-Hall, 1975.

————. *Wrigleyville*. New York: St. Martin's, 1996.

Good, Howard. *Diamonds in the Dark: America, Baseball, and the Movies*. Lanham, MD: Scarecrow, 1996.

Goodwin, Doris Kearns. *Wait till Next Year: A Memoir*. New York: Simon and Schuster, 1997.

Graham, Frank. *Lou Gehrig: A Quiet Hero*. New York: Putnam's, 1942.

Green, Douglas B. "The Singing Cowboy: An American Dream." *Journal of Country Music* 7 (1978): 4–62.

Greenberg, Hank. *Hank Greenberg: The Story of My Life*. Ed. Ira Berkow. New York: Times Books, 1989.

Gregory, Robert. *Diz: Dizzy Dean and Baseball During the Great Depression*. New York: Viking, 1992.

Grella, George. "Harold Seymour (1910–1992)." *The National Pastime: A Review of Baseball History* 17 (1997): 128–130.

Griffey, Ken, Jr. *Junior: Griffey on Griffey*. Ed. Mark Vancil. New York: Collins, 1997.

Gropman, Donald. *Say It Ain't So, Joe: The True Story of Shoeless Joe Jackson and the 1919 World Series*. 1979. Reprint, New York: Lynx, 1988.

Gruver, Edward. *Koufax*. Dallas: Taylor Publishing Company, 2000.

Gulliford, Andrew. *America's Country Schools*. 3d ed. Niwot: University Press of Colorado, 1996.

Guschov, Stephen D. *The Red Stockings of Cincinnati*. Jefferson, NC: McFarland, 1998.

Gutman, Bill. *Ken Griffey, Jr.: Baseball's Best*. Brookfield, CT: Millbrook, 1998.

———. *Sammy Sosa: A Biography*. New York: Pocket Books, 1998.

Gutman, Dan. *Honus and Me: A Baseball Card Adventure*. New York: Avon, 1997.

———. *It Ain't Cheatin' If You Don't Get Caught: Scuffing, Corking, Spitting, Gunking, Razzing, and Other Fundamentals of Our National Pastime*. New York: Penguin, 1990.

Guttmann, Allen. *From Ritual to Record: The Nature of Modern Sports*. New York: Columbia University Press, 1978.

Hageman, William. *Honus: The Life and Times of a Baseball Hero*. Champaign, IL: Sagamore, 1996.

Hall, Donald. "Baseball." *The Museum of Clear Ideas: New Poems*. New York: Ticknor and Fields, 1993, pp. 11–39.

———. *Fathers Playing Catch with Sons: Essays on Sport (Mostly Baseball)*. San Francisco: North Point, 1985.

Hall, Jonathan. *Mark McGwire: A Biography*. New York: Pocket Books, 1998.

Halper, Barry, and Bill Madden. "Baseball Collecting." In *Total Baseball: The Official Encyclopedia of Major League Baseball*. 5th ed. Ed. John Thorn et al. New York: Viking, 1997, pp. 549–553.

Hammer, Trudy J. *The All-American Girls Professional Baseball League*. New York: New Discovery Books, 1994.

Hanchett, Doug. "Welcome to Mudville: A Look at Worcester's Baseball Past." *Worcester Magazine*, April 7–13, 1999, pp. 10–11.

Hano, Arnold. *Greatest Giants of Them All*. New York: Putnam's, 1967.

———. *Sandy Koufax: Strikeout King*. Rev. ed. New York: G. P. Putnam's, 1967.

———. *Willie Mays*. New York: Grosset and Dunlap, 1966.

Harper, William. *How You Played the Game: The Life of Grantland Rice*. Columbia: University of Missouri Press, 1999.

Harris, Mark. *Bang the Drum Slowly*. 1956. Reprint, Lincoln: University of Nebraska Press, 1984.

Hartel, William. *A Day at the Park: In Celebration of Wrigley Field*. Rev. ed. Rock Island, IL: Quality Sports, 1994.

Hatch, Francis W. "Maine's All-Time Great Baseball Player." *Down East* (August 1963): 37–39, 59.

Hathaway, Dale E. *People of Rural America*. Washington, DC: U.S. Department of Commerce, 1968.

Helyar, John. *Lords of the Realm: The Real History of Baseball*. 1994. Reprint, New York: Ballantine Books, 1995.

Hemingway, Ernest. *The Nick Adams Stories*. Ed. Philip Young. New York: Scribner's, 1972.

———. *The Old Man and the Sea*. New York: Scribner's, 1952.

Henderson, Robert William. *Ball, Bat, and Bishop: The Origin of Ball Games*. New York: Rockport, 1947.

———. *Early American Sport: A Check-List of Books by American and Foreign Authors Published in America Prior to 1860, Including Sporting Songs*. 2d ed. New York: A. S. Barnes, 1953.

Henrich, Tommy, with Bill Gilbert. *Five O'-Clock Lightning: Ruth, Gehrig, DiMaggio, and the Glory Days of the New York Yankees*. Carol, 1992.

Hill, Bob. *The Louisville Slugger Story*. Santa Monica, CA: General Publishing Group, 1999.

Hirshberg, Albert. *The Up-to-Date Biography of Henry Aaron, Quiet Superstar*. New York: Putnam's, 1974.

Hittner, Arthur D. *Honus Wagner: The Life of Baseball's "Flying Dutchman."* Jefferson, NC: McFarland, 1996.

Hoffman, Andrew Jay. *Inventing Mark Twain: The Lives of Samuel Langhorne Clemens*. New York: William Morrow, 1997.

Hoie, Bob. "The Minor Leagues." In *Total Baseball*. 6th ed. Ed. John Thorn et al. New York: Total Sports, 1999, pp. 510–526.

Hollander, Zander. *Presidents in Sport*. New York: Associated Features, 1962.

Holmes, Tommy. *Dodger Daze and Knights: Enough of a Ball Club's History to Explain Its Reputation*. New York: D. McKay, 1953.

Holst, David L. "Charles G. Radbourne [sic]: The Greatest Pitcher of the Nineteenth Century." *Illinois Historical Journal* 81(4) (1988): 255–268.

Holtzman, Jerome. *The Chicago Cubs Encyclopedia*. Philadelphia: Temple University Press, 1997.

———. *The Commissioners: Baseball's Midlife Crisis*. New York: Total Sports, 1998.

———. *No Cheering in the Press Box*. New York: Holt, 1974.

Holway, John B. *Blackball Stars: Negro League Pioneers*. Westport, CT: Meckler, 1988.

———. *Josh and Satch*. New York: Meckler, 1991.

———. *Voices from the Great Black Baseball Leagues*. New York: Dodd, Mead, 1975.

Honig, Donald. *The American League: An Illustrated History*. New York: Crown, 1983.

———. *Baseball America: The Heroes of the Game and the Times of Their Glory*. New York: Barnes and Noble, 1997.

Hood, Robert E. *The Gashouse Gang*. New York: Morrow, 1976.

Houk, Ralph. *Season of Glory: The Amazing Saga of the 1961 New York Yankees*. New York: Putnam's, 1988.

Hubbard, Freeman H. *Encyclopedia of North American Railroading*. New York: McGraw-Hill, 1981.

Humber, William. *Cheering for the Home Team: The Story of Baseball in Canada*. Erin, Ontario, Canada: Boston Mills, 1983.

———. *Diamonds of the North: A Concise History of Baseball in Canada*. Toronto: Oxford University Press, 1995.

Hunter, Jim. *Catfish: My Life in Baseball*. New York: McGraw-Hill, 1988.

Hurley, C. Harold. *Hemingway's Debt to Baseball in* The Old Man and the Sea: *A Collection of Critical Readings*. Lewiston, NY: Edwin Mellen, 1992.

Hynd, Noel. *The Giants of the Polo Grounds: The Glorious Times of Baseball's New York Giants*. New York: Doubleday, 1988.

Ivor-Campbell, Frederick. "The All-Star Game." In *Total Baseball*. 6th ed. Ed. John Thorn et al. New York: Total Sports, 1999, pp. 287–305.

———. "1884: Old Hoss Radbourne [sic] and the Providence Grays." In *The National Pastime*. Ed. John Thorn. New York: Warner, 1987, pp. 156–169.

Ivor-Campbell, Frederick, and David Pietrusza. "Postseason Play." In *Total Baseball*. 6th ed. Ed. John Thorn et al. New York: Total Sports, 1999, pp. 306–492.

Ivor-Campbell, Frederick, and Matthew Silverman. "Team Histories." In *Total Baseball*. 6th ed. Ed. John Thorn et al. New York: Total Sports, 1999, pp. 13–71.

Jackson, Carlton. *Zane Grey*. Rev. ed. New York: Twayne, 1989.

Jackson, Reggie, with Mike Lupica. *Reggie: The Autobiography of Reggie Jackson*. New York: Villard Books, 1984.

James, Bill. *Whatever Happened to the Hall of Fame: Baseball, Cooperstown, and the Politics of Glory*. 1994. Reprint, New York: Simon and Schuster, 1995.

Jennings, Kenneth M. *Swings and Misses: Moribund Labor Relations in Professional Baseball*. Westport, CT: Praeger, 1997.

Johnson, Daniel E. *Japanese Baseball: A Statistical Handbook*. Jefferson, NC: McFarland, 1999.

Johnson, Don, ed. *Hummers, Knucklers, and Slow Curves: Contemporary Baseball Poems*. Urbana: University of Illinois Press, 1991.

Johnson, Susan E. *When Women Played Hardball*. Seattle: Seal, 1994.

Jordan, David M. *The Athletics of Philadelphia: Connie Mack's White Elephants, 1901–1954*. Jefferson, NC: McFarland, 1999.

Jordan, David M., Larry R. Gerlach, and John P. Rossi. "A Baseball Myth Exploded: Bill Veeck and the 1943 Sale of the Phillies." *The National Pastime: A Review of Baseball History* 17 (1998): 3–13.

Kahn, Roger. *The Boys of Summer*. New York: Harper and Row, 1972.

Kashatus, William C. *Connie Mack's '29 Triumph: The Rise and Fall of the Philadelphia Athletics Dynasty*. Jefferson, NC: McFarland, 1999.

———. *One-Armed Wonder: Pete Gray, Wartime Baseball, and the American Dream.* Jefferson, NC: McFarland, 1995.

Kavanagh, Jack. *The Heights of Ridiculousness: The Feats of Baseball's Merrymakers.* South Bend, IN: Diamond Communications, 1999.

———. *Walter Johnson: A Life.* 1995. Reprint, South Bend, IN: Diamond Communications, 1996.

Kavanagh, Jack, and Norman Macht. *Uncle Robbie.* Cleveland: SABR, 1999.

Kerrane, Kevin. *Dollar Sign on the Muscle: The World of Baseball Scouting.* 1984. Reprint, Lincoln: University of Nebraska Press, 1999.

Kerrane, Kevin, and Richard Grossinger, eds. *Baseball Diamonds.* Garden City, NY: Doubleday, 1980.

Kessler, Leonard. *Here Comes the Strikeout.* New York: Harper and Row, 1965.

Kimball, Arthur G. *Ace of Hearts: The Westerns of Zane Grey.* Fort Worth: Texas Christian University Press, 1993.

Kindred, Dave. "A Good Man, That Charlie Brown." *The Sporting News,* January 10, 2000, p. 70.

Kiner, Ralph McPherran. *Kiner's Korner: My Quarter Century with the New York Mets.* New York: Arbor House, 1987.

Kinsella, W. P. *Shoeless Joe.* 1982. Reprint, New York: Ballantine, 1996.

"Kinsella, W(illiam) P(atrick) 1935–." In *Contemporary Authors.* New Revision Series. Detroit: Gale Research, 1981–. 21: 217–223.

Kirsch, George B. *The Creation of American Team Sports: Baseball and Cricket.* Urbana: University of Illinois Press, 1989.

Klatell, David A. *Sports for Sale: Television, Money, and the Fans.* New York: Oxford University Press, 1988.

Kneer, Marian E. *Softball: Slow and Fast Pitch.* Dubuque: W. C. Brown, 1987.

Kramer, Barbara. *Ken Griffey, Junior: All-Around All-Star.* Minneapolis: Lerner, 1996.

Kuhn, Bowie, and Martin Appel. *Hardball: The Education of a Baseball Commissioner.* New York: Times Books, 1987.

Kuklick, Bruce. *To Everything a Season: Shibe Park and Urban Philadelphia, 1909–1976.* Princeton: Princeton University Press, 1991.

Kull, Andrew. "Baseball's Greatest Pitcher." *American Heritage* (April-May 1985): 102–106.

Lacy, Sam, with Moses J. Newson. *Fighting for Fairness: The Life Story of Hall of Fame Sportswriter Sam Lacy.* Centreville, MD: Tidewater, 1998.

Ladson, William, ed. *The Yankees: Steinbrenner's 25 Years of Triumph and Turmoil.* Special Collector's Edition of *The Sporting News.* 1998.

Laforse, Martin W. "Baseball and Urbanism." In *Popular Culture and American Life: Selected Topics in the Study of American Popular Culture.* Martin W. Laforse and James A. Drake. Chicago: Nelson-Hall, 1981, pp. 163–228.

Laidlaw, Robert. "Baseball in Australia." In *Total Baseball.* 6th ed. Ed. John Thorn et al. New York: Total Sports, 1999, pp. 549–558.

Landis, D. B. *The Landis Family of Lancaster County, Pa.* Lancaster: Privately printed, 1888.

Lang, Jack. "Baseball Reporting." In *Total Baseball.* 6th ed. Ed. John Thorn et al. New York: Total Sports, 1999, pp. 586–591.

Lapchick, Richard Edward. *The Rules of the Game: Ethics in College Sport.* American Council on Education/Macmillan Series in Higher Education. New York: Macmillan, 1989.

Lardner, Ring W. *The Annotated Baseball Stories of Ring W. Lardner, 1914–1919.* Ed. George W. Hilton. Stanford: Stanford University Press, 1995.

Lardner, Ring, Jr. *The Lardners: My Family Remembered.* New York: Harper and Row, 1976.

Lasorda, Tommy, and David Fisher. *The Artful Dodger.* New York: Avon, 1985.

Leatherstocking Base Ball Club Website. http://www.freeyellow.com/members2/tbone-tabor

Lemke, Bob. *1999 Standard Catalog of Baseball Cards.* 8th ed. Iola, WI: Krause, 1998.

Levine, Peter. *A. G. Spalding and the Rise of Baseball: The Promise of American Sport.* New York: Oxford University Press, 1985.

Levy, Lester S., ed. *Take Me Out to the Ball Game and Other Favorite Song Hits, 1906–1908.* Mineola, NY: Dover, 1984.

Lewis, Allen. *Baseball's Greatest Streaks: The Highs and Lows of Teams, Pitchers, and Hitters in the Modern Major Leagues.* Jefferson, NC: McFarland, 1992.

Libby, Bill. *Catfish: The Three Million Dollar Pitcher.* New York: Coward, McCann, and Geoghegan, 1976.

Lichtenwanger, William. *The Music of the Star-Spangled Banner from Ludgate Hill to Capitol Hill.* Washington, DC: Library of Congress, 1977.

Lieb, Fred. *Connie Mack: Grand Old Man of Baseball.* New York: Putnam's, 1945.

———. *The St. Louis Cardinals: The Story of a Great Baseball Club.* New York: Putnam's, 1944.

The Life and Times of Hank Greenberg (documentary). Dir. Aviva Kempner. Ciesla Foundation, 1999.

Lindberg, Richard. *Sox: The Complete Record of Chicago White Sox Baseball.* New York: Macmillan, 1984.

———. *Stealing First in a Two-Team Town: The White Sox from Comiskey to Reinsdorf.* Champaign, IL: Sagamore, 1994.

Linn, Edward. *Hitter: The Life and Turmoils of Ted Williams.* New York: Harcourt, 1993.

———. *Steinbrenner's Yankees.* New York: Holt, 1982.

Lipman, David, and Ed Wilks. *Bob Gibson: Pitching Ace.* New York: Putnam's, 1975.

Lockwood, Lee. *Castro's Cuba, Cuba's Fidel: An American Journalist's Inside Look at Today's Cuba in Text and Picture.* New York: Vintage, 1969.

Louisville Slugger Museum Website. http://www.slugger.com/museum

Lowenfish, Lee. *The Imperfect Diamond: A History of Baseball's Labor Wars.* Rev. ed. New York: Da Capo, 1991.

Lowry, Philip. *Green Cathedrals.* Reading, MA: Addison-Wesley, 1992.

Lurs, Victor. *The Great Baseball Mystery: The 1919 World Series.* New York: A. S. Barnes, 1966.

Lynn, Kenneth S. *Hemingway.* New York: Simon and Schuster, 1987.

Macht, Norman L. *Cy Young.* New York: Chelsea House, @\Body:1992.

———. *Jim Abbott: Major League Pitcher.* Great Achievers: Lives of the Physically Challenged Series. New York: Chelsea House, 1994.

Mack, Connie. *From Sandlot to Big League: Connie Mack's Baseball Book.* Rev. ed. New York: Knopf, 1960.

———. *My 66 Years in the Big Leagues: The Great Story of America's National Game.* Philadelphia: Winston, 1950.

MacLean, Norman. *Casey Stengel: A Biography.* New York: Drake, 1976.

MacPhail, Lee. *My 9 Innings: An Autobiography of 50 Years in Baseball.* Westport, CT: Meckler, 1989.

Macy, Sue. *A Whole New Ball Game: The Story of the All-American Girls Professional Baseball League.* New York: Holt, 1993.

Madden, Bill. *Damned Yankees: A No-Holds-Barred Account of Life with "Boss" Steinbrenner.* New York: Warner, 1990.

Madden, W. C. *The All-American Girls Professional Baseball League Record Book.* Jefferson, NC: McFarland, 1999.

Malamud, Bernard. *The Natural.* 1952. Reprint, New York: Noonday, 1990.

———. *Talking Horse: Bernard Malamud on Life and Work.* Ed. Alan Cheuse and Nicholas Delhanco. New York: Columbia University Press, 1996.

Manley, Effa, and Leon Herbert. *Negro Baseball . . . Before Integration.* Chicago: Adams, 1976.

Mann, Arthur William. *Baseball Confidential: Secret History of the War Among Chandler, Durocher, MacPhail, and Rickey.* David McKay, 1951.

———. *Branch Rickey: American in Action.* Boston: Houghton Mifflin, 1957.

———. *The Jackie Robinson Story.* New York: Grosset and Dunlap, 1956.

Mantle, Merlyn. *A Hero All His Life.* New York: HarperCollins, 1996.

Mantle, Mickey. *All My Octobers: My Memories of Twelve World Series When the Yankees Ruled Baseball.* New York: HarperCollins, 1994.

———. *The Mick.* Garden City, NY: Doubleday, 1985.

Marichal, Juan. *A Pitcher's Story.* Garden City, NY: Doubleday, 1967.

Maris, Roger. *Roger Maris at Bat.* New York: Duell, Sloan, and Pearce, 1962.

Mark, Stephen. *Double Play: The Economics and Financing of Stadiums for the Yankees and Mets*. New York: Independent Budget Office, 1998.

Markham, Jesse W., and Paul V. Teplitz. *Baseball Economics and Public Policy*. Lexington, MA: Lexington, 1981.

Markusen, Bruce. *Baseball's Last Dynasty: Charles Finley's Oakland A's*. Indianapolis: Masters, 1998.

Marshall, William Leonard. *Baseball's Pivotal Era: 1945–1951*. Lexington: University Press of Kentucky, 1999.

Martin, Mollie. *St. Louis Cardinals*. Mankato, MN: Creative Education, 1982.

Martinez, David H. *The Book of Baseball Literacy*. New York: Plume, 1996.

Mathewson, Christy. *Pitching in a Pinch: Or, Baseball from the Inside*. New York: Grosset and Dunlap, 1912.

May, Stephen. *Zane Grey: Romancing the West*. Athens: Ohio University Press, 1997.

Mays, Willie. *Born to Play Ball*. New York: Putnam's, 1955.

———. *Say Hey: The Autobiography of Willie Mays*. New York: Simon and Schuster, 1988.

McBride, Joseph. *High and Inside: An A-to-Z Guide to the Language of Baseball*. Lincolnwood (Chicago): Contemporary Books, 1997.

McCallum, John Dennis. *The Tiger Wore Spikes: An Informal Biography of Ty Cobb*. New York: Barnes, 1956.

———. *Ty Cobb*. New York: Praeger, 1975.

McCarver, Tim, with Danny Peary. *The Perfect Season: Why 1998 Was Baseball's Greatest Year*. New York: Villard Books, 1999.

McCollister, John. *The Bucs: The Story of the Pittsburgh Pirates*. Lenexa, KS: Addax, 1998.

McCroskey, Dennis. "Fantasy Camps." http://www.HiHard1.com/basfnpg1.html-ssi

McGill, Frances. *Go Not Gently: Letters from a Patient with Amyotrophic Lateral Sclerosis*. New York: Arno, 1980.

McGraw, Blanche Sindall. *The Real McGraw*. New York: D. McKay, 1953.

McGraw, John Joseph. *My Thirty Years in Baseball*. New York: Boni and Liveright, 1923.

McKelvey, G. Richard. *Fisk's Homer, Willie's Catch, and the Shot Heard 'Round the World: Classic Moments from Postseason Baseball, 1940–1996*. Jefferson, NC: McFarland, 1998.

McLain, Denny, with Dave Diles. *Nobody's Perfect*. New York: Dial, 1975.

McLoughlin, William Gerald. *Billy Sunday Was His Real Name*. Chicago: University of Chicago Press, 1955.

Mead, William B. *Baseball Goes to War*. Washington, DC: Farragut, 1985.

Mead, William B., and Paul Dickson. *Baseball: The Presidents' Game*. New York: Walker, 1997

Meany, Thomas. *The Yankee Story*. New York: Dutton, 1960.

Melville, Tom. *Cricket for Americans: Playing and Understanding the Game*. Bowling Green, OH: Bowling Green State University Popular Press, 1993.

———. *The Tented Field: A History of Cricket in America*. Bowling Green, OH: Bowling Green State University Popular Press, 1998.

Mencken, H. L. *The American Language: An Inquiry into the Development of English in the United States*. 4th ed. New York: Knopf, 1936.

Men's Senior Baseball League [also Men's Adult Baseball League] official website: http://www.msbl.com/msbl

Miklasz, Bernie, et al. *Celebrating 70: Mark McGwire's Historic Season*. St. Louis: Sporting News, 1998.

Miller, Marvin. *A Whole Different Ball Game: The Sport and Business of Baseball*. Secaucus, NJ: Carol, 1991.

Miller, Roger W. *Athletes and Steroids: Playing a Deadly Game*. Rockville, MD: Department of Health and Human Services, 1988.

Mitsumoto, Horoshi. *Amyotrophic Lateral Sclerosis*. Philadelphia: F. A. Davis, 1998.

Moore, Jim, and Natalie Vermilyea. *Ernest Thayer's "Casey at the Bat": Background and Characters of Baseball's Most Famous Poem*. Jefferson, NC: McFarland, 1994.

Moore, Joseph Thomas. *Pride against Prejudice: The Biography of Larry Doby*. Westport, CT: Greenwood Press, 1988.

Morris, Timothy. *Making the Team: The Cultural Work of Baseball Fiction*. Urbana: University of Illinois Press, 1997.

Morse, Ann. *Baseball's Record Breaker, Hank Aaron.* Mankato, MN: Children's Press, 1976.

Mote, James. *Everything Baseball.* New York: Prentice Hall, 1989.

Moyers, Bill. "August Wilson's America: A Conversation with Bill Moyers." *American Theatre* (June 1989): 13–17, 54.

MSBL/MABL website: http://www.msblnational.com

Muller, Joseph. *The Star-Spangled Banner.* New York: Da Capo, 1973 (annotated bibliography of versions and arrangements, with notes on music publishers).

Munro, Neil, and STATS, Inc. *Canadian Players Encyclopedia.* Skokie, IL: STATS, 1996.

Murdock, Eugene C. *Mighty Casey: All American.* Westport, CT: Greenwood Press, 1984.

Musial, Stan. *Stan Musial: "The Man's" Own Story, as Told to Bob Broeg.* Garden City, NY: Doubleday, 1964.

Musial, Stan, Jack Buck, and Bob Broeg. *We Saw Stars.* St. Louis: Bethany, 1976.

Musick, Phil. *Who Was Roberto? A Biography of Roberto Clemente.* Garden City, NY: Doubleday, 1974.

Nadel, Alan. "Boundaries, Logistics, and Identity: The Property of Metaphor in *Fences* and *Joe Turner's Come and Gone.*" In *May All Your Fences Have Gates: Essays on the Drama of August Wilson.* Ed. Alan Nadel. Iowa City: University of Iowa Press, 1994, pp. 86–104.

Nagata, Yoichi, and John B. Holway. "Baseball in Japan." In *Total Baseball.* 5th ed. Ed. John Thorn et al. New York: Viking, 1997, pp. 465–472.

National Cancer Institute. *Spitting into the Wind: The Facts about Dip and Chew.* Bethesda, MD: National Cancer Institute, 1999.

Nemec, David. *The Great Encyclopedia of 19th-Century Major League Baseball.* New York: Donald I. Fine, 1997.

New York Daily News Staff. *Joe DiMaggio: An American Icon.* New York: Sports Publishing, 1999.

Newark Eagle Files. Newark Public Library. New Jersey Collection. Newark, NJ.

Nicholson, Lois. *Ken Griffey, Jr.* Philadelphia: Chelsea House, 1999.

Nightengale, Bob. "Nothing Keeps This Man Down: Darryl Strawberry Battles Back from Colon Cancer Surgeries." *USA Today Baseball Weekly,* March 3–9, 1999, pp. 8–11.

Noden, Merrell. *Home Run Heroes: Mark McGwire, Sammy Sosa, and a Season for the Ages.* New York: Simon and Schuster, 1998.

Nutt, Amy Ellis. "Baseball and Softball." In *Nike Is a Goddess: The History of Women in Sports.* Ed. Lissa Smith. New York: Atlantic Monthly, 1998, pp. 33–54.

Obojski, Robert. *Bush League.* New York: Macmillan, 1975.

O'Connor, Gerry. "Bernard Malamud's *The Natural:* 'The Worst There Ever Was in the Game.'" *Arete* 3(2) (1986): 37–42.

Okkonen, Marc. *Baseball Uniforms of the 20th Century: The Official Major League Baseball Guide.* New York: Sterling, 1991.

Oleksak, Michael M., and Mary Adams Oleksak. *Beisbol: Latin Americans and the Grand Old Game.* Grand Rapids, MI: Masters, 1991.

Oliva, Tony, with Bob Fowler. *Tono O! The Trials and Triumphs of Tony Oliva.* New York: Hawthorn, 1973.

Oliver, Robert Tarbell. *A History of the Korean People in Modern Times: 1800 to the Present.* Newark, NJ: University of Delaware Press, 1993.

O'Neil, Buck. *I Was Right on Time: My Journey from the Negro Leagues to the Majors.* 1996. Reprint, New York: Fireside, 1997.

Orodenker, Richard. *The Writers' Game: Baseball Writing in America.* New York: Twayne, 1996.

Overfield, Joseph M. "Tragedies and Shortened Careers." In *Total Baseball.* 5th ed. Ed. John Thorn et al. New York: Viking, 1997, pp. 155–170.

———. "Zane Grey's Redheaded Outfield." In *The National Pastime.* Ed. John Thorn. New York: Warner, 1987, pp. 285–293.

Overmyer, James. *Queen of the Negro Leagues: Effa Manley and the Newark Eagles.* Rev. ed. Lanham, MD: Scarecrow, 1998.

Paige, Leroy. *Maybe I'll Pitch Forever: A Great Baseball Player Tells the Hilarious Story Behind the Legend.* 1962. Reprint, Lincoln: University of Nebraska Press, 1993.

Patrick, Walton R. *Ring Lardner.* New York: Twayne, 1963.

Pelton, Robert W. *Collecting Autographs for Fun and Profit.* White Hall, VA: Betterway, 1987.

Pepe, Phil. *The Wit and Wisdom of Yogi Berra.* New York: Hawthorn, 1974.

Pereira, Kim. *August Wilson and the African-American Odyssey.* Urbana: University of Illinois Press, 1995.

Perry, Thomas K. *Textile League Baseball: South Carolina's Mill Teams, 1880–1955.* Jefferson, NC: McFarland, 1993.

Peterson, Robert. *Only the Ball Was White.* 2d ed. New York: McGraw-Hill, 1984.

Petterchak, Janice A., and Jerome Holtzman. *Jack Brickhouse: A Voice for All Seasons.* Lincolnwood, IL: NTC, 1996.

Phillips, Louis, and Burnham Holmes. *Yogi, Babe, and Magic: The Complete Book of Sports Nicknames.* New York: Prentice-Hall, 1994.

Pietrusza, David. *Baseball's Canadian-American League: A History of Its Inception, Franchises, Participants, Locales, Statistics, Demise, and Legacy, 1936–1951.* Jefferson, NC: McFarland, 1990.

———. *Judge and Jury: The Life and Times of Judge Kenesaw Mountain Landis.* South Bend, IN: Diamond Communications, 1998.

———. *Lights On! The Wild Century-Long Saga of Night Baseball.* Lanham, MD: Scarecrow, 1997.

Pietrusza, David, Lloyd Johnson, and Bob Carroll. *The Total Baseball Catalog.* New York: Total Sports, 1998.

Play Ball! Compact Disc. Telarc, 1998.

Polner, Murray. *Branch Rickey: A Biography.* New York: Atheneum, 1982.

PONY Baseball and Softball Website. http://www.pony.org

Pope, Edwin. *Baseball's Greatest Managers.* Garden City, NY: Doubleday, 1960.

———. *Ted Williams.* Englewood Cliffs, NJ: Prentice-Hall, 1970.

Postema, Pam, and Gene Wojciechowski. *You've Got to Have Balls to Make It in This League.* New York: Simon and Schuster, 1992.

Povich, Shirley. *All These Mornings.* Englewood Cliffs, NJ: Prentice-Hall, 1969.

———. *The Washington Senators.* New York: Putnam's, 1954.

Quirk, James, and Rodney Fort. *Hard Ball: The Abuse of Power in Pro Team Sports.* Princeton, NJ: Princeton University Press, 1999.

Quirk, Robert. *Fidel Castro.* New York: Norton, 1993.

Quisenberry, Dan. Poems in *Spitball: The Literary Baseball Magazine,* No. 51 (1997): 33–40.

Rabin, Roni. *Six Parts Love: One Family's Battle with Lou Gehrig's Disease.* New York: Scribner, 1985.

Rains, Rob. *Mark McGwire: Home Run Hero.* New York: St. Martin's, 1998.

Ralbovsky, Marty. *Destiny's Darlings: A World Championship Little League Team Twenty Years Later.* New York: Hawthorn, 1974.

Reeder, Red. *On the Mound: Three Great Pitchers.* Champaign, IL: Garrard, 1966.

Regalado, Samuel O. *Viva Baseball! Latin Major Leaguers and Their Special Hunger.* Urbana: University of Illinois Press, 1998.

Regan, F. Scott. "The Mighty Casey: Enduring Folk Hero of Failure." *Journal of Popular Culture* 31(1) (1997): 91–109.

Reidenbaugh, Lowell. *Baseball's Hall of Fame: Cooperstown Where the Legends Live Forever.* Rev. by Editors of *The Sporting News.* New York: Crescent Books, 1997.

Reidenbaugh, Lowell, Joe Hoppel, and Mike Nahrstedt. *The Sporting News: First Hundred Years, 1886–1986.* St. Louis: The Sporting News, 1985.

Reiser, Howard. *Nolan Ryan: Strikeout King.* Chicago: Childrens Press, 1993.

Reisler, Jim, ed. *Black Writers/Black Baseball: An Anthology of Articles from Black Sportswriters Who Covered the Negro Leagues.* Jefferson, NC: McFarland, 1994.

Reston, James, Jr. *Collision at Home Plate: The Lives of Pete Rose and Bart Giamatti.* New York: HarperCollins 1991; New York: HarperPerennial, 1992.

Ribowsky, Mark. *The Power and the Darkness: the Life of Josh Gibson in the Shadows of the Game.* New York: Simon and Schuster, 1996.

Rice, Grantland. *The Omnibus of Sport.* New York: Harper, 1932.

———. *Only the Brave and Other Poems*. New York: Barnes, 1941.

———. *The Tumult and the Shouting: My Life in Sport*. New York: Barnes, 1954.

Richmond, Peter. *Ballpark*. New York: Simon and Schuster, 1993.

Rickey, Branch. *The American Diamond: A Documentary of the Game of Baseball*. New York: Simon and Schuster, 1965.

Rielly, Edward J. "Green on Green: Baseball Fiction, Myth, and Money." In *Cooperstown Symposium on Baseball and the American Culture* (1990). Ed. Alvin L. Hall. Westport, CT: Meckler, 1991, pp. 400–417.

Riess, Steven A. *City Games: The Evolution of American Urban Society and the Rise of Sports*. Urbana: University of Illinois Press, 1989.

Riess, Steven A., ed. *Sports and the American Jew*. Syracuse: Syracuse University Press, 1998.

———. *Touching Base: Professional Baseball and American Culture in the Progressive Era*. Rev. ed. Urbana: University of Illinois Press, 1999.

Riley, James A. *The Biographical Encyclopedia of the Negro Baseball Leagues*. New York: Carroll and Graf, 1994.

Ripken, Cal. *The Only Way I Know*. New York: Viking, 1997.

Ritter, Lawrence S. *The Glory of Their Times: The Story of the Early Days of Baseball by the Men Who Played It*. 1984. Reprint, New York: Vintage Books, 1985.

———. *Lost Ballparks: A Celebration of Baseball's Legendary Fields*. 1992. Reprint, New York: Penguin, 1994.

Robertson, John G. *The Babe Chases 60: That Fabulous 1927 Season, Home Run by Home Run*. Jefferson, NC: McFarland, 1999.

Robinson, Frank. *My Life in Baseball*. Garden City, NY: Doubleday, 1968.

Robinson, Jackie. *I Never Had It Made: The Autobiography of Jackie Robinson*. 1972. Reprint, Hopewell, NJ: Ecco, 1995.

———. *Jackie Robinson: My Own Story, as Told to Wendell Smith*. New York: Greenberg, 1948.

———. *Jackie Robinson's Little League Baseball Book*. Englewood Cliffs, NJ: Prentice-Hall, 1972.

Robinson, Ray. *Iron Horse: Lou Gehrig in His Time*. New York: Norton, 1990.

———. *Matty: An American Hero*. New York: Oxford University Press, 1993.

———. *Stan Musial: Baseball's Durable "Man."* New York: Putnam's, 1963.

———. *Yankee Stadium: 75 Years of Drama, Glamour, and Glory*. New York: Penguin Studio, 1998.

Robinson, Sharon. *Stealing Home: An Intimate Family Portrait by the Daughter of Jackie Robinson*. 1996. Reprint, New York: HarperPerennial, 1997.

Rockwell, Norman. *Norman Rockwell: A Sixty Year Retrospective*. New York: Abrams, 1972.

———. *Norman Rockwell: My Adventures as an Illustrator*. New York: Abrams, 1988.

Rogosin, William Donn. *Invisible Men: Life in the Negro Baseball Leagues*. New York: Athenaeum, 1987.

Rooney, John F. *The Recruiting Game: Toward a New System of Intercollegiate Sports*. 2d ed. Lincoln: University of Nebraska Press, 1987.

Rose, Pete, and Roger Kahn. *Pete Rose: My Story*. New York: Macmillan, 1989.

Rosenfeld, Harvey. *Iron Man: The Cal Ripken, Jr. Story*. New York: St. Martin's, 1995.

Rosentraub, Mark. *Major League Losers: The Real Cost of Sports and Who's Paying for Them*. Rev. ed. New York: BasicBooks, 1999.

Ross, Jerry. *Damn Yankees: A New Musical Based on the Novel* The Year the Yankees Lost the Pennant. New York: Random House, 1956.

———. *Damn Yankees: Original Broadway Cast*. RCA Victor, 1988.

Rothel, David. *The Gene Autry Book*. Rev. ed. Madison, NC: Empire, 1988.

Rubinstein, Murray A. *Taiwan: A New History*. Armonk, NY: M. E. Sharpe, 1999.

Ruck, Rob. "Baseball in the Caribbean." In *Total Baseball*. 6th ed. Ed. John Thorn et al. New York: Total Sports, 1999, pp. 536–543.

Rumer, Thomas A. *The American Legion: An Official History, 1919–1989*. New York: M. Evans, 1990.

Runquist, Willie. *Baseball by the Numbers: How Statistics Are Collected, What They*

Mean, and How They Reveal the Game. Jefferson, NC: McFarland, 1995.

Ruth, Claire Merritt. *The Babe and I*. Englewood Cliffs, NJ: Prentice-Hall, 1959.

Ryan, Nolan. *Kings of the Hill: An Irreverent Look at the Men on the Mound*. New York: HarperCollins, 1992.

————. *Miracle Man: Nolan Ryan, the Autobiography*. Dallas: Word, 1992.

————. *Throwing Heat: The Autobiography of Nolan Ryan*. New York: Doubleday, 1988.

Ryczek, William J. *When Johnny Came Sliding Home: The Post–Civil War Baseball Boom, 1865–1870*. Jefferson, NC: McFarland, 1998.

Salin, Tony. *Baseball's Forgotten Heroes: One Fan's Search for the Game's Most Interesting Overlooked Players*. Chicago: Masters, 1999.

Sampson, Arthur. *Ted Williams: A Biography of the Kid*. New York: Barnes, 1950.

Sands, Jack. *Coming Apart at the Seams: How Baseball Owners, Players, and Television Executives Have Led Our National Pastime to the Brink of Disaster*. New York: Macmillan, 1993.

Schaap, Dick. *Steinbrenner!* Rev. ed. New York: Avon, 1983.

Schacht, Alexander. *My Own Particular Screwball: An Informal Autobiography*. Garden City, NY: Doubleday, 1955.

Schneider, Russell, Jr. *Frank Robinson: The Making of a Manager*. New York: Coward, McCann, and Geoghegan, 1976.

Schoenstein, Ralph. *Diamonds for Lori and Me: A Father, a Daughter, and Baseball*. New York: William Morrow, 1988.

Schoor, Gene. *Christy Mathewson: Baseball's Greatest Pitcher*. New York: J. Messner, 1953.

————. *The History of the World Series: 85 Years of America's Greatest Sports Tradition*. New York: Morrow, 1990.

————. *Seaver: A Biography*. Chicago: Contemporary Books, 1986.

————. *The Story of Yogi Berra*. Garden City, NY: Doubleday, 1976.

Schreiber, Lee R. *Race for the Record: The Great Home Run Chase of 1998*. New York: HarperCollins, 1998.

Schulz, Charles M. *The Charlie Brown Dictionary*. New York: Random House, 1973.

————. *Charlie Brown, Snoopy and Me, and All the Other Peanuts Characters*. Garden City, NY: Doubleday, 1980.

————. *It's Baseball Season, Again!* New York: HarperCollins, 1999.

————. *Peanuts Jubilee: My Life and Art with Charlie Brown and Others*. New York: Holt, Rinehart, and Winston, 1975.

Schwartz, Bernard. *A History of the Supreme Court*. New York: Oxford University Press, 1993.

Scully, Gerald W. *The Business of Major League Baseball*. Chicago: University of Chicago Press, 1989.

Seaver, Tom, with Lee Lowenfish. *The Art of Pitching*. New York: Hearst Books, 1984.

Seaver, Tom, with Herb Resnicow. *Beanball*. New York: Morrow, 1989.

Seaver, Tom, with Norman Lewis Smith. *How I Would Pitch to Babe Ruth: Seaver Versus the Sluggers*. Chicago: Playboy, 1974.

Seay, James L. *Who's on First?* Elgin, IL: Performance Publishing, 1975.

Seidel, Michael. *Streak: Joe DiMaggio and the Summer of '41*. New York: McGraw-Hill, 1988.

Seymour, Harold. *Baseball: The Early Years*. 1960. Reprint, New York: Oxford University Press, 1989.

————. *Baseball: The Golden Age*. 1971. Reprint, New York: Oxford University Press, 1989.

————. *Baseball: The People's Game*. 1990. Reprint, New York: Oxford University Press, 1991.

Shannon, Mike. *Diamond Classics: Essays on 100 of the Best Baseball Books Ever Published*. Jefferson, NC: McFarland, 1989.

Shattuck, Debra A. "Women in Baseball." In *Total Baseball*. 6th ed. Ed. John Thorn et al. New York: Total Sports, 1999, pp. 574–577.

Sheed, Wilfrid. *My Life as a Fan*. New York: Simon and Schuster, 1993.

Shissler, Barbara Johnson. *Sports and Games in Art*. Minneapolis: Lerner, 1966.

Silverman, Al. *Heroes of the World Series*. New York: Putnam's, 1964.

Simons, William M. "Hank Greenberg: The Jewish American Sports Hero." In *Sports and the American Jew*. Ed. Steven A. Riess. Syracuse: Syracuse University Press, 1998, pp. 185–207.

Singer, Tom. "The Wide World of Web Sports." *Sport* 90, no. 3 (March 1999): 54–57.

Skipper, John C. *Umpires: Classic Baseball Stories from the Men Who Made the Calls*. Jefferson, NC: McFarland, 1997.

Slide, Anthony. *The Encyclopedia of Vaudeville*. Westport, CT: Greenwood Press, 1994.

Smelser, Marshall. *The Life That Ruth Built: A Biography*. New York: Quadrangle/New York Times Book, 1975.

Smith, Curt. *America's Dizzy Dean*. St. Louis: Bethany, 1978.

———. *The Storytellers: From Mel Allen to Bob Costas—Sixty Years of Baseball Tales from the Broadcast Booth*. New York: Macmillan, 1995.

———. *Voices of the Game*. South Bend, IN: Diamond Communications, 1987.

Smith, David. "The Effect of Artificial Surface." June 17, 1995. Clifford Blau's Website *Original Baseball Research*. http://users.erols.com/brak/index.html

Smith, Red. *The Red Smith Reader*. New York: Random House, 1982.

———. *To Absent Friends*. New York: Atheneum, 1982.

———. *Views of Sport*. New York: Knopf, 1954.

Smith, Robert. *Heroes of Baseball*. Cleveland: World, 1953.

———. *World Series: The Games and the Players*. Garden City, NY: Doubleday, 1967.

Smith, Ronald A. *Sports and Freedom: The Rise of Big-Time College Athletics*. New York: Oxford University Press, 1988.

Smith, Wendell. "Wendell Smith Papers." National Baseball Hall of Fame Library. http://www.baseballhalloffame.org/library/aids/msb1.html

Smizik, Bob. *The Pittsburgh Pirates: An Illustrated History*. New York: Walker, 1990.

Sobel, Lionel S. *Professional Sports and the Law*. New York: Law-Arts, 1977.

Society for American Baseball Research. *Membership Directory 1999–2000*. Cleveland: SABR, 1999.

Society for American Baseball Research. Website www.sabr.org.

Sowell, Mike. *The Pitch That Killed*. New York: Macmillan, 1989.

Spalding, Albert G. *Base Ball: America's National Game*. 1911. Reprint, revised and edited by Samm Coombs and Bob West, San Francisco: Halo Books, 1991.

Spaner, David. "Greenberg to Green: Jewish Ball Players." In *Total Baseball*. 5th ed. Ed. John Thorn et al. New York: Penguin, 1997, pp. 171–180.

Spink, J. G. Taylor. *Judge Landis and Twenty-five Years of Baseball*. 1947. Reprint, St. Louis: Sporting News, 1974.

The Sporting News Website. http://www.sportingnews.com

Sports Turf Managers' Association. Website: http://www.aip.com/SIMA

St. John, Thomas. "History of the Korean Baseball Organization." In *Total Baseball*. 6th ed. Ed. John Thorn et al. New York: Total Sports, 1999, pp. 559–562.

Stainback, Robert D. *Alcohol and Sports*. Champaign, IL: Human Kinetics, 1997.

Stambler, Irwin. *Catfish Hunter: The Three Million Dollar Arm*. New York: Putnam's, 1976.

Staten, Vince. *Ol' Diz: A Biography of Dizzy Dean*. New York: HarperCollins, 1992.

Staudohar, Paul. *The Sports Industry and Collective Bargaining*. 2d ed. Ithaca: ILR, 1989.

Stein, Fred. *Giants Diary: A Century of Giants Baseball in New York and San Francisco*. Berkeley: North Atlantic Books, 1987.

———. *Mel Ott: The Little Giant of Baseball*. Jefferson, NC: McFarland, 1999.

Stevens, David. *Baseball's Radical for All Seasons: A Biography of John Montgomery Ward*. Lanham, MD: Scarecrow, 1998.

Stockton, J. Roy. *The Gashouse Gang and a Couple of Other Guys*. New York: A. S. Barnes, 1945.

Stone, Steve, with Barry Rozner. *Where's Harry? Steve Stone Remembers His Years with Harry Caray*. Dallas: Taylor, 1999.

Stotz, Carl E., as told to Kenneth D. Loss. *A Promise Kept: The Story of the Founding of Little League Baseball*. Jersey Shore, PA: Zebrowski Historical Services, 1992.

Stover, John F. *American Railroads*. Chicago: University of Chicago Press, 1961.

Strazzabosco, Jeanne. *Learning about the Work Ethic from the Life of Cal Ripken, Jr.* New York: PowerKids, 1996.

Stump, Al. *Cobb: A Biography*. Chapel Hill: Algonquin Books, 1994.

Sullivan, George. *The Complete Guide to Soft-ball*. New York: Fleet, 1965.

——. *Detroit Tigers: The Complete Record of Detroit Tigers Baseball*. New York: Collier, 1985.

——. *Home Run!* New York: Dodd, Mead, 1977.

——. *Tom Seaver of the Mets*. New York: Putnam's, 1971.

Sullivan, Neil J. *The Dodgers Move West*. New York: Oxford University Press, 1987.

——. *The Minors: The Struggles and the Triumph of Baseball's Poor Relation from 1876 to the Present*. New York: St. Martin's Press, 1990.

Sunday, Billy. *"Billy" Sunday, the Man and His Message, with His Own Words which Have Won Thousands for Christ*. Philadelphia: John C. Winston, 1914.

Svejda, George J. *History of the Star-Spangled Banner from 1814 to the Present*. Washington, DC: Division of History, Office of Archeology and Historic Preservation, 1976.

"Take Me Out to the Ball Game." *Play Ball!* Compact Disc. Telarc, 1998.

Thomas, Bob. *Bud and Lou: The Abbott and Costello Story*. Philadelphia: J. B. Lippincott, 1977.

Thomas, Henry W. *Walter Johnson: Baseball's Big Train*. 1995. Reprint, Lincoln: University of Nebraska Press, 1998.

Thorn, John. "Jim Creighton: To a Ballplayer Dying Young." *Elysian Fields Quarterly* 11(3) (1992): 59–63.

Thorn, John, and the National Baseball Hall of Fame and Museum. *Treasures of the Baseball Hall of Fame: The Official Companion to the Collection at Cooperstown*. New York: Villard, 1998.

Thorn, John, et al., eds. *Total Baseball*. 6th ed. New York: Total Sports, 1999.

Thorn, John, Pete Palmer, and Joseph M. Wayman. "The History of Major League Baseball Statistics." In *Total Baseball*. 6th ed. Ed. John Thorn et al. New York: Total Sports, 1999, pp. 615–629.

Torre, Joe, with Henry Dreher. *Joe Torre's Ground Rules for Winners*. New York: Hyperion, 1999.

Torre, Joe, with Tom Verducci. *Chasing the Dream: My Lifelong Journey to the World*

Series. 1997. Reprint, New York: Bantam, 1998.

Torres, Angel. *La historia del beisbol cubano, 1878–1976*. Los Angeles: Angel Torres, 1976.

Traubel, Horace. *With Walt Whitman in Camden*. Ed. Sculley Bradley. Carbondale: Southern Illinois University Press, 1959.

Treat, Roger L. *Walter Johnson: King of the Pitchers*. New York: J. Messner, 1948.

Trujillo, Nick. *The Meaning of Nolan Ryan*. College Station: Texas A&M University Press, 1994.

Twain, Mark. *Mark Twain Speaking*. Ed. Paul Fatout. Iowa City: University of Iowa Press, 1976.

Tygiel, Jules. *Baseball's Great Experiment: Jackie Robinson and His Legacy*. New York: Oxford University Press, 1983.

Tygiel, Jules, ed. *The Jackie Robinson Reader: Perspectives on an American Hero*. New York: Dutton, 1997.

Valerio, Anthony. *Bart: A Life of A. Bartlett Giamatti*. New York: Harcourt Brace Jovanovich, 1991.

Vamplew, Wray. *The Oxford Companion to Australian Sport*. 2d ed. New York: Oxford University Press, 1994.

Vamplew, Wray, and Brian Stoddart, eds. *Sport in Australia: A Social History*. New York: Cambridge University Press, 1994.

Van Blair, Rick. *Dugout to Foxhole: Interviews with Baseball Players Whose Careers Were Affected by World War II*. Jefferson, NC: McFarland, 1994.

Van Hyning, Thomas E. *Puerto Rico's Winter League: A History of Major League Baseball's Launching Pad*. Jefferson, NC: McFarland, 1995.

Vanderberg, Bob. *'59: Summer of the Sox*. Champaign, IL: Sports Publishing, 1999.

Vaughan, Roger. *Ted Turner: The Man Behind the Mouth*. Boston: Sail Books, 1978.

Veeck, Bill, with Ed Linn. *The Hustler's Handbook*. New York: Putnam's, 1965.

——. *Veeck—As in Wreck: The Autobiography of Bill Veeck*. New York: Putnam's, 1962.

Verducci, Tom. "The Left Arm of God." *Sports Illustrated*, July 12, 1999, pp. 82–100.

Vlasich, James A. *A Legend for the Legendary: The Origin of the Baseball Hall of Fame.*

Bowling Green, OH: Bowling Green University Popular Press, 1990.

Voigt, David Quentin. *American Baseball*. 3 vols. (1966–1983). University Park: Pennsylvania State University Press, 1983.

———. *American Baseball: From Gentleman's Sport to the Commissioner System*. Norman: University of Oklahoma Press, 1966.

———. "America's Game: A Brief History." In *The Baseball Encyclopedia*. 10th ed. Editorial Director, Jeanine Bucek. New York: Macmillan, 1996, pp. 3–13.

Wagenheim, Kal. *Babe Ruth: His Life and Legend*. New York: Holt, 1992.

———. *Clemente!* New York: Praeger, 1973.

Walker, Paul Robert. *Pride of Puerto Rico: The Life of Roberto Clemente*. San Diego: Harcourt, 1991.

Waller, Spencer Weber, Neil B. Cohen, and Paul Finkelman. *Baseball and the American Legal Mind*. New York: Garland, 1995.

Wallop, Douglass. *The Year the Yankees Lost the Pennant*. New York: Norton, 1954.

Ward, Geoffrey C., and Ken Burns. *Baseball: An Illustrated History*. New York: Alfred A. Knopf, 1994.

Ward, John Montgomery. *Base Ball: How to Become a Player*. Philadelphia: Athletic Publishing Company, 1888.

Warfield, Don. *The Roaring Redhead: Larry MacPhail, Baseball's Great Innovator*. South Bend, IN: Diamond Communications, 1987.

Weiler, Paul, and Gary Roberts. *Sports and the Law*. Westbury, NY: Foundation, 1993.

Weistart, John, and Cym Lowell. *The Law of Sports*. Charlottesville, VA: Michie, 1979.

Wellman, Trina. *Louis Francis Sockalexis: The Life-Story of a Penobscot Indian*. Augusta, ME: Department of Indian Affairs, 1975.

Wendel, Tim. *Castro's Curveball*. New York: Ballantine, 1999.

Westbrook, Deeanne. *Ground Rules: Baseball and Myth*. Urbana: University of Illinois Press, 1996.

Weybright, Victor. *Spangled Banner: The Story of Francis Scott Key*. New York: Farrar and Rinehart, 1935.

Wheeler, Lonnie. *Bleachers: A Summer in Wrigley Field*. Chicago: Contemporary Books, 1988.

Wheeler, Lonnie, and John Baskin. *The Cincinnati Game*. Wilmington, OH: Orange Fraser, 1988.

Wheeler, Robert W. *Jim Thorpe: World's Greatest Athlete*. Rev. ed. Norman: University of Oklahoma, 1979.

White, G. Edward. *Creating the National Pastime: Baseball Transforms Itself, 1903–1953*. Princeton: Princeton University Press, 1996.

Whiteford, Mike. *How to Talk Baseball*. 1983. Reprint, New York: Galahad Books, 1996.

Whiting, Robert. *You Gotta Have WA*. New York: Macmillan, 1989.

Whitman, Walt. *The Works of Walt Whitman*. New York: Funk and Wagnalls, 1968.

Whittemore, Hank. *CNN: The Inside Story*. Boston: Little, Brown, 1990.

Wilbert, Warren, and William Hageman. *Chicago Cubs: Seasons at the Summit*. Champaign, IL: Sagamore, 1997.

Williams, Peter W. *America's Religions: Traditions and Cultures*. Urbana: University of Illinois Press, 1998.

Williams, Ted. *My Turn at Bat: The Story of My Life*. New York: Simon and Schuster, 1969.

———. *The Science of Hitting*. New York: Simon and Schuster, 1971.

Williamson, Juanita V., and Virginia M. Burke. *A Various Language: Perspectives on American Dialects*. New York: Holt, 1971.

Wilson, August. *Fences*. New York: NAL, 1986.

Wilson, Jeffrey. "Baseball in Taiwan." In *Total Baseball*. 6th ed. Ed. John Thorn et al. New York: Total Sports, 1999, pp. 563–569.

Winegardner, Mark. *Prophet of the Sandlots: Journeys with a Major League Scout*. New York: Atlantic Monthly, 1990.

The Winning Team. Dir. Lewis Seiler. Warner Bros., 1952.

Wolfe, Rich, and George Castle. *I Remember Harry Caray*. Champaign, IL: Sports Publishing, 1998.

The World of Abbott and Costello. Narr. by Jack E. Leonard, 1965 (documentary).

Wortman, Marc. "Diamonds Are Forever: Once a Game Only for the Boys of Summer, Amateur Baseball Leagues Are Now Filled with Thousands of Men Over 30."

September/October 1998. *Cigar Aficionado* website: http://www.cigaraficionado.com/Cigar/Aficionado/Archives/199810/fh1098.html

Wright, Russell O. *The Evolution of Baseball: A History of the Major Leagues in Graphs, 1903–1989.* Jefferson, NC: McFarland, 1992.

Yablonsky, Lewis, and Jonathan Brower. *The Little League Game: How Kids, Coaches, and Parents Really Play It.* New York: Times Books, 1979.

Yardley, Jonathan. *Ring: A Biography of Ring Lardner.* New York: Random House, 1977.

Yoggy, Gary A. "Prime-Time Bonanza! The Western on Television." In *Wanted Dead or Alive: The American West in Popular Culture.* Ed. Richard Aquila. Urbana: University of Illinois Press, 1996, pp. 160–187.

———. *Riding the Video Range: The Rise and Fall of the Western on Television.* Jefferson, NC: McFarland, 1995.

Zimbalist, Andrew. *Baseball and Billions: A Probing Look inside the Big Business of Our National Pastime.* Rev. ed. New York: BasicBooks, 1994.

Zoss, Joel, and John Bowman. *Diamonds in the Rough: The Untold History of Baseball.* 1989. Reprint, Chicago: Contemporary Books, 1996.

Zucker, Harvey Marc, and Lawrence J. Babich. *Sports Films: A Complete Reference.* Jefferson, NC: McFarland, 1987.

About the Author

Edward J. Rielly chairs the English Department at Saint Joseph's College in Maine, where he teaches, among many other courses, "The Modern Novel, Baseball, and Society." He holds a doctorate in English from the University of Notre Dame. His previous books include a study of *Gulliver's Travels* and eight books of poetry. A cultural history of the 1960s is forthcoming. Rielly's interest in baseball began on his family's farm in Wisconsin, where he listened to the Chicago White Sox and Milwaukee Braves on radio and devoted many hours to hitting baseballs against the wall of an old barn.

Index